1993

BUSINESS RESEARCH METHODS

THIRD EDITION

BUSINESS RESEARCH METHODS

T H I R D   E D I T I O N

William G. Zikmund
Oklahoma State University

THE DRYDEN PRESS

Chicago Fort Worth San Francisco Philadelphia
Montreal Toronto London Sydney Tokyo

Acquisitions Editor: Robert Gemin
Project Editor: Teresa Chartos
Production Manager: Bob Lange
Permissions Editor: Cindy Lombardo
Director of Editing, Design, and Production: Jane Perkins

Design Supervisor: Rebecca Lemna
Copy Editor: Mary Englehart
Compositor: G & S Typesetters, Inc.
Text Type: 10/12 Sabon

Library of Congress Cataloging-in-Publication Data

Zikmund, William G.
    Business research methods / William G. Zikmund.—3rd ed.
       p.   cm.
    Includes bibliographical references.
    ISBN 0-03-033078-5
    1. Management—Research.   2. Business-Research.   I. Title.
HD30.4.Z54   1991
658.4'03'072-dc20
                                                                90-34781
                                                                  CIP

Printed in the United States of America
012-015-987654321

Address orders:
The Dryden Press
Orlando, FL 32887

Address editorial correspondence:
The Dryden Press
908 N. Elm St.
Hinsdale, IL 60521

The Dryden Press
Holt, Rinehart and Winston
Saunders College Publishing

Cover Illustrator: Rebecca Lemna

To My Parents

THE DRYDEN PRESS
SERIES IN MANAGEMENT

Preface

The third edition of *Business Research Methods* is a comprehensive, practical, and extremely accessible presentation of the field of business research. It emphasizes an applied approach based on practical applications that give students a basic understanding of the scope of business research.

My experience in teaching business research at the university level for 20 years and my experience as a researcher in industry have shown me that a practical and straightforward presentation of business research is necessary. I have tried, therefore, to present a balanced view of the theory of research and its practical applications. My objective in writing this book is to provide a fundamental treatment of business research that stresses the importance of research methods in business and nonprofit organizations.

Business Research Methods seeks to introduce the student to the basic tools of business research by explaining the various research techniques and methodologies. Numerous illustrations, portraying actual research in management, marketing, finance, accounting, and other areas of business, show how to perform the research function.

More than other business research textbooks, the third edition of *Business Research Methods* is written to be topically relevant and to meet the student's need for an overview of the field.

ORGANIZATION OF THE BOOK

The organization of the third edition of *Business Research Methods* follows the logic of the business research process. The book is organized into eight parts. Each of the first seven parts presents the basic research concepts for one of the stages in the research process and discusses how these concepts relate to decisions about conducting specific projects. Part One, "Introduction," discusses the scope of business research and provides an overview of the entire business research process. Part Two, "Beginning Stages of the Research Process," covers problem definition, research proposals, exploratory research, and secondary data. Part Three, "Research Methods for Collecting Primary Data," covers the concepts and issues related to designing and using surveys, observation studies, and experiments. Part Four, "Measurement Concepts," discusses the logic of measurement and the practical issues involved in attitude measurement and questionnaire design. Part Five, "Sampling and Fieldwork," discusses why sampling is required, how to design samples, how to conduct fieldwork, and how to determine sample size. A review of basic statistical concepts appears in this part of the book. Part Six, "Data Analysis and Presentation," covers editing and coding, descriptive data analysis and inferential statistical analysis, and communication of research results. Part Seven, "A Special Topic," discusses ethical issues in business research and ends with a final note on the use of business research. Part Eight, "Cases," provides materials that challenge students to apply the concepts they have learned.

NEW TO THE THIRD EDITION

Chapter 1 has been rewritten to give greater emphasis to business research's role in the generation of vital information and the impact that information has on a firm's decision making.

In Chapter 4 the material on problem definition and the development of research proposals has been greatly expanded. In recent years technological changes have had considerable influence on the way information is gathered, stored, and distributed. The book has been altered to reflect these changes. Decision support systems and database search and retrieval systems are now emphasized in a revised chapter on secondary data, Chapter 6. The section on microcomputers in business research has been updated to reflect the major computer innovations introduced to the market over the last few years.

Chapter 9, dealing with observation studies, has been rearranged and rewritten so that students can more easily understand the importance of observation studies.

Chapter 16 reorganizes the topic of fieldwork into two major sections: fieldwork principles and fieldwork management.

New material on data transformations and the summarization of rank order data has been added to Chapter 18, which deals with basic data analysis and descriptive statistics.

The discussion of the research report (Chapter 23) now gives greater emphasis to oral presentation of the research findings.

The number of cases in Part Eight has been expanded to 18.

FEATURES STUDENTS WILL LIKE

More than other business research textbooks, the third edition of *Business Research Methods* is a book written to meet the student's need for topical relevance and for an overview of the field. To achieve these objectives, the following elements have been emphasized:

Learning objectives outlining key concepts are presented at the beginning of each chapter.

An opening vignette describing an actual situation relevant to the chapter focuses student attention on the pragmatic aspects of each chapter.

Numerous real-world, easy-to-understand examples help the student gain insight into the applications of business research.

A straightforward prose style presents a balanced coverage of business research as it is actually practiced. This is a comprehensive coverage rather than a superficial treatment of topics. Considerable effort has been made to explain topics using examples that clarify rather than mystify.

Statistical concepts are presented in a simple, straightforward manner, as befits the book's managerial orientation. The statistical and quantitative aspects of the book are written for those students who need an understanding of basic concepts, and a separate section is devoted to a review of statistics. Those students who approach the prospect of statistical material with unnecessary trepidation, and especially those who have rusty statistical skills, will benefit from a quick review of the basic statistical concepts. "Statistical Tutor" boxes aid in the learning process by visually reflecting statistical concepts.

The end-of-chapter questions have been designed to stimulate the student's thinking about topics beyond the text's coverage. The student's understanding of key concepts is enhanced by the review materials following each chapter.

The cases at the end of the book present interesting, real-life research situations that require the student to make thoughtful decisions. They offer the opportunity for active participation in a decision-making process, one of the most effective forms of learning.

To enhance the student's understanding of conceptual materials, many exhibits that indicate relationships among variables and that *visually highlight ideas* are included.

Learning the vocabulary of business research is essential to understanding the topic. *Business Research Methods* facilitates this in three ways. First, key concepts are boldfaced and completely defined when they first appear in the textbook. Second, all key terms and concepts are listed at the end of each chapter. Third, a glossary of key terms summarizing all key terms and definitions appears at the end of the book for handy reference. A glossary of frequently used symbols is also included.

FEATURES PROFESSORS WILL LIKE

Materials to supplement the content of the textbook are available to help instructors perform their vital teaching function. The extensive learning package provided with *Business Research Methods* includes a combined test bank and instructor's manual with transparency masters, a floppy disk containing databases for several cases, and other ancillary materials. Special attention has been given to the preparation of the test bank portion because it is one of the most important ancillary materials. The test bank is more extensive than that for any other business research textbook. *Instructor's Manual, Test Bank, and Transparency Masters* provides extensive support for the text. In addition to numerous transparency masters, the *Instructor's Manual* contains solutions to cases, chapter outline lecture notes, and answers to end-of-chapter questions.

Several comprehensive cases appear at the end of the book. Each case discusses an entire research project and includes a database useful for assignments dealing with statistical analysis. These databases are computerized (see below).

Several cases stored on floppy disk are marked with this 🖫 symbol to indicate the data set in the case is also stored on a floppy disk that is available to instructors.

Edu-Stat, a comprehensive package of statistical software, is another teaching and learning supplement to this book. A variety of statistical programs ranging from simple descriptive analysis to complex multivariate statistical analysis are stored on a floppy disk that can be used with an IBM or IBM-compatible personal computer. Edu-Stat allows students to perform statistical tests and to analyze problems in the databased cases that appear in *Business Research Methods*. It is available free to adopters of this text.

ACKNOWLEDGMENTS

I would like to acknowledge the help of the business research muse, who came to me at odd times without any understanding of the requirements of family life. The time required to write a textbook must be paid for by family and friends.

I owe a debt of gratitude to many people who helped me finish this book. Joan Kirkendall cheerfully typed the manuscript and, as always, I am deeply in her debt. John Bush wrote the first draft of Chapter 23, and I sincerely appreciate his contribution. Lorna Brown did the leg work required to research the text, and she also provided considerable help with the *Instructor's Manual*. Her assistance and good humor were greatly appreciated.

I would like to thank Gwenn Grondal, *University of Phoenix;* Jeffrey Jung, *University of Phoenix;* and Ernest Maier, *Lawrence Institute of Technology* for their in-depth reviews of the third edition manuscript.

I also appreciate the reviews of previous editions by Professors Nathan Adams, *Middle Tennessee University;* J. K. Bandyopedyay, *Central Michigan University;* Ralph F. Catalenello, *Northern Illinois University;* James R. Dyprey, *Lawrence Institute of Technology;* Nancie Fimbel, *San Jose State University;* Jim Grimm, *Illinois State University;* Laurie Larwood, *Claremont McKenna College;* Ernie Maier, *Lawrence Institute of Technology;* E. J. Manton, *East Texas State University;* John D. Nicks, Jr., *Pepperdine University;* James Novitzki, *University of Montana;* Marjorie Platt, *Northeastern University;* Arthur Reitsch, *East Washington University;* John P. Tillman, *University of Wisconsin—LaCrosse;* and Gerrit Wolf, *University of Arizona.*

This book could not have been completed without the able assistance of my editor Butch Gemin. Teresa Chartos' constant attention to editorial concerns and her cheerful and efficient performance of the production tasks greatly facilitated the publication of this book. Also, Becky Lemna's help in designing a very attractive cover and text is greatly appreciated. The people at The Dryden Press deserve my sincere gratitude.

William G. Zikmund
October 1990

ABOUT THE AUTHOR

A native of the Chicago area, William G. Zikmund now makes his home in Tulsa, Oklahoma. He is a professor in the College of Business Administration at Oklahoma State University. He received a bachelor of science degree in business from the University of Colorado, a master of science degree in marketing from Southern Illinois University, and a doctor of business administration degree from the University of Colorado.

Before beginning his academic career, Professor Zikmund worked in business research for the Conway/Millikin Company and the Remington Arms Company. Professor Zikmund has also served as a business research consultant to several business and nonprofit organizations. His applied business research experiences range from interviewing and coding to designing, supervising, and analyzing entire research programs.

During his academic career Professor Zikmund has published dozens of articles and papers in a diverse group of scholarly journals, among them the *Journal of Marketing,* the *Accounting Review,* and the *Journal of Applied Psychology.* He is on the editorial review boards of the *Journal of Business Research* and the *Journal of Marketing Education.* In addition to *Business Research Methods,* Professor Zikmund has written *Exploring Marketing Research* and *Marketing* (coauthored with Michael F. d'Amico) and has coedited two other textbooks. His first work of fiction, *A Corporate Bestiary* (Holt, Rinehart and Winston), was written to remind himself and perhaps a few others not to take work too seriously. He is an avid tennis player who follows the adage *mens sana in corpore sano.*

Contents in Brief

Contents

Introduction

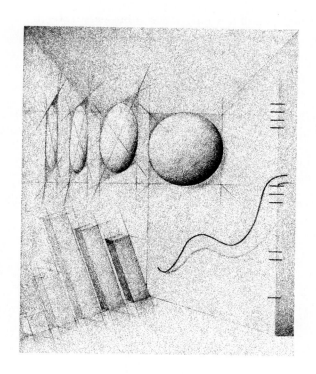

The Role of Business Research

What you will learn in this chapter:

To understand the importance of business research as a management decision-making tool.

To define business research.

To understand the difference between basic and applied research.

To understand the managerial value of business research and the role it plays in the development and implementation of strategy.

To understand when business research is needed and when it should not be conducted.

To identify the various categories of business research activities.

Business research conducted by the Japan Productivity Center refuted the stereotype that Japanese workers and managers work in harmony and without job-induced stress. In recent years, many Japanese companies have experienced rising stress levels among employees. Researchers at the Japan Productivity Center also concluded that "stress diminishes as managers rise on the executive ladder. The company president is a very happy man." The increased level of personal freedom rather than material success or status was found to be the apparent reason for less stress at the top. In Japanese companies, middle managers must conform; they cannot really be themselves.[1]

In thousands of organizations, business research is an important managerial tool that exerts a major influence on decision making. The above example of stress in Japanese companies illustrates how business research can provide insight into organizational problems. The managerial value and diverse nature of business research can be illustrated by the following additional examples. As you read through these examples, imagine that you are an executive and consider the importance of business research in providing information essential for good decision making.

A Midwestern bank investigated tellers' job satisfaction and the relationship of that job satisfaction to turnover, absenteeism, and balance shortages. The researchers, after evaluating the cost of negative performance, suggested that low job satisfaction had the potential to cost the bank more than $1,500 per teller per year.[2]

Clairol's Park Avenue offices include a test salon where the company tries out various home hair-care items on women volunteers. Researchers look on through a two-way mirror as the volunteers shampoo, condition, or color their hair with test products from Clairol or its competitors. The volunteers are given a free hair styling for their help. In return, the company gets to observe how the women react to home hair-care products and to learn whether they understand and correctly follow label directions. Sometimes favorable "verbatims" or comments, from the volunteers are recorded and later used in advertising.[3]

3

Sports Team Analysis and Tracking Systems (STATS), a specialized computer service, analyzes information from baseball records (e.g., how often a single advances a runner from first base to third) to help managers win games. A business researcher in the press box keeps a record of every pitch on a small computer, and after a ball is hit, he records its precise direction, the number of feet it travels, the player who fields the ball, and the outcome of the play. Computerized summaries of play-by-play activities are provided for broadcasters who cover the games. The information is also stored in a master computer that keeps pitch-by-pitch records for the entire season, as well as past seasons. Managers may use this information to have the computer draw a baseball field diagram to indicate where a particular batter has hit against a particular pitcher or a particular type of pitch. Old-time managers like Casey Stengel had to keep this sort of information on paper or in their heads. On the computer screen modern baseball teams, using this research technique, can see the data instantly, then select a pinch hitter or relief pitcher or reposition their fielders accordingly.[4] (See Exhibit 1.1.)

An academic researcher conducted an experiment to determine if workers whose goals are set unattainably high will perform better than workers

EXHIBIT   1 . 1   **A Computer Analysis of the Play-by-Play Data for the Oakland A's**

Source: Doug Wilson/© 1982 Discover Publications and Kevin McKean, "Turning Baseball into a Science," *DISCOVER* Magazine, © 1982 Time Inc. (June 1982), 28. Reprinted with permission.

whose goals are relatively easy to achieve. The experimenter concluded that the higher the intended level of achievement the higher the level of performance.[5]

Each of these examples illustrates a business research problem. All the examples relate to business research, but each illustrates a different form of research. The bank example illustrates how survey findings can be directly translated into cost savings strategy. The Clairol example points out the value of an observation study. The other examples illustrate that researchers use more than surveys. Internal records, government and trade association statistics, psychological tests, and experiments are valuable tools for business research. Inasmuch as these examples illustrate only a few applications of business research, it should not surprise you to learn that the role of business research is growing in importance.

■

SCOPE OF BUSINESS RESEARCH

The scope of business research is limited by one's definition of "business." Certainly research in the production, finance, marketing, or management areas of a for-profit corporation is within the scope of business research. A broader definition of business, however, includes not-for-profit organizations, such as the American Heart Association, the San Diego Zoo, and the Boston Pops Orchestra. Each of these organizations exists to satisfy social needs, and they require business skills to produce and distribute the services that people want. Business research may be conducted by organizations that are not business organizations. (The federal government, for example, performs many functions that are similar, if not identical, to those of business organizations. Federal managers may use research techniques for evaluative purposes much the same way as managers at DuPont or Ford.) The term *business research* is utilized because all its techniques are applicable to business settings.

Business research covers a wide range of phenomena. For managers the purpose of research is to fulfill their need for knowledge of the organization, the market, the economy, or another area of uncertainty. A financial manager may ask, "Will the environment for long-term financing be better two years from now?" A personnel manager may ask, "What kind of training is necessary for production employees?" or "What is the reason for the company's high turnover?" A marketing manager may ask, "How can I monitor my sales in retail trade activities?" Each of these questions requires information about how the environment, employees, customers, or the economy will respond to executives' decisions. Research may be one of the principal tools for answering these practical questions.

The development and implementation of plans and strategies require information, and every day managers translate their experiences with business phenomena into tactics and strategies. Information from a manager's experiences is frequently used in an intuitive manner because of time pressure on a business decision or because the problem is minor. However, the primary task of management is effective decision making. "Flying by the seat of the pants" decision making, without systematic inquiry, is like betting on a long shot at the racetrack because the horse's name is appealing. Occasionally there are successes, but in the long run intuition without research can lead to disappointment. Business research helps decision makers shift from intuitive information gathering to systematic and objective investigation.

A business researcher conducting research within an organization may be referred to as a "marketing researcher," an "organizational researcher," a "director of financial and economic research," or one of many other titles. Although business researchers are specialized, the term *business research* encompasses all of these functional specialties. While researchers in different functional areas may investigate different phenomena, they are similar to one another because they utilize a similar research methodology.

BUSINESS RESEARCH DEFINED

The task of business research is to generate accurate information for use in decision making. As we saw above, the emphasis of business research is on shifting decision makers from intuitive information gathering to systematic and objective investigation. **Business research** is defined as the systematic and objective process of gathering, recording, and analyzing data for aid in making business decisions.

This definition suggests, first, that research information is neither intuitive nor haphazardly gathered. Literally, research (*re-search*) means to "search again." It connotes patient study and scientific investigation wherein the researcher takes another, more careful look at data to discover all that can be known about the subject of study.

Second, if the information generated or data collected and analyzed are to be accurate, the business researcher must be objective. The need for objectivity was cleverly stated by the nineteenth-century American humorist Artemus Ward, who said, "It ain't the things we don't know that gets us in trouble. It's the things we know that ain't so." Thus the role of the researcher is to be detached and impersonal, rather than biased in an attempt to prove preconceived ideas. If bias enters the research process, the value of the data is considerably reduced.

A developer who owned a large area of land on which he wished to build a high-prestige shopping center wanted a research report to demonstrate to prospective retailers that there was a large market potential for such a center. Because he conducted his survey *exclusively* in an elite neighborhood, not surprisingly his findings showed that a large percentage of respondents wanted a "high-prestige" shopping center. Results of this kind are misleading, of course, and should be disregarded. If the user of such findings discovers how they were obtained, the developer loses credibility. If the user is ignorant of the bias in the design and unaware that the researchers were not impartial, his decision may have consequences more adverse than if he had made it strictly on intuition. The importance of objectivity cannot be overemphasized. Without objectivity, research is valueless.

Third, the above definition of business research points out that its objective is to facilitate the managerial decision process for all aspects of a business: finance, marketing, personnel, etc. The definition is not restricted to one aspect of business. An essential tool for management in its problem-solving and decision-making activities, business research generates and provides the necessary information upon which to base decisions. By reducing the uncertainty of decisions, it reduces the risk of making wrong decisions. However, research should be an *aid* to managerial judgment, not a substitute for it. There is more to management than research. Applying research remains a managerial art.

BASIC RESEARCH AND APPLIED RESEARCH

One reason for conducting research is to develop and evaluate concepts and theories, and **basic**—or **pure**—**research** attempts to expand the limits of knowledge. It does not directly involve the solution to a particular, pragmatic problem, but it has been said, "There is nothing so practical as a good theory." Although this statement is true in the long run, *basic* research findings generally cannot be immediately implemented. Basic research is conducted to verify the acceptability of a given theory or to know more about a certain concept.

For example, consider this basic research conducted by a university. Academic researchers investigated whether or not an individual's perception that he or she was doing well on a task would have any influence on future performance. Two nearly identical groups of adults were given ten puzzles to solve. All of the individuals had identical sets of puzzles to solve. After the subjects had given their solutions to the researchers, they were told "how well" they did on the test. All of the persons in the first group were told that they had done well (70 percent correct regardless of the actual percent correct). The members of the other group were told that they had done poorly (30 percent correct). Then both groups were given another set of ten puzzles. The group that had been told they had done well on the first set of puzzles performed better with the second set of puzzles than did the group that had been told they had been relatively unsuccessful with the first puzzle solving.[6] The results of this basic research expands scientific knowledge about theories of general performance behavior. This study was conducted because the researchers thought the theory being tested was far-reaching and applicable to a broad range of situations and circumstances.

Applied research is conducted when a decision must be made about a specific real-life problem. Applied research encompasses those studies undertaken to answer questions about specific problems or to make decisions about a particular course of action or policy. For example, an organization contemplating a paperless office and a networking system for the company's personal computers may conduct research to learn the amount of time its employees spend at personal computers in an average week.

The procedures and techniques utilized by basic and applied researchers do not differ substantially. Both employ the **scientific method** to answer the questions at hand. Broadly characterized, the scientific method refers to techniques and procedures that help the researcher to know and understand business phenomena. The scientific method requires systematic analysis and logical interpretation of empirical evidence (facts from observation or experimentation) to confirm or disprove prior conceptions. In basic research, first testing these prior conceptions or hypotheses and then making inferences and conclusions about the phenomena leads to the establishment of general laws about the phenomena.

Use of the scientific method in applied research assures objectivity in gathering facts and testing creative ideas for alternative business strategies. The essence of research, whether basic or applied, lies in the scientific method, and much of this book deals with *scientific methodology*. The difference in the techniques of basic and applied research is largely a matter of degree rather than substance.

MANAGERIAL VALUE OF BUSINESS RESEARCH

We have argued that research facilitates effective management. At the Ford Motor Company a marketing manager stated, "Research is fundamental to everything we do, so much so that we hardly make any significant decision without the benefit of some kind of market research. The risks are too big."[7] Managers in other functional areas have similar beliefs about research in their specialties.

The prime managerial value of business research is that it reduces uncertainty by providing information that improves the decision-making process. The decision-making process associated with the development and implementation of a strategy involves three interrelated stages:

1. Identifying problems or opportunities
2. Selecting and implementing a course of action
3. Evaluating the course of action

Business research, by supplying managers with pertinent information, may play an important role by reducing managerial uncertainty in each of these stages.

Identifying Problems or Opportunities

Before any strategy can be developed, an organization must determine where it wants to go and how it will get there. Business research can help managers plan strategies by determining the nature of situations by identifying the existence of problems or opportunities present in the organization.

Business research may be used as a diagnostic activity to provide information about what is occurring within an organization or in its environment. The mere description of some social or economic activity may familiarize managers with organizational and environmental occurrences and help them understand a situation. For example, the description of the dividend history of stocks in an industry may point to an attractive investment opportunity.

Information supplied by business research may also indicate problems. For example, employee interviews undertaken to delineate the dimensions of an airline reservation clerk's job may reveal that reservation clerks emphasize competence in issuing tickets over courtesy and friendliness in customer contact. Once business research indicates a problem, managers may feel that the alternatives are clear enough to make a decision based on experience or intuition, or they may decide that more business research is needed to generate additional information for a better understanding of the situation.

Whether an organization recognizes a problem or gains insight into a potential opportunity, an important aspect of business research is its provision of information that identifies or clarifies alternative courses of action.

Selecting and Implementing a Course of Action

After the alternative courses of action have been identified, business research is often conducted to obtain specific information that will aid in evaluating the alternatives and in selecting the best course of action. For example, suppose a facsimile (fax) machine manufacturer must decide to build a factory either in Japan or in South Korea. In such a case, business research can be designed to supply the exact information necessary to determine which course of action is best for the organization.

Opportunities may be evaluated through the use of various performance criteria. For example, estimates of market potential allow managers to evaluate the revenue that will be generated by each of the possible opportunities. A good forecast supplied by business researchers is among the most useful pieces of planning information a manager can have. Of course, complete accuracy in forecasting the future is not possible because change is constantly occurring in the business environment. Nevertheless, objective information generated by business research to forecast environmental occurrences may be the foundation for selecting a particular course of action.

Clearly, the best plan is likely to result in failure if it is not properly implemented. Business research may be conducted with the people who will be affected by a pending decision to indicate the specific tactics required to implement that course of action.

Evaluating the Course of Action

After a course of action has been implemented, business research may serve as a tool to inform managers whether planned activities were properly executed and whether they accomplished what they were expected to accomplish. In other words, business research may be conducted to provide feedback for evaluation and control of strategies and tactics.

Evaluation research is the formal, objective measurement and appraisal of the extent to which a given action, activity, or program has achieved its objectives.[8] In addition to measuring the extent to which completed programs achieved their objectives or to which continuing programs are presently performing as projected, evaluation research may provide information about the major factors influencing the observed performance levels.

In addition to business organizations, nonprofit organizations, such as agencies of the federal government, frequently conduct evaluation research. It is estimated that every year more than 1,000 federal evaluation studies are undertaken to systematically assess the effects of public programs.[9] For example, the General Accounting Office has been responsible for measuring outcomes of the Employment Opportunity Act, the Head Start program, and the Job Corps program.

Performance-monitoring research is a term used to describe a specific type of evaluation research that regularly, perhaps routinely, provides feedback for the evaluation and control of recurring business activity. For example, most firms continuously monitor wholesale and retail activity to ensure early detection of sales declines and other anomalies. In the grocery and retail drug industries, sales research may use the universal product code (UPC) for packages, together with electronic cash registers and computerized checkout counters, to provide valuable market-share information to store and brand managers interested in the retail sales volume of specific products.

United Airline's Omnibus in-flight surveys provide a good example of performance-monitoring research. United routinely selects sample flights and administers a questionnaire about in-flight service, food, and other aspects of air travel. The Omnibus survey is conducted quarterly to determine who is flying and for what reasons. It enables United to track demographic changes and to monitor customer ratings of its services on a continuing basis, allowing the airline to gather vast amounts of information at low cost. The information relating to customer reaction to services can be compared over time. For example, suppose United decided to change its menu for in-flight meals. The results of the Omnibus survey might indicate that shortly after the menu changed, the customers' rating of the airline's food declined. Such information would be extremely valuable, as it would allow management to quickly spot similar trends among passengers in other aspects of air travel, such as airport lounges, gate-line waits, or cabin cleanliness. Thus managerial action to remedy problems could be rapidly taken.

When analysis of performance indicates that all is not going as planned, business research may be required to explain why something "went wrong."[10] Detailed information about specific mistakes or failures is frequently sought. If a general problem area is identified, breaking down industry sales volume and a firm's sales volume into different geographic areas may provide an explanation of specific problems, and exploring these problems in greater depth may indicate which managerial judgments were erroneous.

WHEN IS BUSINESS RESEARCH NEEDED?

A manager faced with two or more possible courses of action faces the initial decision of whether or not research should be conducted. The determination of the need for research centers on (1) time constraints, (2) the availability of data, (3) the nature of the decision that must be made, and (4) the value of the business research information in relation to its costs.

Time Constraints

Systematically conducting research takes time. In many instances management concludes that because a decision must be made immediately, there will be no time for research. As a consequence, decisions are sometimes made without adequate information or thorough understanding of the situation. Although not ideal, sometimes the urgency of a situation precludes the use of research.

Availability of Data

Frequently managers already possess enough information to make a sound decision without business research. When there is an absence of adequate information, however, research must be considered. Managers must ask themselves, "Will the research provide the information needed to answer the basic questions about this decision?" If the data cannot be made available, research cannot be conducted. For example, prior to 1980 the People's Republic of China had never conducted a population census. Organizations engaged in international business often find that data about business activity or population characteristics, found in abundance when investigating the United States, are nonexistent or sparse when the geographic area of interest is an underdeveloped country. Further, if a potential source of data exists, managers will want to know how much it costs to obtain those data.

Nature of the Decision

The value of business research will depend on the nature of the managerial decision to be made. A routine tactical decision that does not require a substantial investment may not seem to warrant a substantial expenditure for business research. For example, a computer company must update its operator's instruction manual when minor product modifications are made. The cost of determining the proper wording for the updated manual is likely to be too high for such a minor decision. The nature of such a decision is not totally independent from the next issue to be considered: the benefits versus the costs of the research. However, in general the more strategically or tactically important the decision, the more likely that research will be conducted.

Benefits versus Costs

Some of the managerial benefits of business research have already been discussed. Of course, conducting research activities to obtain these benefits requires an expenditure; thus there are both costs and benefits in conducting business research. In any decision-making situation, managers must identify alternative courses of action, then weigh the value of each alternative against its cost. It is useful to think of business research as an investment alternative. When deciding whether to make a decision without research or to postpone the decision in order to conduct research, managers should ask: (1) Will the payoff or rate of return be worth the investment? (2) Will the information gained by business research improve the quality of the decision to an extent sufficient to warrant the expenditure? and (3) Is the proposed research expenditure the best use of the available funds?

For example, *TV Cable Week* was not test-marketed before its launch. While the magazine had articles and stories about television personalities and events, its main feature was a channel-by-channel program listing showing the exact programs that a particular subscriber could receive. To produce a "custom" magazine for each individual cable television system in the country re-

EXHIBIT   1 . 2   **Determining When Business Research Should Be Conducted**

Time Constraints		Availability of Data		Nature of the Decision		Benefits versus Costs		
Is there sufficient time available before a managerial decision must be made?	Yes →	Is the information already on hand inadequate for making the decision?	Yes →	Is the decision of considerable strategic or tactical importance?	Yes →	Does the value of the research information exceed the cost of conducting research?	Yes →	Conduct Business Research
↓ No		↓ No		↓ No		↓ No		

Business Research Should Not Be Conducted

quired developing a costly computer system. Because development required a substantial expenditure, one that could not be scaled down for research, the conducting of research was judged to be an improper investment. The value of the research information was not positive, because the cost of the information exceeded its benefits. Unfortunately, pricing and distribution problems became so compelling after the magazine was launched that it was a business failure. Nevertheless, the publication's managers, without the luxury of hindsight, made a reasonable decision not to conduct research. They analyzed the cost of the information (i.e., the cost of business research) relative to the potential benefits. Exhibit 1.2 outlines the criteria for determining when to conduct business research.

MAJOR TOPICS FOR RESEARCH IN BUSINESS

Research is expected to improve the quality of business decisions, but what business-decision topics benefit from research efforts? Exhibit 1.3 lists several major topics for research in business.[11]

SUMMARY

Business research is a management tool that companies use to reduce uncertainty. Business research, the manager's source of information about organizational and environmental conditions, covers topics ranging from long-range planning to the most ephemeral tactical decisions.

Business research is the systematic and objective process of gathering, recording, and analyzing data for decision making. The research must be systematic, not haphazard. It must be objective to avoid the distorting effects of personal bias. The objective of applied business research is to facilitate managerial decision making. Basic or pure research is used to increase the knowledge of theories and concepts.

EXHIBIT   1.3

**Major Topics for
Research in Business**

General Business, Economic, and Corporate Research
Short-range forecasting (up to one year)
Long-range forecasting (over one year)
Studies of business and industry trends
Inflation and pricing studies
Plant and warehouse location studies
Acquisition studies
Export and international studies

Financial and Accounting Research
Forecasts of financial interest-rate trends
Stock, bond, and commodity value predictions
Capital formation alternatives
Research related to mergers and acquisitions
Risk–return trade-off studies
Impact of taxes
Portfolio analysis
Research on financial institutions
Expected-rate-of-return studies
Capital asset pricing models
Credit risk
Cost analysis

Management and Organizational Behavior Research
Morale and job satisfaction
Leadership style
Employee productivity
Organizational effectiveness
Structural studies
Absenteeism and turnover
Organizational climate
Organizational communication
Time and motion studies
Physical environment studies
Labor union trends

Sales and Marketing Research
Measurement of market potentials
Market-share analysis
Market segmentation studies
Determination of market characteristics
Sales analysis
Establishment of sales quotas, territories
Distribution-channel studies
New-product concept tests
Test-market studies
Advertising research
Buyer-behavior studies

Corporate Responsibility Research
Ecological impact studies
Legal constraints on advertising and promotion studies
Sex, age, and racial discrimination worker-equity studies
Social values and ethics studies

Managers can use business research in all stages of the decision-making process: to define problems, to identify opportunities, and to clarify alternatives. Research is also used to evaluate current programs and courses of action, to explain what went wrong with managerial efforts in the past, and to forecast future conditions.

A manager determining whether business research should be conducted considers (1) time constraints, (2) the availability of data, (3) the nature of the decision to be made, and (4) the benefits of the research information in relation to its costs.

There is a broad variety of applied research topics, such as business, economic, and corporate research; financial and accounting research; management and organizational behavior research; sales and marketing research; and corporate responsibility research.

Key Terms

business research	scientific method
basic (pure) research	evaluation research
applied research	performance-monitoring research

Questions

1. What are some examples of business research in your particular field of interest?
2. In your own words, define *business research* and list its tasks.
3. How might a not-for-profit organization use business research?
4. What is the difference between applied and basic research?
5. Discuss how business research can be used in each stage of the decision-making process.
6. In your own words, describe the scentific method and state why it is an essential aspect of business research.
7. Describe a situation where business research *is not* needed and a situation where business research *is* needed. What factors differentiate the two situations?

References

[1] Information adapted from David Cohen, "Japanese Face Up To Stress on the Job," *The APA Monitor* (December 1985), 2.

[2] Adjusted for Inflation. Based on P. H. Mirvis and E. E. Lawler III, "Measuring the Financial Impact of Employee Attitudes," *Journal of Applied Psychology* 62 (1977): 1–8.

[3] Nancy Giges, "No Miracle in Small Miracle: Story Behind Clairol Failure," *Advertising Age*, Aug. 16, 1982, 76.

[4] Kevin McKean, "Turning Baseball into a Science," *Discover*, June 1982, 31.

[5] W. Clay Hamner, "Motivation Theories and Work Applications," in Steve Kerr, ed., *Organizational Behavior* (Columbus, OH: Grid Publishing, 1979), 47.

[6] Russell A. Jones, *Self-Fulfilling Prophecies: Social, Psychological, and Physiological Effects of Expectancies* (Hinsdale, NJ: Lawrence Erlbaum Associates, 1977), 167.

[7] Don Edgar, "Market Research Balances the Risks," *Advertising Age*, Sept. 17, 1979, S33.

[8] J. B. Brent Richie, "Roles of Research in the Management Process," *MSU Business Topics* (Summer 1976), 13–22.

[9] Mark R. Daniels and Clifford J. Wirth, "Paradigms of Evaluation Research: The Development of an Important Policy Making Component," *American Review of Public Administrators* (Spring 1985), 33–45.

[10] David K. Hardin, "Editorial: Marketing Research—Is It Used or Abused?" *Journal of Marketing Research* 6 (1969): 239.

[11] Adapted from Dik Warren Twedt, *Survey of Marketing Research* (Chicago: American Marketing Association, 1983).

Theory Building

To understand the goals of theory.

To define the meaning of theory.

To understand the terms *concept, proposition, variable,* and *hypothesis.*

To understand that because concepts abstract reality, it is possible to discuss concepts at various levels of abstraction.

To understand the scientific method.

To discuss how theories are generated.

Theories are nets cast to catch what we call "the world": to rationalize, to explain, and to master it. We endeavour to make the mesh ever finer and finer.

—*Karl R. Popper,* The Logic of Scientific Discovery

The purpose of science concerns the expansion of knowledge and the discovery of truth. Theory building is the means by which basic researchers hope to achieve this purpose.

■

WHAT ARE THE GOALS OF THEORY?

A scientist, investigating business phenomena, wants to know what produces inflation. Another person wants to know if organizational structure influences leadership style. Both want to be able to predict behavior, to be able to say: If we do such and such, then so and so will happen.[1]

Prediction and understanding are the two purposes of theory.[2] Accomplishing the first goal allows the theorist to predict the behavior or characteristics of one phenomenon from the knowledge of another phenomenon's characteristics. A business researcher may theorize that older investors tend to be more interested in investment income than younger investors.[3] This theory, once verified, should allow researchers to predict the importance of expected dividend yield on the basis of investors' ages. The ability to anticipate future conditions in the environment or in an organization may be extremely valuable, yet prediction alone may not satisfy the scientific researcher's goals. Successfully forecasting an election outcome does not satisfy one's curiosity about the reason *why* a candidate won the election. Understanding is desired. In most situations, of course, prediction and understanding go hand in hand. To predict phenomena, we must have an explanation of why variables behave as they do. Theories provide these explanations.

THE MEANING OF THEORY

Like all abstractions, the word "theory" has been used in many different ways, in many different contexts, at times so broadly as to include almost all descriptive statements about a class of phenomena, and at other times so narrowly as to exclude everything but a series of terms and their relationships that satisfies certain logical requirements.[4]

For our purposes, a **theory** is a coherent set of general propositions, used as principles of explanation of the apparent relationships of certain observed phenomena. A key element in our definition is the term *proposition*. Before a proposition can be explained, the nature of *theoretical concepts* must be understood.

CONCEPTS

Theory development is essentially a process of describing phenomena at increasingly higher levels of abstraction. Things that we observe can be described as ideas or concepts. A **concept** (or construct) is a generalized idea about a class of objects, attributes, occurrences, or processes that has been given a name. If you, as an organizational theorist, describe phenomena such as supervisory behavior, you would categorize empirical events or real things into concepts. Concepts are our building blocks and, in organizational theory, "leadership," "productivity," and "morale" are concepts. In the theory of finance, "gross national product," "asset," and "inflation" are frequently used concepts.

Concepts abstract reality. That is, concepts are expressed in words that refer to various events or objects. For example, the concept "asset" is an abstract term that may, in the concrete world of reality, refer to a specific punch press machine. Concepts, however, may vary in degree of abstraction. The abstraction ladder in Exhibit 2.1 indicates that it is possible to discuss concepts at

E X H I B I T   2 . 1

**A Ladder of
Abstraction
for Concepts**

EXHIBIT   2.2

**Concepts Are
Abstractions
of Reality**

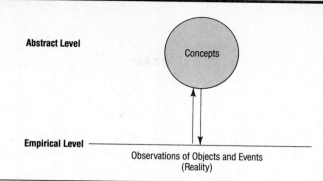

Source: Adapted from Fred N. Kerlinger, *Behavioral Research: A Conceptual Approach* (New York: Holt, Rinehart and Winston, 1979), 42.

various levels of abstraction. Moving up the ladder of abstraction, the basic concept becomes more abstract, wider in scope, and less amenable to measurement. The basic or scientific business researcher operates at two levels: the **abstract level** of concepts (and propositions) and the empirical level of variables (and hypotheses). At the **empirical level,** we "experience" reality, that is, we observe or manipulate objects or events (see Exhibit 2.2).[5]

If the organizational researcher says, "Older workers prefer different rewards than younger workers," two concepts—age of worker and reward preference—are the subjects of this statement made at the abstract level. If the researcher wishes to test this hypothesis, John, age 19, Chuck, age 45, and Mary, age 62—along with other workers—may be questioned about their preferences for salary, retirement plans, intrinsic job satisfaction, and the like. Recording their ages and observing their stated preferences occurs at the empirical level.

Researchers are concerned with the observable world, or what we shall loosely term "reality." Theorists translate their conceptualization of reality into abstract ideas. Thus theory deals with abstraction. Things are not the *essence* of theory, ideas are.[6] Concepts in isolation are not theories. Only when we explain how concepts relate to other concepts do we begin to construct theories.

NATURE OF PROPOSITIONS

Concepts are the basic units of theory development. However, theories require that the relationship among concepts be understood. Thus once reality is abstracted into concepts, the scientist is interested in the relationship among various concepts. **Propositions** are statements concerned with the relationships among concepts. At the explanatory level, a proposition is the *logical* linkage among concepts. A proposition asserts a universal connection between properties. A proposition states that every event or thing of a certain sort either has a certain property or stands in a certain relationship to other events or things that have certain properties.[7]

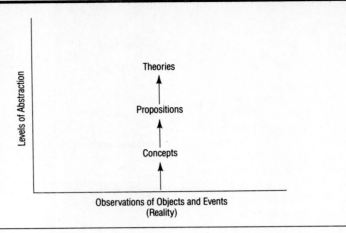

Consider the following behavioral science proposition that permeates many business theories:

> *If reinforcements follow each other at evenly distributed intervals, and everything else is held constant, the resulting habit will increase in strength as a positive growth function of the number of trials.*[8]

This proposition identifies theoretical relationships between the concepts "reinforcements" and "habit." It identifies the direction and magnitude of these relationships.

We have indicated that a theory is an abstraction from observed reality. Concepts are at one level of abstraction (see Exhibit 2.3). Investigating propositions requires that we increase our level of abstract thinking. When we think about theories, we are at the highest level of abstraction because we are investigating the relationship between propositions. Theories are networks of propositions.

THE SCIENTIFIC METHOD

A **scientific method** is the use of a set of prescribed procedures for establishing and connecting theoretical statements about events and for predicting events yet unknown.[9] There is no consensus concerning exact procedures for the scientific method, but most discussions of the scientific method include a reference to "empirical testability." Empirical means that something is verifiable by observation, experimentation, or experience. The process of empirical verification cannot be divorced from the process of theory development.

A **hypothesis** is a proposition that is empirically testable. It is an empirical statement concerned with the relationship among variables. The abstract proposition "Reinforcements will increase habit strength" may be tested empirically with a hypothesis. Exhibit 2.4 shows that the hypothesis "Bonus pay will be associated with sales volume consistently above quota" is an empirical counterpart of the proposition. Bonus pay and sales are **variables**, reflecting con-

R E S E A R C H   I N S I G H T
Ballistic Theory

Ballistic theory is a theory because it deals with measurable factors, because it states their relationships in detail, and because any one factor can be fairly completely determined by a knowledge of all the others. Given all of the factors except the initial speed of the projectile, an engineer can determine what that speed was. Asked to change the point of impact, he can suggest several ways in which this can be accomplished—all of which will work.

It is common knowledge that the behavioral sciences are not as advanced as the physical sciences. What this means, in effect, is that no one has yet defined all of the factors in human behavior or determined the influence

that each has on events. In fact, no one has really done a very good job of determining what an event is, that is, how to measure it or what to consider relevant about it.

Again, an example may help explain the dilemma. It is irrelevant to ballistic theory that John Gingrich is standing beside the 155 mm rifle when it is fired. It may not be irrelevant to consumer behavior theory that he is standing beside the person who selects a necktie. It is not relevant to ballistic theory that the gunner's father once carried an M-1. It may be relevant to consumer behavior theory that the automobile purchaser's grandfather once owned a Ford.

Source: W. T. Tucker, *Foundations for a Theory of Consumer Behavior* (New York: Holt, Rinehart and Winston, 1967), v–vii.

cepts at the empirical level. Variables may be measured. Thus the scientific method has two basic levels:

> ... *the empirical and the abstract, conceptual. The empirical aspect is primarily concerned with the facts of the science as revealed by observation and experiments. The abstract or theoretical aspect, on the other hand, consists in a serious attempt to understand the facts of the science, and to integrate them into a coherent, i.e., a logical, system. From these observations and integrations are derived, directly or indirectly, the basic laws of the science.*[10]

E X H I B I T   2 . 4

Hypotheses Are the Empirical Counterparts of Propositions

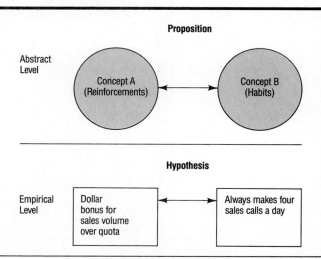

AN EXAMPLE OF A THEORY

Exhibit 2.5 is a simplified portrayal of a theory to explain voluntary job turnover, that is, an individual's movement to another organization or movement to another position within the same organization. Two concepts—(1) the *perceived desirability of movement* to another organization and (2) the *perceived ease of movement* from the present job—are expected to be the primary determinants of *intentions to quit*. This is a proposition. Further, the concept *intentions to quit* is expected to be a necessary condition before the actual *voluntary turnover behavior* occurs. This is a second proposition that links concepts together in this theory. In the more elaborate theory, *job performance* is another concept considered to be the primary determinant influencing both perceived ease of movement and perceived desirability of movement. Moreover, perceived ease of movement is related to other concepts such as labor market conditions, number of organizations visible to the individual, and personal characteristics. Perceived desirability of movement is influenced by concepts such as equity of pay, job complexity, and participation in decision making.

A complete explanation of this theory is not possible; however, this example should help the reader understand the terminology used by theory builders.

E X H I B I T   2 . 5

**A Basic Theory Explaining
Voluntary Job Turnover**

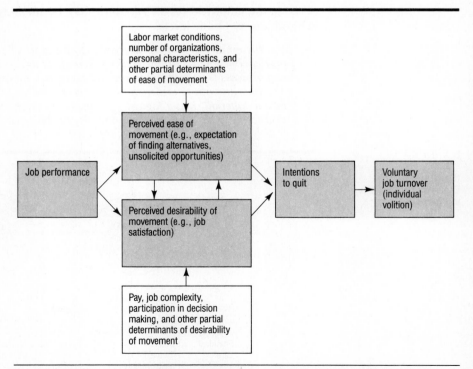

Source: Based on Ellen J. Jackofsky, "Turnover and Job Performance: An Integrated Process Model," *Academy of Management Review* 9, no. 1 (1984): 78; and Paul Solomon, "Reducing Unwanted Staff Turnovers in Public Accounting: An Action Plan," *Northern California Executive Review* (Spring 1986): 22–25.

VERIFYING THEORY

In most scientific situations there are alternative theories to explain certain classes of phenomena. To determine which is the better theory, researchers gather empirical data or observations to verify the theories.

Maslow's hierarchical theory of motivation offers one explanation for behavior. For example, Maslow theorizes that individuals will attempt to satisfy physiological needs before self-esteem needs. An alternative view of motivation is provided by Freudian (psychoanalytic) theory, which suggests that unconscious, emotional impulses are the basic influences on behavior. One task of science is to determine if a given theoretical proposition is false or if there are inconsistencies between competing theories. Just as records are made to be broken, theories are made to be tested.

> It must be possible to demonstrate that a given proposition or theory is false. This may at first glance appear strange. Why "false" rather than "true"? Technically, there may be other untested theories which could account for the results we obtained in our study of a proposition. At the very least, there may be a competing explanation which could be the "real" explanation for a given set of research findings. Thus, we can never be certain that our proposition or theory is the correct one. The scientist can only say, "I have a theory which I have objectively tested with data and the data are consistent with my theory." If the possibility of proving an idea false or wrong is not inherent in our test of an idea, then we cannot put much faith in the evidence that suggests it to be true. No other evidence was allowed to manifest itself. [11]

Business research gathers facts to verify theories. However, the researcher who wishes to identify inconsistency within a particular theory must understand the difference between facts and theories:

> Facts and theories are different things, not rungs in a hierarchy of increasing certainty. Facts are the world's data. Theories are structures of ideas that explain and interpret facts. Facts do not go away when scientists debate rival theories to explain them. Einstein's theory of gravitation replaced Newton's, but apples did not suspend themselves in midair pending the outcome. [12]

HOW ARE THEORIES GENERATED?

Many students ask, "Where do theories come from?" Although this is not an easy question to answer in a short chapter on theory in business research, we shall nevertheless explore this topic briefly.

In this chapter theory has been explained at the abstract, conceptual level and at the empirical level. Theory generation may occur at either level.

At the abstract, conceptual level, theory may be developed with deductive reasoning by going from a general statement to a specific assertion. **Deductive reasoning** is the logical process of deriving a conclusion from a known premise or something known to be true. For example, we know that *all managers are human beings.* If we also know that *Mary Fischer is a manager,* then we can deduce that *Mary Fischer is a human being.*

R E S E A R C H   I N S I G H T
Theory and Song

The following song (attributed to George Schultz, a former secretary of state) goes to the lively tune *Silver Dollar*.

A fact without a theory
Is like a ship without a sail,
Is like a boat without a rudder,
Is like a kite without a tail.
A fact without a figure
Is a tragic final act,
But one thing worse
In this universe
Is a theory without a fact.

Source: George Schultz, quoted in "Another Professor with Power," *Time*, Feb. 26, 1973, 80. Reprinted with permission.

At the empirical level, theory may be developed with inductive reasoning. **Inductive reasoning** is the logical process of establishing a general proposition on the basis of observation of particular facts. All managers that have ever been seen are human beings; therefore all managers are human beings.

Suppose a stockbroker with 15 years experience trading on the New York Stock Exchange repeatedly notices that the price of gold and the price of gold stocks rise whenever there is a hijacking, terrorist bombing, or military skirmish. In other words, similar patterns occur whenever a certain type of event occurs. The stockbroker may project these empirical observations to a more generalizable situation and conclude that the price of gold is related to political stability. Thus the stockbroker states a proposition based on his or her experience or specific observations.

Over the course of time, theory construction is often the result of a combination of deductive and inductive reasoning. Our experiences lead us to draw conclusions that we then try to empirically verify by using the scientific method.

OVERVIEW OF THE SCIENTIFIC METHOD

It is useful to look at the analytic process of scientific theory building as a series of stages. Seven operations may be viewed as the steps involved in the application of the scientific method:

1. Assessment of relevant existing knowledge
2. Formulation of concepts and propositions
3. Statement of hypotheses
4. Design the research to test the hypotheses
5. Acquisition of meaningful empirical data

6.   Analysis and evaluation of data
7.   Provide explanation and state new problems raised by the research [13]

An excellent overview of the scientific method is presented in the book *Zen and the Art of Motorcycle Maintenance:*

> *Actually I've never seen a cycle-maintenance problem complex enough really to require full-scale formal scientific method. Repair problems are not that hard. When I think of formal scientific method an image sometimes comes to mind of an enormous juggernaut, a huge bulldozer—slow, tedious, lumbering, laborious, but invincible. It takes twice as long, five times as long, maybe a dozen times as long as informal mechanic's techniques, but you know in the end you're going to get it. There's no fault isolation problem in motorcycle maintenance that can stand up to it. When you've hit a really tough one, tried everything, racked your brain and nothing works, and you know that this time Nature has really decided to be difficult, you say, "Okay, Nature, that's the end of the nice guy," and you crank up the formal scientific method.*
>
> *For this you keep a lab notebook. Everything gets written down, formally, so that you know at all times where you are, where you've been, where you're going and where you want to get. In scientific work and electronics technology this is necessary because otherwise the problems get so complex you get lost in them and confused and forget what you know and what you don't know and have to give up. In cycle maintenance things are not that involved, but when confusion starts it's a good idea to hold it down by making everything formal and exact. Sometimes just the act of writing down the problems straightens out your head as to what they really are.*
>
> *The logical statements entered into the notebook are broken down into six categories: (1) statement of the problem, (2) hypotheses as to the cause of the problem, (3) experiments designed to test each hypothesis, (4) predicted results of the experiments, (5) observed results of the experiments and (6) conclusions from the results of the experiments. This is not different from the formal arrangement of many college and high-school lab notebooks but the purpose here is no longer just busywork. The purpose now is precise guidance of thoughts that will fail if they are not accurate.*
>
> *The real purpose of scientific method is to make sure Nature hasn't misled you into thinking you know something you don't actually know. There's not a mechanic or scientist or technician alive who hasn't suffered from that one so much that he's not instinctively on guard. That's the main reason why so much scientific and mechanical information sounds so dull and so cautious. If you get careless or go romanticizing scientific information, giving it a flourish here and there, Nature will soon make a complete fool out of you. It does it often enough anyway even when you don't give it opportunities. One must be extremely careful and rigidly logical when dealing with Nature: one logical slip and an entire scientific edifice comes tumbling down. One false deduction about the machine and you can get hung up indefinitely.*
>
> *In Part One of formal scientific method, which is the statement of the problem, the main skill is in stating absolutely no more than you are positive you know. It is much better to enter a statement "Solve Problem: Why doesn't cycle work?" which sounds dumb but is correct, than it is to enter a statement "Solve Problem: What is wrong with the electrical system?" when*

you don't absolutely know the trouble is in the electrical system. What you should state is "Solve Problem: What is wrong with cycle?" and then state as the first entry of Part Two: "Hypothesis Number One: The trouble is in the electrical system." You think of as many hypotheses as you can, then you design experiments to test them to see which are true and which are false.

This careful approach to the beginning questions keeps you from taking a major wrong turn which might cause you weeks of extra work or can even hang you up completely. Scientific questions often have a surface appearance of dumbness for this reason. They are asked in order to prevent dumb mistakes later on.

Part Three, that part of formal scientific method called experimentation, is sometimes thought of by romantics as all of science itself because that's the only part with much visual surface. They see lots of test tubes and bizarre equipment and people running around making discoveries. They do not see the experiment as part of a larger intellectual process and so they often confuse experiments with demonstrations, which look the same. A man conducting a gee-whiz science show with fifty thousand dollars' worth of Frankenstein equipment is not doing anything scientific if he knows beforehand what the results of his efforts are going to be. A motorcycle mechanic, on the other hand, who honks the horn to see if the battery works is informally conducting a true scientific experiment. He is testing a hypothesis by putting the question to nature. The TV scientist who mutters sadly, "The experiment is a failure; we have failed to achieve what we had hoped for," is suffering mainly from a bad scriptwriter. An experiment is never a failure solely because it fails to achieve predicted results. An experiment is a failure only when it also fails adequately to test the hypothesis in question, when the data it produces don't prove anything one way or another.

Skill at this point consists of using experiments that test only the hypothesis in question, nothing less, nothing more. If the horn honks, and the mechanic concludes that the whole electrical system is working, he is in deep trouble. He has reached an illogical conclusion. The honking horn only tells him that the battery and horn are working. To design an experiment properly he has to think very rigidly in terms of what directly causes what. This you know from the hierarchy. The horn doesn't make the cycle go. Neither does the battery, except in a very indirect way. The point at which the electrical system directly causes the engine to fire is at the spark plugs, and if you don't test here, at the output of the electrical system, you will never really know whether the failure is electrical or not.

To test properly the mechanic removes the plug and lays it against the engine so that the base around the plug is electrically grounded, kicks the starter lever and watches the spark-plug gap for a blue spark. If there isn't any he can conclude one of two things: (a) there is an electrical failure or (b) his experiment is sloppy. If he is experienced he will try it a few more times, checking connections, trying every way he can think of to get that plug to fire. Then, if he can't get it to fire, he finally concludes that (a) is correct, there's an electrical failure, and the experiment is over. He has proved that his hypothesis is correct.

In the final category, conclusions, skill comes in stating no more than the experiment has proved. It hasn't proved that when he fixes the electrical system the motorcycle will start. There may be other things wrong. But he does know that the motorcycle isn't going to run until the electrical system is working and he sets up the next formal question: "Solve problem: What is wrong with the electrical system?"

He then sets up hypotheses for these and tests them. By asking the right questions and choosing the right tests and drawing the right conclusions the mechanic works his way down the echelons of the motorcycle hierarchy until he has found the exact specific cause or causes of the engine failure, and then he changes them so that they no longer cause the failure.

An untrained observer will see only physical labor and often get the idea that physical labor is mainly what the mechanic does. Actually the physical labor is the smallest and easiest part of what the mechanic does. By far the greatest part of his work is careful observation and precise thinking. That is why mechanics sometimes seem so taciturn and withdrawn when performing tests. They don't like it when you talk to them because they are concentrating on mental images, hierarchies, and not really looking at you or the physical motorcycle at all. They are using the experiment as part of a program to expand their hierarchy of knowledge of the faulty motorcycle and compare it to the correct hierarchy in their mind. They are looking at underlying form.[14]

PRACTICAL VALUE OF THEORIES

As the above excerpt makes evident, theories allow us to generalize beyond individual facts or isolated situations. Theories provide a framework that can guide managerial strategy by providing insights into general rules of behavior. When different incidents may be theoretically comparable in some way, the scientific knowledge gained from theory development may have practical value. A good theory allows us to generalize beyond individual facts so that general patterns may be predicted and understood. For this reason it is often said there is nothing so practical as a good theory.

SUMMARY

Prediction and understanding are the two purposes of theory. A theory is a coherent set of general propositions used as principles of explanation of the apparent relationships of certain observed phenomena. Concepts and propositions are the elements of theory at the abstract level. At the empirical level, theory is concerned with variables and testable hypotheses, the empirical counterparts of concepts and propositions. The scientific method is a series of stages utilized to develop and refine theory.

Key Terms

theory

concept

ladder of abstraction

abstract level

empirical level

propositions

scientific method

hypothesis

variable

deductive reasoning

inductive reasoning

Questions

1. What are some theories in your field of business?
2. How do propositions and hypotheses differ?
3. How do concepts differ from variables?
4. Comment on: "There is nothing so practical as a good theory."
5. Go to your library and find another definition of *theory*. How is it similar to this textbook's definition of theory? How is it different?

References

[1] Fred N. Kerlinger, *Behavioral Research: A Conceptual Approach* (New York: Holt, Rinehart and Winston, 1979), 3.

[2] Robert Dubin, *Theory Building* (New York: Free Press, 1969), 9.

[3] H. Kent Baker and John A. Haslem, "The Impact of Investor Socioeconomic Characteristic on Risk and Return Preference," *Journal of Business Research* (October 1974): 469.

[4] Reavis Cox, Wroe Alderson, and Stanley J. Shapiro, *Theory in Marketing* (Chicago: American Marketing Association, 1964), 20.

[5] Kerlinger, *Behavioral Research: A Conceptual Approach* (New York: Holt, Rinehart and Winston, 1979), 42.

[6] Robert Bartels, *Marketing Theory and Metatheory* (Chicago: American Marketing Association, 1970), 6.

[7] R. B. Braithwaite, *Scientific Explanation* (London: Cambridge University Press, 1968), 9.

[8] Clark L. Hull, *A Behavioral System* (New York: Wiley, 1952), 6.

[9] Gerald Zaltman, Christian Pinson, and Reinhart Angelmar, *Metatheory and Consumer Research* (New York: Holt, Rinehart and Winston, 1972), 5.

[10] Adapted from Clark L. Hull, *A Behavioral System* (New York: Wiley, 1952), 1.

[11] Gerald Zaltman and Philip C. Burger, *Marketing Research* (Hinsdale, IL: Dryden Press, 1975), 28.

[12] Stephen Jay Gould, "Evolution as Fact and Theory," *Discover,* May 1981, 35.

[13] Gerald Zaltman, Christian Pinson, and Reinhart Angelmar, *Metatheory and Consumer Research* (New York: Holt, Rinehart and Winston, 1972), 12–13.

[14] Excerpts from pp. 107–111 from *Zen and the Art of Motorcycle Maintenance* by Robert M. Pirsig. Copyright © 1974 by Robert M. Pirsig. By permission of William Morrow & Company.

The Research Process: An Overview

What you will learn in this chapter:

To classify business research as either exploratory research, descriptive research, or causal research.

To list the stages in the business research process.

To identify and briefly discuss the various decision alternatives available to the researcher during each stage of the research process.

To explain the difference between a research project and a research program.

In recent years the Immigration and Naturalization Service has been arresting aliens who are illegally working in the United States. The Immigration Reform and Control Act of 1986 established civil and criminal penalties for employers who knowingly hire unauthorized aliens. Furthermore, the antidiscrimination provision of the law requires employers to ask all job applicants for documents verifying either that they are citizens or that they are authorized to work in the United States. Are employers aware of this law? To avoid being sanctioned, will employers not hire foreign-looking or foreign-sounding U.S. citizens or legal aliens? Has the intent of the law been carried out satisfactorily? Has the law created an unnecessary regulatory burden? In what situations is compliance most likely? The research process can answer questions such as these, but what form should the research take? Should a survey of employers be taken? Should an experiment be designed to determine the cause of discrimination or compliance? Should a survey of illegal aliens be part of the research strategy?[1]

This chapter discusses how managers make decisions about planning research strategies and tactics.

∙

TYPES OF BUSINESS RESEARCH

In a number of situations researchers will know exactly what their problems are and will design studies to test specific hypotheses. For example, a brewery introducing a new dry beer might want to know whether gold or silver packaging would be more effective. In this situation the problem is fully defined, and without much preliminary investigation an experiment may be designed to answer the question. In another circumstance—at the other end of the problem—uncertainty continuum—management may be totally unaware of the nature of a problem. For example, a manufacturer may notice that employee turnover has increased dramatically, but the plant manager may be totally ignorant of the reason for the increase. In such a case exploratory research may be necessary to gain insights into the nature of the problem.

Because of the variety of research activity, it will be helpful to categorize the types of business research. Business research can be classified on the basis of either technique or function. Experiments, surveys, and observational studies are just a few common research *techniques*. Classifying them on the basis of *purpose* or function allows us to understand how the nature of the problem influences the choice of research method. The nature of the problem will determine whether the research is (1) exploratory, (2) descriptive, or (3) causal.

Exploratory Studies

Exploratory studies are conducted to clarify the nature of problems. Management may have discovered general problems, but research is needed to gain better understanding of the dimensions of the problems. Management needs information to help analyze a situation, but conclusive evidence to determine a particular course of action is *not* the purpose of exploratory research. Usually, **exploratory research** is conducted with the expectation that *subsequent* research will be required to provide conclusive evidence. It is a serious mistake to rush into detailed surveys before less expensive and more readily available sources of information have been exhausted.

In an organization considering a program to help employees with child-care needs, for example, exploratory research with a small number of employees who have children might determine that many of them are from families in which both parents work and that these employees have a positive reaction to the possibility of an on-site child-care program. In such a case exploratory research helps to crystallize a problem and identify information needs for future research.

Descriptive Research

The major purpose of **descriptive research,** as the term implies, is to describe characteristics of a population or phenomenon. Descriptive research seeks to determine the answers to *who, what, when, where,* and *how* questions. Every month the Bureau of Labor Statistics conducts descriptive research. Official statistics on unemployment and other characteristics of the labor force are derived from the Current Population Survey, which is conducted monthly.

The Wall Street Journal, for example, conducted a survey aimed at describing its subscribers. The study indicated that its readers are wealthy: Individual subscribers have an average income of $108,000, an average household income of $146,300, and an average net worth of $1 million (median $448,700). The average age is 49, and almost 50 percent have at least studied at the postgraduate level. The survey also indicated that 31 percent of subscribers are chief executive officers, 21 percent are chief operating officers, and 15 percent have served as advisers or consultants to governmental bodies.[2] Such a descriptive study, however, gives no *explanation* for the cause of such findings.

Let us consider an additional example of descriptive research. A university placement service may want to determine if its facilities and services are adequate. A descriptive study might be initiated to determine how many inter-

RESEARCH INSIGHT
Poetry and Research: An Odd Couple?

I keep six honest serving men,
(they taught me all I knew),
their names are What, and Why, and When,
and How, and Where, and Who.[a]
Kipling's words can be helpful to the business researcher.
Those who ask the *what, why, when, how, where,* and
who questions will be started on the right road to solving
their business research problems.

[a]*Just So Stories* by Rudyard Kipling.

---

views each student desires, whether students are able to schedule appointments with certain desirable organizations, and if there are any problems with physical facilities. It is clear that mere description of a situation may provide important information and that in many situations descriptive information is all that is needed to solve business problems, even though the answer to *why* is not given.

Accuracy is of paramount importance in descriptive research. Although errors cannot be completely eliminated, good researchers strive for descriptive precision. Suppose the purpose is to describe the market potential of personal photocopying machines. If the study does not present a precise measurement of the sales volume, it will mislead the managers who are making production scheduling, budgeting, and other decisions based on that study.

Unlike exploratory research, descriptive studies are based on some previous understanding of the nature of the research problem. For example, state societies of certified public accountants (CPAs) conduct annual practice management surveys that ask questions such as "Do you charge clients for travel time at regular rates?" "Do you have a program of continuing education on a regular basis for professional employees?" "Do you pay incentive bonuses to professional staff?" Although the researcher may have a general understanding of the situation, the conclusive evidence, answering questions of fact necessary to determine a course of action, has yet to be collected. Frequently, descriptive research will attempt to determine the extent of differences in the needs, perceptions, attitudes, and characteristics of subgroups.

The purpose of many organizational behavior studies, for example, is to describe the reasons employees give for their explanations of the nature of things. In other words, a **diagnostic analysis** is performed when employees in the various subgroups are asked questions such as "Why do you feel that way?" Although the reasons employees feel a certain way are described, the findings of a descriptive study such as this, sometimes called *diagnostics,* do not provide evidence of a causal nature.

Causal Research

The main goal of **causal research** is identification of cause-and-effect relationships between variables. (Exploratory and descriptive research normally precedes cause-and-effect relationship studies.) In causal studies it is typical to have an expectation of the relationship to be explained, such as predicting the influence of price, packaging, advertising, and the like, on sales. Thus researchers must be knowledgeable about the research subject. Ideally, a manager would like to establish that one event (say a new package) is the means for producing another event (an increase in sales).

Causal research attempts to establish that when we do one thing, another thing will follow. The word *cause* is frequently used in everyday conversation, but from a scientific research perspective, a causal relationship is impossible to prove. Nevertheless, researchers seek certain types of evidence to help them understand and predict relationships.

A typical causal study has management change one variable (e.g., training) and then observe the effect on another variable (e.g., productivity). In this situation there is evidence for establishing causality because it appears that the cause precedes the effect. In other words, having an appropriate causal order of events, or temporal sequence, is one criterion for causality that must be met to measure a relationship. If an organizational behavior theorist wishes to show that attitude change *causes* behavior change, one criterion that must be established is that attitude change *precedes* behavior change.

Further, there is some evidence of *concomitant variation* in that, in our example, increased training and increased productivity appear to be associated. Concomitant variation is the occurrence of two phenomena or events that vary together. When the criterion of concomitant variation is not met—that is, when there is no association between variables—reason suggests that no causal relationship exists. If two events vary together, one *may* be the cause. However, this by itself is not sufficient evidence for causality because the two events may have a common cause, that is, both may be influenced by a third variable.

For instance, one morning at Atlantic City's beach a large number of ice cream cones are sold and that afternoon there is a large number of drownings. Most of us would not conclude that eating ice cream cones causes drownings. More likely, the large number of people at the beach probably influenced both ice cream cone sales and drownings. It may be that the "effect" was produced in other ways. Because there is concomitant variation and a proper time sequence between the occurrence of Event A and Event B, causation is not certain. There may be plausible alternative explanations for an observed relationship.[3] A plurality of causes is possible.

Consider a presidential candidate who reduces advertising expenditures near the end of the primary campaign and wins many more delegates in the remaining primaries. To infer causality—that reducing advertising increases the number of delegates—might be inappropriate because the *presumed* cause of the increase may not be the real cause. It is likely that, near the end of a race, marginal candidates withdraw. Thus the real cause may be unrelated to advertising.

In these examples the third variable that is the source of the spurious association is a very salient factor readily identified as the more likely influence on change. However, within the complex environment in which managers operate, it is difficult to identify alternative or complex causal factors.

In summary, research with the purpose of inferring causality should:

1. Establish the appropriate causal order or sequence of events.
2. Measure the concomitant variation between the presumed cause and the presumed effect.
3. Recognize the presence or absence of alternative plausible explanations or causal factors.[4]

Even when these three criteria for causation are present, the researcher can never be certain that the causal explanation is adequate.

Most basic scientific studies in business (e.g., the development of organizational behavior theory) ultimately seek to identify cause-and-effect relationships. When one thinks of science, one often associates it with experiments. Thus to predict a relationship between, say, price and perceived quality of a product, causal studies often create statistical experimental controls to establish "contrast groups." A number of business experiments are conducted by both theory developers and pragmatic businesspeople. (More will be said about experiments and causal research in Chapter 10.)

INFLUENCE OF UNCERTAINTY ON TYPE OF RESEARCH

The uncertainty of the research problem is related to the type of research project. Exhibit 3.1 illustrates that exploratory research is conducted during the early stages of decision making when management is uncertain about the na-

EXHIBIT   3.1

Types of Business Research

	Exploratory Research	Descriptive Research	Causal Research
Degree of Problem Definition	*Unaware of problem*	*Aware of problem*	*Problem clearly defined*
Possible Situation	"Absenteeism is increasing and we don't know why."	"What kind of people favor trade protectionism?"	"Which of two training programs is more effective?"
	"Would people be interested in our new-product idea?"	"Did last year's product recall have an impact on our company's stock price?"	"Can I predict the value of energy stocks if I know the current dividends and growth rates of dividends?"
	"What task conditions influence the leadership process in our organization?"	"Has the average merger rate for savings and loans increased in the past decade?"	"Do buyers prefer our product in a new package?"

Note: The degree of uncertainty about the research problem determines the research methodology.

ture of the problem. When management is aware of the problem but not completely knowledgeable about the situation, descriptive research is usually conducted. Causal studies require sharply defined problems.

STAGES IN THE RESEARCH PROCESS

As previously noted, business research can take many forms, but systematic inquiry is a common thread. Systematic inquiry requires careful planning in an orderly investigation. Business research, like other forms of scientific inquiry, is a sequence of highly interrelated activities. The stages in the research process overlap continuously, and it is somewhat of an oversimplification to state that every research project follows a neat and ordered sequence of activities. Nevertheless, business research often follows a generalized pattern. The stages are: (1) defining the problem, (2) planning a research design, (3) planning a sample, (4) collecting data, (5) analyzing the data, and (6) formulating the conclusions and preparing the report. These six stages are portrayed in Exhibit 3.2 as a cyclical process, as a circular-flow concept, because conclusions from research studies usually generate new ideas and problems that need to be further investigated.

In practice, the stages overlap chronologically and are functionally interrelated. Sometimes the later stages are completed before the earlier ones. The terms *forward* and *backward linkage* are associated with the interrelatedness of the various stages.[5] The term **forward linkage** implies that the earlier stages of research will influence the design of the later stages. Thus the objectives of

E X H I B I T   3 . 2

**Phases of the
Research Process**

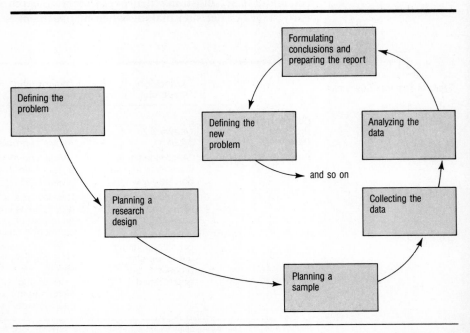

the research outlined in the problem definition will have an impact on the selection of the sample and the way in which the data will be collected. The decision concerning who will be sampled will affect the wording of questionnaire items. For example, if the research concentrates on respondents who have low educational levels, the wording of the questionnaire will be simpler than the language used when the respondents are college graduates. The notion of **backward linkage** implies that the later steps have an influence on the earlier stages in the research process. If it is known that the data will be analyzed by computer, then computer coding requirements are included in the questionnaire design. Perhaps the most important backward linkage is the knowledge that the executive who will read the research report needs certain information. The professional researcher anticipates executives' need for information in the planning process and considers this need during the analysis and tabulation stages.

DECISION ALTERNATIVES IN THE RESEARCH PROCESS

A number of alternatives are available to the researcher during each of the six stages of the research process. The research process can be compared with a guide or a map.[6] On a map some paths are better charted than others. Some are difficult to travel, and some are more interesting and scenic than others. Rewarding experiences may be gained during the journey. It is important to remember there is no right path or best path for all journeys. The road one takes depends on where one wants to go and the resources (money, time, manpower, and so on) one has available for the trip. The map analogy is useful for the business researcher because in each stage of the research process there are several paths to follow. In some instances the quickest path will be the appropriate means of research because of certain time constraints. In other circumstances when money and human resources are plentiful, the path the research takes may be quite different. Exploration of the various paths of business research decisions is our primary purpose.

Each of the six stages in the research process is briefly described below.[7] Exhibit 3.3 shows the decisions that researchers must make in each stage of the research process. Discussion of the research process begins with problem discovery and definition because most research projects, albeit at an earlier moment in time, are initiated because of some uncertainty about some aspect of the firm or its environment.

PROBLEM DISCOVERY AND DEFINITION

In Exhibit 3.3 the research process begins with problem discovery, and identifying the problem is the first step toward its solution. The word *problem,* in general usage, suggests something has gone wrong. Unfortunately, the term *problem* does not connote a business opportunity, such as expanding operations into a foreign country. Nor does it connote the need for evaluation of an existing program, such as employee satisfaction with professional development programs. Actually, the research task may be to clarify a problem, to evaluate a program, or to define an opportunity, and *problem discovery and definition*

E X H I B I T   3 . 3   **Flowchart of the Research Process**

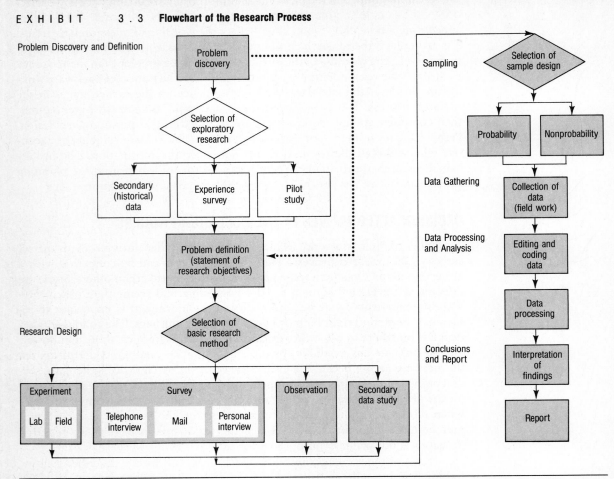

Note: Diamond-shaped boxes indicate a stage of the research design process where a choice of one or more techniques must be made. A dotted line indicates an alternative path when exploratory research is not used.

will be used in this broader context. It should be noted that the initial stage is problem *discovery,* rather than *definition.* (The researcher may not have a clear-cut statement of the problem at the outset of the research process.) Often, only symptoms are apparent to begin with. Profits may be declining, but management may not know the exact nature of the problem. Thus the problem statement is often made only in general terms. What is to be investigated is not yet specifically identified.

It was Albert Einstein who noted that "the formulation of a problem is often more essential than its solution."[8] This is good advice for managers. Too often managers concentrate on finding the right answer rather than asking the right question. Many do not realize that defining a problem may be more difficult than solving it. In business research, if the data are collected before the nature of the business problem is carefully thought out, the data probably will not help solve the problem.

A Problem Well Defined

The adage "a problem well defined is a problem half solved" is worth remembering. This adage emphasizes that an orderly definition of the research problem gives a sense of direction to the investigation. Careful attention to problem definition allows the researcher to set the proper research objectives. If the purpose of the research is clear, the chances of collecting the necessary and relevant information—without collecting surplus information—will be much greater.

To be efficient, business research must have clear objectives and definite designs. Unfortunately, in many cases little or no planning goes into the formulation of a research problem. Consider the case of the Ha-Psu-Shu-Tse (a Pawnee Indian word for red corn) brand of Indian fried bread mix. The owner of the company, Mr. Ha-Psu-Shu-Tse, thought his product, one of the few American Indian food products available in the United States, wasn't selling because it wasn't highly advertised. He wanted a management-consulting group to conduct some research concerning advertising themes. However, the management consultants pointed out to the Ha-Psu-Shu-Tse family that the brand (family) name on the bread might be a foremost source of concern. It was suggested that investigating the brand image and consumer behavior research might be the starting point, rather than advertising copy research. Family management agreed. (It should be emphasized that we are now using "problem" to refer to the managerial problem, which may be a lack of knowledge about consumers or advertising effectiveness and the lack of needed information.) Frequently business researchers will not be involved until line management discovers that information is needed about a particular aspect of the decision at hand. Even at this point the exact nature of the problem may not be well defined. Once a problem area has been discovered, the researcher can begin the process of precisely defining it.

Although the **problem definition** stage of the research process is probably the most important stage, it is frequently a neglected area of research. Too often it is forgotten that the best place to begin a research project is at the end. Knowing what is to be accomplished determines the research process. A problem definition error or omission is likely to be a costly mistake that cannot be corrected in later stages of the process. (Chapter 4 discusses problem definition in greater detail.)

Exploratory Research

Many research projects with clearly defined research problems, such as an annual survey of industry compensation, do not require exploratory research. There are, however, many research studies that would have inadequate problem definitions if exploratory research were not conducted.

Exploratory research is usually conducted during the initial stage of the research process. The preliminary activities undertaken to refine the problem into a researchable one need not be formal or precise. The purpose of the exploratory research process is a progressive narrowing of the scope of the research topic and a transformation of the discovered problems into defined ones, incorporating specific research objectives. By analyzing any existing studies on the subject, by talking with knowledgeable individuals, and by informally investigating the situation, the researchers can progressively sharpen the concepts. After such exploration the researchers should know exactly what data to collect during the formal project and how the project will be conducted. Exhibit 3.3 indicates that a decision must be made regarding the selection of one or more exploratory research techniques.

The business researcher has three basic techniques for discovering insights and gaining a clearer idea of the problem: secondary data, experience surveys, and pilot studies.

Secondary Data

Secondary, or historical, **data** are data previously collected and assembled for some project other than the one at hand. **Primary data** are data gathered and assembled specifically for the project at hand. Secondary information can often be found inside the company or in the library, or it can be purchased from firms that specialize in providing information, such as economic forecasts, that is useful to organizations. The researcher who assembles data from the *Census of Population* or the *Survey of Current Business* is using secondary sources.

A literature research study or a literature survey of published articles and books discussing theories and past empirical studies about a topic is almost universal in academic research projects. It is also common in many applied research studies. Students who have written term papers should be familiar with the process of checking card catalogues, indexes to published literature, and other library resources to establish a bibliography portraying past research. Suppose, for example, a bank is interested in determining the best site for an electronic funds transfer system machine. A logical first step would be to investigate the factors that bankers in other parts of the country consider important. By reading articles in banking journals, the bank management might quickly discover that the best locations are residential areas where people are young, highly educated, and earning higher-than-average incomes. These data might lead the bank to investigate census information to determine where in the city such people live. Reviewing and building upon the work already compiled by others is an economical starting point for most research.

Secondary data can almost always be gathered faster and at a lower cost than primary data. However, secondary data may be outdated or may not exactly meet the needs of the researcher because they were collected for another purpose. Nevertheless, secondary sources often prove to be of great value in exploratory research. Investigating such sources has saved many a researcher from "reinventing the wheel" in primary data collection.

Experience Surveys

People who are knowledgeable about the area to be investigated are often willing to share their experience with others (competitors excluded, of course). Experience surveys consist of talking to people inside and outside the company to obtain insights into the relationships between variables. For example, an organization considering the use of polygraph tests to evaluate the honesty of employees may discuss the general nature of polygraphs in the work environment with managers in other organizations who have already implemented lie detector programs. When the competitive environment is the subject of exploratory research, members of the company's sales force may be a valuable source of information.

The purpose of these conversations in an experience survey is to exhaust the information available from relatively inexpensive sources before gathering expensive primary data. Thus, while the interviews with knowledgeable individuals may reveal nothing conclusive, they may help to define the problem more formally.

Pilot Studies

Pilot studies collect data from the ultimate subject of the research project to serve as a guide for the larger study.[9] When the term *pilot study* is used in the context of exploratory research, the data collection methods are informal and the findings may lack precision because rigorous standards are relaxed. For instance, a downtown association concerned with revitalization of the central business district (CBD) conducted a very flexible survey with questions that were open ended. The interviewers were given considerable latitude to identify executives' (the ultimate subjects) opinions about future requirements in the downtown area. The results of this survey were used to suggest possible topics for formal investigation.

Having researchers or managers experience what employees, consumers, or the general public experience is inexpensive and valuable. Without indicating their real positions with the company, researchers/managers may wait on customers, ride in repair trucks, and answer telephones. For example, the chairman of Avis occasionally gets in line with airport customers who are waiting for rental cars, or may work behind the counter to get customer reactions. This form of pilot study may yield a true comprehension of the situation to be investigated.

The focus group interview is a more elaborate exploratory pilot study (see Exhibit 3.4). Increasingly popular in recent years, the focus group is a group dynamics session with approximately eight people, loosely structured and based on the assumption that individuals are more willing to share their ideas as they share in the ideas of others. Information obtained in these studies is qualitative and serves as a basis for a subsequent quantitative study.

Three basic types of exploratory research have been identified, but there is no standard design for such research. Since the purpose of exploratory research is to gain insights and to discover new ideas, researchers may use considerable creativity and flexibility. It is common to collect data with several exploratory techniques. Exhausting these sources is generally worth the effort because the expense is relatively low. Further, insights into how and how not to conduct research may be gained from activities during the problem definition stage. If the conclusions made during this stage suggest business opportunities,

EXHIBIT   3 . 4

**A Typical Focus
Group Session**

Source: Courtesy of C/J Research, Inc., Arlington Heights, Illinois.

the researcher is in a position to begin planning a formal quantitative research project.

Statement of Research Objectives

A decision must initially be made as to precisely what should be researched. After identifying and clarifying the problem, with or without exploratory research, the researchers should make a formal statement of the problem and the research objectives. This delineates the type of information that should be collected and provides a framework for the scope of the study or **research project.**

The answers to questions such as "To what extent did the new compensation program achieve its objectives?" are a typical research objective. In this sense the statement of the problem is a research question.

The best expression of a research objective is a well-formed, testable research hypothesis, and a *hypothesis* is a statement that can be refuted or supported by empirical data. For example, an exploratory study might lead us to the hypothesis that male-dominated unions discriminate against women who want to enter the trades. In basic research, theory is the guide that helps generate hypotheses. Once the hypothesis has been developed, the researchers are ready to select a research design.

PLANNING THE RESEARCH DESIGN

After the researcher has formulated the research problem, the research design must be developed. A **research design** is a master plan specifying the methods and procedures for collecting and analyzing the needed information. It is a framework of the research plan of action. The objectives of the study determined during the early stages of the research are included in the design to ensure that the information collected is appropriate for solving the problem. The research investigator must also determine the sources of information, the design technique (survey or experiment, for example), the sampling methodology, and the schedule and cost of the research.

Selecting the Appropriate Research Design

Again, the researcher must make a decision. Exhibit 3.3 indicates there are four basic design techniques for descriptive and causal research: survey techniques, experiments, secondary data, and observation. The objectives of the study, the available data sources, the urgency of the decision, and the cost of obtaining the data will determine which design technique is chosen. The managerial aspects of selecting the research design will be considered later.

Surveys

The most common method of generating primary data is through surveys. Most people have seen the results of political surveys by Gallup or Harris, and some have been respondents (members of a sample that supplies answers) to business research questionnaires. A survey is a research technique in which information is gathered from a sample of people by use of a questionnaire. The task of writing a questionnaire, determining the list of questions, and designing the exact format of the printed or written questionnaire is an essential aspect of the development of a survey research design.

Research investigators may choose to contact respondents by telephone, mail, or in person. An advertiser who spends $800,000 for 30 seconds of commercial time during the Super Bowl may telephone people to quickly gather information concerning their response to the advertising. Your congressman may send you a mail questionnaire to learn how he or she should vote on issues. It is an inexpensive method of data collection for a congressman or any person. A forklift truck manufacturer, trying to determine why sales in the wholesale grocery industry are low, might choose a mail questionnaire because the appropriate executives are hard to reach by telephone. A computer manufacturer, wishing to conduct an organizational survey among employees, might determine the need for a versatile survey method whereby an interviewer can ask a variety of personal questions in a flexible format. Although personal interviews are expensive, they are valuable because investigators can utilize visual aids and supplement the interview with personal observations. Each of these survey methods has advantages and disadvantages. The researcher's task is to find the most appropriate way to collect the information that is needed.

Experiments

Business experiments hold the greatest potential for establishing cause-and-effect relationships. The use of experimentation allows investigation of changes in one variable, such as productivity, while manipulating one or two other variables, perhaps social rewards or monetary rewards, under controlled conditions. Ideally, experimental control provides a basis for isolating causal factors because outside (or exogenous) influences do not come into play.

Test marketing is a frequent form of business experimentation. The example of Chelsea, Anheuser-Busch's "not-so-soft soft drink," illustrates the usefulness of experiments. Anheuser-Busch first introduced Chelsea as a socially acceptable alternative to beer for adults who didn't want to get intoxicated. As a result of the natural flavorings used, Chelsea contained a slight amount of alcohol (less than 0.5 percent)—well within the FDA guidelines for classification as a soft drink. During an experiment to test-market the "not-so-soft soft drink," and the not-so-sweet concept, a Virginia nurses' association and some religious groups strongly criticized the company and the new product. These critics suggested that Anheuser-Busch had introduced a product that might encourage children to become beer drinkers. They contended that Chelsea was packaged like beer and looked, foamed, and poured like beer. The criticism led the brewery to suspend production, advertising, and promotion of the drink. It later reintroduced the product as a soft drink, with only "a trace of alcohol" and with not-so-sweet and stylish attributes, as a "natural alternative" to soft drinks. This experiment pointed out to Anheuser-Busch that the variable—alcohol level—caused an inadvertent miscommunication: Consumers confused the original Chelsea with beer.

An experiment controls conditions so that one or more variables can be manipulated in order to test a hypothesis. In the Chelsea situation there was a trial of a proposed course of action and observation of the effect on sales. This case illustrates that extraneous variables are difficult to control and can influence results. It also portrays a field experiment where a deliberate modification of marketing strategy was made. Other experiments—laboratory experiments—are deliberate modifications of an environment created for the research itself. Laboratory experiments are often used in basic research to test theories. The following laboratory experiment concerned a test of equity theory. Student subjects, hired and paid for the task of scoring research questionnaires, were separated into two groups. One group was led to believe that it was less qualified than the other workers because it lacked previous experience in coding questionnaires. The group was also told that even though it was less qualified, its pay would be the same as the pay for experienced workers. Thus the students believed themselves to be overpaid. The other group did not receive any messages about the others' experience and thus was led to believe that the pay was equitable. Both groups coded the questionnaires for two hours. The "equitably" paid group was less productive than the group that believed it was overpaid.[10]

Secondary Data

As in exploratory research, descriptive and causal studies also use previously collected data. Although the terms *secondary* and *historical* are interchangeable, *secondary data* will be used here. An example of a secondary data study is the development of a mathematical model to predict sales on the basis of past sales or on the basis of a correlation with related variables (see Exhibit 3.5). Manufacturers of home computers may find that sales are highly correlated with

EXHIBIT   3 . 5

**Financial Information from a
Secondary Data Source**

Source: Courtesy Standard & Poor's Corporation.

discretionary personal income. To predict future market potential, data concerning projections of disposable personal income may be acquired from the
government or from a university. This information can be mathematically manipulated to forecast sales. Formal secondary data studies have benefits and
limitations similar to exploratory studies that use secondary data. Also, the
analysis of secondary data studies generally requires a greater quantitative
sophistication.

Observation Techniques

In many situations the objective of the research project is merely to record what can be observed—for example, the number of automobiles that pass a site for a proposed gasoline station. This can be mechanically recorded or observed by any person. The amount of time it takes an employee to perform a task may be observed in a time-and-motion study. Research personnel, known as "mystery shoppers," may act as customers to observe the actions of sales personnel or do "comparative shopping" to learn the prices of competitive outlets.

The main advantage of the observation technique is that it records behavior without relying on reports from respondents. Observational methods are often nonreactive because data are collected unobtrusively and passively without a respondent's direct participation. For instance, the A. C. Nielsen Company's people meter is a machine attached to television sets to record the actual programs being watched by various members of the household. This eliminates the possible bias of respondents stating that they watched the president's State of the Union address rather than the situation comedy that was on another channel.

Observation is more complex than mere "nose counting," and the task is more difficult to administer than the inexperienced researcher would imagine. Several things of interest simply cannot be observed. Attitudes, opinions, motivations, and other intangible states of mind cannot be recorded by using the observation method.

Evaluating Research Designs

Researchers argue that there is no one best research design for all situations. There are no hard-and-fast rules for good business research. This does not mean that the researcher, when faced with a problem, is also faced with chaos and confusion. It means that the researcher has many alternative methods for solving the problem. An eminent behavioral researcher has stated this concept quite eloquently:

> There is never a single, standard, correct method of carrying out a piece of research. Do not wait to start your research until you find out the proper approach, because there are many ways to tackle a problem—some good, some bad, but probably several good ways. There is no single perfect design. A research method for a given problem is not like the solution to a problem in algebra. It is more like a recipe for beef Stroganoff; there is no one best recipe.[11]

Knowing how to select the most appropriate research design develops with experience. Inexperienced researchers often jump to the conclusion that the survey method is the best design, because they are most familiar with this method. When Chicago's Museum of Science and Industry wanted to determine the relative popularity of its exhibits, it could have conducted a survey. Instead, a creative researcher, familiar with other research designs, suggested a far less expensive alternative—an unobtrusive observation technique. It was suggested that the museum merely keep track of the frequency with which the floor tiles in front of the various exhibits had to be replaced, indicating where the heaviest traffic occurred. When this was done, it was found that the chick-hatching exhibit was most popular.[12] This method provided the same results as a survey, but at a much lower cost.

Once an appropriate design has been determined, the researcher moves on to the next stage—planning the sample to be used.

SAMPLING

Although the sampling plan is included in the research design, the actual sampling is a separate stage of the research process. However, for convenience, the sample planning and sample generation processes are treated together in this section.

If you take your first bite of a steak and conclude it needs salt, you have just conducted a sample. Sampling involves any procedure that uses a small number of items or that uses parts of the population to make a conclusion regarding the whole population. In other words, a sample is a subset from a larger population. If certain statistical procedures are followed, it is unnecessary to select every item in a population because the results of a good sample should have the same characteristics as the population as a whole. Of course, when errors are made, samples do not give reliable estimates of the population. A famous example of error due to sample selection is the 1936 *Literary Digest* fiasco. The magazine conducted a survey and predicted that Alf Landon would win over Franklin D. Roosevelt by a landslide. History tells us there was an error due to sample selection. The postmortems showed that *Literary Digest* had sampled telephone and magazine subscribers. In 1936 these people were not a representative cross section of voters because a disproportionate number of them were Republicans. (See Exhibit 3.6.)

This famous example teaches that the first sampling question that must be asked is "Who is to be sampled?" The answer to this primary question requires the identification of a target population. Defining the population and determining the sampling units may not be obvious. For example, for answers to image questions a savings and loan company may survey people who already have accounts. The selected sampling units will not represent potential customers who do not have accounts with the savings and loan. Specifying the target population is a crucial aspect of the sampling plan.

The next sampling issue concerns sample size. How big should the sample be? Although management may wish to examine every potential buyer of a product, every employee, or every stock traded on an exchange, it is unnecessary (as well as unrealistic) to do so. Typically, large samples are more precise than small samples, but if proper *probability sampling* is implemented, a small proportion of the total population will give a reliable measure of the whole. (A later discussion will explain how large a sample must be to be a truly representative universe or population.)

The final sampling decision requires the researcher to choose how the sampling units are to be selected. Students who have taken their first statistics course generally are familiar with simple random sampling, where every unit in

EXHIBIT   3 . 6

**Surveys Should Be
Representative**

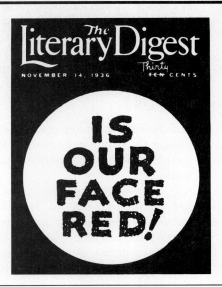

Source: The Literary Digest.

the population has an equal and known chance of being selected. However, this is only one type of sampling. For example, a cluster sampling procedure may be selected because it may reduce costs and make the data gathering procedures more efficient. If members of the population are found in close geographic clusters, a sampling procedure that selects area clusters rather than individual units in the population will reduce costs. In other words, rather than selecting 1,000 individuals throughout the United States, it may be more economical to select 25 counties and then sample within those counties. This substantially reduces travel, hiring, and training costs. In determining the appropriate sample plan, the researcher will have to select the most appropriate sampling procedure to meet established study objectives.

There are two basic sampling techniques: probability and nonprobability sampling. A *probability sample* is defined as a sample in which every member of the population has a known, nonzero probability of selection. If sample units are selected on the basis of personal judgment (e.g., a test plant is selected because it appears to be typical), the sample method is a *nonprobability sample*. In actuality, the sampling decision is not a simple choice between two methods. Simple random samples, stratified samples, quota samples, cluster samples, and judgmental samples are some of the many types of samples that may be drawn. (A full discussion of these techniques must be postponed to Chapter 14.)

DATA COLLECTION

Once the research design (including the sampling plan) has been formalized, the process of gathering information from respondents may begin. Obviously, because there are many research techniques, there are many methods of data collection. When the survey method is utilized, some form of direct participation by the respondent is necessary during the process. The respondent may participate by filling out a questionnaire or by interacting with an interviewer. If an unobtrusive method of data collection is utilized, the subjects do not actively participate. For instance, a simple count of motorists driving past a proposed franchising location is one kind of data collection. However the data are collected, it is important to minimize errors in the data collection process. For example, it is important that the data collection be consistent in all geographic areas. If an interviewer phrases questions incorrectly or records a respondent's statements inaccurately (not verbatim), this will cause major data collection errors. Often there are two phases to the process of collecting data: pretesting and the main study. A *pretesting phase,* using a small subsample, may determine whether the data collection plan for the main study is an appropriate procedure. Thus a small-scale pretest study provides an advance opportunity for the investigator to check the data collection form to minimize errors due to improper design elements, such as question wording or sequence. Additional benefits are discovery of confusing interviewing instructions, learning if the questionnaire is too long or too short, and uncovering other such field errors. Tabulation of data from the pretests provides the researcher with a format of the knowledge that may be gained from the actual study. If the tabulation of the data and statistical tests do not answer the researcher's questions, this may lead the investigator to redesign the study.

DATA PROCESSING AND DATA ANALYSIS

Editing and Coding

Once the field work has been completed, the data must be converted into a format that will answer the decision maker's questions. Data processing generally begins with the editing and coding of the data. Editing involves checking the data collection forms for omissions, legibility, and consistency in classification. The editing process corrects problems like interviewer errors (e.g., an answer recorded on the wrong portion of a questionnaire) before the data are transferred to a computer or readied for tabulation.

Before data can be tabulated, meaningful categories and character symbols must be established for groups of responses. The rules for interpreting, categorizing, recording, and transferring the data to the data storage media are called *codes.*[13] This coding process facilitates computer or hand tabulation. Of course, if computer analysis is to be utilized, the data are entered into the computer and verified. Computer-assisted (on-line) interviewing illustrates the impact of technological change on the research process. Telephone interviewers are seated at a computer terminal. Survey questions are printed out on the screen. The interviewer asks the questions and then types the respondents' answers on the keyboard. Thus answers are collected and processed into the computer at the same time, eliminating intermediate steps where errors could creep in.

Analysis

Analysis is the application of logic to understand and interpret the data that have been collected about a subject. In simple description, analysis may involve determining consistent patterns and summarizing the appropriate details revealed in the investigation. The appropriate analytical technique for data analysis will be determined by management's information requirements, the characteristics of the research design, and the nature of the data collected. Statistical analysis may range from portraying a simple frequency distribution to very complex multivariate analysis, such as multiple regression. Later chapters will discuss statistical analysis under three general categories: univariate analysis, bivariate analysis, and multivariate analysis.

CONCLUSIONS AND REPORT PREPARATION

As mentioned earlier, most business research is applied research. Hence the purpose of the research is to make a business decision. An important but often overlooked aspect of the researcher's job is to look at the analysis of the collected information and ask, "What does this mean to management?" The final stage in the research process is to interpret the information and make conclusions for managerial decisions.

The research report should communicate the research findings effectively. All too often the report is a complicated statement of the study's technical aspects and sophisticated research methods. Often, management is not interested in detailed reporting of the research design and statistical findings but wishes only a summary of the findings. It cannot be overemphasized that if the findings of the research remain unread on the manager's desk, the study is useless. Research is only as good as the applications made of it. Business researchers must communicate their findings to a managerial audience. The manager's information needs will determine how much detail is provided in the written report. The written report serves another purpose: It is a historical document that will be a source of record for later usage, such as repeating the survey or providing a basis for building upon the survey findings.

Now that we have outlined the research process, it should be noted that the logic of the order of this textbook follows the flowchart of the research process presented in Exhibit 3.3. Readers should keep this flowchart in mind as they read future chapters.

RESEARCH PROJECT VERSUS RESEARCH PROGRAM

Discussion of the business research process began with the assumption that the research investigator wished to gather information to achieve a specific objective. We have emphasized the researcher's need to select specific techniques for solving one-dimensional problems, such as identifying the characteristics of productive employees, selecting the best packaging design, or forecasting bond values.

However, when we think about a firm's strategic activity in a given period of time, perhaps a year, we realize that business research is not a one-shot approach. Research is a continuous process. We may conduct an exploratory research study and then conduct a survey. Or it is very likely that a specific research project will be conducted for each aspect of a program. If a new product is being developed, the different types of research might include (1) market potential studies, to identify the size and characteristics of the market; (2) product usage testing, where consumers' reactions to using prototype products will be recorded; and (3) brand-name and packaging research to determine the product's symbolic connotations. Ultimately, the new product may (4) go into a test market.

Because research is a continuous process, management should view research at a strategic planning level. **Research program** strategy refers to a firm's overall plan to utilize business research. This program is a planning activity that places each research project into the company's strategic plan.

ETHICAL DECISIONS IN BUSINESS RESEARCH

Conducting business research often requires that the researcher follow a certain code of ethics. For example, it is generally assumed that the researcher will be objective and will protect both the subjects' and client's right to confidentiality. These issues are dealt with in depth in Chapter 24. The reader may periodically wish to refer to Chapter 24 when studying how researchers determine the appropriate research designs.

SUMMARY

There are three major types of business research projects. Which one is to be used is decided by the clarity with which the research problem is defined. Exploratory research is chosen when management knows only the general problem. It is not conducted to provide conclusive evidence but to clarify problems. Descriptive research is conducted when there is some understanding of the nature of the problem (it is used to provide an accurate description of the problem). Causal research identifies cause-and-effect relationships when the research problem has been narrowly defined.

The research process proceeds in a series of six interrelated phases. The first is problem definition, which may include exploratory research using secondary data, experience surveys, or pilot studies. Once the problem is defined, the researcher selects a research design. The major designs are survey techniques, experiments, secondary data analysis, and observation. Creative selection of the research design can minimize the cost of obtaining reliable results. After the design has been selected, a sampling plan is chosen, using either a probability or a nonprobability sample, or a combination of the two.

The design is put into action in the data collection phase. This phase may involve a small pretest before the main study is undertaken. In the analysis stage the data are edited and coded, then processed, usually by computer. The results are interpreted in light of the decisions that management must make. Finally, the analysis is presented to decision makers in a written or oral report.

This last step is crucial because an excellent project will not lead to proper action if the results are poorly communicated.

Quite often research projects are conducted together as parts of a research program. Such programs can involve successive projects that incorporate earlier findings into later research designs.

A major problem facing students of business research is that each stage in the research process is difficult to consider separately. However, without concentrated emphasis on each stage of the total research process, it is difficult to understand the individual stages in the research process. Thus learning business research is like walking a tightrope between too broad an outlook and too narrow a focus.

Key Terms

exploratory research	problem definition
descriptive research	secondary data
diagnostic analysis	primary data
causal research	pilot studies
forward linkages	research project
backward linkages	research design

Questions

1. For each situation below, decide whether the research should be exploratory, descriptive, or causal:
   a. Establishing the functional relationship between advertising and sales.
   b. Investigating reactions to the idea of a new method of defense budgeting.
   c. Identifying target-market demographics for a shopping center.
   d. Estimating stock prices for IBM two years in the future.
   e. Learning how many organizations are actively involved in just-in-time production.
   f. Learning the extent of job satisfaction in a company.
2. Describe a research situation that allows one to infer causality.
3. A researcher is interested in knowing the answer to a *why* question, but does not know what sort of answer will be satisfying. Is this exploratory, descriptive, or causal research? Explain.
4. Do the stages in the research process follow the scientific method?
5. In the research process, why is the problem-definition stage probably the most important stage?
6. The Department of the Treasury is conducting technological research into creation of a feasible, plastic-like substance upon which currency notes can be printed. Currency printed on this substance would increase the circulation life of low-value currency notes and enhance their utility in vending equipment. What type of research should be conducted?
7. What research design seems appropriate for each of the following studies?

a. The manufacturer and marketer of flight simulators and other pilot-training equipment wishes to forecast sales volume for the next five years.

b. A local chapter of the American Lung Association wishes to identify the demographic characteristics of individuals who donate more than $100 per year.

c. A manager notices the number of grievances is increasing. The manager wishes to investigate this occurrence.

d. A financial analyst wishes to investigate whether load or no-load mutual funds have a higher yield.

e. A corporation wishes to evaluate the quality of its college-recruiting program.

f. An academic researcher wishes to investigate if the United States is losing its competitive edge in world trade.

g. A food company researcher is interested in knowing what types of food are carried in brown-bag lunches to learn if the company can capitalize on this phenomenon.

8. Why is a knowledge of forward and backward linkages in the research process important?

9. Give an example of a program research project in your field of interest.

10. In your field of interest, which research design (surveys, observation studies, experiments, or secondary-data studies) is the most popular?

References

[1] "Study Hints at Job Discrimination Against Foreign-Looking People," *New York Times,* Nov. 20, 1988, 18Y.

[2] Jack Honomichl, "Tapping Its Readers," *Advertising Age,* June 19, 1989, 50.

[3] Claire Selltiz, Lawrence S. Wrightsman, and Stuart W. Cook, *Research Methods in Social Relations* (New York: Holt, Rinehart and Winston, 1976), 114–115.

[4] Paul E. Green, Donald S. Tull, and Gerald Albaum, *Research for Marketing Decisions* (Englewood Cliffs, NJ: Prentice-Hall, 1988), 105–110.

[5] Donald P. Warwick and Charles A. Lininger, *The Sample Survey: Theory and Practice* (New York: McGraw-Hill, 1975), 20–21.

[6] Philip J. Runkel and Joseph E. McGrath, *Research on Human Behavior: A Systematic Guide to Method* (New York: Holt, Rinehart and Winston, 1972), 2.

[7] Each topic is discussed in greater depth in later chapters.

[8] A. Einstein and L. Infeld, *The Evolution of Physics* (New York: Simon & Schuster, 1942), 95.

[9] Pretests of full-blown surveys and experiments are also called pilot studies. These smaller versions of the formal studies generally are utilized for refining techniques rather than for problem definition and clarification of the hypothesis.

[10] R. D. Middlemist and R. B. Peterson, "Test of Equity Theory by Controlling for Comparison Co-Workers' Efforts," *Organizational Behavior and Human Performance* 15 (1976): 335–354; and R. Dennis Middlemist and Michael A. Hitt, *Organizational Behavior: Applied Concepts* (Chicago: Science Research Associates, 1981), 33.

[11] Julian Simon, *Basic Research Methods in Social Science: The Art of Empirical Investigation* (New York: Random House, 1969), 4.

[12] Stewart H. Britt, "Marketing Research: Why It Works and Why It Doesn't Work," Chicago Chapter, American Marketing Association, Conference on Marketing Research, 1972.

[13] John A. Sonquist and William C. Dunkelberg, *Survey and Opinion Research: Procedures for Processing and Analysis* (Englewood Cliffs, NJ: Prentice-Hall, 1977), 9.

Beginning Stages of the Research Process

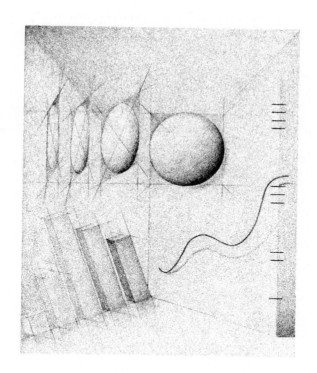

Problem Definition and the Research Proposal

Once upon a time a Sea Horse gathered up his seven pieces of eight and cantered out to find his fortune. Before he had traveled very far he met an Eel, who said,

"Psst. Hey, bud. Where 'ya goin'?"

"I'm going out to find my fortune," replied the Sea Horse, proudly.

"You're in luck," said the Eel. "For four pieces of eight you can have this speedy flipper, and then you'll be able to get there a lot faster."

"Gee, that's swell," said the Sea Horse, and paid the money and put on the flipper and slithered off at twice the speed. Soon he came upon a Sponge, who said,

"Psst. Hey, bud. Where 'ya goin'?"

"I'm going out to find my fortune," replied the Sea Horse.

"You're in luck," said the Sponge. "For a small fee I will let you have this jet-propelled scooter so that you will be able to travel a lot faster."

So the Sea Horse bought the scooter with his remaining money and went zooming through the sea five times as fast. Soon he came upon a Shark, who said,

"Psst. Hey, bud. Where 'ya goin'?"

"I'm going out to find my fortune," replied the Sea Horse.

"You're in luck. If you'll take this short cut," said the Shark, pointing to his open mouth, "you'll save yourself a lot of time."

"Gee, thanks," said the Sea Horse, and zoomed off into the interior of the Shark, there to be devoured.

The moral of this fable is that if you're not sure where you're going, you're liable to end up someplace else—and not even know it.[1]

Before a research design is chosen, managers and researchers need a sense of direction for the investigation. The adage "If you do not know where you are going, any road will take you there" suggests some good advice to managers and researchers: It is extremely important to define the business problem carefully because it determines the purpose of the research and, ultimately, the research design.

This chapter explains how to define a business problem and how to prepare a research proposal.

■

DECISION MAKER'S OBJECTIVES

As a staff person, the research investigator must attempt to satisfy the objectives of the line manager who requested the project. Management theorists suggest the decision maker should express his or her goals to the researcher in measurable terms. Relying on the expectation that a decision maker will follow this recommendation is, unfortunately, somewhat optimistic:

> Despite a popular misconception to the contrary, objectives are seldom clearly articulated and given to the researcher. The decision maker seldom formulates his objectives accurately. He is likely to state his objectives in the form of platitudes which have no operational significance. Consequently, objectives usually have to be extracted by the researcher. In so doing, the researcher may well be performing his most useful service to the decision maker. . . . One effective technique for uncovering these objectives consists of confronting the decision maker with each of the possible solutions to a problem and asking him whether he would follow that course of action. Where he says "no," further probing will usually reveal objectives which are not served by the course of action.[2]

Researchers who must conduct investigations when the line manager wants the information "yesterday" do not usually get a great deal of assistance when management is asked, "What are your objectives for this study?" Nevertheless, both parties should attempt to have a clear understanding of the purpose for undertaking the research. Often exploratory research, by illuminating the nature of the opportunity or problem, helps managers clarify their objectives and decisions.

IMPORTANCE OF PROPER PROBLEM DEFINITION

The formal quantitative research process should not begin until the problem has been clearly defined. Properly and completely defining a business problem is easier said than done. When a problem or opportunity is discovered, managers may have only vague insights about a complex situation. For example, morale may be declining at a West Coast television studio, and management does not know the reason. If quantitative research is conducted before learning exactly what issues are important, false conclusions may be drawn from the investigation. The right answer to the wrong question may be absolutely worthless. Or, a decision made on the basis of a solution to the wrong problem may be harmful.

Consider what happened when Coca-Cola made the decision to change its Coke formula. The company's managers decided to investigate the ultimate consumer reaction to the taste of reformulated Coke and nothing more. (The company carried out a series of taste tests in shopping malls. No take-home taste tests were conducted.) In retrospect we know about the consumer protests associated with dropping the original formula of Coke, and we are aware that there was a larger problem. Coke's business research was too narrow in scope and the problem was not adequately defined. Coca-Cola tested one thing and one thing only.[3] The business research failed to identify consumers' emotional attachment and loyalty to the brand as a problem for investigation. There is a lesson to be learned from the Coca-Cola mistake: Do not ignore investigating the emotional aspects of human behavior.

Just because a problem has been discovered or an opportunity has been recognized does not mean that the problem has been defined. A **problem definition** indicates a specific managerial decision area that will be clarified by answering some research questions.

Iceberg Principle

Why do so many business research projects begin without a definition of the problem? Managers are logical people, and it seems logical that definition of the problem is the starting point for any enterprise. Frequently researchers and managers cannot discover the actual problem because they lack sufficiently detailed information; the **iceberg principle** serves as a useful analogy. A sailor on the open sea notices only a small part of an iceberg. Only 10 percent of it is above the surface of the water, and 90 percent is submerged. The dangerous part of many business problems, like the submerged portion of the iceberg, is neither visible to nor understood by managers. If the submerged portions of the problem are omitted from the problem definition (and subsequently from the research design), the decisions based on the research may be less than optimal. The example of the new Coke is a case in point. Omission of important information or a faulty assumption about the situation can be extremely costly.

Understanding the Background of the Problem

Although no textbook outline exists for identifying the business problem, the iceberg principle illustrates that understanding the background of a problem is vital. Often experienced managers know a great deal about a situation, and can provide the researchers with considerable background information about previous events and why those events happened. In situations in which the decision maker's objectives are clear, the problem may be diagnosed exclusively by exercising managerial judgment. In other situations in which information about what has happened previously is inadequate or if managers have trouble identifying the problem, a **situation analysis** is the logical first step in defining the problem. A situation analysis involves a preliminary investigation or informal gathering of background information to familiarize researchers or managers with the decision area. Gaining an awareness of organizational or environmental conditions and an appreciation of the situation often requires exploratory research. The many exploratory research techniques that have been developed to help formulate clear definitions of problems will be covered in Chapter 5.

Isolating and Identifying the Problem, Not the Symptoms

Anticipating all of the dimensions of a problem is impossible for any researcher or executive. For instance, a firm may have a problem with its advertising effectiveness. The possible causes of this problem may be low brand awareness, the wrong brand image, use of the wrong media, or perhaps too small a budget. Management's job is to isolate and identify the most likely causes. Certain occurrences that appear to be "the problem" may be only symptoms of a deeper problem. Exhibit 4.1 illustrates how symptoms may cause confusion about the nature of the true problem.

Other problems may be identified only after a search of background information and after conducting exploratory research. How does one ensure that the fundamental problem, rather than symptoms associated with the problem, has been identified? There is no easy or simple answer to this question. Executive judgment and creativity must be exercised. The archeological puzzle in Exhibit 4.2 shows that good researchers must be creative in developing problem definitions by investigating situations in new ways.

What Is the Unit of Analysis?

Defining the problem requires that the researcher determine the unit of analysis for study. The researcher must specify whether the level of investigation will focus on the collection of data about organizations, departments, work groups, individuals, or objects. In studies of home buying, for example, the husband–wife dyad rather than the individual typically is the unit of analysis because the purchase decision is jointly made by husband and wife.

E X H I B I T   4 . 1   **Symptoms Can Be Confusing**

Organization	Symptoms	Problem Definition Based on Symptoms	True Problem
20-year-old neighborhood swimming association in a major city	Membership has been declining for years; new water park with wave pool and water slides moved into town a few years ago.	Neighborhood residents prefer the expensive water park and have a negative image of swimming pool.	Demographic changes: Children in the neighborhood have grown up, and older residents no longer swim at all.
Cellular phone manufacturer	Women employees complain that salaries are too low.	Salaries need to be compared to industry averages.	Benefits program is not suited to womens' needs (e.g., maternity leave).
Brewery	Consumers prefer taste of competitor's product.	Taste of brewery's product needs to be reformulated.	Old-fashioned package is influencing taste perception.
Television station	Few employees change retirement plan after money market annuity option becomes available.	Attributes of money market annuity program need to be changed.	Except for those close to retirement, most employees are not highly involved in detailed pension-investment decisions; knowledge about plan is minimal.

E X H I B I T   4 . 2

Look Again

What language is written on this stone found by archeologists?

new way.
to problems. A good researcher creatively develops a hypothesis by looking at problems in a
often they see what they want to expect. They give stereotyped answers
familiar problems. Managers often do not look at these problems in a new light, however. Too
The language is English: TO/TIE/MULES/TO. A great deal of time and effort is spent looking at

Answer (turn book upside down):

Source: Adapted from Robert Ferber, Donald F. Blankertz, and Sidney Hollander, Jr., *Marketing Research* (New York: Ronald Press, 1964), 157. Adapted with permission.

Researchers who think carefully and creatively about situations often discover that a problem may be investigated at more than one level of analysis. Determining the unit of analysis, although relatively straightforward in most projects, should not be overlooked during the problem definition stage of the research. It is a fundamental, crucial aspect of problem definition.

What Are the Relevant Variables?

Another aspect of problem definition is identification of the key variables. The term *variable* is an important one in research. A **variable** is defined as anything that varies or changes in value. Because a variable represents a quality that can exhibit differences in value, usually in magnitude or strength, it may be said that a variable generally is anything that may assume different numerical or categorical values.

Key variables should be identified in the problem definition stage. Attitude toward brokerage firms may be a variable, for example, as people's attitudes may vary from positive to negative. The attitude toward each of the many characteristics of brokerage firms, such as availability of investment advisory services, newsletters, toll-free calls, and the like, would be a variable.

In statistical analysis a variable is identified by a symbol such as X. Categories or numerical values may then be associated with this symbol. The variable "sex" may be categorized as male or female; sex is therefore a **categorical**—or classificatory—**variable** because it has a limited number of distinct values. On the other hand, sales volume may encompass an infinite range of numbers; it is therefore a **continuous variable**—one having an infinite number of values.

To address the specific problem, managers and researchers should be careful to include all of the relevant variables that must be studied. Similarly, variables that are superfluous (i.e., not directly relevant to the problem) should not be included.

In causal research the terms *dependent variable* and *independent variable* are frequently encountered. A **dependent variable** is a criterion or a variable that is to be predicted or explained. An **independent variable** is a variable that is expected to influence the dependent variable. For example, average hourly rate of pay may be a dependent variable that is influenced or can be predicted by an independent variable such as number of years of experience.

These terms are discussed in greater detail in the chapters on experimentation and data analysis.

How Much Time Should Be Spent Defining the Problem?

Budget constraints usually influence the amount of effort that will be spent defining the problem. Most business situations are complex, and numerous variables may have some influence. It is impractical to search for every conceivable cause and minor influence. The importance of the recognized problem will dictate what is a reasonable amount of time and money to determine which explanations or solutions are most likely.

Managers—those responsible for decision making—generally want the problem definition process to proceed quickly, whereas researchers usually take long periods of time to carefully define problems and thereby frequently frustrate managers. Nevertheless, the time spent to identify the correct problem to be researched is time well spent.

How Can the Problem Statement Be Clarified?

Formulating a series of research questions and hypotheses can add clarity to the statement of the business problem. For example, a company made the following statement to define a training problem: In the broadest sense, the business problem is to determine the best ways our company can train existing and potential users of desktop personal computers. This problem statement led to the following research questions: How familiar are employees with the various software applications for personal computers? What attitudes do employees have toward these software packages? How important are the various factors for evaluating the use of a personal computer? How effective are our training efforts in terms of increased knowledge and increased use of the new applications?

The inclusion of research questions makes it easier to understand what is perplexing managers and indicates the issues to be resolved. A research question is the researcher's translation of the business problem into a specific need for inquiry. For example, a research question such as "Is Advertising Copy X better than Advertising Copy Y?" is vague and too general. Advertising effectiveness can be variously measured—by sales, recall of sales message, brand awareness, intentions to buy, and so on. A more specific research question such as "Which advertisement has a higher day-after recall score?" helps the researcher design a study that will produce pertinent information. The answer to the research question should be a criterion that can be utilized as a standard for selecting alternatives. This stage of the research is obviously related to problem definition. The goal of defining the problem is to state the research questions clearly and to have well-formulated hypotheses.

A **hypothesis** is an unproven proposition or possible solution to a problem. Hypothetical statements assert probable answers to research questions. A hypothesis is also a statement about the nature of the world, and in its simplest form it is a guess. A manager may hypothesize that salespersons who show the highest job satisfaction will be the most productive salespersons. An organizational researcher may believe that if workers' attitudes toward an organizational climate are changed in a positive direction, there will be an increase in organizational effectiveness among these workers.

Problems and hypotheses are similar. Both state relationships, but problems are interrogative and hypotheses are declarative. Sometimes they are almost identical in substance. An important difference, however, is that hypotheses are usually more specific than problems; they are usually closer to the actual research operations and testing.[4] Hypotheses are statements that can be empirically tested.

Formal statements of hypotheses have considerable practical value in planning and designing research. They force researchers to be clear about what they expect to find through the study, and further, the formal statement raises crucial questions about the data that will be required in the analysis stage.[5] When evaluating a hypothesis, research management should make sure the information collected will be useful in decision making. Notice how the following hypotheses express expected relationships between variables:

There is a positive relationship between "mail order" catalog buying and the presence of younger children in the home.[6]

Voluntary turnover (quitting) will be higher among employees who perceive themselves to be inequitably paid than among employees who perceive themselves to be equitably paid.[7]

A consumer will distort (shift) his affective reaction (liking) to a specific product characteristic in the negative direction when the characteristic is likened to an unfamiliar (highly ambiguous) brand name.[8]

Common stocks bought at high dividend yields will afford less than average returns than securities bought at lower dividend yields.[9]

Managers with decisive and flexible decision styles will process less accounting data than those with hierarchic and integrative decision styles.[10]

Opinion leaders are more affected than nonleaders by mass media communication sources.[11]

Decision-Oriented Research Objectives

The **research objective** is the researcher's version of the business problem. Once the research questions and/or hypotheses have been stated, the research project objectives are derived from the problem definition. Exhibit 4.3 illustrates how the business problem of a large organization—should the organization offer

E X H I B I T   4 . 3   **Business Problem Translated into Research Objectives**

Management Problem/Questions	Research Questions	Research Objectives
Should the organization offer outplacement?	Are managers aware of outplacement services? How concerned are managers about outplacement services?	To determine managers' awareness using aided recall. To measure managers' satisfaction with existing personnel policies.
Which of the services should be offered? Severance pay? New employment assistance? Personal counseling? Job contacts?	How do managers evaluate the need for severance pay? New-employment assistance? Personal counseling? Job contacts? What are the benefits of each outplacement service?	To obtain ratings and rankings of the various outplacement services. To identify perceived benefits and perceived disadvantages of each outplacement service.
Should the services be provided by in-house personnel or outside consultants?	Would managers prefer in-house personnel or outside consultants? How much would each alternative cost?	To measure managers' perceived benefits and disadvantages of in-house versus outside consultants. To measure managers' preference of alternatives if discharge occurred. To identify costs associated with each alternative.
Do employees with ten or more years of service have different awareness levels, etc. than employees with less than ten years of service?	Do the answers to the above questions differ by employee's years of service?	To compare, using cross-tabulations, levels of awareness, evaluations, etc. of managers with ten or more years of service with managers with less than ten years of service.

Note: For simplification, hypotheses are omitted from the table.

outplacement services (e.g., severance pay) to discharged executives—is translated into research objectives. These objectives explain the purpose of the research in measurable terms and define standards of what the research should accomplish.

In addition to stating the reasons for initiating the research project, outlining objectives helps to ensure that the project will be manageable in size.[12]

In some instances the business problems and the research objectives are the same. The objectives must, however, specify the information needed to make a decision. Identifying the information needed may require managers or researchers to be as specific as listing the exact wording of the question in a survey or explaining exactly what behavior might be observed or recorded in an experiment. Statements about the required precision of the information or the source of the information may be required to clearly communicate exactly what information is needed. Many career decisions, for example, are made by both a husband and wife. If this is the case, the husband—wife decision-making unit is the unit of analysis. The objective of obtaining X information about research questions from this unit should be specifically stated.

EXHIBIT   4.4

**The Statement of the
Business Problem
Influences Other
Activity**

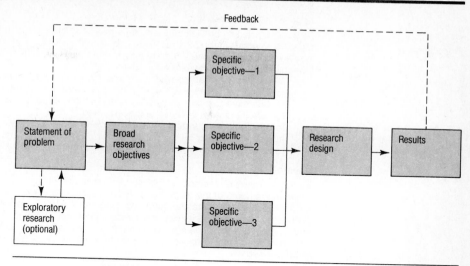

It is useful if the research objective is a managerial action standard. If the criterion to be measured (e.g., absenteeism, sales, or attitude changes) turns out to be X, the management will do A; if it is Y, then management will do B. This type of objective leaves no uncertainty about the decision to be made once the research is finished.

The number of research objectives should be limited to a manageable quantity. The fewer the study objectives, the easier it is to ensure that each will be addressed fully.

Exhibit 4.4 shows that the statement of the management problem influences the research objectives. The specific objectives, in turn, are the basis for the research design.

In our earlier example of an organization's research concerning outplacement services, the broad research objective—to determine managers' perceived need for outplacement services in the organization—was translated into specific objectives, namely to determine ranked preferences for severance pay, new employment assistance, and the like; to compare the needs of employees having more than ten years of service with those having less than ten years of service; and so on. Therefore specific objectives influence the research design. A research objective should identify the information needs. This may be as specific as listing the exact wording of the question in a survey or explaining exactly what behavior might be observed or recorded in an experiment. Once the research is conducted, the results may show an unanticipated aspect of the problem and may suggest that additional research is necessary to satisfy the main objective. Exhibit 4.4 also shows that exploratory research may help in the overall definition of the management problem. In routine situations or when managers are quite familiar with background information, however, it is quite

**An Abbreviated
Version of a Research
Proposal for the IRS**

Purpose of the Research

The general purpose of this study is to determine the taxpaying public's perceptions of the role of the IRS in administering the tax laws. In defining the limits of this study, the IRS identified study areas to be addressed. A careful review of those question areas led to the development of the following specific research objectives:

1.   To identify the extent to which taxpayers cheat on their returns, their reasons for doing so, and approaches which can be taken to deter this behavior.
2.   To determine taxpayers' experience and satisfaction with various IRS services.
3.   To determine what services taxpayers need.
4.   To develop an accurate profile of taxpayers' behavior relative to the preparation of their income tax returns.
5.   To assess taxpayers' knowledge and opinions about various tax laws and procedures.

Research Design

The survey research method will be the basic research design. Each respondent will be interviewed in the home of the respondent. The personal interviews are generally expected to last between 35 and 45 minutes, although the length of the interview will vary depending on the previous tax-related experiences of the respondent. For example, if a respondent has never been audited, questions on audit experience will not be addressed. Or, if a respondent has never contacted the IRS for assistance, certain questions concerning reactions to IRS services will be skipped.

Some sample questions that will be asked are:

Did you (or your spouse) prepare your federal tax return for (year)?

☐ Self
☐ Spouse
☐ Someone else

Did the federal income tax package you received in the mail contain all the forms necessary for you to fill out your return?

☐ Yes
☐ No
☐ Didn't receive one in the mail
☐ Don't know

Source: Based on *A General Taxpayer Opinion Survey,* Office of Planning and Research, Internal Revenue Service, March 1980.

likely the problem definition will be based exclusively on the decision maker's objectives.

THE RESEARCH PROPOSAL

The **research proposal** is a written statement of the research design. It always includes a statement explaining the purpose of the study (research objectives) or a definition of the problem. It systematically outlines the particular research methodology and details the procedures that will be utilized at each stage of the research process. Normally a schedule of costs and deadlines will be included in the research proposal. Exhibit 4.5 illustrates a short research proposal for the Internal Revenue Service that explored public attitudes toward a variety of tax-related issues.

If you were calling the IRS for assistance and someone were not able to help you immediately, would you rather get a busy signal or be asked to wait on hold?

☐ Busy signal

☐ Wait on hold

☐ Neither

☐ Don't know

During the interview a self-administered written questionnaire will be given to the taxpayer. The questionnaire will ask certain sensitive questions such as:

Have you ever claimed a dependent on your tax return that you weren't really entitled to?

☐ Yes

☐ No

Sample Design

A survey of approximately 5,000 individuals located in 50 counties throughout the country will provide the data base for this study. The sample will be selected on a probability basis from all households in the continental United States.

Eligible respondents will be adults, over the age of 18. Within each household an effort will be made to interview the individual who is most familiar with completing the federal tax forms. When there is more than one taxpayer in the household, a random process will be used to select the taxpayer to be interviewed.

Data Gathering

The fieldworkers of a field research organization will conduct the interview.

Data Processing and Analysis

Standard editing and coding procedures will be utilized. Simple tabulation and cross-tabulations will be utilized to analyze the data.

Report Preparation

A written report will be prepared, and an oral presentation of the findings will be made by the research analyst at the convenience of the IRS.

Budget and Time Schedule

[Any complete research proposal should include (1) a schedule of how long it will take to conduct each stage of the research and (2) a statement of itemized costs.]

Preparation of a research proposal forces the researcher to critically think through each stage of the research process. Vague plans, abstract ideas, and sweeping generalizations about problems or procedures must become concrete and precise statements about specific events. What information will be obtained and what research procedures will be implemented have to be clearly specified so others may understand their exact implications. All ambiguities about why and how the research will be conducted must be clarified before the proposal is complete.

Because the proposal is a clearly outlined plan submitted to management for acceptance or rejection, it initially performs a communication function; it serves as a mechanism that allows managers to evaluate the details of the proposed research design and determine if alterations are necessary. The proposal helps managers decide if the proper information wil be obtained and if the proposed research will accomplish what is desired. If the business problem has not been adequately translated into a set of specific research objectives and research design, the client's assessment of the proposal will help ensure that the researchers revise the proposal to meet the client's information needs.

The proposal needs to communicate exactly what information will be obtained, where it will be obtained, and how it will be obtained. For this reason, proposals must be explicit about sample selection, measurement, fieldwork, and so on. For instance, most survey proposals will include a copy of the proposed questionnaire, at bare minimum some sample questions, to ensure that managers and researchers agree on the information to be obtained and how questions should be worded.

The format for the IRS research proposal in Exhibit 4.5 follows the six stages in the research process outlined in Exhibit 3.3. Each stage implies that one or more questions must be answered before selecting one of the various alternatives facing the business researcher. For example, before a proposal can be completed, one has to ask "What is to be measured?" Simply answering "market share" may not be enough—market share may be measured by auditing retailers' or wholesalers' sales, by using trade association data, or by asking consumers what brands they buy. The question of what is to be measured is just one of the important questions that need to be answered before setting the research process into motion. This issue will be addressed in greater detail in Chapter 11; for now, an overview of issues is presented for each stage of the research process. Exhibit 4.6 outlines some of the basic questions that managers and researchers typically have to answer when planning a research design.

Review the IRS research proposal to see how some of these issues were answered in a specific situation.[13] The entire textbook will have to be read before these issues can be fully understood, however.

In business one often hears the adage "Don't say it, write it." This is wise advice for the researcher who is proposing a research project to management. Misstatements and faulty communication may occur if the parties rely only on each individual's memory of what occurred at a planning meeting. Writing the research design in a proposal format, specifying exactly what will be done, creates a record to which everyone can refer and eliminates many problems that might arise after the research has been conducted. Finding out after the fact (after the research) that information related to a particular variable was omitted or that the sample size was too small for a particular subgroup is less likely to occur with written proposals. Further, as a statement of agreement between the executives and researchers, the formal proposal will reduce the tendency for someone reading the results to say, "Shouldn't we have had a larger sample?" or "Why didn't you do it this way?" As a record of the researcher's obligation, the proposal also provides a standard for determining if the actual research was conducted as originally planned.

When a consultant or an outside research supplier will be conducting the research, the written proposal serves as a company's bid to offer a specific service. Typically, a client will solicit several competitive proposals, and these written offers help management judge the relative quality of alternative researcher suppliers.

EXHIBIT   4.6

Basic Questions Typically Asked When Planning a Research Design

Decision to Make in the Research Process	Basic Questions
Problem definition	What is the purpose of the study?
	How much is already known?
	Is additional background information necessary?
	What is to be measured? How?
	Can the data be made available?
	Should research be conducted?
	Can a hypothesis be formulated?
Selection of basic research design	What types of questions need to be answered?
	Are descriptive or causal findings required?
	What is the source of the data?
	Can objective answers be obtained by asking people?
	How quickly is the information needed?
	How should survey questions be worded?
	How should experimental manipulations be made?
Selection of sample	Who or what is the source of the data?
	Can the target population be identified?
	Is a sample necessary?
	How accurate must the sample be?
	Is a probability sample necessary?
	Is a national sample necessary?
	How large a sample is necessary?
	How will the sample be selected?
Data gathering	Who will gather the data?
	How long will data gathering take?
	How much supervision is needed?
	What operational procedures need to be followed?
Data analysis and evaluation	Will standardized editing and coding procedures be utilized?
	How will the data be categorized?
	Will computer or hand tabulation be utilized?
	What questions need to be answered?
	How many variables are to be investigated simultaneously?
	What are the criteria for evaluation of performance?
Type of report	Who will read the report?
	Are managerial recommendations requested?
	How many presentations are required?
	What will be the format of the written report?
Overall evaluation	How much will the study cost?
	Is the time frame acceptable?
	Do we need outside help?
	Will this research design attain the stated research objectives?
	When should the research be scheduled to begin?

One final comment needs to be made about the nature of research proposals: All proposals do not follow the same format. The researcher must adapt his or her proposal to the audience to whom the proposal will be submitted.[14] An extremely brief proposal submitted by an organization's internal research department to its own executives bears little resemblance to a complex proposal submitted by a university professor to an agency of the federal government to test a basic theory about international financial markets.

ANTICIPATING OUTCOMES

The presentation of data processing and analysis in Exhibit 4.5 is extremely brief because this topic will not be discussed until Chapter 17. However, at this stage of our discussion some advice about data analysis needs to be given.

One aspect of problem definition often lacking in research proposals is anticipating the outcome, that is, the statistical findings, of the study. The use of a dummy table in the research proposal often helps the manager gain a better understanding of what the actual outcome of the research will be. **Dummy tables** are representations of the actual tables that will be in the findings section of the final report. They are called *dummy tables* because the researcher fills in or "dummies up" the tables with likely, but fictitious, data. In other words, the researcher anticipates what the final research report will contain (table by table) before the project begins.

A research analyst can present dummy tables to the decision maker and ask, "Given these findings, will you be able to make a decision to solve your managerial problem?" If the decision maker says "Yes," then the proposal may be accepted. However, if the decision maker cannot glean enough information from these dummy tables to make a decision about what the company would do with the hypothetical outcome suggested by the tables, then the decision maker must rethink what outcomes and data analyses are necessary to solve the problem. In other words, the business problem is clarified by deciding on action standards or performance criteria and by recognizing what type of research findings are necessary to make a specific decision.

SUMMARY

The first step in any business research project is to define the problem or opportunity. Decision makers must express their objectives to researchers to avoid getting the right answer to the wrong question. Defining the problem is often complicated in that portions of the problem may be hidden from view. The research must help management isolate and identify the problem to ensure that the real problem, rather than a symptom, is investigated.

A variable is anything that changes in value. Variables may be categorical or continuous. One aspect of problem definition is the identification of the key dependent variables and the key independent variables.

Research questions and hypotheses are translations of the business problem into business research terms. A hypothesis is an unproven proposition or a possible solution to the problem. Hypotheses state relationships between variables that can be empirically tested. Research objectives specify information needs. For the research project to be successful, the research problem must be stated in terms of clear and precise research objectives.

The research proposal is a written statement of the research design that makes the research process operative for the specific problem. The research proposal allows managers to evaluate the details of the proposed research and determine if alterations are needed. Most research proposals will include the following sections: purpose of the research, research design, sample design, data gathering and/or fieldwork techniques, data processing and analysis, budget, and time schedule.

Key Terms

problem definition	dependent variable
iceberg principle	independent variable
situation analysis	hypothesis
variable	research objective
categorical variable	research proposal
continuous variable	dummy table

Questions

1. In its broadest context, what is the task of problem definition?
2. In the nine-dot square below, connect all nine dots using no more than four straight lines and without lifting the pencil from the paper. What analogy can be made from the solution of this problem to the solution of problem definition situations?

          •   •   •

          •   •   •

          •   •   •

3. What is the iceberg principle?
4. State a problem in your field of interest and list some variables that might be investigated to solve this problem.
5. Go to the library, find business journals, and record and evaluate some hypotheses that have been investigated in recent years. Identify the key independent and dependent variables.
6. Evaluate the statement of the business problem in each of the following situations:

   a. *A farm implement manufacturer:* Our objective is to learn the most effective form of capitalization so that we can maximize profits.

   b. *An employees' credit union:* Our problem is to determine the reasons why employees join the credit union, to determine members' awareness of credit union services, and to measure attitudes and beliefs about how effectively the credit union is operated.

   c. *The producer of a television show:* We have a problem: The program's ratings are low. We need to learn how to improve our ratings.

   d. *A soft-drink manufacturer:* The problem is that we do not know if our bottlers are more satisfied with us than our competitors' bottlers are with them.

   e. *A women's magazine:* Our problem is: To document the demographic changes that have occurred in recent decades in the lives of women and to put these changes in historic perspective; to examine several generations of American women through most of this century, tracking their roles as student, worker, wife, and mother and noting the changes in timing, sequence, and duration of these roles; to examine at what age and for how long a women enters each of the various stages of her life: school, work, marriage, childbearing, divorce. This documentation will be accomplished by analyzing demographic data over several generations from this perspective.

f.   *A manufacturer of fishing boats:* The problem is to determine sales trends over the past five years by product category and to determine the seasonality of unit boat sales by quarters by region of the country.

7.   What purpose does the research proposal serve?

8.   What role should managers play in the development of the research proposal?

9.   Comment on the following statement: "The best business researchers are prepared to rethink and rewrite their proposals."

10.   You have been hired by a group of hotel owners, restaurant owners, and other people engaged in businesses that benefit from tourism on South Padre Island, Texas. They wish to learn how they can attract a larger number of college students to their town during spring break. Define the business research problem. (You may substitute a beach town in Florida or California, if you prefer.)

References

[1] From *Preparing Instructional Objectives* by Robert F. Mager. Copyright © 1984 by Lake Publishing Company, Belmont, CA 94002. Reprinted with permission.

[2] Russell L. Ackoff, *Scientific Method* (New York: John Wiley, 1962), 71.

[3] Mitchell J. Shields, "Coke's Research Fizzles, Fails to Factor In Consumer Loyalty," *ADWEEK*, July 15, 1985, 8.

[4] Fred N. Kerlinger, *Behavioral Research: A Conceptual Approach* (New York: Holt, Rinehart and Winston, 1979), 34.

[5] Donald T. Warwick and Charles A. Lininger, *The Sample Survey: Theory and Practice* (New York: McGraw-Hill, 1975), 51.

[6] Fred D. Reynolds, "An Analysis of Catalog Buying Behavior," *Journal of Marketing* (July 1974): 47–51.

[7] R. D. Pritchard, "Equity Theory: A Review and Critique," *Organizational Behavior and Human Performance* 4 (1969): 176–211.

[8] Stephen J. Miller, Michael B. Mazis, and Peter L. Wright, "The Influence of Brand Ambiguity on Brand Attitude Development," *Journal of Marketing Research* (November 1971): 455–459.

[9] Richard W. McEnally, "An Evaluation of Some Costs and Consequences of Dividend-Oriented Investment Strategies," *Journal of Business Research* (January 1974): 59.

[10] Richard S. Savich, "The Use of Accounting Information in Decision Making," *Accounting Review* (July 1977): 645.

[11] Johan Arndt, "A Test of the Two-Step Flow in Diffusion of a New Product," *Journalism Quarterly* (Autumn 1968): 457–465.

[12] William B. Locander and A. Benton Cocanougher, *Problem Definition in Marketing* (Chicago: American Marketing Association, 1975), 4.

[13] Space restrictions do not permit us to present complete research proposals. Often entire questionnaires appear as exhibits in the proposal.

[14] Students interested in additional information on writing the research proposal should review Appendix 23A on writing the research report.

CHAPTER 5

Exploratory Research

What you will learn in this chapter:

To understand the differences between qualitative research and quantitative research.

To explain the purposes of exploratory research.

To identify the three general categories of exploratory research.

To explain the advantages and disadvantages of experience surveys, focus group interviews, projective techniques, case study methods, depth interviews, and other exploratory research techniques.

To understand when exploratory techniques are appropriate and to understand their limitations.

When DeBeers, the diamond firm, conducted qualitative exploratory research, it discovered a surprising finding: The man, rather than the woman, is the key figure in the diamond jewelry acquisition process. The exploratory research techniques employed to draw out the respondents' innermost feelings about diamonds indicated the essence of the transaction is that the diamond is a gift from a man to a woman. Further, the study attempted to examine the curiously semipassive role the woman plays prior to the diamond purchase. The man–woman roles seem to reflect the sexual attitudes in a Victorian novel: Women appear to believe that there is something "improper" about receiving a diamond gift. They speak of large diamonds as "flashy, gaudy, overdone" and otherwise inappropriate. Yet the study also found that women believe diamonds are a traditional and conspicuous signal of achievement, status, and success. The hypothesis resulting from the exploratory research: The element of surprise, even if feigned, plays the same accommodating role in accepting a diamond gift as it does in romantic seductions. It permits the woman to pretend that she is not actively participating in the decision. Thus she both retains her innocence and acquires her diamond.[1] (See Exhibit 5.1.)

This chapter discusses the various exploratory research techniques used in business research.

·

EXPLORATORY RESEARCH: WHAT IT IS AND WHAT IT IS NOT

When a researcher has a limited amount of experience with or knowledge about a research issue, **exploratory research** is a useful preliminary step that helps ensure that a more rigorous, more conclusive future study will not begin with an inadequate understanding of the nature of the management problem. The findings of the DeBeers exploratory research, for instance, would lead the researchers to emphasize learning more about men's purchasing behavior in subsequent conclusive studies. Conclusive research answers questions of fact

necessary to determine a course of action. This is never the purpose of exploratory research.

Much, but certainly not all, exploratory research provides *qualitative* data. Usually, exploratory research provides greater understanding of a concept or crystallizes a problem, rather than providing precise measurement or *quantification*. A researcher may search for numbers to indicate economic trends, but a rigorous mathematical analysis is not performed. Any source of information may be informally investigated to clarify which qualities or characteristics are associated with an object, situation, or issue.

Alternately, the purpose of *quantitative* research is to determine the quantity or extent of some phenomenon in the form of numbers. Most exploratory research is *not* quantitative research. This chapter discusses exploratory research under the assumption that its purpose is qualitative.

Exploratory research may be a single research investigation or a *series* of informal studies to provide background information. Researchers must be creative in the choice of information sources to be investigated. They must be flexible enough to investigate all inexpensive sources that may possibly provide information to help understand a problem. This need to be flexible does not mean that researchers do not have to be careful and systematic when designing exploratory research studies. Most of the techniques discussed in this chapter have limitations. Researchers should be keenly aware of the proper and improper uses of the various techniques.

WHY CONDUCT EXPLORATORY RESEARCH?

The purpose of exploratory research is intertwined with the need for a clear and precise statement of the recognized problem. Three interrelated purposes for exploratory research exist: (1) diagnosing a situation, (2) screening alternatives, and (3) discovering new ideas.

Diagnosing a Situation

Much has already been said about the need for situation analysis to clarify a problem's nature. Exploratory research helps diagnose the dimensions of problems so that successive research projects will be on target. It helps set priorities for research. In some cases exploratory research provides an orientation for management by gathering information on a topic with which management has little experience. Although a research project has not yet been planned, information about an issue is needed before the appropriate action can be developed.

Personnel research managers often conduct exploratory research as a diagnostic tool to point out issues of employee concern or to generate possible explanations for motivational patterns. For example, preliminary interviews with employees may be utilized to learn current "hot" issues, as well as concerns about bread-and-butter issues such as wages, working conditions, career opportunities, and the like.

The experience of an advertising agency executive also illustrates this purpose of exploratory research:

> *The last campaign I directed was Sunrise Coffee, for Nestle. This was a new product—a new kind of instant coffee, containing chicory. So our basic challenge was to develop a creative strategy that would appeal to chicory users as well as nonusers. Right away, we decided on nonbitter. Right away, before even getting into the chicory thing, we figured we at least had to promise people nonbitter coffee. Then we went to our research people to find out about chicory, and what they told us was that almost nobody had ever heard of chicory. I mean, it wasn't being used for this, it wasn't being used for that; in fact, almost nobody seemed to know anything about it from a user point of view. So research said we could say pretty much what we wanted to about it.*[2]

Screening Alternatives

When several opportunities arise but the budget precludes investigating all possible options, exploratory research may be used to determine the best alternatives. Many good investments were not made because a company chose to invest in something better. Some new organizational structures are found to be unworkable. Or, in an exploratory look at market data (size, number, and so on), a product alternative may not be feasible because the market is too small. Although this aspect of exploratory research is not a substitute for conclusive research, certain evaluative information can be acquired in exploratory studies.

The need for concept testing is a frequent reason for conducting exploratory research. **Concept testing** is a general term for many different research procedures, all of which have the same purpose. It refers to those research procedures that test some sort of stimulus as a proxy for a new or revised program, product, or service. Typically, test subjects are presented with an idea and asked if they would use it, if they liked it, and so on.[3] Concept testing is a means of evaluating ideas by providing a "feel" for the merits of an idea prior to the commitment of research and development, manufacturing, or other company resources.[4] Researchers look for trouble signals in evaluations of concepts in order to avoid future problems in business research.

Concept testing may portray the functions, uses, and possible situations for a proposed product. For example, Del Monte conducted a concept test to determine if consumers would accept the idea of shelf-stable yogurt. The plan to produce the yogurt was scrapped after surveys showed that buyers refused to accept the idea that yogurt could be kept unrefrigerated. Early research indicated that such a concept was viewed as desirable and unique, but the cost of achieving believability was finally judged to be too high.[5]

In other cases, when subjects have expressed reservation about certain aspects of the idea but the general concept has not been evaluated negatively, researchers know that the concept needs to be refined. Exhibit 5.2 presents excellent concept statements for two new seafood products made from squid. The intangibles—influencing brand image, product appearance, name, and price—as well as a description of the product simulate reality. Thus, prior to actual product development, the idea expressing the nature of the brand is conveyed to the test subjects.

Discovering New Ideas

Exploratory research is often used to generate new ideas. Perhaps factory workers have suggestions for increasing production, reducing costs, or improving safety. Consumers may suggest new product ideas, or unthought-of problems might be identified.

CATEGORIES OF EXPLORATORY RESEARCH

There are many techniques for investigating undefined research problems. Several of the most popular qualitative techniques are discussed in this section. However, the *purpose,* rather than *technique,* determines whether a study is exploratory, descriptive, or causal. For example, telephone surveys (discussed in Chapter 8) are sometimes used for exploratory purposes, although they are used primarily for descriptive research. The versatile techniques discussed in this chapter allow for an intensive, in-depth questioning of respondents, and these techniques tend to be used *primarily,* though not exclusively, for exploratory purposes.

A manager may choose from three general categories of exploratory research methods: (1) experience surveys, (2) secondary data analysis, and (3) pilot studies. Each category provides various alternative ways of gathering information.

Experience Surveys

In attempting to understand the problems at hand, managers may discuss issues and ideas with top executives and knowledgeable managers who have had personal experience in the field. This constitutes an informal **experience survey.**

For example, a chain saw manufacturer received from its Japanese distributor a recommendation to modify its product with a drilling attachment on the sprocket (replacing the chain and guide bar) and use it as a mushroom-planting device. The distributor indicated that many such units had been sold in Japan. However, an experience survey with only one individual, the president of the Mushroom Growers Association, indicated the product was not feasible in the United States. Americans consume a white cultured mushroom grown in enclosed areas or caves rather than the variety of mushrooms grown on wood in Japan. The mushroom expert indicated Americans believe too many old wives' tales about poison mushrooms and would not change their eating habits to include the Japanese variety.

Exploratory research during the situational analysis may be quite informal. Discussions with knowledgeable people, both inside and outside the company, may not be much more than conversations. This activity, intended only to get ideas about the problem, may be conducted by the line manager rather than the research department. The financial research analyst may have within an industry many contacts that he or she relies on for information. Exploratory information from an experience survey is not expected to be conclusive. Often an experience survey consists of interviews with a small number of experienced people who have been carefully selected. Some formal questions may be asked, but the respondents will generally be allowed to discuss the questions with few constraints. Knowledgeable people should be selected because they are articulate individuals, rather than a representative probability sample. The purpose is to help formulate the problem and clarify concepts, rather than develop conclusive evidence.

Secondary Data Analysis

Another economical and quick source of background information is trade literature in the public library. Searching through such material is exploratory research by means of **secondary data analysis.** Basic theoretical research is rarely conducted without extensive reviews of the literature in the field or similar research. Using secondary data may be equally important in applied re-

a. Squid Concept Alternative 1
CALAMARIOS

CALAMARIOS* are a new and different seafood product made from tender, boneless, North Atlantic squid. The smooth white body (mantle) of the squid is thoroughly cleaned, cut into thin, bite-sized rings, then frozen to seal in their flavor. To cook CALAMARIOS, simply remove them from the package and boil them for only eight minutes. They are then ready to be used in a variety of recipes.

For example, CALAMARIOS can be combined with noodles, cheese, tomatoes, and onions to make "Baked CALAMARIO Cacciatore." Or, CALAMARIOS can be marinated in olive oil, lemon juice, mint, and garlic and served as a tasty squid salad. CALAMARIOS also are the prime ingredient for "Calamary en Casserole" and "Squid Italienne." You may simply want to steam CALAMARIOS, lightly season them with garlic, and serve dipped in melted butter. This dish brings out the fine flavor of squid. A complete CALAMARIOS recipe book will be available free of charge at your supermarket.

CALAMARIOS are both nutritious and economical. Squid, like other seafoods, is an excellent source of protein. CALAMARIOS can be found at your supermarket priced at $2.50 per pound. Each pound you buy is completely cleaned and waste-free.

Because of their convenient versatility, ample nutrition, and competitive price, we hope you will want to make CALAMARIOS a regular item on your shopping list.

Calamario is the Italian word for squid.

Source: Glen L. Urban and John R. Hauser, *Design and Marketing of New Products* © 1980, pp. 35–37. Adapted with permission of Prentice-Hall, Inc., Englewood Cliffs, New Jersey.

**b. Squid Concept Alternative 2
SCLAM CHOWDER**

SCLAM CHOWDER is a delicious new seafood soup made from choice New England clams and tasty, young, boneless North Atlantic squid. Small pieces of clam are combined with bite-sized strips of squid and boiled in salted water until they are soft and tender. Sautéed onions, carrots, and celery are then added together with thick, wholesome cream, a dash of white pepper, and sprinkling of fresh parsley. The entire mixture is then cooked to perfection, bringing out a fine, natural taste that will make this chowder a favorite in your household.

SCLAM CHOWDER is available canned in your supermarket. To prepare, simply combine SCLAM CHOWDER with 1½ cups of milk in a saucepan, and bring to a boil over a hot stove. After the chowder has reached a boil, simmer for 5 minutes and then serve. One can makes 2–3 servings of this hearty, robust seafood treat. Considering its ample nutrition and delicious taste, SCLAM CHOWDER is quite a bargain at 99¢ per can.

Both clams and squid are high in protein, so high in fact that SCLAM CHOWDER makes a healthy meal in itself, perfect for lunches as well as with dinner. Instead of adding milk, some will want to add ⅓ cup of sour cream, and use liquid chowder as an exquisite sauce to be served on rice, topped with grated Parmesan cheese.

However you choose to serve it, you are sure to find SCLAM CHOWDER a tasty, nutritious, and economical seafood dish.

Sclam Chowder

-a delicious blend of
squid & clams

Ingredients: Squid, Clams, Milk, Water, Potatoes, Onion, Seasonings.

search. For example, a personnel manager may want to evaluate her company's formal training programs. A short time in a library may reveal that in companies with more than 50 employees the average executive receives 41.4 hours of training per year while the average office secretarial worker gets 18.8 hours of training per year.[6] Additional information about the types of training, use of computers in training, industry differences in training, and the like may help clarify the issues that need to be researched. If the problem is to determine the reasons for a sales decline of an existing product, the manager's situational analysis might begin with an analysis of sales records by region and by customer or some other source of internal data.

Investigating data that have been compiled for some purpose other than the project at hand, such as accounting records or trade association data, is one of the most frequent forms of exploratory research. Because this is also a technique for both descriptive and conclusive research, a separate chapter (Chapter 6) is devoted to the investigation of secondary sources.

Once a situational analysis using secondary data or experience surveys has been informally carried out, issues that still need clarification may warrant further exploratory investigation beyond the gathering of background information. At this point the research specialist is needed to design a pilot study. The remainder of this chapter presents a number of exploratory and preliminary research techniques that can aid in the definition of the problem.

Pilot Studies

The term *pilot studies* is used as a collective to group together a number of diverse research techniques. When the term **pilot study** is used within the context of exploratory research, it conveys the message that some aspect of the research (e.g., fieldwork) will be on a small scale. Thus a pilot study is a research project that involves sampling, but the rigorous standards used to obtain precise, quantitative estimates from large, representative samples are relaxed.

A pilot study generates primary data, usually for qualitative analysis. This characteristic distinguishes pilot studies from gathering background information using secondary data. The primary data are usually collected from consumers or other subjects of ultimate concern, rather than from a few knowledgeable experts. This distinguishes pilot studies from experience surveys. Four major categories of pilot studies will be discussed in this chapter: focus group interviews, case studies, projective techniques, and depth interviews.

FOCUS GROUP INTERVIEW

Business executives have been hearing a lot about the focus group interview lately. The focus group interview is so popular today that many research agencies consider it to be the "only" exploratory research tool. A **focus group interview** is an unstructured, free-flowing interview with a small group of people. It is not a rigidly constructed question-and-answer session, but a flexible format that encourages discussion of, say, a labor issue, reactions toward a political candidate, or a new-product concept. Participants meet at a central location at a designated time. The group consists of an interviewer or moderator and six to ten participants who discuss a single topic. The participants may be women talking about maternity leave, petroleum engineers talking about problems in the "oil patch," or patients talking about health care. The moderator introduces the topic and encourages the group members to discuss the subject among themselves. Focus groups allow people to discuss their true feelings, anxieties, and frustrations, and to express the depth of their convictions in their own words. Ideally, the discussion proceeds at the group's initiative.

The primary advantages of focus group interviews are that they are relatively brief, easy to execute, quickly analyzed, and inexpensive. In an emergency situation, three or four group sessions can be conducted, analyzed, and reported in less than a week at a cost substantially lower than that of other attitude-measurement techniques.[7] It must be remembered, however, that a small discussion group will rarely be a representative sample, no matter how carefully it is recruited. Focus group interviews cannot take the place of quantitative studies.

The flexibility of group interviews is an advantage, especially when compared with the rigid format of a survey. Numerous topics can be discussed and many insights can be gained, particularly those involving the contingencies of behavior. Responses such as the following, which would be unlikely to emerge in a survey, often come out in a group interview: "If it is one of the three brands I sometimes use and it is on sale, I buy it; otherwise, I buy my regular brand." "If the day is hot and I have to serve the whole neighborhood, I make bug juice; otherwise I give them soda or Coke."[8]

If a researcher is investigating a target group to determine who consumes a particular beverage or why a particular brand is purchased, situational factors must be taken into account. If the researcher does not realize the impact of the occasion on which the particular beverage is consumed, the results of the research may be general and not portray the consumers' actual thought process. A focus group elicits situationally specific responses: hot day, and the "whole neighborhood" gets "bug juice"; a few, and they get soda or Coke.

Focus groups are often used for concept screening and refinement. The concept may be continually modified, refined, and retested until management believes that the concept is acceptable.

The specific advantages of focus group interviews have been categorized as follows:[9]

> Synergism: *The combined effort of the group will produce a wider range of information, insights, and ideas than will the cumulation of separately secured responses of a number of individuals.*
>
> Snowballing: *A bandwagon effect often operates in a group interview situation. A comment by one individual often triggers a chain of responses from the other participants.*
>
> Stimulation: *Usually, after a brief introductory period, the respondents want to express their ideas and expose their feelings as the general level of excitement about the topic increases.*

Security: *In the well-structured group, the individual can usually find some comfort in the fact that his or her feelings are similar to those of others in the group, and that each participant can expose an idea without being obliged to defend it or to follow through and elaborate on it. One is more likely to be candid because the focus is on the group rather than on the individual; the participant soon realizes that the things said are not necessarily being identified with him or her.*

Spontaneity: *Since no individual is required to answer any given question in a group interview, the individual's responses can be more spontaneous and less conventional. A spontaneous answer may provide a more accurate picture of the person's position on some issue. In a group interview people speak only when they have definite feelings about a subject, not because a question requires a response.*

Serendipity: *It is more often the case in a group than in an individual interview that some idea will drop out of the blue. The group also affords the opportunity to develop the idea to its full significance.*

Specialization: *The group interview allows the use of a more highly trained interviewer (moderator) because there are certain economies of scale when a number of individuals are "interviewed" simultaneously.*

Scrutiny: *The group interview permits closer scrutiny in several ways. First, the session can be observed by several people; this affords some check on the consistency of the interpretations. Second, the session can be tape-recorded or videotaped. Later, detailed examination of the recorded session can offer additional insights and help clear up disagreements about what happened.*

Structure: *The group interview affords more control than the individual interview with regard to the topics covered and the depth in which they are treated. The interviewer/moderator is often one of the participants and therefore has the opportunity to reopen topics that received too shallow a discussion when initially presented.*

Speed: *The group interview permits securing a given number of interviews more quickly than does interviewing designated respondents.*

Group Composition

The ideal size of the focus group is six to ten individuals. If the group is too small, one or two members may intimidate the others. Groups that are too large may not permit adequate participation by each group member. Homogeneous groups seem to work best. Selecting homogeneous groups allows researchers to concentrate on individuals with similar lifestyles, job classifications, experiences, and communication skills. The session thus does not become confused with too many arguments and different viewpoints stemming from diverse backgrounds of participants. For example, married women who stay home full time to raise their children are often grouped separately from unmarried working women.

Researchers who wish to collect information from different types of people should conduct several focus groups. For example, one focus group

RESEARCH INSIGHT

Excerpt from a Bank's Focus Group Interview with Newcomers to a Community

Moderator: Undoubtedly, some of you had situations that arose when you got ready to come here, inconveniences that happened to you. They may have been major things or minor things, but no matter what, they were still problems that came about when you got ready to move. I'd like to talk about the problems and inconveniences you had in getting ready to come to San Diego.

Brenda: What do you mean by inconveniences?

Marian: Like changes of addresses in banks or your subscriptions?

Moderator: Things that disrupted your living the way you were living.

Marian: Taking my daughter, who is a senior in high school, away and leaving all her friends. She despises it. That is an inconvenience. The move itself. The movers were late naturally. The furniture was broken. The claim is still not settled.

Moderator: You mentioned banking, was that a problem?

Marian: I've changed banks since I've been here. I don't like the banking hours here. In Kansas City, the banks were open just like department stores, day and night. So the banking was very easy. Here I started with Bank of America, but they were never open so I switched real quick.

Moderator: What do you mean they were never open?

Marian: They didn't open early, the one near me didn't open until 10:00 in the morning and is only open until 3:00 and we're used to 7:00 to 7:00 hours. I'm surprised by the banks. In such a big place, why not open longer and on Saturdays? I found a bank that is open Saturdays for my checking account. I've never seen such long lines in my whole life. With so many working in such a large population you would think they would accommodate more. You could wait an hour just to get a check cashed. I'm trying to get my account going, just to add a name. The drive-up is open, but they can't pass the card. I have to go inside and stand in the hour-long lines to do that, and I'm not willing to do that. I learned a long time ago that anything you open up, use the word *or* not *and*. Like Marty *or* Marian—not *and*. Then you don't have any trouble.

Moderator: Brenda, how about you?

Brenda: Trying to weed out what to bring or throw away. We brought only what we could take in the car. We have a few things in storage but not much. Like everyone, I feel the banks out here are the most horrendous situations I've ever seen. I've never found it so hard to get a check cashed. My husband, in his own bank, has to show his driver's license, and if you don't have a picture ID, you're out of luck. They are too untrusting, it's outrageous. I've been in many cities in many states and have never run into anything so outrageous in my entire life.

Moderator: Then your difficulty in cashing a check is your main difficulty in banking?

Brenda: Just everything . . . people's attitudes. Out here it's like everyone is for themselves, no one wants to help anyone else. Everybody is on their own. The last place I lived was a small town and the people were more willing to help you out. Most people I've run into out here are not willing to be helpful, especially the banks. I haven't been here long enough for firsthand evidence, but from what I've heard, even the residents have trouble. The lady I'm staying near has had to change banks three times in the last year.

Moderator: Lisa, what problems have you encountered?

Lisa: Well, not really very much. I take life as it comes, living day-to-day. I don't have any money in banks. I would never put money in a bank. Why? Because I don't like the way they do business. I don't like what they do with the money while it's in there. I don't like the interest they give you and I don't like the waiting in lines. I don't like anything about it. The banks aren't interested in us, they just want the money so they can use it.

Moderator: Carolyn?

Carolyn: The moving van gave us the most problems. Many of our things were damaged and many stolen. I don't know how to claim these items. We were delayed one day because the vans won't move less than five tons and we only had two. We paid for five. Also the banks . . . cashing out-of-state checks in your own bank. My husband applied for a Visa card here. Our credit is fantastic but we were denied the credit because they say they have no

(continued)

R E S E A R C H   I N S I G H T

(continued)

record of our credit rating. We could not transfer it out here, so fine, they won't use our money, we'll just keep sending it back to Virginia. The service charge out here is outrageous. I had a totally free checking account. No service charge, no minimum balance, everything was free. The checks were free. We figured it will cost about $40 a year to maintain a checking account.

Lisa: So she has the right idea not to put money in the bank, put everything in cash. Also your records are not closed. The government can get your records. They can come in and construct a whole lifestyle by your transactions, so if you want the whole world to know about you, where you bank, where you buy, where you borrow, what church you donate or go to, then just use a bank!

Carolyn: Another thing that surprised me is that when you buy a money order, even in the city, the banks won't cash it. That's wrong. This is just like cash. It was bought and paid for. Where can you cash them? You have to open an account and leave them there for so many days . . . in the city a couple of days, out of the city probably two weeks, and out of state up to eighteen to twenty days. A cashier's check is the same. Nobody trusts nobody. It took a friend about thirty days to cash a cashier's check. It was for $1,000 from Las Vegas so they couldn't cash it. The money is there so why can't they cash it? Travelers checks are not acceptable everywhere. Some stores and gas stations will not accept them.

Moderator: Anna, tell us about your problems.

Anna: You wouldn't believe it. Being a student, I have no credit cards, no credit. I have a driver's license and a military ID and it's impossible to cash a check without a credit card. Also, trying to find a place to live. I'm not twenty-one so they won't let you rent an apartment. They would not take my signature. I had to call my Dad and have him fly down, which is $100 one-way, and sign for me to get the apartment, and then fly back home. My parents send me money each month in a cashier's check, but I go through the problem all the time to cash it. I could get my parents to put me on their Visa card as a signer.

Roger: Couldn't you go to a bank and get a check guarantee card?

Anna: I've heard of it, but I don't have one. I have a military ID and a driver's license. I feel those two should be sufficient.

Moderator: Did you experience any other problems as you were planning the move?

Anna: Yes, getting into school. They sent my application to San Jose instead of San Diego State, so by the time I got it back it was too late to register and I had to go contract register and it cost me $40 more per unit. At the time I was taking fifteen units, so I dropped all but ten units. I paid $400 instead of $100 and after moving down here and everything, I couldn't move back home.

Moderator: Roger, how about you? When you were planning to move from Los Angeles?

Roger: I had no problems moving down as I moved all my own stuff so if anything was broken, it was no one's fault but my own. As far as banking, you just go down and open an account and hope the bank has interest in other personal accounts in California. Most banks don't. I don't feel San Diego is any different than Los Angeles.

Source: Excerpts from "Suncoast National Bank" by Donald Sciglimpaglia, in William G. Zikmund, William J. Lundstrom, and Donald Sciglimpaglia, *Cases in Marketing Research* (Hinsdale, IL: Dryden Press, 1982), 48–51.

consisting only of men and another focus group consisting only of women might be conducted. Thus a diverse sample may be obtained even though each group is homogeneous.

Environmental Conditions

The site of the group session may be at the research agency, an office conference room, a hotel, or one of the subjects' home. One researcher suggests that a "coffee klatch" or "bull session" atmosphere be established to ensure that the mood of the sessions will be as relaxed and natural as possible.[10]

The Moderator

A transcript of a focus group interview appears in the Research Insight on pages 85–86. Notice how the moderator makes sure that everyone gets a chance to speak and how she contributes by asking questions to clarify topics that have been introduced into the discussion. The moderator's job is to develop a rapport with the group and to promote interaction among its members. The combined effort of the group is likely to produce a wider range of information, insights, and ideas than a number of personal interviews would provide.[11] The moderator should be someone who is really interested in people, who listens carefully to what others have to say, and who can readily establish rapport and gain the confidence of people and make them feel relaxed and eager to talk. Careful listening by the moderator is especially important, because the group interview's purpose is to stimulate spontaneous responses. The moderator's role is also to focus the discussion on the problem areas of concern. When a topic is no longer generating fresh ideas, the effective moderator changes the flow of discussion. The moderator does not give the group total control of the discussion, but normally has prepared questions on topics that are of concern to management. However, the timing of these questions and the manner in which they are raised are left to the moderator's discretion. The term *focus group* derives from the moderator's task. He or she starts out by asking for a general discussion but usually focuses in on specific topics during the session.

Shortcomings

The shortcomings of focus groups are similar to those of most qualitative research techniques, and they are discussed at the end of this chapter. However, a specific shortcoming of focus groups should be pointed out here. Without a sensitive and effective moderator, a single, self-appointed participant may dominate the session. Sessions that include a dominant participant may be somewhat abnormal. Participants may react negatively toward the dominant member, causing a "halo" effect on attitudes toward the concept or the topic of discussion. In other words, a negative impression of the individual may be projected to the topic of discussion. Such a situation should be avoided so that a negative impression of an "obnoxious person" does not inhibit other members from being candid and does not influence the statements that other members make.

CASE STUDY METHOD

The purpose of the **case study method** is to obtain information from one or a few situations that are similar to the researcher's problem situation. For example, a bank in Montana may intensively investigate the computer-security activities of an innovative bank in California. An academic researcher, interested in doing a nationwide survey among union workers, may first look at a few union locals to identify the nature of any problems or topics that should be investigated. See Exhibit 5.3 for an interesting example of the case study method used by the Schwinn Bicycle Company.

E X H I B I T   5 . 3

**Case Study Method:
The Salesman Who
Spoke Magic Words
(Schwinn Bicycle
Company)**

A business researcher at Schwinn conducted an observation study for exploratory purposes.
Here is a description of the study in his own words:

> We had a very successful dealer on the West Coast. He sold a lot of bicycles. So it
> occurred to me that we'd go out and find out how he's doing it. We'll use a tape recorder
> and get in the back room where we'll hear these magic words that he says to people to
> make them buy bicycles. We'll take that tape back to the factory. We'll have it all typed
> out. We'll print it in the *Reporter* [dealer newsletter]. We'll send it to all the other dealers
> and everybody can say the same words. And, boy, we'll need another factory! Right? So
> we go out. The guy's got a nice store out in Van Nuys. We sit in the back room and we
> listen. The first customers come in, a man and a woman with a boy about nine or ten
> years old. The dad says, "Which one is it?" The son says, "This one over here." Dad
> looks at it. He says to the clerk, "How much is it?" The clerk says, "$79.95." The father,
> "Okay, we'll take it." It blew the whole bit. So we stand there and we listen to some of
> these conversations going on like this. Suddenly it dawned on us that it was not what
> they say, it's the atmosphere of the store. Here, it was not Joe's old, dirty bike shop, but
> here was a beautiful store on the main street. A big sign was in front, "Valley Cyclery,"
> inside [were] fluorescent lights, carpeting on the floor, high-fi music, air-conditioning, a
> beautiful display of bicycles. It was like a magnet. People came in. So, maybe this is the
> catch. We tried to introduce that idea to other dealers. Put a bigger investment into your
> store and see what happens. Some of them did, and it happened.

This observation study serendipitously led to a discovery that would change Schwinn's
entire channel of distribution strategy. The opportunity was a direct result of being open-minded
in the problem discovery stage of business research.

Source: Ray Burch, "Marketing Research: Why It Works, Why It Doesn't Work," speech to the Chicago Chapter,
American Marketing Association, 1973. Reprinted with permission from Chicago Chapter, American Marketing
Association.

The primary advantage of the case study is that an entire organization or
entity can be investigated in depth and with meticulous attention to detail. This
highly focused attention enables the researchers to carefully study the order of
events as they occur or to concentrate on identifying the relationships among
functions, individuals, or entities.

Conducting a case study often requires the cooperation of the person
whose history is being studied—for example, a franchisee who allows the franchiser access to the former's records and reports. Again, intensive interviews or
long discussions with the franchisee and his or her employees may provide an
understanding of a complex situation. Researchers, however, have no standard
procedures to follow. They must be flexible and attempt to glean information
and insights wherever they find them. The freedom to search for whatever data
an investigator deems important makes the success of any case study highly
dependent on the alertness, creativity, intelligence, and motivation of the individual performing the case analysis.

Like all exploratory research, the results from case analysis should be
seen as tentative. Generalizing from a few cases can be dangerous because most
situations are atypical in some sense. A bank in Montana may not be in a situation comparable to one in California. But even if situations are not directly
comparable, a number of insights can be gained and hypotheses suggested for
future research.

Obtaining information about competitors may be very difficult, because they generally like to keep the secrets of success to themselves. The exact formulation of Coca-Cola Classic, for example, is known by only a few top executives in the firm. Confidentiality, they feel, is a definite competitive edge in their product strategy. Thus researchers may have limited access to information from other firms.

PROJECTIVE TECHNIQUES

There is an old story about asking one's neighbor why he purchased a Cadillac. If you ask the person directly, he will tell you the car holds its value and does not depreciate much, that it gets better gas mileage than you'd expect, or that it has a comfortable ride. But if you ask that same man why the man down the block purchased a Cadillac, he answers, "Oh, that status seeker!" This story illustrates that individuals may be more likely to give a true answer (consciously or unconsciously) if the question is disguised. The purpose of projective techniques is to discover an individual's attitudes, motivations, defensive reactions, and characteristic ways of responding.

The underlying assumption for these methods is contained in Oscar Wilde's phrase: "A man is least himself when he talks in his own person; when he is given a mask he will tell the truth." In other words, advocates of projective techniques assume that when directly questioned, respondents' true feelings are not expressed because they are embarrassed about answers that reflect poorly on their self-concept. They wish to please the interviewer with the "right" answer, or they cannot reveal unconscious feelings of which they are unaware. However, if respondents are presented with unstructured, ambiguous stimuli, such as cartoons or ink blots, and are allowed considerable freedom to respond, their true feelings will be expressed.

A **projective technique** is an indirect means of questioning that enables the respondent to "project" beliefs and feelings onto a third party, to an inanimate object, or into a task situation. Respondents are not required to provide answers in a structured format. They are encouraged to describe a situation in their own words, with little prompting by the interviewer. Individuals are expected to interpret the situation within the context of their own experiences, attitudes, and personality and to express opinions and emotions that may be hidden from others and, possibly, themselves. The most common projective techniques in business research are word association, sentence completion, third-person techniques, and thematic apperception tests.

Word Association

During a **word association** test the subject is presented with a list of words, one at a time, and asked to respond with the first word that comes to his or her mind. Both verbal and nonverbal responses (such as hesitation in responding) are recorded. A researcher who reads a list of job tasks to employees expects that the word association technique will reveal each individual's true feelings about the job task. It is assumed that an employee's first thought is a spontaneous answer because the subject does not have adequate time to think about and avoid making admissions that reflect poorly on himself or herself. This technique is frequently used in testing potential brand names. For example, a liquor manufacturer, attempting to market a light whiskey, tested the brand names Frost, Verve, Ultra, and Master's Choice. Frost was seen as upbeat, modern, clean, and psychologically right. Verve was "too modern," Ultra was "too common," and Master's Choice was "not upbeat enough." [12]

Interpreting word association tests is difficult, and researchers should make sure that they avoid subjective interpretations. When there is considerable agreement in the "free association" process, the researcher assumes that the test has revealed the person's inner feelings about the subject. Word association tests are also analyzed by the amount of elapsed time. For example, if the researcher is investigating sexual harassment, a person's hesitation in responding may indicate that the responses were delayed because the subject is emotionally involved in the expression (possibly seeking an "acceptable" response). Thus analysis of projective technique results takes into account not only what people say but what they *do not say*.

Word association tests can also be used to pretest words or ideas to be used in questionnaires. This enables the researcher to know beforehand whether and to what degree the meaning of a word or phrase is understood in the context of a survey. [13]

Sentence Completion

The **sentence completion** method is also based on the assumptions of free association. Respondents are required to complete a number of partial sentences with the first word or phrase that comes to mind. For example:

People who work late are _____.

A female manager is most liked by _____.

A boss should not _____.

Answers to sentence completion questions tend to be more extensive than answers to word association tests. The intent of these sentence completion questions is more apparent, however.

Third-Person Technique and Role Playing

The Iowa Poll asked, "Will you wind up in heaven or hell?" Nearly all Iowans believed they would be saved, but one-third of them described a neighbor as a "sure bet" for hell. [14]

Almost literally, providing a "mask" is the basic idea behind the **third-person technique**. Respondents are asked why a third person (e.g., one's neighbor) does what he does or thinks what he thinks about a person, event, or concept. For example, investors might be told: "We are talking to a number of investors like you about this money market fund. Some men and women like it the way it is; others believe that it should be improved. Please think of some of

RESEARCH INSIGHT
Cigarette Smoking—Are You Being Honest with Yourself?

Cigarette smoking at the office in public spaces is an emotionally charged and hotly debated issue. Direct, undisguised questioning may not be the best alternative because cigarette smoking is a behavior where ego defense mechanisms seem to operate. Business researchers directly questioned 179 smokers who believed cigarettes to be a health hazard why they continued to smoke. The majority answered, "Pleasure is more important than health," "Moderation is OK," "I like to smoke." Such responses suggest that smokers are not dissatisfied with their habit. However, in another portion of the study, the researchers used a projective method. Respondents were asked to respond with the first thing that came to their mind after hearing the sentence "People who never smoke are _____." The answers were "better off," "happier," "smarter," "wiser," "more informed." "Teenagers who smoke are _____," smokers responded with "foolish," "crazy," "uninformed," "stupid," "showing off," "immature," "wrong." The sentence completion test indicated that smokers are anxious, uncomfortable, dissonant, and dissatisfied with their habit. The sentence completion test elicited responses that the subjects would not have given otherwise.

Source: Adapted from "Projective Methods," by Harold H. Kassarjian, in *Handbook of Marketing Research,* ed. Robert Ferber. Copyright © 1974, McGraw-Hill. Adapted with the permission of McGraw-Hill Book Company.

your friends or neighbors and tell us what it is they might find fault with in this new money market fund." Thus the respondent can transfer his attitudes to his neighbors, to friends, or to people he works with. He is free to agree or disagree with an unknown third party.

The best-known and certainly a classic example of this indirect technique was conducted in 1950 when Nescafe Instant Coffee was new to the market. Two shopping lists, identical except for coffee, were given to two groups of women:

> *Pound and a half of hamburger*
>
> *2 loaves of Wonder bread*
>
> *Bunch of carrots*
>
> *1 can of Rumford's Baking Powder*
>
> *Nescafe Instant Coffee* or *Maxwell House Coffee, drip grind*
>
> *2 cans Del Monte peaches*
>
> *5 pounds potatoes*

The instructions were:

> *Read the shopping list. Try to project yourself into the situation as far as possible until you can more or less characterize the woman who bought the groceries. Then write a brief description of her personality and character. Whenever possible indicate what factors influenced your judgment.*

Forty-eight percent of the housewives who were given the Nescafe list described the Nescafe user as lazy and a poor planner. Others indicated that they felt the instant coffee user was not a good wife and spent money carelessly. The Maxwell House user was thought to be practical, frugal, and a good cook.[15]

Role playing is a dynamic reenactment of the third-person technique in a given situation. The role-playing technique requires the subject to act out someone else's behavior in a particular setting. For example, a worker in a role-playing situation who is instructed to perform a supervisor's task projects herself into a supervisor's role. This projective technique can be used to determine a true feeling about a supervisor or work situation. In role-playing games, persons may become caught up in acting out the roles and thereby reveal their true feelings.

Role playing is particularly useful in investigating situations where interpersonal relationships are the subject of the research, as, for example, salesperson–customer, husband–wife, and worker–supervisor.

Thematic Apperception Test (TAT)

A **thematic apperception test** (TAT) consists of a series of pictures or cartoons in which the research topic (co-workers, job task, and the like) is the center of attention. The investigator asks the subject to tell what is happening in the picture and what the people might do next. Hence themes (*thematic*) are elicited on the basis of the perceptual-interpretive (*apperceptive*) use of the pictures. The researcher then analyzes the content of the stories that the subjects relate.

The picture or cartoon stimulus must be sufficiently interesting to encourage discussion but sufficiently ambiguous not to disclose the nature of the research project.[16] Clues should not be given to the character's positive or negative predisposition. In a preliminary version of a TAT investigating why men might purchase a chain saw, a picture of a man looking at a very large tree was used in a pretest. The subjects of the research were homeowners and weekend woodcutters. When they were confronted with the picture of the extremely large tree, they almost unanimously said they would get professional help from a tree surgeon. Thus early in the pretesting process the researchers found that the picture was not sufficiently ambiguous and that the subjects did not identify with the man in the picture. If subjects are to project their views into the situation, the environmental setting should be a well-defined familiar problem, but the "solution" should be ambiguous.

Frequently a series of pictures with some continuity is presented so that stories may be constructed in a variety of settings. For example, in the first picture a woman might be working at her desk, and the final picture might show her making a presentation at a conference table.

The **picture frustration** version of the TAT uses a cartoon drawing in which the respondent suggests dialogue that the cartoon characters might speak. In Exhibit 5.4, a purposely ambiguous illustration of an everyday occurrence, two co-workers are placed in a situation and the respondent is asked what the woman might be saying.

EXHIBIT   5.4

**Picture Frustration
Version of TAT**

Source: Drawing by Nancy Blackwood.

DEPTH INTERVIEW

Motivational researchers, interested in the "why" of organizational or consumer behavior, may use a relatively unstructured, extensive interview during primary stages of the research process. This **depth interview** is similar to the client interview of a clinical psychologist or a psychiatrist. In the interviewing session the researcher asks many questions and probes for elaboration after the subject answers. Unlike the projective techniques, the subject matter is generally undisguised. The interviewer's role is extremely important in the depth interview. He or she must be a highly skilled individual who can encourage respondents to talk freely without influencing the direction of the conversation. Probing statements, such as "Can you tell me more about that?" "Can you give me an example of that?" "Why do you say that?" are made to stimulate respondents to elaborate on the topic being discussed. An excerpt from a depth interview is given in Exhibit 5.5.

While depth interviewing can be valuable in the early stages of researching a problem, this motivational research technique has lost some popularity in recent years. The depth interview may last more than an hour and it requires

E X H I B I T   5 . 5

**Excerpts from a
Depth Interview**

An interviewer (I) talks with Marsha (M) about furniture purchases. Marsha indirectly indicates she delegates the buying responsibility to a trusted antique dealer. She has already said that she and her husband would write the dealer telling him the piece they wanted (e.g., bureau, table). The dealer would then locate a piece which he considered appropriate and would ship it to Marsha from his shop in another state.

M.   . . . we never actually shopped for furniture since we state what we want and (the antique dealer) picks it out and sends it to us. So we never have to go looking through stores and shops and things.

I.   You depend on his [the antique dealer's] judgment?

M.   Um, hum. And, uh, he happens to have the sort of taste that we like and he knows what our taste is and always finds something that we're happy with.

I.   You'd rather do that than do the shopping?

M.   Oh, much rather, because it saves so much time and it would be so confusing for me to go through stores and stores and stores looking for things, looking for furniture. This is so easy that I just am very fortunate.

I.   Do you feel that he's a better judge than . . .

M.   Much better.

I.   Than you are?

M.   Yes, and that way I feel confident that what I have is very, very nice because he picked it out and I would be doubtful if I picked it out. I have confidence in him, [the antique dealer] knows *everything* about antiques, I think. If he tells me something, why I know it's true—no matter what I think. I know he is the one that's right.

This excerpt is most revealing of the way in which Marsha could increase her feeling of confidence by relying on the judgment of another person, particularly a person she trusted. Marsha tells us quite plainly that she would be doubtful (i.e., uncertain) about her own judgment, but she "knows" (i.e., is certain) that the antique dealer is a good judge, "no matter what I think." The dealer once sent a chair that, on first inspection, did not appeal to Marsha. She decided, however, that she must be wrong, and the dealer right, and grew to like the chair very much.

Source: From Donald F. Cox, *Risk Taking and Information Handling in Consumer Behavior*. Boston: Division of Research, Harvard Business School, 1967, pp. 65–66. Copyright © 1967 by the President and Fellows of Harvard College. Used with permission.

an extremely skilled interviewer; so it is expensive. In addition, because the area for discussion is largely at the discretion of the interviewer, the success of the research is dependent on the interviewer's skill. And, as is so often the case, good people are hard to find. A third major problem stems from the necessity of getting both the surface reactions and the subconscious motivations of the respondent. Analysis and interpretation of such data is highly subjective and it is difficult to determine the "true interpretation." Finally, for most information, alternative techniques, such as focus groups, may be utilized as a substitute for the depth interview.

A WARNING

Exploratory research cannot take the place of quantitative, conclusive research. Nevertheless, a number of firms use what should be exploratory studies as the final, conclusive research project. This has led to incorrect decisions. The most

important thing to remember about exploratory research techniques is that
they have limitations. Most of them are qualitative, and interpretation of the
findings is typically judgmental. For example, the findings from projection
techniques can be vague. They may produce some interesting, and occasionally
bizarre, hypotheses about what was inside a person's mind, such as:

**A woman is very serious when she bakes a cake because unconsciously she is
going through the symbolic act of giving birth.**

A man buys a convertible as a substitute "mistress."

Men who wear suspenders are reacting to an unresolved castration complex.

Conclusions based on qualitative research may also be subject to considerable
interpreter bias.[17]

An example of conflicting claims is illustrated by studies of prunes made
by two organizations. One study, using projective techniques, showed that
people considered prunes to be shriveled, tasteless, and of poor appearance.
The research showed that the prunes were symbolic of old age and of parental
authority (thus disliked), and associated with hospitals, boarding houses, peculiar people, and the army. The other study stated that the principal reason why
people did not like prunes was because of their laxative property.

Findings from focus group interviews may similarly be ambiguous. How
is a facial expression or nod of the head interpreted? Have subjects fully grasped
the idea or concept behind a nonexistent product? Have respondents over-
stated their interest because they tend to like all new products? Because of such
problems in interpretation, exploratory findings should be considered preliminary. Another problem with exploratory studies involves the projectibility of
the findings. Most exploratory techniques utilize small sample sizes, which
may not be representative because they have not been selected on a probability
basis. Case studies, for example, may have been selected because they represent
extremely good or extremely bad examples of a situation rather than average
situations.

Before a scientific decision can be made, a quantitative study with an adequate sample should be conducted to ensure that measurement is precise. This
is not to say that exploratory research lacks value; it simply means that such
research cannot deliver what it does not promise. The major benefit of exploratory research is that it generates insights and clarifies the business problems for
hypothesis testing in future research. One cannot determine the most important attributes of a new program or policy until those attributes have been identified. Thus exploratory research is extremely useful, but it should be used with
caution.

There are some occasions when the research process should stop at the
exploratory stage. If a personnel manager conducted exploratory research to
get a better perspective on employees' reaction to eliminating a group dental
health insurance plan, and if exploratory findings showed an extreme negative
reaction by almost all participants in a focus group, then the personnel manager may no longer wish to continue the project. One researcher suggests that
the greatest danger of utilizing exploratory research to evaluate alternative pro-

grams, new product concepts, and the like is not that a poor idea will be accepted, because successive steps of research will prevent that. The real danger is that a good idea with promise may be rejected because of findings at the exploratory stage. This is the greatest danger.[18] In other situations where everything looks positive in the exploratory stage, there is the temptation to accept the new idea without further research. What management should do after conducting exploratory research is determine whether the benefits of the additional information would be worth the cost of further research. In most cases when a major commitment of resources is at stake, it is well worth the effort to conduct the quantitative study. Many times good business research only documents the obvious. However, the purpose of the business is to make a profit, and decision makers want to be confident that they have made the correct choice.

SUMMARY

Qualitative research is subjective in nature. It leaves much of the measurement process to the discretion of the researcher. This approach does not use rigorous mathematical analysis. Quantitative research determines the quantity or extent of an outcome in numbers. It provides an exact approach to measurement.

The focus of this chapter is on qualitative exploratory research. Exploratory research may be conducted to diagnose a situation, to screen alternatives, or to discover new ideas. It may take the form of gathering background information through investigating secondary data, conducting experience surveys, or utilizing a pilot study. The purpose of the research, rather than the technique, determines whether a study is exploratory, descriptive, or causal. Thus the techniques discussed in this chapter are *primarily* but not exclusively used for exploratory studies.

Focus group interviews are unstructured, free-flowing, group dynamics sessions that allow individuals the opportunity to initiate the topics of discussion. There is a synergistic and spontaneous interaction among respondents that has been found to be highly advantageous.

The case study method involves intensive investigation into one particular situation that is similar to the problem under investigation.

Projective techniques are an indirect means of questioning respondents. Some examples are the word association test, the sentence completion test, the third-person technique, the role-playing technique, and the thematic apperception test.

Depth interviews are unstructured, extensive interviews that encourage a respondent to talk freely and in depth about an undisguised topic.

Although exploratory research has many advantages, it also has several shortcomings and should not take the place of quantitative, conclusive research.

Knowing where and how to use exploratory research is important. Many firms make the mistake of using exploratory studies as the final, conclusive research project. This could lead to decisions based on incorrect assumptions. Exploratory research techniques have limitations: The interpretation of the findings is based on judgment, samples are not representative, and these techniques rarely provide precise quantitative measurement. The ability to generalize results is limited.

Key Terms

exploratory research	word association
concept testing	sentence completion
experience survey	third-person technique
secondary data analysis	role playing
pilot study	thematic apperception test (TAT)
focus group interview	picture frustration
case study method	depth interview
projective technique	

Questions

1. What type of exploratory research would you suggest in each of the following situations?
    a. At an executive meeting a manager suggests the company look into implementing "quality circles" in the factory.
    b. A bank loan officer wishes to forecast the economy of the state in which the bank operates.
    c. A product manager suggests that a nontobacco cigarette, blended from wheat, cocoa, and citrus, be developed.
    d. A research project has the purpose of identifying the labor issues of concern to a union.
    e. A manager must determine the best site for a convenience store in an urban area.
2. Develop a concept statement for a thermometer that consists of a chemically treated plastic strip. The thermometer is placed against a child's forehead and held firmly in place. What are the important characteristics of your concept statement?
3. What is the function of a focus group? What are the advantages and disadvantages of a focus group interview?
4. What benefits can be gained from case studies? What dangers, if any, are there in using them? In what situations are they useful?
5. Investigate the focus group interview on pages 85–86. Evaluate it and generate a number of tentative hypotheses for future quantitative research.
6. A focus group moderator plans to administer a questionnaire before starting the group discussion about several new compensation concepts. Is this a good idea? Explain.
7. Telefocus is a new system that utilizes advanced telephone technology to hold group sessions over the telephone. What advantages and disadvantages do you think this exploratory research technique might have?
8. What are some potential uses of word association tests and sentence completion tests in your particular field of interest?

References

[1] Based on "N. W. Ayer Manipulated Americans' Attitudes Towards Diamonds," *Ad Week,* June 28, 1982, 82.

[2] Reprinted by permission of Farrar, Straus and Giroux, Inc. Excerpts from p. 11 of *Thirty Seconds* by Michael J. Arlen. Copyright © 1979, 1980 by Michael J. Arlen. This material first appeared in *The New Yorker.*

[3] Bill Iuso, "Concept Testing: An Appropriate Approach," *Journal of Marketing Research* (May 1975): 228–231.

[4] *Concept, Product, and Package Testing* (Cincinnati, OH: Burke Marketing Research).

[5] Sally Scanlon, "Calling the Shots More Closely," *Sales and Marketing Management* (March 1979): 90.

[6] Dale Fever, "Where the Dollars Go," *Training* (October 1985): 46.

[7] John M. Hess, "Group Interviewing," in R. L. King, ed., *New Science of Planning* (Chicago: American Marketing Association, 1968), 194.

[8] William D. Wells, "Group Interviewing," in Robert Ferber, ed., *Handbook of Marketing Research* (New York: McGraw-Hill, 1977), 2–133.

[9] John M. Hess, "Group Interviewing," in *New Science of Planning,* ed. R. L. King (Chicago: American Marketing Association, 1968), 194. The general advantages of the focus group interview are based on this source.

[10] Myril D. Axelrod, "Ten Essentials for Good Qualitative Research," *Marketing News,* Mar. 14, 1975, 11.

[11] Wells, "Group Interviewing."

[12] Robert F. Hartley, *Marketing Mistakes* (Columbus, OH: Grid, 1976), 87.

[13] Dietz Leonhard, *The Human Equation in Marketing Research* (New York: American Management Association, 1967), 78.

[14] The Iowa Poll, August 1977.

[15] Mason Haire, "Projective Techniques in Marketing Research," *Journal of Marketing* (April 1950): 649–652.

[16] Leonhard, *Human Equation in Marketing Research,* 73.

[17] Philip Kotler, "Behavioral Models for Analyzing Buyers," *Journal of Marketing* (October 1965): 37–45.

[18] Lee Adler, "To Learn What's on the Consumer's Mind, Try Some Focus Group Interviews," *Sales and Marketing Management,* April 9, 1979, 76–80.

Secondary Data and Database Search and Retrieval Systems

What you will learn in this chapter:

To explain the difference between secondary data and primary data.

To discuss the advantages and disadvantages of secondary data and give examples of each.

To discuss the various internal and external sources of secondary data and give examples of each.

To explain the management information systems concept.

To define a decision support system and list its components.

To understand the process of database searching and retrieving with computers.

To give examples of the major wholesalers of bibliographic databases.

To discuss the channels of distribution for secondary data.

Zoos have learned a lesson from art museums. To increase the public's interest, zoos in different regions of the world are starting to exchange animals. Zoo curators, however, must ask questions such as "Is the gorilla in Seattle related to the one in San Antonio?" Until recently, that question could only be answered with a stack of pedigree charts and the time to study them. Now the answer can be found in seconds, along with other valuable information.

As major zoos around the world become business-oriented, they increasingly use databases and computerized decision support systems to manage their "product lines." The Animal Records Keeping System (ARKS) allows zoos to tap into information about their animal collections, ranging from how inbred an animal is to how much it cost and the number of times it has been on loan. Each program is tailored specifically to the zoo using it, covering only the animals in each particular collection.

Zoos are not just tracking animals on their computers, however. Computers are being used for the storage and retrieval of all kinds of information that will allow zoos to do a better job of marketing. For example, a zoo can learn from its program that 10,000 people attended the zoo on the first Saturday of June 1988 but that only 6,000 attended on the first Saturday of June 1989, and it can also see whether it was raining or whether there was another community event on that day.

ARKS is maintained by the International Species Inventory System (ISIS). The 13-year-old organization, which keeps track of exotic animals in captivity, is now working to develop a second database, called MedARKS, that will store medical information.[1]

Consider another example. The American Medical Association estimates that in the year 2000 pediatricians will face more competitive conditions. There will be half as many children per pediatrician in the United States by the year 2000 compared with 1970. The number of children per pediatrican was 3,098 in 1970, 2,082 in 1983, and is projected to be 1,254 by the year 2000. Since 1970 the number of pediatricians has increased 89 percent, while the *number of children under 19 has dropped 8 percent. By 1990 there will be 41,350 pediatricians in America; the national quota is near 36,400.*[2]

As these examples show, secondary data—groups of factual items that have already been collected for another purpose, often from sources outside the research department—are extremely diverse. They can be extremely useful, and they are used extensively by most business organizations.

This chapter discusses the general nature of secondary data and illustrates many of the diverse sources for secondary data. The chapter also discusses how the searching of computerized databases is changing the way secondary data research is conducted.

■

WHAT ARE SECONDARY DATA?

Secondary data are data gathered and recorded by someone else prior to (and for purposes other than) the current needs of the researcher. Secondary data are usually historical, already assembled, and do not require access to respondents or subjects. For example, there are considerable secondary data concerning financial markets in Standard & Poor's Corporation's Market Value Index, and the Dow Jones industrial averages may be found daily in *The Wall Street Journal* and weekly in *Barron's*. Standard & Poor's *Trade and Security Statistics* contains extensive historical data about financial markets. For instance, a researcher interested in corporate failures can find in this source more than 150 years of secondary data.

Market potential is often estimated with secondary data. In many cases the exact figure may be published by a trade association or found in another source. However, when the desired information is unavailable, the researcher may estimate market potential by converting different types of secondary data that are available from two or more sources. For example, one source reports a survey finding that 10 percent of all electrical contractors intend to buy a drill. Another source indicates there are 80,000 electrical contractors in the market area. To learn how many drills will be sold to electrical contractors, the researcher multiplies 10 percent times 80,000 to convert the data so that an estimate may be made (8,000 drills will be sold to electrical contractors).

ADVANTAGES OF SECONDARY DATA

Fortunately, researchers are able to build on past research—a "body" of business knowledge. "Nowhere in science do we start from scratch."[3] Business researchers use others' experience and data, when these are available, as secondary data. The primary advantage of secondary data is that obtaining secondary data is almost always less expensive than acquiring primary data. In addition, secondary data can usually be obtained rapidly.

One only needs to consider the money and time saved by researchers who obtain updated population estimates for a town between the 1980 and 1990 censuses. Instead of doing the fieldwork themselves, researchers can acquire estimates from a firm that deals in demographic information, or they can make estimates from *Sales and Marketing Management's Survey of Buying Power.* Many of the activities normally associated with primary data collection (e.g., sampling, data processing) are eliminated.

In some instances data cannot be obtained by using primary data collection procedures. For example, a manufacturer of farm implements could not duplicate the information in the *Census of Agriculture* because much of its information (e.g., taxes paid) might not be accessible to a private firm.

DISADVANTAGES OF SECONDARY DATA

An inherent disadvantage of secondary data is that they were not designed specifically to meet the researcher's needs. Thus researchers must ask: "How pertinent are the secondary data?" In addition, to evaluate secondary data, researchers should ask questions such as: "Is the subject matter consistent with our problem definition?" "Do the data apply to the population of interest?" "Is the time period consistent with our needs?" "Do the secondary data appear in the correct units of measurement?" "Do they cover the subject of interest in adequate detail?"

Consider the following typical situations.

A researcher, interested in forklift trucks, finds that the secondary data on the subject are in a broader, less pertinent category, encompassing all industrial trucks and tractors. Furthermore, these data were collected five years earlier.

An investigator, wishing to study those who make more than $75,000 per year, finds the top-end category in a secondary study, reported at $45,000 or more a year.

An investor, wishing to compare dividends of several industrial robot manufacturers, finds that the units of measure differ because stock splits are not provided.

Every business day the Dow Jones Industrial Average, a stock market indicator series, is reported by the local media. This secondary data source reflects the prices of 30 nonrandomly selected "blue chip" stocks. This readily available, and inexpensive, source of information may not suit the needs of the individual concerned with the "typical company listed on the New York Stock Exchange."

Each of these situations shows that even when secondary information is available, it can be inadequate. The most common problems are (1) outdated information, (2) variation in definition of terms, (3) different units of measurement, and (4) lack of information to verify the data's accuracy.

Secondary information quickly becomes outdated in our rapidly changing environment. Since the purpose of most studies is to predict the future, helpful secondary data must be timely.

Each primary researcher has the right to define the terms or concepts under investigation. This is little solace to the investigator of black American labor who finds secondary civilian labor force data reported as "12.5 percent nonwhite." Variances in terms or classifications should be scrutinized to determine if differences are important. Units of measurement may cause problems if they are not identical to the researcher's needs. For example, lumber shipments in millions of board feet are quite different from shipments in billions of ton-miles of lumber transported on freight cars. Head-of-household income is not the same unit of measure as total family income. Often the objective of the original, primary study may dictate that the data be summarized, rounded, or reported in such a way that even though the original units of measurement were comparable, these aggregated or adjusted units of measurement are not suitable in the secondary study.

When secondary data are reported in a format that does not exactly meet the researcher's needs, data conversion may be necessary. **Data conversion** (or data transformation) is the process of changing the original form of the data to a format suitable to achieve the research objective. For example, sales for food products may be reported in pounds, cases, or dollars. An estimate of dollars per pound or pounds per case may be used to convert the data reported as dollar volume to pounds or to another suitable format.

Another disadvantage of secondary data is that the user has no control over their accuracy. Although timely and pertinent secondary data may fit the researcher's requirements, the data could be inaccurate. Research conducted by other persons may be biased to support the vested interest of the source. For example, media often publish data from surveys to identify the characteristics of their subscribers or viewers, but they will most likely exclude derogatory data from their reports. If the possibility of bias exists, the secondary data should not be used.

Investigators are naturally more prone to accepting data from sources such as the U.S. government because of the integrity of the source. Nevertheless, the researcher must assess the reputation of the organization gathering the data and critically assess research design to determine if the research was correctly implemented. Unfortunately, such evaluation may not be possible if the information explaining how the original research was conducted is not available.

Researchers should verify the accuracy of the data whenever possible. Cross-checks of data from multiple sources—that is, comparison of the data from one organization with data from another source—should be made to determine the similarity of independent projects. When the data are not consistent, researchers should attempt to identify reasons for the differences or to determine which data are most likely to be correct. If the accuracy of the data cannot be established, the researcher must determine if using the data is worth the risk. Exhibit 6.1 presents a series of questions that should be asked to evaluate secondary data before use.[4]

CLASSIFICATION OF SECONDARY DATA

Internal Sources

Secondary data come either from *internal* sources or from sources *external* to the organization. Most organizations routinely gather, record, and store internal data for solving future problems. The accounting systems of most firms

EXHIBIT   6 . 1

Evaluating Secondary Data

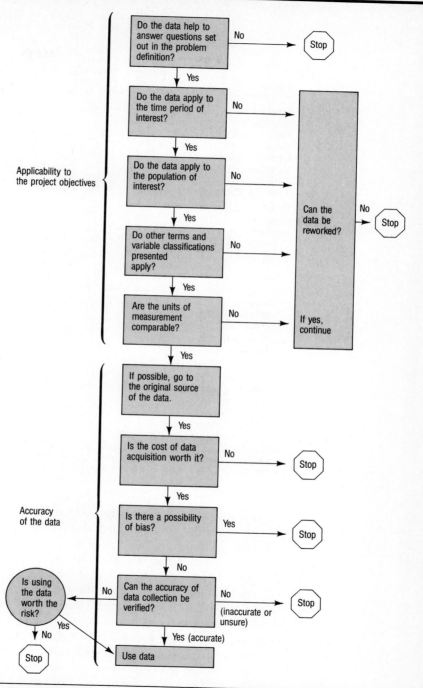

Source: Robert W. Joselyn, *Designing the Marketing Research Project* (New York: Petrocelli/Charter, 1977), 54.
Copyright © 1977 by Petrocelli/Charter Company. Reprinted by permission of Van Nostrand Reinhold.

EXHIBIT   6 . 2

Example of Internal Data from Accounting

Operating Car Loads vs. Forecast
May 15 (Current Year)

Market	Actual Today	Cars Over- (Under-) Forecast	Actual Month to Date	Over- (Under-) Forecast	Gross Rev. Equiv. M-T-D (-000-)	Rate
Automotive	551	49	7067	335	2092	296
Chemicals	540		7285	(6)	2732	375
Food + grain	284	(31)	4333	(352)	1343	310
Metals + coke ferr. ore	308	(1)	4843	33	1753	362
Lumber + paper	534	60	6957	(39)	1725	248
Minerals	475	21	6430	612	1421	221
Consumer + misc. prod.	386	(63)	6016	89	1378	229
Total merchandise	3076	35	42931	722	12444	
Coal—actual cars	3159	(91)	37902	(1118)	10271	271
Coke	29	(11)	500	(100)	108	215
Iron ore	311	66	3555	(120)	700	197
Total coal coke + ore	3499	(36)	41957	(1333)	11079	
Grand total	6575	(1)	84888	(616)	23523	

	C + O	B + O	Chessie
Total merchandise—year to date May 15, 19—			
This year	369,331	497,298	866,629
Last year (includes new rail cars)	406,053	515,841	921,894
% variance from last year	(9.0%)	(3.6%)	(6.0%)
Total merchandise—month to date			
This year	42,931	57,398	100,329
Last year (includes new rail cars)	49,953	59,641	109,594
% variance from last year	(14.91%)	(3.8%)	(8.5%)
Forecast May 19—			
Forecast this month	85,600	114,600	200,200
Revised outlook			
Actual same month year ago	101,300	121,500	222,800
Outlook % variance from last year	(15.5%)	(5.7%)	(10.1%)

Source: David L. Hurwood, E. S. Grossman, and E. L. Bailey, *Sales Forecasting* (New York: Conference Board, 1978), 30. Reprinted by permission of the Conference Board and Chessie System.

provide a wealth of information. The accounting department usually records information from routine source documents, such as sales invoices, for external financial reporting (which can be a source for further analysis). If the data are properly coded into a modular database in the accounting system, researchers may be able to conduct more detailed analyses.

Sales volumes by product and region can be identified; sales information can be broken down for accounts; information related to orders received, back orders, and unfilled orders can be identified; and sales can be forecast on the basis of past data (see Exhibit 6.2). Aggregating or disaggregating internal data is a common form of organizational research. Other useful sources of internal data may be files of salespersons' call reports, employee complaints, personnel records—and any other forms or records that a company may keep.

In large organizations consisting of many divisions, it is not unusual for one division to conduct research that proves useful to another division. One department usually does not know what another department is doing or has done; so, to avoid duplicate efforts, researchers should exhaust all sources within the company before searching elsewhere. Too often, secondary data analysis of internal data is ignored because research practitioners are inclined to design a new study every time management is in a quandary. A research executive at New York Telephone indicates there is a tendency to reinvent the wheel:

> *There is a gold mine of untapped information, direct or inferential, in the files or data banks of most moderate to large-size companies.*
>
> *Three years ago, we set about to examine all routine company reports and data generation processes to see how they could be harnessed for marketing purposes. We discovered that by interfiling or cross-referencing various accounting records, we could significantly disaggregate one standard measure of telephone consumption: the amount of monthly charges for telephone service.*
>
> *Whether you are a residential or business customer, basic consumption, represented by the number of telephones and the grade of service you have, plus all the peripheral equipment, is shown in one lump sum on the first line of the telephone bill.*
>
> *Yet, we have more than 2,000 different products and services that could be part of that single billing. Our new [analytical] tool, customer products database, gives us monthly, for each central office entity, a listing of all these 2,000-odd items.*[5]

External Sources

There are numerous external sources of data, the choice of which will be determined by the objectives of the research project. Of the external sources listed below, libraries, government sources, and commercial sources are the primary sources.

Libraries.   In addition to books and periodicals, libraries stock many bibliographies, abstracts, guides, directories, and indexes.

Professional journals, such as the *Journal of Business Research, Journal of Finance, Journal of Finance and Quantitative Analysis, Financial Analysts Journal, Accounting Review, Journal of Accounting Research, Journal of Marketing Research, Journal of Marketing, Journal of Academy of Management, Organizational Behavior and Human Performance,* and *Public Opinion Quarterly,* as well as commercial business periodicals such as *The Wall Street Journal, Fortune,* and *Business Week,* contain much useful material. *Sales and Marketing Management's Survey of Buying Power* is a particularly useful source for information about consumer markets (Exhibit 6.3). A companion volume, *Sales and Marketing Management's Survey of Industrial Buying Power* is useful for investigating industrial markets. Standard & Poor's stock reports are an important source of financial information about a company.

To locate data in periodicals, indexing services such as the *Business Periodicals Index* and *The Wall Street Journal Index* are very useful. Several guides to data sources are also helpful. For example, the *American Statistical Index* and *Business Information Source* are valuable sources. Also, the University of

The Survey of Buying Power

Colorado

METRO AREA County City	Total Population (Thousands)	% Of U.S.	Median Age Of Pop.	% of Population by Age Group				Households (Thousands)	Total Retail Sales ($000)	Food ($000)	Eating & Drinking Places ($000)	General Mdse. ($000)	Furniture/ Furnish/ Appliance ($000)	Automotive ($000)	Drug ($000)
				18-24 Years	25-34 Years	35-49 Years	50 & Over								
BOULDER–LONGMONT	221.4	.0893	29.9	15.7	24.0	21.4	16.3	86.4	1,729,250	372,211	193,383	169,155	79,603	385,571	36,851
Boulder	221.4	.0893	29.9	15.7	24.0	21.4	16.3	86.4	1,729,250	372,211	193,383	169,155	79,603	385,571	36,851
• Boulder	78.2	.0315	28.5	25.3	25.1	17.8	15.8	31.4	938,898	155,982	114,172	122,702	52,830	205,563	15,802
• Longmont	52.5	.0212	30.6	9.9	22.0	20.8	19.5	20.3	427,218	107,394	37,889	37,224	14,308	108,583	13,105
SUBURBAN TOTAL	90.7	.0366	30.7	10.9	24.2	24.7	14.9	34.7	363,134	108,835	41,322	9,229	12,465	71,425	7,944
COLORADO SPRINGS	400.0	.1613	29.5	14.4	19.9	21.2	17.9	149.9	2,573,497	446,129	256,583	332,176	147,644	599,651	47,740
El Paso	400.0	.1613	29.5	14.4	19.9	21.2	17.9	149.9	2,573,497	446,129	256,583	332,176	147,644	599,651	47,740
• Colorado Springs	290.5	.1172	30.7	12.8	20.1	21.1	20.3	117.0	2,375,521	406,812	225,620	299,649	142,056	597,515	45,401
SUBURBAN TOTAL	109.5	.0441	26.0	18.8	19.1	21.5	11.4	32.9	197,976	39,317	30,963	32,527	5,588	2,136	2,339
DENVER	1,684.5	.6795	31.4	10.6	21.9	22.2	19.9	671.6	11,641,766	2,393,247	1,297,261	1,584,989	659,756	2,440,615	232,365
Adams	285.5	.1152	29.2	12.1	20.6	21.3	16.8	105.1	1,851,219	375,925	149,867	320,074	98,877	456,968	31,984
Thornton	51.6	.0208	27.7	11.3	25.9	18.3	12.7	17.9	433,907	62,231	26,061	88,964	11,832	179,159	5,414
Westminster	66.1	.0267	28.1	11.0	27.4	20.0	11.2	23.2	275,704	68,996	32,114	64,409	17,419	11,532	6,922
Arapahoe	402.8	.1625	31.1	9.4	22.3	24.8	16.5	156.5	3,471,010	571,911	273,074	568,406	136,102	954,004	57,682
Aurora	232.3	.0937	29.8	10.7	25.9	22.0	14.5	87.3	1,785,975	417,487	150,023	345,120	73,534	314,933	28,617
Denver	504.7	.2036	32.6	12.0	23.0	17.5	27.1	230.1	3,310,636	745,595	558,630	344,840	242,934	362,022	74,222
• Denver	504.7	.2036	32.6	12.0	23.0	17.5	27.1	230.1	3,310,636	745,595	558,630	344,840	242,934	362,022	74,222
Douglas	46.5	.0187	32.2	6.0	18.5	30.1	14.8	14.4	173,930	60,706	15,399	8,155	15,110	17,021	5,197
Jefferson	445.0	.1795	31.4	9.3	21.3	24.8	17.6	165.5	2,834,971	639,110	300,291	343,514	166,733	650,600	63,280
Arvada	94.4	.0381	30.6	9.3	20.3	25.7	15.3	33.4	360,870	126,261	42,891	32,827	17,688	31,718	7,227
Lakewood	123.9	.0500	33.4	10.1	18.2	25.9	21.2	47.9	1,319,683	158,082	126,488	121,518	80,370	468,341	21,043
SUBURBAN TOTAL	1,179.8	.4759	30.8	9.9	21.3	24.2	16.9	441.5	8,331,130	1,647,652	738,631	1,240,149	416,822	2,078,593	158,143
DENVER–BOULDER CONSOLIDATED AREA	1,905.9	.7688	31.2	11.2	22.0	22.1	19.5	758.0	13,371,016	2,765,458	1,490,644	1,754,144	739,359	2,826,186	269,216
FORT COLLINS–LOVELAND	187.6	.0756	29.7	16.3	21.9	19.4	18.9	71.6	1,197,147	260,111	122,076	119,626	61,990	251,623	24,804
Larimer	187.6	.0756	29.7	16.3	21.9	19.4	18.9	71.6	1,197,147	260,111	122,076	119,626	61,990	251,623	24,804

Source: 1989 Survey of Buying Power, reprinted by permission of Sales & Marketing Management © Survey of Buying Power, August 7, 1989.

Colorado's business research staff has published a useful data-source guide: "Business Facts: Where to Find Them."[6]

Government Sources. Government agencies are prolific in producing data, and most of the data published by the federal government can be counted on for accuracy and high quality of investigation. Most students are familiar with the *Census of Population,* which provides a wealth of data. (Exhibit 6.4 shows some of the geographic areas in the 1990 census reports.) Of course, the *Census of Population* is only one of the many resources that the government provides. Many companies rely heavily on the *Survey of Current Business, Economic Indicators,* and the *Economic Report of the President* for data relating to research on financial and economic conditions. Builders and contractors utilize information in the *Current Housing Report* and *Annual Housing Survey* for their research. The *Statistical Abstract of the United States* is an extremely valuable source for information about the social, economic, and political organization of the United States. The appendix at the end of this chapter lists and annotates many of these important government documents.

State, county, and local government agencies can also be useful sources of information. Many states publish state economic models and forecasts. Many

EXHIBIT   6 . 4

**Geographic Building
Blocks for Census
Data Reporting**

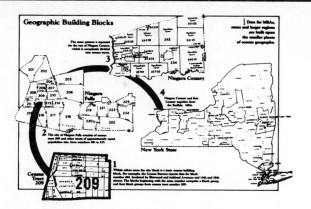

Source: Reproduced with permission from *American Demographics,* © October 1979, 40.

cities have metropolitan planning agencies that provide data about the population, economy, transportation, and the like. These data are similar to federal government data but are more current and structured to suit local needs.

Regional Publications.   In addition to national material issued by the government, regional data and comments on the economy are published by a number of banks.[7] The Federal Reserve system is divided into 12 Federal Reserve districts, with a major Federal Reserve bank in each, as follows:

1. Boston
2. New York
3. Philadelphia
4. Cleveland
5. Richmond
6. Atlanta
7. Chicago
8. St. Louis
9. Minneapolis
10. Denver
11. Dallas
12. San Francisco

Each Federal Reserve district bank has a research department that issues periodic reports. Although most of the publications generated by the various banks differ, monthly reviews, which are available to interested parties, are published by all district banks. In addition to providing descriptive statistics, these reviews typically contain one (or several) articles of interest to those in the region. A major exception is the St. Louis Federal Reserve Bank, which publishes numerous weekly, monthly, and quarterly statistical releases containing extensive national and international data.

Several large commercial banks, such as Chase Manhattan (New York) and Continental Bank (Chicago), prepare weekly or monthly letters that comment on the current and future outlooks.

Commercial Sources.   Numerous firms specialize in selling information. For example, the R. L. Polk Company publishes information in the automotive field: average car values and new-car purchases by zip code. The Petroleum Information Corporation provides information on oil inventories. Several such firms will be discussed here to provide a sampling of the diverse data available.

Market Share Data.   Market tracking refers to the observation and analysis of trends in industry volume and brand share over time. A number of syndicated services supply either wholesale or retail sales volume data based on product movement. Selling Areas—Marketing Incorporated (SAMI) is one of several research suppliers that provide figures on warehouse withdrawals, that is, product movement out of distributor warehouses into retail stores.

The A. C. Nielsen Company performs a wide range of research services. Although it it best known for providing television ratings, the Nielsen Retail Index Service is also a major market-tracking service. It measures consumer response at the point of sale. Using a carefully selected sample of stores (e.g., grocery stores), it tracks volume at the retail level. Nielsen auditors visit the stores at regular intervals. The audits reveal sales to customers, retail inventories' brand distribution, out-of-stock conditions, prices, and the like for competitive brands as well as for the client's own brand. Burgoyne Inc. also supplies retail information, providing audits of food, drug, mass merchandise, hardware, and convenience stores.

Scanner Data.   Advances in market tracking through optical character recognition are occurring with systems such as **universal product code (UPC)**. This system and optical scanners in more than 30,000 supermarkets now provide a wealth of product and brand sales information collectively known as **scanner data.**

Substituting mechanized record keeping for human record keeping results in greater accuracy and more rapid feedback about store activity. The universal product code contains information on the category of goods (e.g., grocery or drug item) and the manufacturer, as well as product identification information such as size, flavor, color, and so on. As the laser beam at the checkout counter reads the code, a computer-assisted sales receipt is printed with price and other descriptive information, and the computer records this in its memory for inventory and analytical purposes.

Information Resources, Inc. uses a national sample of supermarkets with optical scanning checkouts for its syndicated service that provides weekly product item movement, brand share data, and other aggregated product sales information. Organizations such as this enable researchers to monitor sales data before, during, and after the manipulation of advertising frequency, price changes, distribution of free samples, and similar marketing tactical changes. The rapidity of marketplace feedback is a direct result of a new technology that is continually improving.

Systems based on the UPC bar-code technology have been implemented in factories, warehouses, and transportation companies to research inventory levels, shipments, and the like.

Demographic and Census Updates.   A number of firms, such as CACI/Instant Demographics offer computerized U.S. census files and updates of these data by geographic areas, such as ZIP codes.

Attitude and Public Opinion Research.   Many research firms offer special-ized, syndicated services. For example, Yankelovich, Clancy and Schulman provides "custom" research, or research that is tailored for specific projects, and several syndicated services. Public-opinion research studies, such as the voter, executive, and public-attitude surveys in *Time* and *Business Week* maga-zines, are a source of secondary data. One of the more interesting services is offered in the *Yankelovich Monitor,* which is a cost-shared annual census of changing social values and how they can affect consumer marketing. The *Monitor* charts the growth and spread of new social values, the types of cus-tomers who support the new values and the types who support traditional val-ues, and the ways in which people's values affect purchasing behavior.

The Louis Harris Company is another public opinion research firm that provides syndicated and customer-research data for business. One of its ser-vices, the *ABC News/Harris Survey,* is released three times a week and pro-vides information about the American public on a wide variety of topics, such as inflation, unemployment, energy, attitudes toward the president, elections, and so on.

Stock Market Sources.   Numerous firms sell advisory services that supply in-formation on the aggregate market and individual stocks.[8] The following ad-visory services are examples of what is available.

Standard & Poor's *Corporation Records* is a set of seven volumes, the first six of which contain basic information on corporations, arranged alpha-betically. The volumes are updated throughout the year. The seventh volume, a daily news volume, contains recent data on all companies listed in the en-tire set.

Standard & Poor's *Stock Reports* are comprehensive two-page reports on numerous companies with stocks listed on the NYSE and the AMEX, and those traded OTC. They include the near-term sales and earnings outlook, re-cent developments, key income-statement and balance-sheet items, and a chart of stock-price movements (in bound volumes by exchange). A sample page is shown in Exhibit 6.5.

Standard & Poor's *Stock Guide* is a monthly publication that contains, in compact form, pertinent financial data on more than 5,000 common and pre-ferred stocks. It is a very useful quick-reference guide for almost all actively traded stocks. A separate section covers over 400 mutual fund issues. For each stock, the guide contains information on price ranges (historical and recent), dividends, earnings, financial position, institutional holdings, and its ranking for earnings and dividend stability.

Standard & Poor's *Bond Guide,* also published monthly, contains the most pertinent comparative financial and statistical information on a broad list of bonds, including domestic and foreign bonds (about 3,900 issues), 200 foreign-government bonds, and about 650 convertible bonds.

Moody's *Industrial Manual,* similar to the Standard & Poor's service, is currently published once a year in two bound volumes. It covers industrial companies listed on the NYSE and AMEX, as well as companies listed on re-gional exchanges. There is also a section on international industrial firms and

EXHIBIT 6.5 **Sample Page from a Standard & Poor's Stock Report**

Int'l Business Machines — 1210

NYSE Symbol IBM Options on CBOE (Jan-Apr-Jul-Oct) In S&P 500

Price	Range	P–E Ratio	Dividend	Yield	S&P Ranking	Beta
Dec. 27'89	1989					
94¾	130⅞–93⅜	10	4.84	5.1%	A+	0.84

Summary

IBM is the world's dominant manufacturer of mainframe computers and is also a major supplier of minicomputers, computer peripheral equipment, personal computers, networking products, and system software. An earnings recovery is foreseen for 1990, reflecting the absence of restructuring costs, increased global capital expenditures in the second half, and translation gains from a weaker dollar.

Current Outlook

Earnings for 1990 are expected to increase to $10.20 a share from 1989's estimated $6.90, which includes a $2.25 restructuring charge.

The $1.21 quarterly dividend is the minimum expectation.

Gross income should rise over 5% in 1990, benefiting from healthy demand overseas and a modest resurgence in domestic demand for IBM's main hardware products, plus translation gains from a weaker dollar. Profit margins should be stable, with gains from the domestic cost containment program offsetting pricing pressures in the mainframe and minicomputer markets.

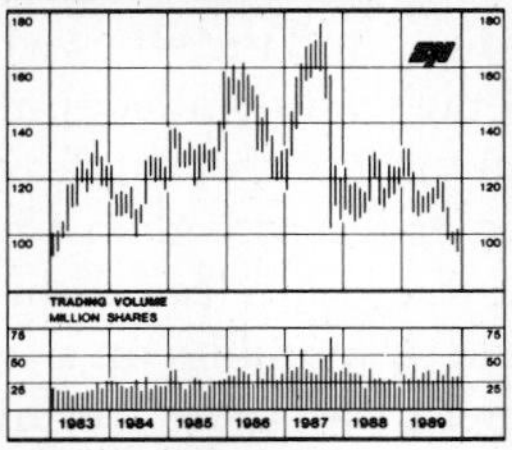

Revenues (Billion $)

Quarter:	1990	1989	1988	1987
Mar.	---	12.73	12.06	10.68
Jun.	---	15.21	13.91	12.80
Sep.	---	14.31	13.71	12.73
Dec.	---	---	20.00	18.01
	---	---	59.68	54.22

Revenues for the first nine months of 1989 advanced 6.5%, year to year, reflecting increased hardware and software sales, both in the U.S. and major international markets, despite the negative impact the stronger dollar had on the reporting of foreign revenues. Despite the absence of onetime manufacturing restructuring charges, net income edged up just 0.7%. Earnings per share were $5.43, compared with $5.30, which was before a $0.53 special credit from an accounting change.

Capital Share Earnings ($)

Quarter:	1990	1989	1988	1987
Mar.	E1.60	1.61	1.57	1.30
Jun.	E2.35	2.31	1.63	1.95
Sep.	E2.00	1.51	2.10	2.00
Dec.	E4.25	E1.47	3.97	3.47
	E10.20	E6.90	9.27	8.72

Important Developments

Dec. '89— The company said it would restructure its domestic operations, resulting in a $2.3 billion pretax charge in the fourth quarter, equal to about $2.25 a share after taxes. Some 10,000 positions would be eliminated. Nonetheless, management expected modest growth in the U.S. in 1990 and continued double digit revenue growth overseas in local currencies. Savings from the restructuring, which would include consolidations, capacity reductions, and technology investment writedowns, could add $1.00 to share earnings by 1991.

Dec. '89— Directors approved the repurchase of $4 billion of IBM stock in addition to the $1 billion previously authorized in October.

Aug. '89— During July and August IBM announced the actual or planned acquisition of minority stakes in a number of computer software concerns as part of an effort to speed development of applications software for IBM computers.

Next earnings report expected in mid-January.

Per Share Data ($)

Yr. End Dec. 31	[1]1988	1987	1986	1985	1984	1983	1982	1981	1980	1979
Tangible Bk. Val.	65.78	62.81	55.40	50.60	41.79	38.02	33.13	30.66	28.18	25.64
Earnings[2]	9.27	8.72	7.81	10.67	10.77	9.04	7.39	5.63	6.10	5.16
Dividends	4.40	4.40	4.40	4.40	4.10	3.71	3.44	3.44	3.44	3.44
Payout Ratio	47%	50%	56%	41%	38%	41%	47%	62%	56%	67%
Prices—High	129½	175⅞	161⅞	158¾	128½	134¼	98	71½	72¾	80½
Low	104¼	102	119¼	117⅜	99	92¼	55⅝	48⅜	50⅜	61⅛
P/E Ratio—	14-11	20-12	21-15	15-11	12-9	15-10	13-8	13-9	12-8	16-12

Data as orig. reptd. Adj. for stk. div(s). of 300% Jun. 1979. 1. Reflects acctg. change. 2. Bef. spec. item(s) of +0.53 in 1988. E-Estimated.

Standard NYSE Stock Reports
Vol. 57/No. 4/Sec. 15

January 5, 1990

Standard & Poor's Corp.
25 Broadway, NY, NY 10004

1210 International Business Machines Corporation

Income Data (Million $)

Year Ended Dec. 31	Revs.	Oper. Inc.	% Oper. Inc. of Revs.	Cap. Exp.	Depr.	Int. Exp.	[1]Net Bef. Taxes	Eff. Tax Rate	[2]Net Inc.	% Net Inc. of Revs.
[3]1988	59,681	12,617	21.1	5,390	3,871	802	9,033	39.2%	5,491	9.2
1987	54,217	11,269	20.8	4,304	3,527	619	8,609	38.9%	5,258	9.7
1986	51,250	11,175	21.8	4,620	3,316	604	8,389	42.9%	4,789	9.3
1985	50,056	14,281	28.5	6,430	3,051	443	11,619	43.6%	6,555	13.1
1984	45,937	14,446	31.4	5,473	3,215	408	11,623	43.4%	6,582	14.3
1983	40,180	13,216	32.9	4,930	3,627	390	9,940	44.8%	5,485	13.7
1982	34,364	11,618	33.8	6,685	3,562	514	7,930	44.4%	[3]4,409	12.8
1981	29,070	9,356	32.2	6,845	3,329	480	5,988	44.8%	3,308	11.4
1980	26,213	8,499	32.4	6,592	2,759	[3]325	5,897	39.6%	3,562	13.6
1979	22,863	7,566	33.1	5,991	2,321	140	5,553	45.8%	3,011	13.2

Balance Sheet Data (Million $)

Dec. 31	Cash	Curr. Assets	Curr. Liab.	Curr. Ratio	Total Assets	Ret. On Assets	Long Term Debt	Common Equity	Total Inv. Capital	% LT Debt of Cap.	Ret. On Equity
1988	6,123	35,343	17,387	2.0	73,037	8.1%	8,518	39,509	52,650	16.2	14.2%
1987	6,967	31,020	13,377	2.3	63,688	8.7%	3,858	38,263	47,271	8.2	14.6%
1986	7,257	27,749	12,743	2.2	57,814	8.7%	4,169	34,374	43,067	9.7	14.5%
1985	5,622	26,070	11,433	2.3	52,634	13.7%	3,955	31,990	39,595	10.0	22.4%
1984	4,362	20,375	9,640	2.1	42,808	16.4%	3,269	26,489	31,815	10.3	26.4%
1983	5,536	17,270	9,507	1.8	37,243	15.6%	2,674	23,219	26,606	10.1	25.2%
1982	3,300	13,014	8,209	1.6	32,541	14.1%	2,851	19,960	23,134	12.3	22.9%
1981	2,029	10,303	7,320	1.4	29,586	11.7%	2,669	18,161	21,082	12.7	19.0%
1980	2,112	9,925	6,526	1.5	26,703	13.9%	2,099	16,453	18,734	11.2	22.7%
1979	3,771	10,851	6,445	1.7	24,530	13.3%	1,589	14,961	16,690	9.5	21.2%

Data as orig. reptd.; finance subs. consol. aft. 1987. 1. Incl. equity in earns. of nonconsol. subs. 2. Bef. spec. item in 1988. 3. Reflects acctg. change.

Business Summary

IBM is the largest manufacturer of data processing equipment and systems. Industry segment contributions in recent years:

Gross Revenues	1988	1987
Processors/peripherals	44%	46%
Workstations	19%	19%
Programs/maint./other	34%	31%
Federal systems	3%	4%

Hardware sales provided 67% of revenues in 1988, software and services 29%, and rentals 4%. Foreign operations contributed 58% of revenues in 1988 and 71% of profits.

Processors manipulate data through the operation of a stored program. Peripherals include printers, storage and telecommunication devices. Workstations include small business computers, intelligent workstations and typewriters. Program products include applications and systems software. Maintenance represents separately billed maintenance services. Other revenues are derived from financing revenue, supplies and miscellaneous support services. The Federal systems group serves the U.S. government's defense, space and other agencies.

Dividend Data

Dividends have been paid since 1916. A dividend reinvestment plan is available.

Amt. of Divd. $	Date Decl.	Ex-divd. Date	Stock of Record	Payment Date
1.10	Jan. 31	Feb. 2	Feb. 8	Mar. 10'89
1.21	Apr. 24	May 4	May 10	Jun. 10'89
1.21	Jul. 25	Aug. 3	Aug. 9	Sep. 9'89
1.21	Oct. 31	Nov. 2	Nov. 8	Dec. 9'89

Next dividend meeting: late Jan.'90.

Finances

Research, development and engineering expense totaled $5.9 billion (9.0% of gross income) in 1988, versus $5.4 billion (9.8%; restated) in 1987.

Capitalization

Long Term Debt: $10,864,000,000, incl. $1.25 billion of 7⅞% debs. conv. into com. at $153.66 a sh.

Capital Stock: 578,846,802 shs. ($1.25 par).
Institutions hold approximately 49%.
Shareholders of record: 833,785.

Office—Armonk, New York 10504. **Tel**—(914) 765-1900. **Stockholder Relations Dept**—590 Madison Ave., NYC 10022. **Tel**—(212) 735-7000. **Chrmn**—J. F. Akers. **Secy**—W. W. K. Rich. **Treas**—D. A. Finley. **Investor Contact**—J. C. Clippard. **Dirs**—J. F. Akers, S. D. Bechtel, Jr., H. Brown, J. E. Burke, F. T. Cary, W. T. Coleman, Jr., T. F. Frist, Jr., F. Gerber, N. deB. Katzenbach, N. O. Keohane, J. D. Kuehler, R. W. Lyman, J. R. Munro, T. S. Murphy, J. R. Opel, H. Sihler, J. B. Slaughter, E. S. Woolard, Jr. **Transfer Agent & Registrar**—Morgan Shareholder Services Trust Co., NYC. **Incorporated** in New York in 1911. **Empl**—387,112.

Information has been obtained from sources believed to be reliable, but its accuracy and completeness are not guaranteed. Robert S. Natale, CFA

Source: Copyright © 1990 Standard & Poor's Corporation. Reprinted with permission.

an "Industrial News Reports" section that contains items on events that occurred after publication of the basic manual.

Moody's also publishes specialized industry books, such as *Moody's OTC Industrial Manual* (limited to stocks traded in the OTC market), *Moody's Public Utility Manual, Moody's Transportation Manual* (the transportation industry includes railroads, airlines, steamship companies, electric railways, bus and truck lines, oil pipelines, bridge companies, and automobile- and truck-leasing companies), *Moody's Bank and Finance Manual,* and *Moody's Municipal and Government Manual* [data on the U.S. government, all the states, state agencies, municipalities (over 13,500), foreign governments, and international organizations].

The *Value Line Investment Survey* is published in two parts. The first volume contains basic historical information on about 1,700 companies, a number of analytical measures of earnings stability and growth rates, a common-stock safety factor, and a timing-factor rating. It also includes extensive two-year projections for the given firms and three-year estimates of performance. In early 1990 it will include projections for 1990, 1991, and 1992–1994. The second volume includes a weekly service that provides general investment advice and recommends individual stocks for purchase or sale.

The *Value Line OTC Special Situations Service* is published 24 times a year for the experienced investor who is willing to accept high risk in the hope of realizing exceptional capital gains. In each issue past recommendations are discussed, and 8 to 10 new stocks are presented for consideration.

Other Financial Sources.   Financial information about other corporations may be obtained from numerous external sources, such as firms' annual reports, brokerage firm reports, and Security and Exchange Commission (SEC) reports.

Media Sources.   Information on a broad range of subjects is available from broadcast and print media. *The Wall Street Journal* is a comprehensive source for information on security-market prices. *Time* magazine commissioned a research study about hotel users, and the report of this survey is available free to potential advertisers. Data about the readers of magazines are typically profiled in media kits and advertisements. For example, for *Manhattan Inc.* the statistics are: median reader age, 41.6; male, 77.5 percent; hold management jobs, 75.5 percent; have investment portfolio, 94.3 percent, with average worth of $386,193.

Data like these are plentiful. The media like to show that their vehicles are viewed or heard by the advertisers' target markets. This type of data should be given careful evaluation, however, because often it covers only limited aspects of a topic. Nevertheless, it can be quite valuable for research, and it is generally free of charge.

SECONDARY DATA RETRIEVED BY COMPUTERS

Our discussion thus far has treated searches for secondary data in a traditional fashion, implying that most searches for secondary data require a trip to the library or to the accounting department to look at a book or a company report. However, recent developments in desktop computers and computer software have had a major impact on the retrieval and use of secondary data. Many manual data retrieval methods are being replaced by computerized **database retrieval systems.**

A **database** is either an internal or external collection of raw or aggregated data that is arranged in a logical manner and organized in a form that can be stored and processed by a computer.[9] Retrieval of secondary data from an internal database is discussed in the following section on decision support systems. Retrieval of secondary data from an external database is discussed in the subsequent section on database searching systems.

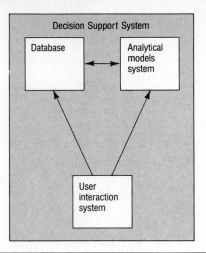

Decision Support Systems

Researchers make a distinction between the terms *data* and *information*. The primary difference between data and information is that **data** are simply facts, recorded measures of certain phenomena, whereas **information** refers to a body of facts that is in a format suitable for making a decision or in a context that defines a relationship between two pieces of data.

The purpose of a decision support system is to store internal data and transform that data into accessible information. A **decision support system** is a computer-based system that helps decision makers confront problems through direct interactions with databases and analytical models.[10]

Internal decision support systems have been developed because managers, with many alternative sources and types of information available to them, realized information had to be managed systematically. These systems are on-line computer systems that have been designed to sort, analyze, evaluate, and distribute pertinent, timely, and accurate information for decision making.

Exhibit 6.6 shows that a decision support system has three major components: database system, analytical models system, and user interaction system.

When internal data from accounting, finance, sales, manufacturing, payroll, and other areas of a business are stored in a computer system and arranged in a logical order, they are called *internal databases*. For example, employment data recorded by state, county, and city may be contained in a database. In a decision support system these databases become accessible to managers on an on-line, real-time basis.

Exhibit 6.7 illustrates the type of data that may be in the internal records system.

EXHIBIT   6 . 7

The Internal Record System Stores Considerable Amounts of Data

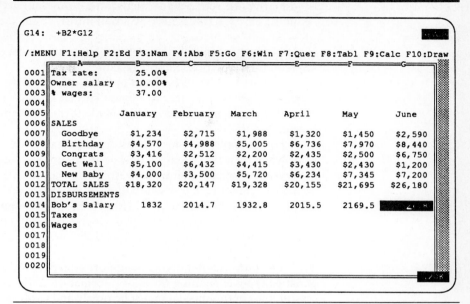

```
G14:   +B2*G12

/:MENU F1:Help F2:Ed F3:Nam F4:Abs F5:Go F6:Win F7:Quer F8:Tabl F9:Calc F10:Draw
        A          B          C          D          E          F          G
0001 Tax rate:      25.00%
0002 Owner salary   10.00%
0003 % wages:       37.00
0004
0005              January   February   March      April      May        June
0006 SALES
0007   Goodbye     $1,234    $2,715     $1,988     $1,320     $1,450     $2,590
0008   Birthday    $4,570    $4,988     $5,005     $6,736     $7,970     $8,440
0009   Congrats    $3,416    $2,512     $2,200     $2,435     $2,500     $6,750
0010   Get Well    $5,100    $6,432     $4,415     $3,430     $2,430     $1,200
0011   New Baby    $4,000    $3,500     $5,720     $6,234     $7,345     $7,200
0012 TOTAL SALES  $18,320   $20,147    $19,328    $20,155    $21,695    $26,180
0013 DISBURSEMENTS
0014 Bob's Salary   1832     2014.7     1932.8     2015.5     2169.5
0015 Taxes
0016 Wages
0017
0018
0019
0020
```

Source: Figure 3–2, "The Sales and Expenses of Gourmet Flakes, Inc." from *Joe Spreadsheet*, p. 84, copyright © 1988 by Goldstein Software, Inc., reprinted by permission of Goldstein Software, Inc.

Analytical Models System.   Computer technology has revolutionized the analysis of data in business. An **analytical models system** contains statistical software systems, spreadsheet software, and decision model banks that combine and restructure databases, diagnose relationships, estimate variables, and otherwise analyze the data within a system. Decision analysts apply complex statistical procedures and computerized decision models to such data. For instance, suppose a bank has a listing of all its customers in a central computer file. Analysts can create a new file of high-volume customers, and by using certain statistical procedures, they can even analyze the demographic structure of this group by zip code.

User Interaction System.   The interactive, on-line processing feature of a decision support system is what makes a decision support system so desirable. Having a system that is user friendly—one that is easy for novices to use yet allows them to maintain direct control over the computer's tasks and their outcomes—requires software to manage the interface between the user and the system. Computer software written to manage this activity is referred to as the **user interaction system.**[11]

The interaction system allows the manager to sit at a computer terminal to retrieve data files and perform recurrent analyses. At K mart a computerized point-of-sale checkout system (UPC scanners) and a satellite communications system linked to a decision support system allow managers at the retailer's headquarters to retrieve and analyze up-to-the-minute sales data on all merchandise for its 2,100 stores.[12] Certain information, such as monthly sales figures, is "fed" to managers on a recurring basis. Further, managers operate an inquiry data terminal in their offices and retrieve databases that provide answers to their questions almost instantly.

A more important function of the user interaction system, however, is the ability it gives the manager to request special analyses that will refine, modify, or generate information in a tailor-made format suitable for evaluating consequences or alternatives.

For example, at American Hoechst managers can obtain automatic solutions when they ask "what if" questions. A computer-mapping system projects the revenue increases that would result from various placements of salespeople. To achieve this, a manager who visualizes an alternative sales force deployment simply touches the map with a light pen and the computer changes the picture to reflect the new alignment of personnel. Company officials estimate that the improved decision making made possible with their decision support system increases sales by $1.3 million a year.

The purpose of a decision support system is to manage information systematically by expediting flows of information to decision makers. To be successful, the continuous data must be timely and easily accessible and must regularly provide adequate assistance to the manager who is making the decisions. Nonrecurring information must also be provided in a format that adequately satisfies the information requirements.

Database Searching Systems

There are numerous database searching systems available in libraries and on a subscription-service basis.

Computer-assisted literature searching has made the traditional method of searching for publications—thumbing through a library card catalog—obsolete. In the modern library patrons command a computer to do the searching. The modern "card catalog" is a computer terminal and modem that enables the computer to transmit and receive information over a telephone line. University students may find these terminals in the main lobby of the library or in many other campus locations. Searchers for secondary data query the library computer to learn whether the library owns a particular book and whether that book is on the shelf or checked out. The process is, of course, much faster than using a card catalog. An added dimension to information search and retrieval within libraries, "on-line search services" use portable computer terminals, acoustical couplers, and a telephone.

Database searching is becoming the most efficient and exhaustive form of search for "published" external secondary data. Several major "wholesalers" (also called on-line vendors) of bibliographic databases include BRS (BRS Information Technologies), DIALOG (DIALOG Information Services, Inc.), NEXIS (Mead Data Central, Inc.), ORBIT (ORBIT Search Services), and Dow Jones News/Retrieval Service. These services provide access to computer-readable databases for business executives and scholars. (See Exhibit 6.8.)

DIALOG, for example, is the distributor of more than 350 databases. A typical database may have a million or more records each consisting of an abstract of a published article, containing one or two paragraphs that give the major points of the article, along with bibliographic information. One of DIALOG's databases, ABI/Inform, abstracts significant articles in more than 80 current journals in business and management.

To illustrate the process, let's use another example. Suppose a large organization subscribes to the ORBIT search system. A business executive might use the computer retrieval system to search the Accountant's Index for articles related to some aspect of auditing. If the executive wants a broader search to look for material not found in the Accountant's Index, the computer may be asked to search a second database, such as ABI Inform, that is also accessible through the ORBIT search system. Searching three or more databases is possible, but it does, of course, increase the cost of the research.

A computerized bibliography is an efficient way to begin the library research process. Exhibit 6.9 shows two references and abstracts obtained in a search that requested from DIALOG all articles on "equity theory published in 1987 and 1988."

Database searching requires the researcher to initiate a *controlled vocabulary search* by indicating specific descriptors or names, such as a company name, or by *free text searching* using pertinent key words. Notice in Exhibit 6.9 that "equity theory" is a descriptor in both article abstracts. The free text searching process can identify other articles on the basis of words in the abstract. Other articles that mention equity theory even though it's not a primary focus may be found this way. Perhaps the major advantage of computerization is the computer's ability to merge or delete references and to obtain precisely what is needed. A researcher interested in site location may use the descriptor "location analysis," which could be restricted to "bank location analysis" with a simple programming change.

To illustrate in greater detail, Exhibit 6.10 takes a step-by-step look at the Compuserve system's IQuest database. Notice that IQuest-I begins with a set of prompts that helps you select an appropriate database to search. If you had in mind a particular database where you expected to find information about your topic, you would select IQuest-II, which would then prompt you for the name of that resource.

Many computerized databases provide information other than abstracts of published journal articles. The Compustat database described in Exhibit 6.11 provides an example of the extensive statistical and financial data that are available. A description of the most popular on-line information services is provided in Exhibit 6.12.[13]

Compact Disk—Read Only Memory systems (CD—ROM systems) provide an alternative technology for databased searching.[14] Large amounts of data (the equivalent of 275,000 printed pages) can be stored on a single compact disk. The database in a CD—ROM system, rather than being stored on-line in a central computer at another location, is stored on a compact disk that can be inserted into the microcomputer work station at the library or wherever the microcomputer is located. Many libraries have CDs that contain bibliographic databases. However, CD—ROM systems are more widely used for the storage of financial, statistical, and market data. For example, Compact Disclosure has financial and management information on more than 12,000 public companies, and the Donnelley Company has demographic data, data on retail sales for hundreds of product categories, physical-distance data, and other types of data stored on CD—ROM systems for every zip code in the

EXHIBIT   6 . 9   **Sample Results from a Computerized Search for Articles on Equity Theory**

89-00794
Title: Equity and Workplace Status: A Field Experiment
Authors: Greenberg, Jerald
Journal: Jrnl of Applied Psychology Vol: 73 Iss: 4 Date: Nov 1988
             pp: 606-613 Jrnl Code: JAP ISSN: 0021-9010
Terms: Equity theory (PER); Job status; Studies; Hypotheses; Work
             environment; Job attitudes; Life insurance companies; Questionnaires;
             Variance analysis
Codes: 2500 (Organizational behavior); 9130 (Experimental/theoretical); 8210
             (Life & health insurance)
Abstract: To investigate whether the characteristics of an employee's workspace
   influence perceptions of equitable treatment on the job, 198 employees in the
   life insurance underwriting department of a large company were temporarily
   reassigned to new offices while their own offices were being refurbished.
   The new offices were those of either higher, lower, or equal-status
   coworkers. The principal dependent measure was job performance. To help
   explain the performance measure, additional information, including a job
   satisfaction rating, was obtained by questionnaire. The equity theory
   hypothesis that the status value of the new offices would influence
   performance was supported by statistical analyses. Specifically, those
   workers who were reassigned to higher status offices increased performance
   whereas those reassigned to lower status offices decreased performance.
   Equity theory is thus a useful tool for explaining workers' reactions to
   temporary working environments. Tables. Graphs. References.

87-14275
Title: A New Perspective on Equity Theory: The Equity Sensitivity Construct
Authors: Huseman, Richard C.; Hatfield, John D.; Miles, Edward W.
Journal: Academy of Mgmt Review Vol: 12 Iss: 2 Date: Apr 1987 pp: 222-234
             Jrnl Code: AMR ISSN: 0363-7425
Terms: Equity; Theory; Organizational behavior; Compensation; Input; Output;
             Psychological aspects; Personality; Studies
Codes: 2500 (Organizational behavior); 9130 (Experimental/theoretical)
Abstract: Equity theory proposes that individuals who perceive themselves as
   either underrewarded or overrewarded will experience distress, which leads to
   efforts to restore equity. There still appear to be individual differences
   in regard to equity, however. To explain these differences a new construct,
   equity sensitivity, is proposed. Equity sensitivity describes 3 classes of
   individuals along a continuum: 1. Benevolents, who prefer their
   outcome/input ratios to be less than the outcome/input ratios of the
   comparison other, 2. Equity Sensitives, who prefer their outcome/input
   ratios to equal those of comparison others, and 3. Entitleds, who prefer
   their outcome/input ratios to exceed the comparison others. These general
   preferences for equity can be traced to internal standards. This construct
   helps explain perceptions of job satisfaction, quantity and quality of work,
   absenteeism, and turnover. Charts. Graphs. Diagrams. References.

United States. The researcher can retrieve these data for any type of geographic area to be investigated.

The 1990 U.S. census will be available from private companies in a CD–ROM format. The U.S. Census' TIGER System (Topologically Integrated Geographic Encoding and Reference System) will be the first computer-mapping system of the entire United States. The database will have the country on the

E X H I B I T   6 . 1 0   **IQuest Sample Search**

IQuest Navigational Command Summary

The same navigational commands you use to travel the CompuServe Information Service are in place in the IQuest database.

Type	Action
B	To back up one screen
T	To return to the IQuest Main Menu
Exit	To leave the IQuest database
H	To display online HELP information
Off	To log off the Information Service
SOS	To summon online assistance from an IQuest research specialist

Step #1

Select IQuest-1 if you don't know which database fits your topic.

PRESS	TO SELECT	
1	IQuest-I	We pick the database
2	IQuest-II	You pick the database
H	Help	

Total charges thus far : $0.00
─⟩ 1

Step #2

Use the menus to describe your topic. In this example we selected Subject.

PRESS	TO SELECT
1	Subject
2	Person
3	Place
4	Organization
H	Help

Total charges thus far : $0.00
─⟩ 1

Step #3

Choose from the main subject topics. Here, we selected Business.

PRESS	TO SELECT
1	Current Events
2	Business, Economics
3	Sci/Tech, Computers, Medicine
4	Law, Trademarks, Patents
5	Social sciences, Education
6	Art, Literature and Entertainment
7	Religion, Philosophy
H	Help

Total charges thus far : $0.00
─⟩ 2

Step #4

Further qualify topic. We chose Economics.

PRESS	TO SELECT
1	Accounting
2	Banking and investment services
3	Corporate information
4	Economics
5	Finance
6	Insurance
7	Other choices
H	Help

Total charges thus far : $0.00
─⟩ 4

Step #5

Select a source of information from various media. We chose Professional journals.

PRESS	TO SELECT
1	Professional journals
2	Popular magazines
3	Books on economics
4	Encyclopedias
H	Help

Total charges thus far : $0.00
─⟩ 1

Step #6

Enter the words you would like to search for. Notice that we have used the wild card ("/") to find variations of "telecommute" (telecommuting, telecommuter, etc.). We also used "and" and "or" to qualify our search. This search will find articles on telecommuting as well as articles with the words "computer," "work" and "home" all included.

Enter your economics topic.

(type H for important examples) or B to back up)

─⟩ TELECOMMUT/ or (COMPUTER/and WORK and HOME)

Is:

TELECOMMUT/ OR (COMPUTER/ AND WORK AND HOME)
Correct? (Yes/No) ─⟩ Y

Step #7

IQuest determines the database to be searched and performs the search. Here, the ABI/INFORM database was accessed and the search found 80 articles.

System is searching the ABI/INFORM database, copyrighted 1986 by Data Courier, Inc., Louisville, KY, and available through BRS Information Technologies.

Accessing Network.(Standby). Connected.

Accessing Database Vendor . . . . Completed.

Submitting User name . . . . Completed.

Submitting Password . . . . Completed.

Selecting Database . . . . Completed.

Each star equals one line of retrieved data. This may take several minutes . . .
****
****
****
****
Search completed . . . .

Source: "CompuServe IQuest," *Online Today,* May 1986, 28–29. Reprinted with permission of *Online Today* Magazine, published by CompuServe, Inc.

There are 80 item(s) which satisfy your search phrase.

We will show you the most recent 10

Step #8

IQuest displays the 10 most recent titles (complete with bibliographic references).

Heading # 1

AN 86-06192. 8602.
AU Grevstad-Eric.
TI Telecommuter: Laptop Meets Desktop.
SO Tele: The Communications Magazine for Business. VOL: v1n4. PAG: 68-71, 4 pages. Jan 1986.

Heading # 10

AN 85-33212. 8510.
AU Antonoff-Michael.
TI The Push for Telecommuting.
SO Personal Computing. VOL: v9n7. PAG: 82-92, 8 pages. Jul 1985.

Press (return) to continue . . . —⟩

Step #9

Abstracts, photocopies of entire articles, or more titles may be selected from this menu. Here we chose to see an abstract.

PRESS	TO
1	Review results again
2	See abstracts (need heading #'s $2.00 each)
3	Order reprints (need heading #'s)
4	See next 10 headings ($7.00 extra)
5	Start a new search
6	Leave System

Total charges thus far : $7.00
—⟩ 2

Step #10

Simply enter the heading number(s) of the title(s) for which you want to see an abstract.

The Heading numbers currently range between 1 and 10

Enter the Heading numbers of the articles for which you wish abstracts. Separate each number by a comma.

Total charges thus far : $7.00
—⟩ 10

Step #11

The abstract is retrieved and then displayed.

Heading # 1

AN 85-33212. 8510.
AU Antonoff-Michael.
TI The Push for Telecommuting.
SO Personal Computing. VOL: v9n7. PAG: 82-92, 8 pages. Jul 1985.
CC 5250.
DE Work-at-home. Trends. Microcomputers. Softwarepackages. Advantages. Productivity. Disadvantages.
AV ABI/INFORM.

AB Telecommuting is gaining momentum as personal computers increasingly gain acceptance. In 1984, there were an estimated 100,000 telecommuters working for 400 companies. According to Gil Gordon, a consultant who publishes a newsletter about telecommuting, 10 million employees may work remotely by 1990. It has also been estimated that up to 20% of the Fortune 500 companies will have formal telecommuting programs by the mid-1990s. Telecommuting affords many benefits to companies, such as the need for less office space. Telecommuting also offers a way to keep skilled workers and reduce recruiting and training costs. For employees, telecommuting reduces transportation costs and makes it easier to take care of family responsibilities. In one study on telecommuters, it was found that telecommuting results in improved employer-employee supervision. However, labor unions have voiced opposition to the telecommuting trend. They fear the electronic cottage may turn into an electronic sweatshop. Tables. Graphs.

E X H I B I T   6 . 1 1   **The Compustat Database Is Stored on Compact Disc**

The first compact disc combining financial and full-text company reports for investment analysis.

WALL ST

"Compustat PC Plus," from McGraw-Hill. Start with 20 years of financial information on over 12,000 U.S. companies. Add word-for-word annual reports, 10K's, 10Q's and proxies for New York and American Stock Exchange companies. Combine with software for comprehensive financial analyses. Now, place it all in the palm of your hand. It fairly boggles the mind.

At McGraw-Hill, being first is almost second nature.

Source: Courtesy of McGraw-Hill, Inc.

same scale—1:100,000—and each map will fit with the segments. Although the map may be useful by itself (e.g., to make transportation and delivery more efficient), the greatest value will probably occur when it is coupled with demographic statistics to provide profiles of any small geographic area such as a zip code or individual block or street.

Macro Perspective of Secondary Sources: Information Reduction, Distribution, and Consumption

As we pointed out, secondary information is available from a number of sources, and Exhibit 6.13 indicates the channels of distribution for the information industry.[15] Just as a consumer may buy furniture directly from the factory or through a retailer, secondary information may be obtained from a number of different information providers.

Initiators of information (Level 1) produce information that may later be submitted for publication. Often, prior to formal publication, research results may be communicated through informal networks of colleague associations.

EXHIBIT   6.12

Selected Information
Retrieval Services and
Selected Examples of
Their Databases

Information Retrieval Service	Selected Sample Databases	Type of Data
BRS Information Technologies	ABI/Inform	Abstracts from business and management journals
	Investext	Full text for reports on companies and industries prepared by investment analysts in financial organizations
DIALOG Information Service	New York Times Information Bank	Abstracts of the *New York Times,* 13 other newspapers, and over 40 magazines
	American Statistical Index	Economic, demographic, agricultural, and other statistical data from government publications
	Standard & Poor's News	Financial and business activity data for 9,000 U.S. companies
ORBIT Search System	Chemical Industry Notes	Abstracts of business and other articles in several chemical industries
	Accountant's Index	Abstracts, articles on auditing, taxation, financial management, and other issues pertinent to CPAs
Compuserve	Disclosure Database	Financial data on more than 12,000 publicly held companies that file reports with the SEC
Dow Jones News/Retrieval	Dow Jones News/Retrieval Service	Complete and abridged articles from *The Wall Street Journal, Barron's,* and the Dow Jones News Service; price quotations on stocks, bonds, options, and mutual funds
DRI/McGraw-Hill	DRI Japanese Forecast	Data on the Japanese economy, including a macroeconomic model and forecasts

At Level 2 the "product" is manufactured. For example, the government puts the information from the census tapes into a formal government report. Scholarly journals or conference proceedings, when they become available for purchase, are another example of information distribution at Level 2.

Many users, such as the Fortune 500 corporations, purchase government documents and other publications. However, many smaller corporations learn about secondary data from an intermediate distributor (Level 3), an intermediary who collects and disseminates information. Abstracting and indexing services condense and cite the location of information.

For example, in chemistry and chemical engineering, one might use *Chemical Abstracts* to locate a specific topic. The abstracting service searches many journals and other publications to accumulate a large number of citations, then lists them by source so the user can have direct and easy access to a given topic. Retrieval-service vendors acquire data primarily from abstracting

Channels of Distribution: Information Industry

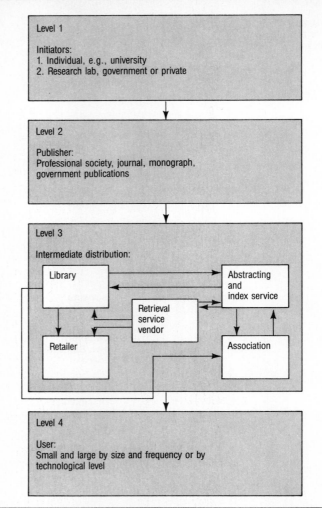

Level 1

Initiators:
1. Individual, e.g., university
2. Research lab, government or private

Level 2

Publisher:
Professional society, journal, monograph, government publications

Level 3

Intermediate distribution:

Library

Abstracting and index service

Retrieval service vendor

Retailer

Association

Level 4

User:
Small and large by size and frequency or by technological level

Source: James M. Comer and Alok K. Chakrabarti, "The Information Industry for the Industrial Marketer," *Industrial Marketing Management*, 7 (1978), 267–270. Copyright 1978 Elsevier North Holland, Inc. Reprinted with permission.

and indexing services, and add them to citation and indexing data that are stored in their computers. These "systems" are then sold to users, who install terminals in their organizations to facilitate usage.

A retailer of secondary data offers a full range of services beyond information retrieval. For example, technical consulting or design may be provided for the research consumer, as well as data.

Trade associations, such as the Food Marketing Institute or the American Petroleum Institute, serve the information needs of a particular industry. The trade association collects data on a number of topics of specific interest to firms, especially market size and market trends. Thus association members have a source of information that is particularly germane to their industry's questions.

For example, the Newspaper Advertising Bureau (NAB) has cataloged and listed on its computer the specialized sections that are currently popular in newspapers. NAB surveys all daily, Sunday, and weekend newspapers in the United States and Canada on their editorial content and stores this information, along with data on rates, circulation, and mechanical requirements, in its computer for the advertiser's use. And libraries, of course, are vast storehouses of information for dissemination to the public.

At Level 4 is the ultimate user of the information. As stated earlier, some users prefer to go directly to the initiator; other, less frequent users of information more than likely will use an intermediary to obtain information.

SUMMARY

Secondary data are data gathered and recorded by "someone else" prior to (and for purposes other than) the current needs of the researcher. Secondary data are usually historical, already assembled, and do not require access to respondents or subjects.

Primary data are data gathered for the specific purpose of the current researcher.

The chief advantage of secondary data is that they are almost always less expensive than primary data. They can generally be obtained rapidly and may include information not otherwise available to the researcher.

The main disadvantage of secondary data is that they were not designed specifically to meet the researcher's needs. Therefore the researcher must examine secondary data for accuracy, bias, and soundness. One method for doing this is to cross-check *different* sources of secondary data.

Data conversion is the process of changing the original form of the data to a format suitable to achieve the research objective.

Secondary data can come from internal sources, such as accounting records, or from external sources. The three primary external sources are libraries, government sources, and commercial sources.

Computerized information retrieval systems are growing rapidly, and computer technology is making significant changes in the means of acquiring and manipulating secondary data.

A decision support system stores internal data and transforms that data into accessible information. Database search and retrieval systems provide an efficient and exhaustive means for searching for published external secondary data.

There are many suppliers of bibliographic and numeric databases. Some of the major wholesalers of bibliographic databases include BRS, DIALOG, ORBIT, Compuserve, and Dow Jones News/Retrieval.

Because secondary data are available through a variety of channels, they may also come directly from the originators, from the publications of those originators, or from intermediate distributors, such as abstracting and index-ing services, retrieval-service vendors, retailers, trade associations, or libraries.

Key Terms

secondary data	database
data conversion	data
cross-checks	information
internal sources	decision support system
universal product code (UPC)	analytical models system
scanner data	user interaction system
databased retrieval systems	

Questions

1. Suppose you wish to learn about bankruptcies, mergers, and acquisi-tions. Indicate probable sources for these secondary data.
2. Over the past five years a manager has noted a steady growth of sales and profits for her division's product line. Is there a need to utilize any sec-ondary data to further evaluate the division's condition?
3. In the U.S. census, are college students counted at their homes or at their school residences?
4. What are the major geographic areas for secondary data reporting?
5. What would be the best source for the following data?
    a. State population, state income, and state employment for Illinois and Indiana.
    b. Maps of U.S. counties and cities.
    c. Demographics in Canada and other countries.
    d. Divorce trends in the United States.
    e. Median weekly earnings of full-time salaried workers for the range 1982–1987.
    f. Annual sales of the top ten fast-food companies.
    g. Brands of beer recently introduced in the United States.
    h. Number of airplane trips made by college students.
6. General Foods Corporation reports internal shipment data by calendar months. SAMI data are reported in "retail months" (13 periods a year). Nielsen retail audit data are reported bimonthly. What problem does this cause? Can it be corrected? Explain.
7. Suppose you are a business research consultant. If a client comes to your office and says, "I must have the latest information on the supply and de-mand of Maine potatoes within the next 24 hours," what would you do?
8. Find the following data in the *Survey of Current Business*, May 1987:
    a. Gross national product for the first quarter of 1987.
    b. Fixed investment for residential structures for the first quarter of 1987.
    c. Exports of goods and services for the first quarter of 1987.

9. Find the following data in the 1987 *Census of Manufacturers,* Industry Series:
   a. Value of shipments (1987, 1977) for industrial trucks and tractors—Standard Industrial Classification (SIC) 3537.
   b. Payroll per employee—industrial trucks and tractors—SIC 3537.
   c. Regional establishments—industrial trucks and tractors—SIC 3537.
10. Use the most recent *Sales and Marketing Management's Survey of Buying Power* to find the total population, median age, and total retail sales for (a) your hometown (or county), and (b) the town (or county) in which your school is located.
11. Use the most recent *Sales and Marketing Management's Survey of Industrial Buying Power* to find (a) the number of aluminum foundries (SIC 3361) in Cook County, Illinois, and in Los Angeles County, California, and (b) U.S. total employment in heating equipment manufacturing (SIC 3433).
12. Go to your library and prepare a list of computerized databases that contain financial data (e.g., stock prices).
13. Using secondary sources, what type of information can you find out about American labor unions? What trends are occurring in the American labor movement?
14. What is the difference between data and information? Provide an example.
15. What is the purpose of a decision support system?

References

[1] Adapted from Hilary Stout, "Getting the Rhino into the Computer," *New York Times,* July 12, 1987, F-15.

[2] AMA estimate reported in Steve Findlay, "More Doctors Make Swing to Pediatrics," *USA Today,* July 10, 1987, A-1.

[3] A. Kaplan, *The Conduct of Inquiry* (Scranton, PA: Chamber Publishing, 1964), 86.

[4] The original idea for this came from Robert W. Joselyn, *Designing the Marketing Research Project* (New York: Petrocelli/Charter, 1977), 54.

[5] "Heavy Regulation Doesn't Cut Need for Research: Harkay," *Marketing News,* Apr. 6, 1979, 11, published by the American Marketing Association.

[6] C. R. Goldner and Laura M. Dirks, "Business Facts: Where to Find Them," *MSU Business Topics* (Summer 1976).

[7] This section is adapted from Frank K. Reilly, *Investment Analysis and Portfolio Management,* 3rd ed. (Hinsdale, IL: Dryden Press, 1989), 184–185.

[8] This section is adapted from Frank K. Reilly, *Investment Analysis and Portfolio Management,* 3rd ed. (Hinsdale, IL: Dryden Press, 1989), 196–201.

[9] H. Webster Johnson, Anthony J. Faria, and Ernest L. Maier, *How to Use the Business Library* (Cincinnati: South-Western Publishing, 1984), 29; and Lorna M. Daniells, *Business Information Sources* (Berkeley, CA: University of California Press, 1985, with a new edition in progress).

[10] Ralph H. Sprague, Jr., and Hugh J. Watson, *Decision Support Systems: Putting Theory into Practice* (Englewood Cliffs, NJ: Prentice-Hall, 1986), 1.

[11] Sprague and Watson, *Decision Support Systems,* 21, 155.

[12] Patricia Strand, "K mart Moving to Scanners," *Advertising Age,* June 8, 1987, 36.

[13] For an extensive listing of databases, see *The Annual Directory of On-Line Data Bases* (New York: Cuadra/Elsevier); see also H. Webster Johnson, Anthony J. Faria, and Ernest L. Maier, *How to Use the Business Library: With Sources of Business Information* (Cincinnati: South-Western Publishing, 1984) for excellent coverage of this topic.

[14]See Ernie Maier, "Comments on Databased Searching," working paper, Lawrence Technological University for a discussion of this technology and how it differs from other forms of on-line databased searching.

[15]This section has been adapted from James M. Comer and Alok K. Chakrabarti, "The Information Industry for the Industrial Marketer," *Industrial Marketing Management* 7 (1978): 267–270. Copyright 1978 by Elsevier North Holland Inc.

Selected Secondary Sources

GOVERNMENT SOURCES

Census Data

- *Census Catalog and Guide.* Published annually. A guide to census data and reports available during the quarter. Issues contain descriptions of publications, data files, and special tabulations.
- *Census of Agriculture.* Compiled every five years (in years ending in 2 and 7). Includes data by state and county of the number, types, and sizes of farms, land use, employment, products, and value of products. Supplemented by *Agricultural Statistics and Commodity Yearbook.*
- *Census of Business.* Compiled every five years (in years ending in 2 and 7). Presented in four units:

    1. *Census of Retail Trade.* Presents statistics on states, Metropolitan Statistical Areas (MSAs), Primary Metropolitan Statistical Areas (PMSAs), Consolidated Metropolitan Statistical Areas (CMAs), counties, and cities. Data include sales, payroll, employees, and number of establishments, sales by merchandise lines, and so forth, arranged by Standard Industrial Classification (SIC) code number. Updated each month by Monthly Retail Trade.

    2. *Census of Wholesale Trade.* Gives data for states, MSAs, and counties on sales, number of establishments, payrolls, warehouse space, expenses, and so forth, arranged by SIC code number. Updated each month by Monthly Wholesale Trade.

    3. *Census of Service Industries.* Gives statistics on retail service organizations like hotels, beauty parlors, laundries, and the like on receipts, employment, number of units, payrolls, and so on for states, MSAs, counties, and cities. Does not include information on the professions, insurance, or real estate. Updated each year by Annual Selected Services Receipts.

4. *Census of Transportation.* Compiled every five years (in years ending in 2 and 7). Presented in three divisions: Truck Inventory and Use Survey, National Travel Survey, and Commodity Transportation Survey.

- *Census of Housing.* Compiled every ten years (in years ending in 0) in conjunction with population estimates and projections, income, mobility, education, migration, birth and death rates, and other information. Contains information about a variety of geographic divisions—in some MSAs, by city block. Housing characteristics include cost of housing, monthly rent, average value, type of structure, size, condition of building, year built, occupancy figures, water and sewer facilities, financial characteristics, average number of rooms, occupancy by nonwhites, and equipment (such as washers, stoves, and air conditioning).

- *Current Housing Report* and *Annual Housing Survey.* Provide updated information between censuses on vacancies, urban and rural housing data, general housing characteristics, and other information. Composed of five volumes: *States and Small Areas, Metropolitan Housing, City Blocks, Components of Inventory Change,* and *Residential Financing.*

- *Census of Manufacturers.* Compiled every five years (in years ending in 2 and 7). Manufacturing industries are grouped into over 450 classes. Information on capital expenditures, value added, employment, payrolls, number of establishments, inventories, and so on is contained in two reports: *Final Area Reports* (with data by geographic region) and *Final Industry Reports* (with data by industry type). *Annual Survey of Manufacturers* and *Current Industrial Reports* update the information between censuses.

- *Census of Population.* Compiled every ten years (in years ending in 0). Presents population characteristics of states, counties, MSAs, urbanized areas, and census tracts. Demographics include age, sex, race, marital status, family composition, national origin, citizenship status, employment, income, level of education, and other characteristics. *Current Population Report,* published annually, updates the information in the *Census of Population* and gives data on family characteristics. The reports from the 1990 census are listed below.

Volume I:
- *Characteristics of the Population.* This volume consists of separate reports for the United States, each of the 50 states, the District of Columbia, Puerto Rico, Guam, the Virgin Islands, American Samoa, and the Trust Territory of the Pacific Islands.

- *Number of Inhabitants.* Final official population counts are presented for states, counties, MSAs, urbanized areas, county subdivisions, incorporated places, and census-designated places.

- *General Population Characteristics.* Statistics on age, sex, race, Spanish origin, marital status, and household relationship are presented for states, counties, MSAs, PMSAs, CMSAs, urbanized areas, county subdivisions, places of 1,000 or more inhabitants, Indian reservations, and Alaskan native villages.

- *General Social and Economic Characteristics*. These reports focus on the population subjects collected on a sample basis. Each subject is shown for some or all of the following areas: states, counties, MSAs, urbanized areas, places of 2,500 or more inhabitants, Indian reservations, and Alaskan native villages.
- *Detailed Population Characteristics*. These reports cover most of the population subjects collected on a sample basis, presenting the data in considerable detail, cross-classified by age, race, and other characteristics. Each subject is shown for states and large MSAs. Some subjects will also be shown for central cities of large MSAs.

Volume II:

- *Subject Reports*. Each report in this volume concentrates on a particular subject. Detailed sample information and cross-relationships are provided on a national and/or regional level; in a few reports, data for states, large cities, MSAs, or Indian reservations are also shown. Some of the characteristics covered are national origin, race, Spanish origin, type of residence, fertility, families, marital status, migration, education, employment, occupation, industry, income, and poverty status.
- *Census of Transportation*. Compiled every five years in years ending in 2 and 7. Provides statistics on the number of trucks, their uses, vehicle miles, etc.

General Information

- *American Statistics Index*. Used to identify, evaluate, and obtain information contained in the myriad statistical publications of more than 500 sources within the federal government. Published monthly in two parts: *Index* and *Abstracts*.
- *Business Statistics*. Biennial supplement to *Survey of Current Business*. Contains extensive historical data, usually monthly, for about 2,100 series contained in survey. An explanatory note for each of the series describes the series and indicates original sources for data.
- *CIS Index*. Used to identify, evaluate, and obtain information contained in the working papers of the U.S. Congress. It covers hearings, prints, documents, reports, and special publications issued as far back as 1970 or as recently as a month ago. Published monthly in two parts: *Index* and *Abstracts*.
- *County Business Patterns*. Published annually by the Department of Commerce. Businesses are classified by type, employment, and payroll, and arranged by SIC code number. Breakdowns are given by county and state, and totals for the United States are presented.
- *County and City Data Book*. Supplement to *Statistical Abstract*, published irregularly (although at least every five years). Provides break-

downs by city and county for income, population, education, employment, housing, banking, manufacturing, capital expenditures, mineral and agricultural production, retail and wholesale sales, voting records, and other categories. Data are taken from censuses and other government publications.

- *Economic Indicators.* Published monthly by the Council of Economic Advisors. Contains current data on prices, wages, money, credit, gross national product, personal consumption, federal finance, production, and other series that indicate the country's economic condition.
- *Economic Report of the President.* Published annually. Review of economic conditions in the United States and the economic policy of the administration, taken from the president's yearly address to Congress on the country's economic outlook. Includes annual report of the Council of Economic Advisors and statistics from other government documents.
- *Federal Reserve Bulletin.* Published monthly by the Board of Governors of the Federal Reserve System. Contains financial and economic data, including interest rates, savings, industrial production, banking, loans, investments, securities prices, fund flows, money market data, and international trade.
- *Historical Statistics of the United States.* Supplements *Statistical Abstract* by presenting general data that allow comparison of figures from colonial times to present (last published in 1970).
- *Index to International Statistics.* Used to identify, evaluate, and obtain information contained in the statistical publications of the world's major intergovernmental organizations (IGOs). These 80–90 IGOs include the United Nations system, the Organization for Economic Development, the European Community, the Organization of American States, commodity organizations, development banks, and other regional and special-purpose organizations. Published monthly in two parts: *Index* and *Abstracts.*
- *Monthly Catalog of United States Government Publications.* Published monthly, with semiannual index. Describes publications of the U.S. government, arranged by publication number. Includes subject and title indexes.
- *Monthly Labor Review.* Published monthly by the Bureau of Labor Statistics. Contains information on nationwide labor conditions and trends, including employment, wage rates, work weeks, collective bargaining, labor turnover, work stoppages, industrial accidents, and so on. Includes relevant data on consumer price indexes and wholesale and retail prices.
- *Selected Publications to Aid Business and Industry.* A one-time publication by the Department of Commerce, International Trade Administration. Presents federal statistical sources (since 1979) that are useful to business and industry.
- *Social Indicators.* Published irregularly (most recently in 1980) by the Bureau of the Census, Department of Commerce. Presents statistics and trends on social conditions: health, public safety, education, employ-

ment, income, housing, leisure and recreation, and population. Can be used for making industry forecasts.

- *Standard Industrial Classification Manual.* Published by the Office of Management and the Budget. Businesses are classified numerically according to product or services they offer (commonly called SIC Code). Useful as a reference when searching other secondary sources.

- *Statistical Abstract of the United States.* Published by the Bureau of the Census on an annual basis. This is one of the most valuable references because it abstracts data from original government reports and serves as a reference for more detailed information about the social, political, and economic organizations in the United States. It is designed to serve as a convenient volume for statistical reference and as a guide to other statistical publications and sources.

- *Statistics of Income.* Published annually by the Internal Revenue Service of the Treasury Department. Data collected from the federal income tax returns of businesses and individuals. Information is contained in three volumes: *Corporations, Sole Proprietorships and Partnerships,* and *Individuals.* Within each volume information is further broken down by industry, assets owned, and so on. Summary reports are included in each volume.

- *Statistical Reference Index.* Used to identify, evaluate, and obtain significant statistical information published by a wide range of U.S. associations and institutes, businesses, commercial publishers, independent research organizations, state governments, and university research centers. Published monthly in two parts: *Index* and *Abstracts.*

- *Survey of Current Business.* Published monthly, with weekly statistical supplements, by the Office of Business Economics. This document is the source of figures for the gross national product, national income, and international balance-of-payments calculations. Also provides statistics on general business conditions, domestic trade, personal-consumption expenditures, and industry (including breakdowns by industry for earnings, employment, labor force, and so on). Most data are for the previous four years.

- *Statistical Bulletin.* Monthly publication of the Securities and Exchange Commission (SEC). Contains data on securities trading in the United States, with emphasis on common stocks. Gives volume of trading on all exchanges and the OTC market, prices on these exchanges, volatility and liquidity measures, and information on new-issue registrations.

- *Annual Report of the SEC.* Published by the SEC for the fiscal year ending in June. Detailed discussion of important developments during year. Also comments on the SEC's disclosure system and regulation of securities markets, and a statistics section contains historical data on many items in the *Statistical Bulletin.*

- *Quarterly Financial Report (QFR).* Published by the Bureau of the Census (was published by the Federal Trade Commission until recently). Up-to-date aggregate statistics on the financial position of U.S. corporations.

Estimated statements of income and retained earnings, balance sheets, and related financial and operating ratios for all manufacturing corporations. Includes data on mining and trade corporations. Statistical data are classified by industry and, within the manufacturing group, by size.

- *U.S. Industrial Outlook.* Published annually by the International Trade Commission. Trends and 10-year projections for approximately 240 U.S. industries are given, as well as detailed information on each industry.

REFERENCE GUIDES

- *Business Information Sources,* rev. ed., by Lorna M. Daniells (Berkeley, CA: University of California Press, 1985). An annotated bibliography of books, periodicals, and reference sources in all important areas of business. Of its 21 chapters, 3 focus on business statistical sources, 2 on investment sources, and 1 on marketing (the latter including handbooks, books, and reference books on marketing, market research, product development, selling, advertising, and retailing. A new edition is in progress with publication planned for 1992.
- *Encyclopedia of Business Information Sources,* 7th ed. (Detroit: Gale Research, 1987). Presents detailed listing of primary subjects of interest to managerial personnel, with a record of source books, periodicals, organizations, directories, handbooks, bibliographies, and other sources of information on each topic.
- *Encyclopedia of Geographic Information Sources,* 4th ed. (Detroit: Gale Research, 1987). Sources of information for cities, states, and regions on such topics as population, taxes, business conditions, communications, transportation facilities, and climate.

MARKET DATA

- *Predicasts Forecast Index.* Published monthly, quarterly, and annually by Predicasts Inc. Reviews business, financial, and trade magazines, newspapers, and newsletters. Information includes statistics and forecasts for product areas, industries, and U.S. economy.
- *Market Guide.* Published annually in October by *Editor and Publisher* magazine. Similar to *Survey of Buying Power.* Provides information on approximately 1,500 newspaper markets in the United States and Canada. Data include population, number of households, transportation, housing, retail outlets, principal industries, banks, automobiles, and so on. Market maps are included.
- *Survey of Buying Power.* Published annually in two parts in special July/August and October/November issues of *Sales and Marketing Management.* Market data are given for states, counties, cities, metropolitan areas, and regions for the United States and Canada. Includes statistics on industrial buying, population, retail sales of many types of products, market potential, individual income, households, and so on. Two indexes

are computed for each area: effective buying income, which is an estimate of personal income, and buying power index, which measures market potential.

ECONOMIC AND INDUSTRY DATA

- *Annual DRI/McGraw-Hill Spring Survey of Business' Plans for New Plants and Equipment.* Published annually by McGraw-Hill. Survey of industrial firms' capital investment plans for the coming four-year period, reported by industry.
- *Standard & Poor's Industry Survey.* Published by Standard & Poor's Corporation. Survey of major U.S. industries, presenting current state of the industry, trends, and projections as well as statistics on each industry group. A "basic analysis" is published annually. A short "current analysis" updates the "basic analysis" three times annually.

CORPORATE DATA

- *Dun's Market Identifiers.* A database directory file produced by Dun's Marketing Services. Contains information about both public and private U.S. companies that have five or more employees, or companies with $1 million or more in sales. The database covers all types of commercial and industrial establishments as well as all product areas. Data on more than 8 million businesses has been gathered via interviews.
- *The Fortune 500.* Published annually in the April-May issues of *Fortune.* Statistics on sales, assets, profits, invested capital, and so on are given for the 500 largest U.S. corporations, 100 diversified service companies, 100 commercial banks, and 100 diversified financial companies, 50 largest (each) life insurance companies, retailing firms, transportation companies, and utilities in the United States. In addition, information on private organizations, exporters, and foreign corporations is provided.
- *Standard & Poor's Corporation Records.* Published semimonthly by Standard & Poor's Corporation, with bimonthly supplements. Contains updated information about corporate earnings, stocks, capitalization, and so forth.
- *Thomas Register of American Manufacturers.* Published annually by Thomas Publishing Company. Lists over 115,000 manufacturers by product classification. Information includes principal products, trademarks, and so on.

MAJOR INDEXES

- *Applied Science Technology Index.* Published monthly except July, with periodic cumulations. Indexes approximately 300 journals in applied sciences, such as geology, oceanography; technological fields, such as petroleum and gas, physics, plastics; and engineering disciplines, including telecommunications and environmental engineering.

- *Business Periodicals Index.* Published monthly, except July, with periodic cumulations. Indexes about 300 U.S. and foreign business publications, including popular periodicals and scholarly journals. Includes business book reviews at the end of each issue. On-line counterpart since 1984 is WILSON LINE.
- *Public Affairs Information Service Bulletin.* Published semimonthly, with periodic cumulations. A subject index compiled by library subject specialists in economics, business, public administration, and social problems. Lists magazine articles, books, pamphlets, U.S. government publications, and foreign government publications written in English. On-line counterpart is PAIS International.
- *Reader's Guide to Periodical Literature.* Published semimonthly, with periodic cumulations. Indexes over 150 general-interest U.S. magazines by subject and author. Does not index any academic or other scholarly business magazines; indexes only those magazines that are popular with lay audiences.
- *Social Sciences Citation Index.* Published triannually, with annual cumulations of over 4,700 periodicals in the social sciences, including economics, management, finance, and marketing. Indexed by subject, author, and citations of article.
- *The Wall Street Journal Index.* Published monthly, with annual cumulations. Lists all articles in *The Wall Street Journal*'s eastern edition by subject.

SELECTED INTERNATIONAL SOURCES

- *Yearbook of International Trade Statistics* (New York: United Nations Publishing Service, New York 10017). An annual two-volume publication. Volume 1 contains statistics on individual countries, and Volume 2 presents statistics by commodities and regions.
- *United Nations Statistical Yearbook* (New York: United Nations Publishing Service, New York 10017). An annual publication presenting statistics on population, agriculture, transportation, manufacturing, employment, wages, and education for a wide range of activities in various countries.
- *United Nations Demographic Yearbook* (New York: United Nations Publishing Service, New York 10017). Presents detailed demographic characteristics of the populations of various countries.
- *UNESCO Statistical Yearbook* (Louvain, Belgium). Detailed statistical tables for education (including educational expenditures); science and technology; culture and communication (including libraries, museums, book production, newspapers and other periodicals, paper consumption, film and cinema, radio and TV broadcasting).
- *Commodity Yearbook* (New York: Commodity Research Bureau Inc., New York 10006). Presents data on prices, production, exports, stocks, and so forth for more than 100 commodities.

INVESTMENT DATA [1]

- *New York Stock Exchange Fact Book.* An annual publication of the New York Stock Exchange. An outstanding source of current and historical data on activity on the NYSE. Also contains comparative data on the AMEX, the OTC market, institutional trading, and investors in general.
- *AMEX Statistical Review.* A comparable data book for the American Stock Exchange. Contains pertinent information on the exchange, its membership, listed companies, administration, trading volume, and monthly AMEX "market indices." The first issue (entitled *AMEX Data-book*) was published in 1969. The data book was originally published biennially; it is now published annually.
- *The Dow-Jones Investor's Handbook.* Contains the complete DJIA results for each year, along with earnings and dividends for the series since 1939. Individual reports on common and preferred stocks and bonds listed on the NYSE and AMEX, including high and low prices, volume, dividends, and the year's most active stocks, are also included. (Prior to 1980 the firm published handbooks on several other topics, including *Barron's Market Laboratory, The Dow-Jones Commodities Handbook,* and *The Dow-Jones Stock Options Handbook.*)
- *S&P Trade and Security Statistics.* A service of Standard & Poor's that includes a basic set of historical data on various economic and security price series and a monthly supplement that updates the series for the preceding period. There are two major sets of data: (1) business and finance and (2) security price index record. Within the business and finance section are long-term statistics on trade, banking, industry, prices, agriculture, and financial trends. The security price index record contains historical data for all of the Standard & Poor's indexes. This includes 500 stocks broken down into 88 individual groups, of which the four main groups—industrial composite, rails, utilities, and the 500 composite—are composed. There are also four supplementary group series: capital goods companies, consumer goods companies, high-grade common stocks, and low-priced common stocks. In addition to the stock price series, Standard & Poor's has derived a quarterly series of earnings and dividends for each of the four main groups. The earnings series includes data from 1946 to the present. The booklet also contains data on daily stock sales on the NYSE from 1918 on and historical yields for a number of bond series, both corporate and government.

References

[1] This section is adapted from Frank K. Reilly, *Investment Analysis and Portfolio Management,* 3rd ed. (Hinsdale, IL: The Dryden Press, 1989), 187–191.

PART 3

Research Methods for Collecting Primary Data

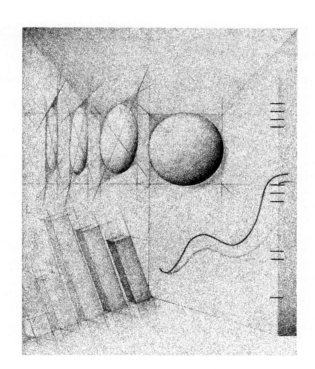

CHAPTER 7

Survey Research: An Overview

What you will learn in this chapter:

To understand the terms *survey, sample survey,* and *respondent.*

To understand the advantage of using surveys.

To discuss the type of information that may be gathered in a survey.

To recognize that very few surveys are error-free.

To distinguish between random sampling error and systematic error.

To classify the various types of systematic error and to give examples of each type.

To discuss how response error may be an unconscious misrepresentation and/or deliberate falsification.

To describe the classification of surveys according to method of communication, according to the degree of structure and disguise in questionnaires, and on a temporal basis.

Shortly *after several Wall Street scandals had made headlines, the television program, "Wall Street Week" commissioned Opinion Research Corporation to conduct a survey.[1] Almost a third of the 1,045 respondents said they were less likely to invest in stocks and bonds because of the scandals about junk bonds and inside trading. Thirty-six percent believed Wall Street was less ethical than it was 10 years ago. The survey revealed that most people (66 percent) think the stock market should be better regulated. However, a minority (16 percent) believed that there is already too much regulation. More than 40 percent thought that the Securities and Exchange Commission was doing a good job, but a third thought that the SEC was ineffective. Overall, the survey showed that 60 percent of the people believed that Wall Street was at least as ethical as other industries.*

A survey to determine airline pilots' major safety concerns found that fatigue in the cockpit, often due to a work load characterized by long hours of boredom, was the pilots' first concern. Indeed, one in five pilots indicated that they had observed fellow crew members sleeping in the cockpit. The second most pressing problem, according to the survey, was the perception that air traffic controllers were inadequately trained.[2] It is somewhat reassuring, however, to learn from the survey that 75 percent of the pilots believed that the day-to-day risk of a midair collision is low.

A survey by an opinion-research firm revealed that three-fourths of Americans reject the prospect of working at a boring job "as long as the pay is good." More than 60 percent felt that an employee has the right to refuse a promotion or refuse to move to another city if his employer asks him. Almost 80 percent would refuse to leave a job they like for one that pays more.[3]

Official statistics on unemployment, earnings, disability, retirement, and other characteristics of the labor force are derived from the Current Population Survey, *a survey of a scientifically selected sample of households conducted monthly by the Bureau of the Census for the Bureau of Labor Statistics.*

Survey research is conducted among voters, investors, consumers, employees, executives, wholesalers, retailers, bankers, students, zoo patrons, and many other people.

*The purpose of survey research is to collect **primary data**—data gathered and assembled specifically for the research project at hand. This chapter is the first of two on survey research: It defines the subject. It also discusses typical research objectives that may be accomplished with surveys and the various advantages of applying the survey method. The chapter provides a detailed explanation of the many potential errors that researchers must be careful to avoid. Finally, it classifies survey research methods.*

■

THE NATURE OF SURVEYS

Surveys require asking people, who are called **respondents,** for information, using either verbal or written questioning. Questionnaires or interviews are utilized to collect data through the mail, on the telephone, or face to face. The more formal term **sample survey** emphasizes that the purpose of contacting respondents is to obtain a representative sample of the target population. Thus a **survey** is defined as a method of primary data collection based on communication with a representative sample of individuals.

Survey Objectives: Type of Information Gathered

The type of information gathered in surveys varies considerably, depending on a survey's objectives. Typically, survey investigations attempt to describe what is happening or to learn the reasons for a particular business activity. Most survey research is therefore descriptive research. Some typical survey objectives are to identify characteristics of a particular group, measure attitudes, and describe behavioral patterns.

Most surveys have multiple objectives; few gather only a single type of factual information. For example, an organizational researcher might conduct a descriptive survey to determine workers' feelings toward a four-day work week. Demographic information might also be collected to determine if younger employees' feelings on the subject are different from those of older employees or if men agree with women on the subject.

Although it has been suggested that surveys are conducted to *quantify* certain factual information, certain aspects of surveys may also be *qualitative.* In new-product development surveys, the qualitative objective of a survey is often to test and refine new-product concepts. Stylistic, aesthetic, or functional changes may be welcome suggestions. Although most surveys are descriptive, they can also be designed to provide causal explanations or to explore ideas.

Advantages of Surveys

Surveys provide a quick, inexpensive, efficient, and accurate means of assessing information about the population.[4] The examples of surveys earlier in this chapter illustrate that surveys are quite flexible and, when properly conducted, extremely valuable to managers.

R E S E A R C H   I N S I G H T

Objectives and Results of a Descriptive Organizational Survey at Sears

Sears conducted a survey of 784 buyers, assistant buyers, and assistant sales managers from eight units of the corporate branch of the company. It was designed to measure the executives' satisfaction levels. Measures were also made of critical job characteristics, organizational environment characteristics, and certain individual characteristics of these executives. The following table lists the variables included in the survey.

Job Satisfaction Facets	Individual Characteristics	Job Characteristics	Organizational Environment Characteristics
1. Supervision	1. Sex	1. Task significance	1. Company support level
2. Career future	2. Age	2. Skill variety	2. Leadership: interpersonal orientation
3. Financial rewards	3. Race	3. Task identity	3. Leadership: task orientation
4. Amount of work	4. Education level	4. Autonomy	4. Work-assignment favorableness
5. Kind of work	5. Company tenure	5. Task feedback	5. Career favorableness
6. Company policies and practices			6. Organizational climate
7. Overall satisfaction			7. Work-group climate

The results of this survey were used to examine the relative levels of satisfaction with different facets and to determine which of the individual, job, and organizational environment variables were related to these satisfaction levels. The accompanying illustration summarizes the overall relationships of these sets of variables to the job satisfaction variables. On the average, individual characteristics accounted for only 2 percent of the variation in job satisfaction scores, while job characteristics and organizational environment characteristics explained 12 percent and 38 percent of the variation, respectively.

The Sears analysis provided some important observations:

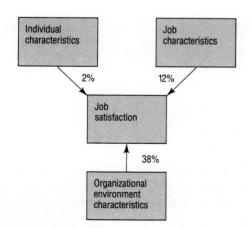

1. Of the individual characteristics, only tenure and age were related to any of the satisfaction variables, and even these were related only to satisfaction with career future and with company policies and practices. Older workers with longer tenure with the company were more satisfied than were younger, newer employees.
2. All five job characteristic variables were related to the job satisfaction variables. By far the strongest relationship was between job characteristics and satisfaction with the kind of work. In general, as the significance, variety, identity, autonomy, and feedback perceived in a job increased, satisfaction with the kind of work increased also—as did, to a lesser extent, satisfaction with supervision and satisfaction with company policies and practices.
3. All organizational environment characteristics were related to one or more job satisfaction variables. Satisfaction with supervision and career future had the strongest relationships to organizational variables while satisfaction with financial aspects and with amount of work had the weakest relationships. Organizational and work-group climate both had a positive impact on satisfaction with company policies and practices. Company support level positively influenced satisfaction with career future more than any other variable. Both interpersonal and task-oriented leadership behavior were very strongly related to satisfaction with

(continued)

R E S E A R C H   I N S I G H T

(continued)

supervision. Descriptions of current work assignments were highly related to satisfaction with the kind of work. Finally, positive descriptions of the career were indicative of satisfaction with career future and with company policies and practices.

Although these data cannot prove cause-effect relationships, they do provide a comprehensive overview of the current state of the organization. Such a perspective is valuable for understanding the interaction of employees, jobs, and elements of the organization.

Source: From *Organizational Surveys: An Internal Assessment of Organizational Health* by Randall B. Dunham and Frank J. Smith, pp. 37–40, published by Scott, Foresman and Company. Copyright © 1979 by Randall B. Dunham and Frank J. Smith. Reprinted with permission from the authors.

As we discussed in Chapter 1, business research has proliferated in recent years. The growth of survey research is related to the simple idea that to find out what people think, one should ask them.[5]

Over the last fifty years, and particularly during the last two decades, survey research techniques and standards have become quite scientific and accurate. When properly conducted, surveys offer managers many advantages. However, survey research can also be used poorly.

> *It may be no exaggeration to say that the greater number of surveys conducted today are a waste of time and money. Many are simply bad surveys. Samples are biased; questions are poorly phrased; interviewers are not properly instructed and supervised; and results are misinterpreted. Such surveys are worse than none at all because the sponsor may be misled into a costly area. Even well-planned and neatly executed surveys may be useless if, as often happens, the results come too late to be of value or converted into a bulky report which no one has time to read.*[6]

The disadvantages of surveys are best discussed in specifics for each form of data collection (mail, personal interview, and telephone). However, a general discussion of errors in surveys is appropriate.

ERRORS IN SURVEY RESEARCH

A manager evaluating the quality of a research project must estimate the accuracy of the survey. Exhibit 7.1 outlines the various forms of survey error. The two major sources of survey error are random sampling error and systematic error.

Random Sampling Error

Most surveys try to portray a representative cross section of a particular target population. Even with technically proper random probability samples, statistical errors will occur because of chance variation. Unless sample size is increased, these statistical problems are unavoidable. However, **random sam-**

EXHIBIT   7 . 1   **Tree Diagram of Total Survey Error**

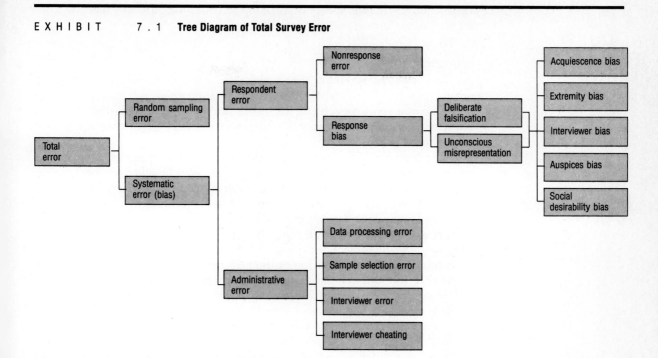

pling errors can be estimated, and they will be discussed in greater detail in Chapters 13 and 14.

Systematic Error

Systematic error results from some imperfect aspect of the research design or from a mistake in the execution of the research. Because all sources of error other than those introduced by the random sampling procedure are included, these errors or biases are also called *nonsampling errors*. A **sample bias** exists when the results of a sample show a persistent tendency to deviate in one direction from the true value of the population parameter. The many sources of error that in some way systematically influence answers can be classified under two general categories: respondent error and administrative error. These are discussed in the following sections.

RESPONDENT ERROR

Surveys are based on asking people for answers. If respondents cooperate and give truthful answers, the survey will likely accomplish its goal. Two disadvantages of survey research that occur if these conditions are not met are non-response error and response bias.

Nonresponse Error

Few surveys have a 100 percent response rate. A researcher who obtains an 11 percent response to a five-page questionnaire concerning trends in pork belly futures faces a serious problem. To utilize the results, the researcher must be sure that those who *did* respond to the questionnaire were representative of those who *did not*.

The statistical differences between a survey that includes only those who responded and a survey that also includes those who failed to respond are referred to as a **nonresponse error.** This problem is especially acute in mail surveys, but it also exists in telephone and face-to-face interviews.

People who are not contacted or who refuse to cooperate are **nonrespondents.** A nonresponse occurs if someone is not at home and a subsequent callback also finds the subject not at home. The number of **not-at-homes** is increasing as more married women (more than 60 percent) work in the labor force. The mother who answers the telephone with a half-diapered child in her arms and refuses to participate in a survey because she is too busy is also a nonresponse. **Refusals** occur because people are unwilling to participate in the research. Not-at-homes and refusals can seriously bias survey data.

Self-selection bias is a problem frequently seen in self-administered questionnaires. A woman who had soup spilled on her at a restaurant, a person who was treated to dinner as a surprise, or others who feel strongly about a restaurant's service are more likely to respond to a self-administered questionnaire left at the table than those individuals who are indifferent about the restaurant. Self-selection biases the survey because it allows extreme positions to be overrepresented while those who are indifferent are underrepresented.

To identify the extent of nonresponse error, business researchers often select a sample of nonrespondents who are then recontacted. Further, researchers have developed systematic callback and follow-up procedures to reduce nonresponse error. These topics are discussed more fully in Chapter 8.

Arbitron, a research firm, had problems getting people to record their radio-listening habits in a diary every day. In one period only 28 percent of a sample filled in the diary. Arbitron conducted a survey to find differences between diary keepers and those who refused. Diary keepers were found to favor middle-of-the-road "beautiful" music, and news/talk stations; nonrespondents favored contemporary and black stations.[7]

Comparing the demographics of the sample with the demographics of the target population is one means of inspecting for possible biases in response patterns. If a particular group, such as older citizens, is underrepresented or if any potential biases seem to appear in a response pattern, additional efforts should be made to obtain data from the underrepresented segments of the population. For example, personal interviews may be used instead of telephone interviews for the underrepresented segments of the population.

After a refusal has been given to an interviewer, nothing can be done except be polite. The respondent who is not at home, or out of the office when called or visited, should be scheduled to be contacted at a different time of day or on a different day of the week.

In a mail survey the researcher never really knows whether a nonrespondent has refused to participate or is just indifferent. Researchers know that those who are most involved in an issue are more likely to respond to a mail survey. The strategy to increase responses in mail surveys is to encourage respondents to reply. Several of these techniques will be discussed in the section on mail surveys in the next chapter.

Response Bias

A **response bias** occurs when respondents tend to answer in a certain direction, i.e., when they consciously or unconsciously misrepresent the truth. If a distortion of the measurement occurs because respondents' answers are falsified or misrepresented, either intentionally or inadvertently, the sample bias that occurs is a response bias.

Consider this modern version of the *Literary Digest* study.[8] In a recent New York City election, all the polls showed David Dinkins, a black candidate, leading Rudolph Giuliani, a white candidate, by 12 to 16 percentage points, but Dinkins won by just 2 percentage points. On the same day, Douglas Wilder, the black candidate who was 9 to 11 percentage points ahead of the white candidate in the polls, won the Virginia governorship by only 0.3 percentage points.[9] After the election, research experts explained that whites who say they are undecided in a black–white race usually vote overwhelmingly for the white candidate. People who plan to vote against a black candidate, for whatever reason, are reluctant to admit their true intentions. Perhaps they fear being labeled a racist or bigot, or wish to have the interviewer think they are socially progressive. The end result is that in elections with racially mixed candidates, the survey results are likely to have response bias. So in order to estimate the true vote, the poll should have included a corrective to allow for this response bias.

The results of a study that checked the accuracy of interview techniques among low-income Mexican Americans, low-income Anglos, and middle-income Anglos indicated that the first group tends to distort its beer purchases by reporting no consumption at all, and the second group misrepresents the quantity. Furthermore, all groups systematically overreported the purchases of products with "positive connotations," such as milk and beef.[10]

Deliberate Falsification.   Occasionally some people deliberately give false answers. It is difficult to assess why people knowingly misrepresent answers. A response bias may occur when people misrepresent answers in order to appear intelligent, to conceal personal information, to avoid embarrassment, and so on. For example, respondents may be able to remember the total amount of money spent grocery shopping, but they may forget the exact prices of individual items that were purchased. Rather than appear stupid or unconcerned with prices, they may provide their best estimate and not tell the truth, namely, that they can't remember.

In employee surveys, employees may believe that their responses, especially those indicating negative feelings, may not be confidential. By falsifying their answers, they may believe they are safeguarding their jobs or chances for advancement. Sometimes employees will not give truthful answers when they think that telling the truth will result in a negative outcome for a supervisor or an organizational unit, ultimately resulting in a less desirable situation for the employees.

Sometimes respondents who become bored with the interview will simply provide answers just to get rid of the interviewer. At other times respondents provide the answers they think are expected of them in order to appear well informed. Sometimes answers are given simply to please the interviewer.

One explanation for conscious and deliberate misrepresentation of facts is the "average man" hypothesis. It may be that individuals prefer to be viewed as average and that respondents alter their reports of the truth to conform more closely to their *perception* of the average man.[11] "Average man effects" have been found to exist in response to questions such as savings account balances, number of hours worked, car prices, voting behavior, and reports of hospitalization.

Unconscious Misrepresentation.   Even when a respondent is consciously trying to be truthful and cooperative, response bias can arise from question format, question content, or some other stimulus. For example, bias can be introduced by the situation in which the survey is administered. The results of two in-flight surveys concerning aircraft preference illustrates this point. Passengers flying on B-747s preferred B-747s to L-1011s (74 percent versus 19 percent), whereas passengers flying on L-1011s preferred L-1011s to B-747s (56 percent versus 38 percent). The reversal in preference between the B-747 and the L-1011 appears to have been largely a function of the aircraft the respondent was flying on when the survey was conducted, although sample differences may have been a factor. A likely influence was the respondent's satisfaction with the plane on which he or she was flying when surveyed. In other words, in the absence of any strong preference, the respondent might simply have been trying to identify the aircraft traveled on and indicated that as his or her preference.[12]

Respondents who misunderstand the question may unconsciously provide a biased answer. Respondents may be willing to answer but unable to do so because they have forgotten the exact details. "When was the last time you received on-the-job training?" may result in a "best guess" estimate because the respondent has forgotten the exact time.

A bias may also occur when a respondent has not thought about the question "sprung" on him or her by an interviewer. Many respondents will answer questions even though they have given them little thought. In most investigations of intentions, the predictability of the intention scales depends on how close the subject is to making a decision. Thus asking if a respondent intends to change jobs will likely bring a biased response unless the decision is extremely close at hand. In a consumer-purchasing survey, the intentions of subjects who have little knowledge of the brand alternatives being surveyed or the intentions of subjects who have not yet made any purchase plans cannot be expected to predict purchase behavior.

Asking respondents how spicy they like their chili is not likely to produce well-articulated answers. In cases like this, respondents cannot adequately express their feelings in words—there is an unconscious communication breakdown. An international business research survey provides a classic example of unconscious misrepresentation due to a communication breakdown. A survey in the Philippines found that, despite seemingly high toothpaste usage, only a tiny percentage of people responded positively when asked, "Do you use toothpaste?" As it turned out, Colgate is a generic name for toothpaste in the Philippines. When researchers returned and asked, "Do you use Colgate?" the positive response soared.

As the time between an activity or behavioral event and the survey contact increases, there is a tendency for underreporting of information about that activity or event. Time lapse influences ability to properly remember and communicate specific factors. Unconscious misrepresentation bias sometimes occurs because people unconsciously avoid facing the realities of a future situation. For example, housing surveys record that Americans overwhelmingly continue to aspire to owning detached, single-family dwellings (preferably single-level, ranch-type structures requiring two to five times the amount of land per unit required for attached homes). However, builders' statistics show that *attached* housing is increasingly what buyers actually select.[13]

Types of Response Bias.   There are five specific categories of response bias: acquiescence bias, extremity bias, interviewer bias, auspices bias, and social desirability bias. These categories overlap and are not mutually exclusive. A single biased answer may be distorted for many complex reasons, some deliberate misrepresentations and some unconscious misrepresentations.

Acquiescence Bias.   Some respondents are very agreeable. They are "yea sayers" who accept all statements they are asked about. This tendency to agree with all or most questions is particularly prominent in research on new products, new programs, or ideas previously unfamiliar to the respondents. When a respondent is faced with a new concept, there is generally some **acquiescence bias,** which gives positive connotations to most new ideas. Some individuals tend to disagree with all questions, but this is also acquiescence. Thus acquiescence bias is a response bias due to respondents' tendency to concur with a particular position.

Extremity Bias.   Some individuals tend to use extremes when responding to questions; others tend to respond neutrally. Responding styles vary from person to person, and they may cause an extremity bias in the data. (This issue is dealt with in Chapter 11.)

Interviewer Bias.   Response bias may occur because of an interplay between interviewer and respondent. If an interviewer's presence influences respondents to give untrue or modified answers, the survey has **interviewer bias.** To many housewives or retired people, the visit of an interviewer is a welcome break in routine activities; so respondents may give the "right" answers—the ones they believe will please the interviewer rather than the truthful response. Or respondents may wish to appear intelligent and wealthy—of course, they read *Fortune* rather than *Reader's Digest.*

All too often socially acceptable responses are provided, rather than actual answers, to "save face" in the presence of an interviewer. The way the interviewer is dressed, the interviewer's age, sex, tone of voice, facial expressions, or other nonverbal characteristics may have some influence on a respondent's answer. If an interviewer smiles and makes a positive statement after a respondent's answer, the respondent will be more likely to give similar responses. In a research study on sexual harassment among women, the use of male interviewers might not yield responses as candid as would the same survey conducted by female interviewers.

Most interviewers, contrary to instruction, shorten or rephrase questions to suit their needs. This potential influence on responses can be avoided (to some extent) if interviewers receive training and supervision that emphasizes the interviewer's necessity to appear neutral.

If interviews continue too long, respondents may feel that their time is being wasted and they may answer as abruptly as possible, without a great deal of forethought.

Auspices Bias.   If the National Riflemen's Association is conducting a study on gun control, answers to its survey may be deliberately or subconsciously misrepresented because respondents are influenced by the organization conducting the study. Again, if a national committee on gun control conducted the same study, respondents' answers might vary from their NRA answers because of **auspices bias.**

Social Desirability Bias.   A **social desirability bias** in a response may occur, either consciously or unconsciously, because the respondent wishes to create a favorable impression. In surveys of outdoor recreational activity, participation rates are based on respondent estimates rather than actual measurement of participation. People may overestimate their recreational activities because recreation is perceived as a socially desirable activity. Similarly, answering that one's income is only $35,000 a year might be difficult for someone whose self-concept is that of an upper middle-class manager "about to make it big." Incomes are inflated, education is overstated, or "respectable" answers are given in order to gain prestige. In contrast, answers to questions that seek factual information or responses in matters of public knowledge (zip code, number of children, and so on) are usually quite accurate.

An interviewer's presence may increase a respondent's tendency to give an inaccurate answer to sensitive questions such as "Did you vote in the last election?" "Do you have termites or roaches in your home?" "Do you dye your hair?" or "Have you ever been fired from a job?"

ADMINISTRATIVE ERROR

The results of improper administration or execution of the research task are **administrative errors.** They are inadvertently (or carelessly) caused by confusion, neglect, omission, or some other blunder. Four types of administrative errors are data processing error, sample selection error, interviewer error, and interviewer cheating.

Data Processing Error

The accuracy of data processed by computer, as with any arithmetic or procedural process, is subject to error, because data must be edited, coded, and entered into the computer by people. The accuracy of data processed by computer depends on correct data entry and programming. Data processing mistakes can be minimized by establishing careful procedures for verifying each step in the data processing stage.

Sample Selection Error

Executing a sampling plan free of procedural error is difficult. A firm that selects its sample from the telephone book will have some systematic error because unlisted numbers are not included. Stopping respondents during daytime hours in shopping centers excludes working women, who may shop by mail or by telephone. In other cases the "wrong person" may be interviewed. For example, consider a political pollster who uses random selection of telephone numbers to select a sample, rather than a list of registered voters. Unregistered 17-year-olds may be willing to give their opinions, but they are the wrong people to ask because they cannot vote. **Sample selection error** is a systematic error that results in an unrepresentative sample because of an error in either the sample design or execution of the sampling procedure.

Interviewer Error

Interviewers' abilities vary considerably. When interviewers record answers, they may check the wrong response, or they may not be able to write fast enough to record answers verbatim. Selective perception may influence the way interviewers record data that are not somewhat supportive of their own attitudes and opinions.

Interviewer Cheating

Interviewer cheating may occur when an interviewer falsifies entire questionnaires or fills in the answers to certain questions. To finish interviews as quickly as possible or to avoid asking questions about sensitive topics, an interviewer may intentionally skip questions. If interviewers are suspected of faking questionnaires, it is wise to let them know that a percentage of respondents will be called upon to confirm that the initial interview was actually conducted. This discourages interviewers from cheating.

R E S E A R C H   I N S I G H T
Semantic Confusion

The misunderstanding of questions by respondents often can be humorous. Consider the following misunderstandings.

During advertising research for a disinfectant, the copy showed a housewife referring to the product as a "bathroom sanitizer." The housewife said: "Yes, I'm certainly for that. I think we so need sanity in the bathroom."

In a consumer survey for a new detergent, the question concerned locations of use of detergents within the home. A specific reference was to "germ-ridden areas." "I want a germ-ridden kitchen," one woman said to the interviewer. "What do you mean by that?" dutifully probed the interviewer. "Well, I want to be ridden of all my germs."

An insecticide marketer wished to learn the meaning attached to the term "residual insecticide." They found out that the term not only meant what they always thought it meant but also:

"has no residual"
"for insects that reside"
"more powerful"
"powdered form"

Research can be fun.

Source: Lee Adler, "Confessions of an Interview Reader," reprinted by permission from the *Journal of Marketing Research,* May 1966, pp. 194–195, published by the American Marketing Association.

RULE-OF-THUMB ESTIMATES FOR SYSTEMATIC ERROR

Sampling error due to random or chance fluctuations may be estimated by calculating confidence intervals with the statistical tools presented in Chapters 14, 17, 18, 19, and 20.

The ways to estimate *systematic* or *nonsampling error* are less precise. To estimate systematic error, many researchers have established conservative rules of thumb based on past experience. They have found it useful to have some benchmark figures or standards of comparison in order to understand how much error can be expected. For example, according to some business researchers in the consumer packaged-goods field, approximately one-half of those who say they "will *definitely buy* within the next three months" actually do make a purchase.[14] In consumer durables, however, the figures are considerably lower: Only about one-third of those who say they definitely will buy a certain durable within the next three months will actually do so. Among those who say they "will *probably buy,*" the number who actually purchase the durable is so much lower that it is scarcely worth including it in the early purchase estimates for new durables. Thus researchers often present actual survey findings *and* their interpretation of estimated purchase response based on estimates of nonsampling error. For example, one cable television company surveys geographic areas it plans to enter and estimates the percentage of people who indicate they will subscribe to its service. Then the company knocks down the percentage by a "ballpark 10 percent," because experience in other geographic areas has indicated that there is a systematic upward bias of 10 percent on this intentions question.

WHAT CAN BE DONE TO REDUCE SURVEY ERROR?

Now that the sources of error in surveys have been presented, you may have lost some of your optimism about survey research. Don't be discouraged! The discussion has emphasized the *bad news* because it is important for managers to realize that surveys are not a panacea. But there are ways of handling and reducing survey errors. For example, Chapter 13, on questionnaire design, discusses the reduction of response bias. Chapters 14 and 15 discuss the reduction of sample selection and random sampling error. Indeed, much of the remainder of this book discusses various techniques for reducing bias in survey research. The *good news* lies ahead.

CLASSIFYING SURVEY RESEARCH METHODS

Now that we have discussed the various advantages and disadvantages of surveys in general, it is appropriate to classify surveys according to several different criteria. Surveys may be classified according to the method of communication, the degree of structure and amount of disguise in a questionnaire, and the time frame in which the data are collected (temporal basis).

Classifying surveys according to methods of communicating with the respondent, such as personal interviews, telephone interviews, and mail surveys, is the subject of the following chapter. The classifications based on structure and disguise and time frame will be discussed in the remainder of this chapter.

Structured and Disguised Questions

In designing a questionnaire (interview schedule), the investigator must decide how much structure or standardization is needed.[15] A **structured question** limits the number of responses available. For example, the respondent may be instructed to give one alternative response, such as "under 17," "18–35," or "over 35," to indicate his or her age. Unstructured questions do not restrict the answers the respondent is allowed. The open-ended, unstructured question "What do you think are the two most important problems facing your company today?" allows the respondent considerable freedom in answering.

The researcher must also decide whether undisguised or **disguised questions** will be utilized. A straightforward question like "Do you smoke marijuana on the job?" assumes that the respondent is willing to reveal the information. However, researchers know that some questions are threatening to a person's ego, prestige, or self-concept. Therefore they have designed a number of techniques that use an indirect approach of questioning to disguise the purpose of the study.

Questionnaires can be categorized by their degree of structure and degree of disguise. For example, interviews in exploratory research might utilize *unstructured-disguised* questionnaires. (The projection techniques discussed in Chapter 5 fall into this category.) Other classifications, typically, are *structured-undisguised, unstructured-undisguised,* and *structured-disguised.*

This classification has two limitations. First, the degree of structure and the degree of disguise vary; they are not clear-cut categories. Second, most surveys are hybrids, asking both structured and unstructured questions.

Recognition of the degree of structure and disguise that is necessary to meet survey objectives will help in the selection of the appropriate communication medium for conducting the survey.

Classifying Surveys on a Temporal Basis

Although most surveys are individual projects conducted only once over a short time period, other projects require multiple surveys to be made over a long period of time. Thus it is possible to classify surveys on a temporal basis.

Cross-Sectional Study.   A nationwide survey was taken to examine the different attitudes of cross sections of the American public toward the arts, and one aspect of the survey dealt with museums. In general, the public's attitudes toward museums were very positive. Museum preferences varied by demographics or cross sections of the population: People in towns and rural areas showed greater interest in historical museums, whereas city and suburban residents leaned more heavily toward art museums. The young (16- to 20-year-olds) were more interested than others in art museums and less interested in historical museums.[16]

This study was a **cross-sectional study** because the data were collected at a single point in time. In such a study, various segments of the population are sampled so that relationships among variables may be investigated by cross-tabulation. Most surveys fall into this category.

The typical means of analysis in the cross-sectional survey is to divide the sample into appropriate subgroups. For example, if the National Association of Accountants expects job title or position to influence attitudes toward continuing-education programs, then the data are analyzed to see if there are any similarities or differences among the subgroups.

Longitudinal Study.   In a **longitudinal study** respondents are questioned at different moments in time. The purpose of longitudinal surveys is to examine continuity of response and to observe changes that occur over time. For example, many syndicated polling services, such as the Gallup Poll and the New York Times/CBS News Poll, are conducted on a regular basis. One regularly asked question in the New York Times/CBS News Poll is "Do you agree or disagree [that] protecting the environment is so important that requirements and standards cannot be too high, and continuing environmental improvements must be made regardless of cost?" The longitudinal results show the percentage of Americans agreeing has grown from 45 percent in 1981 to 57 percent in 1983 to 65 percent in 1986 to almost 80 percent in 1989.[17]

The New York Times/CBS News Poll example above illustrates a longitudinal study that uses successive samples. By taking two or more different samples at different moments in time, researchers can compare trends and identify changes in variables. Longitudinal studies of this type are sometimes called *cohort studies* because similar groups of people (cohorts) are expected to be in each sample.

Studies that monitor voters' attitudes toward issues or awareness of a candidate when a new political campaign is being launched frequently use successive samples. Having two or more sample groups avoids the problem of response bias from a prior interview.

A respondent who had been interviewed in an earlier survey about a certain issue or candidate may become more aware of the issue, or pay more attention to a candidate, after being interviewed. Using different samples eliminates this problem. Of course, one can never be sure whether changes in the variable being measured are due to having different people in the sample or to an actual change in the variable over time.

Panel Study.   A longitudinal study that involves collecting data from the same sample of individuals or households over time is called a **panel study.** Consider the researcher who is interested in learning about brand-switching behavior. A consumer panel, consisting of a group of people who record their purchasing habits in a diary over time, provides the manager with continuous information about the brand and product class. It enables the investigator to track repeat purchase behavior as well as changes in purchasing habits, along with price changes, special promotions, or other changes in marketing strategy.

Panel members may be contacted by telephone, in a personal interview, or by a mail questionnaire. Typically, diaries recording a repetitive behavior are completed by the respondent and mailed back to the research organization. In other cases where panel members have agreed to participate on a recurring basis, such as political polling, personal or telephone interviews may be required. The nature of the research problem dictates which type of communication method is utilized.

Longitudinal panel studies are conducted by educational organizations and government institutions such as the University of Michigan's Panel Study of Income Dynamics, the Census Bureau's Survey of Income and Program Participation, and the Department of Education's National Longitudinal Study of the Class of 1972. The Survey of Income and Program Participation is one of the largest, with about 30,000 households participating.

Because panels are generally expensive to conduct, they are often managed by contractors who offer their services to many organizations. A number of commercial firms, such as National Family Opinion Inc., specialize in maintaining panels and collecting information from panel members about many diverse activities and issues. Clients of these firms find that by "sharing the expenses" with other clients, longitudinal data can be acquired at a reasonable fee.

The typical first questionnaire sent to panel members asks general questions about the survey topic and about family members and household demographic characteristics. The purpose of a particular questionnaire is to gather the behavioral and demographic data that will be used (in conjunction with future surveys) to identify certain types of voters, heavy buyers, difficult-to-reach customers, and the like. (Individuals who are selected as members of commercial panels are generally compensated with cash or an attractive gift for their cooperation.)

SUMMARY

Survey research is a common tool for business research. Surveys can provide a quick, inexpensive, and accurate means to obtain information for a variety of objectives. The typical survey is a descriptive research study that has the objective of measuring awareness, knowledge, behavior, opinions, or the like. The term *sample survey* is often used because a survey is expected to obtain a representative sample of the target population.

There are two major errors common to survey research. The first is random sampling error, caused by chance variation that results in a sample that is not absolutely representative of the target population. These errors are inevitable, but they can also be predicted by using the statistical methods discussed in the chapters on sampling.

The second major form of error is systematic bias, which takes several forms. Nonresponse error is caused by people who are sampled but do not respond and by those who may differ from respondents in some significant way. This error can be reduced by comparing the demographics of the sample population with those of the target population and by making added efforts to contact underrepresented groups.

Response bias occurs when a response to a questionnaire is falsified or misrepresented, either intentionally or inadvertently. There are five specific categories of response bias: acquiescence bias, extremity bias, interviewer bias, auspices bias, and social desirability bias. An additional source of survey error comes from administrative problems such as inconsistencies in interviewers' abilities, cheating, or coding mistakes. Surveys may be classified according to the method of communication, the degrees of structure and disguise in the questionnaire, and the time frame. Questionnaires may be structured, with limited choices of responses, or unstructured, with open-ended responses. Disguised questions may be used to probe sensitive subjects.

Surveys may consider the population at a single point in time or may follow trends over a period of time. The first approach, the cross-sectional study, is usually intended as a basis for separating the population into meaningful subgroups. The second type of study, the longitudinal approach, can reveal important population changes over time. Longitudinal studies may involve different sets of respondents or the same ones contacted repeatedly.

One form of longitudinal study is the panel study. Panels are expensive to operate, so they are often conducted by contractors who provide their service to many companies, thus spreading the cost over many products.

Key Terms

primary data	survey
respondent	random sampling error
sample survey	systematic error

sample bias

nonresponse error

nonrespondent

not-at-home

refusal

self-selection bias

response bias

acquiescence bias

extremity bias

interviewer bias

auspices bias

social desirability bias

administrative error

data processing error

sample selection error

interviewer error

interviewer cheating

structured question

disguised question

cross-sectional study

longitudinal study

panel study

Questions

1. Name several nonbusiness applications of survey research.
2. A major petroleum corporation marketed its gasoline through a franchise dealer organization under a national brand name. The corporation was considering building a number of company-owned stations with a new brand name to market a low-price gasoline product to compete with the independent dealers. Would survey research have been useful? If so, how?
3. What survey research objectives might the Ford Motor Company develop to learn about car buyers?
4. Give an example of each type of error listed in Exhibit 7.1.
5. A bank officer is asked what percentage of the time she spends talking on the telephone, in meetings, working on a computer, and working on other on-the-job activities. What potential sources of error might be associated with asking such questions?
6. Name some common objectives of cross-sectional surveys.
7. Give an example of a political situation in which longitudinal research might be useful. Do the same for a business situation.
8. What topics about organizational behavior (or consumer behavior) might be extremely sensitive issues for directly questioning respondents?
9. In a survey conducted by the National Endowment for the Arts, respondents were asked: "Have you read a book within the last year?" Can you imagine any possible response bias with this question?
10. In what ways might survey results for buying intentions be adjusted for consumer optimism?

References

[1] "Poll: Wall Street Is OK," *USA Today*, June 9, 1989, 1B.

[2] Denise Kalette, "Cockpit Concerns: Airline Pilots' Safety Fears," *USA Today*, Dec. 23, 1987, 4b.

[3] Daniel Yankelovich, *New Rules: Searching for Self-Fulfillment in a World Turned Upside Down* (New York: Random House, 1981), 152.

[4] Paul B. Sheatsley, "Survey Design," in *Handbook of Marketing Research*, ed. Robert Ferber (New York: McGraw-Hill, 1974), 2–66.

[5] The popularity of survey research has had an impact on the willingness of respondents to participate in surveys. People are increasingly refusing to participate in surveys. See Walker Marketing Research, Industry Image Study, 1988.

[6] Sheatsley, "Survey Design," 2–67.

[7] "Arbitron Testing Diary Boosters," *Advertising Age,* Feb. 26, 1979, 81.

[8] The *Literary Digest* study was discussed in Chapter 3.

[9] Adam Clymer, "Election Day Shows What the Opinion Polls Can't Do," *The New York Times,* Nov. 12, 1989, E–4.

[10] William L. Rathje, Wilson W. Hughes, and Sherry L. Jernigan, "The Science of Garbage: Following the Consumer through His Garbage Can," in *Marketing Looks Outward,* ed. William Locander (Chicago: American Marketing Association, 1976), 56–64.

[11] Scott E. Maynes, "The Anatomy of Response Errors: Consumer Savings," *Journal of Marketing Research* (November 1965): 378–387.

[12] Douglas Aircraft Corp., *Consumer Research,* 13.

[13] Lawrence O. Houston, Jr., "A Place to Hang Your Hat: Housing in the Next Decade," *Business Horizons* (January–February 1981): 78.

[14] "VCR/VDP Market Products and Important Research Questions," *Marketing News,* Jan. 6, 1984, 7.

[15] The term *questionnaire* technically refers only to mail surveys, and the term *interview schedule* is used for telephone and face-to-face interviews. However, in this book *questionnaire* is used for all three forms of communication.

[16] *Americans and the Arts: Highlights from a Survey of Public Opinion,* booklet of National Research Center of the Arts, 14.

[17] Robert Suro, "Grass-Roots Groups Show Power Battling Pollution Close to Home," *New York Times,* July 2, 1989, 1, 12.

Survey Research: Basic Methods of Communication with Respondents

To understand when mail, personal interview, or telephone surveys should be conducted.

To discuss the advantages and disadvantages of personal interviews.

To explain when door-to-door personal interviews should be used instead of mall intercept interviews.

To discuss the advantages and disadvantages of telephone surveys.

To discuss random digit dialing and other methods of selecting telphone numbers for surveys.

To discuss the advantages and disadvantages of mail and self-administered questionnaires.

To increase response rates to mail surveys.

To select the appropriate survey research design.

To discuss the importance of pretesting questionnaires.

To provide examples of the influence of modern technology on survey research.

The Ford Motor Company conducts style research clinics to appraise consumer reactions to the exterior styling and interior appearance of its new automotive designs. First, fiberglass prototypes or mock-ups of proposed models are made (see Exhibit 8.1). Then, respondents are recruited (usually after a short telephone interview), brought to a showroom, and exposed to a test car mock-up so it can be compared with competitive models from the world market. Personal interviewers ask about every detail of the car as the would-be prospective buyers pore over it. Ultimately, the results of the style clinics are fed back to designers in Detroit. Millions of dollars were spent, for example, on surveys about the Ford Taurus and Mercury Sable.[1]

Studies of survey research show that approximately three out of four adult Americans have participated in some form of survey in their lives.[2] Survey data are obtained when individuals respond to questions asked by interviewers (interviews) or when individuals respond to questions they have read (questionnaires). Interviewers may communicate with respondents face-to-face or over the telephone. In a sample survey, the use of self-administered questionnaires and distribution by mail is the most common means to obtain a representative sample, although there are other means of distribution.

Personal interviews, telephone interviews, and self-administered mail questionnaires are the three major survey methods of gathering data and communicating with individuals. Each method has its merits and shortcomings. Investigation of these basic methods and their variations is the purpose of this chapter.

■

PERSONAL INTERVIEWS

Although the history of business research is sketchy, the gathering of information through face-to-face contact with individuals has a long history. Periodic censuses were used as a basis for tax rates and military conscription in the an-

This was one of the proposed versions of the Ford Taurus shown to a cross section of the public at research clinics. At the clinics, which lasted up to three hours, participants rated such factors as exterior appearance, exterior size and proportions, interior space, and convenience features. The car shown in this photograph was actually a handmade fiberglass prototype with no transmission, engine, or internal system.

Source: Courtesy Ford Motor Company.

cient empires of Egypt and Rome.[3] Later, during the Middle Ages, the merchant families of Fugger and Rothschild prospered in part because their far-flung organizations enabled them to get information before their competitors.[4] Today it is not uncommon to hear something similar to the following at doorsteps throughout the United States:

Good afternoon, my name is _____. I am with _____ Survey Research Company and we are conducting a survey on _____.

Personal interviews are direct communications wherein interviewers in face-to-face situations ask respondents questions. This versatile and flexible method is a two-way conversation between an interviewer and a respondent.

Personal interviews may take place in a factory, in a homeowner's doorway, in an executive's office, in a shopping mall, or in other settings. Our discussion begins by looking at the general characteristics of all types of personal interviews and then taking a separate look at personal interviews conducted in high-traffic locations, such as shopping malls.

The Opportunity for Feedback

Personal interviews provide the opportunity for feedback to the respondent. For example, in the employee interview the supervisor who is reluctant to provide sensitive information may be reassured that her answers will be strictly confidential. The interviewer may also provide feedback in clarifying any questions an employee or any other respondent has about the instructions or questions. After the interview has been terminated, circumstances may dictate that the employee or other respondent be given additional information concerning the purpose of the study. This is easily accomplished with the personal interview.

Probing Complex Answers

An important characteristic of personal interviews is the opportunity to probe. If a respondent's answer is brief or unclear, the researcher may *probe* for a clearer or more comprehensive explanation. **Probing** refers to interviewers asking for clarification or expansion of answers to standardized questions. Asking "Can you tell me more about what you had in mind?" is an example of a probing question. (See Chapter 16 on field work for an expanded discussion of probing.) Although interviewers are expected to ask questions exactly as they appear on the questionnaire, probing allows the interviewer some flexibility. Depending on the research purpose, personal interviews vary in the degree to which questions are structured and in the amount of probing required. The personal interview is especially useful for obtaining unstructured information. Complex questions that cannot easily be asked in telephone or mail surveys can be handled by skillful interviewers.

Length of Interview

If the research objective requires an extremely lengthy questionnaire, personal interviews may be the only alternative. Generally, telephone interviews last fewer than ten minutes, whereas a personal interview can be much longer, perhaps an hour and a half. A rule of thumb for mail surveys is that they not be more than six pages.

Complete Questionnaires

Social interaction between a well-trained interviewer and a respondent in a personal interview increases the likelihood that a response will be given to all items on the questionnaire. The respondent who grows bored with a telephone interview may terminate the interview at his or her discretion simply by hanging up the phone. A respondent's self administration of a mail questionnaire requires more effort. Rather than write a long explanation, the respondent may fail to complete some of the questions on the self-administered questionnaire. **Item nonresponse,** that is, failure to provide an answer to a question, is less likely to occur when an experienced interviewer is used.

Props and Visual Aids

Interviewing respondents face to face allows the investigator to show the respondent a résumé, a new-product sample, a sketch of a proposed office or plant layout, or some other visual aid. In a survey to determine whether a "super-lightweight" chain saw should be manufactured, visual props were necessary because the concept of weight is difficult to imagine. Two small chain saws (already on the market) and a third wooden prototype, disguised and weighted to look and feel like the proposed model, were put in the back of a station wagon. Respondents were asked to go to the car, pick up each chain saw, and compare them. This research could not have been done in a telephone interview or mail survey.

Anonymity of Respondent

A respondent is not anonymous and may be reluctant to provide confidential information to another person. Researchers often spend considerable time and effort to phrase sensitive questions so that social desirability bias will not occur. For example, the interviewer might show a respondent a card that lists possible answers and ask him or her to read a category number rather than verbalize sensitive answers.

High Participation

The presence of an interviewer generally increases the percentage of people willing to complete the interview. Respondents are generally not required to do any reading or writing—all they have to do is talk. People enjoy sharing information and insights with friendly and sympathetic interviewers.

Personal interviews may be conducted at the respondent's home, office, or in many other places. Increasingly, personal interviews are being conducted in shopping malls. The locale for the interview generally influences the participation rate. For example, the refusal rate is highest when respondents are shopping in a mall.[5]

Door-to-Door Interviews

Door-to-door interviews provide a more representative sample of the population than mail questionnaires. For example, Hispanics, regardless of education, frequently prefer to communicate through the spoken rather than the written word.[6] Response rates to mail surveys are substantially lower among Hispanics, regardless of the questionnaire being printed in English or Spanish. People who do not have telephones, who have unlisted telephone numbers, or who are otherwise difficult to contact may be reached through door-to-door interviews. Such interviews can help solve the problem of nonresponse; however, they may underrepresent some groups and overrepresent others.

Door-to-door interviews may exclude individuals living in multiple-dwelling units with security systems, such as high-rise apartment dwellers, or executives who are too busy to grant a personal interview during business hours. Telephoning individuals in these subgroups to make an appointment may make the total sample more representative; however, it may be difficult to obtain a representative sample of the security-conscious subgroup based on a listing in the telephone directory.

People who are at home and willing to participate, especially if interviews are conducted in the daytime, are somewhat more likely to be over 65 years of age, housewives, or retired people. These and other variables related to respondents' tendencies to stay at home may affect participation.

RESEARCH INSIGHT
Inspector Clouseau or the Crusty French Loaf?

Advertising is a hectic business with tight deadlines and rush jobs. When the Leo Burnett advertising agency suggested using an Inspector Clouseau look-alike for Pillsbury's new crusty French loaf, the idea was enthusiastically supported. What could more perfect for a French bread product than using a spokesperson impersonating the "French" detective character in the Pink Panther movie comedies? Normally, Pillsbury surveys consumer reactions to a "rough" production version of the commercial, featuring either a series of still photographs or live action videotapes that simulate viewing situations of the story. But because the timetable was tight, Pillsbury decided to forgo interviews evaluating a rough commercial and instead prepared a finished commercial.

Ultimately, when personal interviews were used to test reactions to the final commercial, the researchers uncovered a problem: too much character recognition. The researchers discovered that the Clouseau character was so successful that he overshadowed the product. The viewers tended to register high levels of recognition of Clouseau and forgot about the product. Although the character Clouseau connected very well with French bread, eliminating the research on a rough commercial caused a problem. However, because reactions to the finished commercial were tested after production, the research results allowed the advertiser to revise the commercial by giving the product more time and exposure.

Source: Based on "Revised Pillsbury Spot in the Pink," *Advertising Age*, Feb. 13, 1986, 15.

Intercept Interviews in Malls and Other High-Traffic Areas

Personal interviews conducted in shopping malls are referred to as **mall intercept interviews** or *shopping center sampling*. Interviewers generally will intercept shoppers at a central point within or at an entrance to the mall. The main reason these interviews are conducted is their lower cost. No travel is required to the respondent's home—instead, the respondent comes to the interviewer, and many interviews can thus be gathered quickly.[7] The incidence of refusal is high, however, because individuals may be in a hurry to shop or to carry out their personal business.[8]

In mall intercept interviews the researcher must recognize that he or she should *not* be looking for a representative sample of the total population. Each mall will have its own customer characteristics, and there is likely to be a larger bias than with careful household probability sampling. However, personal interviews in shopping malls may be appropriate when demographic factors are not likely to influence the survey's findings or when the target group is a special population segment, perhaps the parents of children of bike-riding age. If the respondent indicates that he or she has a child of this age, the parent can then be brought into a rented space and shown several bikes. Or the mall intercept interview may allow the researcher to show visual materials, such as a videotape, or to give an individual a product to take home and use; then the respondent may be recontacted later by telephone. Mall intercept interviews are also valuable when activities, such as the cooking and tasting of food products, must be closely coordinated and timed to follow each other. They may also be appropriate when something must be demonstrated. For example, when video-cassette recorders and video disk players were innovations in the prototype stage, the extensive space required to set up and properly display these units ruled out door-to-door testing.

An organization's cafeteria, a primary meeting place at a convention, a college's student union, or another location with high pedestrian traffic may be chosen as a site for conducting personal interviews. In general, what we have said about mall intercept interviewing applies to these other, less common, forms of *high-traffic-area interviewing:* Costs are lower but samples may not be as representative as in other types of interviewing.

Disadvantages of Personal Interviews

There are numerous advantages to personal interviews, but there are some disadvantages as well. Respondents are not anonymous and therefore may be reluctant to provide confidential information to another person. Consider this question asked of top executives: "Do you see any major internal instabilities or threats (people, money, material, etc.) to the achievement of your department's objectives?" Many managers may be reluctant to answer this sensitive question honestly in a personal interview where their identity is known.

There is some evidence that the demographic characteristics of the interviewer influence respondents' answers. For example, one research study revealed that male interviewers produced larger variance than females in a survey where 85 percent of the respondents were female. Older interviewers, interviewing older respondents, produced more variance than other age combinations, whereas younger interviewers, interviewing younger respondents, produced the least.[9]

Differential interviewer techniques may be a source of interviewer bias. The rephrasing of a question, the interviewer's tone of voice, and the interviewer's appearance may influence the respondent's answer. Consider the interviewer who has conducted 100 personal interviews. During the next one the interviewer may selectively perceive or anticipate the respondent's answer, so that the interpretation of the response may be somewhat different from the intended response.

Our image of the person who does business research is typically that of the "dedicated scientist." Unfortunately, interviewers who are hired as researchers do not necessarily fit the ideal.[10] Considerable interviewer variability is possible. Cheating is possible. Interviewers may "cut corners" to save time and energy. They may fake parts of their reporting by "dummying up" part or all of the questionnaire. Control over interviewers is important to assure that difficult, embarrassing, and time-consuming questions are handled properly.

Personal interviews are generally more expensive than mail and telephone interviews. The geographic proximity of respondents, the length and complexity of the questionnaire, and the number of people who are nonrespondents because they could not be contacted (not-at-homes) all influence the cost of the personal interview.

Callbacks

When a person selected to be in the sample cannot be contacted on the first visit, a systematic procedure is normally initiated to *call back* at another time. **Callbacks,** or attempts to recontact individuals selected for the sample, are the major means of reducing nonresponse error. The cost of an interviewer calling back on a sampling unit is more expensive (per interview) because subjects who were initially not at home are generally more widely dispersed geographically than the original sample units. Callbacks are important because not-at-home individuals (e.g., working women) may systematically vary from those who *are* at home (nonworking women, retired people, and the like).

TELEPHONE INTERVIEWS

> *"Good evening, I'm with a nationwide survey research company. Are you a registered voter?"*
> *"Yes."*
> *"Do you plan to vote in next week's primary election?"*

Telephone interviewing is becoming increasingly popular, and there is evidence to suggest it is now the prime method of survey research.[11] A study comparing telephone interviews with personal interviews concluded that respondents are willing to provide detailed and reliable information on a variety of personal topics over the telephone.[12] A growing body of research, moreover, supports the conclusion that telephone surveys can provide representative samples of the general population. The quality of data obtained by telephone may be comparable to that collected in personal interviews.[13]

Central Location Interviewing

Research agencies and interviewing services typically conduct all telephone interviews from a central location. WATS (Wide-Area Telecommunications Service) lines are purchased from AT&T Communications or other long-distance telephone services at a fixed charge so that unlimited telephone calls can be made throughout the entire country or within a specific geographic area. Such **central location interviewing** allows firms to hire staffs of professional interviewers and to supervise and control the quality of interviewing more effectively. When telephone interviews are centralized and computerized, additional cost economies are realized.

Computer-Assisted Telephone Interviewing

Advances in computer technology allow telephone interviews to be directly entered into a computer. Exhibit 8.2 illustrates the on-line **computer-assisted telephone interviewing** (CATI) process. Telephone interviewers are seated at a computer terminal. A monitor, similar to a television screen, displays the questionnaire, one question at a time, along with precoded possible responses to each question. The terminal includes a keyboard for entering the response directly into the computer. The interviewer reads each question as it is shown on

Computer-Assisted Telephone Interviewer Seated at Terminal

Source: Courtesy of Walker Research, Inc., Indianapolis, Indiana.

the screen. When the respondent answers, the interviewer enters the response into the computer, and it is automatically transcribed into the computer's memory when the computer displays the next question on the screen. A computer-assisted telephone interview requires that answers to questionnaires be highly structured. For instance, if a respondent gives an answer that is not acceptable (i.e., not precoded and programmed), the computer will reject that answer.

Computer-assisted telephone interviewing systems include telephone management systems that handle telephone number selection, perform automatic dialing, and provide other labor-saving functions. One such system can automatically control sample selection by randomly generating names or fulfilling a sample quota. Another call management system can generate an automatic callback schedule, being programmed to time recontact attempts (e.g., recall no-answers after two hours, recall busy numbers after ten minutes) and allowing the interviewer to enter a time slot (a later day and hour) when a busy respondent indicates that he or she can be interviewed. Still another system can supply daily status reports on the number of completed interviews relative to quotas.

Speed

In telephone interviewing, the speed of data collection is also an advantage. For example, union officials who wish to survey members' attitudes toward a strike may conduct a telephone survey during the last few days of the bargaining process. Rather than requiring several weeks for data collection by mail or personal interviews, hundreds of telephone interviews can be collected literally overnight. When the interviewer enters the respondents' answers directly into a computerized system, data processing is sped up even more.

Cost

As the cost of personal interviews continues to increase, telephone interviews are becoming relatively inexpensive. In a comparison of personal interviews and telephone interviews, it is estimated that the cost differential for telephone interviews is approximately 40 percent of the cost of personal interviews. Travel time and the cost of travel are eliminated, and with interviews centralized and computerized, further cost economies are realized.

Absence of Face-to-Face Contact

Telephone interviews are more impersonal than face-to-face interviews. Embarrassing or confidential questions may be answered more willingly in a telephone interview than in a personal interview. However, a mail survey is the best medium for gathering extremely sensitive information because it is anonymous. Of course, it is not perfect. There is some evidence that income and other financial information is provided only reluctantly even with telephone interviews.[14] Income and wealth questions may be personally threatening for a variety of reasons, and high refusal rates for this type of data occur in all forms of survey research.

Although telephone calls may be less threatening because an interviewer is not present, a limitation of telephone interviewing is the absence of face-to-face contact. The respondent cannot see that the interviewer is still writing down the previous comment and may continue to elaborate on an answer. If the respondent pauses to think about an answer, the interviewer may not realize the person is thinking and go on to ask an additional question. Hence there is a greater tendency for "no answers" and "incomplete answers" to be recorded in telephone interviewing than in personal interviewing.

Cooperation

People in some neighborhoods are reluctant to allow a stranger (interviewer) to come inside the house or to stop on the doorstep. People at work may not wish to be interrupted by a visitor. But these same individuals may be perfectly happy to cooperate with a telephone survey request. Similarly, interviewers may be somewhat reluctant to conduct face-to-face interviews in certain neighborhoods, especially during the evening hours. Of course, some individuals will refuse to participate in a telephone interview, and the researcher should be aware of potential nonresponse bias.

Representative Samples

When an organization's employees are the group of interest, there are few sampling problems in telephone surveys. However, when the group of interest consists of the general population, there are practical difficulties in obtaining a representative sample based on listings in the telephone directory.

Slightly more than 97 percent of all households in the United States have telephones.[15] People without telephones are likely to be poor, aged, rural, or

Southern. People without telephones may be a minor segment of the market, but unlisted numbers and numbers too recently issued to be printed in the directory are a greater problem. Individuals with unlisted numbers are slightly different from individuals with published numbers. The unlisted group tends to be younger; has large families; has fewer professionals and managers and more sales, craft, and service workers; has more low-income households; and has more people in the early cycle of life.[16] Researchers conducting surveys in areas where the proportion of unlisted phone numbers is high, such as Las Vegas (57 percent) or Los Angeles (52 percent), have to pay special attention to making accurate estimates of unlisted numbers.[17] In other areas such as San Antonio, where only 20 percent of the population has unlisted phone numbers, this may not be a major problem.

The problem with unlisted telephone numbers can be partially resolved through **random digit dialing.** Random digit dialing eliminates the "counting of names" in a list (e.g., calling every fiftieth name in a column) and subjectively determining whether a directory listing is a business, institution, or household.[18] In its simplest form, telephone exchanges (prefixes) for the geographic areas in the sample are obtained. Then, using a table of random numbers, the last four digits of the telephone numbers are selected.[19] Telephone directories can be ignored entirely or used in combination with the assignment of one or several random digits. Random digit dialing also helps overcome problems of new listings and recent changes in numbers.

Lack of Visual Medium

Since visual aids cannot be utilized in telephone interviews, research that requires visual material cannot be conducted by phone. Certain attitude scales and measuring instruments, such as the semantic differential (see Chapter 12), cannot be used easily because a graphic scale is needed.

Limited Duration

One disadvantage of the telephone interview is that the length of the interview is limited. Respondents who feel they have spent too much time in the interview will simply hang up.

Refusal to cooperate with interviews is directly related to interview length. A major study on survey research found that for interviews of 5 minutes or less, the refusal rate was 21 percent. For interviews of 6–12 minutes, the refusal rate was 41 percent. For interviews of 13 minutes or more, the refusal rate was 47 percent.[20] Thirty minutes is the maximum time most respondents will spend, unless they are highly interested in the survey subject. (In unusual cases a few highly interested respondents may put up with longer interviews.) A good rule of thumb is to plan telephone interviews to be approximately 10 minutes long.

Callbacks

An unanswered call, a busy signal, or a respondent who is not at home requires a callback. Telephone callbacks are substantially easier and less expensive than personal interview callbacks.

The ownership of telephone-answering machines is growing and, although the effect of these devices on business research has not been studied extensively, it appears unlikely that many individuals would return a call to help someone conduct a survey.

MAIL AND SELF-ADMINISTERED QUESTIONNAIRES

Educational researchers and college professors frequently administer questionnaires to classes of college students. Managers frequently call employees together for group sessions where questionnaires are administered. Self-administered questionnaires are given to exited zoo and museum visitors, toll road users, and many other people who use services. Members of Congress regularly mail questionnaires to registered voters.

Mail surveys and **self-administered questionnaires** present a challenge to the business researcher because they rely on the efficiency of the written word rather than that of an interviewer. This presents several advantages and disadvantages.

Geographic Flexibility

Mail questionnaires can reach a geographically dispersed sample simultaneously and at a relatively low cost because interviewers are not required. Respondents in isolated areas (e.g., farmers) or those who are otherwise difficult to reach (like executives) can easily be contacted by mail. A pharmaceutical firm may find that doctors are inaccessible to personal or telephone interviews. In a mail survey, rural and urban doctors, practicing in widely dispersed geographic areas, can be reached.

Self-administered survey questionnaires can be widely distributed to a large number of employees, so assessing organization problems may be accomplished quickly and inexpensively. For many employee surveys, questionnaires are administered during group meetings. An hour-long period may be scheduled during the working day so that employees can complete a self-administered questionnaire. These meetings generally allow the researcher to provide basic instructions to a large group (generally fewer than 50 people) and to minimize data collection time. They also give the researcher the opportunity to "debrief" subjects without spending a great deal of time and effort.

Cost

Mail questionnaires are relatively low in cost compared with personal interviews and telephone surveys. However, mail surveys are not cheap. Most include a follow-up mailing, which requires additional postage and the printing of additional questionnaires. Questionnaires that are duplicated on poor-quality paper have a greater likelihood of being thrown in the wastebasket than a more expensive, higher-quality printing job.

Respondent Convenience

Mail and self-administered questionnaires can be filled out whenever the respondent has time. Thus there is a better chance that respondents will take time to think about their replies. In some situations, particularly in organizational

RESEARCH INSIGHT
Do You Cheat on Your Income Tax?

During the course of a personal interview concerning tax-payer opinions of the Internal Revenue Service, respondents were requested to provide information on income tax cheating behavior. Needless to say, these are highly sensitive questions. The IRS utilized the locked box technique to ask about tax cheating.

The locked box technique combined two methods of ensuring confidentiality. First, the questionnaire was self-administered. In this way, the respondent was free to reply in a truthful manner without concern about the interviewer's reaction. Second, upon completion of the instru-

ment, the respondent rolled it up, secured it with a rubber band, and placed it in a sealed box (similar to a ballot box). The box was translucent, approximately the size of a shoe box, and designed to hold five or six questionnaires. At all times there was at least one other instrument in the box to further reassure the respondent that his or her response would remain confidential. Once the box was full, the instruments were removed and the box was resealed.

Respondents were given the following instructions and asked ten questions.

Locked Box Instructions

At this point we would like to ask you some specific questions about how you handle your taxes. Because the questions are more personal, and we want you to answer honestly, we are going to let you fill out this part of the questionnaire privately. Once you are finished, you will drop the questionnaire into this box.

As you can see, the box is sealed, so your questionnaire will not be removed until it is sent to our central office in Virginia. I will never see the questionnaire. There is no identifying information on this questionnaire (*show respondent questionnaire*), so your answers will never be identified by name. In fact, we are not interested in individual persons, but in different kinds of people.

Questionnaire

1. Have you ever failed to file a tax return which you think you should have?
   Yes 1
   No 2
2. Have you ever purposely listed more deductions than you were entitled to?
   Yes (Go to Q. 3) 1
   No (Go to Q. 4) 2
3. About how much was the largest amount?
   Amount: _____
4. Have you ever purposely failed to report some income on your tax return—even just a minor amount?
   Yes (Go to Q. 5) 1
   No (Go to Q. 6) 2
5. About how much was the largest amount of income you have not reported?
   Amount: _____
6. How honest do you think you were on filling out your tax return for [year]? Circle the point on the line that best describes how honest you think you were.

Absolutely honest	Pretty honest	Somewhat honest	Not at all honest

7. Have you ever claimed a dependent on your tax return that you weren't really entitled to?
   Yes 1
   No 2

8. Some people pay fewer taxes than are required by the tax code. Below is a list of ways people have avoided paying all their taxes. For each of the ways, show on the scale how often you use each of these methods by circling the appropriate point.

   A. Failing to report some income.

Never	Rarely	Occasionally	Fairly Often	Frequently

   B. Exaggerating medical expenses.

Never	Rarely	Occasionally	Fairly Often	Frequently

   C. Exaggerating charitable donations.

Never	Rarely	Occasionally	Fairly Often	Frequently

9. The following questions ask you about things some people do when filing their tax return. For each one, show on the scale whether your conscience would bother you if you did it. Circle one of the 5 numbers on the line to show whether your conscience would be bothered.

   A. Not filing a return on purpose.

1	2	3	4	5
Not at all		Some		A lot

   B. Understating your income.

1	2	3	4	5
Not at all		Some		A lot

   C. Overstating your medical expenses.

1	2	3	4	5
Not at all		Some		A lot

   D. Claiming an extra dependent.

1	2	3	4	5
Not at all		Some		A lot

   E. Padding business travel expenses.

1	2	3	4	5
Not at all		Some		A lot

   F. Not declaring large gambling earnings.

1	2	3	4	5
Not at all		Some		A lot

   G. Not declaring the value of a service that you traded with someone else.

1	2	3	4	5
Not at all		Some		A lot

10. Did you stretch the truth a little in order to pay fewer taxes for [year]?

    Yes 1
    No 2

Source: *A General Taxpayer Opinion Survey,* Office of Planning and Research, Internal Revenue Service, 1980, 75, A-1, A-2.

research, mail questionnaires allow respondents to collect facts (such as records of absenteeism) that they may not recall accurately. Checking information by verifying records or, in the case of household surveys, consulting with family members should provide more valid, factual information than either personal or telephone interviews.

Sears utilizes mail surveys to estimate sales volume for catalog items by mailing out a "mock" catalog as part of the questionnaire. Respondents are asked to indicate how likely they are to order selected items. Utilizing the mail allows respondents to consult other family members and to make their decisions within a normal time span.

In many situations hard-to-reach respondents who place a high value on responding to surveys at their own convenience are best contacted by mail.

Interviewer's Absence

Although the absence of an interviewer induces respondents to reveal sensitive or socially undesirable information, it can also be a disadvantage. Once the respondent receives the questionnaire, the questioning process is beyond the researcher's control. Although the printed stimulus is the same, each respondent will attach a different personal meaning to each question.

Selective perception operates in research as well as in other areas of daily life. The respondent does not have the opportunity to ask questions of an interviewer. Problems that might be clarified in an interview remain misunderstandings in a mail survey. There is no interviewer who can probe for additional information or clarification of an answer, and the recorded answers must be assumed to be complete.

Standardized Questions

Mail questionnaires are highly standardized, and the questions are quite structured. Questions and instructions must be clear-cut and straightforward. If questions or instructions are difficult to comprehend, respondents must use their own interpretations, which may be wrong. Interviewing, on the other hand, allows for feedback from the interviewer regarding the respondent's comprehension of the questionnaire.

An interviewer who notices that the first 50 respondents are having difficulty understanding a question can report this to the research analyst so revisions can be made. However, once questionnaires are mailed, it is difficult to change the format or questions.

When a respondent self-administers a questionnaire, the entire questionnaire may be read before any answer is given. Thus questions at the end of a questionnaire may bias answers to earlier questions.

Time Is Money

If time is a factor in management's interest in research results or if attitudes are rapidly changing (e.g., toward a political event), mail surveys may not be the best communication medium. A minimum of two to three weeks is necessary to receive the majority of the responses. Follow-up mailings, which are usually sent when returns begin to trickle in, require an additional two or three weeks.

The time between the first mailing and the cutoff date (when questionnaires will no longer be accepted) is usually six to eight weeks.

In a regional or local study, personal interviews can be conducted more quickly. However, conducting a national study by mail might be substantially faster than conducting personal interviews across the nation.

Length of Mail Questionnaire

Mail questionnaires vary considerably in length, ranging from extremely short postcard questionnaires to lengthy, multipaged booklets requiring respondents to fill in thousands of answers. A general rule of thumb is that a mail questionnaire should not exceed six pages in length. When a questionnaire requires a respondent to expend a great deal of effort, an incentive is generally required to induce the respondent to return the questionnaire. The following sections discuss several ways to obtain high response rates even when questionnaires are longer than average.

Response Rates

Surveys that are boring, unclear, or too complex get thrown in the wastebasket. A poorly designed survey may be returned by only 15 percent of those sampled; in other words, it will have a 15 percent response rate. The *basic* calculation for obtaining a **response rate** is to count the number of questionnaires returned or completed, then divide this total by the number of eligible people who were contacted or requested to participate in the survey. Typically, the number in the denominator will be adjusted for faulty addresses and similar problems that reduce the number of "eligible" participants.

The major limitations of mail questionnaires relate to response problems. Respondents who answer the questionnaire may not be typical of all people in the sample. Individuals with a special interest in the topic are more likely to respond to a mail survey than those who are indifferent.

A researcher has no assurance that the intended subject will fill out the questionnaire. The wrong person's answering the questions may be a problem when corporate executives, physicians, and other professionals are surveyed. (A subordinate may be given the mail questionnaire to complete.)

Mail survey respondents tend to be better educated than nonrespondents. Poorly educated respondents who cannot read and write well may skip open-ended questions where respondents are required to write out their answers—if they return the questionnaire at all.

Rarely will a mail survey have the 80 to 90 percent response rate typical of personal interviews. However, the use of follow-up mailings and other techniques may increase the response rate to an acceptable percentage. A noted authority on mail surveys says, "No mail survey can be considered reliable unless it has a minimum of 50 percent response, or unless it demonstrates with some form of verification that the nonrespondents are similar to the respondents."[21]

Increasing Response Rates to Mail Surveys

Nonresponse error is always a potential problem in mail surveys. Individuals who are interested in the subject matter of the survey tend to respond at a higher rate than those with less interest or experience. Thus people who hold extreme positions on an issue are more likely to respond than individuals who are largely indifferent. To minimize this bias, researchers have developed a number of techniques to increase the response rate among sampling units.[22] For example, almost all surveys include a postpaid return envelope. Forcing respondents to pay the postage can substantially reduce the response rate. Designing attractive questionnaires and wording questions so they are easy to understand helps to assure a good response rate. However, special efforts may be required even with a sound questionnaire. Several of these are discussed in the following sections.

Cover Letter.   The **cover letter** that accompanies the questionnaire or that is printed on the first page of the questionnaire booklet is an important means of inducing the reader to complete and return the questionnaire. Exhibit 8.3 illustrates a cover letter and presents some of the points considered by a research professional to be important in gaining respondents' attention and cooperation.

The first paragraph of the cover letter explains *why the study is important*. The basic appeal is social usefulness. Two other frequently used appeals ask the respondent to help the sponsor: "Will you do us a favor?" and to assert themselves (the egotistic appeal): "Your opinions are important! It's important for you to express your opinions so retailers will know the type of products and shopping facilities you would like to have available."[23]

When possible, cover letters should assure confidentiality, indicate a postpaid reply envelope, describe an incentive as a "reward" for participation, explain that answering the questionnaire will not be difficult and will only take a short time, and describe how the person was scientifically selected for participation in the survey.

Monetary Incentives.   The respondent's motivation for returning a questionnaire may be increased by offering monetary incentives or premiums. Although pens, trading stamps, lottery tickets, and a variety of premiums have been utilized, monetary incentives appear to be the most effective and least biasing incentive. Although money may be useful to all respondents, its primary advantage may be as a means of attracting attention. It may be for this reason that monetary incentives work for *all* income categories and not exclusively for the poor.

Often a message such as "We know that the attached dollar (or coin) cannot compensate you for your time. It is just a token of our appreciation" will appear in the cover letter to help increase the response rate. Response rates have increased dramatically when the monetary incentive is to be sent to a charity of the respondent's choice.[24]

Interesting Questions.   The topic of the research cannot be manipulated without changing the definition of the business problem. However, additional "interesting" questions can be added to the questionnaire, perhaps at the beginning, to stimulate the respondent to begin filling out the questionnaire.[25]

EXHIBIT   8.3

**Example of Cover Letter
for Household Survey**

*Official
letterhead*	WASHINGTON STATE UNIVERSITY
PULLMAN, WASHINGTON 99968
DEPARTMENT OF RURAL SOCIOLOGY
ROOM 23, Wilman Hall
Date mailed	April 19, 19xx
*Inside address in
matching type*	Oliver Jones
2190 Fontane Road
Spokane, Washington 99467
*What study is
about; its
social usefulness*	Bills have been introduced in Congress and our State Legislature to encourage the growth of rural and small town areas and slow down that of large cities. These bills could greatly affect the quality of life provided in both rural and urban places. However, no one really knows in what kinds of communities people like yourself want to live or what is thought about these proposed programs.
*Why recipient
is important
(and, if needed,
who should complete
the questionnaire)*	Your household is one of a small number in which people are being asked to give their opinion on these matters. It was drawn in a random sample of the entire state. In order that the results will truly represent the thinking of the people of Washington, it is important that each questionnaire be completed and returned. It is also important that we have about the same number of men and women participating in this study. Thus, we would like the questionnaire for your household to be completed by an <u>adult female</u>. If none is present, then it should be completed by an <u>adult male</u>.
*Promise of
confidentiality;
explanation of
identification
number*	You may be assured of complete confidentiality. The questionnaire has an identification number for mailing purposes only. This is so that we may check your name off of the mailing list when your questionnaire is returned. Your name will never be placed on the questionnaire.
Usefulness of study

*"Token" reward
for participation* | The results of this research will be made available to officials and representatives in our state's government, members of Congress, and all interested citizens. You may receive a summary of results by writing "copy of results requested" on the back of the returns envelope, and printing your name and address below it. <u>Please do not</u> put this information on your questionnaire itself. |
| *What to do if
questions arise* | I would be most happy to answer any questions you might have. Please write or call. The telephone number is (509) 335-8623. |
| *Appreciation* | Thank you for your assistance. |
| | Sincerely, |
| *Pressed blue ball
point signature* | |
| *Title* | Don A. Dillman
Project Director |

Source: Courtesy of Washington State University and Don A. Dillman, *Mail and Telephone Surveys: The Total Design Method* (New York: John Wiley and Sons, 1978), p. 169.

Questions of little interest to the researcher may provide respondents who are indifferent to the major portion of the questionnaire a reason for responding.

Follow-ups.   The graphic plots of cumulative response rates for two mail surveys are shown in Exhibit 8.4. These curves are typical of most mail surveys: The response rate is relatively high for the first two weeks after questionnaires begin to be returned and then gradually trails off.

After responses from the first wave of mailings begin to trickle in, most studies utilize **follow-ups**—letter or postcard reminders. The follow-up letter

**Plot of Actual Response
Patterns for Two
Commercial Surveys**

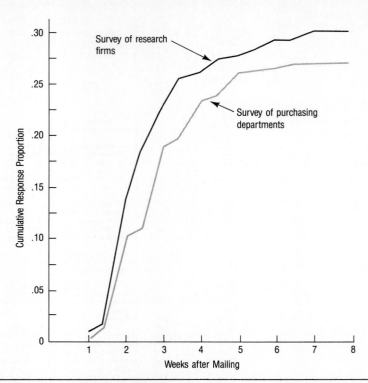

Source: Adapted from A. Parasuraman, "More on the Prediction of Mail Survey Response Rates," *Journal of Marketing
Research*, May 1982, p. 283.

generally requests that the respondent return the questionnaire because a 100
percent response rate is important for the survey's purposes. A follow-up may
include a second questionnaire or merely serve as a reminder for the respondent to fill out the questionnaire that was initially mailed.

For both studies in Exhibit 8.4, a follow-up was mailed. Notice how the
cumulative response rates pick up around Week 4.

Preliminary Notification.   Advance notification, either by letter or telephone,
has been successful in some situations.[26] For example, A. C. Nielsen has utilized this technique to ensure a high cooperation rate in filling out diaries of
television watching. One research practitioner has observed that "advance"
postcards are effective for surveys by publications but not for mailings from a
research consulting firm. Advance notices that go out closer to the questionnaire mailing time produce better results than those sent too far in advance.
The optimal lead time for advanced notification is approximately three days
before the mail survey is to arrive.

Survey Sponsorship.   It has already been suggested that auspices bias may result from the sponsorship of a survey. One industrial company wished to conduct a survey of its wholesalers to learn their stocking policies and their attitudes concerning competitive manufacturers. A mail questionnaire sent under the corporate letterhead very likely would have received a much lower response rate than the questionnaire actually sent, which utilized a commercial survey research firm's letterhead. The sponsorship of well-known and prestigious organizations, such as universities or government agencies, may also significantly influence response rates.

A mail survey sent to members of a longitudinal panel will receive an exceptionally high response rate because panel members have already agreed to cooperate with the organization conducting the survey. For example, the consumer panel sponsored by Market Facts historically has obtained a 75 percent response rate.

Other Techniques.   Researchers have tried numerous other innovations to increase response rate. For example, variations in the type of postage (regular vs. commemorative stamp), personalization of the cover letter (computer-personalized letters vs. printed), color of the questionnaire, and manipulation of many other aspects of the mechanics of mail surveys have been tried. Each has had at least limited success in certain situations. Unfortunately, under other conditions they have failed to increase response rates significantly.

The researcher should consider his particular situation. For example, a researcher investigating consumers has one situation; the researcher involved in surveying corporate executives has quite another.

Keying Mail Questionnaires with Codes.   A survey researcher who is planning a "reminder" follow-up should not disturb respondents who have already returned the questionnaires. The expense of mailing questionnaires to those who have already responded is usually avoidable. One device for eliminating from follow-up mailings those who have already responded is to mark the questionnaires so that they identify members of the sampling frame who are nonrespondents. "Blind" keying of questionnaires on a return envelope (e.g., systematically varying the job number or room number of the business research department) or visible code numbers on the questionnaire have been utilized for these purposes. "Visible" keying is indicated with statements like "The sole purpose of the number on the last page is to avoid sending a second questionnaire to people who complete and return the first one."[27] Ethical researchers key questionnaires strictly to increase response rates. The anonymity of respondents is preserved.

Other Self-Administered Questionnaires

Airlines frequently pass out questionnaires to passengers during a flight. Restaurants, hotels, and other service establishments frequently have short questionnaires printed on a card so customers can evaluate the service. (See Exhibit 8.5.)

Self-Administered Questionnaires on Business Reply Cards

Please help us serve you better by answering these few simple questions.

1. Please rate the level of service provided to you by our lending staff.

	Excellent				Poor
1. Timely	1	2	3	4	5
2. Professional	1	2	3	4	5
3. Informed	1	2	3	4	5
4. Courteous	1	2	3	4	5

2. Would you come back to Chase Manhattan for another loan?
   ☐ Yes   ☐ No

3. Was your loan application: ☐ Approved   ☐ Withdrawn   ☐ Declined

4. Do you have any suggestions regarding the quality of our service?
   _____
   _____
   _____

5. Please tell us how you became aware of Chase Manhattan.
   _____

6. In which city did you apply for a loan? _____

7. Your name (optional) _____

Source: Reprinted courtesy of Chase Manhattan Bank.

Tennis Magazine, Psychology Today, Redbook, and many other magazines have inserted questionnaires into the magazines. This is an inexpensive means of surveying current readers and often provides the source for a magazine article. Many manufacturers utilize their warranty cards to collect demographic information and information about where and why products were purchased. This use of warranty cards is an extremely economical technique for data collection to trace trends in consumer habits. A warranty card questionnaire, in the package with the product, usually has a high response rate.

Extremely long questionnaires may be dropped off by an interviewer and picked up at a later time.

All of these examples illustrate forms of self-administered questionnaires that are very similar to mail questionnaires. Again, problems may arise because those who fill out self-administered questionnaires differ from those who do not.

SELECTING THE APPROPRIATE SURVEY RESEARCH DESIGN

In earlier discussions of research design and problem definition, we emphasized that many research tasks may lead to similar decision-making information. There is no "best" form of survey. Each has advantages and disadvantages. A researcher who must ask highly confidential questions may conduct a mail survey, thus trading off the speed of data collection to avoid any possibility of in-

Exhibit 8.5 *(continued)*

PLEASE COMPLETE AND MAIL AFTER YOUR VISIT TO TEXAS

1. Visited Texas before? Yes ☐   No ☐
2. State (or nation) of residence: _____
3. Number of people in your group: Adults _____   Under 18 _____
   Age group of head of party:
   Under 25 ☐   25–34 ☐   35–49 ☐   50–64 ☐   65 and over ☐
4. Please list up to five of the main Texas cities/towns (or places) you *visited* (not just passed through) this trip: _____
   _____
   During your Texas trip, did you also visit Mexico? Yes ☐   No ☐
5. Purpose of trip (please check as many boxes as appropriate):
   Vacation ☐   Business ☐   Convention ☐   Visit Friends/Relatives ☐
   Moving to Texas ☐   Passing through ☐
6. Time spent in Texas: _____ days.   7. Total miles driven in Texas: _____
8. Please list amounts your group spent in Texas for:
   Lodging $_____   Food $_____   Auto Expense $_____
   Entertainment $_____   Other $_____   TOTAL $_____
9. Accommodations used (please check as many boxes as appropriate):
   Motel ☐   Hotel ☐   Rec. Vehicle ☐   Camping ☐   Apartment ☐
   Private Home ☐
10. Your annual family income: Under $7,000 ☐ $7,000–$12,000 ☐
    $12,000–$16,000 ☐ $16,000–$22,000 ☐   Over $22,000 ☐

Counselor _____   Comments: _____

Bureau _____   _____

Do not write in this space   Thanks for your help!

Source: Courtesy Texas Department of Highways and Public Transportation.

terviewer bias. If a researcher must have considerable control over question phrasing, central-location telephone interviewing may be selected.

To determine the appropriate technique, the researcher must ask questions such as "Is the assistance of an interviewer necessary? Are respondents likely to be interested in the issues being investigated? Will cooperation be easily attained? How quickly is the information needed? Will the study require a long and complex questionnaire? How large is the budget?" The criteria—cost, speed, anonymity, and the like, may be different for each project.

Exhibit 8.6 presents a summary of the major advantages and disadvantages of *typical* personal, mail, and telephone surveys. This summary emphasizes the typical survey. For example, it is possible that a creative researcher might be able to design highly versatile and flexible mail questionnaires, but most of these have standardized questions. An elaborate mail survey may be far more expensive than a short personal interview, but this is generally not the case.

EXHIBIT   8 . 6   **Summary of Advantages and Disadvantages of Three Typical Surveys**

	Personal	**Mail**	**Telephone**
Speed of data collection	Moderate to fast	Researcher has no control over return of questionnaire; slow	Very fast
Geographic flexibility	Limited to moderate	High	High
Respondent cooperation	Excellent, except in shopping malls	Moderate—poorly designed questionnaire will have low response rate	Good
Versatility of questioning	Quite versatile	Highly standardized format	Moderate
Questionnaire length	Long	Varies depending on incentive	Moderate
Item nonresponse	Low	High	Medium
Possibility for respondent misunderstanding	Lowest	Highest—no interviewer available for clarification	Average
Degree of interviewer influence on answers	High	None—interviewer absent	Moderate
Supervision of interviewers	Moderate	Not applicable	High, specially with central-location WATS interviewing
Anonymity of respondent	Low in face-to-face situations	High	Moderate
Ease of callback or follow-up	Difficult	Easy, but takes time	Easy
Cost	Highest	Lowest	Low to moderate
Special features	Visual materials may be shown or demonstrated; extended probing possible	Respondent may answer questions at own convenience; has time to reflect on answers	Simplified field work and supervision of data collection; quite adaptable to computer technology

Note: The emphasis is on *typical*.

NEWER SURVEY RESEARCH METHODS: INFLUENCE OF TECHNOLOGY AND MIXED MODES

Computer-interactive surveys are programmed much the same way as computer-assisted telephone interviewing surveys, except that the respondent interacts directly with an on-site computer. In other words, the respondent self-administers a computer program that asks questions in a sequence determined by the respondent's previous answers. The questions appear on a computer screen and the answers are recorded by simply pressing a key, whereby the data are immediately entered into the computer's memory. Frequently this type of interactive questioning is done at trade shows, at professional conferences, or in research facilities in shopping malls. Exhibit 8.7 illustrates a questionnaire from a computer-interactive survey. Notice that the respondent's name personalizes the questionnaire.

EXHIBIT   8.7

**Questionnaire from a
Computer-Interactive Survey**

Greetings Roxanne,

Thank you for taking a few minutes to help us find out about your reaction to specific conferences.

Please note that this is on conference 30 only, not on any of the other conferences or activities of your group on the system. I will get around to some of the others soon!

Each of the following questions is a seven point scale, with "1" representing the most positive evaluation on your part, "4" the neutral or middle point, and "7" the most negative evaluation.

After the questions and 7 response choices are printed on your terminal, the terminal will print *Response?* Please enter a number from 1 to 7 or a 0 (zero) if you wish to abstain.

If you want to change an answer, you can do so by re-entering,

+Respond, Cthirty

1:
The subject of this conference was intrinsically rewarding for me
: 1 : 2 : 3 : 4 : 5 : 6 : 7 :
very   of no
interesting   interest
Response? 1

2:
My knowledge of the subject made me capable of contributing
: 1 : 2 : 3 : 4 : 5 : 6 : 7 :
a great   nothing at all
deal
Response? 2

3:
I enjoyed participating in this conference
: 1 : 2 : 3 : 4 : 5 : 6 : 7 :
a great   not at all
deal
Response? 3

Thank you!!

If you would like to make any additional comments, please send me a message.

If you would like to see the responses of the members of the conference, type +TAB, CTHIRTY or +GRAPH, CTHIRTY. If at least five participants have responded, you will see a summary of responses. If five have not yet responded, try again in a few days!

THANKS FOR TAKING THE TIME TO RESPOND.

THIS PROCEDURE WAS CREATED BY PETER AND TRUDY JOHNSON-LENZ.

Source: Reprinted by permission of the publisher from "Computerized Conferencing for Opinion Research," by Starr Roxanne Hiltz, *Public Opinion Quarterly,* Winter 1979, pp. 566–567. Copyright 1979 by the Trustees of Columbia University.

One major advantage of computer-assisted surveys is the ability of the computer to sequence questions that are conditional upon previous responses. The computer can be programmed to skip from Question 6 to Question 9 if the answer to Question 6 is no. Furthermore, responses to previous questions can lead to questions that can be personalized for individual respondents (for example, "When you cannot buy your favorite brand, Revlon, what brand of lipstick do you prefer?"). The questionnaire is designed for the research problem, however, and computerization should not compromise this.

In many cases a fieldworker must be at the on-site location to explain how to use the computer system. Most of these technological innovations are in the early stages of development. Nevertheless, they suggest that technology is allowing for creativity in the modes of data collection.

For very short questionnaires, one technological advance is the **computerized voice-activated telephone interviewing** technique. One telephone survey system includes a voice-synthesized module controlled by a microprocessor. With it the sponsor is able to register a caller's single response such as "true/false," "yes/no," "like/dislike," or "for/against." To date, this type of system has been used by television and radio stations to register callers' responses to certain issues. One system, Telsol, begins with the computer tape making an announcement that the respondent is listening to a recorded message. Many people are intrigued with the idea of talking to a robot or a computer, so they stay on the line. The computer then asks questions, leaving blank tape in between to record the answers. If the respondent does not answer the first two questions, the computer disconnects and goes to the next telephone number.

PRETESTS

After questionnaires have been completed or returned, the investigator, who might have surveyed as many as 3,000 people, does not want to find that most respondents misunderstood a question, skipped a series of questions, or misinterpreted the instructions for filling out the questionnaire. To avoid problems like these, screening procedures or *pretests* are often utilized.

Pretests are trial runs with a group of respondents for the purpose of detecting problems in the questionnaire instructions or design. In a pretest the researcher looks for evidence of ambiguous questions and respondent misunderstanding, whether the questions mean the same thing to all respondents, the point at which respondent fatigue sets in, places in the questionnaire where a respondent is likely to terminate, and other considerations. Unfortunately, this stage of research is sometimes eliminated due to cost or time pressure.

Broadly speaking, there are three basic ways to pretest. The first two involve screening the questionnaire with other research professionals, and the third—the one most frequently referred to as "pretesting"—is a trial run with a group of respondents. When screening the questionnaire with other research professionals, the investigator asks them to look for such things as difficulties with question wording, problems with leading questions, and bias due to order. An alternative type of screening might be with a client or with the research manager who has ordered the research.

Many times in research, managers ask for information, but when they have the questionnaire, they find it doesn't meet their needs. Only by checking with the individual who requested the questionnaire do researchers know for sure that they are going to provide the information needed. Once the researcher has decided on the "final questionnaire," data should be collected from a small number of respondents (perhaps 100) to determine if the questionnaire has to be refined.

SUMMARY

There are three methods of collecting survey data. The first is personal interviewing. This flexible method allows the use of visual aids or props. Door-to-door personal interviews get a high response rate, but they are also more costly to administer than the other forms of surveys. The presence of an interviewer may also influence the subjects' responses. When obtaining a sample that is representative of the entire country is not a primary consideration, mall intercept interviews may be conducted to lower costs.

The second method is telephone interviewing. It has the advantages of speed in data collection and lower cost per interview. However, not all households have telephones, and not all telephone numbers are listed in directories. This causes problems in obtaining a representative sampling frame. Absence of face-to-face contact and inability to use visual materials are other limitations of telephone interviewing.

The third method is the self-administered questionnaire, which in the past has most frequently been delivered by mail. However, self-administered questionnaires may be dropped off, administered at a central location, or administered via computer.

Mail questionnaires are generally less expensive than telephone or personal interviews. There is a much larger chance of nonresponse error with mail questionnaires. Several methods can encourage a higher response rate. Mail questionnaires must be more structured than other types of surveys and cannot be changed if problems are discovered in the course of data collection.

Pretesting a questionnaire on a small sample of respondents is a useful way to discover problems while they can still be corrected.

Key Terms

personal interview	random digit dialing
probing	mail survey
item nonresponse	self-administered questionnaire
door-to-door interview	response rate
mall intercept interview	cover letter
callback	follow-up
telephone interview	computer-interactive survey
computer-assisted telephone interview (CATI)	computerized, voice-activated telephone interview
central location interview	pretest

Questions

1. What type of survey (communication medium) would you utilize in each of the following situations?
    a. Survey of achievement motives of industrial engineers.
    b. Survey of satisfactions of rent-a-car users.
    c. Survey of television commercial-advertising awareness.
    d. Survey of top corporate executives.

2. A publisher offers college professors one of a selection of four best-selling mass-market books as an incentive for filling out a ten-page mail questionnaire about a new textbook. What advantages and disadvantages does this incentive offer?

3. "Individuals are less willing to cooperate with surveys today than they were ten years ago." Comment on this statement.

4. What do you think the maximum length of a self-administered questionnaire might be?

5. Do most surveys utilize a single communication mode (e.g., telephone), as most textbooks suggest?

6. A survey researcher reports that "205 usable questionnaires out of 942 questionnaires delivered in our mail survey converts to a 21.7 percent response rate." What are the *subtle* implications of this statement?

7. Evaluate the following survey designs:
    a. A researcher suggests mailing a small safe (metal file box with a built-in lock) without the combination to respondents with a note explaining that respondents will be called in a few days for a telephone interview. During the telephone interview, the combination is given and the safe may be opened.
    b. A shopping center that wishes to evaluate its image places packets containing a questionnaire, cover letter, and stamped return envelope at a central location in the mall where customers can pick them up if they wish.
    c. A questionnaire is programmed on a 5¼-inch floppy disk and then mailed to individuals known to have computers. Respondents put the disk into their computers, answer the questions, and then mail the disk to the research company in a special mailer that has been provided. Each respondent is guaranteed a monetary incentive, and each has the option of increasing it by playing a slot-machine-type game programmed on the disk.
    d. A mall intercept interviewing service is located in a regional shopping center, which contains a small movie theater room for television and movie presentations. Shoppers are used as sampling units, but mall intercept interviewers recruit additional subjects for television commercial experiments relating to the survey by offering shoppers several complementary tickets for a "special sneak preview." Respondents are allowed to bring up to five guests to the preview. The complementary tickets are also offered through local newspaper ads.

e.   A personnel manager places a packet containing a questionnaire, cover letter, and stamped return envelope in the personnel office where employees can pick it up if they wish.

8.   Design a survey to determine if a cable television system (with or without a pay-TV movie channel) should be provided in a rural town of 40,000 people.

References

[1] Information courtesy of Ford Motor Company.

[2] Walker Marketing Research, *Industry Image Study: Research on Research,* 1988.

[3] Donald T. Warwick and Charles A. Lininger, *The Sample Survey: Theory and Practice* (New York: McGraw-Hill, 1975), 2.

[4] L. C. Lockley, "Notes on the History of Marketing Research," *Journal of Marketing* (April 1950): 733.

[5] *Your Opinion Counts, 1986 Refusal Rate Study* (Indianapolis: Walker Marketing Research, 1986), 14.

[6] Rine Anselmo, "Minority Undercount Remains Severe Research Problem," *Advertising Age,* Apr. 16, 1969, s-1; and Richard M. Burr, Pat L. Burr, and Elvin J. Schofield, "An Analysis of Factors Contributing to the Response of a Mail Survey," paper presented to the Southwest Marketing Association, 1975, 4; and Sigfredo A. Hernandes and Carol J. Kaufman, "Marketing Research in Hispanic Barrios: A Guide to Survey Research," *Marketing Research: A Magazine of Management and Applications* (March 1990): 11–27.

[7] Seymour Sudman, "Improving the Quality of Shopping Center Sampling," *Journal of Marketing Research* (November 1980): 423–431.

[8] *Your Opinion Counts.*

[9] John Frieman and Edgar Butler, "Some Sources of Interviewer Variance in Surveys," *Public Opinion Quarterly* (Spring 1976): 79–81.

[10] Julius A. Roth, "Hired Hand Research," *The American Sociologist* (August 1966): 190–196.

[11] *Your Opinion Counts.*

[12] William A. Lucus and William C. Adams, *An Assessment of Telephone Survey Methods,* Rand Report R-2135-NSF, October 1977.

[13] Theresa F. Rogers, "Interviews by Telephone and in Person: Quality of Response and Field Performance," *Public Opinion Quarterly* (Spring 1976): 51–65.

[14] William B. Locander and John P. Burton, "The Effect of Question Form on Gathering Income Data by Telephone," *Journal of Marketing Research* (May 1976): 189–192.

[15] U.S. Bureau of the Census, *Statistical Abstract of the United States: 1982–83* (Washington, DC: Government Printing Office, 1983).

[16] These differences were found in a major investigation of Pacific Telephone subscribers. See Clyde L. Rich, "Is Random Digit Dialing Really Necessary?" *Journal of Marketing Research* (August 1977): 300–305.

[17] Reported by Survey Sampling Inc, 1987.

[18] J. Taylor Sims and John F. Willenborg, "Random-Digit Dialing: A Practical Application," *Journal of Business Research* (November 1976): 371–378.

[19] Seymour Sudman, *Applied Sampling* (New York: Academic Press, 1976), 64–65, or E. Lair Landon, Jr., and Sharon F. Banks, "Relative Efficiency and Bias of Plus-One Telephone Sampling," *Journal of Marketing Research* (August 1977): 294–299.

[20] *Your Opinion Counts.* See also J. M. Struebbe, J. B. Kernan, and T. J. Grogan, "The Refusal Problem in Telephone Surveys," *Journal of Advertising Research* (June/July 1986): 284–287; and M. J. Walters and J. Ferrante-Wallace, "Lessons from Nonresponse in a Consumer Survey," *Journal of Health Care Marketing* (Winter 1985): 17–28.

[21] Paul L. Erdos, *Professional Mail Surveys* (New York: McGraw-Hill, 1970), 144.

[22] For excellent discussions of this topic, see Leslie Kanuk and Conrad Berenson, "Mail Surveys and Response Rates: A Literature Review," *Journal of Marketing Research* (November 1975): 440–453; and Richard T. Hise and Paul J. Solomon, "Improving Response Rates in Mail Surveys," paper presented at Southwest Marketing Association meeting, 1975.

[23] Michael J. Houston and John R. Nevin, "The Effects of Source and Appeal on Mail Survey Response Patterns," *Journal of Marketing Research* (August 1977): 374–378.

[24] Dan H. Robertson and Danny N. Bellenger, "A New Method of Increasing Mail Survey Responses: Contribution to Charity," *Journal of Marketing Research* (November 1978): 632–633.

[25] John A. Clausen and Robert N. Ford, "Controlling Bias in Mail Questionnaires," *Journal of the American Statistical Association* (September 1947): 497–511.

[26] For an empirical research study dealing with this issue, see Ronald D. Taylor, John Beisel, and Vicki Blakney, "The Effect of Advanced Notification by Mails of a Forthcoming Mail Survey on Response Rates, Item Omission Rates and Response to Speed," paper presented at Southern Marketing Association meeting, New Orleans, 1984.

[27] Paul L. Erdos and James Regier, "Visible vs. Disguised Keying on Questionnaires," *Journal of Advertising Research* (February 1977): 15.

CHAPTER **9**

Observation Methods

What you will learn in this chapter:

To distinguish between scientific observation and casual observation.

To discuss what can and cannot be observed.

To understand when observation research is the appropriate research design.

To discuss the characteristics of observation research.

To give examples of nonverbal behavior that can be observed.

To discuss the various situations in which direct observation studies may take place.

To define response latency.

To discuss scientifically contrived observation.

To define physical-trace evidence.

To recognize that content anlysis obtains data by observing and analyzing the content of messages.

To explain the purposes of content analysis.

To describe the various types of mechanical observation and methods for measuring physiological reactions.

To discuss the UPC system and the place of scanner data in observation research.

In conversation one day Sherlock Holmes asked Watson how many steps there were to the Baker Street apartment. Watson responded that he did not know. Holmes replied "Ah, Watson, you see but you do not observe." Although we, like Dr. Watson, are constantly looking around in our daily lives, we often do not observe in a scientific sense. Holmes, on the other hand, trained himself to see what others overlook by systematically observing the environment.

This chapter discusses how the observation method of data gathering is used in business research.

■

WHEN IS OBSERVATION SCIENTIFIC?

Observation becomes a tool for scientific inquiry when it:

1. Serves a formulated research purpose.
2. Is planned systematically.
3. Is recorded systematically and related to more general propositions rather than being presented as reflecting a set of interesting curiosities.
4. Is subjected to checks or controls on validity and reliability.

Scientific observation is the systematic process of recording the behavioral patterns of people, objects, and occurrences without questioning or communicating with them.[1] The researcher utilizing the observation method of data collection witnesses and records information as events occur or compiles evidence from records of past events.

WHAT CAN BE OBSERVED?

A wide variety of information about the behavior of people and objects can be observed. Six kinds of content can be observed: physical actions and evidence, such as work patterns or television viewing; verbal behavior, such as office conversations; expressive behavior, such as tone of voice or facial expressions; spatial relations and locations, such as physical distance between workers and traffic counts; temporal patterns, such as the amount of time spent shopping or time required to perform a work task; and verbal records, such as the content of memoranda. (Although investigation of secondary data uses observation—see Chapter 6—it is not extensively discussed in this chapter.)

Although the observation method may be used to describe a wide variety of behaviors, cognitive phenomena, such as attitudes, motivations, expectations, intentions, and preferences, cannot be observed. Another limitation is that observed behavior is generally of short duration. Observing behavior patterns over a period of several days or several weeks generally is either too costly or too difficult.

NATURE OF OBSERVATION STUDIES

Observation methods may be unobtrusive in that communication with the respondent may not be necessary. Rather than ask customers how much time they spend shopping in a specific supermarket, the supermarket manager might observe and record shopping time by timing the interval between a shopper's entering and leaving the store. The unobtrusive or nonreactive nature of the observation method often generates data without the knowledge of the subjects. Situations where the observer's presence is known to the subject are **visible observation.** Situations where the subject is unaware that observation is taking place are **hidden observation.** With hidden, unobtrusive observation, respondent error is minimized. Asking subjects to participate in the research is not required when those subjects are unaware that they are being observed. However, hidden observation raises an ethical issue concerning respondents' privacy (see Chapter 24 for a discussion of this issue).

The major advantage of observation studies over surveys, which obtain self-reported data from respondents, is that the data do not have distortions, inaccuracies, or other response biases due to memory error, social desirability, and so on. The data are recorded when the actual behavior takes place.

Nonverbal Behavior

Surveys emphasize verbal responses, whereas observation studies emphasize and allow for the systematic recording of nonverbal behavior. Exhibit 9.1 shows some people in working situations. What nonverbal messages are communicated to you?

A French researcher, who regularly visited his wife's office in the early evening, observed a typical pattern: The married men and single women were working overtime, and nearly all of the single men and married women had gone home. This led to the hypothesis that marriage helps men in their careers and hinders women, because the husband receives family support for job ad-

EXHIBIT   9 . 1

**Work Activity
Can Be Observed**

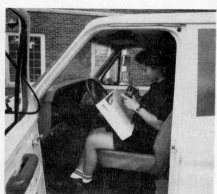

vancement while the married woman does not. This informal observation led to more rigorous quantitative studies.

Toy manufacturers use the observation technique because children often cannot verbally express their reaction to a product. By observing children at play with a proposed toy, doll, or game, business researchers can identify the elements of a potentially successful product. Researchers might observe play with toys to answer the following questions: "How long does the child's attention stay with the toy? Does the child put it down after two minutes or twenty minutes? Are the child's peers equally interested in the product?"

Behavioral scientists have recognized that *nonverbal behavior* can be a communication process by which meanings are exchanged between individuals. Head nods, smiles, raised eyebrows, and other facial expressions or body movements have been recognized as communication symbols. Observation of nonverbal communication may have considerable promise for the business researcher.[2] For example, in customer–salesperson interactions, it has been hypothesized that in low-importance transactions where potential customers are multiple and easily replaced (e.g., a shoe store), salespersons may show definite nonverbal signs of higher status than the customer. When customers are scarce, as in "big ticket" situations (e.g., real estate sales), the opposite should be true, and many nonverbal indicators of deference might be emitted by the salesperson. Observation utilizing the nonverbal communication measures in Exhibit 9.2 could test this hypothesis.

Of course, verbal behavior is not ignored, and in certain cases verbal responses are very important in observation studies.

SUPPLEMENTARY EVIDENCE

The results of observation studies may amplify the results of other forms of research by providing *complementary* evidence concerning individuals' "true" feelings. Role-playing sessions and focus group interviews are often conducted

E X H I B I T   9 . 2   **Nonverbal Communication: Status and Power Gestures**

Behavior	Between Status Equals		Between Status Nonequals		Between Men and Women	
	Intimate	Nonintimate	Used by Superior	Used by Subordinate	Used by Men	Used by Women
Posture	Relaxed	Tense (less relaxed)	Relaxed	Tense	Relaxed	Tense
Personal space	Closeness	Distance	Closeness (optional)	Distance	Closeness	Distance
Touching	Touch	Don't touch	Touch (optional)	Don't touch	Touch	Don't touch
Eye gaze	Establish	Avoid	Stare, ignore	Avert eyes, watch	Stare, ignore	Avert eyes
Demeanor	Informal	Circumspect	Informal	Circumspect	Informal	Circumspect
Emotional expression	Show	Hide	Hide	Show	Hide	Show
Facial expression	Smile[a]	Don't smile[a]	Don't smile	Smile	Don't smile	Smile

[a] Behavior not known.

Source: Nancy M. Henley, *Body Politics: Power, Sex, and Nonverbal Communication* (New York: Simon & Schuster, Inc., 1977), p. 181.

behind two-way mirrors, where researchers observe as well as listen to what is occurring. This allows for the interpretation of such nonverbal behavior as facial expressions or head nods to supplement information from interviews.

It has been recorded that in a focus group session concerning hand lotion, the women's hands were *above* the table while, casually, they were waiting for the session to begin. Seconds after the women were told that the group session was to be about hand lotion, "all hands had been placed *under* the table or out of sight and the women's faces became tense."[3] This observation, along with the group discussion, revealed the women's anger, guilt, and shame about the condition of their hands. Although the women felt they were expected to have soft and pretty hands, housework requires washing dishes, cleaning floors, and other work abusive to hands.

When individual or group behavior is videotaped, observation of nonverbal communication symbols can also add to the researchers' knowledge of the situation.

DIRECT OBSERVATION

Direct observation can produce a detailed record of events or what people actually do. The observer plays a passive role; that is, there is no attempt to control or manipulate a situation. The observer merely *records* what occurs.

Many types of data can be obtained more accurately by direct observation than by questioning. For example, recording traffic counts and/or observing the direction of traffic flows within a factory can be used to design work station layouts. In a time and motion study, an observation study of workers on a loading dock might attempt to break down tasks into component motions (e.g., grasping, picking up, setting down) so that the efficiency of the work process could be cataloged and evaluated. The observer may use a stopwatch to time each of these discrete motions in the work process. Most respondents, if directly questioned in a survey, would be unable to say accurately how much time they spent at each task. If the observation method is used, determination of the time for each task is not difficult.

Researchers using the direct observation method compile data by recording events as they occur. An observation form is often used to help keep the observations consistent and to ensure that all relevant information is recorded. A respondent is not required to recall (perhaps inaccurately) an event after it has occurred. The observation is instantaneous.

In many cases direct observation is the only or the most straightforward form of data collection. The produce manager at a Jewel Food Store may periodically gather competitive price information at the Safeway and IGA stores in the neighborhood. In other situations observation is the most economical technique. In a common observation study, researchers for a shopping center observe the license numbers on cars in the parking lot. This is an inexpensive means of determining where customers live.

Certain data may be more quickly or easily obtained by direct observation. For example, in a quality-of-life survey, respondents were asked a series of questions that were compiled into an index of well-being. Direct observation was also used by the interviewers because the researchers wanted to investigate whether weather conditions influenced people's answers. The researchers quickly and easily observed and recorded outside weather conditions on the day of the interviews, as well as the temperature and humidity in the building where the interviews were taken.[4]

Errors Associated with Direct Observation

Although there is no interaction with the respondent, direct observation is not error-free; the observer may add subjectivity to the recording. The same visual cues that may influence the interplay between an interviewer and respondent (e.g., the subject's age or sex) may also come into play in some types of direct observation settings. For example, the observer may subjectively attribute a particular economic status or educational background to the subject. A distortion of measurement resulting from the cognitive behavior or actions of the witnessing observer is called **observer bias**. In Exhibit 9.3 an excerpt from the observation section of a survey shows how field workers may be required to rely on their own interpretations of people or situations during the observation process.

If the observer does not record every detail that describes the persons, objects, and events in a given situation, accuracy may suffer. As a general guideline, the observer should record as much detail as possible. However, the pace of events, the observer's memory, the observer's writing speed, and other factors will limit the amount of detail that can be recorded.

Interpretation of observation data is another major limitation. Facial expressions and other nonverbal communication may have several meanings.

SECTION M: BY OBSERVATION ONLY

M1.   IF ANYONE WAS PRESENT DURING THE INTERVIEW OTHER THAN R AND INTERVIEWER
      GIVE THE FOLLOWING DETAILS FOR EACH:

		PERSON 1	PERSON 2	PERSON 3
M1a.	Age, approximately			
M1b.	Relationship to R			
M1c.	Present for how much of the interview?			
M1d.	How closely was (s)he listening?	1. CLOSELY 2. CASUALLY 3. HARDLY AT ALL	1. CLOSELY 2. CASUALLY 3. HARDLY AT ALL	1. CLOSELY 2. CASUALLY 3. HARDLY AT ALL
M1e.	Did (s)he make any comments on R's answers?			

M2.   R's Race?   1. WHITE   5. BLACK   OTHER: _____
                                                        (Specify)

M3.   Rate R's physical appearance:

      1. STRIKINGLY HANDSOME OR BEAUTIFUL   2. GOOD-LOOKING (ABOVE AVERAGE
                                                 FOR AGE AND SEX)

      3. AVERAGE LOOKS FOR   4. QUITE PLAIN (BELOW AVERAGE   5. HOMELY
         AGE AND SEX   FOR AGE AND SEX)

M4.   How tall would you say R was? _____ FEET _____ INCHES

M5.   Rate R's apparent intelligence?

      1. VERY   2. ABOVE   3. AVERAGE   4. BELOW   5. VERY
         HIGH   AVERAGE   AVERAGE   LOW

M6.   How suspicious did R seem to be about the study, before the interview?

      1. NOT AT ALL   3. SOMEWHAT   5. VERY SUSPICIOUS

M7.   Overall, how great was R's interest in the interview?

      1. VERY HIGH   2. ABOVE   3. AVERAGE   4. BELOW   5. VERY
                          AVERAGE   AVERAGE   LOW

M8.   How sincere did R seem to be in his answers, especially to the ones using
      the CARD 3?

      1. COMPLETELY SINCERE   2. USUALLY SINCERE   3. OFTEN SEEMED TO
                                                          BE INSINCERE

aR = respondent, DU = dwelling unit

Source: *The Quality of American Life: Perceptions, Evaluations, and Satisfactions,* by Angus Campbell, Phillip E.
Converse, and Willard L. Rogers (New York: Russell Sage Foundation, 1976).

M8a. Were there any particular parts of the interview for which you doubted R's sincerity? If so, name them by section or question numbers: _____

_____

M9. How clean was the interior of the DU?

| 1. VERY CLEAN | | 2. CLEAN | | 3. SO-SO | | 4. NOT VERY CLEAN | | 5. DIRTY |

M10. How much reading material was visible in the DU?

| 1. A LOT | | 2. SOME | | 3. NONE |

M11. TYPE OF STRUCTURE IN WHICH FAMILY LIVES:

01. TRAILER		07. APARTMENT HOUSE (5 OR MORE UNITS, 3 STORIES OR LESS
02. DETACHED SINGLE FAMILY HOUSE		08. APARTMENT HOUSE (5 OR MORE UNITS, 4 STORIES OR MORE)
03. 2-FAMILY HOUSE, 2 UNITS SIDE BY SIDE		09. APARTMENT IN A PARTLY COMMERCIAL STRUCTURE
04. 2-FAMILY HOUSE, 2 UNITS ONE ABOVE THE OTHER		10. OTHER (SPECIFY)
05. DETACHED 3-4 FAMILY HOUSE
06. ROW HOUSE (3 OR MORE UNITS IN AN ATTACHED ROW)

M12. NUMBER OF STORIES IN THE STRUCTURE, NOT COUNTING BASEMENT:

| 1 | | 2 | | 3 | | MORE THAN 3: _____
(SPECIFY)

M13. NEIGHBORHOOD: Look at 3 structures on each side of DU but not more than 100 yards or so in both directions and check as many boxes as apply, below.

00. VACANT LAND ONLY		07. APARTMENT HOUSE (5 OR MORE UNITS, 3 STORIES OR LESS)
01. TRAILER		08. APARTMENT HOUSE (5 OR MORE UNITS, 4 STORIES OR MORE)
02. DETACHED SINGLE FAMILY HOUSE		09. APARTMENT IN A PARTLY COMMERCIAL STRUCTURE
03. 2-FAMILY HOUSE, 2 UNITS SIDE BY SIDE		10. WHOLLY COMMERCIAL OR INDUSTRIAL STRUCTURE
04. 2-FAMILY HOUSE, 2 UNITS ONE ABOVE THE OTHER		11. PARK
05. DETACHED 3-4 FAMILY HOUSE		12. SCHOOL OR OTHER GOVERNMENTAL BUILDING
06. ROW HOUSE (3 OR MORE UNITS IN AN ATTACHED ROW)		13. OTHER (Specify) _____

R E S E A R C H   I N S I G H T
Doctors Should Examine Their Watches

When questioned in a survey, doctors answered they spend about nine times as long informing patients as they actually do. The physicians who were directly questioned answered they spent about 12 minutes giving information to the average patient, but videotapes of the doctor/patient encounters indicated doctors spent only 1.3 minutes giving information. Further, doctors underestimate how much their patients want to know about their illness. When doctors' answers were compared with patients' answers about how much patients wanted to know, doctors underestimated the amount of information two out of three times.

Source: Howard B. Waitzkin, "Information Giving and Medical Care," *Journal of Health and Social Behavior* 26 (1985): 81–101; *U.S.A. Today,* Feb. 10, 1987, d1.

Does a smile always mean happiness? Because someone is standing or seated in close proximity to the president of a company, does that necessarily portray a direct indication of status?

Response Latency

The decision time necessary to make a choice between two alternatives is a relatively simple unobtrusive measure. The term **response latency** refers to the recording of choice time as a measure of the strength of the preference between alternatives.[5] It is hypothesized that the longer a decision maker takes to make a choice between two alternatives, the closer the two alternatives are in terms of preference. However, if a quick decision is made, it is assumed that the "psychological distance" between alternatives is considerable. The response latency measure is growing more popular now that computer-assisted data collection methods are becoming more common (i.e., the computer records the decision time).

Scientifically Contrived Observation

Most observation takes place in a natural setting. Intervention by the investigator to create an artificial environment to test a hypothesis is called **contrived observation**. This increases the frequency of certain behavior patterns. For example, an airline passenger, complaining about a meal or poor service from the flight attendant, may actually be a researcher recording the flight attendant's reactions. If the situation wasn't contrived, the research time spent waiting and observing situations would expand considerably. The term *mystery shopper* is used by a number of retailers to describe this type of research, where an unknown shopper comes into a store and pretends to be interested in a particular product or service. After leaving the store, the shopper (observer) evaluates the performance of the salesperson.

OBSERVING SOCIAL SETTINGS

In many situations the purpose of observation will be to summarize, systematize, and simplify the activities, meaning, and relationships in a social setting. Often, unstructured methods provide the greatest flexibility to the observer. No restrictive checklist or data collection instruments limit the information recorded in the field notes.[6]

What Should Be Observed?

The definition of the problem will, of course, dictate what information is recorded. However, a general list of common elements that will be of interest in most social settings follows:

1. *The participants.* Here one wants to know: Who are the participants? How are they related to one another? How many are there? There are various ways of characterizing the participants, but usually one will want to know at least the following about any person who is being observed: age, sex, official function (teacher, doctor, employee, customer, host, club president) in the situation being observed and in the occupational system of the broader community. One will also want to know how the participants are related to one another: Are they strangers or do they know one another? Are they members of some collectivity, and if so, what kind—an informal friendship group, a fraternity or club, a factory, a church? What structures or groupings exist among the participants: Can cliques, focal persons, or isolates be identified by their spatial groupings or patterns of interaction?

2. *The setting.* Social situations may occur in different settings—a drugstore, a busy street intersection, a factory lunchroom, a nursery school, a slum dwelling, a palatial mansion. About the setting one wants to know, in addition to its appearance, what kinds of behavior it encourages, permits, discourages, or prevents. Or the social characteristics of the setting may be described in terms of what kinds of behavior are likely to be perceived as expected or unexpected, approved or disapproved, conforming or deviant.

3. *The purpose.* Is there some official purpose that has brought the participants together, or have they been brought together by chance? If there is an official purpose, what is it—to attend a funeral, to compete in a boat race, to participate in a religious ceremony, to meet as a committee, to have fun at a party? How do the participants react to the official purpose of the situation—for example, with acceptance or with rejection? What goals other than the official purpose do the participants seem to be pursuing? Are the goals of the various participants compatible or antagonistic?

4. *The social behavior.* Here one wants to know what actually occurs. What do the participants do? How do they do it? With whom and with what do they do it? With respect to behavior, one usually wants to know the following: (a) the stimulus or event that initiated it; (b) its apparent objective; (c) toward whom or what the behavior is directed; (d) the form of

activity entailed in the behavior (talking, typing, driving a car, gesturing, sitting); (e) the qualities of the behavior (its intensity, persistence, unusualness, appropriateness, duration, affectivity, mannerisms); (f) its effects (for example, the behavior it evokes from others).

5. *Frequency and duration.* Here one wants to know the answer to such questions as: When did the situation occur? How long did it last? Is it a recurring type of situation or is it unique? If it recurs, how frequently does it occur? What are the occasions that give rise to it? How typical of such situations is the one being observed?[7]

Participant Observation

Participant observation refers to situations in which an observer gains firsthand knowledge by being in or around the social setting that is being investigated. The individual who joined a management group, for example, may be a known or unknown observer. In either case the observer generally uses a combination of direct observation and interviewing.

Interview questions may be asked during the course of a conversation or discussion, rather than in any structured format. Long and involved personal interaction with the subjects of the research is the prime advantage of participant observation. Increased contact with the subjects allows the subjects to feel comfortable in the participant observer's presence.[8]

The participant observer must develop a system for recording his or her observations. Generally, the observer takes mental notes and jots down field notes where possible. At the end of the day more detailed field notes are recorded to summarize and synthesize the events and activities of the day.

OBSERVATION OF PHYSICAL OBJECTS

Physical phenomena may be the subject of an observation study. **Physical-trace evidence** is a visible mark of some past event or occurrence. For example, the wear on library books indicates which books are actually read (handled most often) after they have been checked out. A classic example of physical-trace evidence in a nonprofit setting investigates erosion traces:

> *The floor tiles around the hatching-chick exhibit at Chicago's Museum of Science and Industry must be replaced every six weeks. Tiles in other parts of the museum need not be replaced for years. The selective erosion of tiles, indexed by the replacement rate, is a measure of the relative popularity of exhibits.*[9]

This research design indicates that a creative business researcher has many options available to determine the solution to the problem.

The counting of the soup cans in the garbage, at the turn of the century, suggests another study of physical traces. (See "Research Insight" box on page 201.) This early study's method is now used in a federally funded scientific project at the University of Arizona, where young archeologists sift through "modern" garbage. They examine cigarette butts, milk cartons, and half-eaten Big Macs in the university's "garbage project."

R E S E A R C H   I N S I G H T
Traces of History

Charles Coolidge Parlin is generally recognized as one of the founders of business research. While working at Curtis Publishing Company early in the century, Parlin designed an observation study to persuade Campbell's Soup Company to advertise in the *Saturday Evening Post*. Campbell was reluctant to advertise because they believed that the *Post* was read primarily by working people who would prefer to make soup from scratch, peeling the potatoes and scraping the carrots, rather than paying 10¢ for a can of soup. To demonstrate that rich people weren't the target market, Parlin selected a sample of Philadelphia garbage routes. Garbage from each specific area of the city that was selected was dumped on the floor of a local National Guard Armory. Parlin had the number of Campbell soup cans in each pile counted. The results indicated that the garbage from the rich people's homes didn't contain many cans of Campbell's soup. Although they didn't make soup from scratch themselves, their servants did. The garbage piles from the blue-collar area showed a large number of Campbell's soup cans. This observation study was enough evidence for Campbell's. They advertised in the *Saturday Evening Post*.

Source: Reprinted with permission from the April 30, 1980, issue of *Advertising Age*. Copyright © 1980 by Crain Communications, Inc.

Investigation of garbage in Tucson has disclosed that the poor eat meat as often as the rich. They drink as much milk as wealthier citizens, consume more vitamins, use more household cleaners, and buy more children's toys and books. Many of the stereotypes don't hold up.[10]

Further investigation has found that (1) Tucson households throw out some 9,500 tons of edible food every year, (2) low-income households utilize food more efficiently than affluent families, (3) more than 80 percent of discarded food consists of "single items" such as a chunk of steak, half a can of beans, or a whole apple, and (4) all income groups have cut back on increasingly costly high-protein foods such as meat, fish, poultry, eggs, and cheese. Yet convenience-food consumption has not decreased. All families shifted their food-purchasing patterns to lower-priced categories, yet poor families went further and chose less expensive items within the categories.

Counting and recording physical inventories by retail or wholesale audits allows researchers to investigate brand sales on regional and national levels, market shares, seasonal purchasing patterns, and the like. In observation studies of the workplace, noise level, temperature, room color, piped-in music, and other physical dimensions may be observed.

Through the use of physical traces an observer can record data that a respondent might not recall accurately. The accuracy of respondents' memory is not a problem for the firm that conducts a "pantry audit," which requires inventory of the brands, quantities, and package sizes of food items in consumers' homes—not responses from individuals. The problem of untruthfulness—or some other form of response bias—is avoided. For example, the pantry audit avoids the problem of respondents' saying they have "prestige" brands in their kitchen cabinets. However, gaining permission to physically check consumers' pantries is not easy, and the fieldwork is expensive. Further, the brand in the pantry may not reflect the brand purchased most often if it was substituted because of a cents-off coupon, an out-of-stock condition, or some other reason.

Actual measurement of the number of ounces of a motor oil used during a test provides a precise physical-trace answer without relying on a respondent's memory.

CONTENT ANALYSIS

Content analysis obtains data by observing and analyzing the content or message of advertisements, union contracts, reports, letters, and the like. It involves systematic analysis, as well as observation, to identify the specific information content and characteristics of the messages.

Content analysis deals with the study of the message itself. Thus content analysis is a research technique for the objective, systematic, and quantitative description of the manifest content of communication.[11] This technique measures the extent of emphasis, or omission of emphasis, on any analytical category.[12] For example, the content of newspaper articles about a company might be investigated with regard to the use of words, themes, characters, or space and time relationships. Investigating the frequency and appearance (or "roles") of blacks, women, and other minorities in mass media has been a research topic that utilizes content analysis.

Content analysis may ask questions such as: "Do certain advertisers use certain types of themes, appeals, claims, or deceptive practices more than other advertisers?" and "Have recent actions by the Federal Trade Commission influenced the content of advertising?" In order to plan effective competition, a cable-television programmer might do a content analysis of network programming to evaluate its competition. For example, sports programs may be analyzed to see how much of the visual material is live action and how much is replay, or how many shots there are of cheerleaders or close-ups of spectators.

Study of the content of communications is more sophisticated than simply counting the items; it requires a system of analysis to secure relevant data. In an employee role-playing session involving "leaders" and "subordinates," videotapes were analyzed to identify categories for verbal behaviors (e.g., positive reward statements, positive comparison statements, and self-evaluation requests). Then trained coders, using a set of specific instructions, recorded and coded the leaders' behavior into specific verbal categories.

The best-selling book *Megatrends* provides an example of the use of content analysis in business research. Its author, John Naisbitt, is a researcher who utilizes newspaper content analysis for the purpose of projecting social trends (or megatrends). His company, The Naisbitt Group, monitors local events throughout the United States by means of a monthly content analysis of 6,000 local newspapers.[13] The results are published in the *Trend Report* on a quarterly basis. For example, the *Trend Report* has used content analysis to predict: (1) a trend toward decentralization in the federal government (power is flowing back to the local community); (2) a trend toward companies becoming more democratic, equalitarian, and spontaneous (there is a move from "organization man" to entrepreneur, with individuals becoming less constrained by layers of management); and (3) a trend toward biology replacing physics and chemistry as the dominant science.

MECHANICAL OBSERVATION

In many situations the primary—and sometimes the sole—means of observation is mechanical rather than human. In **mechanical observation** video-tape cameras, traffic counters, and other machines help observe and record behavior.[14]

Some unusual observation studies have used a motion picture camera and time-lapse photography. An early application of this observation technique, photographing train passengers, determined passenger comfort by observing how the passengers sat and moved in their seats. Another time-lapse study, filming traffic flows in an urban "square," resulted in redesigning the peripheral streets. Similar techniques may be used in research to help design store layouts and to resolve problems dealing with people or objects moving through various spaces over time.

Perhaps the best-known research project involving mechanical observation is the A. C. Nielsen Television Index (NTI), the system for estimating national television audiences. The Nielsen Television Index uses a consumer panel and mechanical observation to obtain ratings for television programs. More than 2,000 households, scientifically selected as representative of the U.S. population, have agreed to have "people meters" (formally "audimeters") placed in their homes and to be members of the consumer panel. The people meter monitors continuously, recording the time a television set is turned on, how long it remains on, which members of the household are watching television, and the channel selections. The data are then fed to the company's central computer via telephone lines, providing program ratings and demographic profiles of specific program audiences for advertisers and networks.

Measuring Physiological Reactions

Business researchers have used a number of other mechanical devices to evaluate physical and physiological reactions to various stimuli. There are four major categories of mechanical devices used to measure physiological reactions: (1) eye-tracking monitors, (2) pupilometers, (3) psychogalvanometers, and (4) voice pitch analyzers.

A magazine or newspaper advertiser may wish to grab the reader's attention with a visual scene and then direct it to a package or coupon. Eye-tracking equipment records how the subject reads the ad (or views a television commercial) and how much time is spent looking at various stimuli. In physiological terms, the gaze movements of the eye are measured with an *eye camera* or *eye view monitor*.

The **oculometer,** a technological advancement in measuring unconscious eye movements, was originally developed to measure astronauts' eye fatigue. It tracks television viewers' eye movements and four focal points through an invisible infrared light beam that "locks" into subjects' eyes. Modern eye

E X H I B I T   9 . 4

An Eye Tracking System

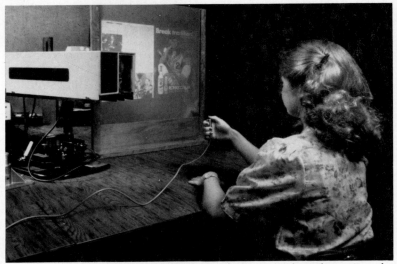

Perception Research Services' eye tracking system projects 35mm slides and pinpoints where the individual is looking.

Source: Courtesy of Perception Research Services, Inc.

tracking systems do not require keeping a viewer's head in a rather stationary position (see Exhibit 9.4). Measuring television commercials (especially animations) with the oculometer should help advertisers to emphasize selling points.

The other devices are based on a common principle:

> *Physiological research depends on the fact that adrenalin is produced when the body is aroused. When adrenalin goes to work the heart beats faster and more strongly, and even enlarges.*
>
> *Blood flows to the extremities and increases capillary dilation at the fingertips and earlobes. Skin temperature increases, hair follicles stand up, skin pores emit perspiration, and the electrical conductivity of the skin surfaces is affected. Eye pupils dilate, electrical waves in the brain increase in frequency, breathing is faster and deeper, and the chemical composition of expired air is altered. This process offers a choice of about 50 different measures—the question of which measure to use is to some extent irrelevant since they are all measuring arousal.[15]*

The **pupilometer** observes and records changes in the diameter of the pupils of a subject's eyes (see Exhibit 9.5). Subjects are instructed to look at a screen on which an advertisement (or other stimulus) is projected. If the brightness and distance of the stimulus from the subject's eyes are held constant, changes in pupil size may be interpreted as changes in cognitive activity, resulting from the stimulus rather than eye dilation and constriction from light intensity, distance from the object, or other physiological reactions to the conditions

EXHIBIT   9.5   **Pupil Response Measurement**

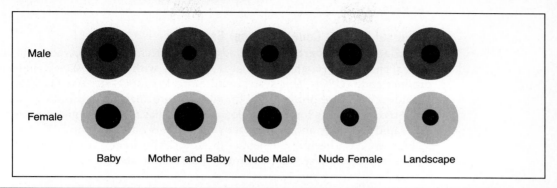

Source: *Psychology Today: An Introduction* (Del Mar, CA: CRM Books, 1970), 44. Reprinted by permission of CRM Books, a division of Random House, Inc.

of observation. This research is based on the assumption that increased pupil size reflects positive attitudes and interests vis-à-vis the stimulus.

The **psychogalvanometer** measures galvanic skin response (GSR), or involuntary changes in the electrical resistance of the skin. Use of this device is based on the assumption that physiological changes, such as increased perspiration, accompany emotional reactions to advertisements, packages, and slogans. Excitement increases the perspiration rate of the body, which increases the electrical resistance of the subject. The test is an indicator of emotional arousal or tension.

Each of these mechanical devices has a limitation in that the subjects are usually placed in an artificial setting (watching television in the laboratory rather than at home) and they know that they are being observed.

Voice pitch analysis measures emotional reactions through physiological changes in a person's voice. Abnormal frequencies in the voice, caused by changes in the autonomic nervous system, are measured with sophisticated audio-adapted computer equipment. This technique does not require subjects to be surrounded by mazes of wires or masses of equipment.

All of the devices described above assume that physiological reactions are associated with persuasiveness or that they predict some cognitive response. But this has not yet been clearly demonstrated.[16] No strong theoretical evidence supports the argument that physiological change is a valid measure of attitude change or behavior change.

Another major problem with physiological research is related to the *calibration,* or sensitivity, of measuring devices. Identifying arousal is one thing, but precisely measuring *levels* of arousal is another. In addition, most of these devices are very expensive. However, as a prominent researcher points out, physiological measurement is coincidental. "Physiological measurement isn't an exit interview. It's not dependent on what was remembered later on. It's a live blood, sweat, and tears, moment-by-moment response, synchronous with the stimulus." [17]

Universal Product Code and Other Bar Codes

As technological progress is made, advances in mechanical observation through optical character recognition are also occurring with systems such as **universal product code** (UPC). This system and optical scanners in supermarkets now provide a wealth of product and brand sales information. Substituting mechanized record keeping for human record keeping has resulted in greater accuracy and rapid feedback about store activity. Systems based on the UPC bar-code technology have been implemented in factories, warehouses, and transportation companies to research inventory levels, shipments, and the like.

SUMMARY

Observation is a powerful tool for the business researcher. Scientific observation is the systematic process of recording the behavioral patterns of people, objects, and occurrences without questioning or communicating with respondents. A wide variety of information about the behavior of people and objects can be observed. Six kinds of content can be observed: physical actions and evidence, verbal behavior, expressive behavior, spatial relations and locations, temporal patterns, and verbal records. Thus both verbal and nonverbal messages may be observed. A major disadvantage of the observation technique is that cognitive phenomena such as attitudes, motivations, expectations, intentions, and preferences cannot be observed. Further, only overt behavior of short duration can be observed. Many types of data can be obtained more accurately through direct observation than by questioning respondents. Observation is often the only or most direct method for collection of certain data.

Observation may be unobtrusive; however, observation is still prone to subjective error, even though the observer does not interact with the respondent.

Observation can sometimes be "contrived" by creating the situations that are to be observed. This is done to reduce the time and expense of obtaining reactions to certain circumstances.

Physical-trace evidence serves as a visible record of past events. Content analysis obtains data by observing and analyzing the content of messages in written and/or spoken communications. Content analysis can be used to determine the information content of phenomena.

Mechanical observation uses a variety of devices to record behavior directly.

Key Terms

scientific observation	observer bias
visible observation	response latency
hidden observation	contrived observation
direct observation	participant observation

physical-trace evidence   pupilometer

content analysis   psychogalvanometer

mechanical observation   voice pitch analysis

oculometer   universal product code (UPC)

Questions

1. Yogi Berra, former New York Yankees baseball player, said, "You can observe a lot just by watching." How does this fit in with the definition of scientific observation?

2. What are the advantages and disadvantages of observation studies relative to surveys?

3. Under what conditions do observation studies seem most appropriate?

4. Suggest some creative new uses for observation studies in your area of business.

5. A multinational fast-food corporation plans to locate a restaurant in Athens, Greece. Secondary data for this city are outdated. Using observation, how might you determine the best location for the restaurant?

6. Researchers plan to utilize voice pitch as an emotional measure of union members' evaluative reactions to a new contract proposal. Computerized analysis compares a respondent's voice pitch during warm-up conversations (normal range) with the same respondent's verbal responses to questions about the new contract. Is this an observation study? Evaluate this research technique.

7. Describe how an observation study might be combined with a personal interview.

8. The "lost letter" technique has been used to predict voting behavior. Letters addressed to various political groups are spread throughout the city. The "respondent" finds an envelope, reads the address of a group supporting (opposing) a candidate, and returns the envelope via the mail (or throws it away). It is assumed that the respondent's action indicates a favorable (unfavorable) attitude toward the political organization. Could this technique be utilized in business research? Explain.

9. Outline a research design using observation for each of the following situations:
   a. A bank wishes to collect data on the number of customer services and the frequency of customer use of these services.
   b. A state government wishes to determine the driving public's use of seat belts.
   c. A researcher wonders how many women have been featured on *Time* magazine covers over the years.
   d. A fast-food franchise wishes to determine how long a customer entering a store has to wait for his or her order.
   e. A magazine wishes to determine exactly what people see and what they pass over while reading the magazine.
   f. A food manufacturer wishes to determine how people use snack foods in their homes.

g.   An overnight package delivery service wishes to observe delivery workers beginning at the point where they stop the truck, continuing to the point where they deliver the package, and finally at the point where they return to the truck.

References

[1] Claire Selltiz, Lawrence S. Wrightsman, and Stuart W. Cook, *Research Methods in Social Relations* (New York: Holt, Rinehart and Winston, 1976), 251.

[2] Thomas V. Bonoma and Leonard C. Felder, "Nonverbal Communication in Marketing: Toward a Communicational Analysis," *Journal of Marketing Research* (May 1977): 169–180.

[3] Glen L. Urban and John R. Hauser, *Design and Marketing of New Products* (Englewood Cliffs, NJ: Prentice-Hall, 1980), 129.

[4] Angus Campbell, Philip E. Converse, and Willard L. Rodgers, *The Quality of American Life* (New York: Russell Sage Foundation, 1976), 112. Although weather conditions did not correlate with perceived quality of life, the comfort variable did show a relationship with the index of well-being. This association might be confounded by the fact that absence of ventilation and/or air-conditioning is more likely to be found in less affluent homes. Income was previously found to correlate with quality of life.

[5] Tyzoon T. Tyebjee, "Response Latency: A New Measure for Scaling Brand Preferences," *Journal of Marketing Research* (February 1979): 96–101.

[6] Claire Selltiz, Lawrence S. Wrightsman, and Stuart W. Cook, *Research Methods in Social Relations*, 3rd ed. (New York: Holt, Rinehart and Winston, 1976), 269–272.

[7] Claire Selltiz, Lawrence S. Wrightsman, and Stuart W. Cook, *Research Methods in Social Relations* (New York: Holt, Rinehart and Winston, 1976), 272.

[8] For a complete discussion of the collection and management of observation data, see John Loflan, *Analyzing Social Settings: A Guide to Qualitative Observation and Analysis* (Belmont, CA: Wadsworth, 1971), 101–109.

[9] Eugene J. Webb, Donald T. Campbell, Richard D. Schwartz, and Lee Sechrest, *Unobtrusive Measures: Nonreactive Research in the Social Sciences* (Chicago: Rand McNally, 1971), 35–36.

[10] "Archaeology Reconstructed Present," *Mosaic* (January/February 1979): 30–37.

[11] Bernard Berelson, *Content Analysis and Communications Research* (Glencoe, IL: Free Press, 1952), 55.

[12] Harold H. Kassarjian, "Content Analysis and Consumer Research," *Journal of Consumer Research* (January 1977): 9.

[13] John Naisbitt, *Megatrends: Ten New Directions Transforming Our Lives* (New York: Warner Communications, 1982).

[14] For an interesting discussion of this topic, see Robert E. Niebuhr, Charles C. Manz, and Kermit R. Davis, Jr., "Using Videotape Technology: Innovations in Behavioral Research," *Journal of Management* 7, no. 2: 43–54.

[15] "Live Simultaneous Study of Stimulus Response Is Physiological Measurement's Greatest Virtue," *Marketing News,* May 15, 1981, 1, 20.

[16] Clark Leavitt, "Physiological Measurers: Is There Hope for Hardware?" paper presented at the 25th Advertising Research Foundation Conference, 1980.

[17] Herbert B. Krugman's statement as quoted in "Live Simultaneous Study of Stimulus Response Is Physiological Measurement's Greatest Virtue," *Marketing News,* May 15, 1981, 1.

Experimental Research

$\mathbf{A}$*T&T conducted an organizational behavior experiment to determine if use of a video display terminal had any influence on employee fatigue or physical discomfort.[1] The experimenter manipulated whether AT&T directory assistance operators used video display terminals or printed paper books to find telephone number listings. When the two groups of directory assistance operators with identical job functions, distinguished only by the method used to retrieve listings, were compared, the groups exhibited no differences in the perception of physical discomfort that lingered after work.*

This experiment was a form of business research. The purpose of this chapter is to explore the use of experiments in business research and the various types of experimental designs.

■

THE NATURE OF EXPERIMENTS

Most students are familiar with the concept of experimentation in the physical sciences. We typically conjure up an image of a chemist, surrounded by bubbling test tubes and Bunsen burners. Indeed, behavioral and physical scientists have been far ahead of business researchers in the uses of experimentation. Nevertheless, the purpose of all experimental research is the same.

The purpose of experimental research is to allow the researcher to *control* the research situation so that *causal* relationships among variables may be evaluated. The experimenter therefore manipulates a single variable in an investigation and holds constant all other relevant, extraneous variables. (Events may be controlled in an experiment in a way that is not possible in a survey.) It has even been stated that "the goal of experimental design is the confidence that it gives the researcher that his experimental treatment is the cause of the effect he measures."[2]

Experiments differ from other research methods in terms of degree of control over the research situation. In an **experiment** one variable (the *indepen-*

dent variable) is manipulated and its effect on another variable (the *dependent variable*) is measured, while all other variables that may confound such a relationship are eliminated or controlled. The experimenter either creates an artificial situation or deliberately manipulates a situation.

Once the experimenter manipulates the independent variable, changes in the dependent variable are measured. The essence of a behavioral experiment is to do something to an individual and observe his or her reaction under conditions where this performance can be measured against a known baseline.

AN ILLUSTRATION: A UNIT-PRICING EXPERIMENT

The concept of experimentation is best illustrated with an extended example concerning unit pricing. Whether or not consumers actually use unit price information is an issue of considerable controversy.[3] The purpose of unit pricing is to help shoppers avoid confusion in attempting to compare prices of comparable products, especially if the products are in different-size packages. There is some evidence that unit pricing has failed to change consumers' purchasing habits. However, much of the research on unit pricing depends on interviewing techniques, question phrasing, and store promotion of unit pricing.

Suppose a researcher argues that unless unit price information is presented in a usable display format, consumers will not use the information. The current form of unit price display is a separate shelf tag for each item. However, this type of information may not facilitate price comparisons. Exhibit 10.1 shows unit prices organized onto a single list.

A survey asking respondents if they use the traditional format of unit pricing and if they have any problems with understanding the traditional unit pricing might not yield truthful responses. It may not be socially desirable for respondents to admit they have problems understanding the traditional format. Or they may be unwilling to provide truthful responses because they are embarrassed that they do not use a procedure that might reduce their grocery bills. Many other limitations of surveys, such as interviewer bias, misunderstanding the question, and so on might also cause errors.

In the simplest form of experiment, the researcher's purpose might be to compare the effectiveness of the traditional shelf tag display and the list format, measuring changes toward the purchase of less expensive brands or sizes. The hypothesis would be that a single list of all brands' sizes and their unit prices is an effective arrangement of unit price information. A shift toward the purchase of less expensive items can be measured by average price paid per unit, the dependent variable.

Let us assume researchers will conduct the experiment in a supermarket chain in a Midwestern city. The supermarket chain has four stores in this city, and none of the stores has previously used unit price information. For a period of five weeks, brand purchases for five product categories may be recorded in every store to indicate sales over a period of time. During the next five weeks, two stores may be assigned unit prices on separate shelf tags and the remaining two stores will display unit price information in the list format (see Exhibit 10.2). This manipulation involves an independent or experimental variable.

EXHIBIT   10.1

**List of Unit Prices:
Dishwashing Detergent
(Order of Increasing
Price per Quart)**

Brand	Price	Unit Price (in quarts)
Par, 48 oz.	$1.08	$0.72
Par, 32 oz.	0.76	0.76
Sweetheart, 32 oz.	1.10	1.10
Brocade, 48 oz.	1.70	1.13
Sweetheart, 22 oz.	0.78	1.13
Super 6, 32 oz.	1.18	1.18
White Magic, 32 oz.	1.18	1.18
Brocade, 32 oz.	1.26	1.26
Brocade, 22 oz.	0.90	1.31
Super 6, 22 oz.	0.90	1.31
White Magic, 22 oz.	0.90	1.31
Brocade, 12 oz.	0.54	1.44
Super 6, 12 oz.	0.58	1.55
Ivory, 32 oz.	1.60	1.60
Dove, 22 oz.	1.12	1.63
Ivory, 22 oz.	1.12	1.63
Lux, 22 oz.	1.12	1.63
Palmolive, 32 oz.	1.70	1.70
Ivory, 12 oz.	0.64	1.71
Palmolive, 22 oz.	1.20	1.75
Palmolive, 12 oz.	0.68	1.81

Source: J. Edward Russo, Gene Krieser, and Sally Mijashita, "An Effective Display of Unit Price Information," reprinted from the *Journal of Marketing,* April 1975, p. 14, published by the American Marketing Association.

EXHIBIT   10.2

Unit Price Experiment

Store	First Five Weeks	Second Five Weeks
1	Record sales	Shelf tag format, record sales
2	Record sales	Shelf tag format, record sales
3	Record sales	List format, record sales
4	Record sales	List format, record sales

EXHIBIT   10.3

**Results of Unit
Price Experiment:
Dishwashing Detergent**

Treatment	Average Price Paid per Unit	
	Five Weeks before Experiment	During Experiment
Shelf tag format (Stores 1 and 2)	65.0¢	61.6¢
List format (Stores 3 and 4)	65.0	60.0
Total all stores	65.0	61.0

Exhibit 10.3 shows that for dishwashing detergent the average price paid per unit purchased was 65.0 cents for all stores before the experiment. After the manipulation of the unit price information, the average price paid per unit in the shelf-tag stores was 61.6 cents, and in the list-format stores the average price paid per unit was 60.0 cents. The results indicate that unit price informa-

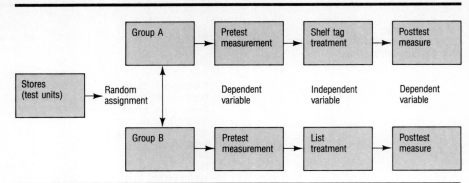

tion is effective in shifting purchases toward less expensive items in both the shelf-tag condition and in the list condition, as opposed to no unit price information displayed before the experiment. Further, the average price paid per unit is lower in the list-format condition than in the shelf-tag condition, suggesting that the list format is more effective than the tag condition.

It might be argued that some of the influence of shifts in purchases may be due to differences in the stores (for example, the stores with the list of unit prices may have shoppers who are generally more sophisticated than those in other stores). To eliminate or minimize this problem, the researchers could randomly assign the experimental condition of unit pricing format to the stores. The randomization minimizes the possibility that changes in the variable under study will be due to forces other than the unit price format. In our example this randomization process resulted in both the shelf-tag and list-format stores having equal (65.0 cents) average prices per unit before the experiment began.

Our experiment has shown that a change in presentation of unit price information (the independent variable) has caused a change in average unit price paid (the dependent variable) when other variables have been controlled for possible causal effects. For example, store image was held constant because the experiment occurred only in stores with the same name. We know that store image may affect sales, but we have controlled for this variable by using only one type of store in one city. We have also assumed invariance for certain variables; that is, we do not expect them to vary appreciably. For example, store temperature may affect the amount of time a shopper would spend in the store, but we are assuming (without checking on or controlling this assumption) that all stores are the same for this variable.

In other cases we assume that some variables are irrelevant. For example, the color of the store managers' eyes may vary but we assume that this does not have any effect on the purchase of products.

This is a simple experiment, intended to introduce some of the concepts of business experimentation. Exhibit 10.4, which diagrams the unit price experiment, can be helpful in the definition of pertinent terminology, which is presented in the next section. The remainder of the chapter explores additional aspects of experimental designs.

About 15 years ago the *New York Herald Tribune* quoted Sir Ronald Fisher, the father of experimental design, on the subject of cigarette smoking and cancer. Fisher pointed out that the only way to establish a causal connection between the two would be to randomly assign a large sample of newborn babies to two groups, those from whom cigarettes would be withheld and those who would be forced to smoke them. Some 70 or 80 years later we *might* have conclusive evidence of the true effects of smoking on death by various causes.

Sir Ronald was simply repeating a lesson that many of us learned in school: to observe a consistent relationship between two variables over time, or over cases at one point in time, does not prove that one causes the other. In its simplest slogan, "correlation is not causation" or "correlation is not *necessarily* causation." As the statistician said when he quit smoking, "I know that correlation is not causation, but in this case I'm willing to take a chance."

He put in a nutshell exactly what we do whenever we put a causal interpretation on *any* result, experimental or nonexperimental: We take a chance. Sometimes we express that chance precisely, as in the confidence level at which we reject a hypothesis in a designed experiment; but usually even then, and virtually always in practical business situations, we really have only a subjective estimate of that chance. We have failed to consider sources of error other than sampling; these must be absent if that confidence level is to be meaningful. Statistics teachers to the contrary, sampling is not always the main source of error in testing hypotheses, and in many business situations it can be unimportant relative to errors due to bias in sample selection.

Source: Excerpted from Charles Ramond, *The Art of Using Science in Marketing* (New York: Harper & Row Publishers, Inc., 1974), 20–21.

BASIC ISSUES IN EXPERIMENTAL DESIGN

Decisions must be made about several basic elements of an experiment: (1) manipulation of the independent variable, (2) selection and measurement of the dependent variable, (3) selection and assignment of test units, and (4) control over extraneous variables.[4]

Manipulation of the Independent Variable

The experimenter has some degree of control over the **independent variable.** The variable is independent because its value can be manipulated by the experimenter to be whatever he or she wishes it to be. Its value may be changed or altered independently of any other variable. The independent variable is hypothesized to be the causal influence.

Experimental treatments are the alternative manipulations of the independent variable that is being investigated. For example, monthly salaries of $2,200, $2,400, and $2,600 might be the treatments in a personnel experiment.

In business research the independent variable is often a categorical or **classificatory variable,** representing some classifiable or qualitative aspects of management strategy. To determine the effects of training, for example, the experimental treatment that represents the independent variable is the training program itself. Alternative financial reporting formats are another example of a categorical or classificatory variable. In other situations the independent variable is a *continuous variable*. The researcher must select the appropriate levels of an independent variable for experimental treatments. For example, the number of dollars that can be spent on training employees may be any number of different values.

Experimental and Control Groups.   In the simplest type of experiment, only two values of the independent variable are manipulated. For example, consider measuring the influence of a change in the work situation, such as piped-in music, on employee productivity. In the experimental condition (treatment administered to the **experimental group**), music is played during working hours. In the control condition (treatment administered to the **control group**), the work situation may remain the same—*without* change. By holding conditions constant in the control group, the researcher controls for potential sources of error in the experiment. Productivity (the dependent variable) in the two treatment groups is compared at the end of the experiment to determine whether playing the music (the independent variable) has had any effect.

Several Experimental Treatment Levels.   The music/productivity experiment, with one experimental and one control group, may not tell the researcher everything he or she wishes to know about the music/productivity relationship. If the researcher wished to understand the functional nature of the relationship between music and productivity at several treatment levels, additional experimental groups, with music played for only two hours, only four hours, and only six hours might be studied. This type of design would allow the experimenter to get a better idea of the impact of music on productivity.

More Than One Independent Variable.   It is possible to assess the effects of more than one independent variable. Perhaps a restaurant chain might wish to investigate the combined effects of increased advertising and a change in prices on sales volume. The more complex experimental designs required for such investigations are discussed later.

Selection and Measurement of the Dependent Variable

The dependent variable is so named because its value is expected to be dependent on the experimenter's manipulation. The **dependent variable** is the criterion or standard by which the results are judged. It is presumed that changes in the dependent variable are a consequence of changes in the independent variable.

Selection of the dependent variable is a crucial decision in the design of an experiment. If we introduce a new pink-grapefruit tea mix in a test market experiment, sales volume is most likely to be the dependent variable. However, if we are experimenting with different forms of training programs, defining the dependent variable may be more difficult. For example, measures of turnover, absenteeism, or morale might be alternate choices for the dependent variable, depending on the purpose of the training. In the unit pricing experiment the dependent variable was the average price per unit. However, the dependent variable might have been preference for the use of pricing information (a cognitive variable); brand-switching behavior, expressed as a percentage of consumers; or attitudes toward the store.

Often the dependent variable selection process, like problem definition, is not as carefully considered by researchers as it should be. The experimenter's choice of a dependent variable determines what type of answer is given to the research question.

In some experiments the time period required for the effects to become evident should be considered in choosing a dependent variable. Productivity may be measured several months after the experiment to determine if there were any carryover effects. Changes that are relatively permanent or more long lasting than changes generated only during the period of the experiment should be considered.

For example, in test market experiments to determine if new products will be successful, it is necessary to think about dependent variables that will identify consumers who initially purchase but do not make repeat purchases over time. In other words, it is necessary to think beyond gross sales or consumers' initial reactions and to select dependent variables that will measure sales behavior over time. Brand awareness, trial purchase, and repeat purchase are all possible dependent variables in such test market experiments. The dependent variable should therefore be carefully considered. Careful problem definition will help researchers select the most important dependent variable(s).

Selection and Assignment of Test Units

Test units are the subjects or entities whose responses to the experimental treatment are measured or observed. Individuals, organizational units, sales territories, or other entities may be the test units. Persons and departments within organizations are the most common test units in most business behaviorial experiments. In the unit pricing example, supermarkets were the test units.

Sample Selection and Random Sampling Error.   As in other forms of business research, random sampling errors and sample selection errors may occur in experimentation. For example, experiments sometimes go awry even when a geographic area is specially chosen for a particular investigation. A case in point was the experimental testing of a new lubricant for outboard motors by Dow Chemical Company. The lubricant was tested in Florida and Michigan. Florida was chosen because researchers thought that a warm-weather state, in which the product would have to stand up under continuous use, would prove the most demanding test. In Florida the lubricant was a success. But the story was quite different in Michigan. Although the lubricant sold well and worked well during the summer, the following spring Dow discovered that in the colder northern climate it had congealed, allowing the outboard motors, idle all winter, to rust. The rusting problem, of course, never came to light in Florida where the motors were in year-round use.[5] Thus some **sample selection error** may occur because of the procedure utilized to assign subjects or test units to either the experimental or the control group.

Random sampling error may occur if repetitions of the basic experiment sometimes favor one experimental condition and sometimes the other on a chance basis. An experiment dealing with video display terminal usage and fatigue may require that the people in both the experimental and control groups be identical with regard to age and experience. However, if subjects are randomly assigned to conditions without consideration of their age or experience, an error resulting from differences in that usage will be a random sampling error. Consider another example. Suppose that a potato chip manufacturer that wishes to experiment with new advertising appeals wants to have the experimental and control groups identical with respect to advertising awareness, media exposure, and so on. The experimenter must decide how to place subjects in each treatment group and which group should receive which treatment. It is generally agreed that the random assignment of participants to groups and experimental treatments to groups is the best procedure.

Randomization.   Random assignment of subjects and treatments is one device for equally distributing or scattering the effects of extraneous variables. Thus the chance of unknown nuisance effects "piling up" in particular experimental groups is identified. The effects of the nuisance variables will not be eliminated, but they will be controlled.

Randomization assures the researcher that repetitions of an experiment— under the same conditions—will show the true effects, if they exist.[6] Random assignment of conditions provides "control by chance."[7] Random assignment of subjects allows the researcher to assume that the groups are identical with respect to all variables except for the experimental treatment.

Matching.   Random assignment of subjects to the various experimental groups is the most common technique used to prevent test units from differing from one another on key variables; it assumes that all characteristics of these subjects have been similarly randomized. If the experimenter believes that certain extraneous variables may affect the dependent variable, he or she can make sure that the subjects in each group are matched on these characteristics. **Matching** the subjects on the basis of pertinent background information is another technique for controlling assignment errors.

For example, an experiment that deals with performing a work task on a word processor may require that the persons in both the experimental and the control groups be matched with regard to employment experience and typing ability (speed). Similarly, if income is expected to influence savings behavior, a savings and loan institution that is conducting an experiment may have greater assurance that there are no intersubject differences if the subjects in all experimental conditions are matched on income.

Although matching assures that the subjects in each group are similar on the matched characteristics, the researcher can never be sure that subjects have been matched on all of the characteristics that could be important to the experiment.

Repeated Measures. In some experiments when the same subjects are exposed to all experimental treatments, the experiment is said to have **repeated measures.** This eliminates any problems due to subject differences, but it causes some other problems (to be discussed later).

Control over Extraneous Variables

The fourth decision about the basic elements of an experiment concerns control over extraneous variables. To understand this issue, the various types of experimental error should be understood.

In Chapter 7 total survey error was classified into two basic categories—random sampling error and systematic error. Although this dichotomy applies to all research designs, the terms *random (sampling) error* and *constant (systematic) error* are utilized more frequently when discussing experiments.

Constant Experimental Error. Random error has already been discussed in the context of experimental selection and assignment of test units. **Constant error** (bias) occurs when the extraneous variables or the conditions of administering the experiment are allowed to have an influence on the dependent variables every time the experiment is repeated. When this occurs, the results will be confounded because the extraneous variables have not been controlled or eliminated.

For example, if subjects in an experimental group are always administered the treatment in the morning and subjects in the control group are always administered the treatment in the afternoon, this will result in a constant, systematic error. Thus in such a situation the time of day is a cause of constant error—an uncontrolled extraneous variable. In a training experiment other sources of constant error might be the persons who do the training (line or external specialists) or whether or not the training is on the employees' own time or on company time. These and other characteristics of the training may have an impact on the dependent variable and will have to be taken into account:

> The effect of a constant error is to distort the results in a particular direction, so that an erroneous difference masks the true state of affairs. The effect of a random error is not to distort the results in any particular direction, but to obscure them. Constant error is like a distorting mirror in a fun house; it produces a picture that is clear but incorrect. Random error is like a mirror that has become cloudy with age; it produces a picture that is essentially correct but unclear.[8]

Extraneous Variables. The experiments discussed so far (and indeed most experiments) concern the identification of a single independent variable and the measurement of its effects on the dependent variable. A number of extraneous variables may affect the dependent variable, thereby distorting the experiment.

An illustration shows how extraneous variables may have an impact on results.[9] Suppose a television commercial for Brand Z gasoline shows two automobiles on a highway. The announcer states that one car has used Brand Z *without* the special additive and the other has used Brand Z *with* the special additive. The car without the special additive comes to a stop first, and the car with the special additive comes to a stop 10 to 15 yards beyond it. (We shall assume that both cars used the same quantity of gasoline.) The implication of this commercial is that the special additive (the independent variable) results in extra mileage (the dependent variable). An experimenter concerned with extraneous variables that could affect the result can raise the following questions:

1. Were the *engines* of the same size and type? Were the conditions of the engines the same (tuning and so on)?
2. Were the *cars* of the same condition (gear ratios, carburetor setting, weight, wear and tear, and so on)?
3. Were the *drivers* different types? Were there differences in acceleration? Were there differences in the drivers' weights?

Because an experimenter does not want extraneous variables to affect the results of an experiment, such variables must be controlled or eliminated.

Demand Characteristics

The term **demand characteristics** refers to experimental design procedures that unintentionally give hints to subjects about the experimenter's hypothesis.[10] Demand characteristics are situational aspects of the experiment that demand the participant to respond in a particular way. Hence they are a source of constant error. If participants recognize the experimenter's expectation or demand, they are likely to act in a manner consistent with the experimental treatment. Even slight nonverbal cues may influence subjects' reactions.

In most experiments, the most prominent demand characteristic is the person who actually administers the experimental procedures. If an experimenter's presence, actions, or comments influence subjects' behavior or influence subjects to slant their answers to cooperate with an experimenter, the experiment has **experimenter bias.**

Subjects in experiments have a tendency to cooperate like guinea pigs and to exhibit behavior that might not be representative of their behavior in the marketplace or workplace. For example, if subjects in a sex discrimination experiment understand that the experimenter is interested in whether or not they changed their attitudes in accord with a given characteristic of a job applicant, they may answer in the desired direction to please the experimenter. This attitude change reflects a **guinea pig effect** rather than a true experimental treatment effect.

A famous management experiment illustrates a common demand characteristic of many experiments. Researchers were attempting to study the effects on productivity of various working conditions, such as hours of work, rest periods, lighting, and methods of pay at the Western Electric Hawthorne plant in Cicero, Illinois. The researchers found that workers' productivity increased whether the work hours were lengthened or shortened, whether lighting was very bright or very dim, and so on. The surprised investigators realized that the workers' morale was higher because they were aware of being part of a special experimental group. This totally unintended effect is now known as the **Hawthorne effect** because researchers realized that subjects will perform differently when they know they are experimental subjects.[11]

If persons in a laboratory experiment interact (i.e., are not relatively isolated), their talk about subjects (for example, résumés) may produce "joint" decisions rather than a desired individual decision. Generally, for this reason, social interaction is restricted in laboratory experiments.

To reduce demand characteristics, steps are taken to make it difficult for subjects to know what the researcher is trying to find in the experiment. Experimenter training and experimental situations are designed to reduce cues that might serve as demand characteristics. For example, the subjects may be told the purpose of the experiment is one thing when the research's purpose is actually something else. If the purpose of the experiment is disguised, the participant does not know how to be a "good subject" to "help" confirm the hypothesis. Of course, the use of deception (for example, if a lie is told to the subject) presents an ethical question that must be resolved by the researcher.

Establishing Control

The major difference between experimental research and other research is the experimenter's ability to "hold constant" conditions and to manipulate the treatment. To conclude that A causes B, a cigarette manufacturer, experimenting with a "new" tobacco's influence on smokers' taste perception, must determine the possible extraneous variables that may affect the results, and attempt to eliminate or control them. We know that brand image and packaging are important factors in smokers' reactions to the products. Wishing to eliminate the effects associated with brand name and packaging, the experimenter may *eliminate* these two extraneous variables by packaging the test cigarettes in plain white packages without brand identification.

When extraneous variables cannot be eliminated, experimenters may strive for **constancy of conditions**.[12] This procedure strives to have all subjects in each experimental group exposed to situations that are exactly alike except for the differing conditions on the independent variable. For example, holding extraneous variables constant might require that all experimental sessions be conducted in the same room at the same time of day.

A supermarket experiment, involving four test products, shows the care that must be taken to hold all factors constant. The experiment required that all factors other than shelf space were to be kept constant throughout the testing period. In all stores the same shelf level that existed before the tests began was maintained throughout the test period. Only the amount of shelf space (shelf treatment) was changed. Another problem involved store personnel accidentally changing shelf spaces when they restocked the test products. This distortion was minimized by auditing each store four times a week. In this way any change could be detected in a minimum amount of time. The experimenter personally stocked as many of the products as possible, and the cooperation of stock clerks also helped lessen treatment deviations.[13]

If the experimental method requires that the same subjects be exposed to two or more experimental treatments, there may be an error due to the **order of**

presentation. An example might be having subjects perform an experimental task that requires a job skill (e.g., assembling a product). Subjects might perform better in a *second* task simply because they acquired experience on the *first* task.

Counterbalancing attempts to eliminate the confounding effects of order presentation by requiring that half the subjects be exposed first to Treatment A and then to Treatment B. The other half receives Treatment B first and then Treatment A.

Blinding is utilized to control subjects' knowledge of whether they have or have not been given a particular experimental treatment. A cola taste test might use two groups of subjects, one group exposed to the new (diet) cola and one group exposed to the regular drink. If all the subjects were "blinded," they may have been told they have *not* been given the diet drink—or that they *have* been given the diet drink. This technique is also used in medical research when chemically inert pills (placebos) are given to those subjects who do not receive any medication.[14]

This technique may also involve the experimenters. Thus if the researchers do not know which toothpastes are in the tubes marked, say, with triangles, circles, or squares, they will not unconsciously influence the subjects. In these circumstances neither the subjects nor the experimenter knows which are the experimental and which are the controlled conditions. Both parties are "blinded"; hence the term **double-blind design.**

Random assignment of subjects to experimental groups and experimental treatment of groups is an attempt to control extraneous variations caused by chance. If extraneous variations *cannot* be controlled, it must be assumed that the confounding effects will be present in all experimental conditions and have approximately the same influence. (This assumption may not be made if assignments are not on a random basis.) In many experiments, especially laboratory experiments, it is important to eliminate or minimize interpersonal contact between members of the various experimental groups and/or the control group. Thus, after the subjects have been assigned to groups, the various individuals should be kept separated so that discussions about what occurs in a given treatment situation does not become an extraneous variable that contaminates the experiment.

Problems with Extraneous Variables

In business experiments it is not always possible to control everything that would be desirable to have the "perfect" experiment. For example, competitors may bring out a new product during the course of an experiment. This form of competitive interference occurred in a Boston test market for Anheuser-Busch's "import" beer, Würzburger Hofbräu, when the Miller Brewing Company introduced its own brand, Munich Oktoberfest, and sent eight salespeople to "blitz" the Boston market.

If a competing firm learns of a test market experiment, it may—knowingly—change its prices or increase its advertising to confuse the test results. This gives a competitor more time to investigate a similar new-product possibility.

Business researchers may also be constrained by management's greater concern with efficiency than with research. In an experiment on the four-day work week (four days—forty hours), researchers planned to investigate employee satisfaction, absenteeism, and leisure-time activity *before* implementation of the four—forty system, *during* the time the system was in effect, and *after* the system was withdrawn.[15] The researchers had planned to investigate the effect of the four—forty schedule over a long period of time, but the organization's management terminated the experiment after one month because of "scheduling difficulties."

FUNDAMENTAL QUESTIONS IN EXPERIMENTATION

Basic versus Factorial Experimental Designs

In *basic experimental designs* a single independent variable is manipulated to observe its effect on a single dependent variable. However, we know that complex dependent variables, such as sales, productivity, preference, and so on are influenced by several factors. A simultaneous change in two independent variables such as price and advertising may have a greater influence on sales than if either variable is changed in isolation.

Factorial experimental designs are more sophisticated than basic experimental designs. They allow for investigation of the interaction of two or more independent variables. Factorial experiments are discussed in the section on complex experimental designs later in this chapter.

Field and Laboratory Experiments

A business experiment can be conducted in a natural setting (**field experiment**) or in an artificial setting, one contrived for a specific purpose (**laboratory experiment**). In a laboratory experiment the researcher has almost complete control over the research setting. For example, subjects for a laboratory experiment investigating whether increasing performance goal difficulty will increase productivity are recruited and brought to a university office, a research agency's office, or perhaps a mobile unit designed for research purposes. These subjects, who have volunteered to work for one hour, are required to perform a task in a setting where they will not be interrupted. Of course, the instructions for the different experimental groups are manipulated by varying the performance goals' level of difficulty.

Let's consider a second example. In a laboratory experiment to measure advertising, subjects are exposed to a television commercial within the context of a program that includes ads for competitive products. Then the subjects are allowed to make a purchase—the advertised product or one of several competitive products—in a simulated store environment. Trial purchase measures are thus obtained. A few weeks later the subjects will be recontacted to measure satisfaction and to determine repeat purchase intentions. This typical laboratory experiment gives subjects an opportunity to "buy" and "invest." In a short time span, the researcher is provided the chance to collect information on decision making.

R E S E A R C H   I N S I G H T
Field Experiment to Evaluate the Impact of Technology on Organizational Changes

A field experiment was conducted in two branches of a large insurance company to assess organizational changes. The organization's executives had decided to replace a paper-record file system used by clerical and semitechnical workers with a computerized system, but they were concerned that increases in technological efficiency might be counterbalanced by negative worker responses to the new system. Thus, the purpose of the research was to determine whether the introduction of this automated system would cause changes in worker attitudes.

The 118 employees involved in the research project were divided into two groups. A control group of 75 employees from one division of the regional office used the old filing system. An experimental group of 43 employees from another division of the same regional office used the new system. A survey questionnaire was administered to both groups of employees one week before the new system was installed. Three months after the change another questionnaire was administered to both groups.

The questionnaire attempted to measure employee satisfaction with the work, with job involvement, and with motivation from the work itself. It evaluated employees' intentions to be absent or to resign as well as attitudes toward absenteeism and resignation. Finally, it assessed perceived job complexity (a combination of variety, autonomy, identity, significance, and feedback). In all cases, employees voluntarily provided individual identification for follow-up purposes.

The control group provided a comparison standard and eliminated many possibly incorrect explanations of the results. For example, if some factor other than the technological change influenced the responses of the experimental group, this extraneous factor might have been falsely interpreted as an effect of the technological change. Most extraneous factors, however, would also influence the control group since the two groups were highly similar. Thus, the organization wanted to know if there were changes in the experimental group that did not occur for the control group.

The results of this series of surveys showed that there were no significant changes in the average responses of the experimental group to questions about satisfaction, motivation, or behavioral intentions after the introduction of the new system. Furthermore, the average responses of the experimental group were not significantly different from those of the control group. Thus, on the average, the anticipated negative effects of the change did not occur.

Another interesting result was detected, however, upon a closer examination of the data. Although on the average there were no significant effects, many workers did perceive changes in job complexity. Because some workers perceived an increase while others perceived a decrease in complexity, there was no average change. The fact that more of these changes occurred in the experimental group than in the control group suggested that the new system did have some effect. Furthermore, those people who perceived decreases in the complexity of the job became less satisfied with the work, less motivated by the work, and more likely to resign. These negative effects were offset by persons who perceived increases in complexity. They became more satisfied with the work, more motivated by the work, and less likely to resign.

Overall, the results of the research indicated that the introduction of the new filing system would have inconsistent effects on workers. The company could proceed to install the system, knowing that it would probably not have a major impact on average worker responses. Because some employees would probably react negatively to these changes, however, the organization would have to be prepared to deal with these individual cases.

EXHIBIT   10.5   **A Tachistoscope Experiment**

Source: Joyce Turovlin, "Paktest's Holistic Approach Helps Package Design Testing," reprinted by permission from the *Marketing News*, Jan. 28, 1977, p. 24, published by The American Marketing Association.

Other laboratory experiments may be more controlled or artificial. Exhibit 10.5 shows a **tachistoscope** in use in a laboratory experiment.[16] The tachistoscope allows researchers to experiment with the visual impact of advertising, packaging, and so on by controlling the amount of time a visual image is exposed to a subject. Each stimulus (e.g., package design) is projected from slides to the tachistoscope at varying exposure lengths (1/10 of a second, 3/10 of a second, etc.). It simulates the split-second duration of a customer's attention in the same way a package might in a mass display.

Field experiments are conducted in natural settings, and they often expose individuals to the treatment for long periods of time. For example, the National Park Service engaged in a field experiment with a computerized reservation service in four national parks. The experiment was conducted to measure public reaction to a system that allowed campers to reserve space in the national parks. As another example, McDonald's conducted a field experiment to test market Triple Ripple, a three-flavor ice cream product. The product was dropped because the experiment showed distribution problems were combined with limited customer acceptance. In the distribution system, the product would freeze, defrost, and refreeze. Solving the problem would have required each McDonald's city to have an ice cream plant with special equipment to roll the three flavors into one. A natural environmental setting for the experiment helped McDonald's executives realize the product was impractical.

These examples illustrate that experiments vary in degrees of artificiality. Exhibit 10.6 shows that as experiments increase in naturalism they begin to approach the pure field experiment, and as experiments become more artificial

E X H I B I T   1 0 . 6   **Artificiality of Laboratory versus Field Experiments**

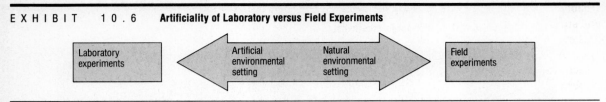

Source: Adapted from Keith K. Cox and Ben M. Enis, *The Marketing Research Process* (Goodyear Publishing, 1972, Scott, Foresman and Company), p. 304. Reprinted with permission.

they approach the laboratory type. The degree of artificiality in experiments refers to the amount of manipulation and control of the situation that the experimenter creates to ensure that the subjects are exposed to the exact conditions the experimenter desires. In the field experiment the researcher manipulates some of the variables but is not able to control all of the extraneous variables. An example would be the National Broadcasting Company's research on new television programs. Viewers who subscribe to a cable television service are asked to view a cable preview on their home television sets at a certain time on a certain cable channel. However, while the program is being aired, telephone calls from the viewers' friends cannot be controlled. Laboratory tests, on the other hand, may show consumers the same program in a movie theater, where the conditions are the same for all of the subjects, without the realistic interruptions of everyday life.

Generally, subjects will be aware of their participation in laboratory experiments. Performance of certain tasks, response to questions, or some form of active involvement are characteristic of laboratory experiments. It is common to *debrief* subjects of laboratory experiments to explain the purpose of the research. In some situations only field studies are usable, because it is not feasible to simulate environmental conditions, such as employees' reactions to a new compensation program.

ISSUES OF EXPERIMENTAL VALIDITY[17]

Internal Validity

Managers must address two fundamental problems in choosing or evaluating experimental research designs: internal validity and external validity. The first has to do with interpretation of the cause-and-effect relationship in the experiment. **Internal validity** refers to whether the experimental treatment was the sole cause of observed changes in the dependent variable. If the observed results are influenced by the confounding effect from extraneous factors (previously discussed), the researcher has problems making valid conclusions about the relationship between the experimental treatment and the dependent variable.

It is helpful to classify the six major types of extraneous variables that may jeopardize internal validity: history, maturation, testing, instrumentation, selection, and mortality.

History.   Suppose an experiment was being conducted by a brokerage firm. If the stock market takes a steep drop just after the beginning of the experiment, this event may jeopardize the validity of the experiment. This is a **history effect.**

A history effect refers to a specific event in the external environment, between the first and second measurements, that is beyond the control of the experimenter. Changes during the course of an organizational behavior field experiment are quite likely. A departmental reorganization, a strike or large layoff, or a change in the economic climate may have an impact on the results of an experiment.

A special case of the history effect sometimes occurs. The *cohort effect* refers to a change in the dependent variable because members of one experimental condition experienced historical situations different from those of members of other experimental conditions. For example, two groups of workers, used as subjects, may be in different "cohorts" because one group of workers experienced the turmoil of long and bitter strikes. Another group of workers, hired after the strikes, may have experienced a different "history" and therefore might behave differently in a workplace experiment.

Maturation.   People change over time; that is, there is a maturing process. During the course of an experiment, subjects may mature or change in some way that will have an impact on the experimental results. The **maturation effect** is a change within respondents that operates as a function of time rather than as a response to a specific event.

During a day-long experiment, subjects may grow hungry, tired, or bored. In an experiment over a longer time span, maturation may influence internal validity because subjects grow older, or become more experienced, or change in other ways that may influence the results.

Suppose an experiment was designed to test the impact of a new compensation program on sales productivity. If the new compensation program were tested over a year's time, it is likely that some of the salespeople would have matured due to increased selling experience or increased knowledge.

Testing.   A **testing effect** is also called a *pretesting effect* because the initial measurement or test alerts respondents to the nature of the experiment. Thus respondents may act differently than they would have if no pretest measure were taken. In a before-and-after study, taking a pretest before the independent variable is manipulated may sensitize respondents when they are taking the test for a second time. For example, students taking achievement and intelligence tests for the second time usually do better than those taking the tests for the first time.[18] Pretesting may increase awareness of socially approved answers, it may increase attention to experimental conditions (i.e., the subject may watch more closely), or it may make the subject more conscious of the dimensions of a problem.

Instrumentation.   Measuring the dependent variable in an experiment requires the use of a questionnaire or other form of measuring instrument. If the identical instrument is used more than once, there may be a testing effect. To avoid the effects of testing, an alternative form of the measuring instrument (for example, questionnaire or test) may be given during the post- (after) measurement. Although this may reduce the effect of testing because of a change in the measuring instrument, it may also result in an **instrumentation effect.**

A change in the wording of questions, a change in interviewers, or a change in other procedures to measure the dependent variable cause an instrumentation effect, which may jeopardize internal validity. For example, if the same interviewers are used to ask questions both before and after measurement, some problems may arise. With practice, interviewers may acquire increased skill in interviewing, or interviewer boredom may cause the instrument to be reworded in the interviewers' own terms. To avoid this problem, new interviewers are hired, but different individuals are a source of extraneous variation due to instrumentation variation. There are numerous sources of instrument decay or variation.

Selection.   The **selection effect** is a sample bias resulting from differential selection of respondents for the comparison groups. This topic has already been addressed.

Mortality.   If an experiment is conducted over a few weeks or more, there may be a sample bias due to *mortality,* or *sample attrition.* Sample attrition occurs when some subjects withdraw from the experiment before it is completed. In an organization behavior experiment, employee turnover may be a factor.

A **mortality effect** may occur if many subjects drop from one experimental treatment group and not from other treatment or control groups. Consider the example of a training experiment that investigates the effects of close supervision (high pressure) versus low supervision (low pressure). The high-pressure condition may misleadingly appear superior if those subjects who completed the experiment did very well but the high-pressure condition caused more subjects to drop out than in other conditions. This apparent superiority may be due to a self-selection bias if only very determined and/or talented salespeople remain throughout the training period.

External Validity

The second validity problem concerns the researcher's ability to generalize the results from the experiment to the external environment, such as other corporate offices or the marketplace. **External validity** is the quality of being able to generalize beyond the data of the experiment to other subjects or other groups in the population under study. In essence, it is a sampling question. To what extent can the results of a simulated negotiating experiment be transferred to the real world of union–management relations? Will a test market in Fort Wayne, Indiana, be representative of a nationwide introduction of the product under study? Can one extrapolate the results of a tachistoscope to an in-store shopping situation? Problems of external validity generally relate to the possibility that a specific but limited set of experimental conditions may not deal with the interactions of untested variables in the real world. In other words, the experimental situation may be artificial and it may not represent the true setting and conditions in which the investigated behavior takes place. If the study lacks external validity, it will be difficult to repeat the experiment if different subjects, settings, or time intervals are used.

Consider a television commercial being pretested by means of personal interviews in a shopping mall. A portable television set simulates an actual television program, with the test commercial inserted along with other commercials. Will respondents view the test commercial exactly as they would if the commercial were viewed on a regular program at home? There probably will be some contamination, but the experiment may still be externally valid if the researchers know how to adjust the results from the artificial settings to the marketplace.

Comparative norms may be established, based on similar, previous studies, so the results can be projected beyond the experiment. Of course, if an experiment lacks internal validity, projecting its result is not possible. Thus the threats to internal validity may also jeopardize external validity.

Student Surrogates.   One issue of external validity concerns the use of college students as experimental subjects. Time, money, and a host of other practical considerations often necessitate the use of students as surrogates for other research subjects.[19] This practice is widespread in academic studies.[20] Some evidence shows that students respond with considerable similarity to groups outside the college or university, but there is also evidence that students do not provide an accurate prediction of other populations. This is particularly true when students are used as substitutes or surrogates for businesspeople.[21] Any researcher who utilizes student surrogates should use considerable caution to ensure that the student subjects and the "real people" they are to portray are similar. This may not be easy, unless the population under study has literacy, alertness, and rationality that parallel these characteristics of the student surrogates.

This issue of external validity should be seriously considered because the student population is likely to be atypical. Students are easily accessible but they often are not representative of the total population.

Trade-offs.   Naturalistic field experiments tend to have greater external validity than artificial laboratory experiments. One of the problems facing the business researcher is that internal validity is generally traded off for external validity. There is more control in a laboratory experiment. The researcher who wishes to test advertising effectiveness via a split-cable experiment has the assurance that the advertisement will be viewed in an externally valid situation, that is, in the respondent's home. However, the researcher has no assurance that some additional information or a distraction (e.g., a telephone call) won't have some influence that will reduce the internal validity of the experiment. Laboratory experiments with many controlled factors are usually high in internal validity. In general, field experiments have less internal validity but greater external validity.

CLASSIFICATION OF EXPERIMENTAL DESIGNS

The design of an experiment may be compared to an architect's plans for a structure, whether it be a skyscraper or a modest home. The basic requirements for the structure are given to the architect by the prospective owner. It is the architect's task to fill these basic requirements, yet the architect has ample room for exercising his ingenuity. Several different plans may be drawn up to meet all the basic requirements. Some plans may be more costly than others. Two plans may have the same cost, but one may offer potential advantages that the second does not.[22]

There are various types of experimental designs. If only one variable is manipulated, the experiment is a **basic experimental design.** If the experimenter wishes to investigate several levels of the independent variable (e.g., four salary levels) or to investigate the interaction effects of two or more independent variables, then the experiment requires a *complex* or *statistical* experimental design.

Symbolism for Diagraming Experimental Designs

The work of Campbell and Stanley has aided many students in understanding the subject of experimental designs.[23] The following symbolism facilitates description of the various experimental designs:

X = exposure of a group to an experimental treatment.

O = observation or measurement of the dependent variable. If more than one observation or measurement is taken, subscripts (that is, O_1, O_2, etc.) will be given to indicate temporal order.[24]

$\boxed{R}$ = random assignment of test units. R symbolizes that individuals selected as subjects for the experiment will be randomly assigned to the experimental groups.

As we diagram the experimental designs with these symbols, the reader should assume a time flow from left to right. The first of the following three examples of quasi-experimental design will make this clearer.

Three Examples of Quasi-Experimental Design

Quasi-experimental designs do not qualify as true experimental designs because they do not adequately control for the problems associated with loss of external or internal validity.

One-Shot Design (After-Only Design).   The **one-shot** (or *after-only*) **design** is diagramed as follows:

$$X \quad O_1$$

Suppose an automobile dealer, after a very cold winter, found himself with a very large inventory of cars. He decided to experiment with a promotional scheme: offering a free trip to New Orleans with every car sold. He experiments with the promotion (X = experimental treatment) and measures his sales (O = measurement of sales after the treatment was administered).

This one-shot design is a case study fraught with problems. In this experiment we do not have any kind of comparison. We have no means of controlling extraneous influences. We need a measure of what would happen when the test units have not been exposed to X to compare with the measure when subjects *have* been exposed to X.

One-Group Pretest-Posttest Design.   Suppose a real estate franchiser wishes to provide a training program for franchisees. If the franchiser measures subjects' knowledge of real estate selling before (O_1) being exposed to the experimental treatment (X) and then measures their real estate selling knowledge after (O_2) they are exposed to the treatment, the design is as follows:

$$O_1 \quad X \quad O_2$$

In this example the trainer is likely to conclude that the difference between O_2 and O_1 ($O_2 - O_1$) is the measure of the influence of the experimental treatment. This **one-group pretest-posttest design** offers a comparison of the same individuals before and after training. Although an improvement over the after-only design, this research still has several weaknesses that may jeopardize internal validity. For example, if the time lapse between O_1 and O_2 was several months, the trainees may have matured (maturation effect) due to experience on the job. The history effect may also have had an influence in this design. Some subjects may have dropped out of the training program (mortality effect). The effect of testing may also have confounded the experiment. For example, taking a test on real estate selling may have made subjects more aware of their lack of specific knowledge. Then, either during the training sessions or on their own, they may have sought to learn material on which, they realized, they were uninformed.

If the second observation or measure (O_2) of salespersons' knowledge was not an identical test, we may have the influence of instrument variation. Or, if we used an identical test but had different graders for the "before" and "after" measurements, the data may not be directly comparable.

Although this design has a number of weaknesses, it is used frequently in business research. Remember, the cost of the research is a consideration in most business research. Although there may be some problems of internal validity, the researcher must always take into account questions of time and cost.

Static Group Design.   In the **static group design,** subjects are identified as either an experimental group or a control group (for example, exposed or not exposed to a fitness program for employees). The experimental group is measured after it has been exposed to the experimental treatment, and the control group is measured without having been exposed to the experimental treatment:

Experimental group: X O_1
Control group: O_2

The results of the static group design are computed by subtracting the observed results in the experimental group from the observed results in the control group ($O_2 - O_1$).

A major weakness of this design is that we have no assurance that the groups were equal on variables of interest before the experimental group received the treatment. If the groups were selected arbitrarily by the investigator or if entry into either group was voluntary, then there may be systematic differences between the groups that could invalidate the conclusions about the effect of the treatment. For example, suppose a corporation that has a fitness program wishes to determine if there is a significant difference in health insurance claims, absenteeism, personnel turnover, and grievances between the group in the program and the group not in the program. If entry into the groups was voluntary, we might find that the group in the fitness program might have some reason for choosing that group (for example, atypical numbers of "health nuts"). Sample attrition of experimental-group members who did not like the program might also be a source of error.

On many occasions *after-only* designs are the only possible design. This is particularly true when "use tests" are conducted for new products or for introducing a new organizational policy. Interpretation and recognition of the design's shortcomings may allow this "necessary evil" to be quite valuable. For example, Airwick Industries conducted in-use tests with Carpet Fresh, a rug cleaner and room deodorizer. Experiments with Carpet Fresh, which was conceived as a granular product to be sprinkled on the carpet before vacuuming, indicated that people were afraid that the granules would lodge under furniture. This research led to changing the product to a powdery texture.

Random assignment of subjects may minimize problems with group differences. If groups can be determined by the experimenter, rather than exist as a function of some other causation, the static-group design is referred to as an *after-only design with control group*.

Three Good Experimental Designs

In a formal, scientific sense, the three designs described above are not true experimental designs. Subjects for the experiments were not selected from a common pool of subjects and randomly assigned to one group or another. The three basic experimental designs discussed below will have the symbol $\boxed{R}$ to the left of the diagram to indicate that the first step in a true experimental design is the randomization of subject assignment.

Pretest-Posttest Control-Group Design (Before-After with Control).   The **pretest-posttest control-group design,** or before-after group with control, is the classic experimental design:

$$\text{Experimental group:} \quad \boxed{R} \quad O_1 \quad X \quad O_2$$
$$\text{Control group:} \quad \boxed{R} \quad O_3 \qquad O_4$$

As the diagram above indicates, the experimental group is tested before and after the subjects are exposed to the treatment. The control group is tested twice, at the same times the experimental group is, but the subjects are not exposed to the experimental treatment. This design has the advantages of the before-after design, with the additional advantages gained by having a control group. The effect of the experimental treatment equals $(O_2 - O_1) - (O_4 - O_3)$.

If there is brand awareness among 20 percent of the subjects ($O_1 = 20\%$, $O_3 = 20\%$) before an advertising treatment and 35 percent awareness in the experimental group after exposure to the treatment ($O_2 = 35\%$) and 22 percent awareness in the control group ($O_4 = 22\%$), the treatment effect equals 13 percent:

$$(.35 - .20) - (.22 - .20)$$
or
$$(.15) - (.02) = .13, \text{ or } 13\%$$

It is assumed that the effect of all extraneous variables will be the same on both the experimental and the control groups. For instance, because both groups receive the pretest, no difference between the groups is expected for the pretest effect. This assumption is also made for effects of other events between the before- and after-measurements (history effects), changes within the subjects that occur with the passage of time (maturation effects), testing effects, and instrumentation effects. Of course, in reality there will be some differences in the sources of extraneous variation. In most cases, however, the assumption that the effect is approximately equal for both groups is a sound premise.

Nevertheless, the interactive testing effect is possible when subjects are sensitized to the subject of the research. This is analogous to a situation in which people learn a new word: They soon discover that they notice the word much more frequently in what they are reading. In an experiment the combination of being interviewed on a subject and the experimental treatment might be a potential source of error. For example, subjects exposed to a certain advertising message in a split-cable experiment might say, "Ah, there is an ad about the product I was interviewed about yesterday!" The respondent pays more attention than normal to the advertisement and may be more prone to change his or her attitude than in a situation where there are no testing effects. This weakness in the *before-after with control group* design can be corrected (see the next two designs).

Testing the effectiveness of television commercials in movie theaters provides an example of the "before-after" with control group design. Subjects are selected for the experiments by being told they are going to preview several new television show pilots. When the subjects enter the theater, they learn that a drawing for several types of products will be held, and they are asked to complete a product preference questionnaire (see Exhibit 10.7). A first drawing is then held. The television commercials and television pilots are shown next. Finally, the "emcee" indicates that there are additional prizes and that a second drawing will be held. Then the same questionnaire about prizes is filled out. The information from the first questionnaire is the "before" measurement and the information from the second questionnaire is the "after" measurement. The control group will receive similar treatment, except that on the day they view the pilot television films, different (or no) television commercials will be substituted for the experimental commercials.

Posttest-Only Control Group Design (After-Only with Control Group).   In some situations pretest measurements are impossible. In other situations selection

E X H I B I T   1 0 . 7   **Product Preference Measure in an Experiment**

We are going to give away a series of prizes. If you are selected as one of the winners, which brand from each of the groups listed below would you truly want to win?

Special arrangements will be made for delivery of any product for which bulk, or one-time, delivery is not appropriate.

Indicate your answers by *filling in* the box like this: ■
Do not "X," check, or circle the boxes please.

Cookies		**Allergy Relief Products**	
(A 3-months' supply, pick *ONE*.)		(A year's supply, pick *ONE*.)	
NABISCO OREO .... □	(1)	ALLEREST .... □	(1)
NABISCO OREO DOUBLE STUFF .... □	(2)	CONTAC .... □	(2)
NABISCO NUTTER BUTTER .... □	(3)	CORICIDIN .... □	(3)
NABISCO VANILLA CREMES .... □	(4)	DRISTAN (Capsule) .... □	(4)
HYDROX CHOCOLATE .... □	(5)	DRISTAN (Tablet) .... □	(5)
HYDROX DOUBLES .... □	(6)	SUPER ANAHIST (Capsule) .... □	(6)
NABISCO COOKIE BREAK .... □	(7)	SUPER ANAHIST (Tablet) .... □	(7)
NABISCO CHIPS AHOY .... □	(8)	OTHER .... □	(8)
KEEBLER E.L. FUDGE .... □	(9)		
KEEBLER FUDGE CREMES .... □	(10)	(Please specify)	
KEEBLER FRENCH VANILLA CREMES ..... □	(11)		

error is not expected to be a problem because the groups are known to be equal. The diagram for the *after-only with control group* is as follows:

Experimental group: $\boxed{R}$ X O_1

Control group: $\boxed{R}$ O_2

The effect of the experimental treatment equals $O_2 - O_1$.

   Consider, for example, the manufacturer of an athlete's foot remedy that wishes to demonstrate by experimentation that the company's product is better than the leading brand. No pretest measure of the effectiveness of the remedy for the fungus is possible. The design is to randomly select subjects, perhaps students, who have contracted athlete's foot and randomly assign them to the experimental or control group. With only the posttest measurement, the effects of testing and instrumentation are eliminated. Further, all the same assumptions about extraneous variables are made; that is, they operate equally on both groups, as in the before-after with control group design.

Solomon Four-Group Design.   By combining the before-after with control group and the after-only with control group designs, the Solomon four-group design provides a means for controlling the interactive testing effect, as well as other sources of extraneous variation. In the diagram below, the two Xs symbolize the same experimental treatment given to each experimental group:

Experimental Group 1 $\boxed{R}$ O_1 X O_2

Control Group 1 $\boxed{R}$ O_3 O_4

Experimental Group 2 $\boxed{R}$ X O_5

Control Group 2 $\boxed{R}$ O_6

Although we will not go through the calculations, it is possible to isolate the effect of the experimental treatment and the effect of interactive testing in this design. Although this design allows for the isolation of the various effects, it is rarely used in business research because of the effort, time, and cost of implementing it. It does point out, however, that there are ways of isolating or controlling most sources of variations.

Compromise Experimental Designs.   In many instances of business research true experimentation is not possible. The best the researcher can do is *approximate* an experimental design. These **compromise designs** may fall short of the requirements to assign subjects randomly to groups or assign treatment randomly to groups.[25]

Consider the situation in which the researcher wishes to implement a pretest-posttest control group design, but it is not possible to assign subjects randomly to the experimental versus the control group. Because the researcher does not have the ability to change a workplace situation, one department of an organization is used as the experimental group and another department of the organization is used as the control group. There is no assurance that the naturally occurring groups are equivalent; the researcher has compromised because of the nature of the situation.

The alternative to the compromise design, when random assignment of subjects is not possible, is to conduct the experiment *without* a control group. Generally this is considered a greater weakness than utilizing nonequivalent groups that have already been established.

When the experiment involves a longitudinal study, circumstances usually dictate a compromise with true experimentation.

Time Series Experimental Designs

Many business experiments may be conducted in a short period of time (a month or less than half a year). However, some business experiments investigate long-term structural change and these experiments may require a time series design. When experiments are conducted over long periods of time, they are most vulnerable to historical changes—in population, attitudes, economic patterns, and the like. Although seasonal patterns and other exogenous influences may be noted, when time is a major factor in design, the experimenter can do little to influence these factors. Hence these designs are quasi-experimental designs, because time series experimental designs generally do not allow the researcher full control over the treatment exposure or the influence of extraneous variables.

Political pollsters provide an example. Pollsters normally utilize a series of surveys to track political candidates' popularity. Consider the political candidate who plans a major speech (the experimental treatment) to refocus the political campaign. The simple **time series design** can be diagrammed as follows:

$$O_1 \quad O_2 \quad O_3 \quad X \quad O_4 \quad O_5 \quad O_6$$

Several observations have been taken before the treatment (X) to identify trends is administered. After the treatment has been administered, several ob-

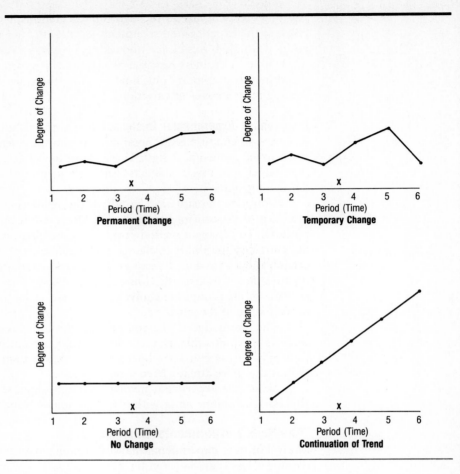

servations are made to determine if the patterns *after* the treatment are similar to the patterns *before* the treatment. Thus if the longitudinal pattern shifts after the political speech, the researcher may conclude that the treatment had a positive impact on the pattern. Of course, this time series design cannot give the researcher complete assurance that the treatment caused the change in the trend. Problems of internal validity are greater here than in more tightly controlled before-and-after designs of shorter durations.

One unique advantage of the time series design is its ability to distinguish temporary from permanent changes. For example, Exhibit 10.8 shows some possible outcomes in a time series experiment.

There is another problem in our political campaign example: Political conversions during August may affect the number of political conversions in September, which may in turn influence what happens in October. In time series designs, there may be carryover effects that cannot be controlled.

An improvement on the basic time series design is to utilize a *time series with control group.* For example, many test markets utilize different geographic areas, which are similar demographically, as a basis for experimental control. Rarely will geographic areas be identical in any characteristic of interest. Thus control is less than perfect.

Complex Experimental Designs

A **complex experimental design** is a statistical design that allows for the isolation of the effects of confounding extraneous variables or allows for manipulation of more than one independent variable in the experiment. *Completely randomized designs, randomized block designs, factorial designs,* and *Latin square designs* are discussed below.

Completely Randomized Design.   The **completely randomized design (CRD)** is an experimental design that uses a random process to assign experimental units to treatments. Randomization of experimental units is the researcher's attempt to control all extraneous variables while manipulating a single independent variable, the treatment variable. Several of the experiments previously discussed are completely randomized designs. As an example, consider an experiment to examine the effects of various incentives on increasing the response rate in a mail survey.[26] Personal monetary payments versus an incentive of monetary contributions to a charity selected by the respondents were the two experimental treatments (see Exhibit 10.9). When a control group is utilized, there are three treatments: (1) control—no incentive, (2) $1 personal incentive, and (3) $1 charity incentive. Suppose the sample was divided into three groups of 150 persons each. Assigning treatments to groups is a relatively simple process. Each treatment is randomly assigned to a group. Exhibit 10.9 shows how we would compare the response rates (dependent variable) of the three treatment groups to determine which method of increasing response was the best.

A pretest-posttest with control group(s) that *replicates,* or repeats, the same treatment on different experimental units is another example of a completely randomized design.

Analysis of variance (ANOVA) involves investigating the effects of one treatment variable on an interval-scaled or ratio-scaled dependent variable. In the completely randomized designs, ANOVA is the appropriate form of statistical analysis when the conditions of randomization and replication are met. This topic is discussed in Chapter 19.

Randomized Block Design.   The **randomized block design (RBD)** is an extension of the completely randomized design (CRD). A form of randomization is utilized to control for *most* extraneous variation. In the randomized block design, however, the researcher has identified a single "extraneous variable" that might affect test units' response to the treatment. The researcher will attempt to isolate the effects of this single variable by blocking out its effects.

The term *randomized block* is derived from agricultural research, where several levels of a treatment variable are applied to each of several blocks of land. Systematic differences in agricultural yields, due to the quality of the blocks of land, may be controlled in the randomized block design.[27] In business research the researcher may wish to isolate "block effects," such as store size,

Response Rate Experiment

Response	Group		
	Control—No Incentive	$1 Personal Incentive	$1 Charity Incentive
Response Rate	23.3%	26.0%	41.3%
Number of Observations	150	150	150

Overall response rate: 136/450 = 30.2%

Source: Dan H. Robertson and Danny N. Bellenger, "A New Method of Increasing Mail Survey Responses: Contributions to Charity," reprinted from the *Journal of Marketing Research,* November 1978, p. 633, published by the American Marketing Association.

Percentage Purchasing Product

Treatment	Mountain	North Central West	North Central East	Mean for Treatments
Package A	14% (Phoenix)	12% (St. Louis)	7% (Milwaukee)	11%
Package B	16% (Albuquerque)	15% (Kansas City)	10% (Indianapolis)	13.6%
Mean for cities	15%	13.5%	8.5%	

plant location, organization size, and so on. By grouping test units into homogeneous blocks on the basis of some relevant characteristic, one known source of extraneous variation may be separately accounted for.

Suppose that a manufacturer of Mexican food is considering two packaging alternatives. It is suspected that regions of the country may confound the packaging experiment. The manufacturer has identified four regions of the country where attitudes toward Mexican food may differ. Within each region it is assumed the relevant attitudinal characteristics are relatively homogeneous. In the randomized block design each block must receive every treatment level. Assigning treatments to each block is a random process. In our example the two treatments will be randomly assigned to two cities within each of these regions. Sales results such as those in Exhibit 10.10 might occur.

The logic behind the randomized block design is similar to the logic underlying the selection of a stratified sample rather than a simple random sample. By isolating the "block effects," one type of extraneous variation is partitioned out and a more efficient experimental design therefore results. This is because experimental error is reduced with a given sample size.

RESEARCH INSIGHT
A Factorial Experiment

A field experiment was undertaken to investigate the possible existence of sex discrimination in the evaluation of job applicant résumés. Scholastic performance was also manipulated in the experiment. Subjects for the experiment were personnel directors in a sample of corporations listed in the *College Placement* annual as seeking accounting students.

A résumé and an attractive cover letter were sent to each personnel director. The résumé provided a complete description of the actual student's personal history, family background, work experience, degrees (e.g., BS and MS degrees in accounting), etc. The sex variable was manipulated, using the first name of the individual. The initials L.C. were used as a neuter indication, and the name Linda was used to indicate female. The variable concerning academic performance was manipulated by using the

GPA of the individual. High academic performance was indicated by a 3.8 GPA (the student's actual GPA). Average academic performance was indicated by a 2.8 GPA.

Each subject was randomly assigned to one of the four treatment groups (n = 25 in each group): initials and high GPA, initials and average GPA, female name and high GPA, and female name and average GPA. Two forms of data were provided by the personnel directors that lent themselves to statistical analysis. The first dependent variable was the number of replies either positive or negative, that is, letters suggesting a personal interview or saying no job was available. A separate analysis was conducted on the number of affirmative responses: those suggesting that the person may have an opportunity for a job at the particular company.

Source: Adapted from William G. Zikmund, Michael A. Hitt, and Beverly Pickins, "Influence of Sex and Scholastic Performance on Reactions to Job Applicants' Résumés," *Journal of Applied Psychology* 63, no. 2 (1978): 252–253. Copyright 1978 by American Psychological Association. Adapted by permission of the publisher and authors.

Factorial Designs.   Even though the single-factor experiments (already considered) may have one specific variable blocked and other confounding sources controlled, they are limited. **Factorial design** allows for testing the effects of two or more treatments (factors) at various levels.

Consider the experimenter who wishes to answer the following questions:

1. What is the effect of varying the salary a new business school graduate is to receive on the probability of accepting a job?
2. What is the effect of varying the number of days per week that a new business school graduate will spend traveling for job purposes?
3. Is the effect of varying salary different if there is a great deal of travel on the job versus very little travel on the job? Is there an interaction between the effect of salaries and much or little travel on the job?

A factorial design might be used to answer these questions because it allows for the simultaneous manipulation of two or more independent variables at various levels. In this example the independent variables are salary and the number of days spent traveling. Increases in the probability of accepting a job, the dependent variable, attributed to each of these variables, considered separately, are referred to as *main effects*. A **main effect** is the influence on the dependent variable by each independent variable.

	Package Design	
Price	Red	Gold
$25	Cell 1	Cell 4
$30	Cell 2	Cell 5
$35	Cell 3	Cell 6

The effects of combinations of these job characteristic variables is the **interaction effect.** A major advantage of the factorial design is its ability to measure the interaction effect, which may be greater than the total of the main effects.

To further explain the terminology of experimental designs, let us use an example of a roller skate marketer who wished to measure the effect of different prices and packaging designs upon the perception of quality of the product. Exhibit 10.11 indicates three experimental treatment levels of price ($25, $30, $35) and two levels of packaging design (gold and red). The exhibit shows that every combination of treatment levels requires a separate experimental group. In this experiment, with three price levels and two packaging design levels, we have a 3 × 2 (read "three by two") factorial design because the first factor (variable) is varied in three ways and the second factor is varied in two ways. A 3 × 2 design requires six cells, or six experimental groups (3 × 2 = 6).

The number of treatments (factors) and the number of levels each treatment has identify the factorial design. A 3 × 3 design incorporates two factors, each having three levels. A 2 × 2 × 2 design has three factors, each having two levels. It is not necessary that the treatments have the same number of levels. For example, a 3 × 2 × 4 factorial design is possible. However, in the factorial experiment each treatment level is combined with each and every other treatment level. A 2 × 2 experiment requires four different subgroups or cells for the experiment. A 3 × 3 experiment requires nine various combinations of subgroups or cells.

In addition to the advantage of investigating two or more independent variables simultaneously, factorial designs allow researchers to measure the interaction effects. In a 2 × 2 experiment the interaction is the effect produced by Treatments A and B simultaneously, which cannot be accounted for by either treatment alone. If the effect of one treatment is different at different levels of the other treatment, interaction occurs.

To illustrate the value of a factorial design, suppose that a researcher is comparing two television commercials. The researcher is investigating the believability of the ads on a scale from 0 to 100 and wishes to consider the gender of the viewer as another factor.

The experiment has two independent variables: gender × ads. This 2 × 2 factorial experiment permits the experimenter to test three hypotheses. Two hypotheses are about the main effects—which ad is more believable and which gender tends to believe magazine advertising more. However, the primary re-

EXHIBIT 1 0 . 1 2

2 × 2 Factorial Design, Illustrating Effects of Gender and Ad on Believability

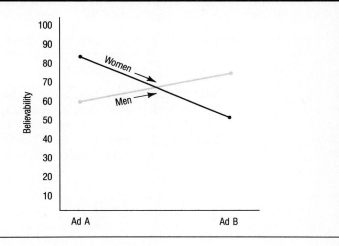

	Ad A	Ad B	
Men	60	70	65 ⎫
Women	80	50	65 ⎭ Main Effects of Gender
	70	60	

Main Effects of Ads

EXHIBIT 1 0 . 1 3

Graphic Illustration of Interaction between Gender and Advertising Copy

search question deals with the interaction hypothesis. A high score indicates a highly believable ad. Exhibit 10.12 shows that the mean believability score for both genders is 65.[28] This suggests that there is no main gender effect, because men and women evaluate believability of the advertisements equally. The main effect for ads indicates that Ad A is more believable than Ad B (70 versus 60). However, if we inspect the data and look within the levels of the factors, we find that men find Ad B more believable and women find Ad A more believable. This is an interaction effect because the believability score of the advertising factor is different at different values of the other independent variable, gender.

Graphic Interaction.　Exhibit 10.13 portrays the results of the believability experiment. The line for men illustrates the two mean believability scores for the advertising copy for Ads A and B. The other line represents the relationship between advertising and believability for women. When there is a difference between the slopes of the two lines, as in this case, the graph indicates interaction between the two treatment variables. What this means is that the believability of the advertising copy "depends" on whether a man or woman is viewing the advertisement.

R E S E A R C H   I N S I G H T
A Lethal Interaction

In pharmacology the interaction effect is usually called a synergistic effect. An example is the lethal combination of barbiturate sleeping pills and alcoholic liquor. Each of these is a drug, and each reduces the number of heartbeats per minute. Their combined effect, however, is a much more severe reduction than one would expect, knowing their individual effects. This is actually a failure of the two treatments to be additive—their combined effect is much more than the sum of their individual effects. Another way of phrasing the synergistic effect is the following: the effect of one treatment differs, depending on the level of the other treatment. That is, the reduction in pulse due to alcohol is different, depending on whether barbiturates are in the person's system or not.

Source: Ya-Lun Chou, *Statistical Analysis with Business and Economic Applications* (New York: Holt, Rinehart and Winston, 1975), 365.

Latin Square Design.   The **Latin square design** attempts to control or block out the effect of two or more confounding extraneous factors. This design is so named because of the layout of the table that represents the design. A Latin square is a balanced, two-way classification scheme.[29] In the 3 × 3 matrix below, each letter occurs only once in each row and only once in each column:

		Order of Usage		
		1	2	3
	1	A	B	C
Subject	2	B	C	A
	3	C	A	B

The capital letters A, B, and C identify the three treatments. The rows and columns of the table identify the confounding factors. For example, a taste test might be confounded by the order of tasting: The first taste may seem better than the last. The taste test might also be confounded by individual taste preferences. To control for these factors, each subject is exposed to every treatment. If all the subjects receive three tastes and the order in which the subjects taste is randomized, neither individual preference nor order effects may confound the experiment. Thus the order of treatment may be randomized under the restriction of balance required for the Latin square. The same type of balance is required for the second confounding factor.

The end result of this design is that each treatment will be administered under conditions involving all levels of both confounding factors. In summary, the Latin square design manipulates one independent variable and controls for two additional sources of extraneous variation by restricting randomization with respect to the row and column effects.

A major assumption of the Latin square design is that interaction effects are expected to be minimal or nonexistent. Thus it is assumed that the first subject does not have a strong preference for the first product used and the third subject does not have a strong preference for the last product used.

A Latin square may have any number of treatments. For example, the arrangement for a five-treatment experiment is given below:

5 × 5

A	B	C	D	E
B	C	D	E	A
C	D	E	A	B
D	E	A	B	C
E	A	B	C	D

Notice that this 5 × 5 matrix requires 25 cells. This matrix also indicates that the number of treatment levels for confounding factors 1 and 2 must be equal in number. This may present certain problems. For example, suppose a retail grocery chain wishes to control for shelf space and city where the product is sold. The chain may be limited in its experiment because it markets in only three cities, but it wishes to experiment with four shelf heights.

Having an unequal number of levels for each factor may be a drawback that will eliminate the Latin square design as a possibility. A second limitation is the assumption that there is no interactive effect. Like most other forms of business research, this research design has its disadvantages, but in certain situations it is advantageous to use the Latin square design.

SUMMARY

The purpose of experimental research is to allow the researcher to control the research situation so that causal relationships among variables may be evaluated. In an experiment one variable (the independent variable) is manipulated to determine its effect on another variable (the dependent variable). The alternative manipulations of the independent variable are referred to as *experimental treatments*.

The choice of the dependent variable is crucial, because this determines the kind of answer given to the research problem. In some situations it is difficult to decide on an appropriate operational measure of the dependent variable.

For experiments, random sampling error is especially associated with selection of subjects and their assignment to the treatments. The best solution to this problem is random assignment of subjects to groups and groups to treatments.

Other errors may arise from using unrepresentative populations as a source of samples (for example, college students) or from sample mortality or attrition, when subjects withdraw from the experiment before it is completed. In addition, in business experiments there are often extraneous variables that may affect the dependent variable and obscure the effect of the independent variable. Experiments may also be affected by demand characteristics, when experimenters inadvertently cue desired responses. Also, the guinea pig effect occurs when subjects modify their behavior because they are being observed.

Extraneous variables can be controlled by eliminating them or by holding them constant for all treatments. Some extraneous error may arise from order of presentation. This can be controlled by counterbalancing the order. Blinding can be used, with subjects being ignorant of what treatment they are receiving. Sometimes the blinding is extended to the person administering the test. Finally, random assignment attempts to control extraneous variables by chance.

Two main types of business experiments are field experiments (such as test markets), which are conducted in a natural environment, and laboratory experiments, which are conducted in an artificial setting contrived for a specific purpose. Experiments are judged by two measures of validity. One is internal validity: whether the independent variable was the sole cause of the change in the dependent variable. There are six different types of extraneous variables that may jeopardize internal validity: history, maturation, testing, instrumentation, selection, and mortality. The second is external validity: the extent to which the results are applicable to the real world. Field experiments are lower than laboratory experiments in internal validity but higher in external validity.

Experimental designs fall into two groups. In basic designs only one variable is manipulated. In complex experimental designs the effects of extraneous variables are isolated or more than one treatment or independent variable is used. Poor basic designs include the one-shot design, the one-group pretest-posttest design, and the static group design. Good basic designs include the pretest-posttest control group design, the posttest-only control group design, and the Solomon four-group design.

Various complex experimental designs are commonly used in business research. These include the completely randomized design, the randomized block design, and various factorial designs. The factorial designs allow for interaction effects between variables. One variation is the Latin square design, which attempts to block out confounding factors.

Key Terms

experiment	demand characteristics
independent variable	experimenter bias
experimental treatment	guinea pig effect
experimental group	Hawthorne effect
control group	constancy of conditions
dependent variable	order of presentation
test unit	counterbalancing
sample selection error	blinding
random sampling error	double-blind design
randomization	laboratory experiment
matching	field experiment
repeated measures	tachistoscope
constant error	internal validity

history effect	pretest-posttest control group design
maturation effect	posttest-only control group design
testing effect	Solomon four-group design
instrumentation effect	compromise design
selection effect	time series design
mortality effect	complex experimental design
external validity	completely randomized design
basic experimental design	randomized block design
quasi-experimental design	factorial design
one-shot design	main effect
one-group pretest–posttest design	interaction effect
static group design	Latin square design

Questions

1. Name some independent and dependent variables frequently studied in your field of interest.
2. What purpose does the random assignment of subjects serve?
3. In a test of a new coffee, three styrofoam cups labeled A, B, and C are placed before subjects. The subjects are instructed to taste the coffee from each cup. What problems might arise in this situation?
4. What are demand characteristics? Give some examples.
5. Do you think the guinea pig effect is a common occurrence in experiments? Why or why not?
6. How may an experimenter control for extraneous variation?
7. Provide an example for each of the six major factors influencing internal validity.
8. Consider the following research project conducted by a company investigating a self-contained heating and light source designed for use during power failures: The product was given to the experimental subjects and they were asked to wait until dark, then turn off their heat and lights, and test the product. A few days later they were telephoned and interviewed about their opinions of the product. Discuss the external and internal validity of this experiment.
9. In a 2 × 2 factorial design there are eight possible patterns of effects. For example, assume Independent Variable A and Independent Variable B have significant main effects but there is no interaction between A and B. Another combination might be no effects of Variable A but a significant effect of Variable B with a significant interaction effect. Try to diagram each of these eight possible effects.
10. In the following situations name the type of experiment described. Evaluate the strengths and weaknesses of each design.
    a. A major automobile manufacturer is considering a drug-testing program for its assembly workers. It selects an Oklahoma City plant, implements the program, and measures the impact on productivity.

b.   The data-processing division of a credit card company conducts an experiment to determine if a flexible work time program (employees choose their own work hours between 6 a.m. and 7 p.m.) is better than the traditional working hours (9 a.m.–5 p.m.). Each employee in the San Jose office is asked if he or she would like to be in the experimental group or in the control group. All employees in the La Jolla office remain on the traditional schedule.

c.   A cigarette manufacturer puts the same brand of cigarette into two differently labeled cigarette packages. Each of two groups is given a package and asked about the cigarette taste. A third group is given the cigarettes in an unlabeled package and asked the same questions.

d.   An advertising agency pretests a television commercial with a portable television set, simulating an actual television program with the test commercial inserted along with other commercials. This program is shown to a focus group, and there is subsequent group discussion.

e.   A manufacturer of a new brand of cat food tests product sampling with a trial-size package versus no sampling and three price levels simultaneously to determine the best market penetration.

11.   Dan Kessler, the manager of an I.G.A. grocery store, had a brother-in-law who supervised a large number of keypunch operators at a public utility company. At a family gathering, Kessler's brother-in-law mentioned that his company had recently begun programming background music into the keypunch operators' room with the result that productivity had increased and number of errors had decreased.

Kessler thought that music within a grocery store might have an impact on customers. Specifically, he thought that customers might stay in the store longer if slow, easy-to-listen-to music were played. After some serious thought, he started thinking that he should hire a business researcher to design an experiment for testing the influence of music tempo on shopper behavior. Operationalize the independent variable music tempo. What dependent variables do you think might be important in this study? Develop a hypothesis for each of your dependent variables.

References

[1] Steven J. Starr, "Effects of Display Terminals in a Business Office," *Human Factors* (1984): 26, no. 3, 347–356.

[2] Seymour Banks, "Designing Marketing Research to Increase Validity," *Journal of Marketing* (October 1964): 32–40.

[3] See J. Edward Russo, "The Value of Unit Price Information," *Journal of Marketing Research* (May 1977): 193–201; and J. Edward Russo, Gene Krieser, and Sally Miyashita, "An Effective Display of Unit Price Information," *Journal of Marketing* (April 1975): 11–19. The example in this section is hypothetical, based on the experiments and material in these two articles.

[4] Vernon Ellingstad and Norman W. Heimstra, *Methods in the Study of Human Behavior* (Belmont, CA: Brooks-Cole Publishing, 1974), 61–62.

[5] "The Most Dangerous Game in Marketing," *Dun's Business Month* (formerly *Dun's Review*), June 1967. Dun & Bradstreet Publications Corp.

[6] William L. Hays, *Statistics* (New York: Holt, Rinehart and Winston, 1963), 450.

[7] Barry F. Anderson, *The Psychological Experiment: An Introduction to the Scientific Method* (Belmont, CA: Brooks-Cole Publishing, 1971), 28.

[8] Ibid., 42–44.

[9] M. Venkatesan and Robert T. Holloway, *An Introduction to Marketing Experimentation: Methods, Applications, and Problems* (New York: Free Press, 1971), 14.

[10] For an excellent discussion of demand characteristics, see Alan G. Sawyer, "Demand Artifacts in Laboratory Experiments in Consumer Research," *Journal of Consumer Research* 1 (March 1975): 20–30; and Alan G. Sawyer, Parker Worthing, and Paul E. Sendak, "The Role of Laboratory Experiments to Test Marketing Strategies," *Journal of Marketing* (Summer 1979): 60–67.

[11] See F. J. Roethlisberger and W. J. Dickson, *Management and the Worker* (Cambridge, MA: Harvard University Press, 1939).

[12] Venkatesan and Holloway, *An Introduction to Marketing Experimentation: Methods, Applications, and Problems,* 36.

[13] Keith K. Cox, *The Relationship between Shelf Space and Product Sales in Supermarkets* (Austin: Bureau of Business Research, University of Texas, 1964), 20.

[14] Anderson, *The Psychological Experiment: An Introduction to the Scientific Method,* 54.

[15] W. Millard, Diane L. Lockwood, and Fred Luthans, "The Impact of a Four Day Work Week on Employees," *MSU Business Topics* (Spring 1980): 33.

[16] Joyce Turovlin, "Paktest's Holistic Approach Helps Package Design Testing," *Marketing News,* Jan. 28, 1977.

[17] This section is based on Donald T. Campbell and Julian C. Stanley, *Experimental and Quasi-Experimental Designs for Research* (Chicago: Rand McNally and Company, 1966), 5–9. Reprinted by permission of the American Educational Research Association, Washington, DC.

[18] Ibid., 9.

[19] Donald E. Vinson and William J. Lundstrom, "The Use of Students as Experimental Subjects in Marketing Research," *Journal of the Academy of Marketing Sciences* (Winter 1978): 114–125.

[20] William H. Cunningham, Thomas W. Anderson, Jr., and John H. Murphy, "Are Students Real People?" *Journal of Business* (July 1974): 399–409; and Ben M. Enis, Keith K. Cox, and James E. Stafford, "Students as Subjects in Consumer Behavior Experiments," *Journal of Marketing Research* (February 1972): 72–74.

[21] Fred W. Morgan, Jr., "Students in Marketing Research: Surrogates vs. Role-Players," *Journal of the Academy of Marketing Science* (Summer 1979): 255–264.

[22] B. J. Winer, *Statistical Principles in Experimental Design* (New York: McGraw-Hill, 1971), 1.

[23] This section is based largely on their classic work: Donald T. Campbell and Julian C. Stanley, *Experimental and Quasi-Experimental Designs for Research* (Chicago: Rand McNally, 1966), 13–25. Reprinted by permission of the American Educational Research Association, Washington, DC.

[24] *Observation* is used in the most general way. Although most business experiments will use some other form of measurement rather than the direct observation of some dependent variable in an experiment, the terminology used by Campbell and Stanley is utilized here because of its traditional nature.

[25] Marjorie B. Platt, "Naturally Occurring Groups Aid Choice of Marketing Mix," *Journal of Business Forecasting Methods and Systems* (Fall 1984): 14–18; and Fred N. Kerlinger, *Foundations of Behavioral Research,* 2d ed. (New York: Holt, Rinehart and Winston, 1973), 341.

[26] Dan H. Robertson and Danny N. Bellenger, "A New Method of Increasing Mail Survey Responses: Contributions to Charity," *Journal of Marketing Research* (November 1978): 633.

[27] Ya-Lun Chou, *Statistical Analysis with Business and Economic Applications* (New York: Holt, Rinehart and Winston, 1975), 355.

[28] The sample size for the experiment is intentionally small and the data are hypothetical for ease of presentation.

[29] B. J. Winer, *Statistical Principles in Experimental Design,* 2d ed. (New York: McGraw-Hill, 1971), 685.

PART 4

Measurement Concepts

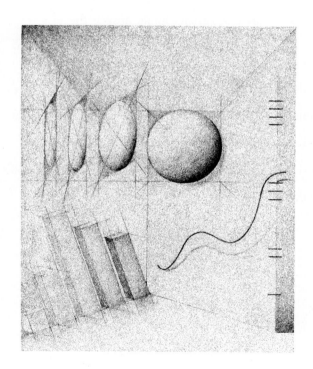

CHAPTER 11

Measurement and Scaling Concepts

What you will learn in this chapter:

To know how a researcher might answer the question "What is to be measured?"

To define the term *operational definition*.

To distinguish among nominal, ordinal, interval, and ratio scales.

To understand the need for index or composite measures.

To define the three criteria for good measurement.

To discuss the various methods for determining reliability.

To discuss the various methods for assessing validity.

For years A. C. Nielsen, the television rating company, was criticized because its audiometer was a passive meter that recorded only which program was being watched. Because it indicated only whether the television set was on a particular channel or was turned off, advertisers did not know if the entire family or just one individual was watching.

The diary system, which required all members of a panel family to log in viewing habits in a "diary," was introduced to supplement the passive meter. However, this system also presented problems: It worked well during the "network only" television era, but recording viewing activity in a diary became increasingly complex in an age of cable television systems with 36 different channels. Many experts also believe diaries exhibit a "halo" bias. When viewers fill out diaries two or three days after watching television, they tend to remember only their favorite shows and forget the others that they had watched. As a result, top-rated programs such as "The Cosby Show" could receive a disproportionately high audience estimate.

So Nielsen set out to make improvements. After spending years developing and testing, the company established a system that promised to be an improvement because information about who was watching which programs would be built into the measuring system.

The people-meter system—a microwave, computerized television-rating system—was designed to use state-of-the-art electronic measuring to replace passive meters and the 30-year-old diary system. When the panel household's television set is turned on, a question mark appears on the television screen to remind viewers to indicate who is watching. Viewers then use a hand-held electronic device—similar to a television's remote control—to record who is watching. A device attached to the television automatically sends the viewer's age and sex and the programs that are watched over telephone lines to Nielsen's computers. People meters thus measure shows' ratings and provide demographic profiles overnight. The people meter is one of a number of innovations aimed at improving the measurement of behavioral phenomena.

This chapter discusses and evaluates the basic forms of measurement used in business research.

■

WHAT IS TO BE MEASURED?

It is possible to measure an object, perhaps your textbook, with either edge of the ruler in Exhibit 11.1. Note that one edge has inches and the other has centimeters; so the scale of measurement will vary, depending on whether the metric edge or the standard edge is used. Many measurement problems in business research are similar to this ruler, with its alternative scales of measurement. The researcher has the opportunity to select a measuring system. Unfortunately, however—unlike the two-edged ruler—many measurement scales in business research are not directly comparable.

The first question the researcher must answer is: "What is to be measured?" This is not as simple a question as it may at first seem. The definition of the problem, based on exploratory research or managerial judgment, indicates the concept to be investigated (for example, sales performance). However, a precise definition of the concept may require a description of how it will be measured. And there is frequently more than one way to measure a particular concept.

For example, if we were conducting research to evaluate what factors influence a sales representative's performance, a number of measures might be used to indicate success. Dollar or unit sales volume or share of accounts lost could be utilized as measures of a salesperson's success. Further, true measurement of concepts requires a process of assigning precise scores or numbers to the attributes of people or objects.[1] The purpose of the assignment of scores or numbers is to convey information about the variable being measured. Hence the key question becomes: "On what basis will scores or numbers be assigned to the concept?" Suppose the task is to measure the height of a boy named Michael.

1. We can create five categories:
   (1) Quite tall for his age
   (2) Moderately tall for his age
   (3) About average for his age
   (4) Moderately short for his age
   (5) Quite short for his age
   Then we can measure Michael by saying that, since he is moderately tall for his age, his height measurement is 2.
2. We can compare Michael to 10 other neighborhood children. We give the tallest child the rank of 1 and the shortest child the rank of 11. Michael's height measurement using this procedure is 4, since he is fourth tallest among the 11 neighborhood children.
3. We can use some conventional measuring unit such as centimeters and, measuring to the nearest centimeter, designate Michael's height as 137.

EXHIBIT 11.1

A Two-Edged Ruler Offers Alternative Scales of Measurement

Source: National Bureau of Standards, Washington, D.C.

4. We can define two categories:
    (1) A nice height
    (2) A not so nice height
    Since by our personal standard Michael's height is a nice height, his height measurement is 1.[2]

In each measuring situation a score has been assigned for Michael's height (2, 4, 137, and 1). In scientific research precision is the goal. The researcher must determine the best way to measure what is to be investigated.

Measurement occurs on campus with girl watching or guy watching. The person who might be a "7" to one person might be a "9" to another. Precise measurement in business research requires a careful conceptual definition, an operational definition, and a system of consistent rules for assigning scores or numbers.

Concepts

Before the measurement process can be initiated, the business researcher must identify the concepts relevant to the problem. A **concept** (or *construct*) is a generalized idea about a class of objects, attributes, occurrences, or processes. Concepts such as age, sex, and number of children are relatively concrete properties and they present few problems in definition or measurement.[3] Other characteristics of individuals or properties of objects may be more abstract. Concepts such as loyalty, power, job involvement, and the like present greater problems in terms of definition and measurement. For example, brand loyalty has been measured utilizing the percentage of a person's purchases going to one brand in a given period of time, sequences of brand purchases, the number of different brands purchased, amount of brand deliberation, and various cognitive measures such as attitude toward a brand.

Operational Definitions

A concept must be made operational in order to be measured. An **operational definition** gives meaning to a concept by specifying the activities or operations necessary to measure it.[4] The concept *nutritional consciousness* might be indicated when a shopper reads the nutritional information on a cereal package. Inspecting a nutritional label is not the same as nutritional consciousness, but it is a clue that a person *may* be nutrition conscious.

EXHIBIT   11.2

**Job Challenge:
An Operational
Definition**

Concept	Conceptional Definition	Operational Definition
Job challenge	This dimension reflects a worker's desire for stimulation and challenge in his or her job and ability to exercise skills in his or her job.	Please tell me how true each statement is about your job. Is it very true, somewhat true, not very true, or not at all true?
		1. The work is interesting.
		2. I have an opportunity to develop my own special abilities.
		3. I am given a chance to do the things I do best.

Source: Based on Angus Campbell, Philip E. Converse, and Willard L. Rodgers, *The Quality of American Life* (New York: Russell Sage Foundation, 1976), 297–298.

A concept like *grievances* may be difficult to operationalize, whereas a concept like *personnel turnover* is less difficult. However, *personnel turnover* may be more difficult to operationalize if the researcher is interested in going beyond the simple ratio of new employees to old employees. Are employees with tenure turning over, or is it the recently hired employees who are constantly turning over?

The operational definition specifies what must be done to measure the concept under investigation. If interest in a specific advertisement is to be measured, *interest* may be operationally defined as a certain increase in pupil dilation. Another operational definition of *interest* might be reliance on direct responses—what persons say they are interested in. Each operational definition has advantages and disadvantages.

An operational definition is like a manual of instructions or a recipe: Even the truth of a statement like "Gaston Gourmet likes Persian lime pie" depends on the recipe. Different instructions lead us to different results.[5] An operational definition tells the investigator, "Do such-and-such in so-and-so manner."[6] Exhibit 11.2 presents the operational definition from a study on quality of work.

Rules of Measurement

A rule is a guide that instructs us on what to do.[7] An example of a **rule of measurement** might be: "Assign the numerals 1 through 7 to individuals according to how productive they are. If the individual is extremely productive, assign a 7 to him or her. If the individual is an unproductive worker with little output, assign the numeral 1."

Operational definitions help the researcher specify the rules for assigning numbers. If, for example, the purpose of an advertising experiment is to increase the amount of time shoppers spend in a department store, "shopping time" must be operationally defined. Once "shopping time" is defined as the interval between entering the door and receiving the receipt from the clerk, assignment of numbers via stopwatch is facilitated. If a study on office computer

R E S E A R C H   I N S I G H T
The Concepts of Employment, Unemployment, and Labor Force

Defining the concepts of *employment, unemployment,* and *labor force* is not as simple as one might first think. The Bureau of Labor Statistics has improved upon early surveys in which the unemployed were defined as those who were not working but were "willing and able to work." This concept, however, did not meet the standards of objectivity that many technicians felt were necessary in order to measure not only the level of unemployment at a moment in time but changes over periods of time. The criterion "willing and able to work," when applied in specific situations, appeared to be too intangible and too dependent on the interpretation and attitude of the person being interviewed.

Out of this experimentation a new set of concepts was developed in the late 1930s that sought to meet these criticisms. According to these concepts, the classification of an individual was to be dependent principally on his actual activity within a designated time period, i.e., whether working or looking for work, or doing something else. These concepts were adopted for the national sample survey in 1940. Although there have been improvements in measurement techniques, these concepts have been used in substantially unchanged form since that date, both in the Current Population Survey and in the decennial censuses.

In measuring activity and status, the time period selected for the monthly survey was a calendar week. The official measures relate to persons 16 years old and over.

The *civilian labor force* comprises all civilians classified as employed or unemployed in accordance with the criteria described below.

The *employed* are all civilians who did any work as paid employees or in their own business during the survey week, or who worked 15 hours or more as unpaid workers in an enterprise operated by a family member. Persons temporarily absent from a job because of illness, bad weather, a strike, or for personal reasons are also counted as employed whether they were paid by their employer or were seeking other jobs.

The *unemployed* are all civilians who did not work during the survey week, made specific efforts to find a job in the prior 4 weeks, and were available for work during the survey week (except for temporary illness). Persons wait-

ing to be recalled to a job from which they had been laid off, and those waiting to report to a new job within the next 30 days, are also counted as unemployed.

Duration of unemployment represents the length of time (through the current survey week) during which persons classified as unemployed have been continuously looking for work. For persons on layoff, duration of unemployment represents the number of full weeks since the termination of their most recent employment. A period of 2 weeks or more during which a person was employed or ceased looking for work is considered to break the continuity of the present period of jobseeking. Duration of unemployment measures the length of a spell of unemployment currently in progress. Hence it should not be confused with a completed spell of unemployment.

Reasons for unemployment are divided into four major groups: (1) Job losers—persons whose employment ended involuntarily and who immediately began looking for work, and persons on layoff; (2) job leavers—persons who quit or otherwise terminated their employment voluntarily and immediately began looking for work; (3) reentrants—persons who previously worked at a full-time job lasting 2 weeks or longer but were out of the labor force before looking for work; and (4) new entrants—persons who never worked at a full-time job lasting 2 weeks or longer.

The *unemployment rate for all civilian workers* represents the number unemployed as a percent of the civilian labor force.

The *civilian labor force participation rate* is the ratio of the civilian labor force to the civilian noninstitutional population.

The *civilian employment–population ratio* is the percentage of all employed civilians in the civilian noninstitutional population.

Hours of work statistics relate to the actual number of hours worked during the survey week. For example, persons who normally work 40 hours a week, but who were off on the Columbus Day holiday, would be reported as working 32 hours even though they were paid for the holiday. For persons working in more than one job, the figures relate to the number of hours worked in all jobs during the survey week with all hours credited to the major job.

RESEARCH INSIGHT
(continued)

The distribution of employment by hours worked relates to persons "at work" during the survey week. At-work data differ from data on total employment because the latter include persons in the zero-hours-worked category, "with a job but not at work." Included in this latter group are persons who were on vacation, ill, involved in a labor dispute, or otherwise absent from their jobs for voluntary, noneconomic reasons.

Persons who worked 35 hours or more in the survey week are designated as working *full time;* correspondingly, persons who worked between 1 and 34 hours are designated as working *part time.* Part-time workers are classified by their usual status at their present job (either full- or part-time) and by their reason for working part time during the survey week (economic or other reasons). "Economic reasons" include: Slack work, material shortages, repairs to plant or equipment, start or termination of job during the week, and inability to find full-time work. Other reasons include: Labor dispute, bad weather, own illness, vacation, demands of home, housework, school, no desire for full-time work, and full-time worker only during the peak season. Persons on full-time schedules include, in addition to those working 35 hours or more, those who worked from 1 to 34 hours for noneconomic reasons and usually work full time.

The *full-time labor force* consists of persons working on full-time schedules, persons involuntarily working part time (part time for economic reasons), and unemployed persons seeking full-time jobs. The *part-time labor force* consists of persons working part time voluntarily and unemployed persons seeking part-time work. Persons with a job but not at work during the survey week are classified according to whether they usually work full or part time.

Source: U.S. Department of Labor, Bureau of Labor Statistics, *How the Government Measures Unemployment,* Report 505 (Washington, DC: U.S. Government Printing Office, 1977), 3; and U.S. Department of Labor, Bureau of Labor Statistics, *Geographic Profile of Employment and Unemployment, 1983,* Bulletin 2216 (Washington, DC: U.S. Government Printing Office, 1984), 118–119.

systems is not concerned with a person's depth of experience but defines people as users or nonusers, a 1 for experience with the system and a 0 for no experience with the system can be used.

The values assigned in the measuring process can be manipulated according to certain mathematical rules. The properties of the scale of numbers may allow the researcher to add, subtract, or multiply answers. In certain cases there may be problems with the simple addition of the numbers or other mathematical manipulations because these are not permissible within the mathematical system.

TYPES OF SCALES

A scale may be defined as "any series of items which is progressively arranged according to value or magnitude into which an item can be placed according to its quantification."[8] In other words, a scale is a continuous spectrum or series of categories. The purpose of scaling is to represent, usually quantitatively, an item's, a person's, or an event's place in the spectrum.

In business research there are a great many scales or number systems. It is traditional to classify scales of measurement on the basis of the mathematical comparisons that are allowable with these scales. The four types of scales are *nominal, ordinal, interval,* and *ratio.*

EXHIBIT   11.3

Nominal, Ordinal, Interval, and Ratio Scales Provide Different Information

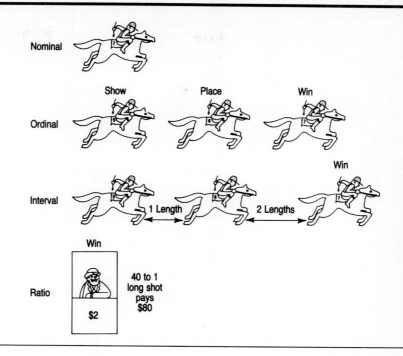

Nominal Scale

Number 23 on the Chicago Cubs represents Ryne Sandberg; Jose Canseco is Number 33 on the Oakland A's. These numbers nominally identify these superstars. A **nominal scale** is the simplest type of scale. The numbers or letters assigned to objects serve as labels for identification or classification. These are scales "in name only." Tulsa's Census Tract 25 and Census Tract 87 are merely labels. The number 87 does not imply that this area has more people or a higher income than the number 25. An example of a typical nominal scale in business research is the coding of males as 1 and females as 2.

The first drawing in Exhibit 11.3 depicts the number 7 on a horse's colors. This is merely a label for the bettors and racing enthusiasts.

Ordinal Scale

At the racetrack we know that when our horse finishes in the "show" position, he has come in third behind the "win" and the "place" horses. An **ordinal scale** arranges objects or alternatives according to their magnitude in an ordered relationship. When respondents are asked to *rank order* their investment preferences, ordinal values are assigned. In our racehorse example, if we assign a 1 to the win position, a 2 to the place position, and a 3 to the show position, we can say that 1 was before 2, and 2 was before 3. However, we cannot say anything about the distance or interval between the win and the show horses or between the show and the place horses.

A typical ordinal scale in business research asks respondents to rate career opportunities, brands, companies, and so on as "excellent," "good," "fair," or "poor." We know "excellent" is higher than "good," but we do not know by how much.

Interval Scale

Exhibit 11.3 depicts a horse race where the win horse is two lengths ahead of the place horse, which is one length ahead of the show horse. Not only is the order of finish known, but the distance between the horses is known.[9] **Interval scales** not only indicate order, they also measure order (or distance) in units of equal intervals.

The location of the zero point is arbitrary. In the consumer price index, if the base year is 1982, the price level during 1982 will be set at 100. Although this is an equal-interval measurement scale, the zero point is arbitrary.

The classic example of an interval scale is the Fahrenheit temperature scale. If a temperature is 80°, it cannot be said that it is twice as hot as 40°. The reason for this is that 0° does not represent the lack of temperature, but a relative point on the Fahrenheit scale. Due to the lack of an absolute zero point, the interval scale does not allow the conclusion that 36 is three times as great as the number 12, only that the interval distance is three times greater.

Similarly, when an interval scale is used to measure psychological attributes, the researcher can comment on the magnitude of differences or compare the average differences on attributes that are measured but cannot determine the actual strength of attitudes toward an object. However, changes in concepts over time can be compared if the researcher continues to use the same scale in longitudinal research.

Ratio Scale

To say that winning tickets pay 40 to 1 or that racehorse Number 7 is twice as heavy as racehorse Number 5, a ratio scale is necessary. **Ratio scales** have absolute rather than relative quantities. For example, money and weight are ratio scales because they possess an absolute zero and interval properties. The absolute zero represents a point on the scale where there is an absence of the given attribute.

When one states that a person has zero ounces of gold, we understand the zero value—for weight and everything else. In the measurement of temperature, the Kelvin scale (a ratio scale) begins at absolute zero, a point that corresponds to −273.16° on the Celsius scale (an interval scale). In distribution or logistical research it may be appropriate to think of physical attributes, such as weight or distance, as ratio scales in which the ratio of scale values is meaningful. Most financial research that deals with dollar values utilizes ratio scales. However, for most behavioral research, interval scales are typically the highest form of measurement.

Mathematical and Statistical Analysis of Scales

The type of scale that is utilized in business research will determine the form of the statistical analysis. For example, a number of operations, such as calculation of the mean (mathematical average), can be conducted only if the scale is

EXHIBIT   11.4

Descriptive Statistics for Types of Scales

Type of Scale	Numerical Operation	Descriptive Statistics
Nominal	Counting	Frequency in each category Percentage in each category Mode
Ordinal	Rank ordering	Median Range Percentile ranking
Interval	Arithmetic operations on intervals between numbers	Mean Standard deviation Variance
Ratio	Arithmetic operations on actual quantities	Geometric mean Coefficient of variation

Note: All statistics that are appropriate for lower-order scales (nominal is the lowest) are appropriate for higher-order scales (ratio is the highest).

of an interval or ratio nature; they are not permissible with nominal or ordinal scales.

Exhibit 11.4 shows the appropriate descriptive statistics for each type of scale. The most sophisticated form of statistical analysis for nominal scale data is counting. Because numbers are merely labels for classification purposes, they have no quantitative meaning. The researcher tallies the frequency in each category and identifies which category contains the highest number of observations (individuals, objects, etc.). An ordinal scale provides data that may be rank-ordered from lowest to highest. Thus observations may be associated with a percentile rank such as the median. Because all statistical analysis appropriate for lower-order scales is appropriate for higher-order scales, an interval scale may be used as a nominal scale to uniquely classify or as an ordinal scale to preserve order. In addition, an interval scale's property of equal intervals allows researchers to compare differences between scale values and to perform arithmetic operations such as addition and subtraction. Numbers may be changed, but the numerical operations must preserve order and relative magnitudes of differences. The mean and standard deviation may be calculated when true interval-scale data are obtained. Ratio scales have all the properties of nominal, ordinal, and interval scales. In addition, researchers may make comparisons of absolute magnitude because the scale has an absolute zero point. Arithmetic operations on actual quantities are permissible. The ratios of scale values are meaningful. Chapters 18 through 22 further explore the limitations of scalar data and their appropriate mathematical analysis.

INDEX MEASURES

This chapter has thus far focused on measuring a concept with a single question or a single observation. A researcher measuring awareness, for example, might use one question, such as "Are you aware of _____?" However, measuring more complex concepts may require more than one question because the concept has several attributes. An **attribute** is a single characteristic or fundamental feature pertaining to an object, person, situation, or issue. Multi-item instruments used to measure a single concept with several attributes are called **index measures** or *composite measures*. One index of social class is based on three weighted variables: residence, occupation, and education.

Measures of cognitive phenomena are often composite indexes of a set of variables or scales. Items are combined into a composite measure. For example, a salesperson's morale may be measured by combining questions such as "How satisfied are you with your job?" "How satisfied are you with your territory?" "How satisfied are you in your personal life?" Measuring a concept by a variety of techniques is one method for increasing precision and accuracy. Asking different questions in order to measure the same thing provides a more accurate cumulative measure than does a single-item estimate.

THREE CRITERIA FOR GOOD MEASUREMENT

There are three major criteria for evaluating measurements: *reliability, validity,* and *sensitivity*.

Reliability

A tailor measuring fabric with a tape measure obtains a "true" value of the fabric's length. If the tailor takes repeated measures of the fabric and each time estimates the same length, it is assumed that the tape measure is reliable. When the outcome of the measuring process is reproducible, the measuring instrument is reliable.

Reliability applies to a measure when similar results are obtained over time and across situations. Broadly defined, **reliability** is the degree to which measures are free from error and therefore yield consistent results.[10] For example, ordinal-level measures are reliable if they consistently rank order subjects in the same manner; reliable interval-level measures consistently rank order and maintain the distance between subjects.

Imperfections in the measuring process that affect the assignment of scores or numbers in different ways each time a measure is taken, such as a respondent who misunderstands a question, are the cause of low reliability. Suppose a respondent understands a question but does not know the real reason for his or her behavior and so cannot give any of several responses with truthfulness. The actual choice between plausible responses may be governed by such transitory factors as mood, whim, or the context set by surrounding questions.[11] Measures of this type will not be error-free and stable over time.

Two dimensions underlie the concept of reliability: *repeatability* and *internal consistency*. Assessing the repeatability of a measure is the first aspect of reliability.

The **test-retest method** involves administering the same scale or measure to the same respondents at two separate times to test for stability. If the measure is stable over time, the reported test, administered under conditions similar to the first test, should obtain similar results. For example, suppose a researcher measures job satisfaction and finds that 64 percent of the population is satisfied with their jobs. If the study is repeated a few weeks later under similar conditions, and the researcher again finds that 64 percent of the population is satisfied with their jobs, it appears that the measure is reliable. The high stability correlation or consistency between the two measures at Time 1 and Time 2 indicates a high degree of reliability.

At the individual (rather than aggregate) level, assume that a person does not change his or her attitude about the job. If repeated measurements of that individual's attitude toward the job are taken with the same attitude scale, a reliable instrument will produce the same results each time the attitude is measured. When a measuring instrument produces unpredictable results from one testing to the next, the results are said to be unreliable because of error in measurement.

There are two problems with measures of test-retest reliability that are common to all longitudinal studies. First, the premeasure (or first measure) may sensitize the respondents to their participation in a research project and subsequently influence the results of the second measure. Further, if the time between measures is long, there may be attitude change or other maturation of the subjects. Thus it is possible for a reliable measure to indicate a low or moderate correlation between the first and the second administration, if this low correlation is due to an attitude change over time rather than to a lack of reliability.

The second dimension of reliability concerns the homogeneity of the measure. An attempt to measure an attitude may require asking several similar (but not identical) questions or presenting a battery of scale items. The three job-challenge items in Exhibit 11.2 represent a battery of scale items. To measure the *internal consistency* of a multiple-item measure, scores on subsets of the items within the scale are correlated.

The technique of splitting halves is the most basic method for checking internal consistency when a measure contains a large number of items. In the **split-half method** the researcher may take the result obtained from one-half of the scale items (e.g., odd-numbered items) and check them against the results from the other half of the items (e.g., even-numbered items).

In the **equivalent-form method** two alternative instruments are designed to be as equivalent as possible. Each of the two measurement scales is administered to the same group of subjects. If there is high correlation between the two forms, the researcher concludes that the scale is reliable. However, there is a problem if there is low correspondence between the two instruments. The researcher will be uncertain whether the measure has intrinsically low reliability or whether a single equivalent form has failed to be similar to the other form.[12]

Both the equivalent-form and the split-half approaches to measuring reliability assume that the concept being measured is unidimensional. They measure homogeneity, or interitem consistency, rather than stability over time.

It should be noted that reliability is a necessary condition for validity, but a reliable instrument may not be valid. For example, a voting-intentions measurement technique may consistently indicate that 20 percent of the sample units are willing to vote for a candidate. Whether or not the measure is valid depends on whether 20 percent of the population do indeed vote for this candidate. A reliable but invalid instrument will yield consistently inaccurate results.

Validity

The purpose of measurement is to measure what we intend to measure—but this obvious goal is not as simple as it sounds at first. Consider the student who takes a test (measurement) in a statistics class. After receiving a poor grade, the student may say: "I really understood that material because I studied hard. The test measured my ability to do arithmetic and to memorize formulas rather than my understanding of statistics." The student's complaint is that the test did not measure her understanding of statistics—what the professor had intended to measure; the test may have measured something else.

One method of measuring the intention to buy is a so-called "gift method." Respondents are told that a drawing will be held at some future time for a year's supply of a certain product. Respondents report which of several brands they would prefer to receive if they win.[13] Do respondents' reports of the brands they prefer to win necessarily constitute a valid measure of the brands they will actually purchase in the marketplace if they don't win the contest? Couldn't there be a systematic bias to identify brands "I wish I could afford" rather than the brands usually purchased? This is a question of validity.

A researcher who wonders if rate of absenteeism might be utilized to measure morale illustrates another validity issue. It is possible that this is not a valid measure of morale because absenteeism might reflect either a wave of illness in the community or unsatisfied workers not coming to work.

Researchers want to know if their measure is valid, and the question of validity expresses their concern with accurate measurement. **Validity** addresses the problem of whether a measure (for example, an attitude measure) measures what it is supposed to measure. If it does not measure what we designate it to measure, there will be problems.

Students should be able to empathize with the following validity problem. Consider the recent controversy about highway patrolmen using radar guns to clock speeders. A "speeder" is clocked at 75 mph in a 55 mph zone. But the same radar gun, aimed at a house, registers 28 mph. (The error occurred because the radar gun had picked up impulses from the squad car's idling engine's electrical system.) The house wasn't speeding—and the test was not valid.

Researchers have attempted to assess validity in a variety of ways, including asking questions such as "Is there a consensus among my colleagues that my attitude scale measures what it is supposed to measure?" "Does my measure correlate with others' measures of the 'same' concept?" or "Does the behavior expected from my measure predict the actual observed behavior?" Researchers expect the answers to provide some evidence of a measure's validity. This section discusses the three basic approaches to dealing with the issue of validity.

Face validity or **content validity** refers to the subjective agreement among professionals that a scale logically appears to accurately reflect what it purports to measure. The content of the scale appears to be adequate. When it appears evident to experts that the measure provides adequate coverage of the concept, a measure has face validity. Clear, understandable questions such as "How many children do you have?" are generally agreed to have face validity. However, in scientific studies researchers generally prefer strong evidence because of the elusive nature of measuring attitudes and other cognitive phenomena. For example, the A. C. Nielsen television-rating system is based on a people meter that mechanically records when a sample household's television is engaged and what channel is selected. If one of the viewers leaves to move to another room or has fallen asleep, the measure is not a valid measure of audience.

Criterion validity is an attempt by researchers to answer the question "Does my measure correlate with other measures of the 'same' construct?" Consider the physical concept of *length*.[14] It is possible to measure length utilizing a tape measure, calipers, odometers, and variations of the ruler. If a new measure of length were developed (for example, through laser technology), finding that the new measure correlated with the other measures of length could provide some assurance that the new measure was valid. A researcher wishing to establish criterion validity for a new measure of absenteeism, such as a measure utilizing co-workers' ratings of employee absenteeism, should correlate it with other traditional measures of absenteeism, such as total days absent.

Criterion validity may be classified as either *concurrent validity* or *predictive validity,* depending on the time sequence of associating the "new" measurement scale and the criterion measure. If the new measure is taken at the same time as the criterion measure, the method is called **concurrent validity.** **Predictive validity** is established when an attitude measure predicts a future event. The two measures differ only on the basis of a time dimension, that is, only if the criterion is separated in time from the predictor measure. A practical example of predictive validity is illustrated by a commercial research firm's testing of the relationship between a rough commercial's effectiveness (for example, recall scores) and a finished commercial's effectiveness (recall scores). Ad agencies often test animatic rough commercials, photomatic rough commercials, or live-action rough commercials before developing the finished commercial. One research consulting firm suggests this testing has high predictive validity. Rough commercial recall scores provide correct estimates of the final, finished commercial recall scores more than 80 percent of the time.[15] While face or content validity is a subjective evaluation, criterion validity provides a more rigorous empirical test.

Construct validity is established by the degree to which the measure confirms a network of related hypotheses generated from a theory based on the concepts. Establishing construct validity occurs during the statistical analysis of the data. In construct validity the empirical evidence is consistent with the theoretical logic about the concepts. In its simplest form, if the measure behaves the way it is supposed to, in a pattern of intercorrelation with a variety of other variables, there is evidence for construct validity.[16]

For example, a consumer researcher developed a personality scale to measure several interpersonal response traits that management theorists had previously related to occupational preference. Testing the new scale against occupational preference would be evidence for construct validity.

To achieve construct validity, the researcher must have already determined the meaning of the measure by establishing what basic researchers call *convergent validity* and *discriminant validity*. **Convergent validity** is synonymous with criterion validity. The criterion may be a construct that one would logically expect to be associated with the new measure. Thus, to establish validity, the new measure should "converge" with other similar measures; a measure of a theoretical concept has convergent validity when it is highly correlated with different measures of similar constructs. A measure has **discriminant validity** when it has a low correlation with measures of dissimilar concepts. This is a complex method of establishing validity and of less concern to the applied researcher than to the basic researcher.

Reliability and Validity.   The concepts of reliability and validity should be compared. Although a tailor, using a ruler, may obtain the same measurements over time, it is possible that he is using a bent ruler. A bent ruler, one that does not provide perfect accuracy, is not a valid measure. Thus reliability, although necessary for validity, is not in itself sufficient. A measure of a subject's physiological reaction to a package (for example, pupil dilation) may be highly reliable, but it does not necessarily constitute a valid measure of purchase intention.

The differences between reliability and validity can be illustrated by the rifle targets in Exhibit 11.5. An expert marksman fires an equal number of rounds with a century-old rifle and with a modern rifle.[17] The shots from the century-old gun are considerably scattered, but the shots from the new gun are closely clustered. The variability of the old rifle, compared to the new weapon, indicates it is less reliable. Target C illustrates the concept of a systematic bias influencing validity. The new rifle is reliable (little variance), but the sharpshooter's vision is hampered by glare from the sun. Although consistent, the marksman is unable to hit the bull's eye.

Sensitivity

The sensitivity of a scale is an important measurement concept, particularly when *changes* in attitudes or other hypothetical constructs are under investigation. **Sensitivity** refers to an instrument's ability to accurately measure variability in stimuli or responses. A dichotomous response category, such as "agree or disagree," does not reflect subtle attitude changes. A more sensitive measure, with numerous items on the scale, may be needed. For example, adding "strongly agree," "mildly agree," "neither agree nor disagree," "mildly disagree," and "strongly disagree" as categories increases a scale's sensitivity.

The sensitivity of a scale based on a single question or single item can also be increased by adding additional questions or items. In other words, because index measures allow for a greater range of possible scores, they are more sensitive than single-item scales.

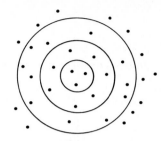 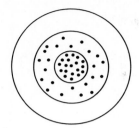 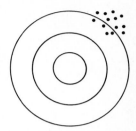

Old Rifle	**New Rifle**	**New Rifle Sunglare**
Low Reliability	High Reliability	Reliable but not Valid
(Target A)	(Target B)	(Target C)

Sources: Adapted from Keith K. Cox and Ben M. Enis, *The Marketing Research Process* (Goodyear Publishing, 1972, Scott, Foresman and Company), pp. 353–355, adapted with permission; and from *Foundation of Behavioral Research*, p. 44, by Fred N. Kerlinger. Copyright © 1973 by Holt, Rinehart and Winston, Inc. Adapted by permission of Holt, Rinehart and Winston.

SUMMARY

Many business research problems require the choice of an appropriate measuring system. The concept to be measured must be given an operational definition that specifies how it will be measured. There are four types of measuring scales. Nominal scales assign numbers or letters to objects only for identification or classification. Ordinal scales arrange objects or alternatives according to their magnitude in an ordered relationship. Interval scales measure order (or distance) in units of equal intervals. Ratio scales are absolute scales, starting with absolute zero—total absence of the attribute. The type of scale determines what numerical and statistical operations can be used in analyzing measurements.

Index or composite measures are often used when measuring complex concepts with several attributes. Asking several questions may yield a more accurate measure than asking a single question.

Measuring instruments are evaluated in terms of reliability, validity, and sensitivity. Reliability refers to the measuring instrument's ability to provide consistent results in repeated uses. Validity refers to the degree to which the instrument measures the concept the researcher wants to measure. Sensitivity is the measuring instrument's ability to accurately measure variability in stimuli or responses.

Reliability may be tested using the test-retest method, the split-half method, or the equivalent-form method. When dealing with issues of validity, the three basic approaches are to establish content validity, to establish criterion validity, or to establish construct validity. The sensitivity of a scale can be increased by allowing for a greater range of possible scores.

Key Terms

concept

operational definition

rule of measurement

nominal scale

ordinal scale

interval scale

ratio scale

attribute

index measures

reliability

test-retest method

split-half method

equivalent-form method

validity

face validity (content validity)

criterion validity (convergent validity)

concurrent validity

predictive validity

construct validity

discriminant validity

sensitivity

Questions

1. What are the permissible descriptive statistics allowable with nominal, ordinal, and interval scales?

2. Discuss the differences between validity and reliability.

3. What is the difference between a conceptual definition and an operational definition?

4. Why might a researcher wish to utilize more than one question to measure satisfaction with a job?

5. Comment on the validity and reliability of the following:

    a. A respondent's reporting of an intention to subscribe to *Consumer Reports* is highly reliable. A researcher believes that this constitutes a valid measurement of dissatisfaction with the economic system and alienation from big business.

    b. A general-interest magazine advertised that the magazine was a better advertising medium than television programs with similar content. Research had indicated that for a soft drink and other test products, recall scores were higher for the magazine ads than for 30-second commercials.

    c. A respondent's report of frequency of magazine reading consistently indicates she regularly reads *Good Housekeeping* and *Gourmet* and never reads *Cosmopolitan*.

6. Indicate whether each of the following measures is a nominal, ordinal, interval, or ratio scale:

    a. Prices on the stock market.

    b. Marital status, classified as married or never married.

    c. Whether or not a respondent has ever been unemployed.

    d. Professorial rank: assistant professor, associate professor, or professor.

7. In the library find out how *Sales and Marketing Management* magazine constructs its buying power index.

8.   Define each of the following concepts and operationally define each concept:
     a.   A good bowler
     b.   A workaholic
     c.   Purchasing intention for a new compact disc player
     d.   A mentor
     e.   Media skepticism
9.   Education is often used as an indicator of a person's socioeconomic status. Historically, in the United States the number of years of schooling completed has been recorded in the population census as a measure of education. Critics say that this measure is no longer accurate as a measure of education. Comment.

References

[1] Jum C. Nummally, *Psychometric Theory* (New York: McGraw-Hill, 1967), 2.

[2] Sarah M. Dinham, *Exploring Statistics: An Introduction for Psychology and Education* (Belmont, CA: Brooks/Cole Publishing Co./Wadsworth, Inc., 1976), 3.

[3] Donald P. Warwick and Charles A. Lininger, *The Sample Survey: Theory and Practice* (New York: McGraw-Hill, 1975), 27.

[4] This definition is adapted from Fred N. Kerlinger, *Foundations of Behavioral Research* (New York: Holt, Rinehart and Winston, 1973), 31.

[5] Barry F. Anderson, *The Psychology Experiment* (Belmont, CA: Brooks/Cole, 1971), 26.

[6] Fred N. Kerlinger, *Behavioral Research: A Conceptual Approach* (New York: Holt, Rinehart and Winston, 1979), 41.

[7] Kerlinger, *Foundations of Behavioral Research,* 428.

[8] Benjamin B. Wolman, ed., *Dictionary of Behavioral Science* (New York: Van Nostrand Reinhold, 1973), 333.

[9] This example assumes a standard measure for the term *length*.

[10] See J. Paul Peter, "Reliability: A Review of Psychometric Basis and Recent Marketing Practices," *Journal of Marketing Research* (February 1979): 6–17, for an excellent review of advanced techniques concerning reliability.

[11] Angus Campbell, Philip E. Converse, and Willard L. Rodgers, *The Quality of American Life* (New York: Russell Sage Foundation, 1976), 45.

[12] Philip J. Runkel and Joseph E. McGrath, *Research on Human Behavior* (New York: Holt, Rinehart and Winston, 1972), 155.

[13] L. J. Rothman, "Foundation of an Index of Propensity to Buy," *Journal of Marketing Research* 1 (1964): 21–25.

[14] Philip J. Runkel and Joseph E. McGrath, *Research on Human Behavior: A Systematic Guide to Method* (New York: Holt, Rinehart and Winston, 1972), 158–161.

[15] Burke Marketing Research, *Rough Commercial Recall Testing.*

[16] John A. Sonquist and William C. Dunkelburg, *Survey and Opinion Research: Procedures for Processing and Analysis* (Englewood Cliffs, NJ: Prentice-Hall, 1977), 335.

[17] Kerlinger, *Foundations of Behavioral Research,* 44.

Attitude Measurement

According to the Times Mirror Company, the conventional labels of liberal and conservative are about as relevant today as Whig and Federalist.[1] *Although Americans may respond to the terms liberal and conservative, the newspaper company believes these expressions no longer come close to defining the polarized positions of American public opinion. Because these terms have lost much of their traditional meaning, the company researched nine basic values and orientations that reflect contemporary American political attitudes:*

- Religious faith—*belief in God*
- Tolerance—*belief in freedom for those who don't share one's values*
- Social justice—*belief in the government's obligation to ensure social justice and social welfare*
- Militant anticommunism—*belief in a strong, aggressive military defense to halt communism*
- Alienation—*belief that the American system does not work for oneself*
- American exceptionalism—*belief that there are no limits to what America can do*
- Financial pressure—*belief about one's financial status*
- Attitudes toward government—*belief about the proper role and effectiveness of government*
- Attitudes toward business corporations—*belief about the goals and effectiveness of business corporations*

The Times Mirror Company investigated these political attitudes because it believed they more clearly define present-day values and political orientations than do the terms conservative and liberal.

Investigating respondent attitudes and the techniques for measuring them is the subject of this chapter.

ATTITUDE DEFINED

There are many definitions for the term *attitude*. An **attitude** is usually viewed as an enduring disposition to consistently respond in a given manner to various aspects of the world, including persons, events, and objects. One conception of attitude is reflected in this brief statement: "Sally loves working at McCartney's. She believes it's clean, conveniently located, and has the best wages in town. She intends to work there until she retires." In this short description three components of attitude have been disclosed: *affective, cognitive,* and *behavioral.*

The **affective component** reflects an individual's general feelings or emotions toward an object. Statements such as "I love my job," "I liked that book, *A Corporate Bestiary,*" or "I hate cranberry juice" reflect the emotional character of attitudes.

The way one feels about a product, person, or object is usually tied to one's beliefs or cognitions. The **cognitive component** represents one's awareness of and knowledge about an object. A woman might feel happy about her job because she "believes that the pay is great" or because she knows "that my job is the biggest challenge in Hinsdale."

The third component of an attitude is the **behavioral component.** Intentions and behavioral expectations are reflected in this component, which therefore reflects a predisposition to action.

ATTITUDE AS A HYPOTHETICAL CONSTRUCT

Many variables that business researchers wish to investigate are psychological variables that cannot be directly observed. For example, someone may have an attitude toward the E. F. Hutton brokerage firm, but we cannot observe this attitude. To measure an attitude, we must infer from the way an individual responds (verbal expression or overt behavior) to some stimulus. The term **hypothetical construct** describes a variable that is not directly observable but is measured by an indirect means, such as verbal expression or overt behavior.[2]

TECHNIQUES FOR MEASURING ATTITUDES

A remarkable variety of techniques have been devised to measure attitudes. In part, this diversity stems from the lack of consensus about the exact definition of the concept. Further, the affective, cognitive, and behavioral components of an attitude may be measured by different means. For example, sympathetic nervous system responses may be recorded using physiological measures to measure affect, but they are not good measures of behavioral intentions. Direct verbal statements concerning affect, belief, or behavior are utilized to measure behavioral intent. However, attitudes may also be measured indirectly by using the exploratory techniques discussed in Chapter 5. Obtaining verbal statements from respondents generally requires that the respondent perform a task such as ranking, rating, sorting, or making a choice or a comparison.[3]

A **ranking** task requires that the respondents rank order a small number of items in overall preference or on the basis of some characteristic of the

RESEARCH INSIGHT

A Hypothetical Construct Is Never Having to Say You're Sorry; or, Love Is a Four-Letter Word

Love Is a Four-Letter Word. It is also a hypothetical construct, that is, a term that psychologists use to describe or explain consistent patterns of human behavior. Love, hate, thirst, learning, intelligence—all of these are hypothetical constructs. They are hypothetical in that they do not exist as physical entities; therefore, they cannot be seen, heard, felt, or measured directly. There is no love center in the brain that, if removed, would leave a person incapable of responding positively and affectionately toward other people and things. Love and hate are constructs in that we invent these terms to explain why, for instance, a young man spends all his time with one young woman while completely avoiding another. From a scientific point of view, we might be better off if we said that this young man's behavior suggested that he had a relatively enduring, positive-approach attitude toward the first woman, a negative-avoidance attitude toward the second.

Source: *Psychology Today: An Introduction* (Del Mar, CA: CRM Books, 1970), 613. Reprinted by permission of CRM Books, a division of Random House, Inc.

---

stimulus. **Rating** asks the respondents to estimate the magnitude of a characteristic or quality that an object possesses. Quantitative scores, along a continuum that has been supplied to the respondents, are used to estimate the strength of the attitude or belief. In other words, the respondents indicate the position, on a scale(s), where they would rate the object.

A **sorting** technique might present respondents with several product concepts, typed on cards, and require that the respondents arrange the cards into a number of piles or otherwise classify the product concepts. The **choice** technique, choosing one of two or more alternatives, is another type of attitude measurement. If a respondent chooses one object over another, it is assumed the chosen object is preferred over the other.

The most popular techniques for measuring attitudes are presented in this chapter.

Physiological Measures of Attitudes

Galvanic skin response, measures of blood pressure, pupil dilations, and other physiological measures may be utilized to assess the affective component of attitudes. They provide a means of measuring attitudes without verbally questioning the respondent. In general, they can provide a gross measure of like or dislike, but they are not sensitive measures for identifying gradients of an attitude. (Each of these measures is discussed elsewhere in the text.)

ATTITUDE RATING SCALES

Using rating scales to measure attitudes is perhaps the most common practice in business research. This section discusses many rating scales designed to enable respondents to report the intensity of their attitudes.

R E S E A R C H   I N S I G H T

Rating Scales Provide Simple Descriptive and Evaluative Measures

Got A Minute?
TELL US HOW WE'RE DOING

Dear Visitor

Thank you for coming and giving us the opportunity of serving you. We know that continued visitor satisfaction is the key to success. With that in mind, we invite your comments and suggestions regarding our SERVICE, CLEANLINESS, ATTITUDE, and EXHIBITS.

We're proud to serve you and we really appreciate your constructive comments. We look forward to serving you again in the very near future.

WE APPRECIATE YOUR OPINION ON THE FOLLOWING
(Please Check boxes below)

	Excl. 1	Good 2	Fair 3	Poor 4	REMARKS
CLEANLINESS					
Grounds	1	2	3	4	
Galleries	1	2	3	4	
Rest Rooms	1	2	3	4	
Exhibits	1	2	3	4	
SERVICE					
Attitude	1	2	3	4	
Courtesy	1	2	3	4	
EXHIBITS					
Appearance	1	2	3	4	
Information	1	2	3	4	
Interest	1	2	3	4	
OVERALL IMPRESSION					
	1	2	3	4	

COMMENTS and SUGGESTIONS _____

Would you like to be contacted about being a volunteer?
☐ Yes   ☐ No

Date _____ Time _____ AM ____ PM

Your Name _____
(optional)

Address _____

City _____ State _____ Zip _____

Telephone Number _____

FOLD HERE
DROP IN THE MAIL ... OR LEAVE IN THE BOX
THANK YOU

Source: Reprinted with permission of the Dallas Museum of Natural History and Dallas Aquarium.

Simple Attitude Scaling

In its most basic form, attitude scaling requires that an individual agree or disagree with a statement or respond to a single question. For example, respondents in a political poll may be asked whether they agree or disagree with the statement "The president should run for re-election." Or an individual might be asked to indicate whether he likes or dislikes labor unions. Because this type of self-rating scale merely classifies respondents into one of two categories, it has only the properties of a nominal scale. This, of course, limits the type of mathematical analysis that may be utilized with the simplified or basic scale. Despite the disadvantages, simple attitude scaling may be used when questionnaires are extremely long, when respondents have little education, or for other specific reasons.

A number of simplified scales are merely checklists. A respondent indicates past experience, preference, and the like merely by checking an item. In many cases these may be adjectives that describe a particular object.

The Job Descriptive Index (JDI) is a modified checklist with a large number of items. The Job Descriptive Index measures several dimensions of satisfaction: pay, promotion, coworkers, supervision, and quality of work. Some sample items appear below.[4]

Directions:

Think of your present work. What is it like most of the time?
Circle YES if it describes your work.
Circle NO if it does NOT describe it.
Circle ? if you cannot decide.

Fascinating	YES	NO	?
Routine	YES	NO	?
Satisfying	YES	NO	?

Most attitude theorists believe that attitudes vary along continua. An early attitude researcher pioneered the view that the task of attitude scaling is to measure the distance between "good to bad," "low to high," "like to dislike," and so on.[5] Thus the purpose of an attitude scale is to find an individual's position on a continuum. If this is the case, simple scales do not allow for making fine distinctions in attitudes. Several other scales have been developed to help make more precise measurements.

Category Scales

Some rating scales have only two response categories: *agree* and *disagree*. Expanding the response categories provides the respondent more flexibility in the rating task. Even more information is provided if the categories are ordered according to a descriptive or evaluative dimension. Consider the questions below:

How often is your supervisor courteous and friendly to you?

- ☐ **Never**
- ☐ **Rarely**
- ☐ **Sometimes**
- ☐ **Often**
- ☐ **Very often**

If you could choose, how much longer would you stay at your present job?

- ☐ **Less than six months**
- ☐ **Six months to one year**
- ☐ **Longer than one year**

Each of these **category scales** is a more sensitive measure than a scale with only two response categories. It provides more information.

Wording is an extremely important factor in the usefulness of these scales. Exhibit 12.1 shows some common wordings for category scales, and question wording is evaluated in Chapter 13.

E X H I B I T   1 2 . 1

Selected Category Scales

Quality

Excellent	Good	Fair	Poor	
Very good	Fairly good	Neither good nor bad	Not very good	Not good at all

Importance

Very important	Fairly important	Neutral	Not so important	Not at all important

Interest

Very interested		Somewhat interested		Not very interested

Satisfaction

Very satisfied	Somewhat satisfied	Neither satisfied nor dissatisfied	Somewhat dissatisfied	Very dissatisfied
Very satisfied	Quite satisfied		Somewhat satisfied	Not at all satisfied

Frequency

All of the time	Very often	Often	Sometimes	Hardly ever
Very often	Often	Sometimes	Rarely	Never
All of the time	Most of the time		Some of the time	Just now and then

Truth

Very true	Somewhat true		Not very true	Not at all true

Summated Ratings Method: The Likert Scale

Business researchers' adaptation of the summated ratings method, developed by Rensis Likert, is extremely popular for measuring attitudes because the method is simple to administer.[6] With the **Likert scale,** respondents indicate their attitudes by checking how strongly they agree or disagree with carefully constructed statements that range from very positive to very negative toward the attitudinal object. Individuals generally choose from five alternatives: strongly agree, agree, uncertain, disagree, and strongly disagree; but the alternatives may number from 3 to 9.[7]

Consider the following example from a study on mergers and acquisitions:

Mergers and acquisitions provide a faster means of growth than internal expansion.

Strongly Disagree (1)	Disagree (2)	Uncertain (3)	Agree (4)	Strongly Agree (5)

To measure the attitude, researchers assign scores or weights to the alternative responses. In this example weights of 5, 4, 3, 2, and 1 are assigned to the answers. (The weights, shown in parentheses, would not be printed on the questionnaire.) Strong agreement indicates the most favorable attitudes on the statement, and the weight of 5 is assigned to this response. The statement used as an example is positive toward the attitude. If a negative statement toward the object (such as "Your access to copy machines is limited") were given, the weights would be reversed, and "strongly disagree" would be assigned the weight of 5. A single scale item on a summated rating scale is an ordinal scale.

A Likert scale may include several scale items to form an index. Each statement is assumed to represent an aspect of a common attitudinal domain. For example, Exhibit 12.2 shows the items in a Likert scale to measure attitudes toward an MBO program. The total score is the summation of the weights assigned to an individual's total response.

In Likert's original procedure a large number of statements is generated and then an *item analysis* is performed. The purpose of the item analysis is to ensure that final items evoke a wide response and discriminate among those with positive and negative attitudes. Items that are poor because they lack clarity or elicit mixed response patterns are eliminated from the final statement list. However, many business researchers do not follow the exact procedure prescribed by Likert. Hence a disadvantage of the Likert-type summated rating method is that it is difficult to know what a single summated score means. Many patterns of response to the various statements can produce the same total score. Thus identical total scores may reflect different "attitudes" because of the different combinations of statements endorsed.

Semantic Differential

The **semantic differential** is a series of attitude scales. This popular attitude-measurement technique consists of identification of a company, product, brand, job, or other concept followed by a series of seven-point bipolar rating scales. Bipolar adjectives, such as "good and bad," "modern and old-fashioned," or "clean and dirty," anchor the beginning and end (or poles) of the scale.

Modern ＿＿ : ＿＿ : ＿＿ : ＿＿ : ＿＿ : ＿＿ : ＿＿ **Old-Fashioned**

The subject makes repeated judgments of the concept under investigation on each of the scales. For example, Exhibit 12.3 shows a series of scales related to measuring attitudes toward jazz saxophonists' recording styles.[8]

The scoring of the semantic differential can be illustrated by using the scale bounded by the anchors "modern" and "old-fashioned." Respondents are instructed to check the place that indicates the nearest appropriate adjective. From left to right, the scale intervals are interpreted as extremely modern, very modern, slightly modern, both modern and old-fashioned, slightly old-fashioned, very old-fashioned, and extremely old-fashioned. A weight is assigned to each position on the rating scale. Traditionally, scores are 7, 6, 5, 4, 3, 2, 1, or +3, +2, +1, 0, −1, −2, −3.

Many researchers find it desirable to assume that the semantic differential provides interval data. This assumption, although widely accepted, has its crit-

---

EXHIBIT   12.2   **Likert Scale: Instructions and Items to Measure Attitudes toward a Management by Objectives (MBO) Program at the Department of Transportation (DOT)**

Here are some statements which describe how employees might feel about the MBO (management-by-objectives) form of management. Please indicate your agreement or disagreement. For each statement please circle the appropriate number to indicate whether you:

1—STRONGLY AGREE
2—AGREE
3—NEUTRAL
4—DISAGREE
5—STRONGLY DISAGREE

Circle one and only one answer for each statement. There are no right or wrong answers to these questions. Just give your opinion.

	Strongly Agree	Agree	Neutral	Disagree	Strongly Disagree
1. MBO is an effective way of planning and organizing the work for which I am responsible.	1	2	3	4	5
2. MBO provides an effective way of evaluating my work performance.	1	2	3	4	5
3. MBO motivates me to do the very best on my job.	1	2	3	4	5
4. MBO is an effective way of coordinating my work with that of other members of my immediate workgroup.	1	2	3	4	5
5. MBO results in good communication between me and my immediate supervisor.	1	2	3	4	5
6. MBO results in regular cooperation between me and my immediate supervisor.	1	2	3	4	5
7. All things considered, I am satisfied with MBO as it relates to my job.	1	2	3	4	5
8. The MBO program has *reduced* cooperation between divisions of DOT.	1	2	3	4	5
9. The MBO program has helped DOT solve some of its serious problems.	1	2	3	4	5
10. The MBO program has had *little effect* on DOT.	1	2	3	4	5
11. The MBO program has improved communications at DOT.	1	2	3	4	5
12. The MBO program has improved the coordination of efforts between divisions.	1	2	3	4	5

Source: Dow Scott, "The Causal Relationship Between Trust and the Assessed Value of Management by Objectives," *Journal of Management* 6, no. 2 (1980): 166.

ics, who argue that the data have only ordinal properties because the weights are arbitrary. Depending on whether or not the data are assumed to be interval or ordinal, the arithmetic mean or the median will be utilized to plot the profile of one concept, product, unit, etc., compared with another concept, product, or unit.

EXHIBIT   12.3

**Semantic Differential
Scales to Measure Attitude
toward Jazz Saxophonists'
Recording Styles**

Fast __ : __ : __ : __ : __ : __ : __ Slow
Intellectual __ : __ : __ : __ : __ : __ : __ Emotional
Contemporary __ : __ : __ : __ : __ : __ : __ Traditional
Composed __ : __ : __ : __ : __ : __ : __ Improvised
Flat __ : __ : __ : __ : __ : __ : __ Sharp
Busy __ : __ : __ : __ : __ : __ : __ Lazy
New __ : __ : __ : __ : __ : __ : __ Old
Progressive __ : __ : __ : __ : __ : __ : __ Regressive

Source: Joel Huber and Morris B. Holbrook, "Using Attribute Ratings for Product Positioning: Some Distinctions Among Compositional Approaches," reprinted from the *Journal of Marketing Research,* November 1979, p. 510, published by the American Marketing Association.

The semantic differential technique was originally developed by Charles Osgood and others as a method for measuring the meaning of objects or the "semantic space" of interpersonal experience.[9] Business researchers have found the semantic differential versatile and have modified the use of the scale for business applications. Replacing the bipolar adjectives with descriptive phrases is a frequent adaptation in image studies.[10] The phrases "aged a long time," "not aged a long time," "not watery looking," and "watery looking" were used in a beer-brand image study. A savings and loan association might use the phrases "low interest on savings," and "favorable interest on savings." These phrases are not polar opposites, but behavioral researchers have found that respondents often are unwilling to use the extreme negative side of a scale. Organizational research with industrial salespeople, for example, found that in rating their own performance, salespeople would not use the negative side of the scale. Hence it was eliminated, and the anchor opposite the positive anchor showed "satisfactory" rather than "extremely poor" performance.

Numerical Scales

Numerical scales have numbers as response options, rather than "semantic space" or verbal descriptions, to identify categories (response positions). If the scale items have five response positions, the scale is called a 5-point numerical scale; with 7 response positions, it is called a 7-point numerical scale; and so on.

Consider the following numerical scale:

Now that you've had your automobile for about one year, please tell us how satisfied you are with your Ford Taurus.

Extremely Satisfied   7   6   5   4   3   2   1   Extremely Dissatisfied

This numerical scale utilizes bipolar adjectives in the same manner as the semantic differential. Exhibit 12.4 shows a measure of leadership effectiveness that combines a semantic differential with an 8-point numerical scale. In practice, researchers have found that for educated populations numerical labels for intermediate points on the scale is as effective a measure as the "true" semantic differential.

EXHIBIT   12.4

LPC: Least-Preferred Co-Worker Scale of Leadership Effectiveness

Think of the person *with whom you can work least well.* The person may be someone you work with now or may be someone you knew in the past. The individual does not have to be the person you like least well, but should be the person with whom you had the most difficulty in getting a job done. Describe this person as he or she appears to you.

	8	7	6	5	4	3	2	1	
Pleasant	__ :	__ :	__ :	__	: __	: __	: __		Unpleasant
Friendly	__ :	__ :	__ :	__	: __	: __	: __		Unfriendly

	1	2	3	4	5	6	7	8	
Rejecting	__ :	__ :	__ :	__	: __	: __	: __		Accepting

	8	7	6	5	4	3	2	1	
Helpful	__ :	__ :	__ :	__	: __	: __	: __		Frustrating

	1	2	3	4	5	6	7	8	
Unenthusiastic	__ :	__ :	__ :	__	: __	: __	: __		Enthusiastic
Tense	__ :	__ :	__ :	__	: __	: __	: __		Relaxed
Distant	__ :	__ :	__ :	__	: __	: __	: __		Close

	8	7	6	5	4	3	2	1	
Cold	__ :	__ :	__ :	__	: __	: __	: __		Warm
Cooperative	__ :	__ :	__ :	__	: __	: __	: __		Uncooperative
Supportive	__ :	__ :	__ :	__	: __	: __	: __		Hostile
Boring	__ :	__ :	__ :	__	: __	: __	: __		Interesting
Quarrelsome	__ :	__ :	__ :	__	: __	: __	: __		Harmonious
Self-assured	__ :	__ :	__ :	__	: __	: __	: __		Hesitant
Efficient	__ :	__ :	__ :	__	: __	: __	: __		Inefficient
Gloomy	__ :	__ :	__ :	__	: __	: __	: __		Cheerful
Open	__ :	__ :	__ :	__	: __	: __	: __		Guarded

Source: Fred E. Friedler, *A Theory of Leadership Effectiveness* (New York: McGraw-Hill, 1967), 40–41. Reprinted with permission.

Stapel Scale

The **Stapel scale** was originally developed in the 1950s to measure the direction and intensity of an attitude simultaneously. Modern versions of the scale use a single adjective as a substitute for the semantic differential when it is difficult to create pairs of bipolar adjectives. The modified Stapel scale places a single adjective in the center of an even number of numerical values (for example, rang-

EXHIBIT   12.5

A Stapel Scale to Measure Attitudes toward a Supervisor

Supervisor's Name

+3
+2
+1

Supportive

−1
−2
−3

Select a *plus* number for words that you think describe the supervisor accurately. The more accurately you think the word describes the supervisor, the larger *plus* number you should choose. Select a *minus* number for words you think do not describe the supervisor accurately. The less accurately you think a word describes the supervisor, the larger the *minus* number you should choose. Therefore, you can select any number from plus 3, for words that you think are very accurate, all the way to minus 3, for words that you think are very inaccurate.

Sources: Based on Irving Crespi, "Use of a Scaling Technique and Surveys," *Journal of Marketing,* July 1961, 69–72, published by the American Marketing Association.

---

ing from +3 to −3).[11] It measures how close to or how distant from the adjective a given stimulus is perceived to be. Exhibit 12.5 illustrates a Stapel scale item used in a measurement of attitudes toward a supervisor.

The advantages and disadvantages of the Stapel scale are very similar to those of the semantic differential. However, the Stapel scale is markedly easier to administer, especially over the telephone.[12] Because the Stapel scale does not call for the construction of bipolar adjectives, as does the semantic differential, the Stapel scale is easier to construct.[13] Research comparing the semantic differential with the Stapel scale indicates that results from the two techniques are largely the same.[14]

Graphic Rating Scales

A **graphic rating scale** presents respondents with a graphic continuum. The respondents are allowed to choose any point on the continuum to indicate their attitude. The scale illustrated in Exhibit 12.6 shows a traditional graphic scale, ranging from one extreme position to the opposite position. Typically, a respondent's score is determined by measuring the length (millimeters) from one end of the graphic continuum to the point marked by the respondent. Many researchers believe scoring in this manner strengthens the assumption that graphic rating scales of this type are interval scales. Alternatively, the researcher

EXHIBIT   12.6

Graphic Rating Scale

Please evaluate each attribute in terms of how important it is to you by placing an "X" at the position on the horizontal line that most reflects your feelings.

Seating comfort	Not Important _____	Very Important
In-flight meals	Not Important _____	Very Important
Air fare	Not Important _____	Very Important

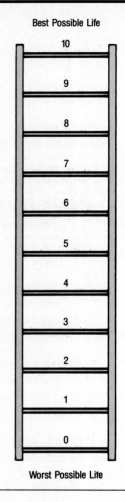

may divide the line into predetermined scoring categories (lengths) and record respondents' marks accordingly. In other words, the graphic rating scale has the advantage of allowing the researchers to choose any interval they wish for purposes of scoring. The disadvantage of the graphic rating scale is that there are no standard answers.

Graphic rating scales are not limited to straight lines as sources of visual communication. The purpose of a graphic rating scale with picture response options or another type of graphic continuum is to enhance communication with respondents. A frequently used variation is the ladder scale, which also includes numerical options:

Here is a ladder scale. [Respondent is shown Exhibit 12.7.] It represents the "ladder of life." As you see, it is a ladder with 11 rungs numbered "0" to "10." Let's suppose the top of the ladder represents the best possible life for you as

EXHIBIT   12.8

**Graphic Rating Scale
Stressing Pictorial
Visual Communications**

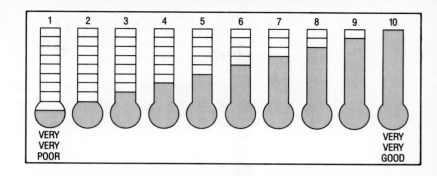

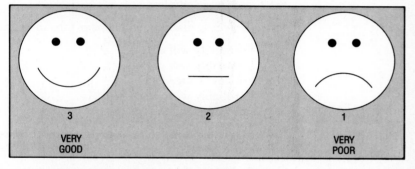

Source: Fred Cutler, "To Meet Criticisms of TV Ads, Researchers Find Ways to Measure Children's Attitudes," reprinted from the *Marketing News*, January 27, 1978, 16, published by the American Marketing Association.

you describe it, and the bottom rung represents the worst possible life for you as you describe it.

On which rung of the ladder do you feel your life is today?

0   1   2   3   4   5   6   7   8   9   10

Research investigating children's attitudes has utilized "happy face" scales (see Exhibit 12.8). With the "happy face" scale, children are asked to indicate which face shows how they feel about candy, a toy, or some other concept. Research with the "happy face" scale indicates that children are prone to choose the faces at the ends of the scale. Although this may be because children's attitudes may fluctuate more widely than those of adults or because they have stronger feelings both positively and negatively, it is a disadvantage of the scale.[15]

Thurstone Equal-Appearing Interval Scale

Louis Thurstone, an early pioneer in attitude research, developed the concept in 1927 that attitudes vary along continua and should be measured accordingly.

Construction of a Thurstone scale is a rather complex process that requires two stages. The first stage is a ranking operation, performed by judges, who assign scale values to attitudinal statements. The second stage consists of asking subjects to respond to the attitudinal statements.[16]

This Thurstone method is time consuming and costly. From a historical perspective it is valuable, but its current popularity is low. Because it is rarely utilized in most applied business research, it will not be discussed further here.

Scales Measuring Behavioral Intentions and Expectations

The behavioral component of an attitude involves the behavioral expectations of an individual toward an attitudinal object. Typically, this represents an intention or a tendency to seek additional information. Category scales that measure the behavioral component of an attitude attempt to determine a respondent's "likelihood" of action or intention to perform some future action, as in the following examples:

How likely is it that you will change jobs in the next six months?

- ☐　I definitely will change.
- ☐　I probably will change.
- ☐　I might change.
- ☐　I probably will not change.
- ☐　I definitely will not change.

I would write a letter to my congressman or other government official in support of this company if it were in a dispute with government.

- ☐　Extremely likely
- ☐　Very likely
- ☐　Somewhat likely
- ☐　Likely, about 50-50 chance
- ☐　Somewhat unlikely
- ☐　Very unlikely
- ☐　Extremely unlikely

The wording of statements used in these scales often include phrases such as "I would recommend," "I would write," or "I would buy" to indicate action tendencies.

The U.S. Bureau of the Census has used a scale of subjective probabilities, ranging from 100 for absolutely certain to 0 for absolutely no chance, to measure expectations. Management researchers have used the following similar subjective probability scale to estimate the chance of job candidates accepting a position:

____ 100% (Absolutely certain) I will accept

____　90% (Almost sure) I will accept

____　80% (Very big chance) I will accept

____　70% (Big chance) I will accept

____　60% (Not so big a chance) I will accept

____　50% (About even) I will accept

EXHIBIT   12.9

**Summary of the Advantages
and Disadvantages
of Rating Scales**

Rating Measure	Subject Must:	Advantages	Disadvantages
Category scale	Indicate response category	Flexible, easy to respond	Items may be ambiguous; with few categories, only gross distinctions can be made
Likert scale	Evaluate statements on 5-point scale	Easiest scale to construct	Hard to judge what a single score means
Semantic differential and numerical scales	Choose points between bipolar adjectives on relevant dimensions	Easy to construct; norms exist for comparison, such as profile analysis	Bipolar adjectives must be found; data may be ordinal, not interval
Stapel scale	Choose points on a scale with a single adjective in center	Easier to construct than semantic differential, easy to administer	Endpoints are numerical, not verbal, labels
Graphic scale	Choose point on a continuum	Visual impact, unlimited scale points	No standard answers
Graphic scale—picture response	Choose visual picture	Visual impact	Hard to attach verbal explanation to response

Source: Based on *Psychology Today: An Introduction* (Delmar, CA: CRM Books, a division of Random House, Inc., 1970), 264.

____   40% (Smaller chance) I will accept

____   30% (Small chance) I will accept

____   20% (Very small chance) I will accept

____   10% (Almost certainly not) I will accept

____   0   (Certainly not) I will accept

Behavioral Differential.   A general instrument, the **behavioral differential,** has been developed to measure the behavioral intentions of subjects toward any object or category of objects.[17] Like the semantic differential, a description of the object to be judged is placed on the top of a sheet, and the subjects indicate their behavioral intentions toward this object on a series of scales. For example, one item might be:

A 25-Year-Old Female Commodity Broker

Would __ : __ : __ : __ : __ : __ : __ : __ : __ Would Not

Ask This Person for Advice

Exhibit 12.9 is a summary of the attitude-rating techniques discussed in this chapter.

RANKING

People often rank order their preferences. An ordinal scale may be developed by asking respondents to rank order (from most preferred to least preferred) a set of objects or attributes. It is not difficult for respondents to understand the task of rank ordering the importance of fringe benefits or arranging a set of job tasks according to preference.

Paired Comparisons

Some time ago a chain-saw manufacturer learned that the competition had introduced a new, lightweight (6½-pound) chain saw. The company's lightest chain saw weighed 9½ pounds. Executives wondered if they needed to introduce a 6-pound chain saw into the product line. The research design was a **paired comparison**. A 6-pound chain saw was designed and a prototype built. To control for color preferences, the competitor's chain saw was painted the same color as the 9½-pound and 6-pound chain saws. Respondents were presented with two chain saws at a time, then asked to pick the one they preferred. Three pairs of comparisons were required to determine the most preferred chain saw.

The following question is the typical format for asking about paired comparisons.[18]

I would like to know your overall opinion of two brands of Product X. They are Brand A and Brand B. Overall, which of these two brands—A or B—do you think is the better one? Or are both the same?

A is better ____

B is better ____

They are the same ____

If researchers wish to compare four brands of pens on the basis of attractiveness or writing quality, six comparisons [(n)(n − 1)/2] are necessary.

Ranking objects with respect to one attribute is not difficult if only a few concepts or items are compared. As the number of items increases, the number of comparisons increases geometrically. If the number of comparisons is too great, respondents may become fatigued and no longer carefully discriminate among them.

SORTING

Sorting tasks require that respondents indicate their attitudes or beliefs by arranging items. Exhibit 12.10 illustrates four cards from a deck of 52 cards in Bruskin's AIM (Association-Identification-Measurement) technique. Each card reflects an element from advertising or the product being measured, and this omnibus service measures how well customers associate and identify these elements with a particular product, company, or advertising campaign.[19] The following (condensed) interviewer instructions illustrate how sorting is utilized in the AIM survey:

EXHIBIT 12.10

**Bruskin Associates—
AIM Syndicated Service**

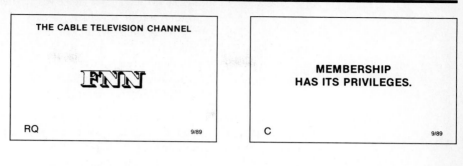

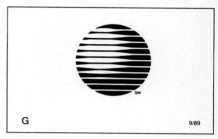

Source: Courtesy of Bruskin Associates, Market Research, New Brunswick, N.J.

Thoroughly shuffle deck.
Hand respondent deck.
Ask respondent to sort cards into two piles:
    Definitely Not Seen or Heard.
    Definitely or Possibly Seen or Heard.
Set aside Definitely Not Seen or Heard *pile.*
Hand respondent the Definitely or Possibly Seen or Heard *pile.*
Have respondent identify the item on each card in the Definitely or Possibly
    Seen or Heard *pile.*
Record on questionnaire.

Constant-Sum Scale

Suppose the manufacturer of Aqua-Fresh toothpaste wished to determine how important the attributes of cavity fighting, breath freshening, and price were to consumers. Respondents might be asked to divide a constant sum to indicate the relative importance of the attributes.[20] For example:

Divide 100 points among the following toothpaste characteristics according to how important each characteristic is to you when selecting a brand of toothpaste:

Cavity fighting ____

Breath freshening ____

Price ____

The **constant-sum scale** works best with respondents having a higher educational level. If respondents follow instructions correctly, the results approximate interval measures. As in the paired-comparison method, as the number of stimuli increases this technique becomes more complex.

Preference may be measured by using this technique in a manner similar to the paired comparison method. Organizational researchers who utilize this technique refer to it as the *cafeteria reward system*. For example:

Suppose you had $3,000 in benefits per month. How much would you like to allocate to salary, medical insurance, and retirement plan? Divide the $3,000 according to your preference.

Salary ____

Medical insurance ____

Retirement plan ____

A variant of the constant-sum technique uses physical counters that the respondent is to divide among the items being tested. In an airline study of customer preferences, the following technique could be used:

Here is a sheet listing several airlines. Next to the name of each airline is a pocket. Here are ten cards. I would like you to put these cards in the pockets next to the airlines you would prefer to fly on your next trip. Assume that all of the airlines fly to wherever you would choose to travel. You may put as many cards as you want in any pocket, or you may put no cards in any pocket.

	Cards
American	____
Delta	____
United	____
Southwest	____
Eastern	____

OTHER METHODS OF ATTITUDE MEASUREMENT

Attitudes, as hypothetical constructs, are not measured directly. Therefore measurement of attitudes is, to an extent, subject to the imagination of the researcher. The traditional methods used for attitude measurement have been presented here, but there are several other techniques in the published literature (e.g., the Guttman scale) that can be utilized when a situation dictates. Advanced students will seek out these techniques when the traditional measures do not apply to the investigator's problem. With the growth of computer technology, techniques such as *multidimensional scaling* and *conjoint analysis* are used more frequently. These are complex techniques that require a knowledge of multivariate statistical analysis (see Chapter 22).

SELECTING A MEASUREMENT SCALE: SOME PRACTICAL DECISIONS

Now that we have illustrated a number of attitude measurement scales, a natural question arises: "Which is most appropriate?" Like the decision that is made in the selection of a basic research design, there is no single best answer that applies to all research projects. The answer to this question is relative, and the choice of scale will be a function of the nature of the attitudinal object to be measured, the manager's problem definition, and the backward and forward linkages to other choices that have already been made (e.g., telephone survey versus mail survey). However, there are several issues that will be helpful to consider when making decisions about the choice of a measurement scale:

1.   Is a ranking, sorting, rating, or choice technique best?
2.   Should a monadic or comparative scale be used?
3.   What type of category labels, if any, should be used?
4.   How many scale positions are needed?
5.   Should a balanced or unbalanced scale be chosen?
6.   Should respondents be given a forced-choice or a nonforced-choice scale?
7.   Should a single measure or an index measure be used?

We shall now discuss each of these issues.

Is a Ranking, Sorting, Rating, or Choice Technique Best?   The answer to this question is largely determined by the problem definition and especially by the type of statistical analysis that is desired. For example, ranking provides only ordinal data, which limits the statistical techniques that may be utilized.

Should a Monadic or Comparative Scale Be Used?   If a scale is other than a ratio scale, the researcher must make a decision whether to use a standard of comparison in the verbal portion of the scale. Consider the following rating scale:

Now that you've had your automobile for about one year, please tell us how satisfied you are with its engine power and pickup?

Completely	Very	Fairly Well	Somewhat	Very
Satisfied	Satisfied	Satisfied	Dissatisfied	Dissatisfied

This is a **monadic rating scale** because it asks about a single concept (the brand of automobile the individual actually purchased) in isolation. The respondent is not given a specific frame of reference. A **comparative rating scale** asks a respondent to rate a concept, such as a specific brand, in comparison with a benchmark—perhaps another similar concept such as a competitive brand—explicitly used as a frame of reference. In many cases the comparative rating scale presents "the ideal situation" as a reference point for comparison with the actual situation. For example:

Please indicate how the amount of authority in your present position compares with the amount of authority that would be ideal for this position.

Too Much	About Right	Too Little

What Type of Category Label, If Any, Will Be Used for the Rating Scale?   We have discussed verbal labels, numerical labels, and unlisted choices. Many rating scales have verbal labels for response categories because researchers believe they help respondents to better understand the response positions. The maturity and educational level of the respondents will influence this decision. The semantic differential, with unlabeled response categories between two bipolar adjectives, and the numerical scale, with numbers to indicate scale positions, are often selected because the researcher wishes to assume interval-scale data.

How Many Scale Categories or Response Positions Are Needed?   Should a category scale have four, five, or seven response positions or categories? Or should the researcher utilize a graphic scale that has an infinite number of positions? The original developmental research on the semantic differential indicated that five to eight points was optimal. However, the researcher must determine the number of meaningful positions that is best for the specific project. This issue of identifying how many meaningful distinctions respondents can practically make is the same issue as sensitivity, but at the operational level rather than the conceptual level.

Should a Balanced or Unbalanced Rating Scale Be Chosen?   The fixed-alternative format may be **balanced** or **unbalanced**. For example, the following "question," which asks about parent–child decisions relating to television program watching, is balanced:

Activity—The television programs your children watch:

Child decides all of the time.
Child decides most of the time.
Child and parent decide together.
Parent decides most of the time.
Parent decides all of the time.[21]

These answers are balanced because a neutral or indifferent point is at the center of the scale. In some cases unbalanced scales are utilized when responses are expected to be distributed at one end of the scale. Unbalanced scales, such as the one below, may eliminate this type of "end piling."

Satisfied
Neither satisfied nor dissatisfied
Quite dissatisfied
Very dissatisfied[22]

The nature of the concept or knowledge about attitudes toward the stimulus to be measured generally will determine the answer to this question.

Should Respondents Be Given a Forced-Choice or a Nonforced-Choice Scale?   In many situations a respondent has not formed an attitude toward a concept and simply cannot provide an answer. If the respondent is forced to answer, the answer is merely a function of the question. If answers are not forced, the midpoint of the scale may be used by the respondent to indicate unawareness as well as indifference.[23] If many respondents in the sample are expected to be unaware of the attitudinal object under investigation, this problem may be eliminated by utilizing a nonforced-choice scale that provides a "no opinion" category. For example:

How does the Bank of Commerce compare with the First National Bank?

Bank of Commerce is better than First National Bank.
Bank of Commerce is about the same as First National Bank.
Bank of Commerce is worse than First National Bank.
Can't say.

Asking this type of question allows the investigator to separate respondents who cannot make an honest comparison from respondents who have had experience with both banks. The argument for forced choice is that people really do have attitudes, even if they are unfamiliar with a bank, and they should be required to answer the question. Higher incidences of "no answer" are associated with forced-choice questions.

Should a Single Measure or an Index Measure Be Used?   How complex is the issue to be investigated? How many dimensions are there to the issue? Are individual attributes of the stimulus part of a holistic attitude or are they seen as separate items? The researcher's conceptual definition will be helpful in making this choice.

The researcher has many scaling options. The choice is generally influenced by what is planned for the later stages of the research project. Again, problem definition becomes a determining factor influencing the research design.

SUMMARY

Attitude measurement is particularly important in behavioral research. Attitudes are enduring dispositions to respond consistently, in a given manner, to various aspects of the world, including persons, events, and objects. Three components of attitudes are: the affective (emotions or feelings involved), the cognitive (awareness or knowledge), and the behavioral (predisposition to action). Attitudes are hypothetical constructs; that is, they are variables that are not directly observable but are measured indirectly.

Many methods have been developed to measure attitudes. Ranking, rating, sorting, and choice techniques are used to measure attitudes.

One class of rating scales, category scales, provides several response categories to allow respondents to indicate the intensity of their attitudes. The simplest is a yes/no or agree/disagree response to a single question. The Likert scale uses a series of statements for which subjects indicate agreement or disagreement. The responses are assigned weights that are summed to indicate the respondents' attitudes.

The semantic differential uses a series of attitude scales anchored by bipolar adjectives. The respondent indicates where his or her attitude falls on the scale between the polar attitudes. Variations on this method, such as numerical scales and the Stapel scale, are also used. The Stapel scale puts a single adjective in the center of numerical values that range from $+5$ to -5.

Graphic rating scales use a continuum on which respondents indicate the position of their attitude. Constant-sum scales require the respondent to divide a constant sum into parts, indicating the weights to be given to various attributes of the item being studied.

Several scales, such as the behavioral differential, have been developed to measure the behavioral component of an attitude.

People often rank order their preferences. Thus ordinal scales may be developed that ask respondents to rank order a set of objects or attributes. In the paired-comparison technique two alternatives are paired and respondents are asked to pick the one preferred. Sorting requires respondents to indicate their attitudes by arranging items into piles or categories.

The business researcher has a number of choices concerning attitude scales. Making a decision among the alternatives requires that the researcher consider several questions, each of which is generally answered by comparing the advantages of each alternative to the problem definition.

A monadic rating scale asks about a single concept. A comparative rating scale asks a respondent to rate a concept in comparison with a benchmark used as a frame of reference.

Scales may be balanced or unbalanced. Unbalanced scales are used to prevent responses from piling up at one end of the scale. Forced-choice scales require the respondent to select an alternative, whereas nonforced-choice scales provide a category indicating inability to select an alternative.

Key Terms

attitude	semantic differential
affective component	numerical scale
cognitive component	Stapel scale
behavioral component	graphic rating scale
hypothetical construct	behavioral differential
ranking	paired comparisons
rating	constant-sum scale
sorting	monadic rating scale
choice	comparative rating scale
category scale	balanced/unbalanced scales
Likert scale	forced-/nonforced-choice scales

Questions

1. What is an attitude? Is there consensus concerning its definition?
2. Distinguish between rating and ranking. Which is a better attitude measurement? Why?
3. In what type of situation would the choice technique be most appropriate?

4. In what type of situation would the sorting technique be most appropriate?
5. What advantages do numerical scales have over semantic differential scales?
6. Identify the issues a researcher should consider when making a decision about the choice of a measurement scale.
7. Name some situations where a semantic differential might be useful.
8. Should a Likert scale ever be treated as if it had ordinal properties?
9. In each of the following indicate the type of scale and evaluate it:

    a. A U.S. congressman's questionnaire to constituents:
        Do you favor or oppose a return of the military draft?
        Favor □   Oppose □   Don't know □

    b. In an academic study on consumer behavior:
        Most people who are important to me think I

        -3 _____ $+3$

        | definitely | definitely |
        | should not buy | should buy |

        (test brand) some time during the next week.

    c. Psychographic statement:
        I shop a lot for specials.

Strongly Agree	Moderately Agree	Neutral	Moderately Disagree	Strongly Disagree
5	4	3	2	1

10. What problems might be involved in attempting to utilize attitude measures to predict specific behavior?
11. If a Likert summated scale has ten scale items, do all ten items have to be phrased as either positive or negative statements, or can both positive and negative statements be used?
12. If a semantic differential has ten scale items, should all the positive adjectives be on the right and all the negative adjectives on the left?
13. A researcher wishes to compare two hotels on the following attributes: convenience of location, friendly personnel, and value for money. To accomplish this task:

    a. Design a Likert scale.
    b. Design a semantic differential.
    c. Design a graphic rating scale.

References

[1] This section is adapted from "The People, Press, and Politics," a report by the Times Mirror Company, September 1987, 4.

[2] Paul F. Secord and Carl W. Backman, *Social Psychology* (New York: McGraw-Hill, 1964), 98.

[3] Donald S. Tull and Gerald S. Albaum, *Survey Research: A Decisional Approach* (New York: Intex Educational Publishers, 1973), 104–107.

[4] P. C. Smith, L. M. Kendall, and C. L. Hulin, *The Measurement of Satisfaction in Work and Retirement* (Chicago: Rand McNally, 1969).

[5] Louis L. Thurstone, "Law of Comparative Judgment," *Psychological Review* 34 (1927): 273–278.

[6] Rensis Likert, "A Technique for the Measurement of Attitudes," *Archives of Psychology* 19 (1932): 44–53.

[7] See Jacob Jacoby and Michael S. Matell, "Three Point Likert Scales Are Good Enough," *Journal of Marketing Research* (November 1971): 495–506; and Roger Best, Del I. Hawkins, and Gerald Albaum, "The Effort of Varying Response Intervals on the Stability of Factor Solutions of Rating Scale Data," in *Advances in Consumer Research,* Vol. 7, ed. Jerry Olson (San Francisco: ACR, 1979), 539–554.

[8] Joel Huber and Morris B. Holbrook, "Using Attribute Ratings for Product Positioning: Some Distinctions Among Compositional Approaches," reprinted by permission from the *Journal of Marketing Research,* November 1979, p. 510, published by the American Marketing Association.

[9] Charles Osgood, George Suci, and Percy Tannenbaum, *The Measurement of Meaning* (Urbana: University of Illinois Press, 1957).

[10] William A. Mindak, "Fitting the Semantic Differential to the Marketing Problem," *Journal of Marketing* (April 1961): 29–33.

[11] Irving Crespi, "Use of a Scaling Technique in Surveys," *Journal of Marketing* (July 1961): 69–72.

[12] D. I. Hawkins, G. Albaum, and R. Best, "Stapel Scale or Semantic Differential in Marketing Research?" *Journal of Marketing Research* (August 1972): 318–322.

[13] Dennis Menezes and Norbert F. Elbert, "Alternate Semantic Scaling Formats for Measuring Store Image: An Evaluation," *Journal of Marketing Research* (February 1979): 80–87.

[14] Ibid. and Hawkins, Albaum, and Best, "Stapel Scale or Semantic Differential in Marketing Research?"

[15] Russell I. Haley, *Developing Effective Communication Strategy: A Benefit Segmentation Approach* (New York: Ronald Press, 1985), 62.

[16] For a complete discussion of the Thurstone scale, see Paul E. Green and Donald S. Tull, *Research for Marketing Decisions* (Englewood Cliffs, NJ: Prentice-Hall, 1978), 180–187.

[17] Harry C. Triandis, *Attitude and Attitude Change* (New York: Wiley, 1971), 50.

[18] Yoram Wind, Joseph Denny, and Arthur Cunningham, "A Comparison of Three Brand Evaluation Procedures," *Public Opinion Quarterly* (Summer 1979): 263.

[19] R. H. Bruskin Associates, 303 George Street, New Brunswick, NJ. Used by permission.

[20] G. David Hughes, "The Measurement of Beliefs and Attitudes," in *Handbook of Marketing Research,* ed. Robert Ferber (New York: McGraw-Hill, 1974), 30–31.

[21] Fred Cutler, "To Meet Criticisms of TV Ads, Researchers Find New Ways to Measure Children's Attitudes," *Marketing News,* Jan. 27, 1976, 16.

[22] *A General Taxpayer Opinion Survey,* Office of Planning and Research, U.S. Internal Revenue Service, March 1980.

[23] C. Campbell and B. L. Joiner, "How to Get the Answer without Being Sure You've Asked the Question," *American Statistician* 27 (December 1973): 229–231.

Questionnaire Design

What you will
learn in this
chapter:

To recognize that questionnaire design is not a simple task and that proper wording of relevant questions can contribute immensely to improving the accuracy of surveys.

To recognize that the type of information needed to answer a manager's questions will substantially influence the structure and content of questionnaires.

To recognize that decisions about the data collection method (mail, telephone, or personal interview) will influence question format and questionnaire layout.

To recognize the difference between open-ended response and fixed-alternative questions.

To understand the guidelines that help to avoid the most common mistakes in questionnaire design.

To discuss how decisions about the sequence of questions may improve questionnaires.

To understand how to plan and design a questionnaire layout.

To understand the importance of pretesting and revising questionnaires.

An early Gallup Poll illustrates that the answer to a question is frequently a function of the question's wording. "People were asked if they owned any stock. A surprisingly high degree of stock ownership turned up in interviews in the Southwest, where respondents were naturally thinking of livestock. The question had to be reworded to make reference to 'securities listed on any stock exchange.'"[1]

Many experts in survey research believe that improving the wording of questions can contribute far more to accuracy than can improvements in sampling. Experiments have shown that the range of error due to vague questions or use of imprecise words may be as high as 20 or 30 percent. Consider the following example, which illustrates the critical consideration of selecting the word with the right meaning. The following questions differ only in the use of the words should, could, *and* might:

> *Do you think anything **should** be done to make it easier for people to pay doctor or hospital bills?*
>
> *Do you think anything **could** be done to make it easier for people to pay doctor or hospital bills?*
>
> *Do you think anything **might** be done to make it easier for people to pay doctor or hospital bills?[2]*

The results from the matched samples: 82 percent replied something should *be done, 77 percent replied something* could *be done, and 63 percent replied something* might *be done. Thus a 19 percent difference occurred between the two extremes,* should *and* might. *Ironically, this is the same percentage point error as that in the* Literary Digest *Poll, which is a frequently cited example of error associated with sampling.*

This chapter outlines a procedure for questionnaire design and illustrates that a little bit of research knowledge can be a dangerous thing.

■

A SURVEY IS ONLY AS GOOD AS THE QUESTIONS IT ASKS

Each stage of the business research process is important because of its inter-dependent nature. However, a research survey is only as good as the questions it asks. The importance of wording questions is easily overlooked, but questionnaire design is one of the most critical stages in the survey research process.

"A good questionnaire appears as easy to compose as does a good poem. The end product should look as if effortlessly written by an inspired child—but it is usually the result of long, painstaking work."[3] Businesspeople who are in-experienced in business research frequently believe that constructing a questionnaire is a simple task. Amateur researchers find it easy to prepare a short questionnaire in a matter of hours. Unfortunately, newcomers who naively believe that common sense and good grammar are all that is needed to construct a questionnaire generally learn that their hasty efforts are inadequate.

While common sense and good grammar are important in question writing, more is required in the art of questionnaire design. To assume that people will understand the questions is a common error. People simply may not know what is being asked. They may be unaware of the product or topic of interest, they may confuse the subject with something else, or the question may not mean the same thing to everyone interviewed. Respondents may refuse to answer personal questions. Further, properly wording the questionnaire is crucial, as some problems may be minimized or avoided altogether if a skilled researcher composes the questions.

QUESTIONNAIRE DESIGN: AN OVERVIEW OF THE MAJOR DECISIONS

Relevance and *accuracy* are the two basic criteria to be met if the questionnaire is to achieve the researcher's purposes.[4] To achieve these ends, a researcher who plans to systematically design a questionnaire will be required to make several decisions, typically but not necessarily in the order listed below:

1. What should be asked?
2. How should each question be phrased?
3. In what sequence should the questions be arranged?
4. What questionnaire layout will best serve the research objectives?
5. How should the questionnaire be pretested? Does the questionnaire need to be revised?

WHAT SHOULD BE ASKED?

During the early stages of the research process, certain decisions will have been made that will influence the questionnaire design. In preceding chapters the need to have a good problem definition and clear objectives of the study was stressed. The problem definition will indicate which type of information must be collected to answer the manager's questions; different types of questions may be better at obtaining certain types of information than others. Further, the communication medium of data collection—telephone interview, personal interview, or mail survey—will have been determined. This decision is another forward linkage that influences the structure and content of the questionnaire. The specific questions to be asked will be a function of the previous decisions. Later stages of the research process also have an important impact on questionnaire wording. For example, determination of the questions that should be asked will be influenced by the requirements for data analysis. As the questionnaire is being designed, the researcher should be thinking about the types of statistical analysis that will be conducted.

Questionnaire Relevancy

A questionnaire is relevant if no unnecessary information is collected and if the information that is needed to solve the business problem is obtained.

Asking the wrong or an irrelevant question is a pitfall to be avoided. If the task is to pinpoint compensation problems, for example, asking for general information about morale may be inappropriate. To ensure information relevancy, the researcher must be specific about data needs, and there should be a rationale for each item of information.

After conducting surveys, many disappointed researchers have discovered that some important questions were omitted. Thus, when planning the questionnaire design, it is essential to think about possible omissions. Is information being collected on the relevant demographic and psychographic variables? Are there any questions that might clarify the answers to other questions? Will the results of the study provide the solution to the manager's problem?

Questionnaire Accuracy

Once the researcher has decided "what should be asked," the criterion of accuracy becomes the primary concern.

Accuracy means that the information is reliable and valid. While it is generally believed that one should use simple, understandable, unbiased, unambiguous, nonirritating words, no step-by-step procedure to ensure accuracy in question writing can be generalized across projects. Obtaining accurate answers from respondents is strongly influenced by the researcher's ability to design a questionnaire that facilitates recall and that will motivate the respondent to cooperate.

Respondents tend to be most cooperative when the subject of the research is interesting. Also, if questions are not lengthy, difficult to answer, or ego threatening, there is a higher probability of unbiased answers. Question wording and sequence substantially influence accuracy. These topics are treated in subsequent sections of this chapter.

PHRASING QUESTIONS

There are many ways to phrase questions, and many standard question formats have been developed in previous research studies. This section presents a classification of question types and provides some helpful guidelines to researchers who must write questions.

Open-Ended Response versus Fixed-Alternative Questions

We may categorize two basic types of questions according to the amount of freedom respondents are given in answering questions. **Open-ended response questions** pose some problem or topic and ask the respondent to answer in his or her own words. For example:

What things do you like most about your job?

What names of local banks can you think of offhand?

What comes to mind when you look at this advertisement?

Do you think that there are some ways in which life in the United States is getting worse? How is that?

If the question is asked in a personal interview, the interviewer may probe for more information by asking such questions as: Anything else? or Could you tell me more about your thinking on that? Open-ended response questions are free-answer questions. They may be contrasted to the **fixed-alternative question,** sometimes called "closed question," in which the respondent is given specific, limited alternative responses and asked to choose the one closest to his or her own viewpoint. For example:

Did you work overtime or at more than one job last week?

Yes ____   No ____

Compared to ten years ago, would you say that the quality of most products made in Japan is higher, about the same, or not as good?

Higher ____   About the same ____   Not as good ____

How much of your shopping for clothes and household items do you do in discount stores? Would you say:

All of it ____

Most of it ____

About half of it ____

About one-quarter of it ____

Less than one-quarter of it ____

In management, is there a useful distinction between what is legal and what is ethical?

Yes ____   No ____

In Aesop's fable "The Ant and the Grasshopper," the ant spent his time working and planning for the future, while the grasshopper lived for the moment and enjoyed himself. Which are you more like?

1. The ant
2. The grasshopper

Open-ended response questions are most beneficial when the researcher is conducting exploratory research, especially if the range of responses is not known. Open-ended questions can be used to learn what words and phrases people spontaneously give to the free-response questions. Respondents are free to answer with whatever is uppermost in their thinking. By gaining free and uninhibited responses, the researchers may find some unanticipated reaction toward the topic. As the responses have the "flavor" of the conversational language that people use in talking about products or jobs, responses to these questions may be a source for effective communication.

Open-ended response questions are especially valuable at the beginning of an interview. They are good first questions because they allow respondents to warm up to the questioning process.

The cost of open-ended response questions is substantially greater than that of fixed-alternative questions, because the job of coding, editing, and analyzing the data is quite extensive. As each respondent's answer is somewhat unique, there is some difficulty in categorizing and summarizing the answers. This process requires an editor to go over a sample of questions to classify the responses into a given scheme. Then all the answers are reviewed and coded according to the classification scheme.

Another potential disadvantage of the open-ended response question is that interviewer bias may influence the responses. While most instructions state that the interviewer is to record answers verbatim, rarely can even the best interviewers get every word spoken by the respondent. Thus there is a tendency for interviewers to take short cuts in recording answers, and a few words that are different from the respondents' may substantially influence the results. Thus the final answer often is a combination of the respondent's and the interviewer's ideas rather than the respondent's ideas alone.

When using open-ended response questions, we find articulate individuals tend to give longer answers. These articulate respondents, who have a tendency to be better educated and in higher-income groups, may not be representative of the entire population. Contrasted with open-ended questions, **fixed-alternative questions** require less interviewer skill, take less time, and are easier for the respondent to answer. This occurs because closed questions require classification of the answer into standardized groupings prior to data collection. Standardizing alternative responses to a question provides comparability of answers, which facilitates coding, tabulating, and, ultimately, interpreting the data.

Our earlier examples of fixed-alternative questions portrayed a variety of this type of question. We will now identify and categorize the various types of fixed-alternative questions.

The **simple-dichotomy** or **dichotomous-alternative question** requires the respondent to choose one of two alternatives. The answer can be a simple "yes" or "no" or a choice between "this" and "that." For example:

Did you make any long-distance calls last week?

☐ **Yes**   ☐ **No**

Several types of questions provide the respondent with *multiple-choice alternatives*. The **determinant-choice question** requires the respondent to choose one—and only one—response from among several possible alternatives. For example:

Please give us some information about your flight. In which section of the aircraft did you sit?

☐   **First class**
☐   **Business class**
☐   **Coach class**

The **frequency-determination question** is a determinate-choice question that asks for an answer about general frequency of occurrence. For example:

How frequently do you watch the MTV television channel?

Every day . . . . ☐
5–6 times a week . . . . ☐
2–4 times a week . . . . ☐
Once a week . . . . ☐
Less than once a week . . . . ☐
Never . . . . ☐

Attitude rating scales, such as the Likert scale, semantic differential, and Stapel scale, are also fixed-alternative questions. These were discussed in Chapter 12.

The **checklist question** allows the respondent to provide multiple answers to a single question. The respondent indicates past experience, preference, and the like merely by checking off an item. In many cases the choices are adjectives that describe a particular object. A typical checklist follows:

Please check which of the following sources of information about investments you regularly use, if any.

☐   **Personal advice of your broker(s)**
☐   **Brokerage newsletters**
☐   **Brokerage research reports**
☐   **Investment advisory service(s)**
☐   **Conversations with other investors**
☐   **Your own study and intuition**
☐   **None of these**
☐   **Other (please specify)** _____

A major problem in developing dichotomous or multiple-choice alternatives is framing the response alternatives. There should be no overlap among categories. Each alternative should be *mutually exclusive,* that is, only one dimension of the issue should be related to that alternative. The following listing of income groups illustrates a common error:

Under $15,000 ___
$15,000–$30,000 ___

$30,000–$55,000 ____
$55,000–$70,000 ____
Over $70,000 ____

How many people with incomes of $30,000 will be in the second group and how many will be in the third group? We would not know the answer. Alternatives grouped without forethought about analysis may cause loss of accuracy.

It should also be noted that few people relish being in the lowest category. Including a category lower than the answers you expect often helps to negate the potential bias caused by respondents avoiding an extreme category.

When the researcher is unaware of the potential responses to a question, fixed-alternative questions obviously cannot be used. If the researcher assumes what the responses might be but is in fact wrong, he or she will have no way of knowing the extent to which the assumption was incorrect.

Unanticipated alternatives emerge when respondents think the closed answers do not adequately reflect their feelings. Comments are made to the interviewer or additional answers are written on the mail questionnaire, indicating that the exploratory research did not yield a complete array of responses. After the fact, not much can be done to correct a closed question with some alternatives missing; therefore the time spent conducting exploratory research with open-ended response questions is well worth the effort. The researcher should strive to ensure that there are sufficient response choices to include almost all possible answers.

Respondents may check off obvious alternatives, such as price or durability, if they do not see their "individualized" answer to a question listed. Thus a fixed-alternative question may tempt respondents to check an answer that is untrue but perhaps more prestigious or socially acceptable. Rather than stating they do not know why they choose a given product, they may select an alternative among those presented. Or, as a matter of convenience, they may select a given alternative rather than give thought to the most correct alternative.

Most questionnaires include a mixture of open-ended and closed questions. Each form has unique benefits; in addition, respondent boredom and fatigue are eliminated with a change of pace.

Phrasing Questions for Mail, Telephone, and Personal Interview Surveys

The means of data collection (mail, telephone, or personal interviews) will influence the question format and question phrasing. In general, mail and telephone questions must be less complex than those utilized in personal interviews. Questionnaires for telephone and personal interviews should be written in a "conversational" manner. Exhibit 13.1 illustrates how a question may be revised for a different medium.

Consider the following question from a personal interview:

Recently there has been a lot of discussion about the potential health threat to nonsmokers from tobacco smoke in public buildings, restaurants, and business

Mail Form:

How satisfied are you with your community?

1. **Very satisfied**
2. **Quite satisfied**
3. **Somewhat satisfied**
4. **Slightly satisfied**
5. **Neither satisfied nor dissatisfied**
6. **Slightly dissatisfied**
7. **Somewhat dissatisfied**
8. **Quite dissatisfied**
9. **Very dissatisfied**

Revised for Telephone:

**How satisfied are you with your community? Would you say you are
very satisfied, somewhat satisfied, neither satisfied nor dissatisfied,
somewhat dissatisfied, or very dissatisfied?**

Very satisfied	**1**
Somewhat satisfied	**2**
Neither satisfied nor dissatisfied	**3**
Somewhat dissatisfied	**4**
Very dissatisfied	**5**

Source: Don A. Dillman, *Mail and Telephone Surveys: The Total Design Method* (New York: John Wiley & Sons, 1978), p. 209. Reprinted with permission.

offices. How serious a health threat to you personally is the inhaling of this secondhand smoke, often called passive smoking: Is it a very serious health threat, somewhat serious, not too serious, or not serious at all?

1. Very serious
2. Somewhat serious
3. Not too serious
4. Not serious at all
5. (Don't know)

You probably noticed that the last portion of the question was a listing of the four alternatives that serve as answers. This listing at the end is often used in interviews to serve as a reminder of alternatives to the respondent who does not have any visual material portraying the choices. The fifth alternative (Don't know) is in parentheses because, although it is known to the interviewer as an acceptable answer, it is not read because the researcher prefers to "force" the respondent to choose among the four listed alternatives.

The data collection technique also influences the layout of the questionnaire. This will be discussed in a later section of this chapter.

THE ART OF ASKING QUESTIONS[5]

In developing a questionnaire, there are no hard-and-fast rules. Fortunately, however, some guidelines that help to avoid the most common mistakes have been developed from research experience.

RESEARCH INSIGHT
"I Don't Understand the Question"

1. The company should continue its excellent fringe benefit programs.
   a. Yes
   b. No

COMMENT: The fringe benefit programs may not be excellent at all. By answering "yes," the respondent is implying that things are just fine as they are. By answering "no," he implies that the company should discontinue the fringe benefits. Don't place the respondent in that sort of a bind.

BETTER: *How satisfied are you with the company's fringe benefit programs?*
   a. *Very satisfied*
   b. *Somewhat satisfied*
   c. *Neither satisfied nor dissatisfied*
   d. *Somewhat dissatisfied*
   e. *Very dissatisfied*

2. Do you understand and like the company's new hiring policy?
   a. Yes
   b. No

COMMENT: There are really two questions here:
(1) Do you understand the company's new hiring policy?
(2) Do you like it?
The answers to the original question are ambiguous.

BETTER: *Do you like the company's new hiring policy?*
   a. *I don't know what the company policy is.*
   b. *I don't like it.*
   c. *I neither like nor dislike it.*
   d. *I like it.*

3. Your supervisor is handling the frequent and serious problems with work quality better now than six months ago.
   a. Strongly disagree
   b. Disagree
   c. Neither agree nor disagree
   d. Agree
   e. Strongly agree

COMMENT: The statement automatically puts respondents in a box, since it assumes that there are frequent serious problems with their work groups' work quality.

BETTER: *Compared with six months ago, how well does your supervisor handle difficult work-related problems?*
   a. *Much better*
   b. *Somewhat better*
   c. *About the same*
   d. *Somewhat worse*
   e. *Much worse*

4. What makes your job a good one?
   a. The good pay
   b. The opportunity for advancement
   c. A good supervisor
   d. Interesting work

COMMENT: This question assumes that the employee's job is a good one, while the employee may not feel that it is particularly good. There is no provision for selecting one or more than one of the choices. If you really want to find out what the employee likes best about his job, you may want to ask an open-ended question. Or you may need to ask a series of questions about different aspects of the job.

BETTER: *What do you like best about your job?*
   a. *The pay*
   b. *The opportunities for advancement*
   c. *The working conditions*
   d. *The people you work with*
   e. *Your supervisor*
   f. *The work*
   g. *The fringe benefits program*

Source: Gloria E. Wheeler, "'Yes; No; All of the Above,' Before You Conduct a Survey," *Exchange* (Spring-Summer 1979), p. 21. Published by Brigham Young University School of Management. Reprinted with permission.

Avoid Complexity: Use Simple, Conversational Language

Words used in questionnaires should be readily understandable to all respondents. The researcher usually has the difficult task of using the conversational language of people from the lowest educational levels without "talking down" to better-educated respondents. Remember, not all people have the vocabulary of a college student. A substantial number of Americans never go beyond high school.

Respondents may be able to tell an interviewer whether they are married, single, divorced, separated, or widowed, but providing their "marital status" may present a problem. Also, the technical jargon of corporate executives should be avoided when surveying retailers, factory employees, or industrial users. Marginal analysis, decision support systems, and words from the language of the corporate staff will not have the same meaning to—or be understood by—the owner-operator in a retail survey. The vocabulary in the following question (from an attitude survey on social problems) is probably confusing for many respondents:

When effluents from a paper mill can be drunk and exhaust from factory smokestacks can be breathed, then man will have done a good job in saving the environment. . . . What we want is zero toxicity; no effluents?

This lengthy question also tends to be a leading question.

Avoid Leading and Loaded Questions

Asking leading and loaded questions is a major source of bias in question wording. **Leading questions** suggest or imply certain answers. In a study of the dry-cleaning industry, this question was asked:

Many people are using dry cleaning less because of improved wash-and-wear clothes. How do you feel wash-and-wear clothes have affected your use of dry-cleaning facilities in the past four years?

    ____ Use less   ____ No change   ____ Use more

The potential "bandwagon effect" implied in this question threatens the study's validity.

Loaded questions are slanted with social desirability or biased with emotional charge. Consider the following:

In light of today's savings and loan crisis, it would be in the public's best interest to have the federal government offer low-interest loans to insolvent savings and loan organizations.

    ____ Strongly   ____ Agree   ____ Uncertain   ____ Disagree   ____ Strongly
    Agree   Disagree

A different answer might be given if the loaded portion of the statement, "savings and loan crisis," had another wording suggesting an insolvency problem of less magnitude than a crisis.

A television station produced a ten-second spot to ask the following question:

We are happy when you like programs on Channel 7. We are sad when you dislike programs on Channel 7. Write us and let us know what you think of our programming.

Most people do not wish to make others sad. This question invites only positive comments.

Some answers to certain questions are more socially desirable than others. For example, a truthful answer to the following classification question might be painful:

Where did you rank academically in your high school graduating class?

Top quarter   2nd quarter   3rd quarter   4th quarter

When taking personality tests, respondents frequently are able to determine which answers are most socially acceptable, even though the answers do not portray the respondents' true feelings. For example, which are the socially desirable answers for the following questions on a self-confidence scale?

I feel capable of handling myself in most social situations.

____ Agree   ____ Disagree

I seldom fear my actions will cause others to have a low opinion of me.

____ Agree   ____ Disagree

Invoking the status quo is a form of loading that results in bias because the majority of respondents tend to be resistant to change.[6]

An experiment conducted in the early days of polling illustrates the unpopularity of *changing*.[7] Comparable samples of respondents were simultaneously asked two questions about the presidential succession. One sample was asked: **"Would you favor or oppose *adding* a law to the Constitution preventing a president from succeeding himself more than once?"** The other sample was asked: **"Would you favor or oppose *changing* the Constitution in order to prevent a president from succeeding himself more than once?"** To the first question 50 percent of the respondents answered in the negative; to the second question 65 percent answered in the negative. Thus the public would rather *add to* than *change* the Constitution.

Partial mention of alternatives is another form of loading.

Building more nuclear power plants, like Three Mile Island, should not be allowed.

How do you generally spend your free time, watching television or what?[8]

Are you familiar with any companies that currently recycle aluminum, such as Coors?

Asking respondents "how often" they use a product or perform a task leads them to generalize about their behavior, because there usually is some variance in their behavior. One is likely to portray one's *ideal* behavior rather than one's average behavior. For instance, brushing one's teeth after each meal ought to be adhered to, but if one is busy, a brushing or two may be skipped. An introductory statement, or preamble, to a question that reassures the respondent that his embarrassing behavior is not abnormal may yield truthful responses: **"Some people have the time to brush three times daily; others do not. Would you please tell me how often you brushed your teeth yesterday?"**

In a survey of college professors, the question below asked them to record both actual and ideal amounts of time they spend on professional activities. This reduces the tendency to idealize the actual amount of time spent in professional activities.

Please indicate (A) your estimate of the actual percentage of time you spend on professional activities during the academic year, and (B) what you consider to be the ideal division of your time as a university professor.

Percentage of Time		
A—Actual	**B—Ideal**	
		Formal instruction (including preparation, presentation, grading, etc.)
		Informal instruction, advisement, student counseling
		Scholarly research and writing
		Academic administration
		Part-time professional employment outside the university (e.g., private practice, consulting)
		Professional activities outside the university (e.g., speaking, conferences, professional association duties)
100%	**100%**	

If a question embarrasses the respondent, it may elicit no answer or a biased response. This is particularly true with personal and classification data such as income and education. This problem may be mitigated by introducing the section of the questionnaire with a **counterbiasing statement** such as: "To help classify your answers, we'd like to ask you a few questions. Again, your answers will be kept in strict confidence."

A positive statement may be leading because it is phrased to reflect either the negative or positive aspects of the issue. To control for this bias, the wording of attitudinal questions may be reversed for 50 percent of the sample. This **split ballot technique** is utilized with the expectation that two alternative phrasings of the same question will yield a more accurate total response than would be possible with only a single phrasing. For example, in a study on small-car-buying behavior, one-half of the imported-car purchasers received a questionnaire in which the statement read: **"Small U.S. cars are cheaper to maintain than small imported cars."** The other half of the imported-car owners received a questionnaire in which the statement read: **"Small imported cars are cheaper to maintain than small U.S. cars."**

Avoid Ambiguity: Be as Specific as Possible

Items on questionnaires are often ambiguous because they are too general. Consider indefinite words such as *often, occasionally, usually, regularly, frequently, many, good, fair,* and *poor.* Each of these words has many meanings. For one person, *frequent* reading of *Fortune* magazine may be six or seven issues a year; for another, twice a year. A great variety of meanings is attributed to *fair.* The same is true for many indefinite words.

Questions such as the following should be interpreted with care:

How often do you feel that you can consider the alternatives before making a decision to follow a specific course of action?

____ **Always**   ____ **Fairly   ____ Occasionally   ____ Seldom   ____ Never**
                 often

In addition to utilizing words like *occasionally,* this question asks the managers to generalize about their decision-making behavior. The question is not specific. What does *consider* mean? The respondents may have a tendency to provide stereotyped "good" management responses rather than to describe their actual behavior. People's memories are not perfect. We tend to remember the good and forget the bad.

Another example of an ambiguous question is: **"Do you usually work alone?"** It would be less ambiguous if the question were restated to something like:

Which of the following best describes your working behavior?

I never work alone.
I work alone less than half the time.
I work alone most of the time.

Similarly, the following question may be important to the researcher: **"How difficult is it for you to get the necessary information about divisional or company objectives or goals for decision making?"** The term *necessary information* is highly subjective. It could be interpreted to mean the *minimum* necessary information or the *optimal* necessary information.

Which of the following is ambiguous?

If something happens that puts your immediate supervisor "on the spot," what is he most likely to do?

Should managers be held personally responsible for the wrongdoings of corporations?

As the reader can tell, question ambiguity is a pervasive problem. It is not easily eliminated.

Some scholars have suggested that the rate of diffusion of an innovation is related to the perception of the innovation's attributes, such as divisibility,[9] which refers to the extent to which an innovation may be tried or tested on a limited scale. An empirical attempt to test this theory by using semantic differentials was a disaster. Pretesting found the bipolar adjectives, *divisible—not divisible,* were impossible for respondents to understand because they did not have the theory in mind as a frame of reference. A revision of the scale used these bipolar adjectives:

Testable __ : __ : __ : __ : __ : __ : __ Not Testable
(sample use   (sample use not
  possible)   possible)

But the question remained ambiguous because the meaning still was not clear.

A brewing industry study on point-of-purchase displays asked:

What degree of durability do you prefer in your point-of-purchase advertising?

____ **Permanent (lasting more than six months)**

____ **Semipermanent (lasting from one to six months)**

____ **Temporary (lasting less than one month)**

Here the researchers clarified the terms *permanent, semipermanent,* and *temporary* by defining them for the respondent. However, the question remains somewhat ambiguous. Beer companies often use a variety of point-of-purchase devices to serve different purposes. Which purpose was the researcher asking about?

Further, a disadvantage in analysis exists because mere preference is given and not any rating of the degree of preference. Thus the meaning of questions may not be clear because there is an inadequate frame of reference for interpreting the context of the question.[10] A student research group asked this question:

What one of these media do you rely on most?

Television ____   AM radio ____   FM radio ____   Newspapers ____

This question is ambiguous because it does not ask about the content of the media. Rely on most for *what*—news, sports, entertainment?

Avoid Double-Barreled Items

A question covering several issues at once is referred to as **double-barreled** and should always be avoided. It's easy to make the mistake of asking two questions rather than one. For example, **"Please indicate your degree of agreement with the following statement: 'Wholesalers and retailers are responsible for the high cost of meat.'"** Which middlemen are responsible, the wholesalers or the retailers? When multiple questions are asked in one question, the results may be exceedingly difficult to interpret. For example, consider the following question from a *Redbook* survey entitled "How Do You Feel about Being a Woman?"

Between you and your husband, who does the housework (cleaning, cooking, dishwashing, laundry) over and above that done by any hired help?

I do all of it	47.0%
I do almost all of it	35.6%
I do over half of it	12.1%

| We split the work fifty-fifty | 4.7% |
| My husband does over half of it | 0.6% |

The answers to this question do not tell us if the wife cooks and the husband dries the dishes.

Another survey, by a university library, asked:

Are you satisfied with the present system of handling "closed-reserve" and "open-reserve" readings? (Are enough copies available? Are the required materials ordered promptly? Are the borrowing regulations adequate for students' use of materials?) ____ Yes ____ No

Here a respondent may feel torn between a "Yes" to one part of the question and a "No" to another part. The answer to this question does not tell the researchers which problem or combination of problems concerns the library user.

Consider this very appropriate comment about double-barreled questions:

Generally speaking, it is hard enough to get answers to one idea at a time without complicating the problem by asking what amounts to two questions at once. If two ideas are to be explored, they deserve at least two questions. Since question marks are not rationed, there is little excuse for the needless confusion that results in the double-barreled question.[11]

Avoid Making Assumptions
Consider the following question:

Should Macy's continue its excellent gift-wrapping program?

☐ **Yes**   ☐ **No**

There is a built-in assumption to this question. The question contains the implicit assumption that people believe the gift-wrapping program is excellent. By answering yes, the respondent implies that things are just fine as they are. By answering no, he or she implies that the store should discontinue the gift wrapping. The researcher should not place the respondent in that sort of bind by including an implicit assumption in the question.[12]

Another mistake that question writers sometimes make is assuming that the respondent has previously thought about an issue. For example, the following question appeared in a survey concerning Jack-in-the-Box restaurants: **"Do you think Jack-in-the-Box restaurants should consider changing their name?"** It is not at all likely that the respondent has thought about this question before being asked to answer it. Most respondents will answer the question even though they had no prior opinion concerning the name change of Jack-in-the-Box. Research that induces people to express attitudes on subjects they do not ordinarily think about is meaningless.

WHAT IS THE BEST QUESTION SEQUENCE?

The order of questions, or the question sequence, may serve several functions for the researcher. If the opening questions are interesting, simple to comprehend, and easy to answer, respondents' cooperation and involvement can be

R E S E A R C H   I N S I G H T
One or Two Questions?

This study was a part of an ongoing series of "research-on-research" investigations. Its purpose was to establish an accurate means of measuring rate of purchase. As in other such studies, it involved demographically matched samples of households, with each sample receiving a different treatment. Self-administered questionnaires were mailed to female heads of households, and purchase data were obtained for the following products: all-purpose white glue, aspirin, replacement automobile tires, and record albums.

Two different ways of asking the purchase incidence questions were investigated. Alternative A was sent to a sample of 1,000 homes; Alternative B was sent to another sample of 1,000 homes. The samples were closely matched in terms of age, income, geography, and city size. Here is a sample pair of questions:

Alternative A

Below are listed several products. Please "X" each product you or anyone in your household *bought* in the PAST THREE MONTHS.

Alternative B

Below are listed several products. Please "X" each product you or anyone in your household *ever bought*. For each product ever bought, "X" the box that best describes when the product was *purchased most recently:*
☐ Within the past 3 months
☐ 4–6 months ago
☐ 7–12 months ago
☐ Over 12 months ago

Here are the results:

Purchase within Past 3 Months

	A 1-Step Question	B 2-Step Question	Percentage Point Difference
White glue	46%	32%	+14
Aspirin	68	57	+11
Replacement auto tires	32	24	+8
Record album	41	32	+9
Number of respondents	(800)	(800)	

Source: Omar J. Bendikas, "One-step Questionnaire May Overstate Response; Two-step Questionnaires Hike Involvement, Accuracy," adapted by permission from the *Marketing News*, May 18, 1979, p. 9, published by the American Marketing Association.

maintained throughout the questionnaire. Asking easy-to-answer questions teaches respondents their role and allows them to build confidence; they know this is a researcher and not another salesperson posing as an interviewer. If respondents' curiosity is not aroused at the outset, they can become disinterested and terminate the interview. A mail research expert reports that a mail survey among department store buyers drew an extremely poor return.[13] However, when some introductory questions related to the advisability of congressional action on pending legislation, of great importance to these buyers, were placed first on the questionnaire, a substantial improvement in response rate occurred. Respondents completed all the questions, not only those of the opening section.

In their attempts to "warm up" respondents toward the questionnaire, student researchers frequently ask demographic or classificatory questions at the beginning of the questionnaire. This is generally not advisable because asking personal information, such as income level or education, may be embarrassing or threatening to respondents. It is generally better to ask embarrassing questions at the middle or end of the questionnaire, after a rapport has been established between respondent and interviewer.

Order Bias

In political elections where candidates do not have high visibility, such as county commissioner and judgeship elections, the first name listed on an election ballot often receives the highest percentage of votes. For this reason many election boards print several ballots so that each candidate's name appears in every possible position (order) on the ballot.

Order bias can distort survey results. **Order bias** results from an alternative answer's position in a set of answers or from the sequencing of questions. If questions about a specific clothing store are asked prior to questions concerning the criteria in selecting a clothing store, respondents who state that they shop at a store where parking needs to be improved may also state that parking is not as important a factor as they really believe it is, to prevent appearing inconsistent. Specific questions may thus influence the more general ones. It is therefore advisable to ask general questions before specific questions in order to obtain the freest of open-ended responses. Known as the **funnel technique,** this procedure allows the researcher to understand the respondent's frame of reference before asking more specific questions about the respondent's particular level of information and intensity of opinions.

Consider the possibility that later answers may be biased by previous questions in this questionnaire on environmental pollution:

Circle the number that best expresses your feelings about the severity of each environmental problem:

Problem	Not a Problem				Very Severe Problem
Air pollution from automobile exhausts	1	2	3	4	5
Air pollution from open burning	1	2	3	4	5
Air pollution from industrial smoke	1	2	3	4	5
Air pollution from foul odors	1	2	3	4	5
Noise pollution from airplanes	1	2	3	4	5
Noise pollution from cars, trucks, motorcycles	1	2	3	4	5
Noise pollution from industry	1	2	3	4	5

It is not surprising that researchers found that responses to each air pollution question were highly correlated, almost identical.

Further, when one is using attitude scales, there may be an *anchoring effect.* The first concept measured tends to become a comparison point with which subsequent evaluations are made.[14] Randomization of these items on a questionnaire of this type helps minimize order bias.

A related problem concerns the order of the alternatives on closed questions. To avoid this problem, the order of these choices should be rotated if alternative forms of the questionnaire are possible. However, business researchers rarely print alternative questionnaires to eliminate problems resulting from order bias. A more common practice is to pencil in Xs or check marks on printed questionnaires to indicate that the interviewer should start a series of repetitive questions at a certain point. For example, the capitalized phrase and sentence in the following question provide instructions to the interviewer to "rotate" brands:

I would like to determine how likely you would be to buy certain brands of candy in the future. Let's start with (X'ED BRAND) in the future. (RECORD BELOW UNDER APPROPRIATE BRAND. REPEAT QUESTIONS FOR ALL REMAINING BRANDS.)

START HERE:	( ) Mounds	(x) Almond Joy	( ) York Peppermint Patties
Definitely would buy	−1	−1	−1
Probably would buy	−2	−2	−2
Might or might not buy	−3	−3	−3
Probably would not buy	−4	−4	−4
Definitely would not buy	−5	−5	−5

Asking a question that doesn't apply to the respondent or that the respondent is not qualified to answer may be irritating or may cause a biased response because the respondent wishes to please the interviewer or to avoid embarrassment. Including a **filter question** minimizes the asking of questions that may be inapplicable. Asking **"Where do you generally have check-cashing problems in Springfield?"** may elicit a response even though the respondent has not had any check-cashing problems and may simply wish to please the interviewer with an answer. A filter question such as

Do you ever have a problem cashing a check in Springfield?

____ Yes   ____ No

would screen out the people who are not qualified to answer. Exhibit 13.2 gives an example of a flowchart plan for a questionnaire that uses filter questions.

Another form of filter question, the **pivot question,** can be used to obtain income information and other data that respondents may be reluctant to provide. For example, a respondent is asked

"Is your total family income over $25,000?" If under, ask, "Is it over or under $15,000?"; If over, ask, "Is it over or under $45,000?"

1. Under $15,000
2. $15,000–$25,000
3. $25,000–$45,000
4. Over $45,000

EXHIBIT   13.2   **Flow of Questions to Determine Level of Prompting Required to Stimulate Recall**

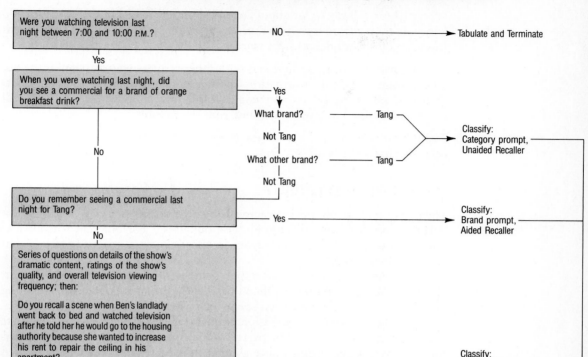

Source: F. Steward DeBruicker and Scott Ward, *Cases in Consumer Behavior,* 1980, p. 217, Prentice Hall, Inc., Englewood Cliffs, NJ. Reprinted with permission of F. Steward DeBruicker.

Structuring the order of questions so that they are logical is another technique to ensure the respondent's cooperation and eliminates any confusion or indecision. The researcher maintains legitimacy when the respondent can comprehend the relationship between a given question (or section of the questionnaire) and the overall purpose of the study. Further, a logical order may aid the individual's memory. Transitional comments explaining the logic of the questionnaire may help guarantee the respondent's continuation. Here are some examples:

We have been talking so far about general shopping habits in this city. Now I'd like you to compare two types of department stores—regular department stores and discount department stores.

So that I can combine your answers with other farmers who are similar to you, I need some personal information about you. Your answers to these questions—as all of the others you've answered—are confidential, and you will never be identified to anyone without your permission.

Thanks for your help so far. If you'll answer the remaining questions, it will help me analyze all your answers.

WHAT IS THE BEST LAYOUT?

The layout and the physical attractiveness of the questionnaire is of crucial importance in self-administered mail questionnaires.[15] For different reasons it is also important to have a good layout in questionnaires designed for personal and telephone interviews.

Exhibit 13.3 presents a short, postcard questionnaire. The layout is neat, attractive, and easy to follow. Often the rate of return can be increased by using the money that might have been spent on an incentive to improve the attractiveness and quality of the questionnaire. An expert in mail surveys suggests questionnaires should never be overcrowded, space should be provided to ensure decent margins, white space should be used to separate solidly printed blocks, and the unavoidable columns of multiple boxes should be kept to a minimum.

Questionnaires should be designed to appear as brief and small as possible. Sometimes it is advisable to use a booklet-form questionnaire, rather than a large number of pages stapled together.

In situations where it is necessary to conserve space on the questionnaire or to facilitate entering the data into a computer or tabulating the data, a multiple-grid layout may be used. In this type of layout, a question is asked, followed by instructions directing the respondent to check the categories as they appear in a grid format. For example:

Airlines often offer special-fare promotions. On a business trip, would you take a connecting flight instead of a nonstop flight if the connecting fare were lower?

	Yes	No	Not Sure
One hour longer?	☐	☐	☐
Two hours longer?	☐	☐	☐
Three hours longer?	☐	☐	☐

Experienced researchers have found it pays to carefully phrase the title to be printed on the questionnaire. In self-administered and mail questionnaires,

EXHIBIT   13.3

**A Good Format for a
Postcard Questionnaire**

Directions: For each question, please check (✔) the appropriate box. Where there is a slash (/) separating two words, circle the appropriate word.

1. Who types your manuscripts?
   ☐ Self   ☐ Word Processing Center   ☐ Secretary
   ☐ Typing Service
   ☐ Other (specify) _____

2. Is Word Processing equipment/service available to you for preparation of your manuscript?
   ☐ YES, what kind? Manufacturer (Model) _____
   ☐ NO   Word Processor software program _____

   If you answered **YES** to Q2—Continue with **Question 3**

   If you answered **NO** to Q2—Go to **Question 6**

3. If Word Processing equipment/service is available to you, do you use it in preparing manuscript?
   ☐ YES   ☐ NO, reason: _____

4. Where is the Word Processing terminal located? ☐ Home   ☐ Office
   ☐ Department (shared/not shared)   ☐ Institution
   ☐ Other (specify): _____

5. Who owns/leases the Word Processing equipment/service?
   ☐ Self   ☐ Institution   ☐ Department   ☐ Dept. rents from institution
   ☐ Other (specify): _____

6. Will Word Processing equipment/service be available to you in the next 18 months?
   ☐ YES, who will own/lease?
          ☐ Self
   ☐ NO   ☐ Department   ☐ Institution
          ☐ Other (specify): _____

Thank You for Your Cooperation

Name: _____
Address: _____
Area(s) of Specialization _____
School: _____ State: _____
Department: _____ Phone: (   ) _____

Source: Holt, Rinehart and Winston, Inc.

a carefully constructed title may underline the importance of the research (Nationwide Study of Blood Donors), emphasize the interesting nature of the study (Study of Women in Accounting), appeal to the respondent's ego (Survey among Top Executives), or emphasize the confidential nature of the study (A Confidential Survey among . . .).

To avoid any negative influence from the wording of the title, the researchers should take steps to ensure that the title does not bias the respondent the same way a leading question may.

When an interviewer is to administer the questionnaire, the analyst can design the questionnaire to make the job of following interconnected questions much easier by utilizing several forms, instructions, and tricks of the trade.

E X H I B I T 1 3 . 4 **Telephone Questionnaire**

1. Did you take the car you had checked to the Standard Auto Repair Center for repairs?
   15 ____ 1 Yes (Skip to Q. 3) ____ 2 No

2. (If no, ask:) Did you have the repair work done?
   16 ____ 1 Yes ____ 2 No
   ↓ ↓

   1. Where was the repair work done?   1. Why didn't you have the car repaired?
   _____ 17   _____ 21
                                                 _____ 22
   2. Why didn't you have the repair work done   _____ 23
       at the Standard Auto Repair Center? ____
   _____ 18
   _____ 19
   _____ 20

3. (If yes to Q. 1, ask:) How satisfied were you with the repair work? Were you . . .
   24 ____ 1 Very satisfied
   ____ 2 Somewhat satisfied
   ____ 3 Somewhat dissatisfied
   ____ 4 Very dissatisfied
   (If somewhat or very dissatisfied:) In what way were you dissatisfied?
   _____ 25
   _____ 26
   _____ 27

4. (Ask everyone:) Do you ever buy gas at the 95th Street Standard Center?
   28 ____ 1 Yes ____ 2 No (Skip to Q. 6)

5. (If yes, ask:) How often do you buy gas there?
   29 ____ 1 Always
   ____ 2 Almost always
   ____ 3 Most of the time
   ____ 4 Part of the time
   ____ 5 Hardly ever

6. Have you ever had your car washed there? 30 ____ 1 Yes ____ 2 No
7. Have you ever had an oil change or lubrication done there? ____ 1 Yes ____ 2 No

---

Exhibits 13.4 and 13.5 illustrate portions of telephone and personal interview questionnaires. Note how the layout and easy-to-follow instructions for interviewers in Exhibit 13.4 (e.g., questions) help the interviewer follow the question sequence. The series of questions in Exhibit 13.4 may facilitate "skip" questions. Either instructions to skip or an arrow drawn to the next question is provided to help the respondent (or the interviewer) know which question comes next.

Note that Questions 3 and 6 in Exhibit 13.5 instruct the interviewer to hand the respondent a card that bears a list of alternatives. Cards may aid respondents to grasp the intended meaning of the question and to help them remember all the brand names or list of items. Also, Questions 2, 3, and 6 instruct the interviewer to start the bank ratings with the bank that has been red-checked in pencil on the printed questionnaire. The name of the red-checked bank is not the same on every questionnaire. By rotating the order of the check marks, the researchers attempt to reduce order bias caused by respondents reacting more

EXHIBIT   13.5   **Personal Interview**

"Hello, my name is _____. I'm a Public Opinion Interviewer with Research Services, Inc. We're making an opinion survey about Banks and Banking, and I'd like to ask you. . . ."

1. What are the names of local banks you can think of offhand? (INTERVIEWER: List names in order mentioned.)
   a. _____
   b. _____
   c. _____
   d. _____
   e. _____
   f. _____
   g. _____

2. Thinking now about the experiences you have had with the different banks here in Boulder . . . have you ever talked to or done business with . . . (INTERVIEWER: Insert name of bank name red-checked below.)
   a. Are you personally acquainted with any of the employees or officers at _____?
   b. (If YES) Who is that?
   c. How long has it been since you have been inside _____?
       (INTERVIEWER: Now go back and repeat 2-2c for all other banks listed.)

	(2) Talked		(2a and 2b) Know Employee or Officer		(2c) Been in Bank in:				
	Yes	No	No	Name	Last Year	1–5	5-Plus	No	DK
Boulder National Bank	1	2	1	_____	1	2	3	4	5
First National Bank	1	2	1	_____	1	2	3	4	5
Arapahoe National Bank	1	2	1	_____	1	2	3	4	5
Security Bank	1	2	1	_____	1	2	3	4	5
United Bank of Boulder	1	2	1	_____	1	2	3	4	5
National State Bank	1	2	1	_____	1	2	3	4	5

3. (HAND BANK RATING CARD.) On this card there are a number of contrasting phrases or statements such as, for example, "Large" and "Small." We'd like to know how you rate (NAME OF BANK RED-CHECKED BELOW) in terms of these statements or phrases. Just for example: Let's use the terms "fast service" and "slow service." If you were to rate the bank #1 on this scale, it would mean you find its service "very fast." On the other hand, a #7 rating would indicate you feel its service is "very slow," whereas a #4 rating means you don't think of it as being either "very fast" or "very slow." Are you ready to go ahead? Good! Tell me then how you would rate (NAME OF BANK RED-CHECKED) in terms of each of the phrases or statements on that card.
   How about (READ NEXT BANK NAME)? . . . Continue on until Respondent has evaluated all six banks.

	Arapahoe National	First National	Boulder National	Security Bank	United Bank	National State
a. Service	_____	_____	_____	_____	_____	_____
b. Size	_____	_____	_____	_____	_____	_____
c. Business vs. family	_____	_____	_____	_____	_____	_____
d. Friendliness	_____	_____	_____	_____	_____	_____
e. Big/small business	_____	_____	_____	_____	_____	_____
f. Rate of growth	_____	_____	_____	_____	_____	_____
g. Moderness	_____	_____	_____	_____	_____	_____
h. Leadership	_____	_____	_____	_____	_____	_____

(continued)

E X H I B I T   1 3 . 5   *(continued)*

	Arapahoe National	First National	Boulder National	Security Bank	United Bank	National State
i. Loan ease	____	____	____	____	____	____
j. Location	____	____	____	____	____	____
k. Hours	____	____	____	____	____	____
l. Ownership	____	____	____	____	____	____
m. Community involvement	____	____	____	____	____	____

4. Suppose a friend of yours who has just moved to Boulder asked you to recommend a bank. Which local bank would you recommend? Why would you recommend that particular bank?

Arapahoe National 1
First National 2
Boulder National 3
Security Bank 4
United Bank of Boulder 5
National State Bank 6
Other (specify)_____
DK/wouldn't 8

5. Which of the local banks do you think of as: (INTERVIEWER: Read red-checked item first. Then read each of the other five.)
   the newcomer's bank? _____
   the student's bank? _____
   the personal banker bank? _____
   the bank where most C.U. faculty and staff bank? _____
   the bank most interested in this community? _____
   the most progressive bank? _____

6. Which of these financial institutions, if any (HAND CARD #2), are you or any member of your immediate family who lives here in this home doing business with now?

   (IF NONE, skip to #19.)

Bank 1
Credit union 2
Finance company 3
Savings and loan 4
Industrial bank 5
None of these 6
DK/not sure 8

7. If a friend of yours asked you to recommend a place where he could get a loan with which to buy a home, which financial institution would you probably recommend? (INTERVIEWER: Probe for specific name.) Why would you recommend (INSTITUTION NAMED IN #7)?

Would recommend: _____
_____
Wouldn't 0
DK/not sure 8

Source: Reprinted by permission from Research Services, Inc., Denver, Colorado, and the United Bank of Boulder, Boulder, Colorado.

favorably to the first set of questions. To facilitate coding, question responses should be precoded when possible, as in Exhibit 13.4.

Layout is especially important when questionnaires are long or require the respondent to fill in a large amount of information.

HOW MUCH PRETESTING AND REVISING IS NECESSARY?

Many novelists write, rewrite, and revise certain chapters, paragraphs, and even sentences of their books. The research analyst lives in a similar world. Rarely does one write only a first draft of a questionnaire. Usually, the questionnaire is "tried out" on a group that is selected on a convenience basis and similar in makeup to the one that ultimately will be sampled. One should select a group that is not too divergent from the actual respondents (e.g., business students as surrogates for businesspeople), but it is not necessary to get a statistical sample for pretesting. The pretesting process allows the researchers to determine if the respondents have any difficulty understanding the questionnaire or if there are any ambiguous or biased questions. This process is exceedingly beneficial. Making a mistake with 25 or 50 subjects can avert the disaster of administering an invalid questionnaire to several hundred individuals.

Tabulating the results of a pretest helps determine whether the questionnaire will meet the objectives of the research. A **preliminary tabulation** often illustrates that while a question is easily comprehended and answered by the respondent, it is an inappropriate question because it does not solve the business problem.

Consider the following example from a survey among distributors of powder-actuated tools concerning the percentage of sales to given industries.

Please estimate what percentage of your fastener and load sales go to the following industries:

____ % **heating, plumbing, and air-conditioning**

____ % **carpentry**

____ % **electrical**

____ % **maintenance**

____ % **other (please specify)** _____

The researchers were fortunate to learn in pretesting that asking the question in this manner made it virtually impossible to obtain the information actually desired. Most respondents' answers did not total 100 percent. The question had to be revised. Usually a questionnaire goes through several revisions.

Getting respondents to "add" everything correctly is a problem. Notice how the questions from a survey on secretarial support in Exhibit 13.6 mitigates this problem.[16] Pretesting difficult questions like this is essential.

What administrative procedures should be implemented to maximize the value of a pretest? Often feedback on a questionnaire administered exactly as planned in the actual study is not possible. For example, mailing out a questionnaire may require several weeks. Pretesting a questionnaire in this manner provides important information on response rate, but it may not point out why questions were skipped or why respondents found certain questions ambiguous or confusing. The ability of a personal interviewer to record requests for additional explanation and to register comments indicating respondents' difficulty with question sequence or other factors is the primary reason why interviewers are often used for pretest work. Of course, self-administered questionnaires are not reworded to be personal interviews, but interviewers are instructed to observe the person filling out the questionnaire and to ask the respondent's comments after completing the questionnaire.[17] When pretesting personal or telephone interviews, interviewers may test alternative wordings

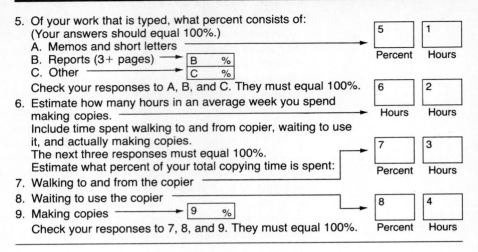

5. Of your work that is typed, what percent consists of:
   (Your answers should equal 100%.)
   A. Memos and short letters
   B. Reports (3+ pages)
   C. Other
   Check your responses to A, B, and C. They must equal 100%.
6. Estimate how many hours in an average week you spend
   making copies.
   Include time spent walking to and from copier, waiting to use
   it, and actually making copies.
   The next three responses must equal 100%.
   Estimate what percent of your total copying time is spent:
7. Walking to and from the copier
8. Waiting to use the copier
9. Making copies
   Check your responses to 7, 8, and 9. They must equal 100%.

and question sequences to determine which format is best suited to the respondents. No matter how the pretest is conducted, the researcher should remember that its purpose is to alert researchers to potential problems that may be caused by the questionnaire. Thus pretests are typically conducted to answer questions about the questionnaire such as:

- Can the questionnaire format be followed by the interviewers?
- Does the questionnaire flow naturally and conversationally?
- Can respondents answer the questions easily?
- Which alternative forms of questions work best?[18]

Pretesting also provides the means to test the sampling procedure. Pretests may determine if interviewers follow the sampling instructions properly and if the procedure is efficient. They also provide estimates for the response rate for mail surveys and the completion rate for telephone surveys.

SUMMARY

Good questionnaire design is a key to obtaining good survey results. The specific questions asked will be a function of the type of information needed to answer the manager's questions and of the communication medium of data collection. Relevance and accuracy are the basic criteria for judging questionnaire results. Relevance means that no unnecessary information is collected and that the information necessary for solving the business problem is obtained. Accuracy means that the information is reliable and valid.

Knowing how each question should be phrased requires familiarity with the different types of questions. Open-ended response questions present some topic or problem and ask the respondent to answer in his or her own words. Fixed-alternative questions require less interviewer skill, take less time, and are

easier to answer. Standardized responses are easier to code, tabulate, and interpret. Care must be taken to formulate the responses so they do not overlap.
Respondents whose answers really don't fit any of the fixed alternatives may be
forced to select alternatives they really don't mean.

In fixed-alternative questions the respondent is given specific limited alternative responses and asked to choose the one closest to his or her viewpoint. Open-ended questions are especially useful in exploratory research or at
the beginning of a questionnaire. Open-ended questions are more costly than
fixed-alternative questions because of the uniqueness of the answers. Interviewer bias can also influence the responses to open-ended questions.

Some guidelines to questionnaire construction have emerged from research experience. The language should be simple to allow for variations in
educational level. Leading or loaded questions suggest answers to the respondents. Other questions induce them to give socially desirable answers. Respondents have a bias against questions suggesting changes in the status quo.
Respondents' reluctance to answer personal questions can be reduced by explaining the need for them and by assuring the respondents of the confidentiality of their replies. Researchers should be careful to avoid ambiguity in
questions. Another common problem is the double-barreled question, which
asks two questions at once.

Question sequence can be very important to the success of a survey. The
opening questions should be designed to interest respondents and keep them
involved. Personal questions should be postponed to the middle or end of the
questionnaire. General questions should precede specific ones. In a series of attitude scales, the first response may be used as an anchor for comparison to the
other responses. The order of alternatives on closed questions can also affect
the results. Filter questions are useful to avoid unnecessary questions that don't
apply to a particular respondent. Such questions may be put into a flowchart
for personal or telephone interviewing.

The layout of a mail or self-administered questionnaire can affect the response rate. An attractive questionnaire encourages a response. A carefully
phrased title can also encourage responses. Finally, pretesting helps reveal
errors while they can still be easily corrected.

Key Terms

open-ended response question

fixed-alternative question

simple-dichotomy (dichotomous-
alternative) question

determinant-choice question

frequency-determination question

attitude rating scale

checklist question

leading question

loaded question

counterbiasing statement

split-ballot technique

double-barreled question

order bias

funnel technique

filter question

pivot question

preliminary tabulation

Questions

1. Evaluate and comment on the following questions from several different questionnaires:

    a. A university computer center survey on TSO (Time Sharing Option) usage:
    How often do you use TSO (access the IBM computer through a computer terminal)? Please check one.
    ____ Infrequently (once a semester)
    ____ Occasionally (once a month)
    ____ Frequently (once a week)
    ____ All the time (daily)

    b. A survey of U.S. congressmen:
    Do you understand and like the current tax laws that allow people who file their federal income tax returns to deduct from their personal income the amount they pay in state and local taxes?
    ____ Yes
    ____ No

    c. A survey on a new small electric car:
    Assuming 90 percent of your driving is in town, would you buy this type of car?
    ____ Yes
    ____ No
    If this type electric car had the same initial cost as a current "Big 3" full-sized, fully equipped car but operated at one-half the cost over a five-year period, would you buy one?
    ____ Yes
    ____ No

    d. A student survey:
    Since the beginning of this semester approximately what percentage of the time did you get to campus using each of the forms of transportation available to you per week?
    Walk ____   Bicycle ____
    Public transportation ____   Motor vehicle ____

    e. A survey of employers:
    Should the company continue its generous medical insurance program?
    ____ Yes
    ____ No

    f. A personnel manager's survey of employees:
    In your opinion, are women discriminated against, treated equitably, or given preference in promotion practices?

Discriminated Against	Treated Equitably	Treated Preferentially
☐	☐	☐

    g. A survey of professors:
    Please check your level of knowledge about microcomputers:
    ☐ Have never used a microcomputer and don't know what most of

the buzz words mean (e.g., software, byte, bus, VLSI, ALU, chip, boot, user-friendly).

☐ Have used a microcomputer for limited, specific tasks requiring minimal knowledge of operation and jargon.

☐ Fairly adept at using user-friendly software packages on one specific microcomputer, but don't really know how the machine works.

☐ Limited programming knowledge in one or more languages (Basic, Fortran, Pascal, etc.) and some experience with large computers. Little or no microcomputer experience.

h.   A government survey of gasoline retailers:

Suppose the full-service selling price for leaded regular gasoline is 62.8 cents per gallon on the first day of the month. Suppose on the tenth of the month the price is raised to 64.9 cents per gallon; and on the twenty-fifth of the month it is reduced to 61.9 cents per gallon. In order to provide the required data, you should list the accumulator reading on the full-service leaded regular gasoline pump when the station opens on the first day, the tenth day, and the twenty-fifth day of the month, and when the station closes on the last day of the month.

i.   An antigun-control group's survey:

Do you believe that private citizens have the right to own firearms to defend themselves, their families, and their property from violent criminal attack?

_____ Yes

_____ No

j.   A survey of the general public:

In the next year, after accounting for inflation, do you think your real personal income will go up or down?

1. Up
2. (Stay the same)
3. Down
4. (Don't know)

k.   A survey of the general public:

Some people say that companies should be required by law to label all chemicals and substances that the government states are potentially harmful. The label would tell what the chemical or substance is, what dangers it might pose, and what safety procedures should be used in handling the substance. Other people say that such laws would be too strict. They say the law should require labels on only those chemicals and substances that the companies themselves decide are potentially harmful. Such a law, they say, would be less costly for the companies and would permit them to exclude those chemicals and substances they consider to be trade secrets. Which of these views is closest to your own?

1. Require labels on all chemicals and substances that the government states are potentially harmful.
2. (Don't know)

   3. Require labels on only those chemicals and substances that companies decide are potentially harmful.

l.   A survey of voters:

Since agriculture is vital to our state's economy, how do you feel about the administration's farm policies?

Strongly favor
Somewhat favor
Somewhat oppose
Strongly oppose
Unsure

2. When the Agency for Consumer Advocacy was under consideration, there was considerable debate regarding the validity of the poll. The Consumer Federation of America charged the following question was loaded: "Those in favor of setting up an additional federal consumer protection agency on top of the other agencies we have say they are not getting the job done by themselves. Those who oppose setting up the additional agency say we already have plenty of government agencies to protect consumers, and it's just a matter of making them work better. How do you feel?" The researchers felt otherwise. How do you feel about this disputed question?

3. How might the wording of a question asking about income influence the answers of respondents?

4. Design an open-ended response question(s) to measure reactions to a Xerox magazine ad.

5. What is the difference between a leading question and a loaded question?

6. Design a complete questionnaire to evaluate job satisfaction.

7. Design a complete (but short) questionnaire to measure student evaluations of a college course.

8. Develop a checklist of things to consider in questionnaire construction.

References

[1] Charles W. Roll, Jr., and Albert H. Cantril, *Polls: Their Use and Misuse in Politics* (New York: Basic Books, 1972), 106.

[2] Stanley L. Payne, *The Art of Asking Questions* (Princeton, NJ: Princeton University Press, 1951), 8–9. The reader who wishes a more detailed account of question wording is referred to this classic book.

[3] Paul L. Erdos, *Professional Mail Surveys* (New York: McGraw-Hill, 1970), 37.

[4] Donald P. Warwick and Charles A. Lininger, *The Sample Survey: Theory and Practice* (New York: McGraw-Hill, 1975), 127.

[5] This heading is borrowed from Payne, *The Art of Asking Questions.*

[6] Payne, *The Art of Asking Questions,* 185.

[7] Roll and Cantril, *Polls,* 106–107.

[8] Warwick and Lininger, *The Sample Survey,* 143.

[9] The others are relative advantage, compatibility, complexity, and communicability. See Thomas S. Robertson, *Innovative Behavior and Communication* (New York: Holt, Rinehart and Winston, 1971), 46–47.

[10] Warwick and Lininger, *The Sample Survey,* 141.

[11] Payne, *The Art of Asking Questions,* 102–103.

[12] Gloria E. Wheeler, "'Yes; No; All of the Above,' Before You Conduct a Survey," *Exchange* (Spring-Summer 1979), 21.

[13] Erdos, *Professional Mail Surveys,* 59.

[14] E. Laird Landon, Jr., "Order Bias, the Ideal Rating, and the Semantic Differential," *Journal of Marketing Research* 8 (August 1971): 375–378.

[15] This section relies heavily on Erdos, *Professional Mail Surveys.*

[16] IBM Management/Staff Booklet for Systems Design, 1975 (Z140-3008-2 U/M 001).

[17] For a detailed discussion of this issue, see S. D. Hunt, R. D. Sparkman, Jr., and J. B. Wilcox, "The Pretest in Survey Research: Issues and Preliminary Findings," *Journal of Marketing Research* (May 1982): 269–273.

[18] Jeffrey L. Pope, *Practical Marketing Research* (New York: AMACOM, 1981), 78.

Sampling and Fieldwork

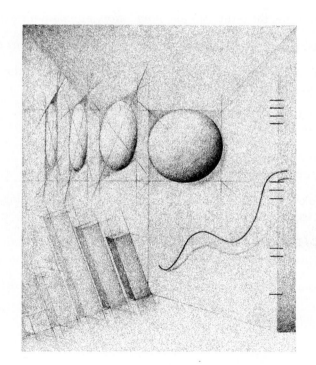

Sample Designs and Sampling Procedures

What you will learn in this chapter:

To define the terms *sample, population, population element,* and *census.*

To explain why a sample rather than a complete census may be taken.

To discuss the issues concerning the identification of the target population and the selection of a sampling frame.

To discuss common forms of sampling frames, such as reverse directories, and to discuss sampling frame error.

To distinguish between random sampling and systematic (nonsampling) errors.

To explain the various types of systematic (nonsampling) errors resulting from sample selection.

To discuss the advantages and disadvantages of the various types of probability and nonprobability samples.

To understand how to choose an appropriate sample design.

We know it's important to make a good first impression because, after a sample exposure, people make judgments about the type of people we are. Unless you are a member of the Polar Bear Swimming Club, you will test the early March water of Lake Michigan with a toe before diving in. Stand in a bookstore and observe the process of sampling. Customers generally pick up a book, look at the cover, and then sample a few pages to get a feeling for the writing style and the content before deciding whether or not to buy. The high school student who visits a college classroom to listen to a professor's lecture is employing a sampling technique. Selecting a college or university on the basis of one classroom visit may not be a scientific sample, but in a personal situation it may be a practical sampling experience. These examples illustrate the intuitive nature of sampling in everyday usages when it is impossible, inconvenient, or too expensive to measure every item in the population.

Although sampling is commonplace in daily activities, most of these familiar samples are not of a scientific nature. The understanding of the concept of sampling may be intuitive, but the actual process of sampling can be quite complex. Because sampling is a central aspect of business research, it requires in-depth examination.

This chapter explains the nature of sampling and how to determine the appropriate sample design.

∎

SAMPLING TERMINOLOGY

The process of **sampling** involves any procedure using a small number of items or parts of the whole population to make conclusions regarding the whole population. A **sample** is a subset or some part of a larger population. The purpose of sampling is to enable researchers to estimate some unknown characteristic of the population.

We have defined sampling in terms of the population to be studied. A **population,** or **universe,** is any complete group of people, companies, hospitals, stores, college students, or the like that share some set of characteristics. When a distinction is made between "population" and "universe," it is on the basis of whether the group is finite (population) or infinite (universe). The term **population element** refers to an individual member of the population. A **census** is an investigation of all the individual elements that make up the population: a total enumeration rather than a sample.

WHY SAMPLE?

At a wine-tasting party we all recognize the impossibility of anything but sampling. But in a scientific study, when the objective is to estimate an unknown population value, why should a sample be taken rather than a complete census?

Pragmatic Reasons

Applied business research projects usually have budget and time constraints. If the U.S. government wished to take a census of federal employees' reactions to a proposed retirement program, millions of workers would have to be contacted. Some of these would be inaccessible (for example, out of the country), and it would be impossible to contact all these people within a short time.

Of course, a researcher investigating a population with an extremely small number of population elements may elect to conduct a census rather than a sample because the cost, manpower, and time constraints are relatively insignificant. Thus a company concerned with programmer satisfaction with its personal computer-networking system may not have any pragmatic reason for avoiding in-house circulation of a questionnaire to all 25 of its employees. In most situations, however, there are many pragmatic reasons for sampling. Sampling cuts costs, reduces manpower requirements, and gathers vital information quickly.[1] Although these advantages may be sufficient in themselves for using a sample rather than a census, there are other reasons.

Accurate and Reliable Results

Another major reason for sampling is that samples, if properly selected, are sufficiently accurate in most cases. If the elements of a population are quite similar, only a small sample is necessary to accurately portray the characteristic of interest. Most of us have had blood samples taken, sometimes from the finger, the arm, or another part of the body. The assumption is that because the blood is sufficiently similar throughout the body, the characteristics of the blood can be determined on the basis of a sample.

When the population elements are highly homogeneous, samples are highly representative of the population. Under these circumstances almost any sample is as good as another.[2] Even when populations have considerable heterogeneity, large samples provide data of sufficient precision to make most decisions.

The well-known research firm A. C. Nielsen has a simple demonstration of how sampling works (see Exhibit 14.1). Four photographs are used to show

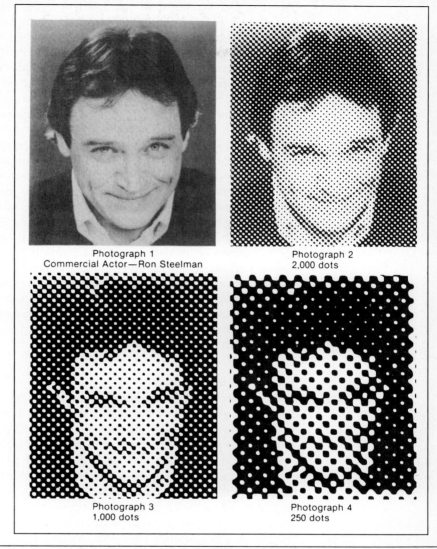

Photograph 1
Commercial Actor—Ron Steelman

Photograph 2
2,000 dots

Photograph 3
1,000 dots

Photograph 4
250 dots

Source: Adapted from A. D. Fletcher and T. A. Bowers, *Fundamentals of Advertising Research* (Columbus, OH: Grid Publishing, 1983), 60–61. Reprinted with permission from John Wiley & Sons, Inc.

how one can take different-size samples and produce a very generalizable conclusion. The first photograph is finely screened and is therefore printed with thousands of dots of ink. Because of the fineness of detail, one might say that this photograph contains nearly all of the detail, or information, that can be provided.

In the other photographs less detail is provided. Photograph 2 is made up of approximately 2,000 dots. The face is still very clear, but not as much so as in the first photograph; some detail is missing, but the face is still recognizable. Photograph 3 is made up of only 1,000 dots, constituting a sample that is only half as large as that in Photograph 2; the face can still be recognized. In Photograph 4 the sample is down to 250 dots—yet if you look at the picture at a distance you can still make out a face and identify it as the same one shown in Photograph 1. The 250-dot sample is still useful despite the fact that it contains only a small fraction of the number of dots in the other photographs. *Precision* has suffered, but *accuracy* has not. Of course, samples are accurate only when researchers have taken care to draw representative samples properly. More will be said about this later in the chapter.

A sample may be more accurate than a census. In a census of a large population there is a greater likelihood of nonsampling errors. In a survey mistakes may occur that are unrelated to the selection of people in the study. For example, a response may be coded incorrectly or the keyboard operator might make a data-entry error. Interviewer mistakes, tabulation errors, and other nonsampling errors may increase during a census because of the increased volume of work. In a sample increased accuracy is possible because the fieldwork and tabulation of the data can be more closely supervised than could be possible in a census. In a field survey a small, well-trained, closely supervised group may do a more careful and accurate job of collecting information than a large group of nonprofessional interviewers trying to contact everyone. An interesting case in point is the fact that the Bureau of the Census uses samples to check the accuracy of the U.S. Census. If the sample indicates a possible source of error, the census is redone.

Destruction of Test Units

Many research projects, especially those in quality control testing, require the destruction of the items being tested. If the manufacturer of firecrackers wishes to find out whether each product met a specific production standard, there would be no product left after the testing. This is the exact situation in many business field experiments. If an experimental treatment were presented to every potential employee or customer, no employees or potential customers would be left uncontacted after the experiment. In other words, if there is a finite population and everyone in the population participated in the research and cannot be replaced, no population elements remain to be selected as sampling units. The test units have been destroyed.

PRACTICAL SAMPLING CONCEPTS

Researchers must make several decisions before a sample is taken. Exhibit 14.2 presents an overview of these decisions as a series of sequential stages, even though the order of decisions does not always follow this particular sequence. These decisions are highly interrelated. The issues associated with each of these stages, except for fieldwork, are discussed in this chapter and in Chapter 15; fieldwork is discussed in Chapter 16.

EXHIBIT   14.2

**Stages in
Selection
of a Sample**

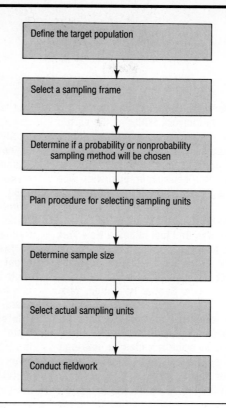

Define the target population

↓

Select a sampling frame

↓

Determine if a probability or nonprobability
sampling method will be chosen

↓

Plan procedure for selecting sampling units

↓

Determine sample size

↓

Select actual sampling units

↓

Conduct fieldwork

Defining the Target Population

Once the decision to sample has been made, the first question related to sampling concerns identifying the **target population,** that is, the specific complete group relevant to the research project. What is the relevant population? In many cases this is not a difficult question. Registered voters may be clearly identifiable. Similarly, if the 206 employees of a company are the population of concern, there are few definitional problems. In other cases the decision may be difficult. One survey concerning industrial buyer behavior incorrectly defined the population as the purchasing agents whom sales representatives regularly contacted. Investigators discovered, after the survey, that industrial engineers within the customer companies had substantial impact on buying decisions, even though they rarely talked with the salespeople. Frequently, the appropriate population element may be the household or organizational unit rather than the individual member of the household or the employee. This presents some problems because household lists or lists of population elements may not be available.

At the outset of the sampling process, it is vitally important to carefully define the target population so the proper source from which the data are to be

R E S E A R C H   I N S I G H T

You Can Learn a Lot from a Few: George Gallup's Nation of Numbers

In the summer of 1932 Iowa Democrats nominated a sixty-year-old widow named Ola Babcock Miller as the party's candidate for secretary of state. It was no big deal. No Democrat had carried the state since the Civil War. But it was a nice thing to do, a gesture of respect for her late husband, a small-town newspaper publisher who had spent his life trying, vainly, to bring down Iowa Republicanism.

Mrs. Miller called in the family for help. Her son-in-law, a college professor who had just joined a New York advertising agency, had some ideas. Why not have some people go door to door, using this "scientific" plan he had, and ask voters what they wanted?

The son-in-law's name was George H. Gallup. Mrs. Miller won.

Young George—he was born in 1901—was a go-getter. His father had been a dreamer, a country schoolteacher who tried to develop what he called "a new logic of lateral thinking" and built an eight-sided house on the theory that it would offer better protection against plains windstorms. But George left the octagonal house and the hometown, Jefferson, as soon as he could find his way in a bigger world. The first stop was Iowa City and the State University of Iowa. Then in 1922, between his junior and senior years, he answered an advertisement for summer employment in St. Louis. The *Post-Dispatch* hired fifty students to survey the city, questioning readers about what they liked and didn't like in the paper.

Each and every reader. The students were hired to go to every door in St. Louis—there were fifty-five thousand homes in the city then—and ask the same questions. Gallup, one hot day, knocked on one door too many, got the same answers one time too many, and decided: There's got to be a better way.

"A New Technique for Objective Methods for Measuring Reader Interest in Newspapers" was the way, and the title of Gallup's Ph.D. thesis at Iowa. Working with the Des Moines *Register* and *Tribune* and the two-hundred-year-old statistical theory probabilities of the Swiss mathematician Jakob Bernoulli, Gallup developed "sampling" techniques. You didn't have to talk to everybody, he said, as long as you randomly selected interviews according to a sampling plan that took into account whatever diversity was relevant in the universe of potential respondents—geographic, ethnic, economic.

Although not everybody understood or believed then—or now—this intellectual invention was a big deal. "Guesswork eliminated in new method for determining reader interest" was the lead headline of the February 8, 1930, issue of the newspaper industry's trade journal, *Editor & Publisher*. There was a photograph of a big, stolid midwesterner above the caption: "George H. Gallup, instructor, U. of Iowa."

The instructor tried to explain what he was talking about and doing. "Suppose there are seven thousand white beans and three thousand black beans well churned in a barrel," he said then, and again more than fifty-two years later as we walked together near his office in Princeton, New Jersey. "If you scoop out one hundred of them, you'll get approximately seventy white beans and thirty black in your hand, and the range of your possible error can be computed mathematically. As long as the barrel contains many more beans than your handful, the proportion will remain within that margin of error nine hundred ninety-seven times out of one thousand."

Well, it seemed to work for newspapers, and George Gallup, instructor, was in great demand around the country. He became head of the journalism department at Drake University and then switched to a professorship at Northwestern—all the while doing readership surveys for papers in Chicago, Cleveland, Buffalo, and points east and west. He was hot, and in that summer of '32 a new advertising agency, Young & Rubicam, invited him to New York to create a research department and procedures for evaluating the effectiveness of advertising. He did that too. One of his first Y&R surveys, based on newspaper experience, indicated that the number of readers of advertisements was proportional to the length of the paragraphs in a piece of copy.

And, of course, by the end of that year, 1932, with his mother-in-law's election, Gallup was confident that his methodology was valid not only for beans and newspaper readers but for voters too. As long as you understood the sampling universe—white, black, male, female, rich, poor, urban, rural, Republican, Democratic—you could predict elections or calculate public attitudes on public questions by interviewing a relatively small number of people.

So Gallup went out and formed the grandly titled American Institute of Public Opinion. Keeping his job at Young & Rubicam, he began syndicating surveys to newspapers under the title: "America Speaks: The National Weekly Poll of Public Opinion." The first Gallup Poll, released in October 1935, focused on the question, asked of three thousand Americans: "Do you think expenditures by the government for relief and recovery are: Too Little? Too Great? About Right?" Three out of five respondents said, "Too Great."

Source: Excerpted from Richard Reeves, "George Gallup's Nation of Numbers," *Esquire*, December 1983, pp. 91–92. Excerpted by permission of International Creative Management © 1983 by Richard Reeves.

collected can be identified.[3] Answering questions about the critical characteristics of the population is the usual technique for defining the target population. Does the term *comic book reader* include children under 6 years who do not actually read the words? Does *all persons west of the Mississippi* include people in east-bank metropolitan areas bordering the river, such as East St. Louis, Illinois?

The question "To whom do we want to talk?" must be answered. It may be users, nonusers, recent employees, or doctors. To implement the sample in the field, tangible characteristics should be used to define the population. A hospital might define the population as all women who are still capable of bearing children. However, a more specific operational definition would be women between the ages of 12 and 50. While this definition by age may exclude a few women who are capable of childbearing and include some who are not, it is still more explicit and provides a manageable basis for the sample design.[4]

The Sampling Frame

In actual practice the sample will be drawn from a list of population elements that is often somewhat different from the target population that has been defined. A **sampling frame** is the list of elements from which the sample may be drawn. A simple example of a sampling frame might be a list of all members of the American Banking Association.

It is generally not feasible to compile a list that does not exclude some members of the population. For example, if the student telephone directory is utilized as a sampling frame listing of your university's student population, it may exclude those students who registered late, students without phones, or those who have their telephones listed only under their roommate's or pet's name.

The sampling frame is also called the *working population* because it provides the list that can be operationally worked with. If a complete list of population elements is not accessible, materials such as maps or aerial photographs may be utilized as a sampling frame.

The discrepancy between the definition of the population and a sampling frame is the first potential source of error associated with selection of a sample. A complete discussion of these errors will be made later in this chapter.

Mailing Lists.   Some firms, called list brokers, specialize in providing **mailing lists** giving the names, addresses, and telephone numbers of specific populations. Exhibit 14.3 shows a page from the catalog of a mailing list company. Companies like this one offer lists based on subscriptions to professional journals, ownership of credit cards, and a variety of other sources. One mailing list company obtained the listing of households with children from an ice cream retailer who gave away a free ice cream cone on a child's birthday (the children filled out cards with their names, addresses, and birthdays, which were then sold to a mailing list company).

A valuable source of information for names is R. L. Polk and Company's series of city directories. A city directory records the name of each resident over 18 years of age and lists pertinent information about each household. A valuable feature is the street directory pages. These pages are a **reverse directory** that provides, in a different format, the same information provided in a telephone directory. Listings may be found by city and street address and/or phone number, rather than in alphabetical order of surnames. This is particularly useful when a researcher wishes to survey only a certain geographic area of the city or when census tracts are to be matched on an income or other basis.

A **sampling frame error** occurs when certain sample elements are excluded or when the entire population is not accurately represented in the sample frame. One city's manager for community development, in preparation for an upcoming bond issue election used telephone numbers (randomly generated) as the basis for a sample survey dealing with attitudes toward capital improvements. When the bond issue failed, consultants pointed out that the appropriate sampling frame would have been a list of registered voters, not any adult with a phone (who might not have voted in this type of election). By including respondents who should not have been listed as members of the population, a sampling frame error occurred.

Population elements can also be overrepresented in a sampling frame. A savings and loan association defined its population as all individuals who had savings accounts. However, when it drew a sample from a list of *accounts,* rather than from a list of names of *individuals,* individuals who had multiple accounts were overrepresented in the sample.

Sampling Units

During the actual sampling process, the elements of the population must be selected according to a certain procedure. The **sampling unit** is a single element or group of elements subject to selection in the sample. For example, if an airline wishes to sample passengers, every twenty-fifth name on a complete list of passengers may be taken. In this case the sampling unit is the same as the element. Alternatively, the airline could first select flights as the sampling unit, then select certain passengers on the flights selected. In this case the sampling unit contains many elements.

EXHIBIT 14.3

Mailing List Directory Page

EXECUTIVES

QUANT	LIST	SIC
33,070	**Structural**(D)	
3,170	Surveying(D)	
900	Textile Engineering(D)	
4,400	Transportation(D)	
6,800	Urban Planning & Development(D)	
20,000	Water Distribution(D)	
21,700	Water Pollution(D)	
	ENGINEERING SERVICES	
580	Architectural	8911B+
14,500	Consulting	8911D+
13,100	Designing	8911E+
1,130	Industrial	7392B+
2,950	Structural	8911C+
117,100	Engineering New Product Service Inq.(D)	
810	Engravers, Photo	2793+
1,300	Engraving & Plate Printers	2753+
8,300	Envelope & Stationery Supply Whls.	5112+
220	Envelope Manufacturers	2642
	ENVIRONMENT	
19,950	Air Pollution Facilities	
21,120	Air Pollution Technicians	
97,000	Clean Earth Booklet Requests(D)	
8,840	Conservation Officials(D)	
4,900	Ecologists(D)	
46,600	Environmental Conservation Experts(D)	
400	Environmental Controls Mfrs.	3822
6,480	Environmental Institution Directors(D)	
57,250	Envir. Protection Officials(D)	
	Executives In(D)	
4,000	Agriculture	
11,500	Air	
5,900	Automobile	
11,500	Energy	
10,000	Land Use	
7,500	Noise	
10,400	Pesticides	
5,800	Radiation	
9,200	Solid Waste	
2,080	Toxic	
12,800	Water	
140,000	Impact Studies Buyers(D)	
12,020	Noise Abatement, Cos. with(D)	
42,000	Solid Waste, Organizations Concerned With(D)	
300	Conservation Groups	
600	Construction Contractors	
5,740	Consulting Engineers	
8,060	Consulting Firms	
1,000	Educational Inst.	
2,720	Federal Government	
2,060	Industrial Firms	

QUANT	LIST	SIC
11,100	Local Government	
1,500	Manufacturers, Equip.	
640	Planning	
800	Regional Governments	
2,860	State Governments	
1,050	Utility Districts	
5,250	Episcopal Churches	866G
12,160	Equipment Rental & Leasing Services	7394+
	ETHNICS *See Page 28 for State Counts*	
6,174,000	Afro-American	
14,579,630	English	
1,174,940	French	
3,356,500	German	
462,540	Italian	
35,490	Japanese	
1,058,720	Jewish	
1,034,280	Scandinavian	
3,228,650	Scottish	
1,167,140	Spanish	
1,300	Evangelical & Covenant Churches	866H
31,100	Excavating & Foundation Contr.	1794+
335,000	Executive Female, The	
	EXECUTIVES	
5,650	Advertising Managers, Big Business	
	Advertisers, National	
11,720	Companies	
36,600	Executives, Total	
3,650	Chairman of Board	
1,210	Chief Exec. Officer	
9,360	President	
6,840	Exec. Vice President	
7,600	Sales	
6,190	Marketing	
580	Merchandising	
4,640	Advertising	
1,780	Public Relations	
	Please inquire for selection by products.	
3,460	**Advertising Agencies, Major**	
3,050	Presidents by Name	
2,280	Art Directors	
1,300	Marketing & P.R. Dirs.	
	Agricultural, Forestry, Fisheries Companies	01 thru 99
3,990	Big Business Cos.	
11,760	Executives of	
	American Stock Exchange	
700	Companies	
7,530	Executives	
	Apparel Mfg. Cos.	2300
2,340	Big Business Cos.	
11,780	Executives of	
	Automotive Mfg.	3700
1,670	Big Business Cos.	
12,880	Executives of	
	Automotive Retailing	5500
3,560	Big Business Cos.	
11,880	Executives of	

QUANT	LIST	SIC
	Bank Executives	
162,500	All Comm'l Banks	
14,730	Presidents	
66,000	Vice-Presidents	
24,900	Branch Managers	
9,520	Chairmen	
9,040	Trust Officers	
8,760	Treasurers	
34,600	Cashiers	
3,820	Secretaries	
5,700	Loan Officers	
930	Marketing/Adv.	
8,000	Saving Bank Execs	
	Banks & Finance Cos.	6000-6200
13,370	Big Business Cos.	
123,330	Executives of	
	Big Business Execs.	
501,210	Total	
83,330	Presidents	
8,480	Owners	
29,230	Chairmen of the Board	
55,220	Treasurers	
7,320	Financial Officers	
15,790	Controllers	
22,620	Exec. Vice-Presidents	
20,890	Sr. Vice-Presidents	
186,400	Vice-Presidents	
61,390	Secretaries	
105,380	Managers	
28,830	Sales Managers	
5,470	Advertising Managers	
191,570	Directors	
15,850	Purchasing Directors	
1,600	International Directors	
9,090	Engineering Mfrs.	
	Board of Directors, Members of	
29,230	Chairmen (Business Addresses only)	
	Directors	
191,570	At Bus. Addresses	
69,730	At Home Addresses	
	By Membership	
39,100	Member of 1 Board	
9,910	Memb. of 2 Boards	
6,760	Memb. of 3 Boards	
4,310	Memb. of 4 Boards	
2,800	Memb. of 5 Boards	
6,560	Member of over 5 Boards	
	By Age	
5,540	Under 40	
15,530	40 to 50	
23,400	50 to 60	
23,990	Over 60	
	This data is available at any cutoff point.	
26,600	Broadcasting Executives (D)	
56,300	Business Advisors, Bus. Research Executives(D)	
24,000	Commerce Bus. Daily Subs.	
27,800	Commodity Future Executives(D)	

Source: Courtesy of Ed Burnett Consultants, Inc., 2 Park Avenue, New York, NY. The *Burnett Guide to Mailing Lists* is available free of charge.

If the target population has first been divided into units, such as airline flights, additional terminology must be used. The term **primary sampling units (PSU)** designates units selected in the first stage of sampling. If successive stages of sampling are conducted, sampling units are called **secondary sampling units,** or **tertiary sampling units.**

EXHIBIT 14.4

**An Operational Definition of
Who Is to Be Included as
a Member of the Household**

**Summary Table for Determining Who Is to Be Included as a Member of the Household
(Control Card Item 14c)**

	Include As Member of Household	

A. PERSONS STAYING IN SAMPLE UNIT AT TIME OF INTERVIEW

Person is member of family, lodger, servant, visitor, etc.

	Yes	No
1. Ordinarily stays here all the time (sleeps here)	Yes	
2. Here temporarily—no living quarters held for person elsewhere	Yes	
3. Here temporarily—living quarters held for person elsewhere		No

Person is in Armed Forces

1. Stationed in this locality, usually sleeps here	Yes	
2. Temporarily here on leave—stationed elsewhere		No

Person is a student—Here temporarily attending school—living quarters held for person elsewhere

1. Not married or not living with own family		No
2. Married and living with own family	Yes	
3. Student nurse living at school	Yes	

B. ABSENT PERSON WHO USUALLY LIVES HERE IN SAMPLE UNIT

Person is inmate of specified institution—Absent because inmate in a specified institution (see listing in Part C, Table A) regardless of whether or not living quarters held for person here .... **No**

Person is temporarily absent on vacation, in general hospital, etc. (including veterans' facilities that are general hospitals)—Living quarters held here for person .... **Yes**

Person is absent in connection with job

1. Living quarters held here for person—temporarily absent while "on the road" in connection with job (e.g., traveling salesperson, railroad person, bus driver)	Yes	
2. Living quarters held here and elsewhere for person but comes here infrequently (e.g., construction engineer)		No
3. Living quarters held here at home for unmarried college student working away from home during summer school vacation	Yes	

Person is in Armed Forces—Was member of this household at time of induction but currently stationed elsewhere .... **No**

Person is a student in school—Away temporarily attending school—living quarters held for person here

1. Not married or not living with own family	Yes	
2. Married and living with own family		No
3. Attending school overseas		No
4. Student nurse living at school		No

C. EXCEPTIONS AND DOUBTFUL CASES

Person with two concurrent residences—Determine length of time person has maintained two concurrent residences

1. Has slept greater part of that time in another locality		No
2. Has slept greater part of that time in sample unit	Yes	

Citizen of foreign country temporarily in the United States

1. Living on premises of an Embassy, Ministry, Legation, Chancellery, or Consulate		No
2. Not living on premises of an Embassy, Ministry, etc.—		
a. Living here and no usual place of residence elsewhere in the United States	Yes	
b. Visiting or traveling in the United States		No

Source: U.S. Department of Commerce, Bureau of the Census, *Current Population Survey, 1982*, Interviewer's Information Card Booklet, 3.

When there is no list of population elements, the sampling unit is generally something other than the population element. For example, in a random-digit dialing study, the sampling unit will be telephone numbers.

Exhibit 14.4 illustrates that the definition of a sampling unit, such as a member of the household, may not be a simple task.

RANDOM SAMPLING ERROR AND NONSAMPLING ERROR

Political pollsters drawing a sample of 1,000 voters to measure if citizens intend to support a bond issue for the construction of a new jail expect the sample to be representative of all voters. However, if there is a difference between the value of a sample statistic of interest (for example, average likelihood of voting for the bond issue) and the corresponding value of the population parameter (again, average likelihood of voting for the bond issue), there has been a *statistical error*.

In Chapter 7 we classified two basic causes of differences between statistics and parameters: random sampling errors and systematic (nonsampling) errors.

An estimation from a sample is not exactly the same as a census count. **Random sampling error** is the difference between the sample result and the result of a census conducted by identical procedures.[5] Of course, the result of a census is unknown unless one is taken, which is rarely done. Other sources of error can also be present (see Exhibit 14.5). Random sampling error occurs because of chance variation in the scientific selection of sampling units.

The sampling units, even though properly selected according to sampling theory, may not perfectly represent the population, but they are generally reliable estimates. It will be seen, in discussion of the process of randomization (a procedure designed to give everyone in the population an equal chance of being selected as a sample member), that because random sampling errors follow chance variations, they tend to cancel each other out when averaged. This means that samples, properly selected, are generally good approximations of the population.

There is almost always a slight difference between the true population value and the sample value, hence a small random sampling error. Thus every once in a while a very unusual sample will be selected, because too many unusual people or companies were included in the sample, and this means there is a large random sampling error.

The theory behind this concept of sample reliability and other basic statistical concepts is reviewed in detail in the next chapter. At this point, recognize *random sampling error* or *sampling error* as a technical term that refers *only* to statistical fluctuations that occur because of chance variations in the elements selected for the sample.

Random sampling error is a function of sample size. As sample size increases, sampling error decreases. The resources available, of course, will influence how large a sample may be. (Sample size is covered in the following chapter.) It is possible to estimate the random sampling error that may be expected with various sample sizes. Suppose a survey of approximately 900 has been

EXHIBIT   14.5

**Errors Associated
with Sampling**

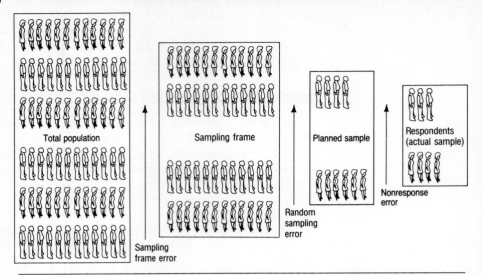

Source: Adapted by permission from Keith K. Cox and Ben M. Enis, *The Marketing Research Process* (Pacific Palisades, Calif.: Goodyear/Scott Foresman and Company, 1972), pp. 377–379, and Danny N. Bellenger and Barnet A. Greenberg, *Marketing Research: A Management Information Approach* (Homewood, Ill.: Richard D. Irwin, 1978), 154–155.

taken among employees to determine the feasibility of moving to a new Sunbelt location. Assume 30 percent of the respondents favor the idea of a new location. The researchers will know, based on the laws of probability, that 95 percent of the time a survey of slightly fewer than 900 people will produce results with an error of approximately plus or minus 3 percent. If the survey had been collected from only 325 people, the margin of error would increase to approximately plus or minus 5 percent.

Systematic (**nonsampling**) **errors** result from nonsampling factors, primarily the nature of a study's design and the correctness of execution. These errors are *not* due to chance fluctuations. For example, in mail surveys highly educated respondents are more likely to cooperate than poorly educated ones, for whom filling out forms is a more difficult and intimidating task.[6] Sample biases such as these account for a large portion of errors in business research. The term *sample bias* is somewhat unfortunate, because many forms of bias are not related to the selection of the sample.

Nonsampling errors have already been discussed in Chapter 7. It should be remembered that error due to sample selection problems, such as sample frame error, are systematic (nonsampling) errors and should not be classified as random sampling errors.

Less Than Perfectly Representative Samples

Random sampling error and systematic error associated with the sampling process may combine to yield a sample that is less than perfectly representative of the population. Exhibit 14.5 illustrates nonsampling errors (sampling frame error and nonresponse error) related to sample design. The total population is represented by the area of the largest rectangle. *Sampling frame errors* eliminate some potential respondents or include respondents who should not be listed as members of the population. Random sampling error (due exclusively to random, chance fluctuation) may cause an imbalance in the representativeness of the group. Additional errors will occur if individuals refuse to be interviewed or cannot be contacted. This **nonresponse error** may also cause the sample to be less than perfectly representative. Thus the actual sample is drawn from a population different from (or smaller than) the ideal.

PROBABILITY VERSUS NONPROBABILITY SAMPLING

There are several alternative ways of taking a sample. The major alternative sampling plans may be grouped into probability techniques and nonprobability techniques. In **probability sampling** every element in the population has a *known nonzero probability* of selection. The simple random sample is the best known probability sample, in which each member of the population has an equal probability of being selected.

In **nonprobability sampling** the probability of any particular member of the population being chosen is unknown. The selection of sampling units in nonprobability sampling is quite arbitrary, as researchers rely heavily on personal judgment. It should be noted that *there are no appropriate statistical techniques for measuring random sampling error from a nonprobability sample. Thus projecting the data beyond the sample is statistically inappropriate.* Nevertheless, there are occasions when nonprobability samples are best suited for the researcher's purpose.

The various types of nonprobability and probability samples will now be explored. Although probability sampling is preferred, nonprobability sampling will be discussed first in order to illustrate some potential sources of error and other weaknesses in sampling.

NONPROBABILITY SAMPLING

Convenience Sampling

Convenience sampling (also called *haphazard* or *accidental sampling*) refers to the procedure of obtaining units or people who are most conveniently available. For example, it may be convenient and economical to sample employees in companies in a nearby area. During election times television channels often present man-on-the-street interviews that are presumed to reflect public opinion. (Of course, the television channel often warns that the survey was "unscientific and random.") The college professor who uses his students has a captive sample—convenient but unrepresentative and perhaps unwilling.

Researchers generally use convenience samples to obtain a large number of completed questionnaires quickly and economically. For example, it was supposedly a man-on-the-street straw poll, conducted by the *Chicago Sun-Times,* that alerted former Senator Charles Percy to his reelection problems in his first reelection campaign. The user of research that is based on a conve-

R E S E A R C H   I N S I G H T

The Dow Jones Industrial Average (DJIA): A Nonprobability Sample

The DJIA has been criticized over time on several counts, the first of which is that the sample used for the series is limited. It is difficult to conceive of how 30 nonrandomly selected blue-chip stocks can be representative of the 1,800 stocks listed on the NYSE. In addition to the fact that their number is limited, the stocks included are, by definition, offerings of the largest and most prestigious companies in various industries. Therefore the DJIA probably reflects price movements for large, mature blue-chip firms rather than for the "typical" company listed on the NYSE. Several studies have pointed out that price movements on the DJIA have not been as volatile as they have been on other market indicator series and that the long-run returns on the DJIA are not comparable to those implied by more representative price indicator series.

In addition, the stocks in the DJIA are weighted on the basis of their relative prices. Therefore, when a high-priced stock such as DuPont moves even a small percent, it has an inordinate effect on the overall index. In contrast, when companies have a stock split, their prices decline and, therefore, their weight in the DJIA is reduced, even though they may be large and important. Therefore, the weighting scheme causes a downward bias in the DJIA because the stocks that have higher growth rates will have higher prices and such stocks tend to consistently split, and thereby consistently lose weight within the index. Irrespective of the several criticisms made of the DJIA, a comparison of short-run price movements of the DJIA and of other NYSE indicators shows a fairly close relationship between the daily percentages of price changes for the DJIA and comparable price changes for other NYSE indicators.

Source: Frank K. Reilly, *Investment Analysis and Portfolio Management*, 3rd ed. (Hinsdale, IL: The Dryden Press, 1989), 153–154.

nience sample should remember that projecting the results beyond the specific sample is inappropriate. Convenience samples are best utilized for exploratory research when additional research will subsequently be conducted with a probability sample.

In many cases a research project using convenience sampling signals that the entire research project may lack objectivity. A supposedly nationwide poll in France was conducted with 1,000 Parisians[7]—an example of how not to select a convenience sample. Not surprisingly, it was conducted by IFOP, a French opinion research firm that had been involved in tampering with survey results.

Judgment or **purposive sampling** is a nonprobability sampling technique in which an experienced individual selects the sample based upon his or her judgment about some appropriate characteristic required of the sample members. The consumer price index (CPI) is based on a judgment sample of market-basket items, housing costs, and other selected goods and services expected to reflect a representative sample of items consumed by most Americans. Test-market cities often are selected because they are viewed as typical cities, with demographic profiles closely matching the national profile. A fashion manufacturer regularly selects a sample of key accounts that it believes are capable of providing the information to predict what will sell in the fall; the sample has been selected to satisfy a specific objective.

Judgment sampling is often used in attempts to forecast election results. People often wonder how, say, a television network can predict the results of an election with only 2 percent of the votes reported. Political and sampling experts judge which small voting districts approximate overall state returns from previous election years. Then these bellwether precincts are selected as the sampling units. Of course, the assumption is that the past voting nature of these districts is still representative of the state's political behavior.

Quota Sampling

Suppose a firm wishes to investigate consumers who currently own videotape recorders. The researchers may wish to ensure that each brand of videotape recorder is proportionately included in the sample. Strict probability sampling procedures would likely underrepresent certain brands and overrepresent other brands. If the selection process were left strictly to chance, some variation would be expected. The purpose of **quota sampling** is to ensure that the various subgroups in a population are represented on pertinent sample characteristics to the exact extent that the investigators desire. Stratified sampling, a probability sampling procedure, also has this objective, and it should not be confused with quota sampling. In quota sampling, the interviewer has a quota to achieve. For example, an interviewer in a particular city may be assigned 100 interviews, 30 of which are with Panasonic owners, 28 with Sony Betamax owners, 10 with Magnavox owners, 7 with Toshiba owners, and the rest with owners of other brands. Aggregating the various interview quotas yields a sample representing the desired proportion of the subgroups.

Possible Sources of Bias.   The logic of classifying the population by pertinent subgroups is essentially sound. However, because respondents are selected according to a convenience sampling procedure, rather than on a probability basis (as in stratified sampling), the haphazard selection of subjects may introduce bias. For example, a college professor hired some of his students to conduct a quota sample based on age. When he analyzed the data, it became apparent that almost all of the people in the "under 25 years" category were college educated. Interviewers are human, and they tend to prefer to interview people similar to themselves. Quota samples have a tendency to include people who are easily found, willing to be interviewed, and middle class.

Fieldworkers are given considerable leeway to exercise their judgment concerning selection of respondents. Interviewers often concentrate their interviewing in heavy pedestrian-traffic areas, such as shopping malls, employee lunchrooms, and college campuses. Those who interview door-to-door learn quickly that quota requirements are difficult to meet by interviewing whoever happens to appear at the door. This tends to overrepresent less active people, who tend to stay at home.

One interviewer related a story of working in an upper-middle class neighborhood. After a few blocks it changed into a neighborhood of "mansions." Feeling that most of these people were above the interviewer's station, these houses were skipped because the interviewer did not feel comfortable knocking on doors that were answered by servants.

Advantages of Quota Samples.   Speed of data collection, lower costs, and convenience are the major advantages of quota sampling compared to probability sampling. Although there are many problems with this method, careful supervision of the data collection may provide a representative sample for analyzing the various subgroups within a population. A number of laboratory experiments rely on quota sampling because it is difficult to find a sample of the general population willing to visit a laboratory for an experiment.

Snowball Sampling

Snowball sampling refers to a variety of procedures in which initial respondents are selected by probability methods, but in which additional respondents are then obtained from information provided by initial respondents.[8] This technique is used to locate members of rare populations by referrals.

Suppose a manufacturer of sports equipment is considering the marketing of a mahogany croquet set for serious adult players. This market is certainly small. An extremely large sample would be necessary in order to find 100 serious adult croquet players. It would be much more economical to survey, say, 300 people and find 15 croquet players and ask them for the names of other players.

Reduced sample sizes and costs are a clear advantage of snowball sampling. Bias is likely to enter into the study, however, because a person who is known to someone (also in the sample) has a higher probability of being similar to the first person. If there are major differences between those who are widely known by others and those who are not, there may be serious problems with snowball sampling.

PROBABILITY SAMPLING

All probability samples are based on chance selection procedures.[9] This eliminates the bias inherent in the nonprobability sampling procedures because the probability sampling process is random. It is frequently forgotten that the term *random* refers to the procedure for selecting the sample; it does not describe the data in the sample.[10] Randomness refers to a procedure the outcome of which cannot be predicted because it is dependent on chance.

The procedure of randomization should not be thought of as unplanned or unscientific. It is the basis of all probability sampling techniques.

Simple Random Sampling

Simple random sampling assures that each element in the population has an equal chance of being included in the sample. Drawing names from a hat or selecting the winning raffle ticket from a large drum is typical of simple random sampling. If the names or raffle tickets are thoroughly stirred, each person (or ticket) should have an equal chance of being selected.

The sampling process is simple because it requires only one stage of sample selection (in contrast to more complex probability samples).

Drawing names or numbers out of a fish bowl, using a spinner, rolling dice, or turning a roulette wheel may be used to draw a sample from small populations. But when populations consist of large numbers of elements, tables of random digits (see Table 1 in the Appendix) or computer-generated random numbers are utilized for sample selection.

Selecting a Random Sample.   A researcher may be interested in selecting a random sample of all presidents of savings and loan associations in New Mexico, Arizona, and Nevada. Each president's name may be assigned a number from 1 to 135. Then each number is written on a separate piece of paper, and all the slips are placed in a large drum. After the slips of paper have been thoroughly mixed, one is selected for each sampling unit. Thus if the sample size is to be 45, the selection procedure must be repeated 44 times after the first slip has been selected. Mixing the slips after each selection will ensure that those at the bottom of the bowl will continue to have an equal chance of being selected in the sample.

To use a table of random numbers, a serial number is assigned to each element of the population. Then, assuming a population of 99,999 or less, five-digit numbers are selected from the table of random numbers merely by reading the numbers in any column or row, by moving upward, downward, left, or right. A random starting point should be selected at the outset. For convenience, we will assume that we have randomly selected the first five digits in Columns 1 through 5, Row 1, of Table 1 in the Appendix as our starting point. The first number in our sample would be 37751; moving downward, our next numbers would be 50915, 99142, and so on.

The random-digit telephone-dialing technique of sample selection requires that researchers identify the exchange or exchanges of interest (the first three numbers) and then use a table of numbers to select the next four numbers.

Systematic Sampling

To illustrate systematic sampling, suppose one wishes to take a sample of 1,000 from a list consisting of 200,000 names of companies. Using **systematic sampling,** every 200th name from the list would be drawn.

The procedure is extremely simple. An initial starting point is selected by a random process, and then every nth number on the list is selected. In a sampling from a rural telephone directory that does not separate business listings from household listings, for example, every 23rd name might be selected as the **sampling interval.** In this sample of consumers it is possible that Mike's Restaurant will be selected. This unit is inappropriate because it is a business listing rather than a consumer listing. Therefore the next eligible name is selected as the sampling unit, and the systematic process is continued.

Although this procedure is not actually a random selection procedure, it yields random results if the arrangement of the items in the list is random in character. The problem of **periodicity** occurs if a list has a systematic pattern, that is, if the list is not random in character. Collecting retail sales information every seventh day would result in a distorted sample because there would be a systematic pattern of selecting sampling units. Sales for only one day of the week, perhaps Monday's sales, would be sampled.

Another periodicity bias might be in a list of contributors to a charity where the first 50 might be extremely large donors. If the sampling interval is every 200th name, this could cause a problem.

Periodicity is rarely a problem for most sampling in business research, but researchers should be aware of its possibility.

Stratified Sampling

The usefulness of dividing the population into subgroups or *strata* that are more or less equal on some characteristic has been illustrated in our discussion of quota sampling. The first step of choosing strata on the basis of existing information, such as classification of retail outlets' size based on annual sales volume, is the same for both stratified and quota sampling. However, the processes of selecting sampling units within the stratum differ substantially. In **stratified sampling** a subsample is drawn utilizing a simple random sample within each stratum. This is not true with quota sampling.

The reason for taking a stratified sample is to have a more efficient sample than could be taken on the basis of simple random sampling. Suppose, for example, that urban and rural groups differ widely on attitudes toward energy conservation, yet members within each group hold very similar attitudes. Random sampling error is reduced because the groups are internally homogeneous but comparatively different between groups. More technically, a smaller standard error may be the result of this stratified sample because the groups are adequately represented when strata are combined.

Another reason for taking a stratified sample is the assurance that the sample will accurately reflect the population on the basis of the criterion or criteria used for stratification. This is a concern because occasionally a simple random sample yields a disproportionate number of one group or another, and the representativeness of the sample could be improved.

A researcher selecting a stratified sample will proceed as follows: First, a variable (sometimes several variables) is identified as an efficient basis for stratification. The criterion for a stratification variable is that it is a characteristic of the population elements known to be related to the dependent variable or other variables of interest. The variable chosen should increase homogeneity within each stratum and increase heterogeneity between strata. The stratification variable is usually a categorical variable or one easily converted into categories, that is, subgroups. For example, a pharmaceutical company interested in measuring how often physicians prescribe a certain drug might choose physicians' training as a basis for stratification. In this example the mutually exclusive strata are M.D.s (medical doctors) and O.D.s (osteopathic doctors).

Next, for each separate subgroup or stratum, a list of population elements must be obtained. If a complete listing is not available, a true stratified probability sample cannot be selected. Then, using a table of random numbers or some other device, a *separate* simple random sample is taken within each stratum. If stratified lists are not available, they can be costly to prepare. Of course, the researcher must determine how large a sample must be drawn for each stratum.

EXHIBIT   1 4 . 6   **Demonstration of Disproportional Sampling Concept**

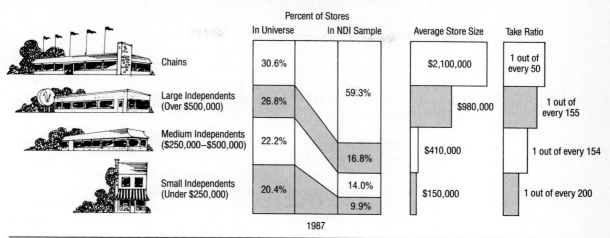

Source: Courtesy of Nielsen Marketing Research, Northbrook, IL.

Proportional versus Disproportional Strata.   If the number of sampling units drawn from each stratum is in proportion to the relative population size of the stratum, the sample is a **proportional stratified sample.** Sometimes, however, a disproportional stratified sample will be selected to ensure an adequate number of sampling units in every strata. Sampling more heavily in a given strata than its relative population size warrants is not a problem if the primary purpose of the research is to estimate some characteristic separately for each stratum, and if researchers are concerned about assessing the differences among strata.

Consider, however, the percentage of stores in Exhibit 14.6. There is a small percentage of large independent stores and a large percentage of other stores. The average store size (in dollar volume) for the chain and large independent store strata varies substantially from the smaller independent stores' average size, again in dollar volume. To avoid overrepresenting medium-size and smaller stores in the sample, a "disproportional" sample is taken.

In a **disproportional stratified sample,** sample size for each stratum is not allocated on a proportional basis with the population size, but by analytical considerations. The logic for this relates to the general argument for sample size. As variability increases, sample size must increase to provide accurate estimates. Thus the strata that exhibit the greatest variability are sampled more heavily in order to increase sample efficiency, that is, smaller random sampling error.

Of course, in the above example previous data have shown there are differences among the strata on average store size. Actually, the A. C. Nielsen example illustrates an **optimal allocation stratified sample** that takes both *varia-*

tion and *size* of each stratum into consideration. Thus the optimal sample size for each stratum may be determined.

Complex formulas (beyond the scope of this book) have been developed to determine the sample size for each stratum. A simplified rule of thumb for understanding the concept of optimal allocation is that stratum sample size increases for strata of larger sizes with the greatest relative variability.

Other complexities arise in determining population estimates. For example, when disproportional stratified sampling is utilized, the estimated means for each stratum have to be weighted according to the number of elements in each stratum in order to calculate the total population mean.

Cluster Sampling

The purpose of **cluster sampling** is to sample economically while retaining the characteristics of a probability sample. Consider the researcher who must conduct 500 interviews with individuals scattered throughout the United States. Travel costs are likely to be enormous because the amount of time spent traveling will be substantially greater than the time spent in the interviewing process.

If an aspirin marketer can assume the product will work as well in Phoenix as it does in Baltimore, or if a frozen-pizza manufacturer can assume employee attitudes toward fringe benefits to be the same in Texas as in Oregon, then cluster sampling may be used. In a cluster sample the primary sampling unit is no longer the individual element in the population (e.g., manufacturing firms) but a large cluster of elements (e.g., cities). The **area sample** is the most popular type of cluster sample. A grocery researcher, for example, may randomly choose several geographic areas as the primary sampling units and then interview all, or a sample, of grocery stores within the geographic clusters. Interviews are confined to these clusters; no interviews occur in other clusters. Cluster sampling is classified as a probability sampling technique either because of the random selection of clusters or the random selection of elements within each cluster.

Cluster samples are frequently utilized when no lists of the sample population are available. For example, in a downtown revitalization investigation of employees and self-employed workers, a list of these people was not available in any comprehensive form. A cluster sample was taken by selecting organizations (business as well as government) as the clusters. A sample of firms within the central business district was developed by using a stratified probability sample to identify clusters. Next, individual workers within the firms (clusters) were selected and interviewed concerning the central business district. (Some examples of clusters are given in Exhibit 14.7.)

Ideally, a cluster should be as heterogeneous as the population itself: a mirror image of the population. Therefore a problem may arise with cluster sampling if the characteristics and attitudes of the elements within the cluster are too similar. For example, geographic neighborhoods tend to have residents of the same socioeconomic status; students at a university tend to share similar beliefs. To an extent this problem may be mitigated by constructing clusters that are composed of diverse elements and by selecting a large number of sampled clusters.

**Examples of
Kinds of Clusters**

Population Elements	Possible Clusters
U.S. adult population	States
	Counties
	Metropolitan statistical areas
	Localities
	Census tracts
	Blocks
	Households
College seniors Professors	Colleges
Manufacturing firms	Counties
	Metropolitan statistical areas
	Localities
	Plants
Airline travelers	Airports
	Planes
Hospital patients Doctors	Hospitals
Sports fans	Stadia

Multistage Area Sampling.   We have described two-stage cluster sampling. **Multistage sampling** involves two or more steps that combine some of the probability techniques already described. Typically, progressively smaller (lower-population) geographic areas will be randomly selected in a series of steps. A political pollster investigating an election in Arizona might first choose counties within the state to ensure that the different areas are represented in the sample. In the second step, precincts within the selected counties may be chosen. As a final step, blocks (or households) within the precincts could be chosen. Then all the blocks (or households) within the geographic area would be interviewed. As many steps as are necessary may be taken to achieve a representative sample.

Exhibit 14.8 portrays a multistage area sampling process frequently used by a major academic research center. Progressively smaller geographic areas are selected until a housing unit is selected for interviewing.[11]

The Census Bureau provides maps, population information, demographic characteristics of the population, and so on by regions, states, counties, cities, and several small geographic areas that may be useful in sampling. Exhibit 14.9 shows how census areas may be progressively broken down into smaller geographic areas.

Census classifications of small geographic areas vary depending on the extent of urbanization within metropolitan statistical areas (MSAs) or counties. Exhibit 14.9 illustrates the geographic hierarchy inside and outside urbanized areas.

EXHIBIT 14.8

An Illustration of Multistage Area Sampling

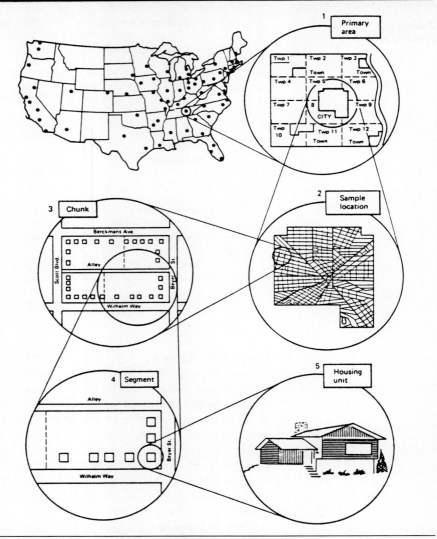

Source: *Interviewer's Manual,* rev. ed. (Ann Arbor, MI: Survey Research Center, Institute for Social Research, University of Michigan, 1976), 36. Reprinted by permission.

WHAT IS THE APPROPRIATE SAMPLE DESIGN?

We have discussed the advantages and disadvantages of each of the various sampling techniques. A summary comparing the sampling techniques is given in Exhibit 14.10. A researcher who must make a decision concerning the most appropriate sample design for a specific project will identify a number of sampling criteria and evaluate the relative importance of each criterion before se-

EXHIBIT   14.9

**Geographic Hierarchy Inside
and Outside Urbanized Areas**

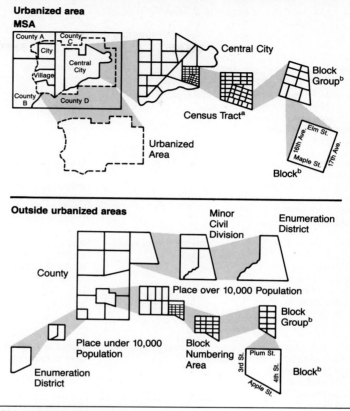

[a] The entire MSA is subdivided into census tracts.

[b] Blocks and block groups do not have symbolized boundaries as do the other areas, but are identified by number.

Source: "Census Geography—Concepts and Products," *U.S. Bureau of the Census—Factfinder for the Nation*, August 1985, 3.

lecting a sample design. This section outlines and briefly discusses the most common criteria.

Degree of Accuracy

Selecting a representative sample is, of course, important to all researchers. However, the degree of accuracy required or the researcher's tolerance for sampling and nonsampling error may vary from project to project, especially when cost savings or another consideration may be a trade-off for a reduction in accuracy.

For example, when the sample is being selected for an exploratory research project, a high priority may not be placed on accuracy because a highly representative sample may not be necessary. For other, more conclusive projects, the sample result must be a precise representation of a population's characteristics, and the researcher must be willing to spend the time and money to achieve accuracy.

E X H I B I T   1 4 . 1 0   **Comparison of Sampling Techniques**

Nonprobability Samples

Description	Cost and Degree of Use	Advantages	Disadvantages
1. *Convenience:* Researcher uses most convenient sample or uses opinion about which sample units are appropriate.	Very low cost, extensively used	No need for list of population.	Variability and bias of estimates cannot be measured or controlled; projecting data beyond sample inappropriate.
2. *Judgment:* An expert or experienced researcher selects the sample to fulfill a purpose, such as ensuring all members have a certain characteristic.	Moderate cost, average use	Useful for certain types of forecasting; sample guaranteed to meet a specific objective.	Bias due to experts' beliefs may make sample unrepresentative; projecting data beyond sample inappropriate.
3. *Quota:* Researcher classifies population by pertinent properties, determines desired proportion of sample from each class, fixes quotas for each interviewer.	Moderate cost, very extensively used	Introduces some stratification of population; requires no list of population.	Introduces bias in researcher's classification of subjects; nonrandom selection within classes means error from population cannot be estimated; projecting data beyond sample inappropriate.
4. *Snowball:* Initial respondents are selected by probability samples; additional respondents are obtained by referral from initial respondents.	Low cost, used in special situations	Useful in locating members of rare populations.	High bias because sample units not independent; projecting data beyond sample inappropriate.

Probability Samples

Description	Cost and Degree of Use	Advantages	Disadvantages
1. *Simple random:* Researcher assigns each member of sampling frame a number, selects sample units by random method.	High cost, not frequently used in practice (except random-digit dialing)	Only minimal advance knowledge of population needed; easy to analyze data and compute error.	Requires sample frame to work from; does not use knowledge of population that researcher may have; larger errors for same sample size than stratified sampling; respondents may be widely dispersed, hence higher cost.
2. *Systematic:* Researcher uses natural ordering or order of sampling frame, selects an arbitrary starting point, then selects items at a preselected interval.	Moderate cost, moderately used	Simple to draw sample; easy to check.	If sampling interval is related to a periodic ordering of the population, may introduce increased variability.
3. *Stratified:* Researcher divides population into groups and selects subsamples from each group. Variations include proportional, disproportional, and optimal allocation of subsample sizes.	High cost, moderately used	Assures representation of all groups in sample. Characteristics of each stratum can be estimated and comparisons made. Reduces variability for same sample size.	Requires accurate information on proportion in each stratum; if stratified lists are not already available, they can be costly to prepare.
4. *Cluster:* Researcher selects sampling units at random, does complete observation of all units in the group.	Low cost, frequently used	If clusters geographically defined, yields lowest field cost. Requires listing of all clusters but of individuals only within clusters. Can estimate characteristics of clusters as well as of population.	Larger error for comparable size than other probability samples; researcher must be able to assign population members to unique cluster, or duplication or omission of individuals results.
5. *Multistage:* Progressively smaller areas are selected in each stage. Researcher performs some combination of the first four techniques.	High cost, frequently used, especially in nationwide surveys	Depends on techniques combined.	Depends on techniques combined.

Resources

The cost associated with the different sampling techniques varies tremendously. If the researcher's financial and human resources are restricted, this limitation of resources will eliminate certain methods. For a graduate student working on a master's thesis, conducting a national survey is almost always out of the question because of limited resources. Managers concerned with the cost of the research versus the value of the information often will opt for a cost savings from a certain nonprobability sample design rather than make the decision to conduct no research at all.

Time

Researchers who need to meet a deadline or complete a project quickly will be more likely to select simple, less time-consuming sample designs. A telephone survey utilizing a sample based on random-digit dialing takes considerably less time than a survey using an elaborate disproportionate stratified sample.

Advance Knowledge of the Population

Advance knowledge of population characteristics, such as the availability of lists of population members, is an important criterion. In many cases, however, a list of population elements will not be available to the researcher. This is especially true when the population element is defined by ownership of a particular product or brand, by experience performing a specific job task, or on the basis of a qualitative dimension. A lack of adequate lists may automatically rule out systematic sampling, stratified sampling, or another sampling design, or it may dictate that a preliminary study, such as a short telephone survey utilizing random-digit dialing, be conducted to generate information to build a sampling frame for the study of primary interest. In smaller towns reverse directories are the exception rather than the rule; thus researchers planning sampling designs will have to work around this limitation.

National versus Local Project

Geographic proximity of population elements will influence sample design. When population elements are unequally distributed geographically, a cluster sampling may become much more attractive.

Need for Statistical Analysis

The need for statistical projections based on the sample is often a criterion. Nonprobability sampling techniques do not allow the researcher to utilize statistical analysis to project the data beyond the sample.

SUMMARY

Sampling is a procedure using a small number of units of a given population as a basis for drawing conclusions about the whole population. Sampling is often necessary because it would be practically impossible to conduct a census to measure characteristics of all elements of a population. Properly taken, samples lead to accurate portrayals of the whole population. Samples are also needed in cases where the measurement involves destruction of the unit measured.

The first problem in sampling is to define the relevant population. Incorrect or vague definition of the population is likely to produce misleading results. A sampling frame is a list of elements, or individual members, of the overall population from which the sample is drawn. A sampling unit is a single element or group of elements subject to selection in the sample.

There are two sources of discrepancy between the sample results and the population parameters. One type of error is random sampling error, arising from the chance variations of the sample from the population. Random sampling error is a function of sample size, and may be estimated using the central limit theorem, to be discussed in Chapter 15. Systematic (nonsampling) errors come from such sources as sample bias, mistakes in recording responses, or nonresponses from persons not contacted or refusing to participate.

The two major sampling methods are probability and nonprobability techniques. The nonprobability techniques include convenience sampling, quota sampling, and snowball sampling. They are convenient, but there are no statistical techniques to measure their random sampling error. Probability samples are based on chance selection procedures. Some of these procedures are simple random sampling, systematic sampling, stratified sampling, and cluster sampling. With these techniques random sampling error can be accurately predicted.

A researcher who must make a decision concerning the most appropriate sample design for a specific project will identify a number of sampling criteria and evaluate the relative importance of each criterion before selecting a sampling design. The most common criteria are accuracy requirements, resources available, time constraints, knowledge availability, and analytical requirements.

Key Terms

sampling	systematic (nonsampling) error
sample	nonresponse error
population (universe)	probability sampling
population element	nonprobability sampling
census	convenience sampling
target population	judgment (purposive) sampling
sampling frame	quota sampling
mailing list	snowball sampling
reverse directory	simple random sampling
sampling frame error	systematic sampling
sampling unit	sampling interval
primary sampling unit (PSU)	periodicity
secondary (tertiary) sampling unit	stratified sampling
random sampling error	proportional stratified sample

disproportional stratified sample   area sample

optimal allocation stratified sample   multistage area sampling

cluster sampling

Questions

1. If we judge whether or not we want to see a new movie or television program on the basis of "coming attractions" or television commercial previews, are we utilizing a sampling technique? A scientific sampling technique? Explain.

2. In what types of situations is conducting a census more appropriate than sampling? When is sampling more appropriate than taking a census?

3. Name some possible sampling frames for the following:
    a. Electric utilities.
    b. Tennis players.
    c. Dog owners.
    d. McDonald's employees.
    e. Wig and hair-goods retailers.
    f. Minority-owned businesses.
    g. Men over 6 feet tall.

4. Describe the difference between a probability sample and a nonprobability sample.

5. Comment on the following sampling designs:
    a. A citizens group, interested in generating public and financial support for a new university basketball arena, has published a questionnaire in area newspapers. Readers return the questionnaires by mail.
    b. A department store that wishes to examine whether it is losing or gaining customers draws a sample from its list of credit card holders by selecting every tenth name.
    c. A motorcycle manufacturer decided to research consumer characteristics by sending 100 questionnaires to each of its dealers. The dealers would then use their sales records to trace buyers of its brand of motorcycle and distribute the questionnaires to them.
    d. In selecting its sample for a focus group, a research company obtains a sample through organized groups such as church groups, clubs, or schools. The organizations are paid for securing a respondent, and no individual is directly compensated.

6. When the National Football League initiated instant replays to help officiate plays on the field, one network announced a viewer preference poll. Viewers who thought that the instant replay should be banned could call a particular 900 number to indicate their preference. Those who thought the instant replay should continue to be used could dial another 900 number to register their preference. At the end of the broadcast segment it was announced that 50 cents would be added to the individual respondent's bill by the telephone company. Evaluate this as a sampling technique.

7. A telephone interviewer asks: "I would like to ask you about race. Are you native American, Hispanic, black, Oriental, or white?" After the respondent replies, the interviewer says: "We have conducted a large number of surveys with people of your background and we do not need to question you further. Thank you for your cooperation." What type of sampling was utilized?

8. What are the benefits of stratified sampling?

9. What geographic units within a metropolitan area are useful for sampling?

10. Outline the step-by-step procedure you would utilize to select the following:
    a. A sample of 150 students at your college or university.
    b. A sample of 50 light users and 50 heavy users of beer in a shopping mall intercept sample.
    c. A sample of 50 mechanical engineers, 40 electrical engineers, and 40 civil engineers from the subscriber list of an engineering journal.
    d. A sample of banks, savings and loans, and other financiers of home mortgage loans.
    e. A sample of male and female workers to compare hourly wages of drill press operators in an industry.

11. In-Home Theatre (IT) is an over-the-air subscription television service operating in a Southwestern city. It receives its signals via a satellite from subscription television, or STV, located in Los Angeles and transmits a UHF signal over the air from a local facility. It broadcasts uncut feature movies through a scrambled television signal that is decoded with sophisticated equipment connected to the subscriber's television set. In-Home Theatre broadcasts over 100 movies per month, ranging from family to adults-only programming. It begins broadcasts at 7 p.m. on weekdays and 1 p.m. on weekends and ends programming at 4 a.m. daily. It shares transmitting facilities with a local station that broadcasts only during daytime hours. It now serves a customer base of approximately 8,000 homes in the urban and rural areas surrounding its headquarters. It plans to conduct a survey to identify the demographic characteristics of its subscribers and to determine their satisfaction with its program selection. What type of survey (mail, telephone, or personal interview) should it utilize? Design a sampling plan for the IT survey. Explain why you chose this sample design.

12. Jury duty is supposed to be a totally random process. Comment on the following computer selection procedures and determine if they are indeed random processes.
    a. A computer program scans the list of names and plucks names that are next to those from the last scan.
    b. Three-digit numbers were randomly generated to select jurors from a list of licensed drivers. If the weight information listed on the license matched the random number, the person was selected.
    c. The juror source list was obtained by merging a list of registered voters with a list of licensed drivers.

References

[1] Morris James Slonim, *Sampling in a Nutshell* (New York: Simon and Schuster, 1960), 3.

[2] Donald T. Warwick and Charles A. Lininger, *The Sample Survey: Theory and Practice* (New York: McGraw-Hill, 1975), 70.

[3] Seymour Sudman, *Applied Sampling* (New York: Academic Press, 1976), 12–13.

[4] Ibid., 14.

[5] This discussion follows Ya-Lun Chou, *Statistical Analysis* (New York: Holt, Rinehart and Winston, 1975), 390–391.

[6] Sudman, *Applied Sampling*, 17.

[7] Carol Pfaff, "French Take Poll-Tampering in Stride," *Advertising Age*, Jan. 15, 1979, 81.

[8] Sudman, *Applied Sampling*, 210–212.

[9] Slonim, *Sampling in a Nutshell*, 7.

[10] Ya-Lun, *Statistical Analysis*, 393.

[11] For additional details see *Interviewer's Manual*, rev. ed., Survey Research Center, Institute for Social Research, University of Michigan, Ann Arbor, 1976, 35–37.

Determination of Sample Size:
A Review of the Statistical Theory

What you will learn in this chapter:

To explain the difference between descriptive statistics and inferential statistics.

To discuss the purpose of inferential statistics by explaining the difference between population parameters and sample statistics.

To make data usable by organizing and summarizing them into frequency distributions, proportions, and measurements of central tendency.

To identify and calculate the various measures of dispersion.

To explain why the standard deviation is such an important measure of dispersion.

To compute the standard deviation.

To identify the characteristics of the normal distribution.

To define the standardized normal curve.

To compute the standardized value, Z, and to use the Z (standardized normal probability curve) tables in the Appendix of this book.

To distinguish among a population distribution, a sample distribution, and a sampling distribution and to identify the mean and standard deviation of each distribution.

To explain the central-limit theorem.

To compute confidence interval estimates.

To understand the three factors required for specifying sample size.

To estimate the same size for a simple random sample when the characteristic of interest is a mean and when the characteristic of interest is a proportion.

To understand which nonstatistical considerations influence the determination of sample size.

The determination of the appropriate sample size is a crucial aspect of business research. To formally identify the proper sample size, statistical theory is utilized. Unfortunately, statistics has a bad image among students.

The fear of statistics is one of the most universal phobias among college students. "Stat is too difficult; I'll never pass" is a lament often heard on campus. Many students postpone their statistics classes until their last semester. Statistics students are frequently subject to mental blocks. They feel like Saint George who must tame the raging statistical dragon. The accompanying cartoon on the next page illustrates the students' fears rather well. There is no need, however, for students to have this dread. Statistics can be easily mastered if one learns the tricks of the trade.

Why are there so many myths about statistics? Statisticians, much like lawyers, medical doctors, and computer scientists, have developed their own jargon. Laymen do not understand the professionals' technical terms. Cynics suspect this terminology ploy is used to impress others and, possibly, to justify higher fees. How many fishermen have you heard say, "Hand me the reticulated lattice joined at the interstices?" Not many, I'll bet. Few fishermen use this terminology when they simply want a net. Then again, when compared to professionals who use complex terminology, fishermen don't make much money.[1]

The point is a simple one. If you don't understand the basics of a language, you'll have problems conversing in that language. Statistics is the language of the researcher. Business researchers use statistics as a means of communication. If administrators and researchers don't speak the same language, there will be a failure to communicate.

This chapter explains how to determine sample size and includes a review of some of the basic terminology involved in statistical analysis.

■

Source: Cartoon by Tony Hall. From *Exploring Statistics: An Introduction for Psychology and Education,* by Sarah M. Dinham. Copyright © 1976 by Wadsworth, Inc. Reprinted by permission of Brooks/Cole Publishing Co., Monterey, CA 93940.

REVIEWING SOME BASIC TERMINOLOGY

The first portion of this chapter summarizes several key statistical concepts necessary for understanding the theory underlying the derivation of sample size. The next 21 pages are intended for students who need to review many of the basic aspects of statistics theory. Many students, even those who received a "good" grade in their elementary statistics class, probably will benefit from a quick review of the basic statistical concepts. Some students will prefer to skim this material and proceed to page 383, where the discussion of the actual determination of sample size begins. Others should study this section with care to acquire an understanding of the purpose of statistics for the first time.

Descriptive and Inferential Statistics

The *Statistical Abstract of the United States* presents table after table of figures associated with the number of births, number of employees of each county of the United States, and other data that the average person calls statistics. These are **descriptive statistics.** Another type of statistics, **inferential statistics,** is used to make an inference about a population from a sample. For example, when a firm test markets a new product in Sacramento and Birmingham, it wishes to make an inference from these sample markets to predict what will happen throughout the United States. Thus there are two applications of statistics: (1) to describe characteristics of the population or sample, and (2) to generalize from the sample to the population.

POPULATION PARAMETERS AND SAMPLE STATISTICS

The primary purpose of inferential statistics is to make a judgment about the population or the collection of all elements about which one seeks information. The sample is a subset or relatively small fraction of the total number of elements in the population. It is useful to distinguish between the data computed in the sample and the data or variables in the population. We use the term **sample statistics** to designate variables in the sample or measures computed from the sample data. The term **population parameters** is used to designate the variables or measured characteristics of the population. Sample statistics are used to make inferences about population parameters. In our notation, we will generally use Greek lower-case letters (μ or σ, for example) to denote population parameters and we will use English letters to denote sample statistics (X or S, for example).[2]

MAKING DATA USABLE

Frequency Distributions

Suppose a telephone survey has been conducted for a savings and loan association. The data have been recorded on a large number of questionnaires. To make the data usable, this information must be organized and summarized. Constructing a **frequency distribution,** or **frequency table,** is one of the most common means of summarizing a set of data. The process begins by recording the number of times a particular value of a variable occurs. This is the frequency of that value. In our survey example, Table 15.1 represents a frequency distribution of respondents' answers to the question asking how much money customers had deposited in the savings and loan.

It is also quite simple to construct a distribution of relative frequency, or a **percentage distribution.** In Table 15.2 the frequency of each value in Table 15.1 has been divided by the total number of observations. Multiplying each of the relative class frequencies by 100, we convert them to percentages and obtain a frequency distribution of percentages.

Probability is the long-run relative frequency with which an event will occur. In inferential statistics, we use the concept of a **probability distribution,** which is conceptually the same as a percentage distribution except that the data have been converted into probabilities (see Table 15.3).

Proportions

When a frequency distribution portrays only a single characteristic as a percentage of the total, the **proportion** of occurrence is defined. A proportion, perhaps the proportion of Hispanic Americans in the work force, may be expressed as a percentage, fraction, or decimal value. A proportion, such as the proportion of tenured faculty at a university, indicates the percentage of population elements that successfully meet some standard on the particular characteristic.

Central Tendency

On a typical day a certain sales manager counts the number of sales calls each of his sales representatives has made. He wishes to inspect the data to see the "center" or "middle area" of the frequency distribution. There are three ways to measure this central tendency, and each of these "averages" has a different meaning.

The Mean.   The mean is an average that all of us have been exposed to. The **mean** is simply the arithmetic average, and it is a very common measure of cen-

Amount	Frequency (Number of People Making Deposits in Each Range)
Less than $3,000	499
$3,000–$4,999	530
$5,000–$9,999	562
$10,000–$14,999	718
$15,000 or more	811
	3,120

Amount	Percent of People Making Deposits in Each Range
Less than $3,000	16%
$3,000–$4,999	17
$5,000–$9,999	18
$10,000–$14,999	23
$15,000 or more	26
	100%

Amount	Probability
Less than $3,000	.16
$3,000–$4,999	.17
$5,000–$9,999	.18
$10,000–$14,999	.23
$15,000 or more	.26
	1.00

tral tendency. At this point it is appropriate to introduce the summation symbol, the Greek capital letter sigma (Σ). A typical use is the following:

$$\sum_{i=1}^{n} X_i$$

This a shorthand way to write the sum:

$$X_1 + X_2 + X_3 + X_4 + X_5 + \cdots + X_n$$

Suppose a sales manager supervises the eight salespeople listed in Table 15.4. Below the Σ is the initial value of an index, usually i, j, or k, and above it

**Number of Sales Calls
per Day by Salespersons**

Salesperson	Number of Sales Calls
Mike	4
Pat	3
Billie	2
Rob	5
John	3
Frank	3
Anne	1
Samantha	5
Total (sum)	26

is the final value, in this case n, the number of observations. The shorthand expression says to replace i in the formula with the values from 1 to 8 and total the observations obtained. The initial and final index values may be replaced by other values to indicate different starting or stopping points without changing the basic formula.

To express the sum of the salespersons' calls in Σ notation, we number the salespersons (this is the index number) and associate subscripted variables with their number of calls:

Index		Salesperson	Variable		Calls
1	=	Mike	X_1	=	4
2	=	Pat	X_2	=	3
3	=	Billie	X_3	=	2
4	=	Rob	X_4	=	5
5	=	John	X_5	=	3
6	=	Frank	X_6	=	3
7	=	Anne	X_7	=	1
8	=	Samantha	X_8	=	5

Then we write an appropriate Σ formula, and evaluate it:

$$\sum_{i=1}^{8} X_i = X_1 + X_2 + X_3 + X_4 + X_5 + X_6 + X_7 + X_8$$
$$= 4 + 3 + 2 + 5 + 3 + 3 + 1 + 5$$
$$= 26$$

The formula for the arithmetic mean is as follows:

$$\text{Mean} = \frac{\sum_{i=1}^{n} X}{n} = \frac{26}{8} = 3.25$$

The sum

$$\sum_{i=1}^{n} X$$

tells us to add all the Xs whose subscripts are between 1 and n inclusive (where n equals the number of observations). The mean number of sales calls in this example is 3.25.

Researchers generally wish to know the population mean, μ (lowercase Greek letter *mu*), which is calculated as follows:

$$\mu = \frac{\sum_{i=1}^{n} X}{N}$$

where

N = number of observations in the population.

Often we will not have enough data to calculate the population mean μ, so we will calculate a sample mean, $\overline{X}$ (read as "X bar"), with the following formula:

$$\overline{X} = \frac{\sum_{i=1}^{n} X}{n}$$

where

n = number of observations in the sample.

More likely than not, you already knew how to calculate a mean. However, distinguishing between the symbols Σ, μ, and $\overline{X}$ is necessary for an understanding of statistics.

Median.   The next measure of central tendency, the **median,** is the midpoint of the distribution, or the fiftieth percentile. In other words, the median is the value below which half the values in the sample fall. In the sales manager example, 3 is the median since half the observations are greater than 3 and half are less than 3.

Mode.   In apparel, "mode" refers to the most popular fashion. In statistics, the **mode** is the measure of central tendency that merely identifies the value that occurs most often. In our example above, Pat, John, and Frank each makes three sales calls per day. The value 3 occurs most often, and thus 3 is the mode. This is determined by listing each possible value and noting the number of times each value occurs.

Measures of Dispersion
The mean, median, and mode summarize the central tendency of frequency distributions. It is also important to know the tendency for observations to depart from the central tendency. Calculating the dispersion of the data, or how the observations vary from the mean, is another means of summarizing the data. Consider, for instance, the 12-month inventory-level patterns of two products shown in Table 15.5. Both have a mean inventory level of 200 units, but the dispersion of observations for Product B is much greater than for Product A. There are several measures of dispersion.

RESEARCH INSIGHT
The Well-Chosen Average

. . . When you read an announcement by a corporation executive or a business proprietor that the average pay of the people who work in his establishment is so much, the figure may mean something and it may not. If the average is a median, you can learn something significant from it: Half the employees make more than that; half make less. But if it is a mean (and believe me it may be that if its nature is unspecified), you may be getting nothing more revealing than the average of one $450,000 income—the proprietor's—and the salaries of a crew of underpaid workers. "Average annual pay of $57,000" may conceal both the $20,000 salaries and the owner's profits taken in the form of a whopping salary.

Let's take a longer look at that one. This shows how many people get how much. The boss might like to express the situation as "average wage $57,000"—using that deceptive mean. The mode, however, is more revealing: most common rate of pay in this business is $20,000 a year. As usual, the median tells more about the situation than any other single figure does; half the people get more than $30,000 and half get less.

Number of People	Title	Salary	
1	Proprietor	$450,000	
1	President	150,000	
2	Vice-presidents	100,000	
1	Controller	57,000	← Arithmetical Average, Mean
3	Directors	50,000	
4	Managers	37,000	(the one in the middle;
1	Foreman	30,000	← Median 12 above him, 12 below)
12	Workers	20,000	← Mode (occurs most frequently)

Source: Adapted from Darrell Huff and Irving Geis, *How to Lie with Statistics* (New York: Norton, 1954), 33. Adapted with permission.

T A B L E   15.5

Inventory Levels for Products A and B (Both Average 200 Units)

	Units Product A	Units Product B
January	196	150
February	198	160
March	199	176
April	200	181
May	200	192
June	200	200
July	200	201
August	201	202
September	201	213
October	201	224
November	202	240
December	202	261

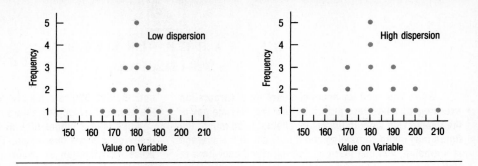

The Range.

The **range** is the simplest measure of dispersion. It is the distance between the smallest and the largest values of a frequency distribution. Thus for Product A the range is between 196 units and 202 units (6 units), whereas for Product B the range is between 150 units and 261 units (111 units). The range does not take into account all the observations. It merely tells us about the extreme values of the distribution.

Just as people may be fat or skinny, distributions may be fat or skinny. For example, for Product A the observations are close together and reasonably close to the mean. While we do not expect all observations to be exactly like the mean, in a skinny distribution they will be a short distance from the mean. In a fat distribution the observations will be spread out. Exhibit 15.1 illustrates this concept with two frequency distributions having identical modes, medians, and means but differing degrees of dispersion.

The *interquartile* range encompasses the middlemost 50 percent of the observations, that is, the range between the bottom quartile (lowest 25 percent) and the top quartile (highest 25 percent).

Deviation Scores.

A method of calculating how far away any observation is from the mean is to calculate individual deviation scores. To calculate a deviation from the mean, we use the following formula:

$$d_i = (X_i - \bar{X})$$

where

$$d_i = \text{a deviation score}$$

If the value of 150 units for Product B represents the month of January, we would calculate its deviation score to be -50; that is, $150 - 200 = -50$. If the deviation scores are large, we will find that we have a *fat* distribution because the distribution exhibits a broad spread.

Why Use the Standard Deviation?

Statisticians have devised several quantitative indexes to reflect a distribution's spread or variability. The **standard deviation** is perhaps the most valuable index of spread or dispersion. Students often have difficulty understanding this concept. Learning about the standard deviation will be easier if we present several other measures of dispersion that may be used. Each of these has certain limitations that the standard deviation does not.

The first of these is the **average deviation**. The average deviation is computed by calculating the deviation score of each observation value, that is, its difference from the mean, and summing up each deviation score. Then we divide by the sample size (n):

$$\text{Average deviation} = \frac{\Sigma(X_i - \bar{X})}{n}$$

While this method of calculating a measure of spread seems of interest, it is never used. The positive deviation scores are always canceled out by the negative deviation scores, thus leaving an average deviation value of zero. Hence the average deviation is useless as a measure of spread.

The disadvantage of the average deviation might be corrected by computing the absolute values of the deviations. In other words, we would ignore all the positive and negative signs and utilize only the absolute value of each deviation. The formula for the *mean absolute deviation* is:

$$\text{Mean absolute deviation} = \frac{\Sigma|X_i - \bar{X}|}{n}$$

While this procedure eliminates the problem of always having a zero score for the deviation measure, it presents some technical mathematical problems that make it less valuable than some other measures. (It is mathematically intractable.)[3]

Variance.   There is another means of eliminating the sign problem caused by the negative deviations canceling out the positive deviations. The procedure is to square the deviation scores. In the formula below, the mean squared deviation is given:

$$\text{Mean squared deviation} = \frac{\Sigma(X_i - \bar{X})^2}{n}$$

This measure is useful to describe the sample variability. However, we typically wish to make an inference about a population from the sample. The divisor n − 1 is used (rather than n) in most pragmatic business research problems.[4] This new measure of spread is called the sample **variance**, and a measure of the formula is given below:

$$\text{Variance, } S^2 = \frac{\Sigma(X_i - \bar{X})^2}{n - 1}$$

The variance is a very good index of the degree of dispersion. The variance, S^2, will be equal to zero if and only if each and every observation in the distribution is the same as the mean. The variance will grow larger as the observations tend to differ increasingly from each other and from the mean.

T A B L E   1 5 . 6

Calculating a Standard Deviation: Number of Sales Calls per Day by Salespersons

	n = 8 $\bar{X}$ = 3.25		
	X	(X − $\bar{X}$)	(X − $\bar{X}$)²
	4	(4 − 3.25) = .75	.5625
	3	(3 − 3.25) = −.25	.0625
	2	(2 − 3.25) = −1.25	1.5625
	5	(5 − 3.25) = 1.75	3.0625
	3	(3 − 3.25) = −.25	.0625
	3	(3 − 3.25) = −.25	.0625
	1	(1 − 3.25) = −2.25	5.0625
	5	(5 − 3.25) = 1.75	3.0625
Σ	a	a	13.5

$$s = \sqrt{\frac{\Sigma(X - \bar{X})^2}{n - 1}} = \sqrt{\frac{13.5}{8 - 1}} = \sqrt{\frac{13.5}{7}} = \sqrt{1.9286} = 1.3887$$

aThe summation of this column is not used in the calculation of the standard deviation.

Standard Deviation.   While the variance is frequently used in statistics, it does have one major drawback. The variance reflects a unit of measurement that has been squared. For instance, if measures of sales in a territory are made in dollars, then the mean number is reflected in dollars but the variance will be in squared dollars. Because of this, statisticians take the square root of the variance. The square root of the variance for distribution is called the *standard deviation*. This eliminates the drawback of having the measure of dispersion in squared units rather than in the original measurement units. The formula for the standard deviation is: [5]

$$S = \sqrt{S^2} = \sqrt{\frac{\Sigma(X_i - \bar{X})^2}{n - 1}}$$

Table 15.6 illustrates that the calculation of a standard deviation requires the researcher to first calculate the sample mean. In the example about 8 salespersons' sales calls (Table 15.4), we calculated the sample mean to be 3.25. Table 15.6 illustrates how to calculate the standard deviation for this data.

At this point, the student should think about the original purpose in looking at measures of dispersion. We have said that we wish to summarize the data from survey research and other forms of business research. Indexes of central tendencies, such as the mean, help us interpret the data. In addition, we wish to calculate a measure of variability that will give us a quantitative index of the dispersion of the distribution. We have looked at several measures of dispersion and have arrived at two very adequate means of measuring dispersion: the variance and the standard deviation.

At this point we should note that the formula is for the sample standard deviation, S. The formula for the population standard deviation, σ, which is conceptually very similar, has not been given. Nevertheless, the reader should

EXHIBIT 15.2

The Normal Distribution: An Example of the Distribution of Intelligence Quotient (IQ) Scores

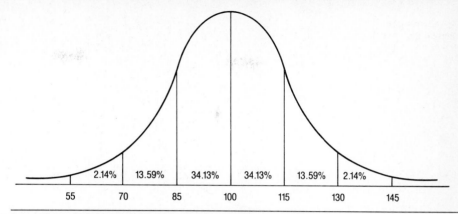

| | 2.14% | 13.59% | 34.13% | 34.13% | 13.59% | 2.14% | |
| 55 | 70 | 85 | 100 | 115 | 130 | 145 |

Source: Thomas H. Wonnacott and Ronald J. Wonnacott, *Introductory Statistics*, 2nd ed. (New York: John Wiley & Sons, 1972), p. 115. Reprinted with permission.

understand that σ measures the dispersion in the population while S measures the dispersion in the sample.

These concepts are crucial to understanding statistics. Remember, the student of statistics must learn the language if he or she is to use it in a research project. If you don't understand the concept at this point, review the material now.

The Normal Distribution

One of the most useful probability distributions in statistics is the **normal distribution,** which is also called the *normal curve*. This mathematical and theoretical distribution describes the expected distribution of sample means and many other chance occurrences. The normal curve is bell-shaped and almost all (99 percent) of its values are within ± 3 standard deviations from its mean. An example of a normal curve, the distribution of IQ scores, appears in Exhibit 15.2. In our example a standard deviation for IQ equals 15. Notice that we can identify the proportion of the curve by measuring a score's (in this case standard deviation) distance from the mean (100).

The **standardized normal distribution** is a specific normal curve that has several characteristics: (1) it is symmetrical about its mean; (2) the mean of the normal curve identifies its highest point (the mode) and vertical line about which this normal curve is symmetrical; (3) the normal curve has an infinite number of cases (it is a continuous distribution), and the area under the curve has a probability density equal to 1.0; and (4) the standardized normal curve has a mean of zero and a standard deviation of 1. Exhibit 15.3 illustrates these properties. Table 15.7 is a summary version of the typical standardized normal table found at the end of most statistics textbooks. A more complete table of areas under the standardized normal distribution appears in Table 2 in the Appendix of Statistical Tables at the end of this book.

E X H I B I T   1 5 . 3

**The Standardized
Normal Distribution**

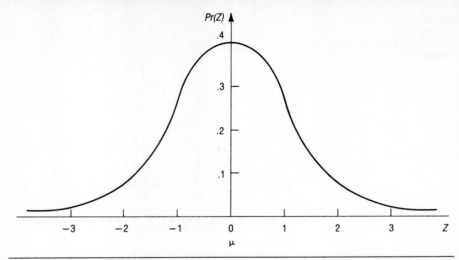

Source: Thomas H. Wonnacott and Ronald J. Wonnacott, *Introductory Statistics,* 2nd ed. (New York: John Wiley & Sons, 1969), p. 67. Reprinted with permission.

T A B L E   1 5 . 7

Standardized Normal Table

Standard Deviation from Mean, in Units of Z	Standard Deviations from Mean, in Tenths of Units of Z									
	—0	—.1	—.2	—.3	—.4	—.5	—.6	—.7	—.8	—.9
	Area under One Half of Normal Curve[a]									
0.—	.000	.040	.080	.118	.155	.192	.226	.258	.288	.316
1.—	.341	.364	.385	.403	.419	.433	.445	.455	.464	.471
2.—	.477	.482	.486	.489	.492	.494	.495	.496	.497	.498
3.—	.499	.499	.499	.499	.499	.499	.499	.499	.499	.499

[a] Area under the normal curve in one direction from the mean to the distance indicated in each row–column combination. For example, the table shows that about 68 percent of normally distributed observations can be expected to fall within one standard deviation on either side of the mean (.341 times 2). An interval of almost 2.0 standard deviations around the mean will include 95 percent of all cases.

The standardized normal distribution is a purely theoretical distribution, yet it is the most useful distribution in inferential statistics. Statisticians have spent a great deal of time and effort making it convenient for researchers to find the probability of any portion of the area under the standardized normal curve. All we must do is transform or convert the data from other observed normal distributions to the standardized normal curve. In other words, the standardized normal distribution is extremely valuable because we can translate or transform any normal variable, X, into the standardized value Z. Exhibit 15.4 illustrates how we can convert either a *skinny* distribution or a *fat* distribution

EXHIBIT   15.4

Linear Transformation of Any Normal Variable into the Standardized Normal Variable

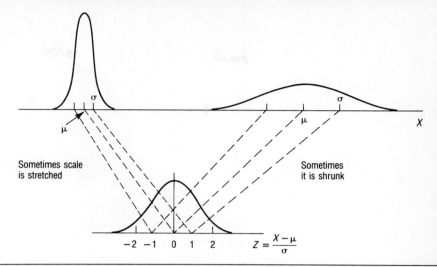

$$Z = \frac{X - \mu}{\sigma}$$

Source: Thomas H. Wonnacott and Ronald J. Wonnacott, *Introductory Statistics* (New York: John Wiley & Sons, 1969), p. 70. Reprinted with permission.

into the standardized normal distribution. This has many pragmatic implications for the business researcher. The standardized normal table at the back of most statistics and research methods books allows us to evaluate the probability of the occurrence of certain events without any difficulty.

The computation of the standardized value, Z, of any measurement expressed in original units is simple. All we need do is subtract the mean from the value to be transformed and divide by the standard deviation (all expressed in original units). The formula for this procedure and its verbal statement follow. In the formula note that σ, the population standard deviation, is utilized for calculation.[6]

$$Z = \frac{X - \mu}{\sigma}$$

where

μ = the hypothesized or expected value of the mean.

$$\text{Standardized value} = \frac{(\text{Value to be transformed}) - (\text{Mean})}{\text{Standard deviation}}$$

Suppose that in the past a toy manufacturer has experienced mean sales, μ, of 9,000 units, $\mu = 9,000$, and a standard deviation, σ, of 500 units during the month of September. The production manager wishes to know if wholesalers will demand between 7,500 and 9,625 units during the month of September in the upcoming year. As there are no tables in the back of our textbook for the distribution where the mean equals 9,000 and a standard deviation

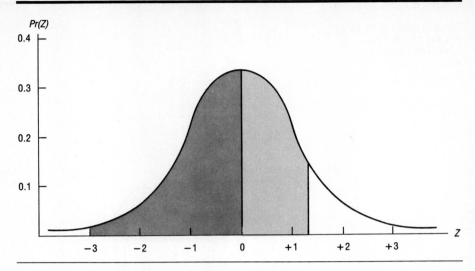

equals 500, we must transform our distribution of sales, X, into the standard-ized form, utilizing our simple formula. The computation below shows that the probability of obtaining sales in this range is probability (Pr) = .893.

$$Z = \frac{X - \mu}{\sigma} = \frac{7,500 - 9,000}{500} = -3.00$$

$$= \frac{9,625 - 9,000}{500} = 1.25$$

Using Table 15.7 (or Table 2 in the Appendix), we find:
When
          Z = 3.00, the area under the curve (probability) equals .499
When
          Z = 1.25, the area under the curve (probability) equals .394
Thus the total area under the curve is .499 + .394 = .893

Thus the area under the curve portraying this computation is the shaded area in Exhibit 15.5. Thus the sales manager knows there is a .893 probability that sales will be between 7,500 and 9,625.

At this point it is appropriate to reiterate that to understand statistics one must understand the language that statisticians use. Each concept that has been discussed thus far is relatively simple. But a clear-cut command of these termi-nologies is essential for understanding what will be discussed later.

Now that certain basic terminology has been covered, we will outline the technique of statistical inference. Three additional types of distribution must be defined: population distribution, sample distribution, and sampling distribution.

POPULATION DISTRIBUTION, SAMPLE DISTRIBUTION, AND SAMPLING DISTRIBUTION

When conducting a research project or a survey, the researcher's purpose is not to describe the sample of respondents but to make an inference about the population. As we have defined previously, a population or universe is the total set or collection of potential units for observation. The sample is a smaller subset of this population.

A frequency distribution of the population elements is called a **population distribution**. The population distribution has its mean and standard deviation represented by the Greek letters μ and σ. A frequency distribution of a sample is called the **sample distribution**. The sample mean is designated $\overline{X}$ and the sample standard deviation is designated S. The concepts of the population distribution and the sample distribution are relatively simple. However, we must now introduce another distribution, the *sampling distribution of the sample mean*. If students forget which distribution is being discussed, there will be some difficulty in learning about statistical inference. One must learn the vocabulary to master a new language.

We are now at a crucial point in understanding statistics. Understanding the sampling distribution is the basis for understanding statistics. The sampling distribution is a theoretical probability distribution that in actual practice would never be calculated. Hence students who are practical and business-oriented have difficulty understanding why the notion of the sampling distribution is discussed. But statisticians, with their mathematical curiosity, have asked themselves the question: "What would happen if we were to draw a large number of samples (say 50,000), each having n elements, from a specified population?" Assuming that the large number of samples were randomly selected, the sample means, $\overline{X}$s, could be arranged in a frequency distribution. Because different people or sample elements will be selected in the different samples, the sample means will not be exactly equal. The shape of the sampling distribution is of considerable importance to statisticians. If the sample size is sufficiently large and if the samples were randomly drawn, we know from the central-limit theorem that the sampling distribution of the mean will be approximately normally distributed.

A formal definition of the sampling distribution is as follows: A **sampling distribution** is a theoretical probability distribution that shows the functional relationship between the possible values of some summary characteristic of n cases drawn at random and the probability (density) associated with each value over all possible samples of size n from a particular population.[7]

The sampling distribution's mean is called the *expected value* of the statistic. The expected value of the mean of the sampling distribution is equal to μ. The standard deviation of the sampling distribution is called the **standard error of the mean** ($S_{\overline{X}}$) and is approximately equal to

$$S_{\overline{X}} = \frac{\sigma}{\sqrt{n}}$$

At this point it is appropriate to review what has just been discussed. There are three important distributions that we must know about if we are to make an inference about a population from a sample. These are the population distribution, the sample distribution, and the sampling distribution. They have the following characteristics:

Distribution	Mean	Standard Deviation
Population	μ	σ
Sample	$\bar{X}$	S
Sampling	$\mu_{\bar{X}} = \mu$	$S_{\bar{X}}$

We now have much of the information that is necessary to understand the concept of statistical inference. To further aid understanding of why the sampling distribution has the characteristic described above, we will elaborate on two concepts: the standard error of the mean and the central-limit theorem. The student may be wondering why the standard error of the mean, $S_{\bar{X}}$, is defined as $S_{\bar{X}} = \sigma/\sqrt{n}$. The reason is based on the notion that the variance or dispersion within the sampling distribution of the mean will be less if we have a larger sample size for independent samples. Intuitively, most students will know that the larger the sample size, the more confident the researcher may be that the sample mean is closer to the population mean. In actual practice the standard error of the mean is estimated by using the sample's standard deviation. Thus $S_{\bar{X}}$ is estimated by using $S/\sqrt{n}$.

Exhibit 15.6 shows the relationship among a population distribution, the sample distribution, and three sampling distributions of varying sample size. In Part *a* of this exhibit we note that the population distribution is not a normal distribution. In Part *b* we note that the sample distribution resembles the distribution of the population; however, there may be some differences. In Part *c* we note that each of the sampling distributions is normally distributed and that the means of each of these sampling distributions is the same. We also note that as sample size increases, the spread of the sample means around μ decreases. Thus with a larger sample size we will have a skinnier sampling distribution.

Central-Limit Theorem

Finding that the means of random samples of a sufficiently large size will be approximately normal in form and that the mean of the sampling distribution will approach the population mean is very useful. Mathematically, this is the assertion of the **central-limit theorem,** which states: As the sample size n increases, the distribution of the means, $\bar{X}_s$, of random samples, taken from practically any population, approaches a normal distribution (with a mean, μ, and a standard deviation $\sigma/\sqrt{n}$).[8]

The central-limit theorem works regardless of the shape of the original population distribution (see Exhibit 15.7). A simple example will demonstrate the nature of the central-limit theorem. Assume that a researcher is interested in the number of dollars children spend on toys each month. Let us further assume that the population the researcher is investigating is 8-year-old children

EXHIBIT   15.6

**Schematic of the Three
Fundamental Types of
Distribution**

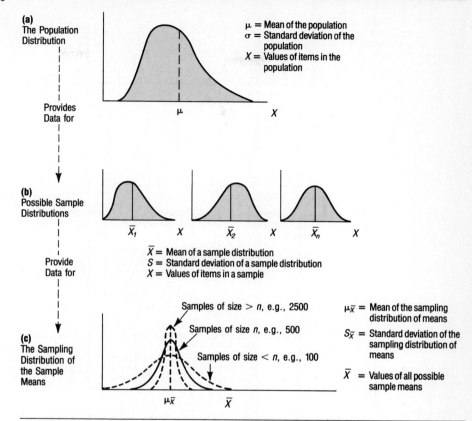

**(a)
The Population
Distribution**

μ = Mean of the population
σ = Standard deviation of the
population
X = Values of items in the
population

Provides
Data for

**(b)
Possible Sample
Distributions**

$\bar{X}$ = Mean of a sample distribution
S = Standard deviation of a sample distribution
X = Values of items in a sample

Provide
Data for

Samples of size $> n$, e.g., 2500

Samples of size n, e.g., 500

Samples of size $< n$, e.g., 100

**(c)
The Sampling
Distribution of
the Sample
Means**

$\mu_{\bar{x}}$ = Mean of the sampling
distribution of means

$S_{\bar{x}}$ = Standard deviation of the
sampling distribution of
means

$\bar{X}$ = Values of all possible
sample means

Source: Adapted from D. H. Sanders, A. F. Murphy, and R. J. Eng, *Statistics: A Fresh Approach*, 123, © 1980
McGraw-Hill. Adapted with the permission of McGraw-Hill Book Company.

in a certain private school. In this example the population consists of only
six individuals. This is a simple example and perhaps somewhat unrealistic.
Nevertheless, let us assume that the population size consists of only six elements. Table 15.8 shows the frequency distribution of the six individuals.

Alice, a relatively deprived child, has only $1 per month, whereas Fat
Freddy, the rich kid, has $6 to spend. The mean expenditure on toys each
month is $3.50; so the population mean, μ, equals 3.5 (see Table 15.9). Now
assume that we do not know everything about the population and we wish to
take a sample size of two, to be drawn randomly from the population of six
individuals. How many possible samples are there? The answer is 15. They are
as follows:

1, 2
1, 3   2, 3
1, 4   2, 4   3, 4
1, 5   2, 5   3, 5   4, 5
1, 6   2, 6   3, 6   4, 6   5, 6

EXHIBIT   1 5 . 7

**Distribution of Sample
Means for Samples of
Various Sizes and Different
Population Distributions**

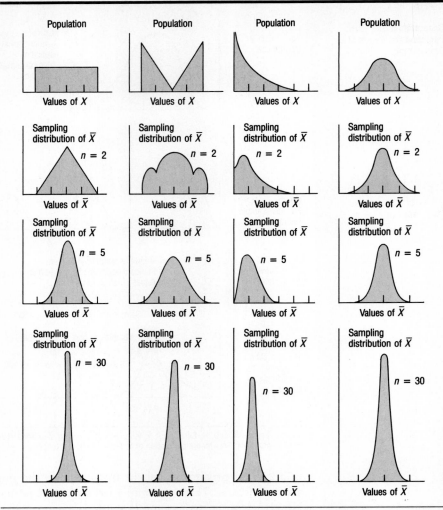

Source: Ernest Kurnow, Gerald J. Glasser, and Frederick R. Ottman, *Statistics for Business Decisions* (Homewood, IL:
Richard D. Irwin, 1959), 182–183. Reprinted by permission.

T A B L E   1 5 . 8

**Hypothetical Population
Distribution of Toy
Expenditures**

Child	Toy Expenditures
Alice	$1.00
Bob	2.00
Chris	3.00
Devin	4.00
George	5.00
Freddy	6.00

TABLE   15.9

Calculation of Population Mean

X
$ 1.00
2.00
3.00
4.00
5.00
6.00

Summation $21.00

Calculation:

$$\mu = \frac{\Sigma X}{N} = \frac{21}{6} = 3.5 = \mu$$

TABLE   15.10

Means of the Samples and Their Frequency Distribution

Sample	ΣX	$\bar{X}$	Probability
$1,$2	$ 3.00	$1.50	1/15
1, 3	4.00	2.00	1/15
1, 4	5.00	2.50	1/15
1, 5	6.00	3.00	1/15
1, 6	7.00	3.50	1/15
2, 3	5.00	2.50	1/15
2, 4	6.00	3.00	1/15
2, 5	7.00	3.50	1/15
2, 6	8.00	4.00	1/15
3, 4	7.00	3.50	1/15
3, 5	8.00	4.00	1/15
3, 6	9.00	4.50	1/15
4, 5	9.00	4.50	1/15
4, 6	10.00	5.00	1/15
5, 6	11.00	5.50	1/15

Sample Mean $(\bar{X})$	Frequency	Probability
$1.50	1	1/15
2.00	1	1/15
2.50	2	2/15
3.00	2	2/15
3.50	3	3/15
4.00	2	2/15
4.50	2	2/15
5.00	1	1/15
5.50	1	1/15

In Table 15.10 we have calculated the sample mean of each of the possible 15 samples. And in Table 15.10 we have a frequency distribution of these sample means with their appropriate probabilities. Note that these sample means consist of a sampling distribution of the mean and that the distribution is *approximately* normal. If we increase the sample size to 3, 4, or more, the distribution of sample means would be a closer approximation to a normal distribution. While this simple example is not a proof of the central-limit theorem, it should give the student a better understanding of the nature of the sampling distribution of the mean.

This theoretical knowledge about distributions can be used to solve these two very practical business research problems: estimating parameters and determining sample size. Estimating parameters is dealt with in this chapter because it will help the student understand the theory of determining sample size.

ESTIMATION OF PARAMETERS

The Ford Motor Company must have a certain number of workers on an assembly line. Making a proper inference about the number of workers expected to show up for work is an important production-planning tool. Statistical analysis of the variance in absenteeism is extremely important.

Suppose that you are a financial analyst and that a planned acquisition is expected to produce cash flows for the next five years. These cash flows are not known with certainty. The financial researcher makes an estimate of cash flows and expected net present value. How could you be sure there were no statistical errors in that estimate? How confident could you be in these figures?[9]

Students often wonder whether statistics are utilized in the business world. The two situations outlined above provide examples of the need for statistical estimation of parameters, and of the value of statistical techniques as managerial tools.

Our goal in utilizing statistics is to make an estimate about the population parameters. The population mean, μ, and the population standard deviation, σ, are constants, but in most instances of business research they are unknown. To estimate the population values, we are required to sample. As we have discussed, X and S are random variables that will vary from sample to sample with a certain probability distribution (sampling distribution). A specific example of statistical inference is a prospective racquetball entrepreneur wishing to estimate the average number of days that players participate in this sport each week. Our previous example was somewhat unrealistic in that the population had only six individuals. When statistical inference is needed, the population mean, μ, is a constant but unknown parameter. To estimate the average number of playing days, we may take a sample of 300 racquetball players throughout the area where our entrepreneur is thinking of building club facilities. If the sample mean, $\overline{X}$, equals 2.6 days per week, we may use this figure as a **point estimate**. This single value, 2.6, is the best estimate of the population mean. However, we would be extremely lucky if the sample estimate were exactly the same as the population value. A less risky alternative would be to calculate a confidence interval.

Confidence Interval

If we specify a range of numbers or an interval within which the population mean should lie, we may be more confident that our inference is correct. Making a **confidence interval estimate** is based on the knowledge that $\mu = \overline{X} \pm$ a small sampling error. After calculating an interval estimate, we will be able to determine how probable it is that the population mean will fall within a range of statistical values. In the racquetball project, the researcher, after setting up a confidence interval, would be able to make a statement such as: "With 95 percent confidence, I think that the average number of days played is between 2.3 and 2.9 per week." This information can be utilized to estimate market demand because the researcher has a certain confidence that the interval contains the value of the true population mean.

The crux of the problem for the researcher is to determine how much random sampling error will be tolerated. In other words, what should the confidence interval be? How much of a gamble should be taken that μ will be included in the range: 80 percent, 90 percent, 99 percent? The **confidence level** is a percentage indicating the long-run probability that the results will be correct. Traditionally, researchers have utilized the 95 percent confidence level. While there is nothing magical about the 95 percent confidence level, it is useful to select 95 percent confidence level in our examples.

Calculating a Confidence Interval.   As we have mentioned, the point estimate does not give us any information about the possible magnitude of random sampling error. The *confidence interval* gives an estimate plus or minus the estimated value of the population parameter. We may express the idea of the confidence interval as:

$$\mu = \overline{X} \pm \text{a small sampling error}$$

More formally, assuming the researchers select a large sample (more than 30 observations), the small sampling error is equal to:

$$\text{Small sampling error} = Z_{c.l.}S_{\overline{X}}$$

where

$$\overline{X} = \text{sample mean}$$
$$Z_{c.l.} = \text{value of Z, our standardized normal variable}$$
$$\text{at a specified confidence level (c.l.)}$$
$$S_{\overline{X}} = \text{standard error of the mean}$$

The precision of our estimate is indicated by the value of $Z_{c.l.}S_{\overline{X}}$. It is useful to define the **range of possible random error, E,** as follows:

$$E = Z_{c.l.}S_{\overline{X}}$$

Thus

$$\mu = \overline{X} \pm E \qquad \text{or} \qquad \mu = \overline{X} \pm Z_{c.l.}S_{\overline{X}}$$

It should be noted that the confidence interval ($\pm E$) is always stated as half of the total interval.

The following is a step-by-step procedure for calculating confidence intervals:

1.   Calculate $\overline{X}$ from the sample.
2.   Assuming σ is unknown, we must estimate the population standard deviation by finding S, the sample standard deviation.
3.   Estimate the standard error of the mean, utilizing the following formula:

$$S_{\overline{X}} = \frac{S}{\sqrt{n}}$$

4. Determine the Z-values associated with the confidence level desired. The confidence level should be divided by 2 to determine what percentage of the area under the curve must be included on each side of the mean.
5. Calculate the confidence interval.

The following example shows how calculating a confidence interval can be utilized in personnel research. Suppose a personnel manager believes age will be a useful criterion for placement. Successful women at the supervisory level are sampled. As the business researcher, you find that the mean age $(\overline{X})$ of 100 women is 37.5 years, with a standard deviation (S) of 12.0 years. Knowing that it would be extremely coincidental if the point estimate from the sample were exactly the same as the population mean age (μ), you decide to construct a confidence interval around the sample mean, using the steps given above:

1. $\overline{X} = 37.5$ years.
2. $S = 12.0$ years.
3. $S_{\overline{x}} = \dfrac{12}{\sqrt{100}} = 1.2.$
4. Suppose you wish to be 95 percent confident, that is, assured that 95 times out of 100 the estimates from the sample will include the population parameter. Including 95 percent of the area requires that 47.5 percent (half of 95 percent) of the distribution on each side be included. From the Z-table (Table 2 in the Appendix) you will find that .475 corresponds to the Z-value 1.96.
5. Substitute the values for $Z_{c.l.}$ and $S_{\overline{x}}$ into the confidence interval formula:

$$\mu = 37.5 \pm (1.96)(1.2)$$
$$= 37.5 \pm 2.352$$

So it is expected that μ is contained in the range from 35.148 to 39.852 years. Intervals constructed in this manner will contain the true value of μ 95 percent of the time.

Step 3 can be eliminated by using S and n directly in the confidence interval formula:

$$\mu = \overline{X} \pm Z_{c.l.} \frac{S}{\sqrt{n}}$$

Remember that

$$\frac{S}{\sqrt{n}}$$

represents the standard error of the mean, $S_{\overline{x}}$. Its use is based on the central-limit theorem.

If the researcher wants to increase the probability that the population mean lies in the confidence interval, he or she can use the 99 percent confidence level, with a Z-value of 2.57. You may want to calculate the 99 percent confidence interval for the example. The answer will be the range between 34.416 and 40.584.

Recapitulation

The basic concept of inferential statistics has now been presented. You should understand the notion that the sample statistics, such as the sample means, $\bar{X}$s, are capable of providing good estimates of population parameters such as μ. You should also realize at this point that there is a certain probability of being in error when you make an estimate of the population parameter from a sample statistic. In other words, there will be a random sampling error that is the difference between the survey results and the results of surveying the entire population. If you have a firm understanding of these basic terms and ideas, the rest of statistics will be relatively simple for you. The concepts already discussed are the essence of statistics. Several ramifications of the simple ideas presented so far will permit better decisions about populations based on surveys or experiments.

SAMPLE SIZE

Random Sampling Error and Sample Size

When asked to evaluate a business research project, most people, even those with little research training, will begin by asking: "How big was the sample?" Intuitively, we know that the larger the sample the more accurate the research. This is in fact a statistical truth; that is, random sampling error varies with samples of different sizes. In statistical terms, increasing the sample size decreases the width of the confidence interval at a given confidence level. When the standard deviation of the population is unknown, a confidence interval is calculated by using the following formula:

$$\bar{X} \pm Z \frac{S}{\sqrt{n}}$$

Observe that the equation for the plus or minus error factor in the confidence interval includes n, the sample size:

$$E = Z \frac{S}{\sqrt{n}}$$

If n increases, E is reduced. Exhibit 15.8 illustrates that the confidence interval (or magnitude of error) decreases as the sample size, n, increases. We have already noted that it is not necessary to take a census of all elements of the population to conduct an accurate study. The laws of probability provide investigators with sufficient confidence regarding the accuracy of collecting data from a sample. Knowledge of the theory concerning the sampling distribution helps researchers make reasonably precise estimates.

Students familiar with the "law of diminishing returns" in economics will easily grasp the concept that increases in sample size reduce sampling error at a *decreasing rate*. For example, doubling a sample of 1,000 will reduce sampling error by 1 percent, but doubling the sampling from 2,000 to 4,000 will reduce sampling error by only another ½ percentage point. More technically, random

EXHIBIT   15.8

**Relationship between
Sample Size and Error**

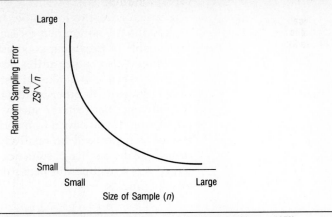

Source: Fred N. Kerlinger, *Foundations of Behavioral Research* (New York: Holt, Rinehart and Winston, 1973).

sampling error is inversely proportional to the square root of n. Exhibit 15.8 gives an approximation of the relationship between sample size and error. Thus the main issue becomes one of determining the optimal sample size.

DETERMINING SAMPLE SIZE

Questions Involving Means

Three factors are required to specify sample size:

1.   Variance or heterogeneity of the population.
2.   Magnitude of acceptable error.
3.   Confidence level.

Suppose a researcher wishes to find out whether 9-year-old boys are taller than 4-year-old boys. Even with a very small sample size, the correct information will probably be obtained. Intuitively, we know this is logical. The logic is based on the fact that the determination of sample size depends on the research question and the variability within the sample.

The *variance* or *heterogeneity* of the population characteristic is the first necessary bit of information. In statistical terms, this refers to the *standard deviation* of the population parameter. Only a small sample is required if the population is homogeneous. For example, predicting the average age of college students requires a smaller sample size than predicting the average age of people visiting the zoo on a given Sunday afternoon. If we are testing the effectiveness of an acne skin-care product, the sample must be large enough to cover the range of skin types because as heterogeneity increases, so must sample size.

The magnitude of error, or the confidence interval, is the second necessary bit of information. Defined in statistical terms as E, the magnitude of error (range of possible random error) indicates how precise the estimate must be.

EXHIBIT 15.9

**Statistical Information
Needed to Determine
Sample Size**

Variable	Symbol	Typical Source of Information
Standard deviation	S	Pilot study or rule of thumb
Magnitude of error	E	Managerial judgment or calculation ($ZS_{\bar{x}}$)
Confidence level	$Z_{c.l.}$	Managerial judgment

From a managerial perspective, the importance of the decision (from a profitability perspective) will influence the researcher's specifications of the range of error. If, for example, favorable results of a test market sample will result in the construction of a new plant and unfavorable results will dictate that it not be built, it is likely that the acceptable range of error will be small. The cost of an error is too great to allow much room for sampling errors. In other cases the estimate need not be extremely precise. Allowing an error of ±$1,000 in total family income, instead of E = ±$50, may be acceptable in most cross-sectional studies.

The third factor of concern is the *confidence level*. In our examples we shall typically use the 95 percent confidence level. This, however, is an arbitrary decision, based on convention. There is nothing sacred about the .05 chance level (i.e., the probability of the true population parameter being incorrectly estimated).[10] Exhibit 15.9 summarizes the information required about these factors to determine sample size.

Estimating the Sample Size

Once the above concepts are understood, determining the actual size for a simple random sample is quite easy. To estimate **sample size,** the researcher does the following:

1. Estimates the standard deviation of the population.
2. Makes a judgment about the desired magnitude of error.
3. Determines a confidence level.

The only problem is that of estimating the standard deviation of the population. Ideally, similar studies conducted in the past will be used as a basis for judging the standard deviation. In practice, researchers without prior information conduct a pilot study for the purpose of estimating the population parameters so that another larger sample, with the appropriate sample size, may be drawn. This procedure is called *sequential sampling* because researchers take an initial look at the pilot study results before deciding on a larger sample that provides more precise information.

A rule of thumb for estimating the value of the standard deviation is to expect it to be one-sixth of the range.[11] In a study on incentive pay, the researcher expected bonus payments to range from $1,000 to $7,000, a $6,000 range. Therefore a rule-of-thumb estimate for the standard deviation would be $1,000.

For the moment, let us assume that the standard deviation has been estimated in some preliminary work. If our concern is to estimate the mean of a particular population, the formula for sample size is derived [12] from our knowledge that $E = ZS_{\bar{x}}$. The formula is:

$$n = \left(\frac{ZS}{E}\right)^2$$

where

$\quad Z =$ standardization value indicating a confidence level
$\quad S =$ sample standard deviation or an estimate of the
$\qquad$ population standard deviation
$\quad E =$ acceptable magnitude of error, plus or minus error factor
$\qquad$ (range is one-half of total confidence interval)

Suppose a survey researcher, studying expenditures on lipstick, wishes to have a 95 percent confidence level (Z) and range of error (E) of less than $2.00. The estimate of the standard deviation is $29.00.

$$n = \left(\frac{ZS}{E}\right)^2 = \left[\frac{(1.96)(29.00)}{2.00}\right]^2 = \left[\frac{56.84}{2.00}\right]^2 = (28.42)^2 = 808$$

If the range of error (E) is acceptable at $4.00, sample size is reduced:

$$n = \left(\frac{ZS}{E}\right)^2 = \left[\frac{(1.96)(29.00)}{4.00}\right]^2 = \left[\frac{56.84}{4.00}\right]^2 = (14.21)^2 = 202$$

Thus, doubling the range of acceptable error reduces sample size to approximately one-quarter its original size, or, stated conversely in a general sense, doubling sample size reduces error by approximately one-quarter.

Influence of Population Size on Sample Size

The A. C. Nielsen Company conducts television ratings. Throughout the years it has been plagued with questions about how it is possible to rate 85-plus million television homes with such a small sample (approximately 2,000 homes). The answer is that in most cases the size of the population does not have a major effect on the sample size. As we have indicated, the variance of the population has the largest effect on sample size. However, a finite correction factor may be needed to adjust the sample size if the sample size is more than 5 percent of a finite population. If the sample is large relative to the population, the above procedures may overestimate sample size and there may be a need to reduce sample size by a certain percentage. The finite correction factor is $\sqrt{(N - n)/(N - 1)}$, where N = population size and n = sample size.

Proportions: Sample Size Determination Requires Knowledge about Confidence Intervals

Researchers are frequently concerned with determining sample size for problems involving estimating population proportions or percentages. When the sample size question involves the estimation of a proportion, the researcher requires some knowledge of the logic for determining a confidence interval around a sample proportion (p) estimation of the population proportion (π). For a confidence interval to be constructed around the sample proportion (p), an estimate of the **standard error of the proportion** (S_p) must be calculated and a confidence coefficient specified.

The precision of our estimate is indicated by the value $Z_{c.l.}S_p$. Thus our *plus or minus* estimate of the population proportion is:

$$\text{Confidence interval} = p \pm Z_{c.l.}S_p$$

If the researcher selects a 95 percent probability for the confidence interval, $Z_{c.l.}$ will equal 1.96 (see Table 2 in the Appendix).

The formula for S_p is:

$$S_p = \sqrt{\frac{pq}{n}} \quad \text{or} \quad S_p = \sqrt{\frac{p(1-p)}{n}}$$

where

S_p = estimate of the standard error of the proportion
p = proportion of successes
$q = (1 - p)$, or proportion of failures

Suppose that in a sample of 1,200, 20 percent of the employees plan to retire in the next five years. The proportion of successes (p) equals .2. The proportion of failures (q) equals .8. To estimate the 95 percent confidence interval:

$$
\begin{aligned}
\text{Confidence interval} &= p \pm Z_{c.l.}S_p \\
&= .2 \pm 1.96\, S_p \\
&= .2 \pm 1.96 \sqrt{\frac{p(1-p)}{n}} \\
&= .2 \pm 1.96 \sqrt{\frac{(.2)(.8)}{1200}} \\
&= .2 \pm 1.96\,(.0115) \\
&= .2 \pm .022
\end{aligned}
$$

Thus the population proportion of the employees who plan to retire next year is estimated to be included in the interval between .178 and .222, or roughly between 18 percent and 22 percent, with a 95 percent confidence coefficient.

To determine *sample size* for a proportion, the researcher must make a judgment about confidence level and the maximum allowance for random sampling error. Further, the size of the proportion influences sampling error; thus an estimate of the expected proportion of successes must be made based on intuition or prior information. The formula is:

$$n = \frac{Z_{c.l.}^2 pq}{E^2}$$

where

        n = number of items in sample

      $Z_{c.l.}^2$ = square of the confidence interval in standard error units

        p = estimated proportion of successes

        q = $(1 - p)$, or estimated proportion of failures

      E^2 = square of the maximum allowance for error between the true proportion and sample proportion, or $Z_{c.l.}S_p$ squared

As an example of this calculation, suppose a researcher believes a simple random sample will show that 60 percent of the respondents (p) will recognize the name of an industrial corporation. The researcher wishes to estimate with 95 percent confidence ($Z_{c.l.}$ = 1.96) that the allowance for sampling error will not be greater than 3.5 percent (E). Substituting these values into the formula above, the researcher finds:

$$n = \frac{(1.96)^2(.6)(.4)}{(.035)^2}$$

$$= \frac{(3.8416)(.24)}{.001225}$$

$$= \frac{.922}{.001225}$$

$$= 753$$

Actual Calculation of Sample Size for a Sample Proportion

A number of tables have been constructed so the determination of sample size may be determined by inspecting the tables. Table 15.11 illustrates a sampling table for problems involving sample proportions (p).

The theoretical principles for calculation of sample size of proportions are similar to those concepts expressed in this chapter. In the example above, suppose researchers wish to take samples of investors in two large cities, New Orleans and Miami. They want no more than 2 percent error and they would be satisfied with a 95 percent confidence level (see Table 15.11).

If we assume all other things are equal, in the New Orleans area where 15 percent of the investors are aware of the corporation and 85 percent are not aware of it, a sample of 1,222 is needed for results with only 2 percent error. However, in the Miami area with 30 percent of the investors aware and 70 percent unaware (a less heterogeneous area), a sample size of 2,009 is required for the same sample reliability.

Table 15.12 shows a sampling error table that is typical of those that accompany research proposals or reports. Most studies will estimate more than one parameter. Thus, in a survey of 100 people in which 50 percent agree with one statement and 10 percent with another, the sampling error is expected to be 10 percentage points and 6 percentage points error, respectively.

Sample Size on the Basis of Judgment

Just as it is easy to select the sample units based on the convenience of the researcher or the judgment of the researcher, sample size may also be determined on the basis of managerial judgment. Using a sample size similar to the sample

TABLE 15.11

Selected Tables for Determining Sample Size When the Characteristic of Interest Is a Proportion

Parameter in Population Assumed to Be over 70 Percent or under 30 Percent and for 95 Percent Confidence Level

Sample Size for Reliabilities of:

Size of Population	±1% Point	±2% Point	±3% Point	±5% Point
1,000	—	—	473	244
2,000	—	—	619	278
3,000	—	1,206	690	291
4,000	—	1,341	732	299
5,000	—	1,437	760	303
10,000	4,465	1,678	823	313
20,000	5,749	1,832	858	318
50,000	6,946	1,939	881	321
100,000	7,465	1,977	888	321
500,000 to ∞	7,939	2,009	895	322

Parameter in Population Assumed to Be over 85 Percent or under 15 Percent and for 95 Percent Confidence Level

Sample Size for Reliabilities of:

Size of Population	±1% Point	±2% Point	±3% Point	±5% Point
1,000	a	a	353	235
2,000	a	760	428	266
3,000	a	890	461	278
4,000	a	938	479	284
5,000	a	984	491	289
10,000	3,288	1,091	516	297
20,000	3,935	1,154	530	302
50,000	4,461	1,195	538	304
100,000	4,669	1,210	541	305
500,000 to ∞	4,850	1,222	544	306

[a] In these cases more than 50 percent of the population is required in the sample. Since the normal approximation of the hypergeometric distribution is a poor approximation in such instances, no sample value is given.

Source: *Foundations of Social Research*, p. 447, by Nan Lin. Copyright © 1976 McGraw-Hill. Used with permission of the McGraw-Hill Book Company.

TABLE 15.12

Allowance for Random Sampling Error (Plus and Minus Percentage Points) at 95 Percent Confidence Level

Response	Sample Size						
	2,500	1,500	1,000	500	250	100	50
10(90)	1.2	1.5	2	3	4	6	8
20(80)	1.6	2	2.5	4	5	8	11
30(70)	1.8	2.5	3	4	6	9	13
40(60)	2	2.5	3	4	6	10	14
50	2	2.5	3	4	6	10	14

sizes used in previous studies provides the inexperienced researcher with a comparison of other researchers' judgment.[13]

Another judgmental factor involving the determination of sample size is the selection of the appropriate item, question, or characteristic for the sample size calculations. In most studies several characteristics are of concern, and the desired degree of precision may vary for these items. The researcher must exercise judgment to determine which item will be utilized. Often the item that will produce the largest sample size will be utilized to determine the ultimate sample size. However, cost of data collection becomes a major consideration and judgment must be exercised concerning the importance of the item information.

Another sampling consideration stems from most analysts' need to analyze the various subgroups within the sample. For example, suppose an analyst wishes to look at a difference in architects' attitudes by geographic region. The analyst will want to make sure that there is an adequate number of sampled architects in the New England region, Mid-Atlantic region, or South Atlantic region, to make sure that subgroup comparisons are reliable. There is a judgmental rule of thumb for selecting minimum subgroup sample size. It has been suggested that each subgroup that will be separately analyzed should have a minimum of 100 or more units in each category of the major breakdowns.[14] According to this procedure, determining the total sample size is computed by totaling the sample size necessary for these subgroups.

Determining Sample Size for Stratified and Other Probability Samples

Stratified sampling involves drawing separate probability samples within the subgroups to make the sample more efficient. With a stratified sample, the sample variances are expected to differ by strata. This makes the determination of sample size more complex. Increased complexity may also characterize the determination of cluster sampling and other probability sampling methods. These formulas are beyond the scope of this research book. Students interested in these advanced sampling techniques should investigate advanced sampling textbooks.

SUMMARY

Determination of sample size requires a knowledge of statistics. Statistics is the language of the researcher, and this chapter introduces its vocabulary. Descriptive statistics describe characteristics of a population or sample, while inferential statistics use a sample to draw conclusions about a population.

A frequency distribution summarizes data by showing how frequently each response or classification occurs. A proportion indicates the percentage of a group having a particular characteristic.

Three measures of central tendency are commonly used: the mean, or arithmetic average; the median, or halfway value; and the mode, or most frequently observed value. Each of these values may be different, and care must be taken to understand distortions that may occur when the wrong measure of central tendency is used.

Measures of dispersion are used along with the measures of central tendency to describe a distribution. The range is the difference between the largest and smallest values observed. The variance and standard deviation are the most useful measures of dispersion.

The normal distribution fits many observed distributions. It is symmetrical about its mean, with equal mean, median, and mode. Almost all the area of the normal distribution lies within ±3 standard deviations of the mean. Any normal distribution can easily be compared to the standardized normal, or Z, distribution, whose mean is 0 and whose standard deviation is 1. This allows easy evaluation of the probability of many occurrences.

The techniques of statistical inference are based on the relationship of the population distribution, the sample distribution, and the sampling distribution. This relationship is expressed in the central-limit theorem.

Estimating a population mean with a single value is a point estimate. A range of numbers within which the researcher is confident the population mean will lie is a confidence interval estimate. The confidence level is a percentage indicating the long-run probability that the confidence interval estimate is correct.

The statistical determination of sample size requires knowledge of (1) the variance of the population, (2) the magnitude of acceptable error, and (3) the confidence level. Several computational formulas are available for determining sample size. Further, a number of easy-to-use tables have been compiled to help calculate sample size. The main reason why a large sample size is desirable is that sample size is related to random sampling error. The smaller the sample, the larger the error one would expect in making estimates.

Many research problems involve the estimation of a proportion. Statistical techniques may be used to determine a confidence interval around a sample proportion. Calculation of sample size for a sample proportion is not difficult. In fact, most researchers use tables that indicate predetermined sample sizes.

A Reminder about the Language of Statistics.   The terms and symbols defined in this chapter provide the basics of the language for statisticians and researchers. In order to learn more about the pragmatic use of statistics in business research, it is essential that this vocabulary be mastered. The speller who forgets "i before e except after c" will have trouble every time the spelling of a word with the "i e" or "e i" combination must be tackled. The same is true for the student who forgets the basics of the "foreign language" of statistics.

Key Terms

descriptive statistics	probability distribution
inferential statistics	proportion
sample statistic	mean
population parameter	median
frequency distribution (table)	mode
percentage distribution	range

standard deviation	standard error of the mean
average deviation	central-limit theorem
variance	point estimate
normal distribution	confidence interval
standardized normal distribution	confidence level
population distribution	magnitude of error
sample distribution	sample size
sampling distribution	standard error of the proportion

Questions

1. What is the difference between descriptive and inferential statistics?
2. The highway speed limits for 14 countries are as follows:

Country	Highway Miles per Hour
Italy	87
France	81
Hungary	75
Belgium	75
Portugal	75
Britain	70
Spain	62
Denmark	62
Netherlands	62
Greece	62
Japan	62
Norway	56
Turkey	56
U.S.	55

   Calculate the mean, median, and mode for these data.
3. Prepare a frequency distribution for the data in Question 2.
4. Why is the standard deviation typically utilized, rather than the average deviation?
5. Calculate the standard deviation for the data in Question 2.
6. Draw three distributions that have the same mean value but different standard deviation values. Draw three distributions that have the same standard deviation but different mean values.
7. A manufacturer of stereo tape players surveyed 100 retail stores in each of its sales regions. An analyst noticed that in the South Atlantic region the average retail price was $165 (mean) and the standard deviation was $30. However, in the Mid-Atlantic region the mean price was $170, with a standard deviation of $15. What do these statistics indicate about these two sales regions?
8. Coastal Star Sales Corporation is a West Coast wholesaler that markets products to several manufacturers of leisure products. Coastal Star has an 80-person sales force that sells to wholesalers in a six-state area divided into two sales regions. The tabulation below gives the names from

a sample of 11 salespersons, some descriptive information about each salesperson, and the sales performance of each for the past two years.

Region	Sales-person	Age	Years of Experience	Sales	
				Previous Year	Current Year
Northern	Jackson	40	7	$ 412,744	$ 411,007
Northern	Gentry	60	12	1,491,024	1,726,630
Northern	La Forge	26	2	301,421	700,112
Northern	Miller	39	1	401,241	471,001
Northern	Mowen	64	5	448,160	449,261
Southern	Young	51	2	518,897	519,412
Southern	Fisk	34	1	846,222	713,333
Southern	Kincaid	62	10	1,527,124	2,009,041
Southern	Krieger	42	3	921,174	1,030,000
Southern	Manzer	64	5	463,399	422,798
Southern	Weiner	27	2	548,011	422,001

Calculate a mean and a standard deviation for each variable and set a 95 percent confidence interval around the mean for each variable.

9. Calculate the median, mode, and range for each variable in Question 8.

10. Organize the data for the variable current sales in Question 8 into a frequency distribution having classes (a) under $500,000, (b) $500,001 to $999,999, and (c) $1,000,000 and over.

11. Organize the data for years of selling experience in Question 8 into a frequency distribution consisting of two classes, one less than five years and the other five or more years.

12. What is the sampling distribution? How does it differ from the sample distribution?

13. What would happen to the sampling distribution of the mean if we increased sample size from 5 to 25?

14. Suppose a fast-food restaurant wishes to estimate average sales volume for a new menu item. The restaurant has observed the sales of the item at a similar outlet and has determined the following results:

$\bar{X} = 500$ (mean daily sales)
$S = 100$ (standard deviation of sample)
$n = 25$ (sample size)

The restaurant manager wants to know into what range the mean daily sales would fall 95 percent of the time. Perform this calculation.

15. In the text example of research on lipstick (page 386) where E = $2.00 and S = $29.00, what sample size would be required if a 99 percent confidence level were desired?

16. Suppose you are planning a sample of transportation employees to determine average annual sick days. The following standards have been set: a confidence level of 99 percent and an error of fewer than 5 days. Past research has indicated the standard deviation should be 6 days. What would be the required sample size?

17. In a survey of 500, 60 percent responded positively to an attitude question. Calculate a confidence interval at 95 percent to get an interval estimate for a proportion.

18. In a nationwide survey a researcher expects that 30 percent of the population will agree with an attitude statement. She wishes to have less than 2 percent error and to be 95 percent confident. What sample size is needed?

19. City Opera, a local opera company, wishes to take a sample of its subscribers to learn the average number of years people have been subscribing to it. The director of research expects the average number of years to be 12 and believes the standard deviation would be about 2 years (approximately one-sixth of the range). She wishes to be 95 percent confident in her estimate. What is the appropriate sample size?

20. A researcher expects the population proportion of Cubs fans in Chicago to be 80 percent. The researcher wishes to have an error of less than 5 percent and to be 95 percent confident of an estimate to be made from a mail survey. What sample size is required?

21. An automobile dealership plans to conduct a survey to determine what proportion of new-car buyers continue to have their cars serviced at the dealership after the warranty period ends. It estimates that 30 percent of customers do so. It wants the results of its survey to be accurate within 5 percent, and it wants to be 95 percent confident of the results. What sample size is necessary?

22. To understand how sample size is conceptually related to random sampling error, costs, and nonsampling errors, graph these relationships.

References

[1] Morris James Slonim, *Sampling in a Nutshell* (New York: Simon & Schuster, 1960), 1–2.

[2] Most of the statistical material in this book assumes the population parameters are unknown, which is the typical situation in most applied research projects.

[3] For a discussion of this problem, see Thomas H. Wonnacott and Ronald J. Wonnacott, *Introductory Statistics* (New York: Wiley, 1969), 6–7.

[4] The reasons for this are related to the concept of degrees of freedom, which will be explained later. At this point, disregard the intuitive notion of division by n, because it produces a biased estimate of the population variance.

[5] An alternative version of this formula is easier to use in computation:

$$S = \sqrt{\frac{\sum\limits_{i=1}^{n} X_i^2 - \left(\sum\limits_{i=1}^{n} X_i\right)^2}{n}}{n = 1}$$

Rather than computing each deviation and summing, one can find the sum and sum of squares of the observations, substitute them into the formula, and evaluate. Many pocket calculators have features that make it easy to accumulate $\sum\limits_{i=1}^{n} X_i$ and $\sum\limits_{i=1}^{n} X_i^2$ at the same time.

[6] In practice, most survey researchers will not utilize this exact formula. A modification of the formula, $Z = (X - \mu)/S$, utilizing the sample standard deviation in an adjusted form is frequently used.

[7] William L. Hayes, *Statistics* (New York: Holt, Rinehart and Winston, 1963), 193.

[8] Thomas H. Wonnacott and Ronald J. Wonnacott, *Introductory Statistics*, 2nd ed. (New York: Wiley, 1972), 125.

[9] James H. Bowman, "Test Marketing Remains the Ol' Standby," *Advertising Age,* Feb. 19, 1979, 24–25.

[10] See, for example, James K. Skipper, J. R. Anthony Guenther, and Gilbert Mass, "The Sacredness of .05 Levels of Significance in Social Science," *American Sociologist* 2 (1967): 16–18.

[11] Walter B. Wentz, *Marketing Research: Management and Methods* (New York: Harper & Row, 1972), 145.

[12] Note that the derivation of this formula is (1) $E = ZS_{\bar{x}}$, (2) $E = ZS/\sqrt{n}$, (3) $\sqrt{n} = ZS/E$, (4) $n = (ZS/E)^2$.

[13] Seymour Sudman, *Applied Sampling* (New York: Academic Press, 1976), 86–87.

[14] Ibid., 30.

Fieldwork

*U*nfortunately, but perhaps predictably, many foul-ups helped the 1990 census get off to a poor start. The Census Bureau, which had 78 percent of its forms returned in 1980, had expected more that 70 percent of its questionnaires to be returned by mail in 1990. However, four weeks after mailing questionnaires and one day before it was to begin sending enumerators (fieldworkers) into the field, the Bureau had received only 63 percent of the questionnaires. Four million forms were undeliverable. In Houston, the census hotline got 900 calls per day from people complaining that they had not received their questionnaires. In Detroit and Baltimore, 10 percent of the households did not get questionnaires; nineteen percent of the households in Los Angeles did not receive forms because of addressing problems; and entire blocks in New York City did not appear on the census address list.

To complicate matters, the hiring, supervision, and retention of fieldworkers (enumerators) who visited households that did not return questionnaires were fraught with problems. Census enumerators used to be housewives, but now most of these women are employed in the workplace. Hiring good people who are not working, who are not happy with their work, or who are willing to work for a short term—five to eight weeks—is difficult. The Census Bureau could attract only 60 percent of the desired number of applicants (paid from $5.50 per hour in Kentucky to $8.00 per hour in New York City). Furthermore, there was a time lag between application and hiring because the Federal Bureau of Investigation, which must screen applicants so that convicted felons are not sent into people's homes, required several weeks to investigate applicants' backgrounds. The turnover rate of field-workers exceeded 60 percent.[1]

The Census Bureau's fieldwork problem may be summarized by the following stanza from Robert Burns's poem "To a Mouse":

The best laid schemes o' mice and men/Gang aft a-gley;
An' lea'e us nought but grief and pain,/For promis'd joy.

The best-laid plans of mice, men, and business researchers *may go astray. An excellent research plan may go astray if the field operations are not performed correctly. A proper research design will eliminate numerous sources of error, but careful execution of the fieldwork is necessary to produce results without substantial error.*

This chapter discusses the nature of an effective fieldwork operation and the procedures fieldwork managers follow to minimize errors.

■

THE NATURE OF FIELDWORK

A personal interviewer administering a questionnaire door to door, a telephone interviewer calling from a central location, an observer counting pedestrians in a shopping mall, and others involved in the collection of data and the supervision of that process are all **field-workers.**

The activities they perform vary substantially. The supervision of data collection for a mail survey will differ from the data collection in an observation study as much as the factory production process for a cereal will differ from the factory production process for a pair of ski boots. Nevertheless, just as production quality control is basic to each production operation, there are some basic fieldwork issues. For ease of presentation, this chapter focuses on the interviewing process conducted by personal interviewers. However, many of the issues apply to all field-workers when translated into their specific setting.

WHO CONDUCTS THE FIELDWORK?

Data collection is rarely done by the person who designs the research project. However, this stage is crucial because the research project is no better than the data collected in the field. Therefore it is important that the research administrator select capable people who may be entrusted to collect the data. An irony of business research is that highly educated and trained individuals will design the research, but the people who collect the data typically have little research training or experience. Knowing that research is no better than the data collected in the field, research administrators must concentrate on performing a good job in the selection of field-workers.

Much fieldwork is conducted by research suppliers who specialize in data collection (see Exhibit 16.1). When a second party is employed, the job of the study designer at the parent firm is not only to hire a research supplier but also to establish supervisory controls over the field service.

In some cases a third party is employed. For example, a firm may contact

When You Need to Ask America...
ASK AMERICA

- Coast to Coast Coverage
- Experienced Professional Affiliates
- Monitored Quality

800-334-0808

A National Network
of Independent Field Services

ASK AMERICA

Source: Courtesy of ASK AMERICA INC., Greensboro, NC.

a survey research firm, which in turn subcontracts the fieldwork to a field service. Under these circumstances it is still desirable to know the problems that might occur in the field and the managerial practices implemented to minimize them.

There are a number of **field interviewing services** and full-service research agencies that perform door-to-door surveys, central location telephone interviewing, and other forms of fieldwork for a fee. These agencies typically employ field supervisors who oversee and train interviewers, edit completed questionnaires in the field, and confirm that the interviews have been conducted by telephoning or recontacting a certain percentage of respondents.

Whether the research administrator hires in-house interviewers or selects a field interviewing service, it is desirable to have field-workers meet certain job requirements. Although the job requirements for different types of surveys will vary, normally interviewers should be selected who are healthy, outgoing, and of pleasing appearance, that is, well groomed and tailored. Fieldwork may be strenuous. The interviewer may be walking from house to house for four or more hours a day. Healthy individuals between 18 and 55 years of age generally seem to have the proper stamina. People who enjoy talking with strangers usually make better interviewers. An essential part of the interviewing process is establishing a rapport with the respondent. Having interviewers who are outgoing helps ensure that the respondent's full cooperation will be elicited. Interviewer bias may enter in if the field-worker's clothing or physical appearance is unattractive or unusual. Suppose that a male interviewer, wearing a dirty T-shirt, interviews subjects in an upper-income neighborhood. They may consider him slovenly and be less cooperative than with a person dressed more appropriately.

Interviewers and other field-workers are generally paid an hourly rate or a per-interview fee. Often interviewers are part-time workers from a variety of backgrounds. Both men and women are employed as field-workers, but the majority are women. Housewives, graduate students, secondary school teachers, and people from diverse backgrounds are frequently hired as field-workers. Primary and secondary school teachers are an excellent source for temporary interviewing work during the summer, especially when they work outside the school districts where they teach. Teachers' educational backgrounds and experiences with the public make them excellent candidates for fieldwork.[2]

IN-HOUSE TRAINING FOR INEXPERIENCED INTERVIEWERS[3]

After personnel are recruited and selected, they must be trained. Suppose a woman who has just sent her youngest child off to first grade is hired by an interviewing firm. She has decided to become a working mother by becoming a professional interviewer. The training that she will receive after being selected by a company may vary from virtually no training to a three-day program if she is selected by one of the larger survey research agencies. Almost always there will be a **briefing session** on the particular project. Typically, the recruits will record answers on a practice questionnaire during a simulated **training interview.**

The objective of training is to ensure that the data collection instrument is administered uniformly by all field-workers. The goal of these training sessions is to ensure that each respondent is provided with common information. If the data are collected in a uniform manner from all respondents, the training session will have been a success.[4]

In the more extensive training programs the following topics are likely to be covered:

1.   How to make initial contact with the respondent and secure the interview.
2.   How to ask survey questions.
3.   How to probe.
4.   How to record responses.
5.   How to terminate the interview.

Making Initial Contact and Securing the Interview

Interviewers will be trained to make appropriate opening remarks that will convince the person that his or her cooperation is important. For example:

Good afternoon, my name is _____ **and I'm from a national survey research company. We are conducting a survey concerning** _____**. I would like to get a few of your ideas.**

When one is making the initial contact in a telephone interview, the introduction might be:

Good evening, my name is _____**. I'm calling from Burke Research in Cincinnati, Ohio.**

By indicating that the telephone call is long distance, interviewers attempt to impress respondents because most people feel a long-distance call is something special or unusual or important. Even though the calls are normally WATS-line calls, it is a subtle way of impressing the respondent.

By giving one's name, the call is personalized. Personal interviewers may carry a letter of identification or an ID card that will indicate that the study is a bona fide research project and not a sales call. Use of the name of the research agency assures the respondent that the caller is trustworthy.

The Survey Research Center at the University of Michigan in its *Interviewer's Manual* recommends avoiding questions that ask permission for the interview, such as "May I come in?" and "Would you mind answering some questions?" In some cases the person will refuse to participate or state an objection to being interviewed. Interviewers should be instructed on handling objections. For example, if the respondent says, "I'm too busy right now," the interviewer might be instructed to respond, "Will you be in at 4 o'clock this afternoon? I would be happy to come back then." In other cases client companies will not wish to offend any individual. The interviewers will be instructed to merely say, "Thank you for your time." This might be the case with a telephone company or an oil company that is sensitive to its public image.

Foot-in-the-Door/Door-in-the-Face.   There is evidence that the **foot-in-the-door** and the **door-in-the-face compliance techniques** are useful in securing interviews.[5] Foot-in-the-door theory attempts to explain compliance with a large or difficult task on the basis of respondents' earlier compliance with a smaller initial request. One experiment has shown that compliance with a minor telephone interview (that is, a small request that few people refuse) will lead to greater compliance with a second, larger request to fill out a long mail questionnaire. When the interviewer begins with an initial request so large that nearly everyone refuses it (that is, the door is slammed in his or her face), the interviewer then requests a small favor, to comply with a "short" survey. This research is in its infancy, but it presents some interesting considerations for improvement of fieldwork. It also presents an ethical consideration if the respondent is deceived.

Asking the Questions

The purpose of the interview is, of course, to have the interviewer ask questions and record the respondent's answers. Training in the art of stating questions can be extremely beneficial because this form of interviewer bias can be a source of considerable error in survey research.

The major principles for asking questions are:

1. Ask the questions exactly as they are worded in the questionnaire.
2. Read each question very slowly.
3. Ask the questions in the order in which they are presented in the questionnaire.
4. Ask every question specified in the questionnaire.
5. Repeat questions that are misunderstood or misinterpreted.[6]

Although interviewers may be trained in these procedures, when working in the field many interviewers do not follow them exactly. Inexperienced interviewers may not understand the importance of strict adherence to the instructions. Even professional interviewers take short cuts when the task becomes monotonous. Interviewers may shorten questions or rephrase unconsciously when they rely on their memory of the question rather than reading the question as it is worded. Even the slightest change in wording can distort the meaning of the question and cause some bias to enter into the study. By reading the question the interviewer may be reminded to concentrate on the avoidance of slight variations in the tone of voice on particular words or phrases in the question.

If respondents do not understand a question, they will usually ask for some clarification. The recommended procedure is to repeat the question, or if the person does not understand a word, such as *nuclear* in the question "Do you feel nuclear energy is a safe energy alternative?" the interviewer should respond with "Just whatever it means to you." However, interviewers often supply their own personal definitions and ad lib clarifications. Their personal interpretation may include words that are not free from bias. One of the reasons why interviewers do this is that field supervisors have a tendency to reward people for completed questionnaires. They tend to be less tolerant of blanks that are due to alleged misunderstandings.

In a number of situations respondents will volunteer information relevant to a question that is supposed to be asked at a later point in the interview. In this situation the response should be recorded under the question that deals specifically with that subject. However, rather than skipping the question that was answered out of sequence, the interviewers should be trained to say something like: "We have briefly discussed this, but let me ask you. . . ." By asking every question, complete answers are recorded. If the partial answer to a question answered out of sequence is recorded on the space reserved for the earlier question, and if the subsequent question is skipped, an omission error will occur when the data are tabulated.

Probing

General training of interviewers should include instructions on how to *probe*.[7] Inexperienced interviewers must be trained to understand that respondents may give no answer, incomplete answers, or answers that require clarification. **Probing** may be needed for two types of situations. First, it is necessary when the respondent must be motivated to enlarge on, clarify, or explain his or her answers. It is the interviewer's job to probe for complete, unambiguous answers. The interviewer must encourage the respondent to clarify or expand on answers by providing a stimulus that will not suggest the interviewer's own ideas or attitudes. The ability to probe with neutral stimuli is the mark of an experienced interviewer. Second, probing may be necessary in situations in which the respondent begins to ramble or lose track of the question. In such cases the respondent must be led to focus on the specific content of the interview and avoid irrelevant and unnecessary information.

The interviewer will have several possible probing tactics to choose from, depending on the situation:

1. *Repetition of the question.* When the respondent remains completely silent, he or she may not have understood the question or may not have decided how to answer it. Mere repetition may encourage the respondent to answer in such cases. For example, if the question is "What is there that you do not like about your supervisor?" and the respondent does not answer, the interviewer may probe: "Just to check, is there anything you do not like about your supervisor?"

2. *An expectant pause.* If the interviewer believes the respondent has more to say, the "silent probe," accompanied by an expectant look, may motivate the respondent to gather his or her thoughts and give a complete response. Of course, the interviewer must be sensitive to the respondent so that the silent probe does not become an embarrassed silence.[8]

3. *Repetition of the respondent's reply.* As the interviewer records the response, he or she may repeat verbatim the respondent's reply. This may stimulate the respondent to expand on the answer.

4. *Neutral questions or comments.* Asking a neutral question may indicate the type of information that the interviewer is seeking. For example, if the interviewer believes that the respondent's motives should be clarified, he or she might ask, "Why do you feel that way?" If the interviewer feels that there is a need to clarify a word or phrase, she might ask, "How do you mean _____?" (Exhibit 16.2 lists some standard interviewer probes and the standard abbreviations that are recorded on the questionnaire with the respondent's answer.)

Interviewer's Probe	Standard Abbreviation
Repeat question	(RQ)
Anything else?	(AE or Else?)
Any other reason?	(AO?)
Any others?	(Other?)
How do you mean?	(How mean?)
Could you tell me about your thinking on that?	(Tell more)
Would you tell me what you have in mind?	(What in mind?)
What do you mean?	(What mean?)
Why do you feel that way?	(Why?)
Which would be closer to the way you feel?	(Which closer?)

Source: Survey Research Center, Institute for Social Research, The University of Michigan, *Interviewer's Manual*, rev. ed. (Ann Arbor: Institute for Social Research, The University of Michigan, 1976), 16. Reprinted with permission.

The purpose of asking questions as probes is to encourage responses. These probes should be neutral and not leading. They may be general, such as "Anything else?" or they may be questions designed by the interviewer to clarify a statement by the respondent.

Recording the Responses

The analyst who does not instruct field-workers in the techniques of recording during the first study rarely forgets to do so in the second study. Although the concept of recording an answer seems extremely simple, mistakes can be made in the recording phase of the research. All field-workers should use the same mechanics of recording. For example, it may appear insignificant to the interviewer whether she uses a pen or pencil. But to the editor who must erase and rewrite illegible words, using a pencil is extremely important. The rules for recording responses to closed questionnaires will vary with the specific questionnaire. The general rule, however, is to place the check in the correct box that reflects the respondent's answer. All too often interviewers will skip recording the answer to a filter question because they believe that the subsequent answer will make the answer to the filter question obvious. However, editors and coders do not know how the respondent was actually answering a question.

The general instruction for recording answers to open-ended-response questions is to record the answer verbatim, a task that is difficult for most people. Inexperienced interviewers should be given the opportunity to practice verbatim recording of answers before being sent into the field.

The *Interviewer's Manual* of the Survey Research Center provides detailed instructions on the recording of interviews. Some of its suggested rules for recording answers to open-ended response questions are:

1.   Record responses during the interview.
2.   Use the respondent's own words.
3.   Do not summarize or paraphrase the respondent's answer.
4.   Include everything that pertains to the question objectives.
5.   Include all of your probes.[9]

EXHIBIT   16.3

**Example of Completed
Questionnaire Page**

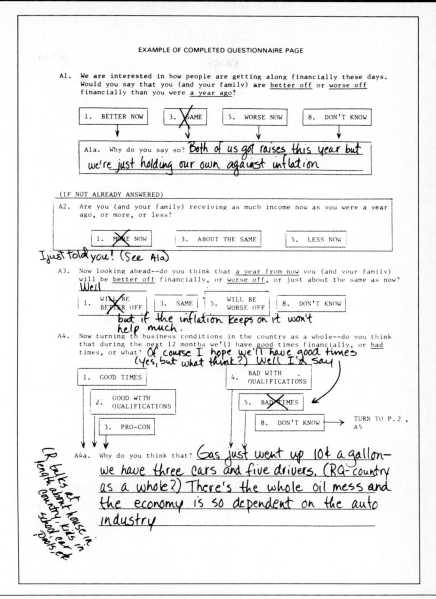

EXAMPLE OF COMPLETED QUESTIONNAIRE PAGE

A1. We are interested in how people are getting along financially these days. Would you say that you (and your family) are <u>better off</u> or <u>worse off</u> financially than you were <u>a year ago</u>?

| 1. BETTER NOW | 3. SAME ✗ | 5. WORSE NOW | 8. DON'T KNOW |

A1a. Why do you say so? *Both of us got raises this year but we're just holding our own against inflation*

(IF NOT ALREADY ANSWERED)

A2. Are you (and your family) receiving as much income now as you were a year ago, or more, or less?

| 1. MORE NOW ✗ | 3. ABOUT THE SAME | 5. LESS NOW |

I just told you! (See A1a)

A3. Now looking ahead--do you think that <u>a year from now</u> you (and your family) will be <u>better off</u> financially, or <u>worse off</u>, or just about the same as now? *Well*

| 1. WILL BE BETTER OFF ✗ | 3. SAME | 5. WILL BE WORSE OFF | 8. DON'T KNOW |

but if the inflation keeps on it won't help much.

A4. Now turning to business conditions in the country as a whole--do you think that during the next 12 months we'll have <u>good</u> times financially, or <u>bad</u> times, or what? *Of course I hope we'll have good times (Yes, but what think?) Well I'd say*

1. GOOD TIMES		4. BAD WITH QUALIFICATIONS
2. GOOD WITH QUALIFICATIONS		5. BAD TIMES ✗
3. PRO-CON		8. DON'T KNOW → TURN TO P.2, A5

A4a. Why do you think that? *Gas just went up 10¢ a gallon— we have three cars and five drivers. (RQ—country as a whole?) There's the whole oil mess and the economy is so dependent on the auto industry*

(R talks at length about house in school, car in suburbs, etc.)

Source: Survey Research Center, University of Michigan, *Interviewer's Manual,* rev. ed. (Ann Arbor: University of Michigan, 1976), 26. Reprinted with permission.

Exhibit 16.3 shows a completed questionnaire page. Note how the interviewer adds supplementary comments to the answers to fixed-alternative questions and indicates probing questions by placing them in parentheses. The answers have been recorded without paraphrasing. The interviewer has resisted the temptation to conserve time and space by filtering comments. The RQ recorded in Question A4a indicates a repeat-question probe.

Terminating the Interview

The final aspect of training deals with instructing the interviewers on how to close the interview and exit the household. Field-workers should not close the interview before all pertinent information has been secured. The interviewer whose departure is hasty may not be able to record those spontaneous comments respondents offer after all formal questions have been asked. Recording just one of these comments may result in a new idea or creative solution to some organizational problem. Avoiding hasty departures is also a matter of courtesy.

Field-workers should also answer to the best of their ability any questions the respondent has concerning the nature and purpose of the study. Because the field-worker may be required to reinterview the respondent at some future time, the respondent should be left with a positive feeling about having cooperated in a worthwhile undertaking. It is extremely important to thank the respondent for his or her cooperation.

PRINCIPLES OF GOOD INTERVIEWING[10]

Yankelovich, Clancy, and Shulman is one of the nation's top business research organizations. One reason for its success is its careful attention to fieldwork. This section presents this organization's principles of good interviewing.

These principles apply no matter what the nature of the specific assignments may be; they are universal and represent the essence of sound data collection for business research purposes. For clarity, they have been divided into two categories: (1) *the basics*—the interviewing point of view and (2) *required practices*—standard inquiry premises and procedures.

The Basics

Interviewing is a skilled occupation; not everyone can do it, and even fewer can do it extremely well. The basic qualities of a good interviewer are these:

1. *Have integrity and be honest.* This is the cornerstone of all professional inquiry, regardless of its purpose.
2. *Have patience and tact.* Interviewers ask for information from people they have not previously known. Thus all the rules of human relations that apply to inquiry situations—patience, tact, and courtesy—apply "in spades" to interviewing. Standard business conventions controlling communications and contact are to be observed at all times.
3. *Pay attention to accuracy and detail.* Among the greatest of interviewing "sins" are inaccuracy and superficiality, for the professional analyst can misunderstand, and in turn mislead, a client. A good rule to follow is not to record a response unless you fully understand it yourself. Probe for clarification and detailed, full answers. Record responses verbatim:

Never assume you know what a respondent is thinking or jump to conclusions as to what he or she might have said but did not.

4. *Exhibit a real interest in the inquiry at hand, but keep your own opinions to yourself.* Impartiality is imperative—if your opinions were wanted, *you* would be asked, not your respondent. You are an asker and a recorder of other people's opinions, not a contributor to the study data.

5. *Be a good listener.* Too many interviewers talk too much, wasting time when respondents could be supplying more pertinent facts or opinions on the study topic.

6. *Keep inquiry and respondents' responses confidential.* Do not discuss the studies you are doing with relatives, friends, or associates—it is not acceptable to either the research agency or its clients. Above all, *never* quote one respondent's opinion to another—that is the greatest violation of privacy of all.

7. *Respect others' rights.* Survey research depends on the good will of others to provide contributory information. There is a "happy medium" path to pursue in obtaining this information. On the one hand is failure to get it all; on the other hand is unnecessary coercion. The middle road is one of clear explanation, friendliness, and courtesy—carried out in an interested and persuasive way. Impress upon prospective respondents that their cooperation is important and valuable.

Required Practices

Presented below are the practical rules of business research inquiry that are to be followed without exception:

1. *Complete the number of interviews according to the sampling plan assigned to you.* Both are calculated with the utmost precision so that when assignments are returned the study will benefit from having available that amount and type of information originally specified.

2. *Follow directions provided.* Remember that there are many other interviewers working on the same study in other places. Lack of uniformity in procedure can spell disaster for later analysis. Each direction has a purpose, even though it may not be completely evident to you.

3. *Make every effort to keep schedules.* Schedules range from "hurry up" to "there should be plenty of time," but there is always a good reason, and you should be as responsive as possible. If you foresee problems, inform your supervisor.

4. *Keep control of each interview you do.* It is up to you to determine the pace of a particular interview, keeping several points in mind:
    a. There is an established *average* length of interview from the time you start to talk to the respondent to the time you finish. It represents a *guideline*, but some interviews will be shorter and some longer.
    b. Always "get the whole story" from the respondent and write it all down in the respondent's own words. Also remember to keep the

interview to the subject at hand and not let it wander off into unnecessary small talk.

c.   Avoid offending the respondent by being too talkative yourself. Executives and other businesspeople have schedules to keep and are not impressed by small talk.

5.   *Complete the questionnaires sent to you meticulously.* This means:

a.   Follow exactly all instructions that appear on the questionnaire. Learn in advance what these instructions direct you to do.

b.   Ask the questions from the first to the last in the exact numerical order (unless directed to do otherwise in particular instances). Much thought and effort go into determining the order of the questioning to avoid bias or to set the stage for subsequent questions.

c.   Ask each question exactly as it is written. There is never a justifiable reason for rephrasing a question. The cost would be lack of uniformity—the research agency would never know whether all respondents were replying to the same question or replying to 50 different interviewers' interpretations of the question.

d.   Never leave blank the answer to a question. It will be difficult to tell whether you failed to ask it, whether the respondent could not answer it due to lack of knowledge or certainty, or whether the respondent refused to answer it for personal reasons. If none of the answer categories provided proves suitable, write in what the respondent said, in his or her own words.

e.   Use all the props provided to aid both interviewers and respondents—show cards, pictures, descriptions, sheets of questions for the respondents to answer themselves, and so on. All have a specific interview purpose. Keys to when and how to use them appear on the questionnaire at the point at which they are to be used.

6.   *Check over each questionnaire you have completed.* This is best done directly after it has been completed. If you find something you have done wrong or omitted, set about correcting it. Often you can call back a respondent, admit you missed something (or are unclear about a particular response), and thereby straighten out the difficulty.

7.   *Compare your sample execution and quota assigned with the total number of questionnaires you have completed.* Do this before you consider your assignments finished.

8.   *Clear up any questions with the research agency.* If questions arise either at the start or during an assignment for which you can find no explanatory instruction, call the agency to get the matter clarified (many agencies provide toll-free numbers so that there will be no expense to you).

FIELDWORK MANAGEMENT

Managers of the field operation select, train, supervise, and control fieldworkers. Our discussion of fieldwork principles mentioned selection and training. This section investigates the tasks of the fieldwork manager in greater detail.

Briefing Session for Experienced Interviewers

After the interviewers have been trained in fundamentals or when they have become experienced, there is always a need to inform workers about the individual project. Both experienced and inexperienced field-workers must be instructed on the background of the sponsoring organization, sampling techniques, asking questions, callback procedures, and other matters specific to the project.

If there are special instructions, such as the utilization of show cards, video cassette equipment, or restricted interviewing times, these will also be covered during the briefing session.

Instructions for handling certain key questions are always important. For example, the following field-worker instructions appeared in a survey of institutional investors who make buy-and-sell decisions with respect to stocks for banks, pension funds, and the like:

> Questions 10, 11:
> *These questions provide verbatim comments for the report to the client.* Probe for more than one- or two-word answers *and record verbatim. Particularly, probe for more information when respondent gives a* general *answer—e.g., "Poor management," "It's in a good industry." Ask: "In what ways is management poor?" "What's good about the industry?" etc.*

The briefing session for experienced interviewers might go something like this: All interviewers are called to the central office, where a brief explanation of the background of the firm is given. The general aims of the study are briefly explained. Interviewers are not provided with too much information about the purpose of the study, thus ensuring that they will not transmit any preconceived notions to respondents. For example, in a survey about the banks in a community, the interviewers should be told that the research is a banking study, but not the name of the sponsoring bank. To train the interviewers about the questionnaire, a field supervisor conducts an interview with another field supervisor who acts as a respondent. The trainees observe the interviewing process. After the demonstration interview, the trainees are instructed to personally interview and record the responses of another field-supervisor respondent. Then additional instructions are given to the trainee after the interview.

Training to Avoid Procedural Errors in Sample Selection.   The briefing session will also cover the sampling procedure. A number of research projects allow the interviewer to be at least partially responsible for selection of the sample. When the field-worker has some discretion in the selection of respondents, the potential for selection bias exists. This is obvious in the case of the quota sample, but less obvious in other cases. For example, in a probability sample where every *n*th house is selected, the field-worker uses his or her discretion in identifying housing units. Avoiding this may not be as simple as it sounds. For example, in an older, exclusive neighborhood, a mansion's coach house or servants' quarters may have been converted into an apartment that should be identified as a housing unit. This type of dwelling and other unusual housing units (alley entrance only, lake cottages, rooming houses) may be sources of selection errors. Errors in the selection or dialing of random-digit dialing samples may also occur. Considerable effort in training and supervisory control should be expended to minimize these errors.

Another selection problem is contacting a respondent when and where it is convenient for both parties. Consider the following anecdote from an interviewer:

> *Occasionally, getting to the interview is half the challenge and tests the interviewer's ingenuity. Finding your way around a huge steel mill is not easy. Even worse, trying to find a correct turn-off to gravel pit D when it's snowing so hard that most direction signs are obliterated. In arranging an appointment with an executive at a rock quarry outside Kansas City, he told me his office was in "Cave Number 3." It was no joke. To my surprise, I found a luxurious executive office in a cave, which had long ago been hollowed by digging for raw material.*[11]

Finding the sample unit was half the battle.

Supervision of Field-Workers

Although briefing and training of interviewers will minimize the probability of interviewing the wrong households or asking biased questions, there is still considerable potential for errors in the field. Direct supervision of personal interviewers, telephone interviewers, and other field-workers is necessary to ensure that the techniques communicated in the training sessions are implemented in the field.

The supervision of interviewers, like other forms of supervision, refers to controlling the efforts of workers. Field supervision of interviewers requires checking to see that field procedures are properly followed. Supervisors check field operations to ensure that the interviewing schedule is being met. They daily collect the questionnaires or other instruments and edit them for completeness and legibility. (See Chapter 17 on editing for more detail.) If there are problems, supervisors discuss them with the field-workers, providing additional training when necessary.

In addition to quality control, field supervision may provide continual training. For example, a telephone supervisor may notice that interviewers are allowing the phone to ring more than eight times before the call is considered a no-answer. The supervisor can instruct the interviewer that the research firm believes that if a phone is allowed to ring too long and then is answered, the individual may be annoyed.[12]

Sampling Verification.   Another important job of the supervisor is to **verify** that the interviews are being conducted according to the **sampling** plan rather than the selection of households most accessible to the interviewer. An interviewer might be tempted to go to the household next door for an interview rather than record that the sampling unit was "not at home," which would require a callback.

Closer supervision of the interviewing procedure occurs in central-location telephone interviewing. The supervisor may be able to listen to the actual interview by "switching in" to an interviewer's line. This, of course, cannot be done if interviewers make calls from their homes.

Interviewing the Right Person.   Supervisors must make sure that the right person within the household or sampling unit is being contacted. One research project for a children's cereal required that several cereal products be placed in the home.[13] The children were expected to record in a diary their daily consumption of and reactions to each cereal. A field supervisor observed that several mothers were filling out the diaries because their children had not done so. An investigation disclosed that although the interviewers were supposed to contact the children to remind them to fill out the diaries, in almost half the cases the mothers filled out the diaries after the children left for school. The novelty of the research project wore off after a few days. The test of eating a specific cereal each day wasn't fun after the first few times and the children stopped keeping the diaries.

This situation may also occur with physicians, executives, and other busy people. The interviewer may find it easier to interview a nurse, secretary, or other assistant rather than wait to interview the right person.

Interviewer Cheating.   **Interviewer cheating** in its most blatant form occurs when an interviewer falsifies interviews. The field-worker merely fills in fake answers rather than contacting respondents. Although this situation does occur, it is not common if the job of selection has been properly accomplished.

However, less obvious forms of interviewer cheating occur with greater frequency. Quota samples are often seen as time-consuming. Quota sample requirements may be stretched a bit to obtain almost-qualified respondents. In the interviewer's eyes, a young-looking 36-year-old is the same as a 30-year-old who fits the quota requirement. Checking the under-30 category "isn't really cheating."

Consider the field-worker who must select only heavy users of a certain brand of hand lotion that the client says is used by 15 percent of the population. But the interviewer is finding only 3 percent of the consumers qualify as heavy users. The interviewer may be tempted to interview an occasional user to stretch the quota somewhat.

Interviewers may fake part of the questionnaire to make it acceptable to the field supervisor. In a survey on flex-time, interviewers might be requested to ask for five reasons why employees prefer flexible working-hour programs. Finding that most people typically give one or two, perhaps three answers, and even with extensive probing can't think of five reasons, interviewers might be tempted to cheat. If they rarely got people to give five reasons, the interviewers, rather than have the supervisor think they were goofing off on the probing, may fill in all five blanks, based on past interviews.[14] In other cases they may cut corners to save time and energy.

Interviewers may fake answers when they find questions embarrassing or troublesome. Thus cheating occurs because an interviewer will complete most of the questionnaire but leave out a question or two because she found it troublesome or time-consuming. For example, in a survey among physicians an interviewer might find questions about artificial-insemination-donor programs embarrassing, skip these questions, and fill in the partial gaps later.

What appears to be interviewer cheating is often caused by improper training or inexperienced field-workers. A field-worker who does not understand the instructions may skip or miss a portion of the questionnaire.

Interviewers may be reluctant to interview sampling units who they feel may be difficult or undesirable to interview. It is the supervisor's function to motivate the interviewers to carefully follow the sampling plan. Sometimes field-workers are instructed to say, at the conclusion of each interview, "Thank you for your time, and by the way, my supervisor may call you to ask you about my work. Please say whatever you wish." Not only does this or a similar statement increase the number of respondents who are willing to cooperate with the verification process, but it also improves the quality of fieldwork.

Careful recording of the number of completed interviews will help to ensure that the sampling procedure is being conducted correctly.

Verification by Reinterviewing.   Supervision for quality control attempts to ensure that the interviewers are following the sampling procedure and to detect interviewers who falsify interviews. Supervisors **verify** approximately 15 percent of the interviews by **reinterviewing.** Normally the interview itself is not repeated, but supervisors recontact respondents and ask about the length of the interview and the respondent's reaction to the interviewer, as well as collect basic demographic data to check for interviewer cheating. Verification can indicate when the interviewer has falsified interviews without contacting the potential respondents. However, it does not detect the more subtle form of cheating in which only portions of the interview are falsified. Telephone validation and postcard validation checks often remind interviewers to be conscientious in their work. A validation check may simply point out that an interviewer contacted the proper household but interviewed the wrong individual in that household. This, of course, can be a serious error.

Field-workers should be aware of supervisory verification practices. The interviewer who is conducting a quota sample and needs an upper-income Hispanic male will be less tempted to interview a middle-income Hispanic man and to falsify the income data in this situation.

SUMMARY

The activities to collect data in the field may be performed by the organization needing information, by research suppliers, or by third-party field service organizations. Proper execution of fieldwork is essential for producing research results without substantial error.

Proper control of fieldwork begins with interviewer selection. Field-workers should generally be healthy, outgoing, and well-groomed. New field-workers must be trained in opening the interview, asking the questions, probing for additional information, recording the responses, and terminating the interview. Experienced field-workers are briefed for each new project so that they are familiar with its specific requirements. A particular concern of the briefing session is close adherence to the prescribed sampling procedures.

Careful supervision of field-workers is also necessary. Supervisors gather and edit questionnaires each day. They check to see that field procedures are properly followed and that interviews are on schedule. Supervisors check to be sure that the proper sampling units are used and that the proper people are responding in the study. Supervisors check for interviewer cheating and verify a portion of the interviews by reinterviewing a certain percentage of each field-worker's respondents.

Key Terms

field-workers	door-in-the-face compliance technique
field interviewing service	probing
training interviews	sampling verification
briefing session	interviewer cheating
foot-in-the-door compliance technique	verification by reinterviewing

Questions

1. What qualities should field-workers possess?
2. What impact have changing women's life-styles had on fieldwork in the past decade?
3. What is the proper method for asking questions? What should be done if a question is misunderstood? What should be done if a respondent answers a question before it is encountered in the questionnaire?
4. When should interviewers probe? Give some examples of how probing should be done.
5. How should respondents' answers to open-ended-response questions be recorded?
6. When the interview is over, how should the field-worker terminate it?
7. Why is it important to be sure field-workers adhere to the sampling procedure specified for a project?
8. What forms does interviewer cheating take? How can these forms of cheating be prevented or detected?
9. Contacting every individual in the United States is a problem for the Census Bureau. List other fieldwork problems that might arise in conducting the U.S. census. What might be done to mitigate these problems?

10. Comment on the following field situations:
    a. After conducting a survey with about ten respondents, an interviewer noticed that many of the respondents were saying, "Was I right?" after a particular question.
    b. A questionnaire asking about a new easy-opening can has the following instructions to interviewers: "(Hand respondent can and matching instruction card.) 'Would you please read the instructions on this card and then open this can for me.' (Interviewer: Note any comments respondent makes. Do not under any circumstances help her to open the can or offer any explanation as to how to open it. If she asks for help, tell her that the instructions are on the card. Do not discuss the can or its contents.)"
    c. A researcher gives balloons to children of respondents to keep them occupied during the interview.
    d. An interviewer tells the supervisor: "With the price of gas, this job isn't paying as well as before!"
    e. When a respondent asks how much time the survey will take, the interviewer responds that it will take 15 to 20 minutes. Then the respondent says, "I'm sorry I have to refuse. I can't give you that much time right now."
11. Write interviewer instructions for a telephone survey.

References

[1] Information compiled from a variety of sources. See, for example, Felicity Barringer, "Census Problems Linked to New Methods," *The New York Times,* April 15, 1990, 10-y; Felicity Barringer, "The Making of the '90 Census," *The New York Times,* March 18, 1990, 1-Y; Susan Everly-Douze, "Census Bureau Screens Applicants Thoroughly," *Tulsa World,* March 18, 1990, A-1; Rob Martindale, "Taking Census to Cost $10 for Each American," *Tulsa World,* March 16, 1990, A-1; and William Dunn, "Cities Seek More Time, Assistance for Census," *USA Today,* April 18, 1990, 3A.

[2] Donald P. Warwick and Charles A. Lininger, *The Sample Survey: Theory and Practice* (New York: McGraw-Hill, 1975), 221.

[3] This section relies heavily on the work of the Survey Research Center, Institute for Social Research, at the University of Michigan. For an excellent treatment of fieldwork procedures, see Survey Research Center, *Interviewer's Manual,* rev. ed. (Ann Arbor: University of Michigan, 1976).

[4] Ibid., 11.

[5] John C. Mowen and Robert B. Cialdini, "On Implementing the Door-in-the-Face Compliance Technique in a Business Context," *Journal of Marketing Research* (May 1980): 253–258; and Robert A. Hansen and Larry M. Robinson, "Testing the Effectiveness of Alternate Foot-in-the-Door Manipulations," *Journal of Marketing Research* (August 1980): 359–364.

[6] Survey Research Center, *Interviewer's Manual,* 11–13.

[7] For an extensive treatment of probing, see ibid., 15–19.

[8] Warwick and Lininger, *The Sample Survey,* 213.

[9] Survey Research Center, *Interviewer's Manual,* 19–21.

[10] This section is adapted with permission from Yankelovich, Skelly and White, Inc., *Interviewing Handbook for Senior Council Interviewers.*

[11] G. Birch Ripley, "Confessions of an Industrial Marketing Research Executive Interviewer," *Marketing News,* Sept. 10, 1976, 20.

[12] A. B. Blankenship, *Professional Telephone Surveys* (New York: McGraw-Hill, 1977), 129.

[13] Shirley Colby, "The Lonely Field Interviewer: Why and How Your Research with Her Is Going Wrong," *Advertising Age,* June 30, 1975, 33–35.

[14] Based on Julius A. Roth, "Hired Hand Research," *American Sociologist* (August 1966), 190–196.

Data Analysis and Presentation

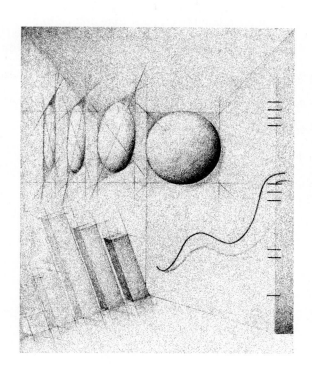

Editing and Coding: Beginning to Transform Raw Data into Information

What you will learn in this chapter:

To define and explain the terms *editing* and *coding*.

To discuss the purposes of field editing and in-house editing.

To describe the different tasks performed by the in-house editor.

To code fixed-alternative questions.

To code open-ended questions.

To define the terms *code book* and *production coding*.

To understand how computerized data processing influences the coding process.

In a managerial survey, respondents were asked:

Relative to other companies in the industry, is your company:

- ☐ *One of the largest*
- ☐ *About average in size*
- ☐ *Small*

One respondent checked both the category "one of the largest" and the category "about average in size." Next to the question the respondent wrote: "average in retailing, one of the largest in drugstore chains." The editor must make the decision whether the industry should be categorized as "retailing" or "drugstore chain industry" and then edit in the appropriate category. A numerical code is then assigned so that researchers, often with the aid of a computer, may analyze the data.

This chapter discusses how editing and coding transform raw data into a format suitable for analysis.

AN OVERVIEW OF THE STAGES OF DATA ANALYSIS

The process of analysis begins after the data have been collected. During the analysis stage several interrelated procedures are performed to summarize and rearrange the data. The research steps related to processing and analysis are presented in Exhibit 17.1. We now turn our attention to this process of data reduction and analysis.

The goal of most research is to provide information. There is a difference between raw data and information. **Information** refers to a body of facts that are in a format suitable for decision making, whereas **data** are simply recorded measures of certain phenomena. The raw data collected in the field must be transformed into information that will answer the manager's questions. The

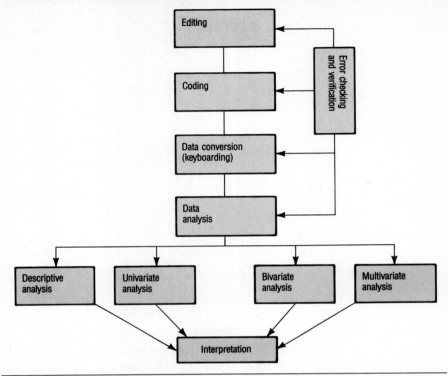

Source: Adapted from John A. Sonquist and William C. Dunkelberg, *Survey and Opinion Research: Procedures for Processing and Analysis,* © 1977, p. 8. Adapted by permission of Prentice-Hall, Inc., Englewood Cliffs, NJ.

conversion of raw data into information requires that the data be edited and coded so the data may be transferred to a computer or other data storage medium.

If the data base is large, there are many advantages to utilizing a computer. Assuming a large database, entering the data into the computer follows the coding procedure.

EDITING

Occasionally, a field-worker makes a mistake and records an impossible answer (e.g., birth year: 1843) or interviews an ineligible respondent (e.g., too young to qualify). Seemingly contradictory answers, such as "no automobile ownership" but an expenditure on automobile insurance, may appear on a questionnaire. There are many problems like these that must be dealt with before the data can be coded. *Editing* procedures are conducted to make the data ready for coding and transfer to data storage. **Editing** is the process of checking and adjusting the data for omissions, legibility, and consistency.

Editing may be differentiated from *coding,* which is the assignment of categories or classifying symbols to previously edited data. Careful editing makes the coding job easier. The purpose of editing is to ensure completeness, consistency, and readability of the data to be transferred to data storage.[1] The editor's task is to check for errors and omissions on the questionnaires or other data collection forms. When a problem is discovered, the editor adjusts the data to make it more complete, consistent, or readable.

The editor may have to reconstruct some data. For instance, a respondent may indicate weekly income rather than monthly income, as requested on the questionnaire. The editor must convert the information to monthly data without adding any extraneous information. The process of editing has been compared to the process of restoring a work of art. The editor "should bring to light all the hidden values and extract all possible information from a questionnaire, while adding nothing extraneous."[2]

Field Editing

Field supervisors are often responsible for conducting a preliminary field edit. The purpose of **field editing** on the same day as the interview is to catch technical omissions (such as a blank page on the interview questionnaire), check legibility of handwriting, and clarify responses that are logically or conceptually inconsistent. If a daily field edit is conducted, a supervisor who edits completed questionnaires will frequently be able to question the interviewers, who may be able to recall the interview well enough to correct the problem. The number of "no answers" or incomplete responses to some questions can be reduced with the rapid follow-up stimulated by a field edit. The daily field edit also allows possible recontacting of the respondent to fill in omissions before the situation has changed. Moreover, the field edit may indicate the need for further interviewer training. For example, the field editor should check open-ended responses for thoroughness of probing and correct following of skip patterns. When poor interviewing is reflected by the lack of probing, supervisors may further train the interviewer. Of course, field editing does not occur with mail surveys.

In-House Editing

Although almost simultaneous editing in the field is highly desirable, in many situations (particularly with mail questionnaires), early reviewing of the data is not always possible. **In-house editing** rigorously investigates the results of data collection. The research supplier or the research department normally has a centralized office staff to perform the editing and coding function.

Arbitron measures radio audiences by having respondents record in diaries their listening behavior in time, station, and place (home or car). After the diaries are returned by mail, in-house editors perform a "usability edit," which checks to make sure the postmark is after the last day of the survey week, checks the legibility of station call letters (station WXXX could look like WYYY), looks for completeness of entries on each day of the week, and performs other editing activities. If the age or sex questions are not filled in, the respondent is called to ensure that this information is included.

Editing for Consistency.   The in-house editor's task is to ensure that inconsistent or contradictory responses are adjusted and that the answers will not be a problem for coders and keyboard operators. Consider the situation in which a telephone interviewer has been instructed to interview only registered voters in a state that requires voters to be 18 years old. The editor's reviewing of a questionnaire indicates that the respondent was only 17 years of age. The editor's task here is to eliminate this obviously incorrect sampling unit. Thus, in this example, the editor's job is to make sure that the sampling unit is consistent with the objectives of the study. The editor checks for adherence to the data collection framework. A survey on in-house versus outside training programs might have a question such as the following:

Does your department utilize in-house training or training by outside consultants? Please check the programs in which your employees participated last month.

A respondent who attended in-house training exclusively might have accidentally checked a program listed under training by outside consultants. The answer must be edited.

Editing requires checking for logically consistent responses. The in-house editor must determine if the answers given by a respondent to one question are consistent with those given to other, related questions. Many surveys utilize filter questions or skip questions that direct the sequence of questions, depending on the respondent's answer. In some cases the respondent will have answered a sequence of questions that should not have been asked. The editor should adjust these answers, usually to "no answer" or "inapplicable," so that the responses will be consistent. In other cases illogical answers will signal that a recording error has been made. For example, a respondent's salary may be listed at $10,000. This may be inconsistent with the 45-year-old respondent's occupational listing as executive vice-president. Or the editor may find it highly unlikely that the answers to two questions could simultaneously be true if both are correct. Judgment is necessary under these conditions.

Editing for Completeness.   In other cases the respondent may have answered only the second portion of a two-part question. The following question indicates the situation where an in-house editor may adjust the questionnaire for completeness.

Does your organization have more than one computer installation?

Yes ＿＿   No ＿＿

If yes, how many?

In this instance it is possible that the respondent checked neither "yes" nor "no" but indicated three computer installations. Here the editor may use her colored pencil to check the "yes" to ensure that this datum is not missing from the questionnaire.

Item nonresponse is the technical term for an unanswered question on an otherwise complete questionnaire. Specific decision rules for handling this problem should be meticulously outlined in the editor's instructions. In many situations the decision rule will be to do nothing with the unanswered question: The editor merely indicates an item nonresponse by writing a message instructing the coder to record a "missing value" or a "blank" as the response. However, when the relationship between two questions is important, such as that of number of sick days to education, it may be necessary for the editor to insert a **plug value**. The decision rule may be to "plug in" an average or neutral value in each case of missing data. Another decision rule may be to alternate the choice of the response categories used as plug values (for example, "yes" the first time, "no" the second time, "yes" the third time, and so on). Still another decision rule might be to randomly select an answer. For example, suppose a respondent has indicated her first compensation preference to be "adequate salary" but has given "retirement program" and "insurance benefits" the same second-preference ranking. The editor may randomly select the second and third choices so that data analysis may be performed as planned.

The editor must also decide whether or not an entire questionnaire is "usable." When a questionnaire has too many answers missing, it may not be suitable for the planned data analysis. In such a situation the editor simply records the fact that a particular incomplete questionnaire has been dropped from the sample.[3]

Editing Questions Answered Out of Order.   Another situation faced by an editor may be the need to rearrange the answers to an open-ended response questionnaire. For example, a respondent may have provided the answer to a subsequent question in her answer to an earlier open-end response question. Because the respondent had already clearly identified her answer, the interviewer may have avoided asking the subsequent question. The interviewer may have wanted to avoid hearing "I already answered that earlier" and, to maintain rapport with the respondent, skipped the question. To make the response uniform with other questionnaires, the editor may move the out of order answer to the section related to the subsequent question.

Facilitating the Coding Process.   While all the previously described editing activities will help coders, several editing procedures are specifically designed to simplify the coding process. For example, the editor checks to make sure every circled response is clearly definable. A response that overlaps two numbers and could be either 3 or 4 is judged by the editor. The editor edits missing information and determines if the answer is "don't know" (DK) or "not ascertained" (NA). These and other decisions by the editor should not be arbitrary but should be based on a systematic procedure of fixed rules for making decisions.

Editing and Tabulating "Don't Know" Answers.   In many situations the respondent will answer "don't know." On the surface this response seems to indicate that the respondent is not familiar with the individual, object, or situation asked about or that he or she is uncertain and has not formulated a clear-cut opinion. This *legitimate* "don't know" means the same as "no opinion." Although the respondent may be unfamiliar with or uncommitted to the topic, there may be reasons other than the legitimate "don't know" answer. The *reluctant* "don't know" is given when an individual simply does not want to answer a question and wishes to stop the interviewer from asking more. For example, asking for information about family income from an individual who is not the head of the household may elicit a "don't know" answer meaning "This is personal, and I really do not want to answer the question." If the individual does not understand the question, he or she may give a *confused* "don't know" answer.

In some situations it is possible for the editor to separate the legitimate "don't know" ("no opinion") answers from the other "don't know" answers. The editor may try to identify the meaning of a "don't know" answer from other data provided on the questionnaire. For instance, the approximate value of a home could be derived from a knowledge of the zip code and the average value of homes within that area.

The tabulation of "don't know" answers requires the researcher to make a decision. One alternative is to record all "don't know" answers as a separate category. This provides for all of the actual response categories, but it may cause some problems with percentage calculation. Another alternative is to eliminate the "don't know" answers from the percentage base. The third alternative is to distribute the "don't know" answers among the other categories, usually on a proportionate basis. Although this is a simple procedure, it is criticized because it assumes that people who give "don't know" answers are the same as those who provide actual answers to a question such as income. In many situations this is not the case, and those who give "don't know" responses are actually a highly homogeneous group.

Mechanics of Editing.   Frequently, the editor's changes to data are written with a colored pencil. When space on the questionnaire permits, the original data are not deleted by eraser, to ensure that a subsequent edit can identify the original concepts. In the author's experience, blue or green pencils have been used for editing and red pencils for coding.

Pretesting Edit.   Editing the questionnaires during the pretest stage can prove to be very valuable. For example, certain slight changes in the questionnaire, such as increasing the space for an open-ended answer because respondents' answers in the pretest were longer than anticipated, will be appreciated during the actual analysis. Answers become more legible because the writers have enough space, answers will be more complete, and answers will be verbatim rather than summarized. Poor instructions or inappropriate question wording on the questionnaire may be identified when editors examine answers to pretests.

Pitfalls of Editing.   Subjectivity can easily enter into the editing job. To do a proper editing job, the editor must be intelligent, experienced, and objective. It is highly recommended that a systematic procedure for assessing the questionnaires be developed by the research analysts, so that the editors may follow clearly defined rules.

EXHIBIT   17.2

Example of a File, Record, and Field on Magnetic Tape

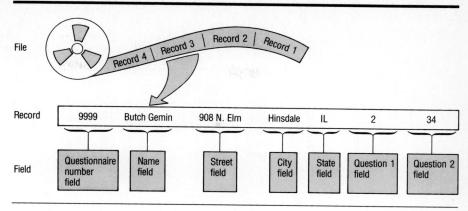

CODING

The process of identifying and classifying each answer with a numerical score or other character symbol is called **coding.** Assigning numerical symbols permits the transfer of data from the survey to the computer. Although **codes** are generally considered to be numerical symbols, they are more broadly defined as the rules for interpreting, classifying, and recording data.[4]

Codes allow data to be processed in a computer. Researchers organize coded data into fields, records, and files. A **field** is a collection of characters (a character is a single number, letter of the alphabet, or special symbol such as the question mark) that represents a single type of data. A **record** is a collection of related fields. A **file** is a collection of related records. Files, records, and fields are stored on magnetic tapes, floppy disks, or hard disks. Each research study is recorded in a file (which is perhaps stored on tape) of all completed questionnaires (see Exhibit 17.2). The file contains a record for each respondent's questionnaire. Each record has a field for various types of information about each respondent and for his or her answers to each question.

The Data Matrix

A **data matrix** is a rectangular arrangement of data into rows and columns. The accountant's spreadsheet, using traditional row-and-column accounting paper, is one example of a data matrix.

Exhibit 17.3 illustrates a data matrix from a secondary-data study investigating each state's population (in millions), average age of the state's residents, and automobile registrations (per 1,000 residents). Each row in the matrix represents one state. In other words, the rows represent records for individual cases, reflecting the fundamental units of analysis. Each column represents a particular field. In our example the columns represent variables that reflect data about each state. The first column contains an abbreviation of the state name. The second column contains the state's population in millions. The third column contains the average age in the state. And the fourth column con-

		Fields			
		State	Population (Millions)	Average Age	Cars per 1,000
	Row	Column 1	Column 2	Column 3	Column 4
Alabama	Row 1	ALAB	3.9	29.3	543
Alaska	Row 2	ALAS	0.4	26.1	387
Arizona	Row 3	ARIZ	2.7	29.2	485
Arkansas	Row 4	ARK	2.3	30.6	442
	.	.	.	.	.
	.	.	.	.	.
	.	.	.	.	.
	.	.	.	.	.
	.	.	.	.	.
Wyoming	Row 50	WYO	0.5	27.1	609

(*Records* labels the vertical axis at left.)

tains the number of automobile registrations per 1,000 residents for each state. The intersection of a row and column indicates a place to enter a number or other code assigned to one state on a particular variable.

In the past the data storage medium used most frequently was the standard-size 80-column punch card. Today the use of an on-line computer terminal for **direct data entry** is the most common input device for data storage, and punch cards are rarely used. Nevertheless, the terminology of direct data entry coding systems is based on the terminology of the traditional punch card system.

Code Construction

Exhibit 17.4 portrays a typical survey question and its associated codes. When the question has a fixed-alternative (closed) format, the number of categories requiring codes is determined during the questionnaire design stage. The codes 8 and 9 are conventionally given to the respective "don't know" (DK) and "no answer" (NA) responses. However, many computer programs recognize a blank field or a certain character symbol, such as a period (.), as indicating a missing value (no answer). The computer program should be considered when selecting codes for "no answer" responses.

There are two basic rules for code construction. First, the coding categories should be *exhaustive*. That is, coding categories should be provided for all subjects or objects or responses. With a categorical variable such as sex, the exhaustiveness of categories is not a problem. However, when the response represents a small number of subjects or when responses might be categorized in a class not typically found, there may be a problem. For example, when questioned about automobile ownership, an antique car collector might men-

EXHIBIT   17.4

**Coding for an
Attitude Statement**

Fixed-Alternative Question

In general, self-regulation by business itself is preferable to stricter control of business by the government.

1. Strongly agree
2. Mildly agree
3. Mildly disagree

4. Strongly disagree
8. Don't know
9. No answer

---

tion he drives a Packard Clipper. This may present a problem if separate categories are developed for all possible makes of cars.

Second, the coding categories should also be *mutually exclusive* and *independent*. This means that there should be no overlap between the categories so that a subject or response can be placed in only one category. This frequently requires that an "other" code category be included to ensure that the categories are all inclusive and mutually exclusive. For example, managerial span of control might be coded: 1, 2, 3, 4, and "5 or more." The "5 or more" category ensures everyone a place in a category.

When a questionnaire is highly structured, precoding of the categories typically occurs before the data are collected. Exhibit 17.5 presents a questionnaire with the precoded response categories that were determined before the start of data collection.

In many cases, such as when researchers are using open-ended response questions to explore an unfamiliar topic, a framework for classifying responses to questions cannot be established before data collection. This situation requires some careful thought concerning the determination of categories after the editing process has been completed. This is called **postcoding,** or simply *coding.*

Precoding Fixed-Alternative Questions

Exhibit 17.5 shows the last page of a questionnaire asking several demographic questions that will be used to classify individuals' scores. Question 29 has three possible answers, and they are precoded 1, 2, 3. Question 30 asks a person to respond "yes" (1) or "no" (2) to the question "Are you the male or female head of the household?" These small numbers slightly raised to the left of the boxes indicate the codes for each response and will be used by the keyboard operator when entering the data into the computer. For example, for Question 30 a field, perhaps Column 32, in the data matrix may be assigned for the answer. If the respondent replies "yes," a "1" will be entered. Question 31 will require a larger field, because there are a large number of possible answers.

The Automarket Research questionnaire shown in Exhibit 17.6 illustrates another form of coding. Question 1a shows that there are five possible answers: completely satisfied, coded 001; very satisfied, coded 002; fairly well satisfied, coded 003; somewhat dissatisfied, coded 004; and very dissatisfied,

29. Do you—or does anyone else in your immediate household—belong to a labor union?
    1☐ <u>Yes</u>, I personally belong to a labor union.
    2☐ <u>Yes</u>, another member of my household belongs to a labor union.
    3☐ <u>No</u>, no one in my household belongs to a labor union.

30. Are you the male or female head of the household—that is, <u>the person whose income is the chief source of support of the household?</u>
    1☐ Yes   2☐ No

31. Would you please check the approximate combined yearly income (*before income taxes and any other payroll deductions*) from <u>all sources of all those</u> in your immediate household? *(Please include income from salaries, investments, dividends, rents, royalties, bonuses, commissions, etc.)* <u>Please remember that your individual answers will not be divulged.</u>

1☐ Less than $4,000	7☐ $8,000–8,999	13☐ $25,000–$29,999
2☐ $4,000–4,999	8☐ $9,000–9,999	14☐ $30,000–$39,999
3☐ $5,000–5,999	9☐ $10,000–12,499	15☐ $40,000–$49,999
4☐ $6,000–6,999	10☐ $12,500–$14,999	16☐ $50,000–$74,999
5☐ $7,000–7,499	11☐ $15,000–$19,999	17☐ $75,000–$99,999
6☐ $7,500–7,999	12☐ $20,000–$24,999	18☐ $100,000 or more

32a. Do you personally own corporate stocks?   1☐ Yes   2☐ No
  b. Do you own stocks in the corporation for which you work?— Do you own them in a corporation for which you do <u>not</u> work? *(Please check as many as apply.)*

    Own <u>STOCK</u> in:
    1☐ Company for which I work   2☐ Other company
    THANK YOU VERY MUCH FOR YOUR COOPERATION
    If you would like to make any comments on any of the subjects covered in this study, please use the space below:

coded 005. The codes for Question 1b begin with 006 and end with 010. This questionnaire gives each possible answer an individual code number. This system of coding is used when the computer has been programmed to change these codes into traditional codes or categorical answers for each question.

The partial questionnaire in Exhibit 17.7 shows a precoding format for a telephone interview. In this situation the interviewer circles the coded numerical score as the answer to the question.

Precoding can be used if the researcher knows what the answer categories will be before data collection occurs. Thus once the questionnaire has been designed and the structured (or closed-form) answers are identified, coding becomes a routine process. In fact, in some cases the predetermined responses are

EXHIBIT   17.6

A Precoded Fixed Alternative Questionnaire

Automarket Research

This questionnaire should be completed by the **principal driver** of the vehicle indicated. Thank you for taking time to answer these questions.

1. Now that you've had your vehicle for about one year, please tell us how satisfied you are in the following areas.	Completely satisfied	Very satisfied	Fairly well satisfied	Somewhat dissatisfied	Very dissatisfied
a. Exterior quality of workmanship (fit and finish)?	001 ☐	002 ☐	003 ☐	004 ☐	005 ☐
b. Interior quality of workmanship (fit and finish)?	006 ☐	007 ☐	008 ☐	009 ☐	010 ☐
c. Engine power and pickup?	011 ☐	012 ☐	013 ☐	014 ☐	015 ☐
d. Smoothness of transmission?	016 ☐	017 ☐	018 ☐	019 ☐	020 ☐
e. Riding comfort?	021 ☐	022 ☐	023 ☐	024 ☐	025 ☐
f. Ease of handling?	026 ☐	027 ☐	028 ☐	029 ☐	030 ☐
g. Fuel economy?	031 ☐	032 ☐	033 ☐	034 ☐	035 ☐
h. Quietness?	036 ☐	037 ☐	038 ☐	039 ☐	040 ☐
i. Operation of the accessories (e.g., radio, air conditioner, heater, defroster, etc.)?	041 ☐	042 ☐	043 ☐	044 ☐	045 ☐
j. Overall satisfaction with the vehicle?	046 ☐	047 ☐	048 ☐	049 ☐	050 ☐

2a. Since the time of purchase, have you taken your Ford Motor Company vehicle to your selling dealer for any kind of service, including warranty work or repairs that you paid for? .... Yes 051 ☐ No 052 ☐ If no, please skip to question 5.

2b. If yes, what was the nature of the service? Check those that apply.

053 ☐ Paint/exterior moldings   056 ☐ Brakes/steering   059 ☐ Electrical system   062 ☐ Other (please describe)
054 ☐ Other body   057 ☐ Engine   060 ☐ Wheels/tires
055 ☐ Interior   058 ☐ Transmission   061 ☐ Maintenance service

	Completely satisfied	Very satisfied	Fairly well satisfied	Somewhat dissatisfied	Very dissatisfied
2c. How satisfied were you with the service you received?	063 ☐	064 ☐	065 ☐	066 ☐	067 ☐

3. Based on your visit(s) to your selling dealership for service, how satisfied would you say you are with each of the following? Mark one box across.	Completely satisfied	Very satisfied	Fairly well satisfied	Somewhat dissatisfied	Very dissatisfied
a. The attitude of service department personnel (their interest in you and your problems)	068 ☐	069 ☐	070 ☐	071 ☐	072 ☐
b. Their overall treatment of you as a customer	073 ☐	074 ☐	075 ☐	076 ☐	077 ☐
c. Their promptness in writing up your order	078 ☐	079 ☐	080 ☐	081 ☐	082 ☐
d. Their politeness	083 ☐	084 ☐	085 ☐	086 ☐	087 ☐
e. Their understanding of your problem(s)	088 ☐	089 ☐	090 ☐	091 ☐	092 ☐
f. Convenience of scheduling the work	093 ☐	094 ☐	095 ☐	096 ☐	097 ☐
g. Convenience of service hours	098 ☐	099 ☐	100 ☐	101 ☐	102 ☐
h. Length of time to complete the work	103 ☐	104 ☐	105 ☐	106 ☐	107 ☐
i. Availability of needed parts	108 ☐	109 ☐	110 ☐	111 ☐	112 ☐
j. Their completing all the work you requested	113 ☐	114 ☐	115 ☐	116 ☐	117 ☐
k. The quality of work done (was it fixed right?)	118 ☐	119 ☐	120 ☐	121 ☐	122 ☐
l. Explanation of work and charges (if any)	123 ☐	124 ☐	125 ☐	126 ☐	127 ☐
m. Fairness of prices (if you were charged)	128 ☐	129 ☐	130 ☐	131 ☐	132 ☐
n. Appearance of service department	133 ☐	134 ☐	135 ☐	136 ☐	137 ☐

4. For the most recent service work	Yes	No	
a. Was the vehicle ready when promised?	138 ☐	139 ☐	
b. Did anyone at the dealership follow up with you after your service visit to see if you were satisfied?	140 ☐	141 ☐	
c. Did the dealership do any repeat work on a problem which they themselves previously tried to but couldn't fix?	142 ☐	143 ☐	If no, please skip to question 5.

d. If yes, what was the nature of the service? Check those that apply.

144 ☐ Paint/exterior moldings   147 ☐ Brakes/steering   150 ☐ Electrical system   153 ☐ Other (please describe)
145 ☐ Other body   148 ☐ Engine   151 ☐ Wheels/tires
146 ☐ Interior   149 ☐ Transmission   152 ☐ Maintenance service

(over please)

1

Source: A. R. Automarket Research, Post Office Box 5021, Southfield, Michigan 48086-5021.

EXHIBIT   17.7

**Precoded Format for
Telephone Interview**

Study #45641   For office use only
Travel (Telephone Screening)   Respondent #_____
City:
Chicago
Gary
Ft. Wayne
Bloomington
Hello, I'm _____ from _____, a national
survey research company. We are conducting a study and would like to ask
you a few questions.

A. Before we begin, do you, or any member of your family, work for . . .

    1 A travel agency   2 An advertising agency   3 A survey research
                                                         company

    (If "yes" to any of the above, terminate and tally on contact sheet)

B. By the way, have you been interviewed as part of a survey research study
   within the past month?

    1 Yes — (Terminate and tally on contact sheet)
    2 No — (Continue)

1. Have you yourself made any trips of over 100 miles within the
   continental 48 states in the past 3 months?

    1 Yes
    2 No — (Skip to Question 10)

2. Was the trip for business reasons (paid for by your firm), vacation, or
   personal reasons?

	Last Trip	Second Last Trip	Other Trips
	( )	( )	( )
Business	1	1	1
Vacation	2	2	2
Personal (excluding a vacation)	3	3	3

---

based on standardized classification schemes. A coding framework that standardizes occupation is given below:

What is your occupation? (*PROBE:* What kind of work is that?)

01   **Professional, technical, and kindred workers**

02   **Farmers**

03   **Managers, officials, and proprietors**

04   **Clerical and kindred workers**

05   **Sales workers**

06   **Craftsmen, foremen, and kindred workers**

07   **Operatives and kindred workers**

08   **Service workers**

09   **Laborers, except farm and mine**

10   **Retired, widow**

11   **Student**

12   **Unemployed, on relief, laid off**

13   **Housewife**

14   **Other (specify)** _____

99   **No occupation given**

Computer-assisted telephone interviewing (CATI) and computer-interactive surveys require precoding. Changing the coding framework after the interviewing process starts is extremely difficult because it requires changes in the computer programs.

Coding Open-Ended Response Questions

The usual reason for using open-ended response questions is that the researcher has no clear hypotheses regarding the answers, which will be numerous and varied. The purpose of coding such questions is to reduce the large number of individual responses to a few general categories of answers that can be assigned a numerical score. Code construction in these situations necessarily must reflect the judgment of the researcher. A major objective in the code-building process is to accurately transfer the meaning from written responses to numeric codes. Experienced researchers recognize that the key to this process is basing code building on thoughts, not just words. The end result of code building should be a list, in abbreviated and orderly form, of all comments and thoughts given in answer to each question.

Differentiating categories of answers for the coding of open-ended response questions is more difficult than coding fixed-alternative questions. Developing an appropriate code from the respondent's exact comments is somewhat of an art. Researchers generally perform a **test tabulation** to identify verbatim responses from approximately 20 percent of respondents' questionnaires and then construct coding categories reflecting the judgment of the person constructing the codes. The test tabulation is a small sample of the total number of replies to a particular question. Its purpose is preliminary identification of the stability and distribution of the answers that will determine how to set up a coding scheme.

The second stage, after tabulating the basic responses, is to determine how many answer categories will be acceptable. This decision will be influenced by the purpose of the study and the limitations of the computer program and plan for data entry. For example, if only one single-digit field is assigned to the particular survey question, the number of possible categories is limited to 10 (0–9). In fact, if an "other" or "miscellaneous" code category appears along with a "don't know/no answer" code category, the code construction would be additionally limited.

T A B L E   1 7 . 1

**Open-Ended Responses
to a Wine Industry Survey:
Women's Suggestions
(Based on 100 Interviews)**

	Number of Women Reporting
Promote through recipe ideas for women	24
Use more advertising	21
Promote through wine tasting parties	13
Tell what to serve the wine with	11
Use magazine ads	9
Have written explanations of different wines	9
Use television ads	8
Advertise more in women's magazines	6
Cut the price on good wines	4
It won't matter; wine drinkers will buy, others won't	4
Show illustrations of dinner tables with wine glasses	3
Make small bottles for first try	3
Stress the health aspect	2
Eliminate the elegant image, wine is for every day	2
Emphasize the elegant image, for gracious living	2
Make wine a family beverage	2
Use newspapers to advertise	2
Make wines more available	2
Emphasize that it's not a dangerous alcohol	2
Make up packages of 2 or 3 types for housewives	1
Don't use TV—too many ads there already	1
Run coupon to send in for recipe book	1
Play up the dinner party angle	1
Educate the public about the different brands	1
Educate the public about the cost of wine	1
Have more articles in women's magazines	1
Write a book on the history and romance of wine	1
Educate the people who are selling the wines	1
Emphasize that it completes a meal	1
Use more catchy tunes in ads	1
Support cooking schools	1
Have restaurants suggest a wine or two with each entree	1
Publish a wine cookbook	1
Use grocery store displays	1
Advertise the excellence of domestic wines	1
Tell of different ways to serve it before dinner	1
Place it near the meat counter	1
Use radio ads	1
Alert the younger generation to its uses	1

Source: *Ladies Home Journal*. Reprinted by permission of Charter Publishing Company.

Devising the Coding Scheme.   The coding scheme should not be too elaborate. The coder's task is to summarize the data. Table 17.1 shows a test tabulation for women's responses to a question about what the wine industry could do to increase people's interest in buying wine. A large number of answers were given to the question. After the "first cut" at devising the coding scheme, it must be decided if it should be revised. The researcher must decide if the codes are appropriate to answer the managerial questions. Preliminary schemes having "too many" categories can always be collapsed or reduced at a later time in the analysis. If initial coding is at too abstract a level and only a few categories are established, it will be difficult to revise the codes to more concrete statements unless the raw data are recoded.

In the wine industry example the preliminary tabulation, with "too many" codes, could be reduced to a smaller number of categories. For example, the heading "Increased Advertising" could include the responses "Use more advertising," "Use magazine ads," "Use television ads," "Advertise more in women's magazines," "Use newspapers to advertise," "Advertise the excellence of domestic wines," and "Use radio ads." Experienced coders group answers under generalized headings that are pertinent to the research question. It is important to make the codes consistent. Individual coders should give the same code to similar responses. The categories should be sufficiently unambiguous so that coders will not classify items in different ways.

The coding of open-ended-response questions is a very complex issue. Certain technical treatises concerning this subject may be referred to if complex problems develop.[5]

Code Book

Up to this point it has been implied that each code's position in the data matrix has already been determined. However, this plan generally occurs only after the coding scheme has been designed for every question.

The **code book** identifies each variable in the study and its location on the magnetic tape or other input medium. With the code book the researcher can identify any variable's description, code name, and field. Exhibit 17.8 illustrates a portion of a code book for the travel study illustrated in Exhibit 17.7. Notice that the first few fields record the study number, city, and other information used for identification purposes. Researchers commonly identify individual respondents by giving each an identification number or questionnaire number. When each interview is identified with a number entered into each computer record, errors discovered in the tabulation process can be checked on the questionnaire to verify the answer.

Production Coding

Transferring the data from questionnaire or data collection form after the data have been collected is called **production coding.** Depending on the nature of the data collection form, codes may be written directly on the instrument or on a special **coding sheet,** which is multi-column ruled paper that is a facsimile of the data matrix. It is best to have coding done in a central location, where a supervisor may help to solve interpretation problems. The value of training coders should not be overlooked.

> *The research staff should prepare one or two practice interviews-questionnaires made up by the research staff in duplicate so that all coders working on the study will be practice-coding the same interviews. The few hours of time invested in training pay off highly in the reduction of coding errors. The objectives of coder training are to demonstrate the consistent and proper application of codes and to encourage the proper use of administrative procedures.[6]*

**Portion of a Code Book
from a Travel Study**

**Study #45641
January 19_____
N = 743**

Question Number	Field or Column Number	Description and Meaning of Code Values
—	1–5	Study number (45641)
—	6	City 1. Chicago 2. Gary 3. Ft. Wayne 4. Bloomington
—	7–9	Interview number (3 digits on upper left-hand corner of questionnaire)
A	Not entered	Family, work for 1. Travel agency 2. Advertising agency 3. Survey research company
B	Not entered	Interviewed past month 1. Yes 2. No
1.	10	Traveled in past 3 months 1. Yes 2. No
2.	11	Purpose last trip 1. Business 2. Vacation 3. Personal
	12	Purpose second last trip 1. Business 2. Vacation 3. Personal
	13	Purpose other trips 1. Business 2. Vacation 3. Personal

Editing and Coding Combined.   Frequently, certain editing functions will be performed by the person coding the questionnaire. For example, the respondent may be asked to indicate an occupational title that may be subsequently coded for socioeconomic status. Often a question asking for a description of the job or business is used as a check to make certain there is no problem with classifying the response. For example, persons who indicate "salesperson" could write their job description as "selling shoes in a shoe store" or "selling IBM computers to the Defense Department." Generally, coders will perform this type of editing function. If questions arise, the help of a tabulation supervisor will be requested.

RESEARCH INSIGHT
Difficulties Faced by the Coder

A common coding problem related to question order is illustrated by the first series of questions and hypothetical answers presented below:

Q.1 Do you think we will have good times in the economy soon?

☐①YES☐   ☐5 NO☐   GO TO Q.4.   ☐8 DK: Uncertain☐

Q.2 About when will that happen?

IN THE NEXT FEW MONTHS

Q.3 Why is that?

(A) BECAUSE WE ARE ALREADY IN AN UPSWING

(B) BECAUSE THE GOVERNMENT IS SPENDING A LOT OF MONEY

Q.4 Do you think that over the next few months the rate of inflation will be reduced or that the level of unemployment will rise?   NO

Q.5 Have you heard any favorable news about the stock market lately?   NO

Q.6 Do you think we might have a recession next year?   YES

The hypothetical intent of the first question is to find out why people think that we will have an economic recovery in the near future. Those who do not expect a recovery are not asked questions 2 and 3 (although, in principle, they could be). The problem here is that the question structure does not make it clear whether or not Q.3 relates back to Q.1 or to Q.2. Thus, answer B is a meaningful answer to Q.3 and could easily be coded (assuming a well-defined code) as an answer to it. Answer A, however, relates to the timing of the upswing and is not really a good answer to the question. This presents the coder with difficulties that take extra time to resolve and could have been avoided simply with better question construction. Placing Q.3 ahead of Q.2 would avoid this problem, making the coding easier and obtaining better data. Answers such as "I heard it on TV" would still result, but the probability of a meaningful answer would be raised. Good question structuring leads to clearer and more easily codable responses, fewer coding errors, and minimizes coder judgment.

Another coding nightmare is posed by Q.4. How is the coder to view this? NO, the rate of inflation will not be reduced? NO, the level of unemployment will not rise? NO, neither will happen? NO, both will happen?

Q.5 is an example of what happens when the likely response pattern of the respondent is not considered. There are many interesting possibilities: NO, heard nothing about the stock market lately; NO, heard nothing favorable about the stock market lately; NO, don't pay any attention to news about the stock market. Whatever the results, they surely must be interpreted in light of the troubles with the question used to generate them. The problems could be discovered through the coder-message technique or by pre-testing the questionnaire.

The way in which people use verb tenses can create problems for the coder also. For example, consider the meaning of the answer to Q.6: YES, we might, but it is very unlikely; YES, it is sure to happen; and everything in between. A NO answer would have similar interpretational problems: NO, we'll never have one; NO, not next year, but perhaps the year after that; NO, not next year, but we'll definitely have one soon.

Source: John A. Sonquist and William C. Dunkelberg, *Survey and Opinion Research: Procedures for Processing and Analysis*, © 1977, pp. 100–101. Adapted by permission of Prentice-Hall, Inc., Englewood Cliffs, NJ.

COMPUTERIZED DATA PROCESSING

Input Medium

Most studies having large sample sizes use a computer for data processing. Magnetic tape is widely used as a data storage medium. However, technological changes now offer researchers several alternative means of putting data into

18. LINE NUMBER

19. What was . . . doing most of LAST WEEK—

Working
Keeping house
Going to school
or something else? ■

Working *(Skip to 20A)* .... WK ○
With a job but not at work .... J ○
Looking for work .... LK ○
Keeping house .... H ○
Going to school .... S ○
Unable to work *(Skip to 24)* .... U ○
Retired .... R ○
Other *(Specify)* .... OT ○
↓

20C. Does . . . USUALLY work 35 hours or more a week at this job?
Yes ○ What is the reason . . . worked less than 35 hours LAST WEEK?
No ○ What is the reason . . . USUALLY works less than 35 hours a week?
(Mark the appropriate reason)

Slack work .... ○
Material shortage .... ○
Plant or machine repair .... ○
New job started during week .... ○
Job terminated during week .... ○
Could find only part-time work .... ○
Holiday *(Legal or religious)* .... ○
Labor dispute .... ○
Bad weather .... ○
Own illness .... ○
On vacation .... ○
Too busy with housework, school, personal bus., etc. .... ○
Did not want full-time work .... ○
Full-time work week under 35 hours ... ○
Other reason *(Specify)* .... ○
↓

(Skip to 23 and enter job worked at last week)

20. Did . . . do any work at all LAST WEEK, not counting work around the house? *(Note: If farm or business operator in hh., ask about unpaid work)*
Yes ○   No ○   *(Go to 21)*

20A. How many hours did . . . work LAST WEEK at all jobs?

0 0
1 1
2 2
3 3
4 4
5 5
6 6
7 7
8 8
9 9

20B. INTERVIEWER CHECK ITEM
49' ○ *(Skip to item 23)*
1-34 ○ *(Go to 20C)*
35-48 ○ *(Go to 20D)*

20D. Did . . . lose any time or take any time off LAST WEEK for any reason such as

---

21. *(If 1 in 19, skip to 21A.)* Did . . . have a job or business from which he was temporarily absent or on layoff LAST WEEK?
Yes ○   No ○   *(Go to 22)*

21A. Why was . . . absent from work LAST WEEK?
Own illness .... ○
On vacation .... ○   ■
Bad weather .... ○
Labor dispute .... ○
New job to begin within 30 days ○   *(Skip to 22B and 22C2)*
Temporary layoff *(Under 30 days)* ○   *(Skip to 22C3)*
Indefinite layoff *(30 days or more or no def. recall date)* ○
Other *(Specify)* .... ○
↙

21B. Is . . . getting wages or salary for any of the time off LAST WEEK?
Yes .... ○
No .... ○
Self-employed .... ○

21C. Does . . . usually work 35 hours or more a week at this job?
Yes ○
No ○   ■

(Skip to 23 and enter job held last week)

22A. What has . . . been doing in the last 4 weeks to find work? *(Mark all methods used; do not read list.)*
Checked with—
pub. employ. agency .... ○
pvt. employ. agency .... ○
employer directly .... ○
friends or relatives .... ○
Placed or answered ads .... ○
Nothing *(Skip to 24)* .... ○
Other *(Specify in notes, e.g., MDTA, union or prof. register, etc.)* .... ○

22B. Why did . . . start looking for work? ■ Was it because . . . lost or quit a job at that time *(pause)* or was there some other reason?
Lost job .... ○
Quit job .... ○
Left school .... ○
Wanted temporary work .... ○
Other *(Specify in notes)* .... ○

22C.
1) How many weeks has . . . been looking for work?
2) How many weeks ago did . . . start looking for work?
3) How many weeks ago was . . . laid off?

0 0
1 1   ■
2 2
3 3
4 4
5 5
6 6
7 7
8 8
9 9

22D. Has . . . been looking for full-time or part-time work?
Full ○   Part ○   ■
●

22E. Is there any reason why . . . could not take a job LAST WEEK?
Yes ○   Already has a job .... ○
                Temporary illness .... ○
                Going to school .... ○
No ○   Other *(Specify in notes)* ..... ○

22F. When did . . . last work at a full-time job or business lasting 2 consecutive weeks or more?
1971 or later *(Write month and year)* ... ○
↙

24A. When did . . . last work for pay at a regular job or business, either full- or part-time?
Within past 12 months ○
1 up to 2 years ago .... ○
2 up to 3 years ago .... ○   *(Go to 24B)*
3 up to 4 years ago .... ○
4 up to 5 years ago .... ○
5 or more years ago .... ○
Never worked .... ○   *(Skip to 24C)*

24B. Why did . . . leave that job?
Personal, family *(Incl. pregnancy)* or school .... ○
Health .... ○
Retirement or old age .... ○
Seasonal job completed .... ○
Slack work or business conditions .... ○
Temporary nonseasonal job completed .... ○
Unsatisfactory work arrangements *(Hours, pay, etc.)* ..... ○
Other .... ○

24D. What are the reasons . . . is not looking for work? *(Mark each reason mentioned)*
● **Believes no work** available in line of work or area .... ○
● **Couldn't find** any work .... ○
● **Lacks nec. schooling,** training, skills or experience .... ○
● Employers think **too young** or **too old** .... ○
● **Other pers. handicap** in finding job. ○
● Can't arrange **child care** .... ○
● **Family** responsibilities............. ○
● **In school** or other training .... ○
● **Ill health,** physical disability ...... ○
● Other *(Specify in notes)*............ ○
● **Don't know** .... ○

the computer. Computer-assisted telephone interviewing is one advance in equipment that is rapidly changing the form of data processing employed in marketing research.

A research system using microcomputers or on-line direct data entry equipment can reduce a three- to four-week research study to a few days. This type of on-line tabulating automatically stores and tabulates responses as they are collected, which substantially reduces clerical errors that occur during the editing and coding process. Also, for highly structured questionnaires **optical scanning systems** may be used to directly read material from *mark sensed* questionnaires onto magnetic tape. This type of system requires the mark sensing of "small squares" on a special sheet of paper devised for optical scanning (see Exhibit 17.9).

Data Entry (Keyboarding)

The process of transforming data from a research project, such as answers to a survey questionnaire, to computers is referred to as **data entry** or **data conversion.** Years ago keypunch machines were used to put the data on computer cards. As computers have become more sophisticated, data entry is either instantaneous, as in computer-assisted telephone interviewing, or converted to magnetic media, such as disks or tape, for storage.

When data are not directly entered into the computer the moment they are collected, data processing for the computer begins with keyboarding. This keyboard equipment transfers coded data from the questionnaires or coding sheets onto a magnetic tape or floppy disk. As in every stage of the research process, there is some concern as to whether the data entry job has been done correctly. Keyboard operators, like anyone else, may make errors. To ensure 100 percent accuracy in transferring the codes to the tape, the job is *verified* by a second keyboard operator who checks the accuracy of the data entered. If an error has been made, the verifier corrects the data entry. This process of verifying the data is never performed by the same person who entered the original data. A person who misread the coded questionnaire during the keyboarding operation might make the same mistake during the verifying process. The mistake might not be detected if the same person is used for both operations.

Keyboard operators prefer to have the data on coding sheets so that they do not have to page through the questionnaire to punch the data. However, this usually increases the time and effort required for coding. Coding on the actual questionnaire eliminates the need for transferring the answers to coding paper. The particular resources of the project will dictate which source is used as input to the keyboard operators. Several of the questionnaires illustrated in this chapter indicate how coding may be placed on the questionnaire itself.

Recoding

It is sometimes easier to enter the raw data into the computer using the precoding on the questionnaire and then programming the computer to recode certain data. This situation often occurs when a researcher measures attitudes with a series of both positive and negative statements. Reversing the order of the codes for negative statements so that their codes reflect the same direction and order or magnitude as the positive statements requires only a simple data transformation. For instance, if a seven-point scale for variable 1 (VAR1) is to be recoded, the following programming statement that subtracts the original code score from eight might be used: $VAR1 = 8 - VAR1$.

Collapsing the number of categories or values of a variable, or creating new variables (e.g., creating an index based on several variables) also require recoding.

Error Checking

The final stage in the coding process is the error checking and verification stage or "data cleaning" stage, which is a check to make sure that all codes are legitimate. For example, if sex is coded 1 = male and 2 = female and a 3 code is found, it is obvious that a mistake has been made that requires an adjustment.

SUMMARY

Raw data must be edited and coded to be put into a form suitable for analysis. Editing involves checking and adjusting for errors or omissions on the questionnaires or other data-collecting forms. Its purpose is to ensure completeness, consistency, and readability of the data. Field supervisors are responsible for preliminary editing. The daily field edit allows rapid follow-up of errors; interviewers may recall responses omitted or be able to recontact respondents. The in-house editor checks for consistency among answers and for completeness or may rearrange responses on an open-ended response questionnaire. The editor's task includes being sure material is ready for coding.

Coding is the process of identifying and classifying each answer with a numerical score or other character symbol. It usually involves entering the data for computer storage. The coding categories should be exhaustive, providing for all responses. They should also be mutually exclusive and independent so that there is no overlap between categories. On highly structured questionnaires, the categories may be precoded. With open-ended-response questions, the answers are postcoded. This means the categories are assigned after the data have been collected. The categories must be assigned according to the researcher's judgment. It is better to assign too many categories than too few, and it is easier to collapse several categories into one than to increase the number of categories. A code book is prepared that identifies each variable and the codes for responses.

Production coding is the actual process of transferring the data from the questionnaire to the storage medium. Data are commonly keyboarded onto magnetic tape. However, other possibilities include on-line computer systems for entering data directly into computer storage as they are collected. After the raw data are in the computer, programs may be used to recode variables or to check for errors.

Key Terms

information	data matrix
data	direct data entry
editing	postcoding
field editing	test tabulation
in-house editing	code book
item nonresponse	production coding
plug value	coding sheet
coding	optical scanning system
code	data entry
field	data conversion
record	recoding
file	error checking

Questions

1. What is the purpose of editing?
2. Suppose respondents in a political survey were asked if they favored or opposed the Agricultural Trade Act. Edit the following open-ended responses:
   a. I don't know what it is, so I'll oppose it.
   b. Favorable, though I don't really know what it is.
   c. You caught me on that. I don't know but from the sound of it I favor it.
3. Comment on the coding scheme for this question: "In which of these groups did your total *family* income, from all sources, fall last year—1989—before taxes, that is? Just tell me the code number."

Response	Code	Response	Code
Under $1,000	01	$25,000 to $29,999	07
$1,000 to $3,999	02	$30,000 to $39,999	08
$4,000 to $9,999	03	$40,000 to $49,999	09
$10,000 to $14,999	04	$50,000 or over	10
$15,000 to $19,999	05	Refused to answer	11
$20,000 to $24,999	06	Don't know	98
		No answer	99

4. Suppose the following information had been gathered about the occupation of several respondents. How would you classify the following respondents' answers in the occupational coding scheme presented in the chapter: plumber, butcher, retail sales, X-ray technician, and veterinarian?
5. A frequently asked question on campus is "What is your major?" Suppose a survey researcher wishes to develop a coding scheme for the answer to this question. What would the scheme look like?
6. A researcher asks the question "What do you remember about advertising for Bic disposable razors?" How should the code book for this question be structured? What coding problems does the question present?

7.   During the month of October a sales manager records the number of days worked, the number of sales calls made, and the actual sales volume for each of his 15 sales representatives. Outline a data matrix for this database.

8.   Design a short questionnaire with fewer than five fixed-alternative questions to measure student satisfaction with your college bookstore. Interview five classmates, then arrange the database into a data matrix.

References

[1] John A. Sonquist and William C. Dunkelberg, *Survey and Opinion Research: Procedures for Processing and Analysis* (Englewood Cliffs, NJ: Prentice-Hall, 1977), 41–72. This is an excellent source for the data processing of survey data.

[2] Paul L. Erdos, *Professional Mail Surveys* (New York: McGraw-Hill, 1970), 176.

[3] D. W. Stewart, "Filling the Gap: A Review of the Missing Data Problem," in Bruce J. Walker et al., *An Assessment of Marketing Thought and Practice* (Chicago: American Marketing Association, 1982), 395–399.

[4] Sonquist and Dunkelberg, *Survey and Opinion Research*, 9.

[5] Philip S. Sibel, "Coding," in *Handbook of Marketing Research*, ed. Robert Ferber (New York: McGraw-Hill, 1974), 181.

[6] Sonquist and Dunkelberg, *Survey and Opinion Research*, 9.

CHAPTER **18**

Basic Data Analysis: Descriptive Statistics

What you will learn in this chapter:

To understand that analysis consists of summarizing, rearranging, ordering, or manipulating data.

To define descriptive analysis.

To compute and explain the purpose of simple tabulations and cross-tabulations.

To discuss how the calculation of percentages helps the researcher understand the nature of relationships.

To discuss the relationship between two variables with cross-tabulation procedures.

To elaborate and refine basic cross-tabulations.

To define and explain spurious relationships.

To discuss data transformations.

To calculate an index number.

To explain some of the computer programs for analyzing descriptive data.

To explain the purpose of interpretation.

To discuss how computer mapping aids descriptive analysis.

According to the Bureau of Labor Statistics, at least 98 percent of employees working for medium-size and large firms have paid vacations and holidays, 92 percent get time off for jury duty, 72 percent get coffee breaks, and 67 percent get sick leave.[1]

These findings illustrate the results of a typical descriptive analysis. This chapter explains how to perform descriptive analysis.

∎

THE NATURE OF DESCRIPTIVE ANALYSIS

Business researchers edit and code data to provide input that results in tabulated information that will answer the research questions. With this input researchers logically and statistically describe project results. Within this context the term *analysis* is difficult to define because it refers to a variety of activities and processes. One form of analysis is summarizing large quantities of raw data so the result can be interpreted. Categorizing, or separating out the components or relevant parts of the whole data set, is also a form of analysis to make the data easily manageable. Rearranging, ordering, or manipulating data may provide descriptive information which answers questions posed in the problem definition. All forms of analysis attempt to portray consistent patterns in the data so the results may be studied and interpreted in a brief and meaningful way.

Descriptive analysis refers to the transformation of the raw data into a form that will make them easy to understand and interpret. Describing responses or observations is typically the first form of analysis. The calculation of averages, frequency distributions, and percentage distributions is the most common form of summarizing data.

As the analysis progresses beyond the descriptive stage, researchers generally apply the tools of inferential statistics. *Univariate analysis,* which is cov-

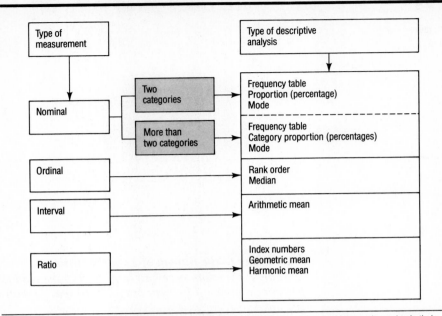

All statistics appropriate for lower-order scales (nominal is the lowest) are appropriate for higher-order scales (ratio is the highest).

ered in Chapter 19, allows researchers to assess the statistical significance of various hypotheses about a single variable.

In Chapter 11 we saw that the type of measurement scale used determines the permissible arithmetic operations. Exhibit 18.1 outlines the most common descriptive statistics associated with each type of scale. It is important to remember that all descriptive statistics appropriate for a lower-order scale are also appropriate for higher-order scales.

TABULATION

Tabulation refers to the orderly arrangement of data in a table or other summary format. Counting the number of responses to a question and putting them in a frequency distribution is a **simple,** or *marginal,* **tabulation.** Simple tabulation of the responses or observations on a question-by-question or item-by-item basis provides the most basic form of information for the researcher and in many cases the most useful information. It tells the researcher how frequently each response occurs. This starting point for analysis requires the counting of responses or observations for each of the categories or codes assigned to a variable. Table 18.1 illustrates a **frequency table.** When this tabulation process is done by hand, it is called *tallying.* Large sample sizes generally require computer tabulation of the data.

T A B L E   1 8 . 1

Frequency Table

Do You Shop at IGA?

Response	Frequency
Yes	330
No	120
Total	450

T A B L E   1 8 . 2   Usefulness of Percentages in the Interpretation of Cross-Tabulation Tables

A. Minority Populations in Five Western States

State	Blacks	Hispanics	Other	Total Population
Arizona	91,500	533,200	213,300	3,100,000
California	2,000,000	5,800,000	2,300,000	26,300,000
Nevada	61,000	69,700	44,300	940,000
Oregon	41,100	76,000	96,500	2,600,000
Washington	122,400	142,000	241,000	4,400,000

B. Minority Populations and Percentages in Five Western States

State	Blacks		Hispanics		Other		Total Population
	No.	%	No.	%	No.	%	
Arizona	91,500	3.0%	533,200	17.2%	213,300	6.9%	3,100,000
California	2,000,000	7.6	5,800,000	22.0	2,300,000	8.7	26,300,000
Nevada	61,000	6.5	69,700	7.4	44,300	4.7	940,000
Oregon	41,100	1.5	76,000	2.9	96,500	3.7	2,600,000
Washington	122,400	2.8	142,000	3.2	241,000	5.5	4,400,000

Source: U.S. Bureau of the Census, *Population Estimates by Race and Hispanic Origin for States, Metropolitan Areas, and Selected Counties* (Washington, DC: Government Printing Office, 1989).

Percentages.   Whether the data are tabulated by computer or by hand, it is useful to have **percentages** and **cumulative percentages** as well as **frequency distributions.** For example, most people find part A of Table 18.2 easier to interpret than part B because the percentages are useful for comparing the trend over the years.

MEASURES OF CENTRAL TENDENCY

In 1986 the Internal Revenue Service calculated that the average deduction for self-employment retirement (Keogh) plans was $8,003.[2] This is a measure of central tendency. Describing central tendencies of the distribution with the mean, median, or mode is another basic form of descriptive analysis. Of course, these measures are most useful when the purpose is to identify typical values of a variable or the most common characteristic of a group. If knowing the average or typical performance will satisfy the information need, the measures described in Chapter 15 should be considered.

CROSS-TABULATION

The mere tabulation of data may answer many research questions. In fact, many studies do not go beyond examining the simple tabulation of the question-by-question responses to a survey. On the other hand, although frequency counts and percentage distributions, or averages, summarize a considerable amount of information, stopping at simple tabulation may not yield the full value of the research. Most data can be further organized in a variety of ways. For example, in a survey that samples both men and women, it is common to analyze the data by separating the respondents into groups or categories based on gender. Analyzing results by groups, categories, or classes is the technique of **cross-tabulation.**

The purpose of categorization and cross-tabulation is to allow the inspection of differences among groups to make comparisons. This form of analysis also allows for determination of the form of relationship between two variables. Cross-tabulating the results of business research helps clarify the research findings as they pertain to industry, market, and organizational segments.

Table 18.3 presents a summary of several cross-tabulations from American citizens' responses to a questionnaire on ethical behavior in the United States. A researcher interested in the relative ethical perspectives of business executives and the general public can inspect this table and easily compare the two groups. The percentage table illustrates the added value of calculating percentages.

Another example of the usefulness of categorization and cross-tabulation can be found in most experiments. It is obvious that the data from the experimental and control groups should be separated or partitioned because researchers wish to compare the effects of a treatment.

Contingency Table

Part A of Table 18.4 shows how the cross-tabulation of two survey questions (or variables) results in a **contingency table,** or data matrix. The frequency counts for the question "Do you shop at IGA?" are presented as column totals. The total number of men and women in the sample are presented as row totals. These row and column totals are often called *marginals,* because they appear in the table's margin. There are four *cells* within Part A, each representing a specific combination of the two variables. The cell representing women who said they do not shop at IGA has a frequency count of 45.

The contingency table in Part A is referred to as a "2 × 2" table because it has two rows and two columns. Any cross-tabulation table may be classified according to the number of rows by the number of columns (R by C). Thus a 3 × 4 table is one with three rows and four columns.

TABLE   18.3   **Cross-Tabulation Table from a Survey on Ethics in America**

| | Reported Behavior by General Public (Percentage Who Have Ever Done Each Activity) | | | | | |
| | General Public | | | | | |
Activity	Under 50 Years Old	Over 50 Years Old	Men	Women	College Graduate	High School Graduate
Taken home work supplies	50%	26%	47%	33%	58%	21%
Called in sick to work when not ill	50	18	Not reported		36	21

| | Reported Behavior (Percentage Who Have Ever Done Each Activity) | |
Activity	Business Executives	General Public
Taken home work supplies	74%	40%
Called in sick to work when not ill	14	31
Used company telephone for personal long-distance calls	78	15
Overstated deductions somewhat on tax forms	35	13
Driven while drunk	80	33
Saw a fellow employee steal something at work and did not report it	7	26

Source: Roger Ricklefs, "Ethics in America," *The Wall Street Journal,* Oct. 31, 1983, 33, 42; Nov. 1, 1983, 33; Nov. 2, 1983, 33; and Nov. 3, 1983, 33, 37.

TABLE   18.4

Possible Cross-Tabulations of One Question

A. Cross-Tabulation of Question "Do You Shop at IGA?" by Sex of Respondent

	Yes	No	Total
Men	150	75	225
Women	180	45	225
Total	330	120	450

B. Percentage Cross-Tabulation of Question "Do You Shop at IGA?" by Sex of Respondent, Row Percentage

	Yes	No	Total (Base)
Men	66.7%	33.3%	100% (225)
Women	80.0	20.0	100 (225)

C. Percentage Cross-Tabulation of Question "Do You Shop at IGA?" by Answer, Column Percentage

	Yes	No
Men	45.5%	62.5%
Women	54.5	37.5
Total	100	100
(base)	(330)	(120)

Percentage Cross-Tabulation

When cross-tabulating data from a survey, calculation of percentages helps the researcher understand the nature of the relationship by making a relative comparison. The total number of respondents or observations may be utilized as a **base** for computing the percentage in each cell. When the objective of the research is to identify a relationship between the two questions (or variables), it is common to choose one of the questions as a base for determining percentages. For example, look at the data in Parts A, B, and C of Table 18.4. Compare Part B with Part C. Selecting either the row percentages or the column percentages will emphasize a particular comparison or distribution. The nature of the problem the researcher wishes to investigate will determine which marginal total will be used as a base for computing percentages.

Fortunately, there is a conventional rule for determining the direction of percentages if the researcher has identified which variable is the independent variable and which is the dependent variable: The percentages should be computed *in the direction of the independent variable.* That is, the margin total of the independent variable should be used as the base for computing the percentages. Although survey research does not identify cause-and-effect relationships, one might argue that it is logical to assume that a variable such as one's gender might predict shopping behavior. Therefore independent and dependent variables may be established for the purpose of presenting the most useful information.

Elaboration and Refinement

The Oxford Universal Dictionary defines analysis as "the resolution of anything complex into its simplest elements." This suggests that once the basic relationship between two variables has been examined, the researcher may wish to investigate this relationship under a variety of different conditions. Typically, a third variable is introduced into the analysis to elaborate and refine the researcher's understanding by specifying the conditions under which the relationship is strongest and weakest.[3] In other words, a more elaborate analysis asks: "Will interpretation of the relationship be modified if other variables are simultaneously considered?"

Performing the basic cross-tabulation within various subgroups of the sample is a common form of **elaboration analysis.** The researcher breaks down the analysis for each level of another variable. For example, if the researcher has cross-tabulated shopping behavior by sex (see Table 18.4) and wishes to investigate another variable (perhaps marital status) that may modify the original relationship, a more elaborate analysis may be conducted. Table 18.5 breaks down the responses to the question "Do you shop at IGA?" by sex and marital status. The data show that marital status does not change the original cross-tabulation relationship among women, but it does change that relationship among men. The analysis suggests that we retain the original conclusion about the relationship between sex and shopping behavior for women; the data confirm our original interpretation. However, our refinements in analysis have

TABLE   18.5

Cross-Tabulation of Marital
Status, Sex, and Responses
to the Question "Do
You Shop at IGA?"

	Married		Single	
	Men	Women	Men	Women
"Do you shop at IGA?"				
Yes	55%	80%	86%	80%
No	45	20	14	20

pointed out a relationship among men that was not immediately discernible in the two-variable case. It may be concluded that marital status modifies the original relationship among men, that is, that there is an interaction effect. In this situation marital status is a moderator variable. A **moderator variable** is a "third" variable that, when introduced into the analysis, alters or has a contingent effect on the relationship between an independent variable and a dependent variable.

In other situations the adding of a third variable to the analysis may lead us to reject the original conclusion about the relationship. When this occurs, the elaboration analysis will have indicated a **spurious relationship**—the relationship between the original two variables was not authentic. Our earlier example of high ice cream cone sales and drownings at the beach (Chapter 3) illustrated a spurious relationship. Additional discussion of this topic, dealing with measures of association, appears in Chapter 21.

Elaborating on the basic cross-tabulation is a form of *multivariate analysis,* because more than two variables are simultaneously analyzed to identify complex relationships. When a breakdown of the responses to three or more questions is required, there is usually a multivariate statistical technique for investigating the relationship. Such techniques are discussed in Chapter 22.

Establishing Categories

In the examples that have been discussed, the variables for cross-tabulating have had standard categories. But in many cases the establishment of categories requires careful thought. For example, how does one categorize women on their orientation toward the feminist movement?

The first rule for identifying categories, as in other aspects of business research, is that the categories should be related to the research problem and purpose. Although this is logical, we often find computer-assisted business researchers going on "fishing expeditions," cross-tabulating every question on a survey with every other question. Thus every possible response becomes a category. All too often this activity only provides reams of extra computer output of no value to management. Further, the categories should conform to the requirements for coding. That is, the researcher should strive for exhaustive categories and mutually exclusive categories to ensure that independent categories will be provided for every answer.

E X H I B I T   1 8 . 2

**Collapsing a
Five-Category
Likert Scale**

Likert Scale As It Appeared on the Questionnaire

Increased foreign investment in the United States poses a threat to our economic independence.

Strongly Agree   Agree   Neither Agree or Disagree   Disagree   Strongly Disagree

Tabulation of Responses in Original and Collapsed Versions

5-Point Scale	Percentage	Collapsed Scale	Percentage
Strongly Agree	3	Strongly Agree/Agree	15
Agree	12		
Neither Agree or Disagree	30	Neither Agree or Disagree	30
Disagree	45	Strongly Disagree/Disagree	55
Strongly Disagree	10		

DATA TRANSFORMATION

Data transformation is the process of changing data's original form to a format that is more suitable to perform a data analysis that will achieve the research objectives. Researchers often modify the values of scalar data or create new variables. For example, many researchers believe that response bias will be less if interviewers ask consumers for their years of birth rather than their ages even though the objective of the data analysis is to investigate respondents' ages in years. This does not present a problem for the research analyst because a simple data transformation is possible. The raw data coded as birth year can be easily transformed to age by subtracting the birth year from the current year.

Collapsing or combining adjacent categories of a variable is a common data transformation that reduces the number of categories. Exhibit 18.2 shows an example of a Likert scale item that has been collapsed. The "strongly agree" response category and "agree" response category have been combined. The "strongly disagree" response category and the "disagree" response category have also been combined into a single category. The result is the "collapsing" of the five-category scale down to three.

Creating new variables by respecifying the data with numeric or logical transformations is another important data transformation. For example, Likert's summated scales reflect the combination of scores (raw data) from each of the attitudinal statements. The summative score for an attitude scale with three statements is calculated in the following manner:

$$\text{Summative Score} = \text{Variable 1} + \text{Variable 2} + \text{Variable 3}$$

This can be accomplished by using simple arithmetic or by programming the computer with a data transformation equation that creates the new variable "summative score."

**Hours of Television
Usage per Week**

Household Size	Hours:Minutes
1	41:01
2	47:58
3+	60:49
Total U.S. average	52:36

Source: Adapted from 1987 Nielsen Television Report.

Index Numbers

The consumer price index and the wholesale price index are secondary data sources frequently used by business researchers. These price indexes, like other index numbers, allow researchers to compare a variable or set of variables in a given time period with another variable or set of variables in another time period. Scores or observations are recalibrated so that they may be related to a certain base period or base number.

Consider the information in Table 18.6 related to weekly television viewing (hours:minutes) by household size. **Index numbers** are computed in the following manner. First, a base number is selected; in this example the U.S. average of 52 hours and 36 minutes is used. The index numbers are computed by dividing the score for each category and multiplying by 100. The index shows percentage changes from base number. For example,

$$1 \qquad \frac{41:01}{52:36} = .7832 \times 100 = 78.32$$

$$2 \qquad \frac{47:58}{52:36} = .9087 \times 100 = 90.87$$

$$3+ \qquad \frac{60:49}{52:36} = 1.1553 \times 100 = 115.53$$

$$\text{Total U.S. average} \qquad \frac{52:36}{52:36} = 1.0000 \times 100 = 100.00$$

If the data are time-related, a base year is chosen. The index numbers are then computed by dividing each year's activity by the base year activity and multiplying by 100. Index numbers require a ratio scale of measurement.

Calculating Rank Order

Respondents often indicate a rank ordering of brand preference or some other variable of interest to researchers. To summarize these data for all respondents, analysts perform a data transformation by multiplying the frequency times the rank (score) to develop a new scale that represents the summarized rank ordering.

For example, suppose the president of a company had ten executives rank their preferences for "dream destinations" that would be the prize in a productivity contest. Table 18.7 shows how ten executives ranked each of four locations: Hawaii, Greece, Paris, and China. Table 18.8 provides a tabulation of

Person	Hawaii	Paris	Greece	China
1	1	2	4	3
2	1	3	4	2
3	2	1	3	4
4	3	4	3	1
5	2	1	3	4
6	3	4	3	4
7	2	3	1	4
8	1	4	2	3
9	4	3	2	1
10	3	1	3	4

Destination	Preference Rankings			
	1st	2nd	3rd	4th
Hawaii	3	3	3	1
Greece	1	2	5	2
Paris	3	1	3	3
China	2	1	2	5

the frequencies of these rankings. To calculate a summary rank ordering, the destination with the first (highest) preference was given the lowest number (1) and the least preferred destination (lowest preference) was given the highest number (4). The summarized rank ordering is obtained with the following calculation:

$$\text{Hawaii: } (3 \times 1) + (3 \times 2) + (3 \times 3) + (1 \times 4) = 22$$
$$\text{Greece: } (1 \times 1) + (2 \times 2) + (5 \times 3) + (2 \times 4) = 28$$
$$\text{Paris: } (3 \times 1) + (1 \times 2) + (3 \times 3) + (3 \times 4) = 26$$
$$\text{China: } (2 \times 1) + (1 \times 2) + (2 \times 3) + (5 \times 4) = 30$$

The lowest total score indicates the first (highest) preference ranking. The results show the following rank ordering (1) Hawaii, (2) Paris, (3) Greece, and (4) China.

TABULAR AND GRAPHIC METHODS OF DISPLAYING DATA

Tables and graphs (pictorial representations of data) may simplify and clarify the research data. Tabular and graphic representations of the data may take a number of forms, ranging from direct computer printouts of the data to elaborate pictographs. The purpose of each table or graph, however, is to facilitate the summarization and communication of the meaning of the data. For example, Table 18.9 illustrates the relationship between education, income, and

T A B L E   1 8 . 9

Regional Airplane Usage for Vacation/Pleasure by Income Classes

	Total	Under $10,000	$10,000–$19,000	$20,000–$39,000	$40,000 and Over
All Consumers					
% Expenditures	100	10	7	16	67
% Consumer units	100	42	19	16	23
Index	100	26	36	100	291
Not High School Grad					
% Expenditures	8	1	2	1	4
% Consumer units	35	21	6	4	4
Index	21	5	33	25	100
High School Grad					
% Expenditures	29	4	2	8	15
% Consumer units	30	11	6	6	7
Index	96	36	33	133	214
Att./Grad. College					
% Expenditures	63	5	3	7	48
% Consumer units	35	10	6	6	13
Index	180	50	50	116	369
				% Pop.	% Expen.
				32 =	78

regional airline usage (expenditures) for vacation/pleasure trips. Note that the shaded boxed area emphasizes a key conclusion with respect to market share (summarizing the information in the box indicates slightly more than 30 percent of the population makes 78 percent of the expenditures). The form of presentation simplifies interpretation. Although there are a number of standardized forms for presenting data in tables or graphs, the researcher may use his creativity to increase the effectiveness of a particular presentation. Bar charts, pie charts, curve diagrams, pictograms, and other graphic forms of presentation create a visual impression. (See Chapter 23.)

COMPUTER PROGRAMS FOR ANALYSIS

The proliferation of computer technology in businesses and universities has greatly facilitated tabulation and statistical analysis. Many collections or packages of computer programs have been designed to tabulate and analyze numerous types of data. Computer program packages such as the Statistical Analysis System (SAS), Statistical Package for the Social Sciences (SPSSX), and the BMD Biomedical Computer Programs (BMDP) are widely available software program packages for mainframe computers. These eliminate the need to write a computer program every time the researcher wants to analyze data on the computer. Most of these computer packages consist of a sizable array of programs for univariable, bivariate, and multivariate statistical analysis.

EXHIBIT   18.3

Selected Examples of Personal Computer Software for Tabulation and Statistical Analysis

Type	Description
Statistical Packages	
ABTAB EDU-STAT MINI TAB SAS-PC SPSS-PC STATPAK SYSTAT	These user-friendly packages emphasize programs for statistical calculations. They also provide computer programs for entering and editing data. They have programs for performing descriptive analysis and hypothesis testing. Output is easily interpreted.
Spreadsheet Packages	
ENABLE EXCELL LOTUS 1-2-3 QUATTRO	These packages emphasize database management and are designed to allow for entering and editing data with minimal effort. They also perform and incorporate some programs for descriptive analysis, graphic analysis, and limited statistical analysis.

EXHIBIT   18.4   **SAS Output of Descriptive Statistics**

STATE=NY

VARIABLE	N	MEAN	STANDARD DEVIATION	MINIMUM VALUE	MAXIMUM VALUE	STD ERROR OF MEAN	SUM	VARIANCE	C.V.
EMP	10	142.930000	232.66490	12.8000000	788.80000	73.575100	1429.30000	54133.0	162.782
SALES	10	5807.800000	11905.12701	307.0000000	39401.00000	3764.731718	58078.00000	141732049.1	204.985N

Key: EMP = Number of employees (000)
     SALES = Sales (000)

A wide variety of software for personal computers is available for applications in business research. There are also many software programs available for use on personal computers.

Exhibit 18.3 lists some of the more popular software products for statistical analysis and database management. Most of these packages consist of a sizable array of programs for descriptive analysis and univariate, bivariate, and multivariate statistical analysis. Several later examples in the text will give illustrations of output from these statistical packages. Additional information about microcomputer software is given in this chapter's appendix on microcomputers in business research.

Exhibit 18.4 shows an SAS computer printout of descriptive statistics for two variables: EMP (number of employees working in an MSA, or Metropolitan Statistical Area) and SALES (sales volume in dollars in an MSA). The numbers of data elements (N), the mean, the standard deviation, and other descriptive statistics are calculated.

EXHIBIT   18.5

**SPSSX Computer Output
Showing Frequencies**

Have you ever been unable to find some of the records you needed
when it's time to prepare your tax return?

	ABSOLUTE FREQUENCY	REL. FREQ. (PCT)	ADJ. FREQ. (PCT)
Yes	102	19.3	19.4
No	423	80.1	80.6
Don't know	1	0.2	MISSING
Blank	2	0.4	MISSING
	- - -	- - - -	- - - -
	528	100.0	100.0

EXHIBIT   18.6

SPSSX Histogram Output

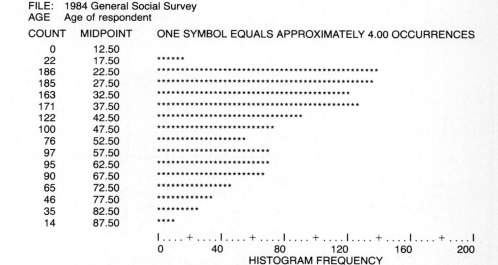

FILE: 1984 General Social Survey
AGE   Age of respondent

COUNT	MIDPOINT	ONE SYMBOL EQUALS APPROXIMATELY 4.00 OCCURRENCES
0	12.50	
22	17.50	******
186	22.50	**
185	27.50	***
163	32.50	***
171	37.50	**
122	42.50	********************************
100	47.50	**************************
76	52.50	*******************
97	57.50	*************************
95	62.50	************************
90	67.50	***********************
65	72.50	****************
46	77.50	************
35	82.50	*********
14	87.50	****

```
            I....+....I....+....I....+....I....+....I....+....I
            0       40       80      120      160      200
                         HISTOGRAM FREQUENCY
```

VALID CASES   1467   MISSING CASES   6

Source: Marija J. Norusis, *The SPSS Guide to Data Analysis* (New York: McGraw-Hill, 1986), Chap. 8.

Exhibit 18.5 presents the output from the SPSSX package showing the results of a question on an Internal Revenue Service survey in a frequency table. This SPSSX output shows the absolute frequency of observations, the relative frequency as a percentage of all observations, and the adjusted frequency as a percentage of the number of respondents who provided a recorded answer rather than answering "don't know" or leaving the question blank.

A histogram is similar to a bar chart. Exhibit 18.6 shows an SPSSX histogram plot of the age data from a survey. In this histogram each asterisk indicates four individuals.

E X H I B I T   1 8 . 7

SPSS/PC Cross-
Tabulation Output

CROSSTABULATION WITH ROW PERCENTS

SPSS/PC Release 1.0

Crosstabulation: JOBCAT   Employment Category
                          By EDLEVEL   Education Level

EDLEVEL→	Count Row Pct	High School 1	High School 2	Some College 3	College Degree 4	Advanced Degree 5	Row Total
JOBCAT	1	115	160	20	5		300
Clerical		38.3	53.3	6.7	1.7		71.4
	2			70	25	15	110
White Collar				63.6	22.7	13.6	26.2
	3				5	5	10
Management					50.0	50.0	2.4
Column		115	160	90	35	20	420
Total		27.4	38.1	21.4	8.3	4.8	100.0

Number of Missing Observations = 80

Source: Used with permission from SPSS Inc. SPSS/PC is a trademark of SPSS Inc. of Chicago, Illinois, for its proprietary computer software.

E X H I B I T   1 8 . 8

Output from Edu-Stat's
Descriptive Data
Analysis Program

Edu-Stat Frequency Analysis
Data Set = Example Commuter Data Set
Variable = MARRIED; 1 = Yes, 2 = No

Value	Frequency	Cum. Freq.	Percent	Cum. Pct.
1	104	104	46.43	46.43
2	120	224	53.57	100.00

Source: Clifford E. Young, *Edu-Stat* (Hinsdale, IL: The Dryden Press, 1989).

Exhibit 18.7 shows an SPSS/PC cross-tabulation of two variables: education (EDLEVEL) and job category (JOBCAT), with the row total utilized as a basis for percentages. (Note: The program identifies the number of respondents for whom data were not provided for both variables as missing observations.)

Exhibit 18.8 shows a simple descriptive data output from Edu-Stat. Exhibit 18.9 shows a graph drawn by a microcomputer using another software package. As you can see, microcomputers are quite versatile, and they are rapidly gaining popularity in business research.

EXHIBIT   18.9

**A Graph Drawn by a
Microcomputer**

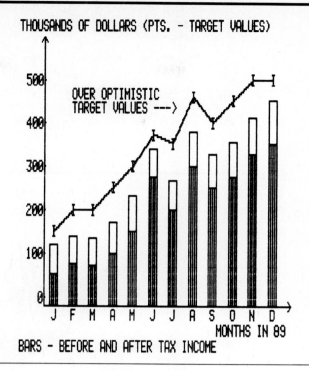

COMPUTER GRAPHICS/COMPUTER MAPPING

Graphic aids prepared by computers are rapidly replacing graphic aids drawn by artists. They are extremely useful for descriptive analysis. (See Exhibit 18.10.) Computer-generated graphics and charts may be created inexpensively and quickly with easy-to-use computer software programs such as *Lotus 1-2-3* or *Print Shop*. These software programs are both user friendly and versatile. The versatility of these programs allows researchers to explore many alternative ways of visually communicating their findings.

An innovation that has shown tremendous potential is **computer mapping,** which is based on geographic information systems. Computer maps portray demographic, sales, or other data on two- or three-dimensional maps generated by a computer. For example, General Motors' Cadillac division uses secondary data and computer graphics to help select locations for new dealers:

Graphics plotters generate maps with dots showing where current and potential customers are located. The computer-linked system also lets Cadillac use the vast banks of vehicle registration data gathered on the auto industry. So instead of asking where Cadillac owners are located, managers might request a map showing where their competitors are or which areas have the largest concentration of high-income households. Cadillac now generates about 75 maps a year, and on the average each leads to two or three decisions to move dealerships.[4]

Firms such as Demographic Research Company specialize in helping clients illustrate statistical material geographically according to county lines, metropolitan areas, zip codes, or other geographic boundaries so that visual, easily recognized patterns of usage are presented. Census data are now geographically coded so that they can be utilized in computer maps.

E X H I B I T   1 8 . 1 0

Examples of Computer Mapping

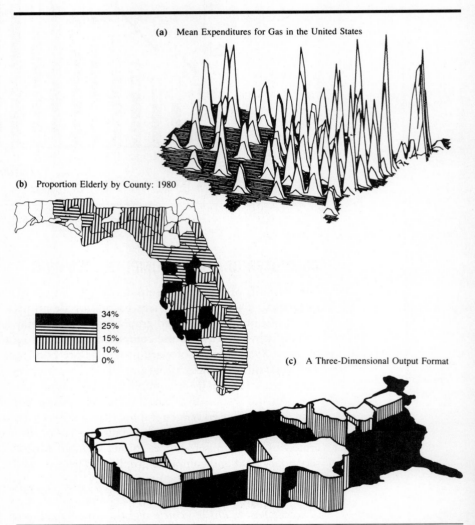

(a) Mean Expenditures for Gas in the United States

(b) Proportion Elderly by County: 1980

34%
25%
15%
10%
0%

(c) A Three-Dimensional Output Format

Sources: (a) SAS Institute Inc. (b) *American Demographics*, January 1985. (c) Reprinted by permission of Harvard Business Review. Exhibit from "New Promise of Computer Graphics" by Hirotaka Tekeuchi and Allan H. Schmidt (January–February 1980). Copyright © 1980 by the President and Fellows of Harvard College; all rights reserved.

Geographic information systems and computer maps have many other uses. Researchers at the World Bank may want to see how cattle might be displaced by a pipeline in Tanzania. When a 911 emergency call comes in, a fire department may use its computer to locate the fire hydrant nearest the fire's location. A city's water department might get a call reporting a water leak near a given intersection and use the geographic information system to map all the water lines and pumps in the area. Further requests could obtain a detailed maintenance history on any segment of the water system.[5]

INTERPRETATION

An interpreter at the United Nations translates a foreign language into a native language to explain the meaning of a foreign diplomat's speech. In business research the interpretation process also has the purpose of explaining the meaning of the data. After the statistical analysis of the data, researchers and managers begin to make inferences and formulate conclusions about their meaning.

A distinction can be made between *analysis* and *interpretation*. **Interpretation** refers to making inferences pertinent to the meaning and implications of the research investigation and the drawing of conclusions about the managerial implications of the variables thereof. Of course, the logical interpretation of the data and the statistical analysis are closely intertwined. Researchers interpret and analyze at the same time—that is, when a researcher calculates, say, a t-test of two means, one almost immediately infers group differences or the existence of a relationship. Almost automatically researchers seek out the significance of the statistical analysis for the research problem as they order, break down, and manipulate the data.[6]

However, from a management perspective the qualitative meaning of the data and the managerial implications are important aspects of the interpretation. Consider the crucial role interpretation of the research results played in investigating a new product—a lip stain that would color the lips a desired shade semipermanently, say, a month at a time:

> *The lip stain idea, among lipstick wearers, received very high scores on a rating scale ranging from "excellent" to "poor," presumably because it would not wear off. However, it appeared that even among routine wearers of lipstick the idea was being rated highly more for its interesting, even ingenious, nature than for its practical appeal to the consumer's personality. They liked the idea, but for someone else, not themselves. . . . [Careful interpretation of the data] revealed that not being able to remove the stain for that length of time caused most women to consider the idea irrelevant in relation to their own personal needs and desires. Use of the product seems to represent more of a "permanent commitment" than is usually associated with the use of a particular cosmetic. In fact, women attached overtly negative meaning to the product concept, often comparing it with hair dyes instead of a long-lasting lipstick.[7]*

This example shows that interpretation is crucial. However, this process is difficult to explain in a textbook because there is no one best way to interpret data.

There are many possible interpretations of data that may be derived from a number of thought processes. Experience with selected cases will help students develop their own interpretative ability.

It should be pointed out that in all too many instances data are merely reported and not interpreted. Research firms may provide reams of computer output that do not state what the data mean. At the other extreme there are researchers who tend to analyze every possible relationship between each and every variable in the study; they usually have not defined the problem during the earlier stages of research. Researchers who have a clear sense of the purpose of the research do not request statistical analysis of data that may have little or nothing to do with the primary purpose of the research.

SUMMARY

Descriptive analysis refers to the transformation of the raw data into an understandable form so that their interpretation will not be difficult. Descriptive information is obtained by summarizing, categorizing, rearranging, and other forms of analysis.

Tabulation refers to the orderly arrangement of data in a table or other summary format. It is useful for indicating percentages and cumulative percentages as well as frequency distributions. The data may be described by measures of central tendency, such as the mean, median, or mode. Cross-tabulation shows how one variable relates to another variable to reveal differences between groups. Such cross-tabulations should be limited to categories related to the research problem and purpose. It is also useful to put the results into percentage form to facilitate intergroup comparisons.

Performing the basic cross-tabulation within various subgroups of the sample is a common form of elaboration analysis. Elaboration analysis often identifies moderator variables or spurious relationships. A moderator variable is a third variable that, when introduced into the analysis, alters or has a contingent effect on the relationship between an independent variable and a dependent variable. A spurious relationship is indicated when the addition of a third variable to the analysis indicates that the relationship between the original two variables was not authentic.

Tables and graphs help to simplify and clarify the research data. Computer software greatly facilitates descriptive analysis. Many programs are available that facilitate the construction of graphs and charts. Data transformation is the process of changing data's original form to a format that is more suitable to perform a data analysis. Index numbers relate data for a particular time period to that of a base year.

Computer mapping portrays demographic, sales, and other data on two- or three-dimensional maps that aid interpretation of descriptive data.

The interpretation of data uses the results of descriptive analysis. It involves making inferences about the real world and drawing conclusions about the data's managerial implications.

Key Terms

descriptive analysis

simple tabulation

frequency table

percentage

cumulative percentage

frequency distribution

cross-tabulation

contingency table

base

elaboration analysis

moderator variable

spurious relationship

data transformation

index numbers

computer mapping

interpretation

Questions

1. In a survey respondents were asked to respond to a statement asking if their work was interesting. Interpret the frequency distribution in the SPSSX output below:

"My work is interesting."

Category Label	Code	Absolute Frequency	Relative Frequency (Percent)	Adjusted Frequency (Percent)	Cum Frequency (Percent)
Very true	1.	650	23.9	62.4	62.4
Somewhat true	2.	303	11.2	29.1	91.5
Not very true	3.	61	2.2	5.9	97.3
Not at all true	4.	28	1.0	2.7	100.0
	0.	1,673	61.6	Missing	
	Total	2,715	100.0	100.0	100.0

Valid cases   1,042   Missing cases   1,673

2. Using the data in the table below, perform these tasks:
    a. Prepare a frequency distribution of respondents' ages.
    b. Cross-tabulate the respondents' sex with cola preference.

Individual	Sex	Age	Cola Preference	Weekly Unit Purchases
John	M	19	Coke	2
Al	M	17	Pepsi	5
Bill	M	20	Pepsi	7
Mary	F	20	Coke	2
Jim	M	18	Coke	4
Karen	F	16	Coke	4
Tom	M	17	Pepsi	8
Dawn	F	19	Pepsi	1

3. The computer output below shows a cross-tabulation of frequencies and provides frequency number (N) and row (R), column (C), and total (T) percentages. Interpret this output.

ACROSS—E2   —HAVE HIGH SCHOOL DIPLOMA?
DOWN—G28   —HAVE YOU READ A BOOK IN PAST 3 MOS?

```
         YES
              : NO
N;R,C,T%    1.      2.        TOTAL

      1.   489     174   :     663     YES
           73.8    26.2  :
           50.8    31.5  :     43.8
           32.3    11.5  :

      2.   473     378   :     851     NO
           55.6    44.4  :     56.2
           49.2    68.5  :
           31.2    25.0  :
          ......  ......       ......
TOTAL      962     552   :    1514
           63.5    36.5  :
```

4. Interpret the following table:

Estimates of Percent of Net Undercount of the Population by Sex, Race, and Selected Broad Age Groups: 1970 Census

	All Races		White		Black	
Age	Male	Female	Male	Female	Male	Female
All ages	3.3	1.8	2.5	1.4	9.9	5.5
20–24 years	3.3	1.4	2.5	1.1	12.1	5.2
25–34 years	5.7	2.8	4.3	2.4	18.5	6.7
35–44 years	5.3	0.9	3.6	0.5	17.7	4.0

5. Visit your computer center and find out if it has SPSS, SAS, or BMD computer packages.

6. What type of scalar data (that is, nominal, ordinal, interval, or ratio) is typically utilized in cross-tabulation analysis?

7. It has been argued that the analysis and interpretation of data is a managerial art. Comment.

8. The data in the following tables are some of the results of an Internal Revenue Service survey of taxpayers. Analyze and interpret the data.

The last year you filed an income tax return, did you get any suggestions or information that was especially helpful to you in filing?

	Absolute Frequency	Relative Frequency (Percent)	Adjusted Frequency (Percent)
Yes	156	29.5	29.8
No	368	69.7	70.2
Don't know	1	0.2	Missing
Not ascertained	1	0.2	Missing
Blank	2	0.4	Missing
	528	100.0	100.0

What kind of information was it?

	Absolute Frequency	Relative Frequency (Percent)	Adjusted Frequency (Percent)
Learned about energy credit	8	1.5	5.4
Learned about another deduction	46	8.7	31.3
Obtained info. about forms to use	9	1.7	6.1
Received pamphlets/forms	40	7.6	27.2
Other	44	8.3	29.9
Don't know	6	1.1	Missing
Not ascertained	2	0.4	Missing
Blank	373	70.6	Missing
	528	100.0	100.0

References

[1] "Break Time," *American Demographics* (February 1987), 1B.

[2] *Statistical Abstract of the United States,* 1989, 10th ed. (Washington, D.C.: U.S. Department of Commerce, 1990), 315.

[3] Herman J. Loether and Donald G. McTavish, *Descriptive Statistics for Sociologists: An Introduction* (Boston: Allyn & Bacon, Co., 1974), 265–266.

[4] "The Spurt in Computer Graphics," *Business Week,* June 16, 1980, 104–106.

[5] Peter H. Lewis, "When Maps Are Tied to Data Bases," *New York Times,* May 28, 1989, 10.

[6] Fred N. Kerlinger, *Foundations of Behavioral Research,* 2d ed. (New York: Holt, Rinehart and Winston, 1973), 134–135.

[7] Bill Iuso, "Concept Testing: An Appropriate Approach," *Journal of Marketing Research* (May 1975): 230, published by the American Marketing Association.

Microcomputers in Business Research

Microcomputers, also called personal computers, are changing the way much business research data are processed and analyzed. This appendix is a brief description of microcomputers and some of the data-processing software systems available to operators.

THE BASICS

There are five general components in the organization of the basic microcomputer. These are conceptually portrayed in Exhibit 18A.1. A photograph of an IBM computer with its five basic components identified is shown in Exhibit 18A.2.

The **input component** transfers data into the computer from some external source. On most microcomputers the input device is a keyboard that looks pretty much like that of an ordinary typewriter. The IBM personal computer keyboard is shown in Exhibit 18A.3.

The **central processing unit** (CPU) is the computer hardware (physical machinery) that controls data flows and executes instructions. The CPU consists of the memory, the control, and the arithmetic/logic circuitry. The **memory** of the computer holds two kinds of information: the program and the data the researcher wishes to process.

The **control unit** is the component that executes or performs the programming instructions. The **arithmetic/logic unit** facilitates the execution of the program. The **program** is a set of instructions describing actions for the computer to perform.

EXHIBIT 18A.1

The Components of a Microcomputer

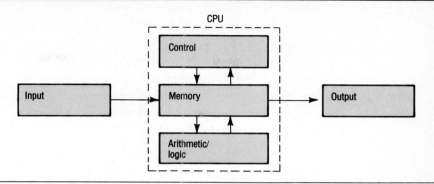

Source: Alan B. Tucker, Jr., *Basic/Apple II: A Programming Guide* (New York: Holt, Rinehart and Winston, 1983), 1.

EXHIBIT 18A.2

Components of a Personal Computer

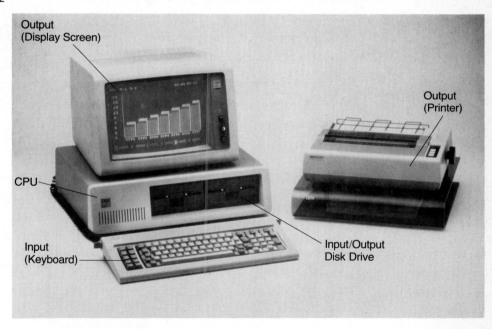

Source: Courtesy of International Business Machines Corporation.

Output refers to the transferring of information from the central processing unit to the user. The output information is usually presented on a display screen, printer, or magnetic disk.

The **disk drive** is both an input and an output device. The floppy disk put into the disk drive is one of the basic magnetic media for storing information

E X H I B I T 1 8 A . 3 **The IBM Personal Computer Keyboard**

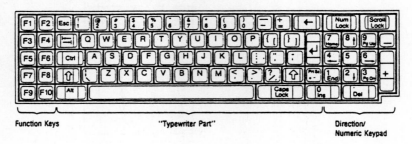

Function Keys

"Typewriter Part"

Direction/
Numeric Keypad

Special Keys in Typewriter Part

Escape

Tab
(also Backtab
with Shift)

Control Shift

Shift

Alternative Shift

Space Bar

Destructive
Backspace

Enter
(or Return)

Asterix
also Print Screen
(with Shift or Ctrl)

Shift

Capitals Lock

Function Key Meanings in 1-2-3

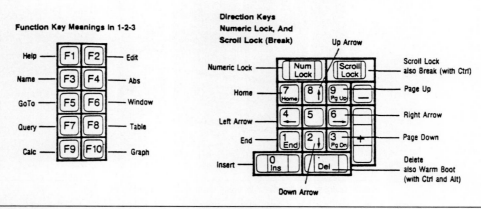

Help — F1 F2 — Edit

Name — F3 F4 — Abs

GoTo — F5 F6 — Window

Query — F7 F8 — Table

Calc — F9 F10 — Graph

**Direction Keys
Numeric Lock, And
Scroll Lock (Break)**

Up Arrow

Numeric Lock

Home

Left Arrow

End

Insert

Scroll Lock
also Break (with Ctrl)

Page Up

Right Arrow

Page Down

Delete
also Warm Boot
(with Ctrl and Alt)

Down Arrow

Source: Darral G. Clarke, *Marketing Analysis and Decision Making: Text and Cases with Lotus 1-2-3* (Redwood City, CA: The Scientific Press, 1986).

when using a microcomputer. The main purpose of the disk drive is to read and write information that will be repeatedly used. It causes the magnetic disk to spin, and in this respect its operation is similar to that of a tape recorder in recording and playing back music.

MENU-DRIVEN SYSTEMS

Many organizations offer microcomputer software systems that perform tasks in much the same way as SAS, SPSSX, and other mainframe computer packages discussed in Chapter 18. Although microcomputer systems have less capacity than the SAS and SPSSX mainframe programs, they are more convenient to use.

Most systems utilize a **start-up disk,** which is a self-contained disk that has an operating system on it.[1] A program on the start-up disk tells the control unit exactly what should be done with the input data in order to produce a particular output. Within several seconds after the start-up disk has been placed in the disk drive, the display screen shows the **main menu.**

Many microcomputer systems, such as Lotus 1-2-3 and Edu-Stat, are **menu-driven systems,** which means that the computer will automatically list everything it can do on the screen. The computer menu, like a restaurant menu, shows the options that are available. The user then chooses from the menu what he or she wants to do merely by inputting a code by pressing the appropriate keys and then the return key. After the user has selected the menu option, the computer then asks him or her to input the data for analysis. Then the central processing unit performs its computations, and the results are displayed, either on the **video display screen** or on the **printer.**[2]

The main menu for the Edu-Stat statistical system for microcomputers is shown in Exhibit 18A.4. If Option B was selected, the Edu-Stat program would then display the statistics menu shown in Exhibit 18A.5. The process would move from menu to menu until the calculations were performed.

Microcomputer software systems are *interactive,* that is, they operate on the basis of a dialogue between computer and user. The dialogue may be a series of questions and answers or of **commands** directing the computer to perform some action and the computer's response. For example, a number of computer software packages have a "help" command that allows the user to request information about an action that may be performed. In the SPSS/PC

E X H I B I T   1 8 A . 4

Edu-Stat Main Menu

Edu-Stat Master Menu
A — Data Base Management Module.
B — Statistics Module.
C — Text Editor Module.
Select Option:

Source: Clifford E. Young, *Edu-Stat* (Hinsdale, IL: The Dryden Press, 1989).

Main Menu

A   Frequencies, Crosstabs, Means, T-Tests
B   Correlation, Covariance, Cronbach Alpha
C   Regression, Analysis of Variance
D   Miscellaneous Probability Distributions
E   Specify Edu-Stat Data Set for Analysis
F   Specify Output Print File for Results
G   View Output Print File of Results

Submenu A: Descriptive Statistics

A   Frequency Listings
B   Cross Tabulations
C   Means and Other Univariate Statistics
D   Breakdown of Means by Categories
E   Tests of One and Two Proportions
F   T-Test of Two Means

Submenu B: Correlation, Covariance, Cronbach Alpha

A   Correlations
B   Correlations, Pairwise Deletion of Cases
C   Covariances
D   Covariances, Pairwise Deletion of Cases
E   Cronbach Alpha

Submenu C: Regression, Analysis of Variance

A   Regression
B   Stepwise Regression
C   Analysis of Variance

Submenu D: Miscellaneous Probability Distributions

A   Factorials
B   Permutations
C   Combinations
D   Hypergeometric Distribution
E   Binomial Distribution
F   Poisson Distribution
G   Exponential Distribution
H   Chi Square Probability
I   Normal Probability
J   Student's t Probability
K   F Probability
L   Specify New Output Print File for Results

Source: Clifford E. Young, *Edu-Stat* (Hinsdale, IL: The Dryden Press, 1989).

program, the user enters the "help" command followed by the name of the command and/or subcommand being asked about. For example, the keyboarding of

HELP IF

would produce the output shown in Exhibit 18A.6.[3]

There is a wide variety of microcomputer software available for applications in business research.[4] This appendix has provided a description of only a

EXHIBIT 18A.6

**SPSS/PC Output for
the Help Command**

SPSS/PC: help if.

IF

Function: Create new variables or replace existing variables with arithmetic expressions
conditionally.

IF (REVENUES GE EXPENSES) PROFITS = 1.
IF (REVENUES LT EXPENSES) PROFITS = − 1.
IF (RECEIVE GT DUE OR (REVENUES GE EXPENSES AND BALANCE GT 0))
STATUS = 1.
IF (STATE EQ 'IL') COST = COST + .07*COST

Syntax: Specify a logical expression followed by an arithmetic assignment. The logical
expression must be enclosed in parentheses.

Notes: Missing values encountered in logical expressions can make the expression false.
The assignment portion follows the same rules for missing values as the COMPUTE
command. Use HELP IF OPERATORS to obtain a list of operators and operands in
logical expressions.

SPSS/PC:

Source: Used with permission from SPSS Inc. SPSS/PC is a trademark of SPSS Inc. of Chicago, Illinois, for its
proprietary computer software.

few sources. In order to actually run a program, you will have to refer to the
operator's manual for the software that is available to you.

References

[1] *Apple IIe Owners Manual* (Cupertino, CA: Apple Computer Co., 1983), 53.

[2] Harold R. Strang and Allison Hinnes, *The Users' Guide for Keystat: A Statistical System for
Microcomputers* (Monterey, CA: Brooks/Cole Publishing, 1982), 1.

[3] SPSS/PC, Operations Overview, prepared June 14, 1984, 33.

[4] See, for example, the excellent review by Robert H. Collins, "Microcomputer Software Application Packages for the Marketing Research Course," *Proceedings,* American Marketing Association
Conference, 1984.

Univariate Statistics

In the last chapter we saw that the figure $8,003 described the IRS calculation of the average deduction for a self-employment retirement (Keogh) plan contribution in 1986. This figure is the finding of descriptive analysis. How reliable is this estimate? Suppose a tax accountant assumed that the average deduction was $9,500. Would this assumption be untenable? Is it reasonable to accept that figure from descriptive analysis? Is it possible to go beyond the simple tabulation of frequencies and the calculation of averages to find some sort of criterion for answering questions about differences between what one expected to find and the actual results of research? This chapter attempts to provide answers to questions such as these.

As has already been discussed, analysis begins for most projects with some form of descriptive analysis to reduce the raw data into a summary format. Often researchers wish to go beyond the simple tabulation of frequency distributions and the calculation of averages: They frequently conduct univariate tests of statistical significance. *The foundation of univariate statistical estimation of parameters involves hypothesis testing when the research focuses on* one variable at a time.

■

STATING A HYPOTHESIS

What Is a Hypothesis?

In statistical theory a **hypothesis** is an unproven proposition or supposition that tentatively explains certain facts or phenomena. A hypothesis is a statement, an assumption, about the nature of the world. In its simplest form a hypothesis is a guess. An R&D manager may hypothesize that engineers highest in technical knowledge will be the most productive. A personnel manager may believe that if attitudes toward job security are changed in a positive direction, there will be an increase in employee retention. With statistical techniques we are able to decide whether or not our theoretical hypotheses are confirmed by the empirical evidence.

The Null Hypothesis and Alternative Hypothesis

Because scientists should be bold in conjecturing but extremely cautious in testing, statistical hypotheses are generally stated in a null form. A **null hypothesis** is a statement about a *status quo*. It is a conservative statement which communicates the notion that any change from what has been thought to be true or observed in the past will be due entirely to random error. In fact, the true purpose of setting up the null hypothesis is to provide an opportunity to nullify it. For example, the academic researcher who expects that highly dogmatic (i.e., closed-minded) individuals will be less likely to try an innovative management technique than less dogmatic individuals will generally formulate a conservative null hypothesis. The null hypothesis in this case would be that there is no difference between "high dogmatics" and "low dogmatics" in their willingness to try an innovation. The **alternative hypothesis** states that there is a difference between "high" and "low" dogmatics, that is, it states the opposite of the null hypothesis.

Hypothesis Testing

We generally assign the symbol H_0 to the null hypothesis and the symbol H_1 to the alternative hypothesis. The purpose of hypothesis testing is to determine which of the two hypotheses is correct. The procedure of hypotheses testing is slightly more complicated than estimating parameters because the decision maker must make a choice between the two hypotheses. However, the student need not worry, because the mathematical calculations are not more difficult than the calculations we have already made.

Hypothesis-Testing Procedure.   The process of hypothesis testing goes as follows. First, a statistical hypothesis is determined. We then imagine what the sampling distribution of the mean would be if this hypothesis were a true statement of the nature of the population. Next, an actual sample is taken and the sample mean (or appropriate statistic, if we are not concerned about the mean) is calculated. We know from our previous discussions of the sampling distribution of the mean that obtaining a sample value exactly the same as the population parameter would be highly unlikely. We expect some small (although it may be large) difference between the sample mean and the population mean. We then must determine if the deviation between the obtained value of the sample mean and its expected value (based on the statistical hypothesis) would have occurred by chance alone, say 5 times out of 100, if the statistical hypothesis were true.

To repeat, we ask the question: "Has the sample mean deviated substantially from the mean of the hypothesized sampling distribution by a large enough value to conclude that this large a deviation would be somewhat rare if the statistical hypothesis were true?" Suppose we observe that the sample value differs from the expected value. Before we can conclude that these results are

STATISTICAL TUTOR
Typical Hypothesis Test

The situation:

A hardware franchise has almost 1,000 retail outlets. Monthly sales of a particular tool averaged 612 units for each franchise. The sales manager believed a competitor's new price on a similar item may have an impact on sales. Based on a random sample of 64 franchises, the sales manager wishes to test if the observed sample mean differs from the benchmark figure.

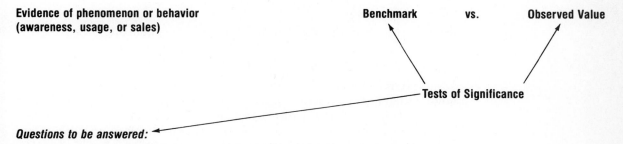

Evidence of phenomenon or behavior   Benchmark   vs.   Observed Value
(awareness, usage, or sales)

Tests of Significance

Questions to be answered:

1. Is the difference between the benchmark and observed value statistically significant?
2. Does the *magnitude* of the increase (or decrease) in phenomenon or behavior justify a change in business strategy?

---

improbable (or possibly probable), we must have some standard or decision rule to determine if, in fact, we should reject the null hypothesis and accept the alternative hypothesis. Statisticians have defined the decision criterion as the *significance level.*

The **significance level** is a critical probability in choosing between the null hypothesis and the alternative hypothesis. The level of significance determines the probability level, say .05 or .01, that is to be considered too low to warrant support of the null hypothesis. On the assumption that the hypothesis being tested is true, if the probability of occurrence of the observed data is *smaller* than the level of significance, then the data suggest the null hypothesis should be rejected. In other words, there is evidence to support contradiction of the null hypothesis, which is equivalent to supporting the alternative hypothesis.

The terminology utilized in discussing confidence intervals identifies what we call the *confidence level* or a *confidence coefficient*. The confidence interval may be regarded as the set of acceptable hypotheses or the level of probability associated with an interval estimate. However, when discussing hypothesis testing, statisticians change their terminology and call this the level of significance α (Greek letter alpha).

Example of Hypothesis Testing.   An example should clarify the nature of hypothesis testing. Suppose that the Red Lion restaurant is concerned about its image. One aspect of its image deals with the amount of friendly service within the restaurant. In a personal interview customers were asked to indicate their perception of service on a five-point scale, where 1 indicated very unfriendly service and 5 indicated very friendly service. The scale was assumed to be an interval scale, and experience has shown that previous distribution of this attitudinal measurement for assessing the service dimension was approximately normal. Now suppose that the researcher entertains the hypothesis that customers feel the restaurant has neither friendly nor unfriendly service. The researcher formulates the null hypothesis that the mean is equal to 3.0:

$$H_0: \mu = 3.0$$

The alternative hypothesis is that the mean does *not* equal 3.0:

$$H_1: \mu \neq 3.0$$

Next, the researcher must decide upon a region of rejection. Exhibit 19.1 shows a sampling distribution of the mean assuming the null hypothesis, that is, assuming $\mu = 3.0$. The shaded area shows the region of rejection when $\alpha =$ .025 in each tail of the curve. In other words, the *region of rejection* shows those values that are very unlikely to occur if the null hypothesis is true but relatively probable if the alternative hypothesis is true. The values within the unshaded area are called acceptable at the 95 percent confidence level (or 5 percent significance level, .05 alpha level), and if we find that our sample mean lies within this region of acceptance, we would conclude that the null hypothesis is true. More precisely, we fail to disprove the null hypothesis. In other words, the range of acceptance (1) identifies those acceptable values with a difference between the hypothesized mean in the null hypothesis and (2) shows a difference in this range to be so minuscule that we would conclude that this difference was due to random sampling error rather than a false null hypothesis.

In our example the Red Lion restaurant hired research consultants who collected a sample of 225 interviews. The mean score on the five-point scale, $\bar{X}$, equaled 3.78. If σ is known, then this is utilized in the analysis; however, this is rarely true, and was not true in this case.[1] The sample standard deviation was $S = 1.5$. Now we have enough information to test the hypothesis.

The researchers decided that the decision rule would be to set the significance level at the .05 level. This means that in the long run the probability of making an erroneous decision when H_0 is true will be fewer than 5 times in 100 (.05). From the table of standardized normal distribution, the researchers find that the Z-score of 1.96 represented a probability of .025 that a sample mean will lie above 1.96 standard errors from μ. Likewise, the table shows that about .025 of all sample means will fall below -1.96 standard errors from μ.

The values that lie exactly on the boundary of the region of rejection are called the **critical values** of μ. Theoretically, the critical values are $Z = -1.96$

EXHIBIT   19.1

A Sampling Distribution of the Mean Assuming $\mu = 3.0$

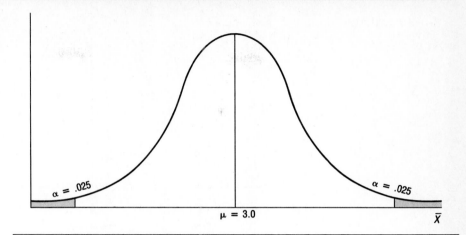

and $+1.96$. Now we must transform these critical Z-values to the sampling distribution of the mean for this image study. The critical values are:

$$\text{Critical value—lower limit} = \mu - ZS_{\bar{X}} \quad \text{or} \quad \mu - Z\frac{S}{\sqrt{n}}$$

$$= 3.0 - 1.96 \left(\frac{1.5}{\sqrt{225}}\right)$$

$$= 3.0 - 1.96\,(.1)$$

$$= 3.0 - .196$$

$$= 2.804$$

$$\text{Critical value—upper limit} = \mu + ZS_{\bar{X}} \quad \text{or} \quad \mu + Z\frac{S}{\sqrt{n}}$$

$$= 3.0 + 1.96 \left(\frac{1.5}{\sqrt{225}}\right)$$

$$= 3.0 + 1.96\,(.1)$$

$$= 3.0 + .196$$

$$= 3.196$$

Based on the survey, $\bar{X} = 3.78$. In this case the sample mean is contained in the region of rejection (see Exhibit 19.2). Thus, since the sample mean is greater than the critical value, 3.196, the researchers say that the sample result is statistically significant beyond the .05 level. In other words, fewer than 5 of each 100 samples would show results that deviate this much from the hypothesized null hypothesis, when in fact the H_0 is actually true.

What does this mean to the management of the Red Lion? The results indicate that customers believe the service is friendly. It is unlikely (less than 5 times in 100) that this result would occur because of sampling error. It means

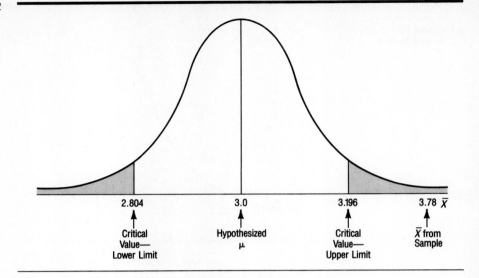

2.804	3.0	3.196	3.78 X̄
↑	↑	↑	↑
Critical Value—Lower Limit	Hypothesized μ	Critical Value—Upper Limit	X̄ from Sample

that the restaurant should worry about factors other than the friendliness of the service personnel.

An alternative way of testing the hypothesis is to formulate the decision rule in terms of the Z-statistic. Using the formula below, we can calculate the observed value of the Z-statistic, given a certain sample mean, X̄:

$$Z_{obs} = \frac{\bar{X} - \mu}{S_{\bar{X}}}$$

$$Z_{obs} = \frac{3.78 - \mu}{S_{\bar{X}}}$$

$$Z_{obs} = \frac{3.78 - 3.0}{.1} = \frac{.78}{.1} = 7.8$$

In this case the Z-value is 7.8, and we find that we have met the criterion of statistical significance at the .05 level. As a matter of fact, this is statistically significant at the .000001 level.

Type I and Type II Errors

Hypothesis testing, as we have previously stated, is based on probability theory. Because we cannot make any statement about a sample with complete certainty, there is always the chance that an error can be made. In fact, the researcher runs the risk of committing two types of errors. Exhibit 19.3 summarizes the state of affairs in the population and the nature of Type I and Type II errors. The four possible situations in the table result because the null hypothesis can be either true or false, and the statistical decision will be either to accept or to reject the null hypothesis.

EXHIBIT   19.3

Type I and Type II Errors in Hypothesis Testing

State of Null Hypothesis in the Population	Decision	
	Accept H_0	Reject H_0
H_0 is true	Correct—no error	Type I error
H_0 is false	Type II error	Correct—no error

If the decision has been made to reject the null hypothesis and, in fact, the null hypothesis is true, we have made what is called a **Type I error.** A Type I error has the probability of alpha (α), the level of statistical significance that the decision maker has set up. If the alternative hypothesis is, in fact, true and the null hypothesis is actually false but the decision maker concludes that he should not reject the null hypothesis, then we have made what is called a **Type II error.** The probability of making this incorrect decision is called *beta* (β). No error is made if the null hypothesis is true and the decision is made to accept it. A correct decision is also made if the null hypothesis is false and the decision is made to reject the null hypothesis.

Unfortunately, without increasing sample size, the researcher cannot simultaneously reduce Type I and Type II errors because there is an inverse relationship between these two types of errors. Thus reducing the probability of a Type II error increases the probability of a Type I error. In business problems Type I errors are generally more serious than Type II errors and there is greater concern with determining the significance level with alpha than with beta.[2]

CHOOSING THE APPROPRIATE STATISTICAL TECHNIQUE

Now that one statistical technique for hypothesis testing has been illustrated, it should be noted that there are a number of appropriate statistical techniques to assist the researcher in interpreting data. The choice of the method of statistical analysis depends on (1) the type of question to be answered, (2) the number of variables, and (3) the scale of measurement.

Type of Question to Be Answered

The type of question the researcher is attempting to answer is a consideration in the choice of statistical technique. For example, a researcher may be concerned about the central tendency of a variable or the distribution of that variable. Comparison of two divisions' average sales will require a t-test of two means, whereas a comparison of the quarterly sales distributions over a year's period will require a chi-square test.

The choice of research design and the type of data to collect should anticipate the method of statistical analysis. Once the data are collected, the initial orientation toward analysis of the problem is reflected in the research design.

R E S E A R C H   I N S I G H T
Type I and Type II Errors in the Legal Profession

Although most attorneys and judges do not concern them-selves with the statistical terminology of Type I and Type II errors, they do follow this logic. For example, our legal system is based on the concept that a person is innocent until proven guilty. Assume that the null hypothesis is that the person is innocent. If we make a Type I error, we send an innocent person to prison. Our legal system takes many cautions to avoid Type I errors. A person is innocent until proven guilty. A Type II error would occur when a guilty party is set free (the null hypothesis is accepted). Our society places such a high value on avoiding Type I errors that Type II errors are more likely to occur.

Number of Variables

The number of variables that will be simultaneously investigated is a primary consideration in the choice of statistical techniques. A researcher who is inter-ested only in the average number of times a prospective home buyer visits financial institutions to shop for interest rates concentrates on investigating only one variable at a time. **Univariate data analysis** is conducted when the re-searchers wish to generalize from a sample about one variable at a time.

Statistically describing the relationship between two variables at one time, such as the relationship between gross national product (GNP) and sales volume, requires **bivariate data analysis.** Tests of differences and measuring the association between variables are bivariate topics, discussed in Chapters 20 and 21.

Multivariate data analysis is the simultaneous investigation of more than two variables. Predicting sales volumes on the basis of advertising expenditure and other variables, such as gross national product and numbers of people in the sales area, is an example of multivariate analysis.

Scale of Measurement

The scale of measurement on which the data are based or the type of measure-ment reflected in the data determines the permissible statistical technique and the appropriate empirical operation that may be performed (see Exhibit 19.4). Testing a hypothesis about a mean, as we have just discussed, requires interval- or ratio-scaled data. Suppose a researcher is concerned with a nominal scale that identifies members versus nonmembers of the teamsters. The researcher must use the mode as the measure of central tendency, because of the type of scale.

In other situations the median may be used as the average, or percentile may be used as a measure of dispersion because the data are measured on an ordinal scale. For example, the ranking of the riskiness of securities is generally an ordinal scale.

Type of Scale	Measure of Central Tendency	Measure of Dispersion
Nominal	Mode	None
Ordinal	Median	Percentile
Interval or ratio	Mean	Standard deviation

Parametric versus Nonparametric Hypothesis Tests

The terms **parametric statistics** and **nonparametric statistics** refer to the two major groupings of statistical procedures. The major distinction between these two groups of procedures lies in the underlying assumptions about the data to be analyzed. When the data are interval- or ratio-scaled and the sample size is large, parametric statistical procedures are appropriate. These procedures are based on the assumption that the data in the study are drawn from populations with normal (bell-shaped) distributions and/or normal sampling distribution. When researchers do not make this assumption of normality, it is appropriate to use nonparametric methods. When data are either ordinal or nominal, it is generally inappropriate to make the assumption that the sampling distribution is normal (thus nonparametric statistics are referred to as distribution-free).[3]

Data analysis of both nominal and ordinal scales typically uses nonparametric statistical tests. If an investigator has two interval- or ratio-scaled measures, such as gross national product and industry sales volume, it is appropriate to use parametric tests to make a comparison of the intervals. Among the possible statistical tests are Z-test (or t-test) for a hypothesis about a mean, product-moment correlation analysis, and analysis of variance tests.

Exhibit 19.5 presents some guidelines for selecting the appropriate univariate statistical method. Although you may not be familiar with most of the statistical tests, the table is meant to illustrate that there are a number of statistical techniques that vary according to the properties of the scale. Further, similar tables showing examples of the selection of appropriate bivariate and multivariate statistical techniques will be shown in the next three chapters. The appropriate technique will vary according to both the properties of the scale and the number of variables investigated. The actual selection of a univariate statistical test consists of many potential choices because there are more alternatives than illustrated in Exhibit 19.5. A complete discussion of all the relevant techniques is beyond the scope of the discussion at this point.

t-DISTRIBUTION

There are a number of situations where researchers wish to test a hypothesis concerning the population mean with a sample size that is not large enough to be approximated by the normal distribution. In situations where the sample size is small ($n \leq 30$) and the population standard deviation is unknown,

EXHIBIT   19.5

**Examples of Selecting the
Appropriate Univariate
Statistical Method**

Business Problem	Statistical Question to Be Asked	Possible Test of Statistical Significance
Interval or Ratio Scale		
Compare actual and hypothetical values of average salary	Is the sample mean significantly different from the hypothesized population mean?	Z-test (if sample is large) t-test (if sample is small)
Ordinal Scale		
Compare actual and expected evaluations	Does the distribution of scores for a scale with the categories *excellent, good, fair,* and *poor* differ from the expected distribution?	Chi-square test
Determine ordered preferences for all brands in a product class	Does a set of rank-orderings in a sample differ from an expected or hypothetical rank ordering?	Kolmogorov-Smirnov test
Nominal Scale		
Identify sex of key executives	Is the number of female executives equal to the number of male executives?	Chi-square test
Indicate percentage of key executives who are male	Is the proportion of male executives the same as the hypothesized proportion?	t-test of a proportion

EXHIBIT   19.6

**The t-Distribution for
Various Degrees of Freedom**

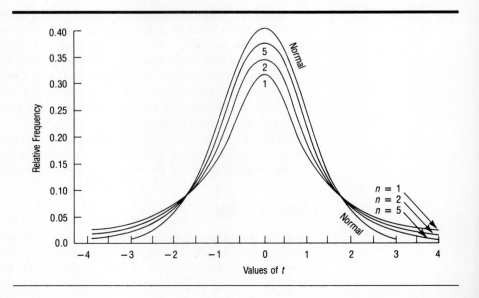

we use the t-distribution (also called the student's t-distribution). The **t-distribution,** like the standardized normal distribution, is a symmetrical, bell-shaped distribution with a mean of zero and a standard deviation of 1. When sample size (n) is larger than 30, the t-distribution and Z-distributions may be considered to be almost identical. Since the t-distribution is contingent on sample size, there is a family of t-distributions. More specifically, the shape of the t-distribution is influenced by its **degrees of freedom (d.f.).** Exhibit 19.6 illustrates t-distributions for 1, 2, 5, and an infinite number of degrees of freedom. The number of degrees of freedom is equal to the number of observations minus the number of constraints or assumptions needed to calculate a statistical term. Another way of looking at degrees of freedom is to think of adding four numbers together when you know their sum, for example:

$$
\begin{array}{r}
4 \\
2 \\
1 \\
\underline{X} \\
10
\end{array}
$$

The value of the fourth number has to be 3. In other words, there is a freedom of choice for the first three digits, but the fourth value is not free to vary. In this example there are three degrees of freedom.

Calculation of a t closely resembles the calculation of the Z-value. To calculate t:

$$
t = \frac{\bar{X} - \mu}{S_{\bar{X}}}
$$

with n − 1 degrees of freedom.

The researcher asks two questions to determine whether the Z-distribution or the t-distribution is the more appropriate for calculating a confidence interval or conducting a test of statistical significance. The first question is: "Is the population standard deviation (σ) known?" If the answer is yes, the Z-distribution is appropriate. The second question is also asked when σ is unknown (the situation in most business research studies); it is: "Is the sample size greater than 30?" If the answer is no, the t-distribution should be used; if it is yes, the Z-distribution may be used because as sample size increases, the t-distribution becomes increasingly similar to the Z-distribution.

Calculating a Confidence Interval Estimate Using the t-Distribution

Suppose a business organization is interested in how long newly hired MBA graduates remain on their first job. On the basis of a small sample of employees with MBAs, the researcher wishes to estimate the population mean with 95 percent confidence. The data from the sample are presented in Table 19.1, which indicates sample mean $\bar{X}$ = 3.7 years with a sample standard deviation S = 2.66.

Length of Initial Employment of MBA Graduates

Number of Years on First Job
3
5
7
1
12
1
2
2
5
4
2
3
1
3
4
2
6

$\Sigma X = 63$ $n = 17$ $\bar{X} = 3.7$ $S = 2.66$ $S_{\bar{X}} = .645$

To find the confidence estimates of the population mean for this small sample, we calculate:

$$\mu = \bar{X} \pm t_{c.l.} S_{\bar{X}}$$

or

$$\text{Upper limit} = \bar{X} + t_{c.l.} \frac{S}{\sqrt{n}}$$

$$\text{Lower limit} = \bar{X} - t_{c.l.} \frac{S}{\sqrt{n}}$$

where

μ = population mean
$\bar{X}$ = sample mean
$t_{c.l.}$ = critical value of t at a specified confidence level
$S_{\bar{X}}$ = standard error of the mean
S = sample standard deviation
n = sample size

More specifically, the step-by-step procedure for calculating the confidence interval is:

1. Calculate $\bar{X}$ from the sample.
2. Since σ is unknown, estimate the population standard deviation by finding S, the sample standard deviation.
3. Estimate the standard error of the mean using the following formula: $S_{\bar{X}} = S/\sqrt{n}$.

4. Determine the t-values associated with the confidence level desired. To do this, go to Table 3 in the Appendix of Statistical Tables. Although the t-table provides information similar to that in the Z-table, it is somewhat different. The t-table format emphasizes the chance of error or significance level (α) rather than the 95 percent chance of including the population mean in the estimate. Our example is a two-tailed test. Thus, since a 95 percent confidence level has been selected, the significance level equals .05 $(1.00 - .95 = .05)$. Once this has been determined, all we have to do to find the t-value is look under the .05 column for *two-tailed tests* at the row in which degrees of freedom (d.f.) equals the appropriate value $(n - 1)$.

5. Calculate the confidence interval.

In the example about the MBA students, we know $\bar{X} = 3.7$, $S = 2.66$, and $n = 17$.

To calculate the confidence interval, we must go to Table 3 in the Appendix and look under 16 degrees of freedom $(n - 1, 17 - 1 = 16)$ for the t-value at the 95 percent confidence level (.05 level of significance), in this case $t = 2.12$. Thus

$$\text{Upper limit} = 3.7 + 2.12(2.66/\sqrt{17}) = 5.07$$

$$\text{Lower limit} = 3.7 - 2.12(2.66/\sqrt{17}) = 2.33$$

In our hypothetical example it may be concluded with 95 percent confidence that the population mean for the number of years spent on the first job by MBAs is between 5.07 and 2.33 years.

Univariate Hypothesis Test Utilizing the t-Distribution

The step-by-step procedure for a **t-test** is conceptually similar to that for hypothesis testing with the Z-distribution. To illustrate, suppose a production manager believes the average number of defective assemblies (assemblies not meeting quality standards) each day to be 20. The factory records the number of defective assemblies for each of the 25 days it was open during a given month. The researcher calculates a sample mean, $\bar{X} = 22$, and a sample standard deviation, $S = 5$.

The first step is to state the null hypothesis and the alternative hypothesis:

$$H_0: \mu = 20$$
$$H_1: \mu \neq 20$$

Next, the researcher must calculate $\bar{X}$, S and estimate the standard error of the mean $(S_{\bar{X}})$:

$$S_{\bar{X}} = S/\sqrt{n}$$

$$= 5/\sqrt{25}$$

$$= 1$$

S T A T I S T I C A L   T U T O R
Chi-Square Test

The situation:

A private art museum sponsoring a program of summer art classes for children expects an equal number of boys and girls to be enrolled in its classes. A random sample from its list of students shows that there are more girls than boys.

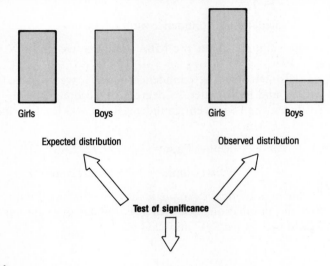

Questions to be answered:

1. **Is the difference between the expected (hypothetical) distribution and the observed distribution statistically significant?**
2. **If statistically significant, is the nature of the difference in distributions of any managerial value?**

Then, the researcher must find the t-value associated with the desired level of statistical significance. If a 95 percent confidence level is desired, the significance level is .05. Next, he or she must formulate a decision rule specifying the critical values by computing the upper and lower limits of the confidence interval to define the regions of rejection. This requires determining the value of t. For 24 degrees of freedom (n − 1, 25 − 1), the t-value is 2.064. These critical values are:

$$\text{Lower limit: } \mu - t_{\text{c.l.}}S_{\bar{X}} = 20 - 2.064\,(5/\sqrt{25})$$
$$= 20 - 2.064\,(1)$$
$$= 17.936$$
$$\text{Upper limit: } \mu + t_{\text{c.l.}}S_{\bar{X}} = 20 + 2.064\,(5/\sqrt{25})$$
$$= 20 + 2.064\,(1)$$
$$= 22.064$$

Finally, the researcher makes the statistical decision by determining if the sample mean falls between the critical limits. Based on the sample, $\overline{X} = 22$. In this case the sample mean is *not* included in the region of rejection. Even though the sample result is only slightly less than the critical value at the upper limit, the null hypothesis cannot be rejected. In other words, the production manager's assumption appears to be correct.

As with the Z-test, there is an alternative way of testing a hypothesis with the t-statistic. This is by using the formula:

$$t_{obs} = \frac{\overline{X} - \mu}{S_{\overline{X}}}$$

$$= \frac{22 - 20}{1} = \frac{2}{1} = 2$$

We can see that the observed t-value is less than the critical t-value of 2.064 at the .05 level when there are 24 $(25 - 1)$ degrees of freedom.

CHI-SQUARE TEST FOR GOODNESS OF FIT

Table 19.2 shows the responses to a survey investigating awareness of a particular brand of automobile tire. This frequency distribution, or one-dimensional table from a sample of 100, suggests that the majority of the population (60 percent) is aware of the brand.

The **chi-square (χ^2) test** allows us to test for significance in the analysis of frequency distributions. Thus categorical data on variables such as sex, education, or dichotomous answers may be statistically analyzed. Suppose, for example, that we wish to test the null hypothesis that the number of consumers aware of a certain tire brand equals the number unaware of the brand. The logic inherent in the χ^2 test allows us to compare the observed frequencies (O_i) with the expected frequencies (E_i) based on our theoretical ideas about the population distribution or our presupposed proportions. In other words, the technique tests whether the data come from a certain probability distribution. It tests the "goodness of fit" of the observed distribution with the expected distribution.

Calculation of the Univariate χ^2

Calculation of the chi-square statistic allows us to determine if the difference between the observed frequency distribution and the expected frequency distribution can be attributed to sampling variation. The steps in this process are:

1. Formulate the null hypothesis and determine the expected frequency of each answer.
2. Determine the appropriate significance level.
3. Calculate the χ^2 value using the observed frequencies from the sample and expected frequencies.
4. Make the statistical decision by comparing the calculated χ^2 value with the critical χ^2 value. (It will soon be explained that this value is found in Table 4 in the Appendix.)

T A B L E   1 9 . 2

One-Way Frequency Table
for Brand Awareness

Awareness of Tire Manufacturer's Brand	Frequency
Aware	60
Unaware	40
	100

To analyze the brand awareness data in Table 19.2, we start with the null hypothesis suggesting that the number of respondents aware of the brand will equal the number of respondents unaware of it. Thus the expected probability of each answer (aware or unaware) is .5; in a sample of 100, 50 people would be expected to respond yes, or be aware, and 50 would be expected to respond no, or be unaware. After we have determined that the chi-square test is appropriate at the .05 level of significance (or some other probability level), the chi-square statistic may be calculated.

To calculate the chi-square statistic, the following formula is used:

$$\chi^2 = \sum \frac{(O_i - E_i)^2}{E_i}$$

where

χ^2 = chi-square statistic
O_i = observed frequency in the ith cell
E_i = expected frequency in the ith cell

We sum the squared differences:

$$\chi^2 = \frac{(O_1 - E_1)^2}{E_1} + \frac{(O_2 - E_2)^2}{E_2}$$

Thus we determine that the chi-square value equals 4:

$$\chi^2 = \frac{(60 - 50)^2}{50} + \frac{(40 - 50)^2}{50}$$
$$= 4$$

Table 19.3 shows the detailed calculation of this statistic.

Like many other probability distributions, the χ^2 distribution is not a single probability curve but a family of curves. These curves, although similar, vary according to the number of degrees of freedom (k − 1). Thus we must calculate the number of degrees of freedom. Remember, "degrees of freedom" refers to the number of observations that can be varied without changing the restraints or assumptions associated with a numerical system. We calculate the degrees of freedom as follows: d.f. = k − 1, where k = the number of cells associated with column or row data.[4] In the brand awareness problem there are only two categorical responses. Thus degrees of freedom equals 1 (d.f. = 2 − 1 = 1).

TABLE   19.3

Calculating the
Chi-Square Statistic

Brand Awareness	Observed Frequency (O_i)	Expected Probability	Expected Frequency (E_i)	($O_i - E_i$)	$\dfrac{(O_i - E_i)^2}{E_i}$
Aware	60	.5	50	10	$\dfrac{100}{50} = 2.0$
Unaware	40	.5	50	−10	$\dfrac{100}{50} = 2.0$
Total	100	1.0	100	0	$\chi^2 = 4.0$

Now it is necessary to compare the computed chi-square value with the critical chi-square values associated with the .05 probability level with one degree of freedom. In Table 4 of the Appendix the critical chi-square value is 3.84. Thus the calculated chi-square is larger than the tabular chi-square, and the null hypothesis—that the observed values are comparable to the expected values—is rejected.[5]

The chi-square test is discussed further in Chapter 20, as it is also frequently utilized in the analysis of contingency tables.

HYPOTHESIS TEST OF A PROPORTION

The population proportion (π) can be estimated on the basis of the sample proportion (p). Researchers often test univariate statistical hypotheses about population proportions. The procedure for the **hypothesis test of a proportion** is conceptually similar to hypothesis testing when the mean is the characteristic of interest. However, the formulation of the standard error of the proportion is mathematically different.

Consider the following example. A state legislature is considering a proposed right-to-work law. One legislator has hypothesized that 50 percent of the state's labor force is unionized. In other words, the null hypothesis to be tested is that the proportion of union workers in the state is .5.

The researcher formulates the statistical null hypothesis that the population proportion (π) equals 50 percent (.5):

$$H_0: \quad \pi = .5$$

The alternative hypothesis is that π does not equal .5:

$$H_1: \quad \pi \neq .5$$

Suppose the researcher conducts a survey with a sample of 100 workers and calculates p = .6. Even though the population proportion is unknown, a large sample allows the use of the Z-test (rather than the t-test). If she decides that the decision rule will be set at the .01 level of significance, the critical Z-value of 2.57 is used for the hypothesis test. Using the following formula, we can calculate the observed value of Z, given a certain sample proportion:

$$Z_{obs} = \frac{p - \pi}{S_p}$$

where

p = sample proportion
π = hypothesized population proportion
S_p = estimate of the standard error of the proportion

The formula for S_p is:

$$S_p = \sqrt{\frac{pq}{n}} \quad \text{or} \quad \sqrt{\frac{p(1 - p)}{n}}$$

where

S_p = estimate of the standard error of the proportion
p = proportion of successes
$q = (1 - p)$, proportion of failures

In our example:

$$S_p = \sqrt{\frac{(.6)(.4)}{100}}$$

$$= \sqrt{\frac{.24}{100}}$$

$$= \sqrt{.0024}$$

$$= .04899$$

The Z_{obs} can now be simply calculated:

$$Z_{obs} = \frac{p - \pi}{S_p}$$

$$= \frac{.6 - .5}{.04899}$$

$$= \frac{.1}{.04899}$$

$$= 2.04$$

The Z_{obs} value of 2.04 is less than the critical value of 2.57, so the null hypothesis cannot be rejected.

In our example the researcher drew a large sample and had to estimate the standard error of the proportion. When the sample size is small, the Z-test is not appropriate and the t-test should be used. The standard rule of thumb for determining if the sample size is too small is to (1) multiply n times π and (2) multiply n times $(1 - \pi)$. If either product is 5 or below, the sample size is considered to be too small to use the Z-test.

ADDITIONAL APPLICATIONS OF HYPOTHESIS TESTING

The discussion of statistical inference in this chapter has been restricted to setting up a confidence interval around the sample mean to estimate the population mean, to chi-square tests to test for the significance in the analysis of frequency distribution, and to Z-tests to test a hypothesis about a sample proportion when the sample size is large. As our discussion of the population proportion suggests, there are other hypothesis tests concerning population parameters estimated from sample statistics. Many of these other tests not mentioned here are conceptually no different in the methods of hypothesis testing. However, the formulas for conducting statistical tests are mathematically different. While these formulations may be important to the reader, the purpose of this chapter has been to discuss basic statistical concepts. The reader has learned the basic terminology in this chapter and should have no problem generalizing to other statistical problems.

As was emphasized in Chapter 15, the key to understanding statistics is learning the basics of the language. This chapter has presented verbs, nouns, and some of the rules of the grammar of statistics. It is hoped that some of the myths about statistics have been shattered.

SUMMARY

This chapter discusses univariate statistical procedures for hypothesis testing when the research focuses on one variable. A hypothesis is a statement of assumption about the nature of the world. A null hypothesis is a statement about the status quo. The alternative hypothesis is a statement indicating the opposite of the null hypothesis.

In hypothesis testing a researcher states a null hypothesis about a population mean and then attempts to disprove it. The Z-test defines a region of rejection based on a significance level on the standardized normal distribution beyond which it is unlikely that the null hypothesis is true. If a sample mean is contained in the region of rejection, the null hypothesis is rejected.

There are two possible types of error in statistical tests: Type I, rejecting a true null hypothesis, and Type II, accepting a false null hypothesis.

A number of appropriate statistical techniques are available to assist the researcher in interpreting data. The choice of the method of statistical analysis depends on (1) the type of question to be answered, (2) the number of variables, and (3) the scale of measurement.

Univariate statistical analysis allows the researcher to assess the statistical significance of various hypotheses about a single variable. Bivariate or multivariate analysis is used when two or more variables are to be analyzed. Nonparametric statistical tests are used on nominal and ordinal data, and parametric tests are used for interval or ratio scales. However, if a researcher cannot reasonably assume a normal population or sampling distribution, nonparametric tests may be used.

This chapter presents the technique for using the t-distributions in estimating confidence intervals for the mean. Calculation of the confidence interval uses the central-limit theorem to estimate a range around the sample mean, which should contain the population mean.

The t-distribution is used for hypothesis testing with small samples when the population standard deviation is unknown. The hypothesis test is analogous to the Z-test. The chi-square test allows the testing of statistical significance in the analysis of frequency distributions: An observed distribution of categorical data from a sample may be compared with an expected distribution for goodness of fit. Conceptually, the hypothesis test of a proportion follows a method similar to the Z-test for mean.

Key Terms

hypothesis	multivariate data analysis
null hypothesis	parametric statistics
alternative hypothesis	nonparametric statistics
significance level	t-distribution
critical values	degrees of freedom (d.f.)
Type I error	t-test
Type II error	chi-square (χ^2) test
univariate data analysis	hypothesis test of a proportion
bivariate data analysis	

Questions

1. What is the purpose of a statistical hypothesis?
2. What is the significance level? How does a researcher choose a significance level?
3. List the steps in the hypothesis-testing procedure.
4. Distinguish between a Type I and a Type II error.
5. What are the factors that determine the choice of the appropriate statistical technique?
6. After a bumper crop a mushroom grower hypothesizes that mushrooms will remain at the wholesale average price of $1 per pound. State the null hypothesis and the alternative hypothesis.
7. Assume you have the following data: H_0: $\mu = 200$, $S = 30$, $n = 64$, and $\bar{X} = 218$. Conduct a hypothesis test at the .05 significance level.
8. Assume you have the following data: H_0: $\mu = 2450$, $S = 400$, $n = 100$, and $\bar{X} = 2300$. Conduct a hypothesis test at the .01 significance level.
9. If the data in Question 8 had been generated with a sample of 25 ($n = 25$), what statistical test would be appropriate?
10. How does the t-distribution differ from the Z-distribution?
11. The answers to a researcher's question will be nominally scaled. What statistical test is appropriate to compare the sample data with hypothesized population data?
12. A researcher plans to ask employees if they favor, oppose, or are indifferent to a change in their company's retirement program. Formulate a

null hypothesis for a chi-square test and determine the expected frequencies for each answer.

13. Give an example of a circumstance in which a Type I error may be more serious than a Type II error.

14. Refer to the brand awareness χ^2 data on pages 447–448. What statistical decisions could be made if the .01 significance level were selected rather than the .05 level?

15. Determine a statistical hypothesis and perform a chi-square test on the following survey data.

 a.   Easy-to-listen-to music should be played on the office intercom:

Agree	40
Neutral	35
Disagree	25
	100

 b.   Demographic characteristics of a group indicate:

Republicans	100
Democrats	100
	200

16. Quality Motors is an automobile dealership that regularly advertises in its local market area. It has claimed that a certain make and model of car averages 30 miles to a gallon of gas and mentions that this figure may vary with driving conditions. A local consumer group wishes to verify the advertising claim. To do so, it selects a sample of recent purchasers of this make and model. It asks them to drive their cars until two tanks of gasoline are used up and to record the mileage. Then the group calculates and records the miles per gallon for each car. The following data portray the results of the tests:

Purchaser	Miles per Gallon	Purchaser	Miles per Gallon
1	30.9	14	27.0
2	24.5	15	26.7
3	31.2	16	31.0
4	28.7	17	23.5
5	35.1	18	29.4
6	29.0	19	26.3
7	28.8	20	27.5
8	23.1	21	28.2
9	31.0	22	28.4
10	30.2	23	29.1
11	28.4	24	21.9
12	29.3	25	30.9
13	24.2		

 a.   Formulate a statistical hypothesis to test the consumer group's purpose.

 b.   Calculate the mean for miles per gallon. Compute the sample variance and sample standard deviation.

 c.   According to your hypothesis, construct the appropriate statistical test using a .05 statistical significance level.

17. A personnel researcher hypothesizes that 15 percent of employees eligible for early retirement will actually choose to retire early. In a sample of 1,200 employees, 20 percent say they plan to retire early. Perform a hypothesis test.

18. In Chapter 15 see Question 8 about Coastal Star Sales Corporation for a description of the data.
    a. Develop a hypothesis concerning the average age of the sales force and test the hypothesis.
    b. Calculate the mean for the previous year's sales and use this as the basis for formulating a hypothesis about current-year sales. Test the hypothesis.

References

[1] Technically the t-distribution should be used when the population variance is unknown and the standard deviation is estimated from sample data. However, with large samples it is convenient to use the Z-distribution, because the t-distribution approximates the Z-distribution.

[2] A complete discussion of this topic is beyond the scope of this book. See almost any statistics textbook for a more detailed discussion of Type I and Type II errors.

[3] A more complete discussion of the differences between parametric and nonparametric statistics is given in Appendix 20A.

[4] The reader with an extensive statistics background will recognize that there are a few rare cases in which the degrees of freedom is not equal to $k - 1$. These cases are infrequently encountered by readers of this level of book, and to present them would only complicate the presentation offered here.

[5] An example of how to use the chi-square table is given in Table 4 of the Appendix of Statistical Tables.

CHAPTER 20

Bivariate Analysis: Tests of Differences

What you will learn in this chapter:

To understand that bivariate statistics deals with the simultaneous investigation of two variables.

To discuss reasons for conducting tests of differences.

To understand how the type of measurement scale will influence the bivariate test of difference selected.

To calculate a chi-square test for a contingency table.

To understand the difference between observed and expected frequencies and how to calculate the expected frequencies for a chi-square test.

To calculate a t-test for two independent samples for differences of means.

To calculate a Z-test for two independent samples for comparing differences between two proportions.

To understand the concept of analysis of variance (ANOVA).

To state a null hypothesis in a test of differences among three or four group means.

To interpret analysis of variance summary tables.

The Center for Creative Leadership compared 21 derailed executives with 20 executives who had made it to the top of their company. Derailed executives, who had been expected to go far because of prior success but who either had been fired, had been forced to retire early, or had reached a job plateau, were similar in many ways to the executives who had arrived at the top. They were bright, worked diligently, and excelled in a technical area, such as accounting or engineering. They had made sacrifices and had established good track records. But the successful executives had more diverse career histories and did not rely on a single functional area. Moreover, they had excellent interpersonal skills. They were able to laugh at themselves and handle mistakes with poise and grace. They maintained composure under stress. They could focus on problems and solve them. They were conceptually strong. On the other hand, derailed executives were unable to think strategically with a broad, long-term view. The most striking difference between the two groups, however, was in their ability to deal with others. The derailed executives were insensitive to others; some were abrasive, aloof, and arrogant.[1]

*Making comparisons such as those listed above involves bivariate analysis—the topic of this chapter. The purpose of descriptive analysis, as we saw in Chapter 18, is to summarize data. After this has been accomplished, the researcher may wish to measure the association between variables or test the difference between groups or objects. The purpose of this chapter is to go beyond univariate statistics, in which the analysis focuses on one variable at a time. Tests of differences and measures of association are in the realm of **bivariate statistics,** where scores on two variables are of concern to the researcher.*

Before we explore the actual statistical tests, an example will be discussed to explain and help us understand the concepts behind difference tests.

■

T A B L E   2 0 . 1   **Client Data (Unseparated): CETA Title III Program**

Client Characteristics

Client Number	Education	Marital Status	Age	Number of Weeks Unemployed	Number of Dependents	Previous Wage
1	X	X	20	X	1	X
2	14	M	32	X	1	X
3	10	M	29	10	3	4.60
4	4	X	55	X	1	X
5	X	X	24	X	1	4.20
6	15	S	22	52	1	3.60
7	12	S	18	X	1	5.00
8	12	M	24	4	2	X
9	12	D	23	16	2	4.20
10	13	S	21	28	1	4.70
11	12	S	20	X	1	X
12	10	X	18	3	1	X
13	13	M	29	5	1	4.00
14	12	S	20	52	2	3.50
15	12	M	36	X	1	4.20
16	12	M	23	36	1	4.20
17	10	S	17	3	1	X
18	13	S	25	0	2	5.00
19	11	D	24	0	2	X
20	13	Sep	25	52	2	X
21	12	M	62	3	1	X
22	14	Sep	25	30	1	X
23	12	M	24	X	1	X
24	13	S	22	X	1	X
25	8	M	19	52	1	X
Average or Total	11.70	9—M 8—S 2—D 2—Sep	26.28	24.71	1.32	4.30

Note: X means the information was not recorded for that client.

[a]S means satisfactory; U means unsatisfactory.

CETA PROGRAM: A CASE EXAMPLE

A program for upgrading the effectiveness of CETA employment and training programs utilized a number of comparisons between two groups: CETA clients who are successful in maintaining employment and those who are not. This section shows how to make comparisons between groups *without statistical tests*. However, this material was written after statistical tests (e.g., t-tests) were used to detect significant differences.[2]

Our example is based on information gathered on clients at a CETA Title III program in a rural community with a population under 25,000. The program served a seven-county area and had a grant of approximately $200,000. The clients on whom data were gathered had been trained in secretarial work and all were female. Table 20.1 shows the client characteristics, program services, and outcome criteria that were recorded. Many other client characteris-

	Program Services				Outcome Criteria	
Hours Week during Training	Own Transportation	Type of Training	Weekly Allowance	Training Site	Weeks Employed	Employer Rating[a]
40	X	WE	84	A	12	S
40	Yes	WE	94	B	12	S
40	Yes	WE	92	X	12	S
40	X	WE	84	X	12	S
40	X	WE	84	X	12	S
40	Yes	PSE	140	X	12	S
40	Yes	OJT	X	D	8	U
40	Yes	WE	92	E	6	U
40	X	WE	84	A	8	U
40	Yes	WE	92	A	12	S
40	X	WE	84	A	12	S
40	X	WE	92	X	1	U
40	Yes	WE	92	E	1	U
40	X	WE	92	E	8	U
40	X	WE	92	D	5	U
40	Yes	WE	92	E	3	U
40	No	WE	92	E	12	U
40	Yes	WE	92	X	4	U
40	X	WE	84	E	2	U
40	X	WE	92	X	10	U
40	X	WE	84	E	3	U
40	No	WE	84	A	2	U
40	X	WE	84	E	7	U
40	X	WE	92	E	1	U
40	Yes	WE	92	A	6	U
40.00	10—Yes 2—No	23 WE 1 OJT 1 PSE	91.08	6—A 1—B 2—D 9—E	X	X

tics and program services are not shown because of inconsistent recording of these factors. Twenty-five clients are included in the sample.

Client Characteristics

Education data were available on 23 clients, and the average education level of these clients was 11.70 years. Marital status was available on 21 clients. The data showed: married = 42.86 percent, single = 38.10 percent, divorced and separated = 19.04 percent; total: 100 percent.

Age data were available on all 25 clients, whose average age was 26.28 years. Data were available only on 16 clients regarding the length of their unemployment prior to training; the average length was 24.71 months. Data on number of dependents were available on all 25 clients; the average number was 1.32.

Wages earned prior to training were available only on 11 clients; the average hourly salary was $4.30. All 25 clients worked 40 hours per week during

T A B L E   20.2   **Client Data by Successful and Unsuccessful Groupings: CETA Title III Program**

Client Characteristics

Client Number	Education	Marital Status	Age	Number of Weeks Unemployed	Number of Dependents	Previous Wage
Successful						
1	X	X	20	X	1	X
2	14	M	32	X	1	X
3	10	M	29	10	3	4.60
4	4	X	55	X	1	X
5	X	X	24	X	1	4.20
6	15	S	22	52	1	3.60
10	13	S	21	28	1	4.70
11	12	S	20	X	1	X
Average or Total	11.33	2 — M 3 — S	25.63	30	1.25	4.28
Unsuccessful						
7	12	S	18	X	1	5.00
8	12	M	24	4	2	X
9	12	D	23	16	2	4.20
12	10	X	18	3	1	X
13	13	M	29	5	1	4.00
14	12	S	20	52	2	3.50
15	12	M	36	X	1	4.20
16	12	M	23	36	1	4.20
17	10	S	17	3	1	X
18	13	S	25	0	2	5.00
19	11	D	24	0	2	X
20	13	Sep	25	52	2	X
21	12	M	62	3	1	X
22	14	Sep	25	30	1	X
23	12	M	24	X	1	X
24	13	S	22	X	1	X
25	8	M	19	52	1	X
Average or Total	11.8	7 — M 5 — S 2 — D 2 — Sep	23.59	23.27	1.35	4.30

Note: X means the information was not recorded for that client.

[a] S means satisfactory; U means unsatisfactory.

training. Since no differences existed between any clients, this factor is not carried through the analysis.

It was recorded that only 13 clients had their own cars, but 83.33 percent of these clients had their own transportation (see Table 20.1). Twenty-three of the clients had received work-experience training, one received on-the-job training, and one received public service employment training. The average weekly allowance received by 24 clients was $91.08 (data were not available for one client). Five basic-training sites were used for training purposes. These training sites are labeled A, B, C, D, and E to maintain program confidentiality. The proportions of clients trained at each site were A, 33 percent; B, 6 percent; C, 0 percent; D, 11 percent; and E, 50 percent.

| | Program Services | | | Outcome Criteria | |
Own Transportation	Type of Training	Weekly Allowance	Training Site	Weeks Employed	Employer Rating[a]
X	WE	84	A	12	S
Yes	WE	94	B	12	S
Yes	WE	92	X	12	S
X	WE	84	X	12	S
X	WE	84	X	12	S
Yes	PSE	140	X	12	S
Yes	WE	92	A	12	S
X	WE	84	A	12	S
4 — Yes	7 WE	94.25	3 — A	Successful	
	1 PSE		1 — B		
Yes	OJT	X	D	8	U
Yes	WE	92	E	6	U
X	WE	84	A	8	U
X	WE	92	X	1	U
Yes	WE	92	E	1	U
X	WE	92	E	8	U
X	WE	92	D	5	U
Yes	WE	92	E	3	U
No	WE	92	E	12	U
Yes	WE	92	X	4	U
X	WE	84	E	2	U
X	WE	92	X	10	U
X	WE	84	E	3	U
No	WE	84	A	2	U
X	WE	84	E	1	U
X	WE	92	E	1	U
Yes	WE	92	A	6	U
6 — Yes	16 WE	89.50	3 — A	Unsuccessful	
2 — No	1 OJT		2 — D		
			9 — E		

Outcome Criteria

Two criteria were used to determine success of the client on the unsubsidized job. If the client had been employed for 12 weeks or more and was rated satisfactorily by the employer at the time of last follow-up, the client was termed successful. Eight clients met these criteria, for a success rate of 32 percent.

Formation of Two Comparison Groups

The client data were separated into two comparison groupings on the basis of the outcome criteria that were described. Table 20.2 shows the resultant groups. The purpose of the first part of the analysis is to determine whether the two groups of clients are similar in personal characteristics. A comparison of personal characteristics is presented below:

	Successful		**Unsuccessful**
Average education	11.33 yr.		11.80 yr.
Marital status			
Single[a]	60%	————	32%
Married[a]	40%	————	43%
Divorced or separated[a]	0%	————	25%
Average age	25.63 yr.		23.59 yr.
Number of weeks unemployed[a]	30.00	————	23.27
Number of dependents	1.25		1.35
Previous wage (hourly)	$4.28		$4.30

[a] The two groups differ on these personal characteristics.

It appears that the clients may be different on two sets of characteristics. First, the composition of marital status is considerably different; however, data are missing on three successful clients (over one-third of the successful cases). Second, the average number of weeks unemployed prior to training seems to be different between the groups. However, five cases in the successful group have missing data (over one-half of the cases).

When so many data are missing, it is unwise to conclude that the groups are dissimilar. It is equally ill advised to conclude that they are similar. If the data were available, the differences could be considerably closer to, or different from, what they appear to be. Therefore the analysis cannot proceed further.

If it cannot be determined whether the two groups are similar or dissimilar, there is no way to compare program services. If we assume the clients are similar and compare program services at this point, we may make some serious mistakes in our conclusions. If we assume the clients are dissimilar and create two more comparison groups, we may make equally serious mistakes in our conclusions.

This case, while unfortunately not allowing a complete comparison of groups, does illustrate the *vital importance of recording full and complete information* on all clients served. An occasional missing piece of data may be handled, but a poorly designed recording procedure will make effectiveness evaluation of any sort an impossibility.

WHAT IS THE APPROPRIATE TEST OF DIFFERENCES?

One of the most frequently tested hypotheses states that two groups are different with respect to a certain behavior, characteristic, or attitude. For example, in the classical experimental design, researchers test differences between subjects assigned to the experimental group and subjects assigned to the control group. Or researchers may be interested in determining if males and females

EXHIBIT 20.1

Common Bivariate Tests of Differences

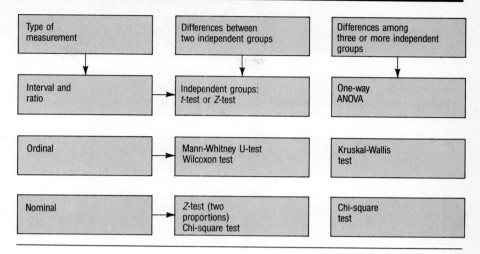

Type of measurement	Differences between two independent groups	Differences among three or more independent groups
Interval and ratio	Independent groups: t-test or Z-test	One-way ANOVA
Ordinal	Mann-Whitney U-test Wilcoxon test	Kruskal-Wallis test
Nominal	Z-test (two proportions) Chi-square test	Chi-square test

perform a task or hold an attitude with the same frequency. In statistical terminology the null hypothesis is that the two groups are the same.

Exhibit 20.1 illustrates that both the type of measurement and the number of groups to be compared influence the type of bivariate statistical test. Often researchers are interested in testing differences in mean scores between groups or in comparing how two groups' scores are distributed across possible response categories. We will focus our attention on these issues.[3] Construction of contingency tables and chi-square analysis is a procedure for comparing the distribution of one group with the distribution of another group. This is a good starting point for discussing testing of differences.

Cross-Tabulation Tables: Using the Chi-Square Test for Goodness of Fit

One of the simplest techniques for describing sets of relationships is the cross-tabulation. A *cross-tabulation*, or *contingency table*, is a joint frequency distribution of observations on two or more sets of variables. This generally means that tabulation of subgroups will be conducted for purposes of comparison. The chi-square distribution provides a means for testing the statistical significance of contingency tables. This allows us to test for differences in two groups' distribution across categories. (Another reason for concern is whether two or more variables are interrelated or associated; this will be discussed in Chapter 21.)

As mentioned in Chapter 19, the logic involved in the **chi-square test** is that of comparing the observed frequencies (O_i) with the expected frequencies (E_i). It tests the "goodness of fit" of the observed distribution with the expected distribution.

T A B L E   2 0 . 3

One-Way Frequency Table for Brand Awareness

Awareness of Tire Manufacturer's Brand	Frequency
Aware	60
Unaware	40
	100

T A B L E   2 0 . 4

Contingency Table (Cross-Tabulation) for Brand Awareness by Sex

Awareness of Tire Manufacturer's Brand	Men	Women	Total
Aware	50	10	60
Unaware	15	25	40
	65	35	100

Table 20.3 reproduces Table 19.2. This one-dimensional table suggests that the majority of the population (60 percent) is aware of the brand. However, if we analyze the data by subgroups based on sex of respondent, as we have in Table 20.4, we can see the logic of cross-classification procedures. Inspection of Table 20.4 suggests that most men are aware of the brand of tires, whereas most women are not. Thus in our simple analysis we conclude that there is a difference in brand awareness between men and women. (It might also be stated that brand awareness may be associated with sex of respondent.)

So far we have not discussed the notion of statistical significance. Is the observed difference between men and women the result of chance variation due to random sampling? Or is the discrepancy more than sampling variation? The chi-square test allows us to conduct tests for significance in the analysis of an R × C contingency table (where R = row and C = column). The formula for the chi-square statistic is the same as that for one-way frequency tables (see Chapter 19):

$$\chi^2 = \sum \frac{(O_i - E_i)^2}{E_i}$$

where

$$\chi^2 = \text{chi-square statistic}$$
$$O_i = \text{observed frequency in the ith cell}$$
$$E_i = \text{expected frequency in the ith cell}$$

Again, as in the univariate chi-square test, a frequency count of data that nominally identify or categorically rank groups is acceptable for the chi-square test for contingency tables. Both variables in the contingency table will be categorical variables rather than interval- or ratio-scaled continuous variables.

We begin, as in all hypothesis-testing procedures, by formulating the null hypothesis and selecting the level of statistical significance for the particular problem. Suppose, for example, that we wish to test the null hypothesis that an equal number of men and women are aware of the brand in the example given above and that the hypothesis test will be made at the .05 level of statistical significance.

In managerial terms the research asks whether men and women have different levels of brand awareness, and the problem is translated into a statistical question: "Is brand awareness independent of the respondent's sex?" Table 20.4 is a 2 × 2 (R × C) contingency table that cross-classifies answers to the awareness question (rows) and the respondent's sex (columns).

To compute the chi-square value for the 2 × 2 contingency table (Table 20.4), the researcher must first identify an expected distribution for that table. Under the null hypothesis that men and women would be equally aware of the tire brand, the same proportion of positive answers (60 percent) should come from both groups. In other words, the proportion of men who are aware of the brand would be the same as the proportion of women who are aware of it. Likewise, the proportion of men who are unaware of the brand would equal the proportion of women who are unaware.

There is an easy way to calculate the expected frequencies for the cells in a cross-tabulation table. To compute an expected number for each cell, the following formula is used:

$$E_{ij} = \frac{R_i C_j}{n}$$

where

R_i = total observed frequency in the ith row
C_j = total observed frequency in the jth column
n = sample size

A calculation of the expected values does not utilize the actual observed numbers of respondents in each individual cell—only the total column and total row values are used in this calculation. The expected cell frequencies are calculated as shown in Table 20.5.

To compute a chi-square statistic, the same formula as before is used, except that we calculate degrees of freedom as the number of rows minus one (R − 1) times the number of columns minus one (C − 1):

$$\chi^2 = \sum \frac{(O_i - E_i)^2}{E_i}$$

with (R − 1)(C − 1) degrees of freedom.

Awareness of Tire Manufacturer's Brand	Men	Women	Total
Aware	50(39)[a]	10(21)	60
Unaware	15(26)	25(14)	40
	65	35	100

[a]Expected frequencies are in parentheses. They were calculated as follows:

$$E_{ij} = \frac{R_i C_j}{n}$$

$$E_{11} = \frac{(60)(65)}{100} = 39$$

$$E_{12} = \frac{(60)(35)}{100} = 21$$

$$E_{21} = \frac{(40)(65)}{100} = 26$$

$$E_{22} = \frac{(40)(35)}{100} = 14$$

Table 20.5 shows the observed versus the expected frequencies for the brand awareness question. Using the data in Table 20.5, the chi-square statistic is calculated as follows:

$$\chi^2 = \frac{(50 - 39)^2}{39} + \frac{(10 - 21)^2}{21} + \frac{(15 - 26)^2}{26} + \frac{(25 - 14)^2}{14}$$
$$= 3.102 + 5.762 + 4.654 + 8.643$$
$$= 22.161$$

The number of degrees of freedom equals 1:

$$(R - 1)(C - 1) = (2 - 1)(2 - 1) = 1$$

From Table 4 in the Appendix of Statistical Tables at the end of the book, we see that the critical value at the .05 probability level with 1 d.f. is 3.84. Thus the null hypothesis is rejected because 22.161 is much greater than 3.84. The brand awareness does not appear to be independent of respondent's sex—in fact, the tabular value for the .001 level is 10.8, and the calculated value of 22.1 far exceeds this critical value.

Proper use of the chi-square test requires that each expected cell frequency (E_{ij}) have a value of at least 5. If this sample size requirement is not met, the researcher may take a larger sample or combine ("collapse") response categories.

t-TEST FOR COMPARING TWO MEANS

The t-test may be used to test a hypothesis stating that the mean scores on some variable will be significantly different for two independent samples or groups. It is used when the number of observations (sample size) is small and the population standard deviation is unknown. To use the **t-test for difference of means**,

S T A T I S T I C A L   T U T O R

Chi-Square Test: A Test of Differences among Groups

The situation:

A survey among Democrats, Republicans, and independents asked: "How often do you contribute money to candidates of an opposition party?"

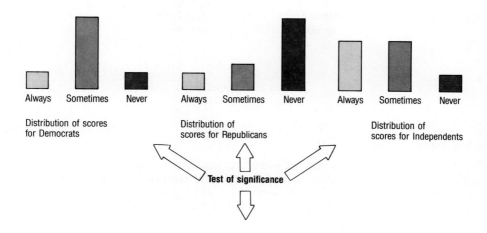

Distribution of scores for Democrats

Distribution of scores for Republicans

Distribution of scores for Independents

Test of significance

Questions:

1. Is the difference between the distributions statistically significant?
2. If statistically significant, is the nature of the difference in distributions of any managerial value?

---

we assume the two samples are drawn from normal distributions and because σ is unknown, we assume the variances of the two populations or groups are equal (homoscedasticity). Further, we assume interval data.

The null hypothesis about differences between groups is normally stated: $\mu_1 = \mu_2$ or $\mu_1 - \mu_2 = 0$. In most cases comparisons are between two sample means ($\overline{X}_1 - \overline{X}_2$). A verbal expression of the formula for t is:[4]

$$t = \frac{\text{Mean 1} - \text{Mean 2}}{\text{Variability of random means}}$$

Thus the t-value is a ratio between the information about the difference between means (provided by the sample) and the random error in the denominator. The question is whether the observed differences have occurred by chance alone. To calculate t, the following formula is used:

$$t = \frac{\overline{X}_1 - \overline{X}_2}{S_{\overline{X}_1 - \overline{X}_2}}$$

STATISTICAL TUTOR
t-Test for Difference of Means

The situation:

A bank takes a sample to compare the annual salaries (dollars) of professional women employees with professional male employees.

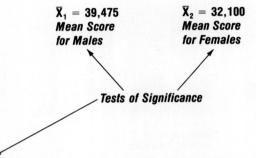

$\bar{X}_1 = 39,475$
Mean Score for Males

$\bar{X}_2 = 32,100$
Mean Score for Females

Tests of Significance

Questions to be answered:

1. Is the difference between the means of men and women *statistically significant*?
2. Is the magnitude of difference large enough to justify a differential treatment strategy?

---

where

$$\bar{X}_1 = \text{mean for Group 1}$$
$$\bar{X}_2 = \text{mean for Group 2}$$
$$S_{\bar{X}_1 - \bar{X}_2} = \text{the pooled or combined standard error} \\ \text{of difference between means}$$

A **pooled estimate of the standard error** is a better estimate of the standard error than one based on the variance from either sample. This requires the assumption that variances of both groups (populations) are equal. To calculate the pooled standard error of the difference between means of independent samples:

$$S_{\bar{X}_1 - \bar{X}_2} = \sqrt{\left(\frac{(n_1 - 1)S_1^2 + (n_2 - 1)S_2^2}{n_1 + n_2 - 2}\right)\left(\frac{1}{n_1} + \frac{1}{n_2}\right)}$$

where

$$S_1^2 = \text{the variance of Group 1}$$
$$S_2^2 = \text{the variance of Group 2}$$
$$n_1 = \text{the sample size of Group 1}$$
$$n_2 = \text{the sample size of Group 2}$$

TABLE   20.6

Comparison of Student Attitudes toward Business

Business Students	Sociology Students
$\bar{X}_1 = 16.5$	$\bar{X}_2 = 12.2$
$S_1 = 2.1$	$S_2 = 2.6$
$n_1 = 21$	$n_2 = 14$

To illustrate the t-test, suppose a researcher wants to test the difference of sociology majors and business majors on scores on a scale measuring attitudes toward business. We will assume that the attitude scale is an interval scale. The result of the simple random sample of these two groups of college students is presented in Table 20.6. A high score equals a favorable attitude toward business. The null hypothesis is that there is no difference in attitudes toward business (mean score) between the two groups. The relevant data computation is as follows:

$$S_{\bar{X}_1 - \bar{X}_2} = \sqrt{\left(\frac{(n_1 - 1)S_1^2 + (n_2 - 1)S_2^2}{n_1 + n_2 - 2}\right)\left(\frac{1}{n_1} + \frac{1}{n_2}\right)}$$

$$S_{\bar{X}_1 - \bar{X}_2} = \sqrt{\left(\frac{(20)(2.1)^2 + (13)(2.6)^2}{33}\right)\left(\frac{1}{21} + \frac{1}{14}\right)} = .797$$

To calculate the t-statistic:

$$t = \frac{\bar{X}_1 - \bar{X}_2}{S_{\bar{X}_1 - \bar{X}_2}} = \frac{16.5 - 12.2}{.797} = \frac{4.3}{.797} = 5.395$$

In a test of two means, degrees of freedom are calculated as follows:

$$d.f. = n - k$$

where

$$n = n_1 + n_2$$
$$k = \text{number of groups}$$

In our example d.f. equals 33. If the .01 level of significance is selected, reference to Table 3 in the Appendix yields the critical t-value. The t-value of 2.75 must be surpassed by the observed t-value if the hypothesis test is to be statistically significant at the .01 level. The calculated t of 5.39 far exceeds the critical value of t for statistical significance, so it is significant at $\alpha = .01$. In other words, this research shows that business students' attitude scores are significantly higher than those of sociology students.

As another example, 11 sales representatives are categorized as either young (1) or old (2) on the basis of their age in years, as shown in Exhibit 20.2. The exhibit presents an SAS computer output comparing the mean sales volume for these two groups.

E X H I B I T   2 0 . 2   **SAS t-Test Output t-Test Procedure Variable: CR Sales**

Age	N	Mean	Standard Deviation	Standard Error	Minimum	Maximum	Variances	t	d.f.	Prob. >|t|
1	6	61879.33333	22356.20845	9126.88388	41152.00000	103059.0000	Unequal	−0.9758	5.2	0.3729
2	5	86961.80000	53734.45098	24030.77702	42775.00000	172530.0000	Equal	−1.0484	9.0	0.3218

For H_0 variances are equal, $F' = 5.78$ with 4 and 5 d.f. Prob > $F' = 0.0815$.

If σ is known or if σ is unknown, but the number of observations in both groups is large, the appropriate test of mean differences between two groups is a Z-test rather than a t-test. The procedure is conceptually identical to the one just discussed.

Z-TEST FOR COMPARING TWO PROPORTIONS

What type of statistical comparison can be made when the observed statistics are proportions? A researcher may wish to test a hypothesis that the proportion of engineers in the research laboratory exposed to a management-by-objectives (MBO) program will differ from the proportion of accounting personnel exposed to an MBO program. Testing the null hypothesis that the population proportion for Group 1 (π_1) equals the population proportion for Group 2 (π_2) is conceptually the same as the t-test of two means.

Again, sample size is the appropriate criterion when selecting either a t-test or a Z-test. This section illustrates a **Z-test for difference of proportions**, which requires a sample size greater than 30.

Our hypothesis, which is:

$$H_0: \pi_1 = \pi_2$$

may be restated as:

$$H_0: \pi_1 - \pi_2 = 0$$

The comparison between the observed *sample proportions p_1 and p_2* allows the researcher to ask whether the differences from two large random samples occurred due to chance alone. To test a Z-test statistic, we use the following formula:

$$Z = \frac{(p_1 - p_2) - (\pi_1 - \pi_2)}{S_{p_1 - p_2}}$$

where

p_1 = sample proportion of successes in Group 1
p_2 = sample proportion of successes in Group 2
$(\pi_1 - \pi_2)$ = hypothesized population proportion 1 minus hypothesized population proportion 2
$S_{p_1 - p_2}$ = pooled estimate of the standard error of difference of proportions

STATISTICAL TUTOR
A Z-Test for Difference of Proportions

The situation:

The proportion of respondents in a survey of top executives (n = 50) with an annual income of $140,000 or over was 10 percent. A follow-up check of nonrespondents indicated the proportion of nonrespondents with an income over $140,000 was 21 percent.

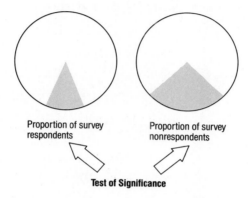

Proportion of survey
respondents

Proportion of survey
nonrespondents

Test of Significance

Questions to be answered:

1. Is the difference in proportion of those with incomes over $140,000 between survey respondents and survey non-respondents statistically significant?
2. If the difference is statistically significant, is the magnitude of this difference large enough to distort the representativeness of the survey?

Normally the value of $(\pi_1 - \pi_2)$ is expected to be 0. So this formula is actually much simpler than it looks at first inspection.

To calculate the standard error of the difference of proportions:

$$S_{p_1 - p_2} = \sqrt{\bar{p}\bar{q}\left(\frac{1}{n_1} + \frac{1}{n_2}\right)}$$

where

$\bar{p}$ = pooled estimate of proportion of success in a sample of both groups

$\bar{q}$ = $(1 - \bar{p})$ or a pooled estimate of proportion of failures in a sample of both groups

n_1 = sample size for Group 1

n_2 = sample size for Group 2

Because π under the null hypothesis is unknown, a weighted average of the sample proportion ($\bar{p}$) is calculated. To calculate the pooled estimator, $\bar{p}$:

$$\bar{p} = \frac{n_1 p_1 + n_2 p_2}{n_1 + n_2}$$

Suppose the survey data were as follows:

Engineers	Accountants
$p_1 = .35$	$p_2 = 40$
$n_1 = 100$	$n_2 = 100$

First, the standard error of the difference of proportions is:

$$S_{p_1 - p_2} = \sqrt{\bar{p}\bar{q}\left(\frac{1}{n_1} + \frac{1}{n_2}\right)}$$

$$= \sqrt{(.375)(.625)\left(\frac{1}{100} + \frac{1}{100}\right)}$$

$$= .068$$

where

$$\bar{p} = \frac{(100)(.35) + (100)(.40)}{100 + 100} = .375$$

If we wish to test the two-tailed hypothesis of no difference, an observed Z-value must be calculated. Thus:

$$Z = \frac{(p_1 - p_2) - (\pi_1 - \pi_2)}{S_{p_1 - p_2}}$$

$$= \frac{(.35 - .40) - (0)}{.068}$$

$$= -.73$$

In this example we accept the null hypothesis of no difference at the .05 level because the calculated Z-value is less than the critical Z-value of 1.96.

ANALYSIS OF VARIANCE (ANOVA)

When the means of more than two groups or populations are to be compared, one-way **analysis of variance (ANOVA)** is the appropriate statistical tool. This bivariate statistical technique is referred to as "one-way" because there is only one independent variable (even though there may be several levels of that variable).[5] An example of an ANOVA problem is to compare women who are working full time outside the home, part time outside the home, and not employed outside the home on their willingness to purchase a personal computer. Here there is *one* independent variable—working status. The independent variable, working status, is said to have three levels: full-time employment,

STATISTICAL TUTOR
Analysis of Variance

The situation:

An experiment is conducted with four groups. Each group receives a different written instruction for performing a task, and the average productivity for each group is recorded.

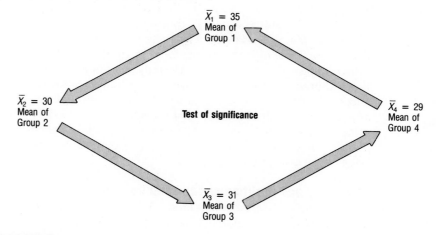

Questions to be answered:

1. **Are the differences among the four groups statistically significant?**
2. **Is the magnitude of difference between Group 1 and Group 4 large enough to justify a differential strategy?**

part-time employment, and not working outside the home. Because there are three groups (levels), a t-test cannot be used for the testing of statistical significance.

If we have three groups or three levels of the independent variable, the null hypothesis is stated as follows:

$$\mu_1 = \mu_2 = \mu_3$$

The null hypothesis is that all the means are equal. In the personal computer example, we are concerned with the average purchasing intention of three different types of women. As the name *analysis of variance* suggests, the problem requires comparing variances to make inferences about the means. The logic of this technique is as follows. The variance of the means of the three groups will be large if these women differ from each other in terms of purchasing intentions. If we calculate this variance within groups and compare it to the variance of the group means about a grand mean, we can determine if the means are significantly different. This will become clearer as we investigate the F-test.

F-Test

The **F-test** is a procedure for comparing one sample variance to another sample variance. (The principle is similar to the chi-square test, where a sample variance is compared to a population variance.) The F-test determines whether there is more variability in the scores of one sample than in the scores of another sample. The key question is whether the two sample variances are different from each other or are from the same population.

The F-test utilizes measures of sample variance rather than the sample standard deviation because standard deviations cannot be summed. Summation is allowable with the sample variance.

To obtain the **F-statistic** (or F-ratio), the larger sample variance is divided by the smaller sample variance. To test the null hypothesis of no difference between the sample variances, a table of the F-distribution is necessary. Using Table 5 (or Table 6) in the Appendix is much like using the tables of the Z- and t-distributions that we have previously examined. This table portrays the F-distribution, which is a probability distribution of the ratios of sample variances. This table of F-distributions indicates that the distribution of F is actually a family of distributions that changes quite drastically with changes in sample sizes. Thus degrees of freedom must be specified. Inspection of an F-table allows the researcher to determine the probability of finding an F as large as the calculated F.

Identifying and Partitioning the Total Variation

In the analysis-of-variance situation, the basic consideration for the F-test is to identify the total variation. There will be two forms of variation: (1) variation of scores due to random error or within-group variation due to individual differences, and (2) systematic variation of scores between the groups due to the manipulation of an independent variable or due to characteristics of the independent variable. Thus we can partition total variance into *with-group variance* and *between-group variance*.

The F-distribution is the ratio of these two sources of variances. That is, F is defined as:

$$F = \frac{\text{Variance between groups}}{\text{Variance within groups}}$$

The larger the ratio of variance between groups to variance within groups, the greater the value of F. If the F-value is large, it is likely that the results are statistically significant.

Calculation of the F-Ratio

The data in Table 20.7 represent a hypothetical packaged-goods company's test-market experiment on pricing. Three pricing treatments are administered in four separate areas (that is, 12 test areas, A–L, were required). These data will be used to illustrate ANOVA.

Terminology for the variance estimates is derived from the calculation procedures. An explanation of the terms used to calculate the F-ratio should

TABLE   20.7

**A Test Market
Experiment
on Pricing**

	Sales in Units (000)		
	Regular Price 99¢	Reduced Price 89¢	Cents-off Coupon Regular Price
Test Market A, B, or C	130	145	153
Test Market D, E, or F	118	143	129
Test Market G, H, or I	87	120	96
Test Market J, K, or L	84	131	99
Mean	$\bar{X}_1 = 104.75$	$\bar{X}_2 = 134.75$	$\bar{X}_3 = 119.25$
Grand mean	$\bar{\bar{X}} = 119.58$		

clarify the meaning of the analysis of variance. The calculation of the F-ratio requires that we partition the total variation into two parts:

$$\text{Total sum of squares} = \frac{\text{Within-group}}{\text{sum of squares}} + \frac{\text{Between-group}}{\text{sum of squares}}$$

or

$$SS_{total} = SS_{within} + SS_{between}$$

The total sum of squares or SS_{total} is computed by squaring the deviation of each score from the grand mean and summing these squares:[6]

$$SS_{total} = \sum_{i=1}^{n} \sum_{j=1}^{c} (X_{ij} - \bar{\bar{X}})^2$$

where

X_{ij} = individual score, i.e., the ith observation or test unit in the jth group
$\bar{\bar{X}}$ = grand mean
n = number of all observations or test units in a group
c = number of jth groups (or columns)

In our example:

$$\begin{aligned}
SS_{total} = {} & (130 - 119.58)^2 + (118 - 119.58)^2 + (87 - 119.58)^2 \\
& + (84 - 119.58)^2 + (145 - 119.58)^2 + (143 - 119.58)^2 \\
& + (120 - 119.58)^2 + (131 - 119.58)^2 + (153 - 119.58)^2 \\
& + (129 - 119.58)^2 + (96 - 119.58)^2 + (99 - 119.58)^2 \\
= {} & 5948.93
\end{aligned}$$

SS_{within}, the variability that we observe within each group, is calculated by squaring the deviation of each score from its group mean and summing these scores:

$$SS_{within} = \sum_{i=1}^{n} \sum_{j=1}^{c} (X_{ij} - \bar{X}_j)^2$$

where

$$X_{ij} = \text{individual score}$$
$$\overline{X}_j = \text{group mean for the ith group}$$
$$n = \text{number of observations in a group}$$
$$c = \text{number of jth groups}$$

In our example:

$$
\begin{aligned}
SS_{within} = {} & (130 - 104.75)^2 + (118 - 104.75)^2 + (87 - 104.75)^2 \\
& + (84 - 104.75)^2 + (145 - 134.75)^2 + (143 - 134.75)^2 \\
& + (120 - 134.75)^2 + (131 - 134.75)^2 + (153 - 119.25)^2 \\
& + (129 - 119.25)^2 + (96 - 119.25)^2 + (99 - 119.25)^2 \\
= {} & 4148.25
\end{aligned}
$$

The sum of squares, between which is the variability of the group means about a grand mean, is calculated by squaring the deviation of each group mean from the grand mean:

$$SS_{between} = \sum_{j=1}^{c} n_j (\overline{X}_j - \overline{\overline{X}})^2$$

where

$$\overline{X}_j = \text{group mean}$$
$$\overline{\overline{X}} = \text{grand mean}$$
$$n_j = \text{number of items in jth group}$$

In our example:

$$
\begin{aligned}
SS_{between} = {} & 4(104.75 - 119.58)^2 + 4(134.75 - 119.58)^2 \\
& + 4(119.25 - 119.58)^2 \\
= {} & 1800.68
\end{aligned}
$$

The next calculation requires dividing the various sums of squares by their appropriate degrees of freedom. The result of these divisions produces the variances, or *mean squares*.

To obtain the mean square between groups, $SS_{between}$ is divided by $c - 1$ degrees of freedom:

$$MS_{between} = \frac{SS_{between}}{c - 1}$$

In our example:

$$MS_{between} = \frac{1800.68}{3 - 1} = \frac{1800.68}{2} = 900.34$$

To obtain the mean square within groups, SS_{within} is divided by $cn - c$ degrees of freedom:

$$MS_{within} = \frac{SS_{within}}{cn - c}$$

In our example:

$$MS_{within} = \frac{4148.25}{12 - 3} = \frac{4148.25}{9} = 460.91$$

Finally, the F-ratio is calculated by taking the ratio of the mean square between groups to the mean square within groups. The between-groups mean square is used as the numerator and the within-groups mean square is used as the denominator:

$$F = \frac{MS_{between}}{MS_{within}}$$

In our example:

$$F = \frac{900.34}{460.91} = 1.95$$

There will be $(c - 1)$ degrees of freedom in the numerator and $(cn - c)$ degrees of freedom in the denominator:

$$\frac{c - 1}{cn - c} \quad \text{or} \quad \frac{3 - 1}{3(4) - 3} = \frac{2}{9}$$

In Table 5 in the Appendix, the critical value of F at the .05 level for 2 and 9 degrees of freedom indicates an F of 4.26 would be required to reject the null hypothesis.

In our example we conclude that we cannot reject the null hypothesis. It appears that all the price treatments produce approximately the same sales volume.

The information produced from an analysis of variance is traditionally summarized in table form. Tables 20.8 and 20.9 summarize the formulas and data from our example.

T A B L E   2 0 . 8

Summary for Analysis of Variance

Source of Variation	Sum of Squares	Degrees of Freedom	Mean Square	F-Ratio
Between groups	$SS_{between}$ or $\sum_{j=1}^{c} n_j(\bar{X}_j - \bar{\bar{X}})^2$	$c - 1$	$MS_{between}$ or $\dfrac{SS_{between}}{c - 1}$	—
Error within groups	SS_{within} or $\sum_{i=1}^{n}\sum_{j=1}^{c}(X_{ij} - \bar{X}_j)^2$	$cn - c$	MS_{within} or $\dfrac{SS_{within}}{cn - c}$	$F \doteq \dfrac{MS_{between}}{MS_{within}}$
Total	SS_{total} or $\sum_{i=1}^{n}\sum_{j=1}^{c}(X_{ij} - \bar{\bar{X}})^2$	$cn - 1$	—	—

where c = number of groups
n = number of observations in a group

Source of Variation	Sum of Squares	Degrees of Freedom	Mean Square	F-Ratio
Between groups	1800.68	2	900.34	—
Within groups	4148.25	9	460.91	1.953
Total	5948.93	11		

Appendix 20B at the end of this chapter provides additional information on analysis of variance in complex experimental designs.

SUMMARY

Bivariate statistical techniques analyze scores on two variables at a time. Tests of differences investigate hypotheses stating that two (or more) groups are different with respect to a certain behavior, characteristic, or attitude. Both the type of measurement and the number of groups to be compared influence researchers' choice of the type of statistical test of differences.

The chi-square statistic allows the testing of whether an observed sample distribution fits some given distribution. It can be used to analyze contingency, or cross-tabulation, tables. In this case the test allows determination of whether two groups are independent. If they are not, then the variables are interrelated. For example, a business researcher may wish to determine if the respondent's sex makes a difference for some observed variable. The t-test for two independent samples is used to determine if the means of two independent samples are significantly different. An example would be the comparison of two populations' characteristics using the same measure of an attribute on samples from each population.

The t-test is appropriate when the population standard deviation is unknown. The t-test should be chosen over the Z-test if the sample size is small. A Z-test for two independent samples is typically used if a large sample has been drawn from each group, because the t-distribution approximates the Z-distribution when a sample is large. A Z-test for two independent samples may be used to determine if two proportions are significantly different.

One-way analysis of variance (ANOVA) compares the means of samples from more than two populations to determine if their differences are statistically significant. The technique is one-way because it deals with only one independent variable, although several levels of that variable may be used. The total variance in the observations is partitioned into two parts, that from within-group variation and that from between-group variation. The ratio of the variance between groups to the variance within groups gives an F-statistic. The F-distribution is a measure used to determine whether the variability of two samples differs significantly. In ANOVA, if the observed statistic is greater than the test value for some level of significance, the hypothesis that there is no significant difference in the means of the sample groups may be rejected.

Key Terms

bivariate statistical analysis

tests of differences

chi-square test for contingency tables

t-test for difference of means

pooled estimate of the standard error

Z-test for differences of proportions

analysis of variance (ANOVA)

F-test

F-statistic

total variance

between-group variance

within-group variance

Questions

1. What test of differences is appropriate in each of the following situations?
    a.   Average campaign contributions of Democrats, Republicans, and independents are to be compared.
    b.   Managers and supervisors respond "yes," "no," or "not sure" to an attitude question. Their answers are to be compared.
    c.   One-half of a sample receives an incentive in a mail survey. The other half does not. A comparison of response rates is desired.
    d.   Stockbrokers in the East, Midwest, and West were asked their annual incomes. Regional comparisons are to be made.
2. Perform a chi-square test on the following data:

a.

Regulation Best Way to Ensure Safe Workplace	Managers	Blue-Collar Workers
Agree	58	66
Disagree	34	24
No opinion	8	10
Totals	100	100

b.

Ownership of Residence	Male	Female
Yes	25	16
No	7	8
Totals	32	24

c.

Age of Shopper	Store A	Store B
20–34	27	73
35–54	31	82
55 and over	11	93
Totals	69	248

3. Collapse the response categories in the following table so that it meets the assumption of the chi-square test. Then perform the test.

	Ownership	
Education	Owners	Nonowners
Less than Grade 8	0	8
Some high school	5	9
High school graduate	30	25
Some college	10	11
College graduate	12	15
Master's degree	3	6
Ph.D. degree	2	1

4. Interpret the SPSSX computer output for the chi-square test below. Variable F7 is "How did you get to work last week?" Variable E6 is "Do you have a college degree?"

SPSS Test Run on State Data
File   State Survey
Cross-Tabulation of How Did You Get to Work Last Week?
by E6. Have College Degree

Count	E6		
Row percent	Yes	No	Row
Column percent			Total
Total percent	1.	2.	
	159	248	407
F7	39.1	60.9	78.6
Driver 1.	74.0	81.8	
	30.7	47.9	
	15	19	34
	44.1	55.9	6.6
Passenger 2.	7.0	6.3	
	2.9	3.7	
	5	4	9
	55.6	44.4	1.7
Bus 3.	2.3	1.3	
	1.0	0.8	
	13	6	19
	68.4	31.6	3.7
Walked 6.	6.0	2.0	
	2.5	1.2	
	9	19	28
	32.1	67.9	5.4
At home 7.	4.2	6.3	
	1.7	3.7	
	14	7	21
	66.7	33.3	4.1
Other 8.	6.5	2.3	
	2.7	1.4	
Column	215	303	518
Total	41.5	58.5	100.0

Chi-square = 13.98101 with 5 degrees of freedom
    significance = 0.0157
Number of missing observations = 2,197

5. A personnel manager has a computerized list of all employees that indicates 70 percent are full-time employees, 20 percent are part-time employees, and 10 percent are furloughed or laid-off employees. A sample of

50 employees from the list indicates 40 full-time employees, 6 part-time employees, and 4 furloughed/laid-off employees. Conduct a statistical test to determine if the sample is representative of the population.

6. Test the hypothesis of no differences for average payback period (years) necessary to justify solar systems for residences.

Savings and Loans	Other Financiers
$\bar{X}_1 = 8.7$	$\bar{X}_2 = 7.7$
$S_1^2 = 0.5$	$S_2^2 = 0.6$
$n_1 = 100$	$n_2 = 64$

7. The managers in a company's East and West regions were rated on the basis of the company's evaluation system. A researcher wishes to conduct a t-test of means to determine if there is a difference between the East and West regions. Perform this calculation.

Region	Manager	Rating	Region	Manager	Rating
West	1	74	East	1	81
West	2	88	East	2	63
West	3	78	East	3	56
West	4	85	East	4	68
West	5	100	East	5	80
West	6	114	East	6	79
West	7	98	East	7	69

8. Given the following data, is there a difference between means?

	Sample 1	Sample 2
Sample mean	324	301
Sample variance	166.41	81
Sample size	44	56

9. A sales force (n = 67) received some management-by-objectives training. Are the before-after mean scores for salespeople's job performance statistically significant at the .05 level?

Skill	Before	After	t
Planning ability	4.84	5.43	4.88
Territory coverage	5.24	5.51	1.89
Activity reporting	5.37	5.42	0.27

10. The incomes of owners of trash compactors were compared with the incomes of nonowners. The average income was as follows:

	Owners	Nonowners
$\bar{X}$	4.6	3.5

Higher values represent higher levels of income. (Actual scaled average; scale is less than \$7,500 = 1, \$7,500–\$20,000 = 2, \$20,000–\$35,000 = 3, \$35,000–50,000 = 4, \$50,000–80,000 = 5, greater than \$80,000 = 6.) Is a t-test appropriate?

11. Test the hypothesis of no difference for the following two groups on credit union usage:

Women under 35	Women 35–54
$P_1 = 13\%$	$P_2 = 23\%$
$S_p = .04$	$S_p = .04$
$n = 144$	$n = 169$

12. Conduct a Z-test to determine if the following two samples indicate the population proportions are significantly different at the .05 level:

	Sample 1	Sample 2
Sample proportion	.77	.68
Sample size	55	46

13. Interpret the t-test results below. Are they statistically significant?

GROUP 1: E2 EQ 1.00
GROUP 2: E2 NE 1.00

VARIABLE	GRP	N	MEAN	STD DEV	STD ERR
D2	1	935	2.282	1.406	.046
	2	529	2.297	1.525	.066

SEPARATE VARIANCE

VARIABLE	MEAN	STD ERR	DIFFERENCE T	DF	PROB
D2	−.014	.081	−.18	1024	.858

POOLED VARIANCE

VARIABLE	MEAN	STD ERR	DIFFERENCE T	DF	PROB
D2	−.014	.079	−.18	1462	.855

14. Suppose a researcher has one nominally scaled variable and one interval-scaled variable. The researcher wishes to use a chi-square test. What can be done?

15. An organizational researcher conducts an experiment to measure perception of task difficulty and level of aspiration for performing the task a second time. Group 1 was told the task was very difficult, Group 2 was told the task was somewhat difficult but attainable, and Group 3 was told the task was easy. Perform an ANOVA on the following data:

Subjects' Level of Aspiration (10-point scale):

Subject	Group 1	Group 2	Group 3
1	6	5	5
2	7	4	6
3	5	7	5
4	8	6	4
5	8	7	2
6	6	7	3
Cases	6	6	6

16. A researcher was concerned with the characteristics of the clientele at a Hard Rock Cafe at lunchtime and in the evenings. On a Saturday in July the researcher collected the following age data by randomly sampling table numbers at the cafe and then obtaining the age of everyone sitting at the table.

	Lunch		**Evening**
Table 1	11	Table 1	26
	9		26
	43		27
	39		28
Table 2	40	Table 2	21
	42		23
	13		21
	9		
Table 3	12	Table 3	24
	13		24
	44		23
	47		
Table 4	44	Table 4	24
	10		22
	12		21
	11		24
Table 5	9	Table 5	22
	39		23
	46		27
	11		
Table 6	32	Table 6	22
	9		18
Table 7	39	Table 7	22
	13		19
	11		
Table 8	43	Table 8	23
	5		24
	12		24
Total number of people	28		25

How would you analyze the differences between the evening and the lunchtime clientele? Perform the statistical analysis that you conclude is the best.

References

[1] Richard L. Daft, *Management* (Hinsdale, Il: Dryden Press, 1988), p. 24–25.

[2] This example is adapted from R. Dennis Middlemist, *Client Oriented Effectiveness Evaluation* (Stillwater, OK: Native American Manpower Training Project, 1977), 28–37. A report performed pursuant to contract 99-6-78-36-141 with the Division of Indian and Native Programs, Department of Labor, Employment and Training Administration, Washington, DC 20213.

[3] Three nonparametric tests, the Wilcoxon matched-pairs signed-ranks test, the Kruskal-Wallis test, and the Mann-Whitney U test, and Anova for complex experimental designs are covered in the appendixes to this chapter.

[4] Fred N. Kerlinger, *Behavioral Research: A Conceptual Approach* (New York: Holt, Rinehart and Winston, 1979), 313.

[5] A one-way analysis of variance may also be referred to as a *single-factor analysis of variance* because only one variable (factor) is manipulated.

[6] At first, $\sum_{i=1}^{n} \sum_{j=1}^{c}$ looks complicated. Our example shows that the procedure is not difficult, but it does require that each observation within a group (n) is summed up, then these totals be summed for all groups (c).

Nonparametric Statistics for Tests of Differences

For many of the statistical tests you have learned to use, it has been necessary to assume that the population (or sampling distribution) is normally distributed.[1] If it is normal, the error made in making inferences about the population from sample data can be estimated. But if it is not normal, the error may be large and cannot be estimated. It is therefore valuable to know some tests in which such a strong assumption as normality does not need to be made about the population distribution; these are called *nonparametric* tests. You have already studied one of them: the χ^2 test. There are many others, but only three of them are included here.

The term *nonparametric* is confusing. It was originally applied when no assumption needed to be made about the population distribution (as in the χ^2 tests) and when there was no estimate of a population parameter. Almost always, however, some assumption needs to be made. So *nonparametric* is now used to mean that a less stringent requirement than normality is made for the population distribution. Also, the meaning of the phrase *nonparametric test* has been extended to include any test that uses nominal-scaled or ordinal-scaled data. Thus a comparison of the heights of two samples of women is made with a nonparametric test if, instead of measuring each person's height, all the women are simply arranged in order of height in a row (the two tallest come from Sample 1, the third tallest comes from Sample 2, and so on). Then, because the data are ranked and not ratio- or interval-scaled, a nonparametric test is used—even if it is known that the heights in both populations from which the samples were chosen are normally distributed.

Nonparametric tests have many advantages: The error caused by assuming a population is normally distributed when it is not is avoided; the computations that need to be made are often very simple; and the data may be easier to collect (almost certainly so when categorical or ranked rather than ratio- or interval-scaled). Why are nonparametric tests not always used, then? The answer is that you don't get something for nothing. If the population distribution is normal, so that, say, a t-test or a nonparametric test may be chosen, the former will generally give a smaller value of β *Type II* error (i.e., a smaller error) than the latter for a given, fixed level of *Type I* error (value of α). If this is the case, sample size will have to be larger for the nonparametric test if the same limits on α and β are to be attained as with a t-test. For the same sample size, then, the t-test results usually will be more reliable. Also, the null hypotheses are sometimes more general; rejection may imply "two population distributions are different," but it is not known whether they have different means, different variances, or different shaped distributions (e.g., one normal and the other not).

WILCOXON MATCHED-PAIRS SIGNED-RANKS TEST

The *Wilcoxon matched-pairs signed-ranks test* is a good measure of differences when the researcher wishes to test the hypothesis $\mu_1 = \mu_2$ and the researcher knows that the samples are not independent, or when the researcher wishes to compare magnitude of differences in ordinal rankings, such as preference ratings between two alternatives. A common situation is the "before/after" experiment, where the same subjects are measured twice.

Suppose a manager wishes to know if a training program will have a positive impact on attitude toward advancement within the organization. Table 20A.1 shows attitude ratings before and after a training program for 11 managers. The Wilcoxon matched-pairs signed-ranks test begins by calculating the signed difference for each matched pair of observations. If the two observations in a pair of observations are the same, this pair is dropped from the analysis. Next, these differences are rank-ordered according to their absolute size. If there are two (or more) pairs with identical absolute-difference values, such as for Manager 2 and Manager 9, an average rank score is given to each of the pairs. Finally, the positive or negative sign is assigned to the rank scores, and the scores for the positive and negative groups are separately totaled. The symbol T_p is the summed ranks for the positive differences, and the symbol T_n is the summed ranks for the negative differences.[2] T represents the *smaller* of T_p or T_n, and for small samples T is the test statistic.

In our example T_n has the smaller value. Thus the calculated value of T is 17. In the Wilcoxon matched-pairs signed-ranks test, the null hypothesis is rejected if the calculated value of T is *equal to or less than* the critical T-value that can be found in Table 8 in the Appendix of Statistical Tables at the end of the book. In that table N represents the number of pairs. At N = 10 (because the tied pair is discarded from the analysis) the critical T-value is 8 at the .05 level of statistical significance. Because the calculated value of T (17) is greater than 8, we cannot reject the null hypothesis. When the sample size is large, the sampling distribution is approximately normal, and the Z-value may be calculated using the following formula:

$$Z = \frac{T - \dfrac{N(N + 1)}{4}}{\sqrt{\dfrac{N(N + 1)(2N + 1)}{24}}}$$

T A B L E   2 0 A . 1   **Training Program Example**

Manager	"Before" Score	"After" Score	Sign of Difference	Absolute Difference	Rank	Signed Rank Position	Negative
1	56	71	+	15	10	10	
2	46	49	+	3	3.5	3.5	
3	74	73	−	1	1		1
4	66	72	+	6	8	8	
5	59	55	−	4	5.5		5.5
6	45	40	−	5	7		7
7	85	87	+	2	2	2	
8	63	67	+	4	5.5	5.5	
9	67	66	−	3	3.5		3.5
10	79	79		0	—	—	—
11	70	78	+	8	9	9	
						$T_p = 38$	$T_n = 17$

MANN-WHITNEY TEST

Many tests of group differences concern comparing two sample means to determine if there is a statistically significant difference between the two population means. The Mann-Whitney (or ranked sum) test allows for testing group differences when the populations are not normally distributed or when it cannot be assumed that the samples are from populations that are equal in variability. It is an alternative to the t-test for two independent samples.

To illustrate how this test is used, consider the following data on the number of minutes needed by two groups of factory workers to learn to assemble a chain saw.[3] Group A received classroom training, whereas Group B received only on-the-job training.

		Average
Group A	35, 39, 51, 63, 48, 31, 29, 41, 55	43.56
Group B	85, 28, 42, 37, 61, 54, 36, 57	50

The means of these two samples are 43.56 and 50. In this case we wish to decide whether the difference between the means is significant.

The two samples are arranged jointly, as if they were one sample, in order of increasing time, and we get the rank-sum test:

Time	Group	Rank
28	B	1
29	A	2
31	A	3
35	A	4
36	B	5
37	B	6
39	A	7
41	A	8
42	B	9

Time	Group	Rank
48	A	10
51	A	11
54	B	12
55	A	13
57	B	14
61	B	15
63	A	16
85	B	17

We indicate each value, whether it belongs to Group A or to Group B. Then we assign the ranks 1, 2, 3, 4, . . . , 17 to the scores, in this order, as shown.

Notice that the Group A scores occupy the ranks of 2, 3, 4, 7, 8, 10, 11, 13, and 16. The Group B scores occupy the ranks of 1, 5, 6, 9, 12, 14, 15, and 17. Now we sum the ranks of the group with the smaller sample size, in this case Group B, and get:

$$1 + 5 + 6 + 9 + 12 + 14 + 15 + 17 = 79$$

The sum of the ranks is denoted by R. In this case R = 79.

We always let n_1 and n_2 denote the sizes of the two samples, where n_1 represents the smaller of the two sample sizes. Thus R represents the sum of the ranks of this smaller group. If both groups are of equal size, then either one is called n, and R represents the sum of the ranks of this group. Statistical theory tells us that if both n_1 and n_2 are large enough, each equal to 8 or more, then the distribution of R can be approximated by a normal distribution. The test statistic is given by the formula:

$$Z = \frac{R - \mu_R}{\sigma_R}$$

where

$$\mu_R = \frac{n_1(n_1 + n_2 + 1)}{2} \quad \text{and} \quad \sigma_R = \sqrt{\frac{n_1 n_2(n_1 + n_2 + 1)}{12}}$$

In our case R = 79, n_1 = 8, and n_2 = 9, so that

$$\mu_R = \frac{n_1(n_1 + n_2 + 1)}{2}$$

$$= \frac{8(8 + 9 + 1)}{2}$$

$$= 72$$

and

$$\sigma_R = \sqrt{\frac{n_1 n_2(n_1 + n_2 + 1)}{12}}$$

$$= \sqrt{\frac{8(9)(8 + 9 + 1)}{12}} = \sqrt{108}$$

$$= 10.39$$

The test statistic then becomes

$$Z = \frac{R - \mu_R}{\sigma_R} = \frac{79 - 72}{10.39} = 0.67$$

Using a .05 level of significance, we reject the null hypothesis of equal means if $Z > 1.96$ or $Z < -1.96$. Since the value of $Z = 0.67$ falls in the acceptance region, we do not reject the null hypothesis. There is no significant difference between the means of these two groups.

Comment.   The method that we have just described is called the *Mann-Whitney* test. Statisticians have constructed tables that give the appropriate critical values when both sample sizes, n_1 and n_2, are smaller than 8. The interested reader can find such tables in many books on nonparametric statistics. The corresponding exact statistic is called the *Mann-Whitney U test*.

THE KRUSKAL-WALLIS TEST FOR SEVERAL INDEPENDENT SAMPLES

When a researcher wishes to compare three or more groups or populations and the data are ordinal, the Kruskal-Wallis test is the appropriate statistical technique. This test may be thought of as a nonparametric equivalent of analysis of variance. However, as with all nonparametric tests, the assumptions are less restricting: The researcher does not have to assume that the underlined populations are normally distributed or that equal variances are shared by each group. If there are three groups, the null hypothesis is that Population 1 equals Population 2, which equals Population 3. In other words, the Kruskal-Wallis test is a technique to determine if the three populations have the same distribution shape and dispersion.

The test requires that the data be ranked from lowest to highest or that the original data be converted so that a numerical rank may be assigned to every observation. If two observations are ranked the same (i.e., when ties occur), the mean rank score is assigned to both of the observations. To illustrate the calculation of the H-statistic, consider the following example. An advertising agency employs three different film production companies to produce its television commercials. The advertising agency has taken a sample of five commercials from each of the production houses, and agency executives have ranked the production quality of the commercials from best quality (1) to lowest quality (15). These ranks are shown in Table 20A.2.

Notice that the advertising agency considered two commercials to be ranked of equal quality. Hence, rather than being ranked a 3 and a 4, the two commercials are each ranked 3.5.

The Kruskal-Wallis test statistic is the H-statistic and is calculated as follows:

$$H = \frac{12}{n(n + 1)}\left[\Sigma\frac{R_i^2}{n_i}\right] - 3(n + 1)$$

	Rank	
Production Company 1	**Production Company 2**	**Production Company 3**
9	6	1
5	13	7
3.5	10	15
14	2	12
8	3.5	11
$R_1 = 39.5$	$R_2 = 34.5$	$R_3 = 46$

where

R_i = sum of the ranks of the ith group
n_i = sample size of the ith group
n = combined sample sizes of all groups

$$H = \frac{12}{n(n + 1)}\left(\frac{R_1^2}{n_1} + \frac{R_2^2}{n_2} + \frac{R_3^2}{n_3}\right) - 3(n + 1)$$

$$= \frac{12}{15(15 + 1)}\left[\frac{(39.4)^2}{5} + \frac{(34.5)^2}{5} + \frac{(46)^2}{5}\right] - 3(15 + 1)$$

$$= \frac{12}{240}\left(\frac{2560.25}{5} + \frac{1190.25}{5} + \frac{2116}{5}\right) - 48$$

$$= .05(973.3) - 48$$

$$= 48.665 - 48$$

$$= 0.665$$

When the sample size (n_i) from each group or population exceeds four observations, the H is approximately the same as the χ^2 with degrees of freedom equal to $K - 1$, where K equals the number of groups.

In our example degrees of freedom equals 2 (3 − 1). Table 4 in the Appendix shows that the critical value at the .05 level with two degrees of freedom is 5.991. Since the calculated H-value is .665, we cannot reject the null hypothesis.

References

[1] This section is reprinted with minor adaptations from Norma Gilbert, *Statistics* (Philadelphia: Saunders College Publishing, 1931), 380–381.

[2] If a completely random relationship between the observations in each pair exists, the values of T_p and T_n are expected to be equal.

[3] This example is modified from Joseph Newmark, *Statistics and Probability in Modern Life,* 2d ed. (New York: Holt, Rinehart and Winston, Inc., 1977), pp. 434–436.

ANOVA for Complex Experimental Designs

ANOVA FOR A RANDOMIZED BLOCK DESIGN

To test for statistical significance in a randomized block design (mentioned in Chapter 10), another version of analysis of variance is utilized. The linear model for the randomized block design for an individual observation is:[1]

$$Y_{ij} = \mu + \alpha_j + \beta_i + \epsilon_{ij}$$

where

Y_{ij} = individual observation on the dependent variable
μ = grand mean
α_j = jth treatment effect
β_i = ith block effect
ϵ_{ij} = random error or residual

The statistical objective is to determine if significant differences among treatment means and block means exist. This will be done by calculating an F-ratio for each source of effects.

The same logic and assumptions that apply in single-factor ANOVA, to use variance estimates to test for differences among means, also apply in the ANOVA for randomized block designs (see Chapter 20). Thus, to conduct the ANOVA, the total sum of squares (SS_{total}) is partitioned into nonoverlapping components.[2]

$$SS_{total} = SS_{treatments} + SS_{blocks} + SS_{error}$$

The various sources of variance are defined below:

- Total sum of squares:

$$SS_{total} = \sum_{i=1}^{r} \sum_{j=1}^{c} (Y_{ij} - \bar{\bar{Y}})^2$$

where

Y_{ij} = individual observation
$\bar{\bar{Y}}$ = grand mean

$$r = \text{number of blocks (rows)}$$
$$c = \text{number of treatments (columns)}$$

- Treatment sum of squares:

$$SS_{treatments} = \sum_{i=1}^{r} \sum_{j=1}^{c} (\overline{Y}_j - \overline{\overline{Y}})^2$$

where

$$\overline{Y}_j = \text{jth treatment mean}$$
$$\overline{\overline{Y}} = \text{grand mean}$$

- Block sum of squares:

$$SS_{blocks} = \sum_{i=1}^{r} \sum_{j=1}^{c} (\overline{Y}_i - \overline{\overline{Y}})^2$$

where

$$\overline{Y}_i = \text{ith block mean}$$
$$\overline{\overline{Y}} = \text{grand mean}$$

- Sum of squares error:

$$SS_{error} = \sum_{i=1}^{r} \sum_{j=1}^{c} (Y_{ij} - \overline{Y}_i - \overline{Y}_j + \overline{\overline{Y}})^2$$

The SS_{error} may also be calculated in the following manner:

$$SS_{error} = SS_{total} - SS_{treatments} - SS_{blocks}$$

The degrees of freedom for $SS_{treatments}$ are equal to $c - 1$ because $SS_{treatments}$ reflects dispersion of treatment means from the grand mean, which is fixed. Degrees of freedom for blocks are $r - 1$ for similar reasons. SS_{error} reflects variations from both treatment and block means; thus d.f. $= (r - 1)(c - 1)$.

Mean squares are calculated by dividing the appropriate sum of squares by the corresponding degrees of freedom.

Table 20B.1 is an ANOVA table for the randomized block design. It summarizes what has been discussed and illustrates the calculation of mean squares.

T A B L E   2 0 B . 1

ANOVA Table for Randomized Block Design

Source of Variation	Sum of Squares	Degrees of Freedom	Mean Squares
Between blocks	SS_{blocks}	$r - 1$	$\dfrac{SS_{blocks}}{(r - 1)}$
Between treatments	$SS_{treatments}$	$c - 1$	$\dfrac{SS_{treatments}}{(c - 1)}$
Error	SS_{error}	$(r - 1)(c - 1)$	$\dfrac{SS_{error}}{(r - 1)(c - 1)}$
Total	SS_{total}	$rc - 1$	—

F-ratios for treatment and block effects are calculated as follows:

$$F_{treatment} = \frac{\text{Mean square treatment}}{\text{Mean square error}}$$

$$F_{blocks} = \frac{\text{Mean square blocks}}{\text{Mean square error}}$$

FACTORIAL DESIGN

There is considerable similarity between the factorial design (mentioned in Chapter 10) and the one-way analysis of variance. The sum of squares for each of the treatment factors (rows and columns) is similar to the between-groups sum of squares in the single-factor model; that is, each treatment sum of squares is calculated by taking the deviation of the treatment means from the grand mean. Of course, calculating the sum of squares for the interaction is a new calculation because this source of variance is not attributable to the treatments as sum of squares or the error sum of squares.

ANOVA for a Factorial Experiment

In a two-factor experimental design the linear model for an individual observation is:

$$Y_{ijk} = \mu + \beta_i + \alpha_j + I_{ij} + \epsilon_{ijk}$$

where

Y_{ijk} = individual observation on the dependent variable
Y_{ijk} = individual observation on the dependent variable
μ = grand mean
β_i = ith effect of Factor B—row treatment
α_j = jth effect of Factor A—column treatment
I_{ij} = interaction effect of Factors A and B
ϵ_{ijk} = random error or residual

Partitioning the Sum of Squares for a Two-Way ANOVA

Again, the total sum of squares can be allocated into distinct and nonoverlapping portions:

Sum of squares total	=	Sum of squares rows (Treatment B)	+	Sum of squares columns (Treatment A)	+	Sum of squares interaction	+	Sum of squares error

or

$$SS_{total} = SSR_{Treatment\ B} + SSC_{Treatment\ A} + SS_{interaction} + SS_{error}$$

The formulas for calculation are given below. Symbol notation is summarized in Table 20B.2.

T A B L E   2 0 B . 2

**Symbol Notation for
Two-Factor ANOVA**

Y_{ijk} = individual observation on the dependent variable
$\bar{\bar{Y}}$ = grand mean
$\bar{Y}_i$ = mean of the ith treatment—Factor B
$\bar{Y}_j$ = mean of the jth treatment—Factor A
$\bar{Y}_{ij}$ = mean of the interaction effect
j = level of Factor A
i = level of Factor B
k = number of an observation in a particular cell
r = total number of levels for Factor B (rows)
c = total number of levels for Factor A (columns)
n = total number of observations in the sample

T A B L E   2 0 B . 3   **ANOVA Table for Two-Factorial Design**

Source of Variation	Sum of Squares	Degrees of Freedom	Mean Square	F-Ratio
Treatment B	$SSR_{Treatment\ B}$	$(r-1)$	$MSR_{Treatment\ B} = \dfrac{SSR_{Treatment\ B}}{r-1}$	$\dfrac{MSR_{Treatment\ B}}{MS_{error}}$
Treatment A	$SSC_{Treatment\ A}$	$(c-1)$	$MSC_{Treatment\ A} = \dfrac{SSC_{Treatment\ A}}{c-1}$	$\dfrac{MSC_{Treatment\ A}}{MS_{error}}$
Interaction	$SS_{interaction}$	$(r-1)(c-1)$	$MS_{interaction} = \dfrac{SS_{interaction}}{(r-1)(c-1)}$	$\dfrac{MS_{interaction}}{MS_{error}}$
Error	SS_{error}	$rc(n-1)$	$MS_{error} = \dfrac{SS_{interaction}}{rc(n-1)}$	
Total	SS_{total}	$rcn-1$	—	

- Sum of squares total:

$$SS_{total} = \sum_{i=1}^{r} \sum_{j=1}^{c} \sum_{k=1}^{n} (Y_{ijk} - \bar{\bar{Y}})^2$$

- Sum of squares for the row treatment—Factor B:

$$SSR_{Treatment\ B} = \sum_{i=1}^{r} (\bar{Y}_i - \bar{\bar{Y}})^2$$

- Sum of squares column treatment Factor A:

$$SSC_{Treatment\ A} = \sum_{j=1}^{c} (\bar{Y}_j - \bar{\bar{Y}})^2$$

- Sum of squares interaction, although $SS_{interaction}$ may be calculated:

$$SS_{interaction} = \sum_{i=1}^{r} \sum_{j=1}^{c} \sum_{k=1}^{n} (\bar{Y}_{ij} - \bar{Y}_i - \bar{Y}_j + \bar{\bar{Y}})^2$$

- $SS_{interaction}$ is generally indirectly computed in the following manner:

$$SS_{interaction} = SS_{total} - SSR_{Treatment\ B} - SSC_{Treatment\ A} - SS_{error}$$

- Sum of squares error:

$$SSE = \sum_{i=1}^{r} \sum_{j=1}^{c} \sum_{k=1}^{n} (Y_{ijk} - \bar{Y}_{ij})^2$$

These sums of squares are summarized in Table 20B.3 along with their respective degrees of freedom and mean squares.

References

[1] We assume no interaction effect between treatments and blocks.

[2] In the ANOVA table it is conventional to place the treatments in columns and the blocks in rows. Because of this, $SS_{treatment}$ may be referred to as $SS_{columns}$ and SS_{blocks} SS_{rows} in some research reports.

Bivariate Analysis: Measures of Association

What you will learn in this chapter:

To give examples of the types of business questions that may be answered by analyzing the association between two variables.

To list the common procedures for measuring association and to discuss how the measurement scale will influence the selection of statistical tests.

To discuss the concept of the simple correlation coefficient.

To calculate a simple correlation coefficient and a coefficient of determination.

To understand that correlation does not mean causation.

To interpret a correlation matrix.

To explain the concept of bivariate linear regression.

To identify the intercept and slope coefficients.

To discuss the least-squares method of regression analysis.

To draw a regression line.

To test the statistical significance of a least-squares regression.

To calculate the intercept and slope coefficients in a bivariate linear regression.

To interpret the analysis of variance summary tables for linear regression.

If you found a variable that has forecasted the next year's direction of the stock market with an accuracy of better than 95 percent, would you be interested in its prediction? If so, watch the Super Bowl. In the 23 Super Bowls from 1967 to 1989, 22 out of 23 times the market rose by year-end when a team from the original NFL won the championship or fell by year-end when a team from the old American Football League (now the NFL's American football conference) won the championship. The value of stock market indexes are associated with the football league winning the Super Bowl. Most likely, this is mere coincidence, but many investors root for teams from the original NFL.

Many business questions are concerned with the association between two (or more) variables. Questions such as "Is the prime interest rate associated with federal deficit spending?" "What is the relationship between inventory and sales?" "Is socioeconomic status associated with the likelihood of purchasing a preferred stock?" or "Does work status relate to attitudes toward the role of women in society?" can be answered by statistically investigating the relationships between the two variables in question. The purpose of this chapter is to investigate questions like these.

■

THE BASICS

Suppose sales is the dependent variable that we wish to predict. The independent variables that we may find associated with the dependent variable "sales" may be aspects of the marketing mix, such as price, number of salespeople, amount of advertising, and/or uncontrollable environmental variables such as population or gross national product. For example, most managers would not be surprised that the sale of baby carriages is associated with the number of babies born a few months prior to the sales period. In this case the dependent variable is the sales volume of baby carriages. The independent variable is the number of babies born.

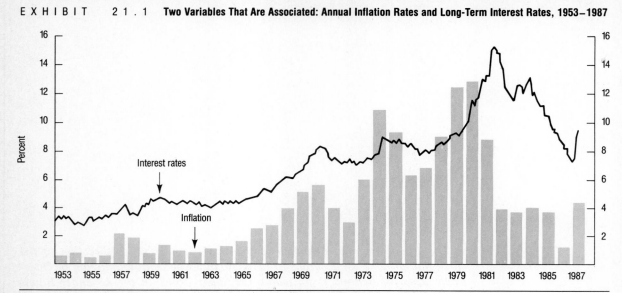

EXHIBIT   21.1   **Two Variables That Are Associated: Annual Inflation Rates and Long-Term Interest Rates, 1953–1987**

Note: Interest rates are those on AAA long-term corporate bonds. Inflation is measured as the annual rate of change in the Consumer Price Index (CPI).
Source: Federal Reserve Bulletin. Also see Eugene F. Brigham and Louis C. Gapenski, *Financial Management: Theory and Practice,* 5/e (Hinsdale, IL: The Dryden Press, 1988).

The mathematical symbol X is commonly used for the independent variable, and Y is typically used for the dependent variable. It is appropriate to label dependent and independent variables only when it is assumed that the independent variable caused the dependent variable.

Exhibit 21.1 compares the annual inflation rate with the long-term interest rate. "Eyeballing" this chart suggests these two financial variables are associated. However, we do not have any mathematical measure of the strength of the relationship.

In many situations, measures of differences, such as the chi-square test, provide information on whether two or more variables are interrelated or associated. For example, a chi-square test between a measure of computer literacy and a measure of education provides some information about the independence or interrelationship of the two variables. Although measures such as the chi-square are useful sources of information about association, statisticians have developed several techniques to estimate the strength of association.

Exhibit 21.2 shows that the type of measures utilized will influence the choice of statistical **measures of association.** This chapter describes simple correlation[1] (Pearson's product-moment correlation coefficient, r) and bivariate regression. Both techniques require interval-scaled or ratio-scaled data. The other techniques are for advanced students who have a specific requirement for these tests.[2]

EXHIBIT   21.2

**Bivariate Analysis—
Common Procedures for
Testing Association**

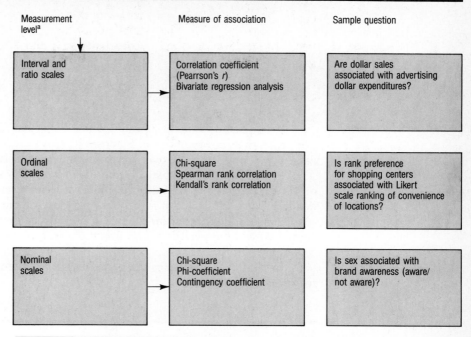

Measurement level[a]	Measure of association	Sample question
Interval and ratio scales	Correlation coefficient (Pearrson's *r*) Bivariate regression analysis	Are dollar sales associated with advertising dollar expenditures?
Ordinal scales	Chi-square Spearman rank correlation Kendall's rank correlation	Is rank preference for shopping centers associated with Likert scale ranking of convenience of locations?
Nominal scales	Chi-square Phi-coefficient Contingency coefficient	Is sex associated with brand awareness (aware/not aware)?

[a] If at least one of the two variables has a given level of measurement, the appropriate procedure is the one with the fewest assumptions about the data.

SIMPLE CORRELATION COEFFICIENT

The most popular technique that indicates the relationship of one variable to another is simple correlation analysis. The **simple correlation coefficient** is a statistical measure of the covariation or association between two variables. The correlation coefficient (r) ranges from +1.0 to −1.0. If the value of r is 1.0, there is a perfect positive linear (straight-line) relationship. If the value of r is −1.0, a perfect negative linear relationship or a perfect inverse relationship is indicated. No correlation is indicated if r = 0. A correlation coefficient indicates both the magnitude of the linear relationship and the direction of the relationship. For example, if we find that the value of r = −.92, we know we have a relatively strong inverse relationship. That is, the greater the value measured by variable X, the less the value measured by variable Y.

The formula for calculating the correlation coefficient for two variables X and Y is:

$$r_{xy} = r_{yx} = \frac{\Sigma(X_i - \bar{X})(Y_i - \bar{Y})}{\sqrt{\Sigma(X_i - \bar{X})^2 \Sigma(Y_i - \bar{Y})^2}}$$

where the symbols $\bar{X}$ and $\bar{Y}$ represent the sample means of X and Y, respectively.

An alternative way of expressing the correlation formula is:

$$r_{xy} = r_{yx} = \frac{\sigma_{xy}}{\sqrt{\sigma_x^2 \sigma_y^2}}$$

where

$$\sigma_x^2 = \text{variance of X}$$
$$\sigma_y^2 = \text{variance of Y}$$
$$\sigma_{xy} = \text{covariance of X and Y}$$

with

$$\sigma_{xy} = \frac{\Sigma(X_i - \bar{X})(Y_i - \bar{Y})}{N}$$

If associated values of X_i and Y_i differ from their means in the same direction, then their covariance will be positive. Covariance will be negative if the values of X_i and Y_i have a tendency to deviate in opposite directions.

In actuality, the simple correlation coefficient is a standardized measure of covariance. In the formula the numerator represents covariance and the denominator is the square root of the product of the sample variances. Researchers find the correlation coefficient useful because two correlations can be compared without regard to the amount of variation exhibited by each variable separately.

Exhibit 21.3 illustrates the correlation coefficients and scatter diagrams for several sets of data.

E X H I B I T   2 1 . 3

Scatter Diagrams Illustrating Correlation Patterns

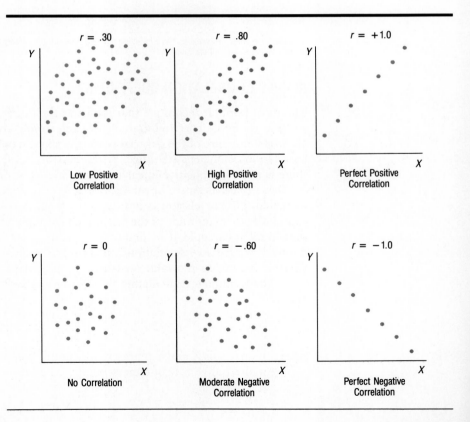

$r = .30$ — Low Positive Correlation

$r = .80$ — High Positive Correlation

$r = +1.0$ — Perfect Positive Correlation

$r = 0$ — No Correlation

$r = -.60$ — Moderate Negative Correlation

$r = -1.0$ — Perfect Negative Correlation

Unemployment Rate (X_i)	Number of Hours Worked (Y_i)	$X_i - \bar{X}$	$(X_i - \bar{X})^2$	$Y_i - \bar{Y}$	$(Y_i - \bar{Y})^2$	$(X_i - \bar{X})(Y_i - \bar{Y})$
5.5	39.6	0.51	.2601	−0.71	.5041	−.3621
4.4	40.7	−0.59	.3481	0.39	.1521	−.2301
4.1	40.4	−0.89	.7921	0.09	.0081	−.0801
4.3	39.8	−0.69	.4761	−0.51	.2601	.3519
6.8	39.2	1.81	3.2761	−1.11	1.2321	−2.0091
5.5	40.3	0.51	.2601	−0.01	.0001	−.0051
5.5	39.7	0.51	.2601	−0.61	.3721	−.3111
6.7	39.8	1.71	2.9241	−0.51	.2601	−.8721
5.5	40.4	0.51	.2601	0.09	.0081	.0459
5.7	40.5	0.71	.5041	0.19	.0361	.1349
5.2	40.7	0.21	.0441	0.39	.1521	.0819
4.5	41.2	−0.49	.2401	0.89	.7921	−.4361
3.8	41.3	−1.19	1.4161	0.99	.9801	−1.1781
3.8	40.6	−1.19	1.4161	0.29	.0841	−.3451
3.6	40.7	−1.39	1.9321	0.39	.1521	−.5421
3.5	40.6	−1.49	2.2201	0.29	.0841	−.4321
4.9	39.8	−0.09	.0081	−0.51	.2601	.0459
5.9	39.9	0.91	.8281	−0.41	.1681	−.3731
5.6	40.6	0.61	.3721	0.29	.0841	.1769

$$\bar{X} = 4.99$$
$$\bar{Y} = 40.31$$
$$\Sigma(X_i - \bar{X})^2 = 17.8379$$
$$\Sigma(Y_i - \bar{Y})^2 = 5.5899$$
$$\Sigma(X_i - \bar{X})(Y_i - \bar{Y}) = -6.3389$$

$$r = \frac{\Sigma(X_i - \bar{X})(Y_i - \bar{Y})}{\sqrt{\Sigma(X_i - \bar{X})^2\Sigma(Y_i - \bar{Y})^2}}$$

$$= \frac{-6.3389}{\sqrt{(17.837)(5.589)}}$$

$$= \frac{-.63389}{\sqrt{99.712}}$$

$$= -.635$$

An Example

To illustrate the calculation of the correlation coefficient, an investigation is made to determine if the average number of hours worked in manufacturing industries is related to unemployment. A correlation analysis on the data in Table 21.1 is used to determine if the two variables are associated.

The correlation between the two variables is −0.635, which indicates an inverse relationship. Thus when the number of hours worked is high, unemployment is low. This makes intuitive sense. If factories are increasing output, regular workers typically work more overtime and new employees are hired (reducing the unemployment rate). Both variables are probably related to overall economic conditions.

Correlation and Causation

It is important to remember that correlation does *not* mean causation. No matter how highly correlated the rooster's crow is to the rising of the sun, the rooster does not cause the sun to rise. It has been pointed out that there is a high correlation between teachers' salaries and the consumption of liquor over a period of years. The approximate correlation coefficient is r = .9. This high correlation does not indicate that teachers drink, nor does it indicate that the sale of liquor increases teachers' salaries. It is more likely that both teachers' salaries and liquor sales covary because they are both influenced by a third variable, such as long-run growth in national income and/or population.

In this example relationship between the two variables is apparent but not real. Even though the variables are not *causally* related, they can be *statistically* related. This can occur because both are caused by a third (or more) factor(s). When this is so, the variables are said to be spuriously related.

Coefficient of Determination

If we wish to know the proportion of *variance* in Y explained by X (or vice versa), we can calculate the **coefficient of determination** by squaring the correlation coefficient (r^2):

$$r^2 = \frac{\text{Explained variance}}{\text{Total variance}}$$

The coefficient of determination, r^2, measures that part of the total variance of Y that is accounted for by knowing the value of X. In the example showing the correlation between unemployment and hours worked, r = −0.635. Therefore r^2 = .403. About 40 percent of the variance in unemployment can be explained by the variance in hours worked, and vice versa.

Correlation Matrix

The **correlation matrix** is the standard form of reporting correlation results. It may be compared to a between-cities mileage table, except that instead of cities the research variables are substituted and instead of mileage a coefficient of correlation is substituted. Table 21.2 shows a correlation matrix, including some measures of sales force performance and satisfaction as they relate to characteristics of the sales force and job attitudes from the Role Orientation Index and a measure of job satisfaction.[3] The student will be faced with this type of matrix on many occasions. Note that the main diagonal (Table 21.2) consists of correlations of 1.00. This will always be the case when a variable is correlated with itself.

The data in this example are from a survey of industrial salespeople selling steel and plastic strapping and seals used in shipping. Performance (S) was measured by identifying the salesperson's actual annual sales volume in dollars. Notice that the performance variable has a .45 correlation with the work load variable, which was measured by recording the number of accounts in the sales territory. Notice also that the salesperson's perception of job-related tension

T A B L E   2 1 . 2   **Pearson Product-Moment Correlation Matrix for Sales Management Example [a]**

Variables		S	JS	GE	SE	OD	VI	JT	RA	TP	WL
S	Performance	1.00									
JS	Job satisfaction	.45[b]	1.00								
GE	Generalized self-esteem	.31[b]	.10	1.00							
SE	Specific self-esteem	.61[b]	.28[b]	.36[b]	1.00						
OD	Other-directedness	.05	−.03	−.44[b]	−.24[c]	1.00					
VI	Verbal intelligence	−.36[b]	−.13	−.14	−.11	−.18[d]	1.00				
JT	Job-related tension	−.48[b]	−.56[b]	−.32[b]	−.34[b]	.26[b]	−.02	1.00			
RA	Role ambiguity	−.26[c]	−.24[c]	−.32[b]	−.39[b]	.38[b]	−.05	.44[b]	1.00		
TP	Territory potential	.49[b]	.31[b]	.04	.29[b]	.09	−.09	−.38[b]	−.26[b]	1.00	
WL	Workload	.45[b]	.11	.29[c]	.29[c]	−.04	−.12	−.27[c]	−.22[d]	.49[b]	1.00

[a] Numbers below the diagonal are for the sample. Those above the diagonal are omitted.
[b] $p < .001$.
[c] $p < .01$.
[d] $p < .05$.

(JT), as measured on an attitude scale, has a −.48 correlation with performance (S). Thus when perceived job tension is high, performance is low. Of course, the correlation coefficients in these examples are moderate.

Another question researchers ask concerns statistical significance. The procedure for determining statistical significance is the t-test of the significance of a correlation coefficient. Typically, it is hypothesized that r = 0 and then a t-test is performed. The logic behind the test is similar to the significance tests already considered. In a large correlation matrix such as Table 21.2, it is customary to footnote each statistically significant coefficient.[4]

REGRESSION ANALYSIS

Regression is another technique for measuring the linear association between a dependent and independent variable. Although regression and correlation are mathematically related, regression assumes the dependent (or criterion) variable, Y, is predictively linked to the independent (or predictor) variable, X. Regression analysis attempts to predict the values of a continuous, interval-scaled dependent variable from the specific values of the independent variable. For example, the amount of external funds required (the dependent variable) might

S T A T I S T I C A L   T U T O R
Regression: One Step Backward

The essence of a dictionary definition of the word "regression" is a going back or moving backward. This notion of regressing, that things "go back to previous conditions," was the source for the original concept of statistical regression. Galton, who first worked out the concept of correlation, got the idea from thinking about "regression toward mediocrity," a phenomenon observed in studies of inheritance. "Tall men will tend to have shorter sons, and short men taller sons. The sons' heights, then, tend to 'regress to,' or 'go back to,' the mean of the population. Statistically, if we want to predict Y and X and the correlation between X and Y is zero, then our best prediction is to the mean."[a] (Incidentally, the symbol r, used for the coefficient of correlation, was originally chosen because it stood for "regression.")

[a] Frederick Kerlinger, *Foundations of Behavioral Research* 2d ed. (New York: Holt, Rinehart and Winston, 1985), 528. Reprinted with permission.

be predicted on the basis of sales growth rates (independent variable). Although there are numerous applications of regression analysis, forecasting sales is by far the most common.

The discussion here concerns **bivariate linear regression.** This form of regression investigates a *straight-line relationship* of the type $Y = a + \beta X$, where Y is the dependent variable and X is the independent variable and a and β are two constants to be estimated. The symbol a represents the Y intercept and β is the slope coefficient. The slope β is the change in Y due to a corresponding change in one unit of X. The slope may also be thought of as "rise over run" (the rise in units on the Y axis divided by the run in units along the X axis). (The Δ is the notation for "a change in.")

Suppose a researcher is interested in forecasting sales for a construction distributor (wholesaler) in Florida. Further, the distributor believes a reasonable association exists between sales and building permits issued by counties. Using bivariate linear regression on the data in Table 21.3, the researcher will be able to estimate sales potential (Y) in various counties based on the number of building permits (X).

For a better understanding of the data in Table 21.3, the data can be plotted on a scatter diagram (Exhibit 21.4). In the diagram the vertical axis indicates the value of the dependent variable Y and the horizontal axis indicates the value of the independent variable X. Each point in the diagram represents an observation of the X and Y at a given point in time, that is, the paired values of Y and X. The relationship between X and Y could be "eyeballed," that is, a straight line could be drawn through the points in the figure. However, such a line would be subject to human error. Two researchers might draw different lines to describe the same data.

Relationship of Sales Potential to Building Permits Issued

Dealer	Y Dealer's Sales Volume (000)	X Building Permits
1	77	86
2	79	93
3	80	95
4	83	104
5	101	139
6	117	180
7	129	165
8	120	147
9	97	119
10	106	132
11	99	126
12	121	156
13	103	129
14	86	96
15	99	108

Scatter Diagram and Eyeball Forecast

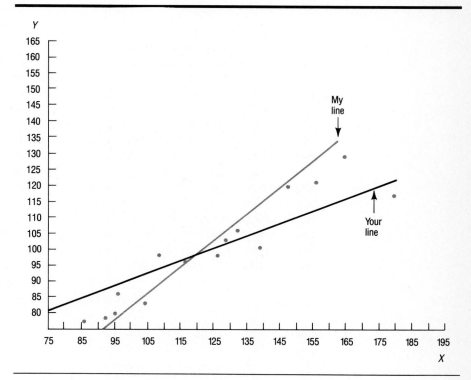

S T A T I S T I C S   T U T O R
Walkup's First Laws of Statistics

Law No. 1
Everything correlates with everything, especially when the same individual defines the variables to be correlated.

Law No. 2
It won't help very much to find a good correlation between the variable you are interested in and some other variable that you don't understand any better.

Law No. 3
Unless you can think of a logical reason why two variables should be connected as cause and effect, it doesn't help much to find a correlation between them. In Columbus, Ohio, the mean monthly rainfall correlates very nicely with the number of letters in the names of the months!

Source: Lewis E. Walkup, "Walkup's First Five Laws of Statistics," *The Bent*, a publication of Tau Beta Pi, Summary 1974 issue, 43; as quoted in Robert W. Joselyn, *Designing the Research Project* (New York: Petrocelli/Charter, 1977), 175. Used by permission.

Least-Squares Method of Regression Analysis

The task of the researcher is to find the best means for fitting a straight line to the data. The **least-squares method** is a relatively simple mathematical technique that ensures that the straight line will best represent the relationship between X and Y. The logic behind the least-squares technique goes as follows. No straight line can completely represent every dot in the scatter diagram. Unless there is a perfect correlation between two variables, there will be a discrepancy between most of the actual scores (each dot) and the predicted score based on the regression line. Simply stated, any straight line that is drawn will generate errors. The method of least squares uses the criterion of attempting to make the least amount of total error in prediction of Y from X. More technically, the procedure used in the least-squares method generates a straight line, which minimizes the sum of squared deviations of the actual values from this predicted regression line. Using the symbol e to represent the deviations of the dots from the line, the least-squares criterion is:

$$\sum_{i=1}^{n} e_i^2 \text{ is minimum}$$

where

$e_i = Y_i - \hat{Y}_i$ (the "residual")
Y_i = actual value of the dependent variable
$\hat{Y}_i$ = estimated value of the dependent variable (Y hat)
n = number of observations
i = number of the observation

TABLE   21.4

Least-Squares Computation

Dealer	Y	Y²	X	X²	XY
1	77	5,929	86	7,396	6,622
2	79	6,241	93	8,649	7,347
3	80	6,400	95	9,025	7,600
4	83	6,889	104	10,816	8,632
5	101	10,201	139	19,321	14,039
6	117	13,689	180	32,400	21,060
7	129	16,641	165	27,225	21,285
8	120	14,400	147	21,609	17,640
9	97	9,409	119	14,161	11,543
10	106	11,236	132	17,424	13,992
11	99	9,801	126	15,876	12,474
12	121	14,641	156	24,336	18,876
13	103	10,609	129	16,641	13,287
14	86	7,396	96	9,216	8,256
15	99	9,801	108	11,664	10,692
Σ	ΣY = 1,497	ΣY² = 153,283	ΣX = 1,875	ΣX² = 245,759	ΣXY = 193,345
	$\bar{Y}$ = 99.8		$\bar{X}$ = 125		

The general equation of a straight line equals $Y = a + \beta X$, whereas a more appropriate equation includes an allowance for error:

$$Y = \hat{a} + \hat{\beta}X + e$$

The symbols $\hat{a}$ and $\hat{\beta}$ are utilized when the equation is a regression estimate of the line. Thus, to compute the estimated values of $\hat{a}$ and $\hat{\beta}$, we use the following formulas:

$$\hat{\beta} = \frac{n(\Sigma XY) - (\Sigma X)(\Sigma Y)}{n(\Sigma X^2) - (\Sigma X)^2}$$

and

$$\hat{a} = \bar{Y} - \hat{\beta}\bar{X}$$

where

$\hat{\beta}$ = estimated slope of the line (the "regression coefficient")
$\hat{a}$ = estimated intercept of the y axis
Y = dependent variable
$\bar{Y}$ = mean of the dependent variable
X = independent variable
$\bar{X}$ = mean of the independent variable
n = number of observations

These equations may be solved by simple arithmetic (see Table 21.4). To estimate the relationship between the distributor's sales to a dealer and the number of building permits, the following manipulations are performed:

$$\hat{\beta} = \frac{n(\Sigma XY) - (\Sigma X)(\Sigma Y)}{n(\Sigma X^2) - (\Sigma X)^2}$$

$$= \frac{15(193,345) - 2,806,875}{15(245,759) - 3,515,625}$$

$$= \frac{2,900,175 - 2,806,875}{3,686,385 - 3,515,625}$$

$$= \frac{93,300}{170,760} = .54638$$

$$\hat{a} = \bar{Y} - \hat{\beta}\bar{X}$$

$$= 99.8 - .54638(125)$$

$$= 99.8 - 68.3$$

$$= 31.5$$

The formula $\hat{Y} = 31.5 + 0.546X$ is the regression equation used for the prediction of the dependent variable. Suppose the wholesaler considers a new dealership in an area where the number of building permits equals 89. Sales may be forecast in this area as:

$$\hat{Y} = 31.5 + .546 \ (X)$$
$$= 31.5 + .546 \ (89)$$
$$= 31.5 + 48.6$$
$$= 80.1$$

Thus our distributor may expect sales of 80.1 in this new area.[5]

Calculation of the correlation coefficient gives an indication of how accurate the predictions may be. In this example the correlation coefficient is $r = .9356$, and the coefficient of determination is $r^2 = .8754$.

Drawing a Regression Line

To draw a regression line on the scatter diagram, only two predicted values of Y need plotting. For example, if Dealer 7 and Dealer 3 are used, $\hat{Y}_7$ and $\hat{Y}_3$ will be calculated to be 121.6 and 83.4:

$$\text{Dealer 7 (actual Y value} = 129): \hat{Y}_7 = 31.5 + .546(165)$$
$$= 121.6$$
$$\text{Dealer 3 (actual Y value} = 80): \hat{Y}_3 = 31.5 + .546(95)$$
$$= 83.4$$

Once the two Y values have been predicted, a straight line connecting the points $\hat{Y}_7 = 121.6$, $X_7 = 165$, and $\hat{Y}_3 = 83.4$, $X_3 = 95$ can be drawn.

Exhibit 21.5 shows the regression line. If it is desirable to determine the error (residual) of any observation, the predicted value of Y is first calculated. The predicted value is then subtracted from the actual value. For example, the actual observation for Dealer 9 is 97 and the predicted value is 96.5. Thus only a small margin of error, $e = .5$, is involved in this regression line:

EXHIBIT   21.5

**Least-Squares
Regression Line**

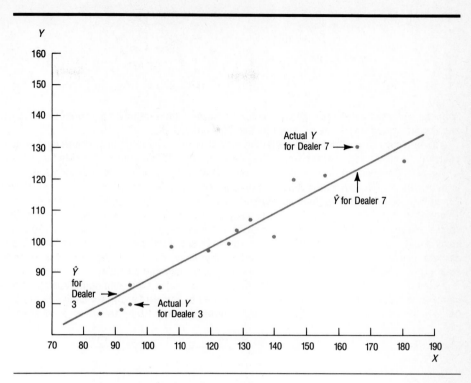

$$e_i = Y_9 - \hat{Y}_9$$
$$= 97 - 96.5$$
$$= 0.5$$

where

$$\hat{Y}_9 = 31.5 + .546(119)$$

Test of Statistical Significance

Now that the error term has been illustrated, a more detailed look at explained and unexplained variation is possible. Exhibit 21.6 gives some additional information about the fitted regression line. If a researcher wishes to predict any dealer's sales volume (Y) without knowing the number of building permits (X), the best prediction would be the average sales volume ($\bar{Y}$) of all dealers. Suppose, for example, a researcher wished to predict Dealer 8's sales without knowing the value of X. The best estimate would have been 99.8 ($\bar{Y}$ = 99.8). An inspection of Exhibit 21.6 shows that this would have been a large error because Dealer 8's actual sales were 120.0. After the regression line has been fitted, it is possible to reduce this error. With the regression equation, Dealer 8's sales are predicted to be 111.8, thus reducing the error to only 8.2

S T A T I S T I C A L   T U T O R

The Concept of Beta When Investing in Stocks

Suppose a regression was run with the historic realized rate of return on a particular stock ($\overline{K}_J$) as the dependent variable and the historic realized rate of return on the stock market ($\overline{K}_m$).

The tendency of a stock to move with the market is reflected in its *beta coefficient,* which is a measure of the stock's *volatility* relative to an average stock. Betas are discussed at an intuitive level in this section.

An *average risk stock* is defined as one which tends to move up and down in step with the general market as measured by some index such as the Dow Jones or the New York Stock Exchange Index. Such a stock will, by definition, have a beta (β) of 1.0, which indicates that, in general, if the market moves up by 10 percent, the stock will also move up by 10 percent, while if the market falls by 10 percent, the stock will likewise fall by 10 percent. A portfolio of such $\beta = 1.0$ stocks will move up and down with the broad market averages and will be just as risky as the averages. If $\beta = 0.5$, the stock is only half as volatile as the market—it will rise and fall only half as much—and a portfolio of such stocks is half as risky as a portfolio of $\beta = 1.0$ stocks. On the other hand, if $\beta = 2.0$, the stock is twice as volatile as an average stock, so a portfolio of such stocks will be twice as risky as an average portfolio.

Betas are calculated and published by Merrill Lynch, Value Line, and numerous other organizations. The beta coefficients of some well-known companies, as calculated by Merrill Lynch, are shown in the table below. Most stocks have betas in the range of 0.75 to 1.50. The average for all stocks is 1.0 by definition. A list of beta coefficients is given below:

Stock	Beta
Apple Computer	1.60
Union Pacific	1.43
Georgia-Pacific	1.36
Mattel	1.15
General Electric	1.09
Bristol Myers	1.00
General Motors	0.94
McDonald's	0.93
Procter & Gamble	0.80
IBM	0.70
Anheuser-Busch	0.58
Pacific Gas & Electric	0.47

Source: Merrill Lynch, *Monthly Research Review,* January 1987.

If a high-beta stock (one whose beta is greater than 1.0) is added to an average risk ($\beta = 1.0$) portfolio, then the beta and consequently the riskiness of the portfolio will increase. Conversely, if a low-beta stock (one whose beta is less than 1.0) is added to an average risk portfolio, the portfolio's beta and risk will decline. Thus, *because a stock's beta measures its contribution to the riskiness of a portfolio, beta is the appropriate measure of the stock's riskiness.*

Source: Excerpt from *Financial Management: Theory and Practice,* 5/e, by Eugene F. Brigham and Louis C. Gapenski, pp. 189–191, copyright © 1988 by The Dryden Press, a division of Holt, Rinehart and Winston, Inc., reprinted by permission of the publisher.

EXHIBIT   21.6

**Scatter Diagram of
Explained and
Unexplained Variation**

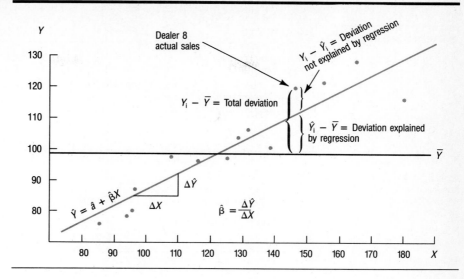

$(120 - 111.8)$ rather than 20.2 $(120 - 99.8)$. That is, error is reduced by using $Y_i - \hat{Y}_i$ rather than $Y_i - \overline{Y}$. This is the "explained" deviation due to the regression. The smaller number 8.2 is the deviation not explained by the regression.

Thus the total deviation can be partitioned into two parts:

$$(Y_i - \overline{Y}) \;=\; (\hat{Y}_i - \overline{Y}) \;+\; (Y_i - \hat{Y}_i)$$

Total		Deviation		Deviation
deviation	=	explained by	+	unexplained by
		the regression		the regression
				(residual error)

where

$$\overline{Y} = \text{mean of the total group}$$
$$\hat{Y} = \text{value predicted with regression equation}$$
$$Y_i = \text{actual value}$$

For Dealer 8 the total deviation is $120 - 99.8 = 20.2$, the deviation explained by the regression is $111.8 - 99.8 = 12$, and the deviation unexplained by the regression is $120 - 111.8 = 8.2$. If these values are summed over all values of Y_i (i.e., all observations) and squared, these deviations provide an estimate of the variation of Y explained by the regression and unexplained by the regression:

$$\Sigma(Y_i - \overline{Y})^2 = \Sigma(\hat{Y}_i - \overline{Y})^2 + \Sigma(Y_i - \hat{Y}_i)^2$$

Total		Explained		Unexplained
variation	=	variation	+	variation
explained				(residual)

Source of Variation	Degrees of Freedom	Sum of Squares	Mean Square (Variance)
Explained by regression	k − 1	$SSr = \Sigma(\hat{Y}_i - \bar{Y})^2$	SSr/k − 1
Unexplained (error)	n − k	$SSe = \Sigma(Y_i = \hat{Y}_i)^2$	SSe/n − k

where k = number of estimated parameters (variables)
       n = number of observations

Source of Variation	Sum of Squares	d.f.	Mean Square	F-Value
Explained by regression	3398.49	1	3398.49	
				91.30
Unexplained by regression (error)	483.91	13	37.22	
Total	3882.4	14		

We have thus partitioned the total sum of squares, SSt, into two parts: the regression sum of squares, SSr, and the error sum of squares, SSe:

$$SSt = SSr + SSe$$

An **F-test** or an *analysis of variance* applied to regression can be used to test relative magnitude of the SSr and SSe with their appropriate degrees of freedom. Table 21.5 indicates the technique for conducting the F-test.

For the example on sales forecasting, the **analysis of variance summary table,** comparing relative magnitudes of the mean square, is presented in Table 21.6. From Table 6 in the Appendix we find that the F-value 91.3, with 1 degree of freedom in the numerator and 13 degrees of freedom in the denominator, exceeds the probability level of .01. The *coefficient of determination, r^2,* reflects the proportion of variation explained by the regression line. To calculate r^2:

$$r^2 = \frac{SSr}{SSt} = 1 - \frac{SSe}{SSt}$$

In our example, r^2 is calculated to be .875:

$$r^2 = \frac{3398.49}{3882.4} = .875$$

The coefficient of determination may be interpreted to mean that 87 percent of the variation in sales was explained by associating the variable with building permits.

S T A T I S T I C A L   T U T O R

A Note of Caution

The nonstatistical definition of regression is moving backward or reverting to an earlier form. This definition emphasizes the past nature of the data and hints that forecasting with statistical regression analysis should be cautiously utilized. Past data may not necessarily reflect future trends. In *Life on the Mississippi,* Samuel Clemens illustrated this concern about forecasting rather well:

"In the space of one hundred and seventy-six years the Lower Mississippi has shortened itself two hundred and forty-two miles. This is an average of a trifle over one mile and a third per year. Therefore, any calm person, who is not blind or idiotic, can see that in the Old Oölitic Silurian Period, just a million years ago next November, the lower Mississippi River was upward of one million three hundred thousand miles long, and stuck out over the Gulf of Mexico like a fishing-rod. And by the same token any person can see that seven hundred and forty-two years from now the Lower Mississippi will be only a mile and three-quarters long, and Cairo and New Orleans will have joined their streets together, and be plodding comfortably along under a single mayor and a mutual board of aldermen. There is something fascinating about science. One gets such wholesale returns of conjecture out of such a trifling investment of fact."[a]

[a] *Life on the Mississippi* by Mark Twain (Samuel Clemens).

SUMMARY

In many situations two variables are interrelated or associated. Many bivariate statistical techniques can be used to measure association. Researchers select the appropriate technique on the basis of each variable's scale of measurement.

The correlation coefficient (r), a statistical measure of association between two variables, ranges from $r = +1.0$ for a perfect positive correlation to $r = -1.0$ for a perfect negative correlation. No correlation is indicated for $r = 0$. Simple correlation is the measure of the relationship of one variable to another. The correlation coefficient indicates the strength of the association of two variables and the direction of that association. It must be remembered that correlation does not prove causation, as variables other than those being measured may be involved. The coefficient of determination (r^2) measures the amount of the total variance in the dependent variable that is accounted for by knowing the value of the independent variable. The results of correlation computations are often presented in a correlation matrix.

Bivariate linear regression investigates a straight-line relationship between one dependent variable and one independent variable. The regression can be done intuitively by plotting a scatter diagram of the X and Y points and drawing a line to fit the observed relationship. The least-squares method mathematically determines the best-fitting regression line for the observed data. The line determined by this method may be used to forecast values of the dependent variable, given a value for the independent variable. The goodness of the line's fit may be evaluated by a variant of the ANOVA (analysis of variance) technique or by calculating the coefficient of determination.

Key Terms

measures of association

simple correlation coefficient

coefficient of determination

correlation matrix

bivariate linear regression

least-squares method

residual slope intercept

analysis of variance summary table

F-test

Questions

1. The discussion in this chapter is limited to linear relationships. Try to diagram some nonlinear relationships that would show an r of zero, using the tests shown in the text.

2. Comment on the following:

    a. A few years ago the Food and Drug Administration issued a strong warning against Procter & Gamble's Rely™ tampons. A study of toxic-shock syndrome (TSS) indicated that of 42 TSS patients, 71 percent of the women had used the Rely tampon. What are the causal implications concerning the Rely tampon and TSS?

    b. Suppose Abraham Lincoln had answered a survey questionnaire and indicated he had not received a grade school diploma. The researcher found that Lincoln's educational score did not correlate highly with the expected variables. What was wrong?

    c. Ted Turner is owner of both the Atlanta Braves baseball team and the Turner Broadcasting System (TBS). During the first few weeks of the 1982 baseball season the stock value of TBS was highly correlated with the Braves' won–loss record. When the Braves won, the TBS stock value increased. Was there a causal relationship?

3. The management of a regional bus line thought its price of gas might be correlated with its passenger/mile ratio. Comment on the data and correlation matrix below.

Avg. Wholesale Price of Gas	Passenger/Mile Ratio
56.5	8.37
59.4	8.93
63.0	9.15
65.6	9.79
89.0	11.20

Correlation Coefficients/Probability > |R| under HO: RHO = O/N = 5

	Year	Price	Mile
Year	1.00000	0.87016	0.95127
	0.0000	0.0551	0.0128
Price	0.87016	1.00000	0.97309
	0.0551	0.0000	0.0053
Mile	0.95127	0.97309	1.00000
	0.0128	0.0053	0.0000

4. A correlation matrix (correlation coefficients and probability level under the hypothesis rho = 0) for a company's sales force (age, years of service, and current sales) is given below. Comment.

Age	1.00000	0.68185	0.21652
	0.0000	0.0208	0.5225
Years of service	0.68185	1.00000	0.64499
	0.0208	0.0000	0.0321
Current sales	0.21652	0.64499	1.00000
	0.5225	0.0321	0.00000

5. Interpret the following:
   a. $\hat{Y} = \hat{a} + \hat{\beta}X$; $\hat{Y} = 3.5 + .7X$, where $\hat{Y}$ = likelihood of buying a new car and X = total family income.
   b. $\hat{Y} = \hat{a} + \hat{\beta}X$; $\hat{Y} = 3.5 - .4X$, where $\hat{Y}$ = likelihood of buying tickets to a rock concert and X = age.

6. The ANOVA summary table below is the result of a regression of sales on year of sales. Is the relationship statistically significant at .05? Comment.

Source of Variation	Sum of Squares	d.f.	Mean Square	F-Value
Explained by regression	605,370,750	1	605,370,750	3.12
Unexplained by regression	1,551,381,712	8	193,922,714	
Total error		9		

7. A metropolitan economist is attempting to predict Phoenix retired couples' average total budget, based on U.S. urban average retired couples' total budget. An r^2 of .7824 is obtained. Will the regression be a good predictive model?

8. A football team's season ticket sales, percentage of games won, and number of active alumni are given below:

Year	Season Ticket Sales	Percentage of Games Won	Number of Active Alumni
1982	4,995	40	NA
1983	8,599	54	NA
1984	8,479	55	NA
1985	8,419	58	NA
1986	10,253	63	NA
1987	12,457	75	6,315
1988	13,285	36	6,860
1989	14,177	27	8,423
1990	15,730	63	9,000

   a. Interpret the correlation between each variable.
   b. Calculate: Regression sales = Percentage of games won.
   c. Calculate: Regression sales = Number of active alumni.

9. Are the different forms of consumer installment credit in the table below highly correlated? Explain.

Credit Card Debt Outstanding (Millions of Dollars)

Year	Gas Cards	Travel and Entertainment Cards	Bank Credit Cards	Retail Cards	Total Credit Cards	Total Installment Credit
1	$ 939	$ 61	$ 828	$ 9,400	$11,228	$ 79,428
2	1,119	76	1,312	10,200	12,707	87,745
3	1,298	110	2,639	10,900	14,947	98,105
4	1,650	122	3,792	11,500	17,064	102,064
5	1,804	132	4,490	13,925	20,351	111,295
6	1,762	164	5,408	14,763	22,097	127,332
7	1,832	191	6,838	16,395	25,256	147,437
8	1,823	238	8,281	17,933	28,275	156,124
9	1,893	273	9,501	18,002	29,669	164,955
10	1,981	238	11,351	19,052	32,622	185,489
11	2,074	284	14,262	21,082	37,702	216,572

10. A manufacturer of disposable washcloths/wipes told a retailer that sales for this product category closely correlated with the sales of disposable diapers. The retailer thought he would check this out for his own sales-forecasting purposes. Where might a researcher find data to make this forecast?

11. The Springfield Electric Company manufactures electric pencil sharpeners. The company believes that sales are correlated with the number of workers employed in specific geographic areas. The following table presents Springfield's sales of electric pencil sharpeners and the total number of employees in 17 Metropolitan Statistical Areas (MSAs) in New York State and New Jersey. Calculate and interpret the correlation coefficient data in the table.

MSA—New York	Number of Employees (000)	Sales	MSA—New Jersey	Number of Employees (000)	Sales
Albany—Schenectady—Troy	58.3	3,749	Allentown—Bethlehem—Easton	110.7	6,123
Binghamton	37.0	2,695	Atlantic City	8.7	2,666
Buffalo	135.6	4,926	Jersey City	74.2	3,210
Elmira	12.8	2,808	Long Branch—Asbury Park	22.8	2,078
Nassau—Suffolk	149.0	7,423	New Brunswick—Perth Amboy—Sayreville	78.9	2,894
New York	788.8	43,401			
Poughkeepsie	24.3	3,254	Newark	252.1	14,989
Rochester	139.1	8,924	Paterson—Clifton—Passaic	60.1	3,806
Syracuse	53.6	13,119			
Utica—Rome	30.8	3,151			

12. Using the data in Question 11, estimate the regression equation coefficients for the data (assuming sales is the independent variable).

13. Using the regression equation from Question 12, forecast sales for the MSAs in the table below:

MSA—Washington	Number of Employees (000)	MSA—Oregon	Number of Employees (000)
Richland—Kennewick	7.8	Eugene—Springfield	18.2
Seattle—Everett	123.6	Portland	90.5
Spokane	11.1	Salem	12.5
Tacoma	18.7		
Yakima	8.8		

MSA—California	Number of Employees (000)
Anaheim—Santa Ana—Garden Grove	149.0
Bakersfield	7.1
Fresno	20.5
Los Angeles—Long Beach	750.3
Modesto	18.7
Oxnard—Simi Valley—Ventura	14.9
Riverside—San Bernardino—Ontario	51.8
Sacramento	20.5
Salinas—Seaside—Monterey	8.0

References

[1] The symbol for the correlation coefficient of a population is the Greek letter rho.

[2] For a discussion of the other measures of association, see the appendix to this chapter and Jean Dickinson Gibbons, *Nonparametric Methods for Quantitative Analysis* (New York, Holt, Rinehart and Winston, 1976).

[3] See Richard P. Bagozzi, "Salesforce Performance and Satisfaction as a Function of Individual Difference, Interpersonal and Situational Factors," *Journal of Marketing Research* (November 1978): 517–531.

[4] To calculate a t-test under the null hypothesis rho = 0, t is distributed with d.f. = n − 2:

$$t = \frac{r}{s_r}, \text{ where } s_r = \sqrt{\frac{1 - r^2}{n - 2}}$$

Table 7 in the Appendix of Statistical Tables at the back of the book provides the critical values of r for the Pearson correlation coefficient to test the null hypothesis that rho equals zero.

[5] This is a point estimate. It is possible to calculate a confidence interval for this sales estimate; however, the topic is beyond the scope of this book.

Nonparametric Measures of Association

In a number of situations the assumption that a researcher's data are metric (interval- or ratio-scaled) cannot be met.[1] A nonparametric correlation technique may be utilized as a substitute for the Pearson correlation technique.

A group of correlation measures deals with rank-order data. Two groups of consumers might be asked to rank, in order of preference, the brands of a product class. The researcher wishes to determine the agreement or correlation between the two groups. Two possible statistics can be computed to accomplish this purpose: the Spearman rank-order correlation coefficient, r_s, and the Kendall rank correlation coefficient, τ (tau).

The *Spearman rank-order correlation coefficient* is computed by

$$r_s = 1 - \frac{6 \sum_{i=1}^{n} d_i^2}{n^3 - n}$$

where d_i is the difference between the ranks given to the ith brand by each group. Thus if Brand B were ranked first by Group 1 and sixth by Group 2, d_b^2 would be equal to $(1 - 6)^2$, or 25. In some cases two brands may be given equal scores by a group or be tied for a certain rank. If the number of ties is not large, their effect is small, and we simply assign the average of the ranks that would have been assigned had no ties occurred for each brand. We then calculate r_s as before. If the number of ties is large, however, a correction factor can be introduced to offset their effect on r_s.

Consider the sales aptitude relationship between a sales manager's ratings of employees and their years of service with the organization. The data are portrayed in Table 21A.1, which illustrates how r_s (rho) is calculated. The highest rating is given the highest ranking (10).

$$r_s = 1 - \frac{6 \sum_{i=1}^{n} d_i^2}{n^3 - n} = 1 - \frac{6(68)}{(10)^3 - 10} = 1 - .412 = .588$$

TABLE 21A.1

Example of Spearman Rank-Order Correlation

Employee	Raw Data		Ranking Values		Differences	
	Sales Aptitude Ratings	Years Service (Y)	Rank of X (X_r)	Rank of Y (Y_r)	d_i ($X_r - Y_r$)	d_i^2
1	3	5	3.5	4.5	−1.0	1.00
2	5	11	6.5	9.0	−2.5	6.25
3	1	1	1.0	1.0	0.0	0.00
4	4	3	5.0	2.0	3.0	9.00
5	8	5	10.0	4.5	5.5	30.25
6	3	4	3.5	3.0	0.5	0.25
7	6	13	8.0	10.0	−2.0	4.00
8	2	6	2.0	6.0	4.0	16.00
9	5	9	6.5	7.0	0.5	0.25
10	7	10	9.0	8.0	1.0	1.00
						$\Sigma d^2 = 68$

The answer $r_s = .588$ is interpreted in a manner similar to the Pearson correlation coefficient.

The Kendall rank correlation coefficient, *Kendall's tau,* is useful for the same type of situation as is appropriate for the Spearman coefficient, but its computation is not quite so straightforward and may best be explained by an example. Suppose two groups have ranked Brands A, B, C, and D in the following way:

Brand	A	B	C	D
Group I	3	4	2	1
Group II	3	1	4	2

Rearranging the items so that Group I's ranks appear in order, we see the following:

Brand	D	C	A	B
Group I	1	2	3	4
Group II	2	4	3	1

To determine the degree of consistency between the two rankings, we examine Group II's rankings to see how many are in the correct order vis-à-vis one another. The first pair, D and C, are in natural order; that is, 2(D) comes before 4(C), and we assign a score of +1 to this pair. We proceed to compare the rank for Brand D with the ranks of the other brands. The second pair, D and A, is assigned a score of +1, while the pair D and B is assigned a score of −1 because Groups I and II do not agree. The total so far is +1. Each rank in turn is compared similarly, with the resulting final total of −2. (Rank of C versus A = −1, C versus B = −1, A versus B = −1, yielding a final real value of −2.) The next step is to compare this actual total with the maximum possible total. A maximum value would occur if Group II rankings were identical to those of Group I, which is found by taking four things, two at a time, or:

$$\binom{N}{2} = \binom{4}{2} = \frac{4!}{2!(4-2)!} = 6$$

Tau is therefore equal to the ratio of the actual total over the maximum possible total:

$$\tau = \frac{\begin{array}{c}\text{Actual}\\\text{total}\\\text{score}\end{array}}{\binom{N}{2}} = \frac{-2}{6} = -0.33$$

and is the measure of correlation between the two ranks. Tied observations are treated in the same way as for the Spearman coefficient. Values obtained for r_s and τ from the same data will not be equal and are not comparable to one another.

These measures of correlation can be subjected to tests of significance to determine whether the correlations are sufficiently different from chance expectations and thus are not due to random sampling error alone. However, the types of tests to be utilized and the rules governing their use are of such magnitude as to be beyond the scope of this appendix. The reader should refer to specialized statistics texts for the appropriate tests.[2]

The *contingency coefficient* is intended to measure association of nominal data recorded in bivariate contingency tables.[3] It is the only correlation coefficient appropriate for use with nominal data, with the possible exception of the phi coefficient, which is limited to 2×2 tables. There is no restriction on the number of categories, provided the number of measures is quite large.

The magnitude of a chi-square statistic calculated from a contingency table is a function of the relationship between the row and column variables. This fact is utilized to develop a formula for the calculation of the contingency coefficient:

$$C = \frac{\chi^2}{n + \chi^2}$$

where

C = contingency coefficient
χ^2 = calculated chi-square value
n = sample size or total number of observations

The test for statistical significance is the same as in the chi-square test of independence.

Unfortunately, the size of the contingency coefficient is a function of the number of cells in the table, and under no circumstances is it possible for the coefficient to be unity, even though a perfect relationship may exist. The maximum value of the contingency coefficient for a 2×2 table is .707, for a 3×3 table .816, and for a 4×4 table .866.

References

[1] Portions of this section are reprinted, with adaptations, from Gerald Zaltman and Philip Burger, *Marketing Research* (Hinsdale, IL: Dryden Press, 1976), 448–449.

[2] For more detail see A. M. Mood and F. A. Graybill, *Introduction to the Theory of Statistics*, 2nd ed. (New York: McGraw-Hill, 1963), and Jean Dickinson Gibbons, *Nonparametric Methods for Quantitative Analysis* (New York: Holt, Rinehart and Winston, 1976).

[3] This material is based on John T. Roscoe, *Fundamental Research for Behavioral Science* (New York: Holt, Rinehart and Winston, 1975), 260–261.

Multivariate Analysis

The U.S. Army's recruiting command has an extensive database of applicant information that comes from tests and forms completed by recruits before they make a binding commitment to enlist. By the time a recruit signs a contract, the army has a record with more than 330 pieces of personal information, such as whether he or she is a high-school graduate. Another characteristic the army monitors is weight. When a military policy for "leaner and meaner" weight requirements was considered, the management information system allowed the army to forecast a 30 percent decrease in the number of new recruits if the suggestion was implemented. By monitoring the numerous characteristics of enlisted men and women, the army can make projections about its recruits based on multivariate analysis. These are some of the same forecasting and analysis techniques used by effective managers in business organizations.[1]

Most business problems are inherently multidimensional. Corporations can be described along a wide variety of dimensions. The price of domestic crude oil can be simultaneously influenced by rate of inflation, political instability, and the balance of payments. Individuals can evaluate various investments on the basis of many different attributes. As researchers increasingly become aware of the multidimensional nature of their problems, they will increasingly utilize multivariate analysis to help them solve complex problems.

As discussed earlier, the investigation of one variable at a time is referred to as univariate analysis. *Investigation of the relationship between two variables is* bivariate analysis. *When problems are multidimensional and three or more variables are involved, we utilize* **multivariate analysis.** *Multivariate statistical methods allow the effects of more than one variable to be considered at one time. For example, suppose a forecaster wished to estimate oil consumption for the next five years. While consumption might be predicted by past oil consumption records alone, adding additional variables, such as average number of miles driven per year, coal production, and nuclear plants under construction, might give greater insight into the determinants of oil consumption.*

To evaluate the probability of corporate bankruptcy, a researcher may select multiple financial ratios, such as current ratio, debt/assets ratio, and return on assets. Consumers, evaluating grocery stores, may be concerned with distance to each store, perceived cleanliness, price levels, and many other attributes of these stores. To understand problems like these, researchers need multivariate analysis.

The computer has influenced the rapid diffusion of multivariate analysis in business research. A number of "canned computer programs" have changed techniques that were once expensive and exotic into affordable and regular forms of analysis. With the multivariate statistical revolution, students need an understanding of these powerful tools of analysis. This chapter presents a non-technical description of some multivariate methods. Computational formulas are not presented.

■

CLASSIFYING MULTIVARIATE TECHNIQUES

A useful classification of most multivariate statistical techniques is presented in Exhibit 22.1.[2] Two basic groups of multivariate techniques are classified: *dependence methods* and *interdependence methods*.

Analysis of Dependence

If the technique attempts to explain or predict the dependent variable(s) on the basis of two or more independent variables, then we are attempting to analyze dependence. An instance where the researcher is interested in specifying a relationship between one dependent variable and several independent variables is illustrated by a common judgment: Is a person a good or a poor credit risk

EXHIBIT   22.1

A Classification of Multivariate Methods

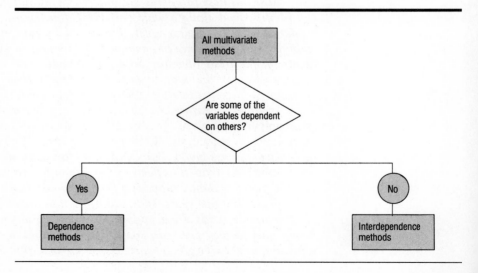

based on age, income, and marital status? Another example of the analysis of dependence would be forecasting the dependent variable sales on the basis of numerous independent variables. *Multiple regression analysis, multiple discriminant analysis, multivariate analysis of variance,* and *canonical correlation analysis* are all dependence methods.

Analysis of Interdependence
The goal of interdependence methods is to give meaning to a set of variables or to seek to group things together. No one variable or variable subset is to be predicted from the others or explained by them. The most common of these methods of interdependence are *factor analysis, cluster analysis,* and *multidimensional scaling.* A manager attempting to identify profitable market segments or market clusters might utilize these techniques. Another example might be to identify and classify similar cities on the basis of population size, income distribution, race and ethnic distribution, and consumption of the manufacturer's product in selecting comparable test markets.

Influence of Measurement Scales
As in other forms of data analysis, the nature of the measurement scales will determine which multivariate technique is appropriate for the data. Exhibits 22.2 and 22.3 shows that selection of the multivariate technique requires consideration of the types of measures used for both independent and dependent sets of variables. For ease of diagraming, Exhibits 22.2 and 22.3 refer to nominal and ordinal scales as *nonmetric* and interval and ratio scales as *metric.*

ANALYSIS OF DEPENDENCE
Multiple Regression Analysis
Multiple regression is an extension of bivariate regression analysis, which allows for the simultaneous investigation of the effect of two or more independent variables on a single interval-scaled dependent variable. In the last chapter bivariate linear regression analysis was illustrated with an example concerning a construction dealer's sales volume. In this bivariate regression example, variations in the dependent variable were attributed to changes in a single independent variable. Yet reality suggests that several factors are likely to affect such a dependent variable. For example, sales volume might be hypothesized to depend not only on the number of building permits but also on price levels, amount of advertising, and the income of families in the area. Thus the problem requires identification of a linear relationship with multiple regression analysis. The multiple regression equation is:

$$Y = a + \beta_1 X_1 + \beta_2 X_2 + \beta_3 X_3 \ldots + \beta_n X_n$$

Another forecasting example is useful in illustrating multiple regression. Assume a toy manufacturer wishes to forecast sales by sales territory. It is thought that retail sales, the presence or absence of a company salesperson in the territory (a binary variable), and grammar school enrollment are the inde-

E X H I B I T   2 2 . 2   **Multivariate Analysis: Classification of Dependence Methods**

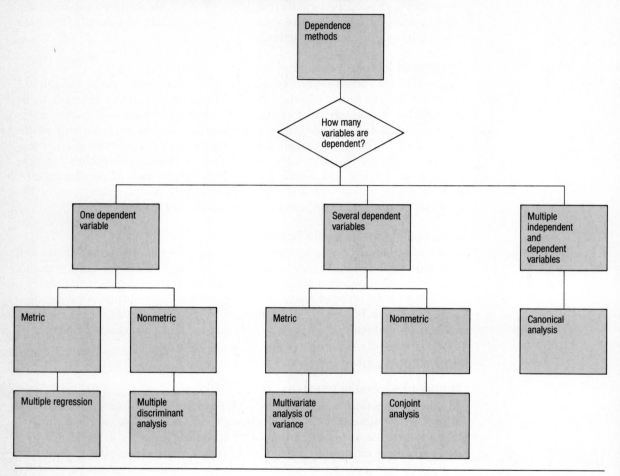

pendent variables that might explain the variation in the sales of a toy. The data appear in Table 22.1. Table 22.2 shows the statistical results from the multiple regression after mathematical computations have been made. The regression equation

$$Y = 102.18 + .387X_1 + 115.20X_2 + 6.73X_3$$

indicates sales are positively related to X_1 and X_2 and X_3. The coefficients (βs) show the effect on the dependent variable of a unit increase in any of the independent variables. The value of $\beta_2 = 115.2$ indicates that an increase of $115,200 (000 included) in toy sales is expected with each additional unit of X_2. Thus it appears that adding a company salesperson has a very positive

E X H I B I T   2 2 . 3   Multivariate Analysis: Classification of Independence Methods

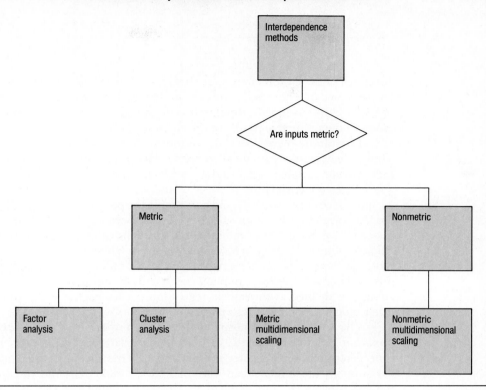

T A B L E   2 2 . 1

Data for a Multiple Regression Problem

Y Sales (000)	X₁ Retail Sales (000)	X₂ Salesman (1) or Agent (0)	X₃ Grammar School Enrollment (000)
222	106	0	23
304	213	0	18
218	201	0	22
501	378	1	20
542	488	0	21
790	509	1	31
523	644	0	17
667	888	1	25
700	941	1	32
869	1066	1	36
444	307	0	30
479	312	1	22

$$Y = 102.18 + .387X_1 + 115.20X_2 + 6.73X_3$$

| Coefficient of determination (R^2) | .845 |
| F-value | 14.6 |

effect on sales. Grammar school enrollments also help predict sales. An increase of one unit of enrollment (a thousand students) indicates a sales increase of \$6,730 (000 included). Retail sales volume (X_1) in the territory does not add much to the predictive power of the equation (\$387).

In multiple regression the terminology for β_1, β_2, and so on is changed. These coefficients are now called **coefficients of partial regression** because the independent variables are usually correlated with the other independent variables. Thus the correlation between Y and X_1 with the correlation that X_1 and X_2 have in common with Y held constant is the partial correlation. Because the partial correlation between sales and X_1 has been adjusted for the effect produced by variation in X_2 (and other independent variables), the correlation coefficient obtained from the bivariate regression will not be the same as the partial coefficient in the multiple regression. Stated differently, the original value of β is the simple bivariate regression coefficient. In multiple regression the coefficient β_1 is defined as the partial regression coefficient for which the effects of other independent variables are held constant.

The **coefficient of multiple determination** or the *multiple index of determination* is shown in Table 22.2. As in the bivariate case, the coefficient of multiple determination indicates the percent of variation in Y explained by the variation in the independent variables. $R^2 = .845$ tells the researcher that the variation in the independent variables accounted for 84.5 percent of the variance in the dependent variable. Typically, adding additional independent variables in the regression equation explains more of the variation in Y than with fewer variables. In other words, the amount of variation explained by two independent variables in the same equation usually explains more variation in Y than either one explains separately.

To test for statistical significance, an F-test, comparing the different sources of variation, is necessary. The F-test allows for testing of the relative magnitudes of the sum of squares due to the regression (SSr) and the error sum of squares (SSe), with their appropriate degrees of freedom:

$$F = \frac{(SSr)/k}{(SSe)/(n - k - 1)}$$

where

k = number of independent variables
n = number of respondents or observations

Table 5 in the Appendix of Statistical Tables at the end of the book shows the F-distributions for hypothesis testing at the .05 significance level. In the preceding example the F-ratio equals 14.6. Degrees of freedom (d.f.) are calculated as follows:

$$\text{d.f. for the numerator} = k$$
$$\text{d.f. for the denominator} = n - k - 1$$

In this example:

$$\text{d.f. (numerator)} = 3$$
$$\text{d.f. (denominator)} = 12 - 3 - 1 = 8$$

Table 5 in the Appendix indicates that an F-value of 4.26 or more is necessary to reject the null hypothesis at the .05 level of statistical significance. Thus it can be concluded that the estimated functional relationship is not due to chance or random variation. There does appear to be an association between the dependent variable and the independent variables other than random variation in the data.

A continuous, interval-scaled dependent variable is required in multiple regression, as it is in bivariate regression. Interval scaling is also a requirement for the independent variables; however, dummy variables, such as the binary variable in our example, may be utilized. A dummy variable is a variable that has two (or more) distinct levels, which are coded 0 and 1. There are several other assumptions for multiple regression (and other multivariate techniques) that require advanced study. Several excellent technical books deal with this topic.[3] The growing use of canned computer programs allows the researcher to compute multiple regressions without a great deal of effort. Managers should be aware of the appropriateness of this technique in using their databases.

Discriminant Analysis

A myriad of situations exist where the researcher's purpose is to classify objects, by a set of independent variables, into two or more mutually exclusive categories. A physician can record a person's blood pressure, weight, and blood cholesterol level and then categorize that person as having a high probability of a heart attack or a low probability. Researchers interested in small-business failures may be able to group firms as to whether they eventually failed or did not fail on the basis of independent variables—location, financial ratios, management changes. A bank may want to be able to discriminate between potentially successful and unsuccessful sites for electronic fund-transfer-system machines. A personnel manager may want to distinguish between applicants to hire and those not to hire. The challenge is to find the discriminating variables to be utilized in a predictive equation that will produce better than chance assignment of the individuals to the two groups.

The prediction of a categorical variable (rather than a continuous, interval-scaled variable as in multiple regression) is the purpose of **multiple discriminant analysis.** In each of the above problems the researcher must determine which variables are associated with the probability of an object falling into one of several groups or categories. In a statistical sense, the problem of studying the direction of group differences is a problem of finding a linear combination of independent variables, the discriminant function, that shows large differences in group means. *Discriminant analysis* is a statistical tool for determining such linear combinations. Deriving the coefficients of the discriminant function (a straight line) is the task of the researcher.

Our example will concentrate on the two-group discriminant analysis problem where the dependent variable, Y, is measured on a nominal scale. (It should be noted that n-way discriminate analysis is possible, but it is beyond the scope of this discussion.) Suppose a personnel manager for an electrical-equipment wholesaler has been keeping records on successful versus unsuccessful sales employees. The personnel manager believes it is possible to predict whether an applicant will be successful on the basis of age, mechanical-ability test scores, and sales-aptitude test scores. As stated at the outset, the problem is to find a linear function of the independent variables that shows large differences in group means. The first task is to estimate the coefficients of the individual applicant's discriminant functions. To calculate the individual's discriminant scores, the following linear function is used:

$$Z_i = b_1 X_{1i} + b_2 X_{2i} \cdots + b_n X_{ni}$$

where

X_{ji} = applicant's value on the jth independent variable
b_j = discriminant coefficient for the jth variable
Z_i = ith applicant's discriminant score

Using all the individuals in the sample, a discriminant function is determined based on the criterion that the groups be maximally differentiated on the set of independent variables.

Returning to the example with three independent variables, suppose the personnel manager calculates the standardized weights in the equation to be:

$$Z = b_1 X_1 + b_2 X_2 + b_3 X_3$$
$$Z = .069 X_1 + .013 X_2 + .0007 X_3$$

This means that age (X_1) is much more important than sales-aptitude test scores (X_2). Mechanical ability (X_3) has relatively minor discriminating power.

In the computation of the linear discriminant function, weights are assigned to the variables such that the ratio of the difference between the means of the two groups to the standard deviation within groups is maximized. The standardized discriminant coefficients or weights provide information about the relative importance of each of these variables in discriminating between the two groups.

An important purpose of discriminant analysis is to perform a classification function. The object of classification in our example is to predict which applicants will be successful and which will be unsuccessful, and to group them accordingly. To determine if discriminant analysis can be used as a good predictor, information provided in the "confusion matrix" is utilized. Suppose the personnel manager has 40 successful and 45 unsuccessful employees in the sample. The confusion matrix in Table 22.3 shows that the number of correctly classified employees (76 percent) in the example is much higher than would be expected by chance. Tests can be performed to determine if the rate of correct classification is statistically significant.

A second example will allow us to portray discriminant analysis from a graphic perspective.[4] Suppose a bank loan officer wants to segregate corporate loan applicants into those likely to default and those likely not to default. As-

T A B L E   2 2 . 3

Confusion Matrix

		Predicted Group	
Actual Group		**Successful**	**Unsuccessful**
Successful		34	6	40
Unsuccessful		7	38	45

T A B L E   2 2 . 4

Data on Bankrupt and Solvent Firms

Firm Number (1)	Current Ratio (2)	Debt/Assets (Percent) (3)	Did Firm Go Bankrupt? (4)	Z- Score (5)	Probability of Bankruptcy (6)
1	3.6	60%	No	-0.780	17.2%
2	3.0	20	No	-2.451	0.8
3	3.0	60	No	-0.135	42.0
4	3.0	76	Yes	0.791	81.2
5	2.8	44	No	-0.847	15.5
6	2.6	56	Yes	0.062	51.5
7	2.6	68	Yes	0.757	80.2
8	2.4	40	Yes[a]	-0.649	21.1
9	2.4	60	No[a]	0.509	71.5
10	2.2	28	No	-1.129	9.6
11	2.0	40	No	-0.220	38.1
12	2.0	48	No[a]	0.244	60.1
13	1.8	60	Yes	1.153	89.7
14	1.6	20	No	-0.948	13.1
15	1.6	44	Yes	0.441	68.8
16	1.2	44	Yes	0.871	83.5
17	1.0	24	No	-0.072	45.0
18	1.0	32	Yes	0.391	66.7
19	1.0	60	Yes	2.012	97.9

[a]Denotes a misclassification. Firm 8 had Z = -0.649, so multiple discriminant analysis predicted no bankruptcy, but the firm *did* go bankrupt. Similarly, multiple discriminant analysis predicted bankruptcy for Firms 9 and 12, but they did *not* go bankrupt. The following tabulation shows bankruptcy and solvency predictions and actual results:

	Z Positive: Multiple Discriminant Analysis Predicts Bankruptcy	Z Negative: Multiple Discriminant Analysis Predicts Solvency
Went bankrupt	8	1
Remained solvent	2	8

Had the multiple discriminant analysis been "perfect" as a bankruptcy predictor, all the firms would have fallen in the diagonal cells. The model did not perform perfectly, as two predicted bankrupts remained solvent, while one firm that was expected to remain solvent went bankrupt. Thus the model misclassified 3 out of 19 firms, or 16 percent of the sample.

sume that data for some past period are available on a group of firms that went bankrupt and on another group that did not. For simplicity, we assume that only the current ratio and the debt/assets ratio are analyzed. These ratios for our sample of firms are given in Columns 2 and 3 of Table 22.4.

The data in Table 22.4 are plotted in Exhibit 22.4. The Xs represent firms that went bankrupt and the dots represent firms that remained solvent. For ex-

EXHIBIT   2 2 . 4

Discriminant Boundary between Bankrupt and Solvent Firms, Based on Current and Debt Ratios

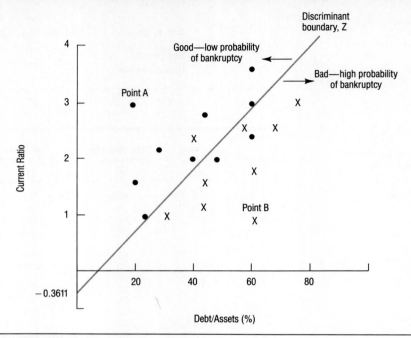

X = firms that went bankrupt
• = firms that remained solvent

ample, Point A in the upper left section is the point for Firm 2, which had a current ratio of 3.0 and a debt/assets ratio of 20 percent. The dot at Point A indicates that the firm did not go bankrupt. Point B, in the lower right section, represents Firm 19, which had a current ratio of 1.0 and a debt/assets ratio of 60 percent. It *did* go bankrupt. From a graphic perspective (the discriminant function), we construct a boundary line through the graph such that if the firm is to the left of the line, it is not likely to become insolvent. In our example it takes this form:

$$Z = a + b_1 \text{ (current ratio)} + b_2 \text{ (debt/assets ratio)}$$

Here a is a constant term and b_1 and b_2 indicate the effect that the current ratio and the debt/assets ratio have on the probability of a firm's going bankrupt.

The following discriminant function is obtained:

$$Z = -0.3877 - 1.0736 \text{ (current ratio)} + 0.0579 \text{ (debt/assets ratio)}$$

This equation may be plotted in Exhibit 22.4 as the locus of points for which $Z = 0$. All combinations of current ratio and debt/assets ratio shown on the line result in $Z = 0$.[5] Companies that lie to the left of the line are not likely to go bankrupt, while those to the right are likely to fail. It may be seen from the graph that one X, indicating a failed company, lies to the left of the line, while two dots, indicating nonbankrupt companies, lie to the right of the line. Thus the discriminant analysis failed to classify properly three companies.

If we have determined the parameters of the discriminant function, we can calculate the Z-score for other companies, say loan applicants at a bank. The Z-scores for our hypothetical companies are given in Column 5 of Table 22.4, and they may be interpreted as follows:

$Z = 0$: 50-50 probability of future bankruptcy (say within two years). The company lies on the boundary line.

$Z < 0$: If Z is negative, there is less than a 50 percent probability of bankruptcy. The smaller the Z-score, the lower the probability of bankruptcy. It is shown in Column 6 of Table 22.4.

$Z > 0$: If Z is positive, the probability of bankruptcy is greater than 50 percent. The larger Z is, the greater the probability of bankruptcy.

The mean Z-score of our companies that did not go bankrupt is -0.583, while that for the bankrupt firms is $+0.648$. These means, along with approximations of the Z-score probability distributions of the two groups, are shown in Exhibit 22.5. We may interpret this graph as indicating that if Z is less than about -0.3, there is a very small probability that a firm will turn out to be in the bankrupt group, while if Z is greater than $+0.3$, there is only a small probability that it will remain solvent. If Z is in the range ± 0.3, we are highly uncertain about how the firm should be classified. This range is called "the zone of ignorance."

The signs of the coefficients of the discriminant function are logical. Since its coefficient is negative, the larger the current ratio, the lower a company's Z-score, and the lower the Z-score, the smaller the probability of failure. Similarly, high debt ratios produce high Z-scores, and this is directly translated into a higher probability of bankruptcy.

E X H I B I T   2 2 . 5

Probability Distributions of Z Scores

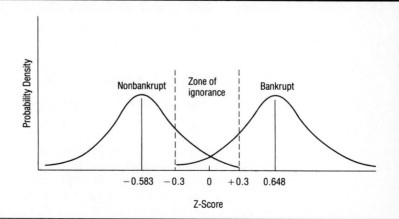

Our illustrative discriminant function has only two variables, but other characteristics could be introduced. For example, we could add such variables as the rate of return on assets (ROA), the times-interest-earned ratio, the quick ratio, and so forth.[6] Had the rate of return on assets been introduced, it might have turned out that Firm 8 (which failed) had a low ROA, while Firm 9 (which did not fail) had a high ROA. A new discriminant function would be calculated:

$$Z = a + b_1 \text{ (current ratio)} + b_2 \text{ (D/A)} + b_3 \text{(ROA)}$$

Firm 8 might now have a positive Z, while Firm 9's Z might become negative. Thus it is quite possible that by adding more characteristics we could improve the accuracy of our bankruptcy forecasts.

In terms of Exhibit 22.5, this would spread the probability distributions apart and narrow the zone of ignorance, while in terms of the confusion matrix in Table 22.4, more firms would fall on the diagonal and fewer in the off-diagonal cells.

Canonical Correlation

Canonical correlation, a very complex statistical technique that is not extensively used, is briefly examined here. When the research analyst has two or more criterion variables (dependent variables) and multiple predictor variables (independent variables), canonical correlation analysis is an appropriate statistical technique. Multiple regression analysis investigates the linear relationship between a single dependent or criterion variable and multiple independent variables. **Canonical correlation** is an extension of multiple regression. The focus of canonical correlation is upon the relationship between two sets of interval-scaled variables.

To illustrate canonical correlation, suppose a researcher wishes to specify the correlation between a set of shopping behavior variables (the criterion set) and some personality variables (the predictor set). The researcher is interested in knowing how several personality traits influence grocery-shopping behavior, such as list preparation, use of store coupons, number of stores visited, and number of trips per week. The researcher is attempting to find personality profiles that tend to be associated with various shopping patterns.

Calculation of the canonical correlation maximizes the correlation between two linear combinations. For example, the linear combinations for shopping behavior might be:

$$Z = a_1X_1 + a_2X_2 \cdots + a_nX_n$$

and the linear combination for the personality variables might be:

$$W = b_1Y_1 + b_2Y_2 \cdots + b_nY_n$$

As in regression analysis, a set of canonical coefficients or weights is identified for the predictor set of variables.

Further, a set of canonical coefficients or weights is identified for the criterion set. To interpret the canonical analysis, the researcher examines the relative magnitude and the signs of the several weights defining each equation, and sees if a meaningful interpretation can be given.

E X H I B I T   2 2 . 6   Summary of Multivariate Techniques for the Analysis of Dependence

Technique	Purpose	Number of Dependent Variables	Number of Independent Variables	Type of Measurement	
				Dependent	Independent
Multiple regression	To simultaneously investigate the effect of several independent variables on a dependent variable	1	2 or more	Interval or ratio	Interval or ratio
Discriminant analysis	To predict the probability of objects or individuals belonging in two or more mutually exclusive categories based on several independent variables	1	2 or more	Nominal	Interval or ratio
Canonical correlation	To determine the degree of linear association between two sets of variables, each consisting of several variables	2 or more	2 or more	Interval or ratio	Interval or ratio
MANOVA	To determine if statistically significant differences of means of several variables occur simultaneously between two levels of a variable	2 or more	1	Interval or ratio	Nominal

Source: The idea for this table was generated from information from p. 218 in *Survey Research: A Decisional Approach,* by D. S. Tull and G. Albaum. Copyright 1973 by Intext Educational Publishers. Reprinted by permission of Harper & Row, Publishers, Inc.

Multivariate Analysis of Variance (MANOVA)

As in canonical correlation, MANOVA is used when there are multiple dependent variables that are interval- or ratio-scaled variables. There may be one or more nominally scaled independent variables. A researcher conducting an experiment by manipulating the sales compensation system in an experimental situation and by holding the compensation system constant in a controlled situation may be interested in identifying the effect of the new compensation system on sales volume, as well as job satisfaction and turnover. With MANOVA a significance test of mean difference between groups can be made simultaneously for two or more dependent variables.

A summary of the multivariate techniques for analysis of dependents appears in Exhibit 22.6.

ANALYSIS OF INTERDEPENDENCE

Attention is now turned to the analysis of interdependence. Rather than attempting to predict a variable or set of variables from a set of independent variables, the purpose of techniques such as factor analysis, cluster analysis, and multidimensional scaling is to further understand the structure of a set of variables or objects.

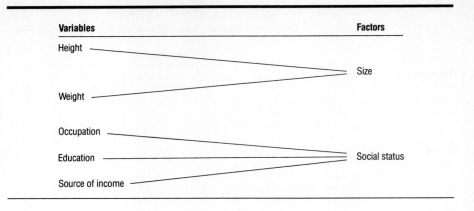

Factor Analysis

Suppose that we measure the height, weight, occupation, education, and source of income for 50 men. The results of a factor analysis might indicate that height and weight may be summarized by the underlying dimension of size. The variables—occupation, education, and source of income—may be summarized by the underlying concept of social status. In this example two new variables, or *factors,* explain the five variables at a more generalized level (Exhibit 22.7).

The general purpose of **factor analysis** is to summarize the information contained in a large number of variables into a smaller number of factors. Factor analysis refers to a diverse number of techniques used to discern the underlying dimensions or regularity in phenomena.[7]

If a researcher has a set of variables and suspects that these variables are interrelated in a complex fashion, then factor analysis may be used to untangle the linear relationships into their separate patterns. The statistical purpose of factor analysis is to determine linear combinations of variables that aid in investigating the interrelationships. For example, a researcher may collect a variety of data on middlemen's attitudes toward their working relationship with a manufacturer. Numerous questions about delivery, pricing arrangements, discounts, sales personnel, repair service, and other relevant issues might be asked. The researcher, however, may want to reduce the large number of variables to certain underlying constructs or dimensions that will summarize the important information contained in the variables. Thus the researcher's purpose is to discover the basic structure of a domain and to add substantive interpretation to the underlying dimensions. Factor analysis accomplishes this by combining these questions to create new, more abstract variables called factors. In general, the goal of factor analysis is parsimony: to reduce a large number of variables to as few dimensions or constructs as possible.

Interpreting Factor Results.   How factor analysis can be used to reduce a large number of variables to a few interpretable dimensions is illustrated in the following consumer behavior example in a health-care setting.[8] With advances in medical science, there has been an increased demand for nonregenerative body

Variable and Factor Descriptions	Factor Loadings		
	Factor 1	Factor 2	Factor 3
Blood, Skin, Marrow			
I would be willing to donate *blood* at least once every two months.	[.3807][b]	.1646	.2009
If I witnessed a traffic accident, I would not be willing to donate *blood* to a victim.	[−.4244]	−.0304	−.1503
If needed, I am willing to give *blood* to a relative or close friend.	[.6339]	.0988	.0517
I would give a piece of my *skin* to a relative who has been seriously burnt.	[.4556]	.1405	.1356
If necessary, I would donate some *bone marrow* to be extracted from my breastbone to a relative.	[.5377]	.3440	.2681
Death Donation			
I am willing to donate both my eyes to a stranger upon my *death*.	.1412	[.7944]	.2946
I am willing to arrange an agreement to donate my heart or any other vital organ for use after my *death*.	.2410	[.7582]	.1664
Kidney Donation			
I would never donate one of my *kidneys* to someone outside of my family, not even to a close friend.	−.1669	−.2544	[−.6770]
If needed, I would donate one of my *kidneys* to a stranger at this very moment.	.1641	.1486	[.6584]
If at this moment I learned that a relative desperately needed a *kidney* to survive, I would not donate one of mine.	−.3814	−.1596	[−.5272]
Explained Variance per Factor	36.9%	12.2%	10.2%
Cumulative	36.9	49.1	59.3

[a] 377 respondents.

[b] [   ] indicates the highest loading in each row.

Source: Edgar A. Pessemier, Albert C. Bemmaor, and Dominique Hanssens, "Willingness to Supply Human Body Parts: Some Empirical Results," *Journal of Consumer Research,* December 1977, p. 134. Reprinted with permission.

parts, such as kidneys, and regenerative body parts, such as blood. The researchers were attempting to investigate whether willingness to donate body parts was a unidimensional domain. Based on factor analysis (Table 22.5), there appear to be three separate underlying dimensions of willingness to donate: Factor 1, blood, skin, and marrow donations; Factor 2, death (cadaver) donation; and Factor 3, kidney donation.

Factor Loadings. The factor loadings in Table 22.5 are roughly analogous to the correlation (or a set of the correlations) of the original variable with the factor. Each **factor loading** is a measure of the importance of the variable in measuring each factor. In the example the statement "If needed, I am willing to give blood to a relative or close friend" has a high factor loading (.6339) on the first factor and a relatively low loading on Factors 2 and 3. Inspection of the table indicates that for each of the variables loading on the blood, skin, marrow factor (Factor 1), the loadings are much higher on Factor 1 than on Factors 2 and 3. Factor loadings provide a means for interpreting and labeling the factors.

Total Variance Explained. In addition to the factor loadings, Table 22.5 portrays a percentage of total variance of the original variables as explained by each factor. The first factor summarizes 36.9 percent of the variance and the second factor summarizes 12.2 percent of the variance. Together the two factors summarize 49.1 percent of the total variance. This explanation of variance is equivalent to the R^2 in multiple regression.

Factor Scores. Each individual observation has a score or value associated with each of the original variables. Factor analysis procedures derive **factor scores** that represent each observation's calculated value or score on each of the factors. The factor score will represent an individual's combined response to the several variables representing the factor.

The factor scores may be used in subsequent analysis. When the factors are to represent a new set of variables that may predict or will be dependent on some phenomenon, the new input may be factor scores.

In addition to reducing a large number of variables to a manageable number of dimensions, factor analysis may also reduce the problem of multicollinearity in multiple regression.[9] If several independent variables are highly correlated, a factor analysis as a preliminary step prior to regression analysis and use of factor scores may reduce the problem of having several intercorrelated independent variables. Thus factor analysis may be utilized to meet the statistical assumptions of various models.

Communality. A researcher may wish to know how much a variable has in common with all factors. **Communality** is a measure of the percentage of a variable's variation that is explained by the factors. A relatively high communality indicates that a variable has much in common with the other variables taken as a group.

How Many Factors? This discussion has concentrated on summarizing the patterns in the variables with a reduced number of factors. The question arises, "How many factors will be in the problem's solution?" This question requires a lengthy, complex answer. It is complex because there can be more than one possible solution to any factor analysis problem, depending on factor rotation. The technical aspects of the concept of factor rotation are beyond the scope of this book. However, the term *rotation* is important in factor analysis and it should be briefly explained. Solutions to factor analysis problems may be portrayed by geometrically plotting the values of each variable for all respondents or observations. Geometric axes may be drawn to represent each factor. New solutions are represented geometrically, by rotation of these axes. Hence a new solution with fewer or more factors is called a **rotation.**

Although the concept of factor analysis is relatively easy to grasp, the technical vocabulary of factor analysis includes a number of unusual terms, such as *eigenvalues, rotated matrix,* and *orthogonal.* Because this is a simplified introduction to the topic of multivariate statistics, we will not define these terms. Competent statisticians should be consulted when working on problems involving factor analysis.

Cluster Analysis

Cluster analysis is a term given to a body of techniques used to identify objects or individuals that are similar with respect to some criterion. The purpose of cluster analysis is to classify individuals or objects into a small number of mutually exclusive and exhaustive groups. The researcher's focus is to determine how objects or individuals should be assigned to groups to ensure that there will be as much likeness within groups and as much difference among groups as possible. The cluster should have high internal (within cluster) homogeneity and high external (between cluster) heterogeneity.

A typical use of cluster analysis is facilitating market segmentation by identifying subjects or individuals who have similar needs, life-styles, or responses to marketing strategies. Clusters or subgroups of recreational vehicle owners may be identified on the basis of their similarity of usage of and benefits sought from recreational vehicles. Alternatively, the researcher might use demographic variables or life-style variables to group individuals into clusters identified as market segments.

Cluster analysis is illustrated by a hypothetical example of the nature of vacations taken by 12 individuals. Vacation behavior is represented on two dimensions: number of vacation days and dollar expenditures on vacations during a given year. Exhibit 22.8 is a scatter diagram that represents the geometric distance between the 12 individuals in two-dimensional space. The scatter dia-

EXHIBIT   2 2 . 8

**Cluster of Individuals
on Two Dimensions**

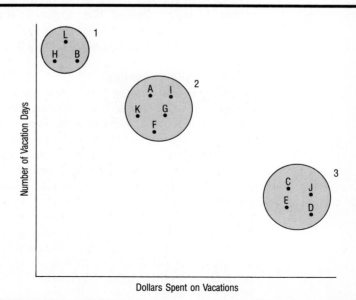

gram portrays three clear-cut clusters. The first subgroup, consisting of individuals L, H, and B, suggests a group of individuals who have many vacation days but do not spend much money on their vacations. The second cluster, consisting of individuals A, I, K, G, and F, represents intermediate values on both variables: an average number of vacation days and an average dollar expenditure on vacations. The third group consists of a cluster of individuals who have relatively few vacation days but spend a large amount on these outings.

In this hypothetical example individuals are grouped on the basis of similarity or proximity of the individual. The logic of cluster analysis is to group individuals or objects on the bases of their similarity or distance from each other. The actual mathematical procedures for deriving clusters will not be dealt with here, as our purpose is only to introduce the technique.[10]

A study by Green, Frank, and Robinson provides a pragmatic example of the use of cluster analysis. Managers are frequently interested in finding test-market cities that are sufficiently similar so that no extraneous variation causes a difference between the experimental and control markets. In this example the objects to be clustered were cities. The characteristics of the cities, such as population, retail sales, number of retail outlets, and percentage of nonwhites, were used to identify the groups. Cities such as Omaha, Oklahoma City, Dayton, Columbus, and Fort Worth and cities such as Newark, Pittsburgh, Cleveland, Buffalo, and Baltimore were similar; but individual cities in each group of cities were dissimilar. See Exhibit 22.9 for additional details.

This example should clarify the difference between factor analysis and cluster analysis. In factor analysis the researcher might search for constructs underlying the variables (population, retail sales, number of retail outlets); in cluster analysis the researcher searches for constructs underlying the objects (cities).

Cluster analysis differs from multiple discriminant analysis in that the groups are not predefined. The purpose of cluster analysis is to determine how many groups really exist and to define their composition. It describes a sample of objects after examining only a sample. It does not predict relationships.

Multidimensional Scaling

Multidimensional scaling provides a means for measuring objects in multidimensional space on the basis of respondents' similarity of judgments of objects. The perceptual difference between objects is reflected in the relative distance between objects in multidimensional space.

Traditionally, attitudes have been measured by using a scale to measure each component of an attitude and then combining the individual's scores into an aggregate score. In the most common form of multidimensional scaling, the subject is asked to evaluate an object's similarity to other objects. For example, in a career orientation study the respondent may be asked to rate the similarity of a certified public accountant to a management consultant.[11] Then the analyst attempts to explain the differences between the objects on the basis of the components of attitudes. The unfolding of the attitude components aids in an understanding of why objects are judged to be similar or dissimilar.

EXHIBIT 22.9

Cluster Analysis of Test-Market Cities

Cluster Number	City	Cluster Number	City	Cluster Number	City
1	Omaha	7	Sacramento	13	Allentown
	Oklahoma City		San Bernardino		Providence
	Dayton		San Jose		Jersey City
	Columbus		Phoenix		York
	Fort Worth		Tucson		Louisville
2	Peoria	8	Gary	14	Paterson
	Davenport		Nashville		Milwaukee
	Binghamton		Jacksonville		Cincinnati
	Harrisburg		San Antonio		Miami
	Worcester		Knoxville		Seattle
3	Canton	9	Indianapolis	15	San Diego
	Youngstown		Kansas City		Tacoma
	Toledo		Dallas		Norfolk
	Springfield		Atlanta		Charleston
	Albany		Houston		Ft. Lauderdale
4	Bridgeport	10	Mobile	16	New Orleans
	Rochester		Shreveport		Richmond
	Hartford		Birmingham		Tampa
	New Haven		Memphis		Lancaster
	Syracuse		Chattanooga		Minneapolis
5	Wilmington	11	Newark	17	San Francisco
	Orlando		Cleveland		Detroit
	Tulsa		Pittsburgh		Boston
	Wichita		Buffalo		Philadelphia
	Grand Rapids		Baltimore	18	Washington
6	Bakersfield	12	Albuquerque		St. Louis
	Fresno		Salt Lake City		
	Flint		Denver		
	El Paso		Charlotte		
	Beaumont		Portland		

Note: Points not in a cluster—Honolulu, Wilkes-Barre.

Source: Paul E. Green, Ronald E. Frank, and Patrick J. Robinson, "Cluster Analysis in Test Market Selection," *Management Science,* Volume 13, April, 1967, p. B393 (Table 2). Copyright 1967 by The Institute of Management Science. Reprinted with permission.

An illustration of the ways that MBA students perceive six graduate schools of business also helps to explain multidimensional scaling. The students were asked to provide their perceptions of relative similarities among the set of graduate schools. Next, the overall similarity scores for all possible pairs of objects were aggregated for all individual respondents and arranged in a matrix. With the aid of a complex computer program, the similarity judgments were statistically transformed into distances by placing the graduate schools of business into a specified multidimensional space. The distance between similar objects on the perceptual map is small. Dissimilar objects are not close together.

Exhibit 22.10 is a perceptual map in two-dimensional space. Inspection of the map illustrates that Harvard and Stanford were perceived to be quite similar to each other, and that MIT and Carnegie were perceived to be very

E X H I B I T   2 2 . 1 0

**Perceptual Map of Six
Graduate Business
Schools—Simple Space**

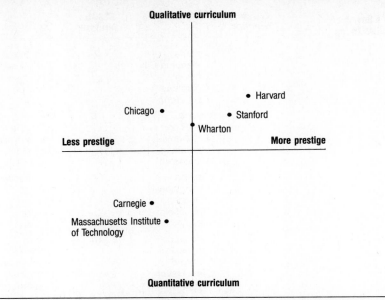

Source: Paul E. Green, F. J. Carmone, and P. J. Robertson, "Nonmetric Scaling Methods: An Exposition and Overview," *Wharton Quarterly*, 2 (1968): 159–173. Reprinted with permission.

similar. However, MIT and Chicago were perceived to be dissimilar. The researchers identified the two axes as "quantitative versus qualitative curriculum" and "less versus more prestige." The labeling of the dimension axes is a task of interpretation for the researcher and is not statistically determined. As with other multivariate techniques in the analysis of interdependence, there are several alternative mathematical techniques for multidimensional scaling.

Automatic Interaction Detection (AID)

Automatic interaction detection (AID), which may be utilized as a clustering method, was originally developed to investigate the interaction of a large set of independent variables.[12] The computer-assisted analysis begins with a total group. The objective is to form subgroups by a number of sequentially generated binary splits. The procedure begins when the researcher selects a dependent variable. The AID program then "tears down" the groups by searching through the various categorical independent variables to obtain a split on a single independent variable that will account for the largest variation in the dependent variable.

Exhibit 22.11 shows an example of AID analysis in the savings and loan industry. "Average savings account balance" was selected as the dependent variable. This means that the analysis attempts to explain the shared characteristics of the major segments associated with "average savings account balance."[13]

EXHIBIT 22.11

"Average Savings Account Balance" AID Analysis

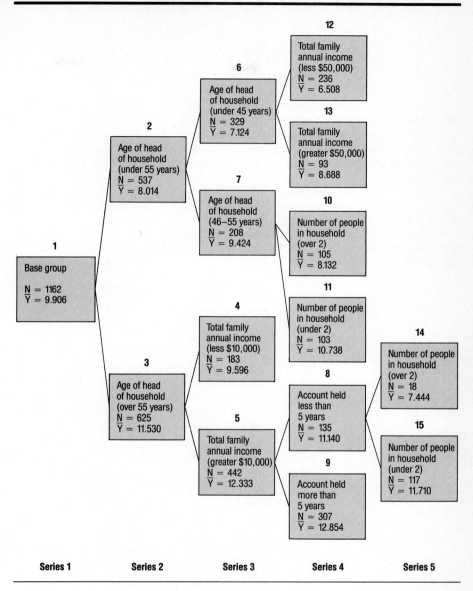

| Series 1 | Series 2 | Series 3 | Series 4 | Series 5 |

Thus, in the box labeled base group, the average savings account balance for all customers observed ($\overline{Y}$) was 9.906, or approximately $10,000 per account. The AID algorithm searches all of the independent variables and attempts to find the variables that have the largest difference in terms of mean value and sum of squares. It picks the variable that contributes most to the

R E S E A R C H   I N S I G H T

Seven Commandments for Users of Multivariate Methods

1. Do not be technique oriented—focus on management's needs, then choose an appropriate analytical tool.

2. Consider multivariate models as information for management—multivariate models (equations, or perceptual maps) are an aid to, not a substitute for, managerial judgment.

3. Do not substitute multivariate methods for researcher skill and imagination—statistics do not assure causality and are not substitutes for common sense.

4. Develop communication skill—management seldom accepts findings based on methods [it doesn't] understand.

5. Avoid making statistical inferences about the parameters of multivariate models—we are seldom certain of the distribution of a population due to nonsampling and measurement errors.

6. Guard against the danger of making inferences about the market realities when such inference may be due to the peculiarities of the method—be sure the statistical findings are consistent with sound theory and common sense.

7. Exploit the complementary relationship between functional and structural methods—use one method to support another.

Source: Jagdish N. Sheth, "Seven Commandments for Users of Multivariate Methods," in *Multivariate Methods for Market and Survey Research*, 1977, pp. 333–335, edited by Jagdish N. Sheth. Reprinted by permission of the American Marketing Association.

---

splitting to be the first variable of the split. In our example the first binary split is based on age. The first split is based on people under 55 and people over 55 years of age. People under 55 have a mean balance value of 8.014 and people over 55 have a different mean balance of 11.530. Hence it appears that older individuals have larger savings and loan balances.

As the sequence progresses to the next split, we find that, for individuals over 55, this group is split into two subgroups. This splitting is based on differences in the mean of the dependent variable between the two new groups that differ in income level. Further splits in the AID tree are based on the two other independent variables, "years account has been held" and "number of people in household." The value of the AID program becomes evident when the interaction effect with the predictor variable "total annual family income" is scrutinized. It appears at first glance that the higher the total family income, the higher the savings balance. However, closer inspection of the diagram reveals that the "over $10,000" mark is prevalent only for people who are 55 years and older. For younger savers the income requirement for greater savings balance is at the $50,000 mark, as seen by the splitting of Group 6 into Groups 12 and 13 in the fourth series.

AID is a very interesting and logical way of breaking a large nonhomogeneous group into various homogeneous subgroups. It is also a logical first step in doing several kinds of multivariate analysis when the homogeneity of the sample is in serious question.

A summary of the multivariate techniques for analysis of interdependence appears in Exhibit 22.12.

Technique	Purpose	Type of Measurement
Factor analysis	To summarize the information contained in a large number of variables into a reduced number of factors	Interval or ratio
Cluster analysis	To classify individuals or objects into a smaller number of mutually exclusive and exhaustive groups, ensuring that there will be as much likeness within groups and as much difference between groups as possible	Interval or ratio
Multidimensional scaling	To measure objects in multidimensional space on the basis of respondents' similarity judgments of objects	Varies depending on technique

SUMMARY

Multivariate analysis is used in problems involving three or more variables. The availability of canned computer programs, prepared to process multivariate statistics, has made such usage more practical in recent years. The dependence method uses two or more independent variables to predict a dependent variable(s). The interdependence method groups subsets of the variables.

A common dependence method is multiple regression. It is an extension of bivariate linear regression using more than one independent variable. The coefficients of partial regression obtained in multiple regression hold all other independent variables constant, and thus they are not identical to the corresponding simple regression coefficients. The coefficient of multiple determination (R^2) represents the portion of the variance in the dependent variable accounted for by the model. An F-test can be used to determine statistical significance.

Another dependence technique is discriminant analysis. It uses the independent variables to classify observations into one of a set of mutually exclusive categories.

Canonical correlation and multivariate analysis of variance are more complex dependence techniques. Canonical correlation uses two criterion variables (dependent variables) and multiple predictor variables (independent variables). Multivariate analysis of variance, or MANOVA, allows significance tests of mean differences between groups for two or more dependent variables.

The first interdependence method is factor analysis. It is used to summarize the information contained in a large number of variables into a smaller number of factors. A second method is cluster analysis, which classifies observations into a small number of mutually exclusive and exhaustive groups. These should have as much likeness within groups and as much difference between groups as possible. In cluster analysis the groups are not predefined.

A third interdependence method is multidimensional scaling. It measures objects in a multidimensional space, based on respondents' similarity judgments. The procedure explains the perceived relationships by unfolding the attitude components making up the judgments.

The purpose of AID (automatic interaction detection) analysis is to form subgroups by searching through the various categorical independent variables to obtain a split on a single independent variable that will account for the largest variation in the dependent variable.

Key Terms

multivariate analysis	factor analysis
analysis of dependence	factor loadings
analysis of interdependence	factor scores
multiple regression analysis	communality
coefficient of partial regression	rotation
coefficient of multiple determination	cluster analysis
multiple discriminant analysis	multidimensional scaling
canonical correlation	automatic interaction detection (AID)
multivariate analysis of variance (MANOVA)	

Questions

1. How do multivariate statistical methods differ from univariate and bivariate methods?
2. What is the distinction between dependence methods and interdependence methods?
3. What is the aim of multiple linear regression? Discriminant analysis? Canonical correlation? Multivariate analysis of variance?
4. Give an example of a situation for which each of the techniques mentioned in Question 3 might be used.
5. What is the aim of factor analysis? Cluster analysis? Multidimensional scaling?
6. Give an example of a situation for which each of the techniques mentioned in Question 5 might be used.
7. Why have canned computer programs increased the use of multivariate analysis?
8. Why might a researcher want to use a multivariate analysis rather than a univariate or bivariate analysis?
9. Using the data from Question 8 in Chapter 15, answer the following questions:
    a. Calculate all bivariate regression equations that will predict current sales. Which is the best one?
    b. Using multiple regression, find a model that will help explain current sales.
    c. Conduct a multiple discriminant analysis to see if you can predict the region in which a salesperson works.

d.   Use cluster analysis to see if there are any natural groupings among the salespeople.

References

[1] Today's Army Relying on Marketing Research to Obtain Recruitment Goals," *Marketing News,* July 6, 1983, 1, 16.

[2] For excellent discussions of multivariate analysis, see Joseph F. Hair, Jr., Rolph E. Anderson, and Ronald L. Tatham, *Multivariate Data Analysis with Readings,* 2nd ed. (New York: Macmillan, 1987); and Jagdish N. Sheth, "The Multivariate Revolution in Marketing," *Journal of Marketing Research* 35 (January 1971): 13–19.

[3] Ibid.

[4] This example is adapted from Eugene F. Brigham and Louis C. Gapenski, *Financial Management: Theory and Practice* 5/e (Hinsdale, IL: The Dryden Press, 1988), pp. 801–805.

[5] To plot the boundary line, let $D/A = 0\%$ and 80%; then find the current ratio that forces $Z = 0$, for example, at $D/A = 0$.

$$Z = -0.3877 - 1.0736(\text{current ratio}) + 0.0579(0) = 0$$
$$-1.0736(\text{current ratio}) = 0.3877$$
$$\text{Current ratio} = 0.3877/-1.0736 = -0.3611$$

Thus -0.3611 is the vertical axis intercept. Similarly, the current ratio at $D/A = 80$ percent is found to be 3.3633. Plotting these two points in Exhibit 22.4 and then connecting them provides the discriminant boundary line. It is the line that best partitions the companies into bankrupt and nonbankrupt. It should be noted that nonlinear discriminant functions may also be used.

[6] With more than two variables, it is difficult to graph the function, but this presents no problem in actual usage because graphs are only used to explain multiple discriminant analysis.

[7] The purpose of this section is to discuss factor-analytic techniques at an intuitive level. The discussion is not complicated by the various mathematically complicated differences between the techniques. An excellent discussion of the mathematical aspects of factor analysis can be found in R. J. Rummel, "Understanding Factor Analysis," *Journal of Conflict Resolution* 11, no. 4: 444–480.

[8] Edgar A. Pessemier, Albert C. Bemmaor, and Dominique M. Hanssens, "Willingness to Supply Human Body Parts: Some Empirical Results," *Journal of Consumer Research* 4, no. 3 (December 1977): 131–140. Used by permission.

[9] The multiple regression model assumes the independent variables are independent of each other. *Multicollinearity* is the technical term used when some of the predictor variables are correlated with each other. For example, the consumer price index and the federal mortgage rate both show a similar historical trend. Thus it would be difficult to appraise their individual influence on a dependent variable, as opposed to their joint influence.

[10] Ronald E. Frank and Paul E. Green, "Numerical Taxonomy in Marketing Analysis: A Review Article," *Journal of Marketing Research* (February 1968): 83–98.

[11] For a discussion of this measuring process, see Lester A. Neidell, "The Use of Nonmetric Multidimensional Scaling in Market Analysis," *Journal of Marketing* (October 1969): 37–43; and Richard S. Blackburn, "Multidimensional Scaling and the Organizational Sciences," *Journal of Management* 8, no. 1: 95–103.

[12] John A. Sonquist and James N. Morgan, *The Source of Interaction Effects,* University of Michigan, Institute of Social Research, 1969 (IS Project 719 MRT 33); and John A. Sonquist, Elizabeth L. Baker, and James N. Morgan, *Searching for Structure* (Ann Arbor: Institute for Social Research, 1973).

[13] This discussion follows the logic of Gerald Zaltman and Philip Berger, *Marketing Research* (Hinsdale, IL: Dryden Press, 1973), 511–512. This example is taken from James Richard Darnaby, "Bank Marketing: Market Segmentation Aimed at Increasing Consumer Profitability" (Master's thesis, Oklahoma State University, July 1979), 31–34.

CHAPTER **23**

Communicating Research Results: Research Report, Oral Presentation, and Research Follow-up[1]

What you will learn in this chapter:

To explain how the research report is the crucial means for communicating the whole research project.

To discuss the research report from a communications model perspective.

To define the research report.

To outline the research report format and its parts.

To discuss the importance of using graphics in research reporting.

To explain how tables and charts are useful for presenting numerical information and how to interpret the various portions of tables and charts.

To identify the various types of research charts.

To discuss how the oral presentation may be the most efficient means of supplementing the written report.

To understand the importance of the research follow-up.

$\mathbf{A}$*fter spending days, weeks, or even months working on a project, a researcher is likely to feel that preparation of a report on that project is an anticlimactic formality. After all, it seems the real work has all been done; it just has to be put on paper. This attitude can be disastrous. The project may have been well designed, the data carefully obtained and analyzed by sophisticated statistical methods, and important conclusions reached, but if the project is not effectively reported, all the preceding effort has been wasted. Many times the research report is the only part of the project that others will ever see. Users of the report cannot separate the* content *of the project and the* form *in which it is presented. If people who need to use the research results have to wade through a disorganized presentation, or are detoured by technical jargon they don't understand, or find sloppiness of language or thought, they will probably discount the report and make decisions without it—just as if the project had never been done. Thus the research report is the crucial means for communicating the whole project—the medium by which it makes an impact on decisions.*

This chapter explains how research reports, oral presentations, and follow-up conversations help communicate research results.

■

COMMUNICATIONS MODEL INSIGHTS

Some insights from the theory of communications help clarify the importance of the research report. Exhibit 23.1 illustrates one view of the **communication process.** Several elements enter into successful communication:

1. The *communicator,* the source or sender of the message (the writer of the report).
2. The *message,* the set of meanings being sent to or received by the audience (the findings of the research project).

EXHIBIT   23.1

The Communication Process—I

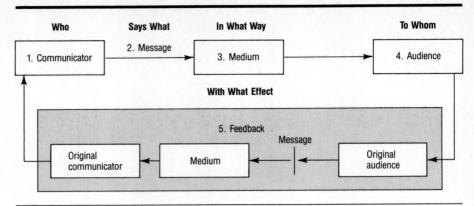

3.   The *medium,* or the means by which the message is carried or delivered to the audience (the oral or written report itself).
4.   The *audience,* the receiver or destination of the message (the manager who will make a decision based, we hope, on the report finding).
5.   *Feedback,* a reverse flow of communication also involving a message and channel, from the audience to the original communicator, which may be used to modify subsequent communications (the manager's response to the report).

This model of communication, though, overstates the case of the communication. It seems that the message flows smoothly along from the writer to the reader, who in turn promptly provides the writer with feedback. Actually, things are more complex, and Exhibit 23.2 emphasizes one of the difficulties.

The communicator and the audience each has a field of experience. These overlap to some extent; otherwise, no communication would be possible. Nevertheless, there is much experience that is not common to both parties. As the communicators send a message, they code it in terms that make sense to them, based on their fields of experience. As the audience receives the message, individuals decode it, based on their own fields of experience. The message is successfully communicated only if there is enough common experience that it may be encoded, transmitted, and decoded with roughly the same meaning.

In the research setting we have a communicator (the researcher) who has spent a great deal of time studying a problem. The researcher has looked at secondary sources, gathered primary data, used statistical techniques to analyze the data, and reached conclusions. When the report on the project is written, all this baggage affects its content. Researchers may assume the reader has a lot of background information on the project. The researchers produce pages of unexplained tables, assuming the reader will dig out from them the same patterns they have observed. The report may use technical terms, such as *parameter, F-distribution, hypothesis test, correlation,* or *eigenvalue,* assuming the reader will understand. Or, on the other hand, the report may go over-

EXHIBIT   23.2

**The Communication
Process—II**

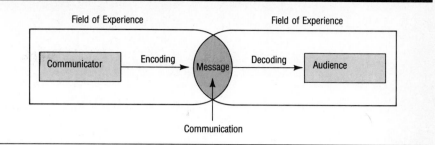

board, explaining everything in sixth-grade terms to make sure the reader is not lost, thereby insulting the reader in the process.

In reality, when the reader receives the report, he or she usually hasn't thought much about the project. The reader may or may not know anything about statistics. In addition, the reader may have many other responsibilities, and if the report can't be understood quickly, it may be added to the stack of things to do "someday."

Under these circumstances, which are certainly not unusual, it can be seen that delivering the report to an audience is not sufficient. It needs to be written to hit the area of common experience between the researcher and the manager. And, to be realistic, the effort to hit that common zone of experience is the responsibility of the writer, not the reader. Unless the report is of a really crucial nature, a busy reader will not spend time and effort struggling through an inadequate report.

THE REPORT IN CONTEXT

A **research report** has been defined as an oral presentation and/or a written statement that has the purpose of communicating research results, strategic recommendations, and/or other conclusions to management and/or other specific audiences.[2] This chapter deals primarily with the final *written report,* with one section on the oral presentation of the research findings. The chapter emphasizes the sort of written report that is needed in an extensive research project. It is easy to adapt the chapter's suggestions for a shorter, less formal report. It is worth remembering, however, that the final report may not be the only kind prepared. For a small project a short oral or written report on the results may be all that is needed. On the other hand, in extensive conferences many written documents, interim reports, and a long, final, written report, with several oral presentations, may be involved.[3]

The emphasis on the final report in this chapter should not be taken to mean that other communications, such as progress reports, during the project are any less important to its eventual success. An appendix on the writing process appears at the end of this chapter, where several principles for organizing, writing, and rewriting are discussed in detail.

EXHIBIT   23.3   **The Makeup of the Report**

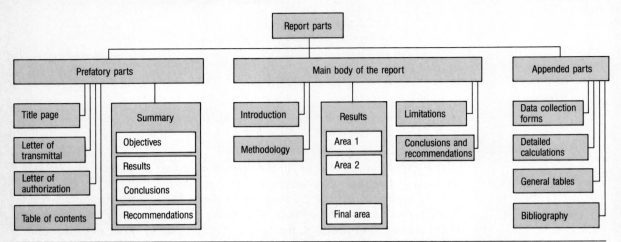

Source: Adapted from Jessamon Dawe and William Jackson Lord, Jr., *Functional Business Communication,* 2d ed., © 1974, 195. Adapted by permission of Prentice-Hall Inc., Englewood Cliffs, NJ, 289.

REPORT FORMAT

Although every research report is custom-made for the project it represents, some conventions of report format are universal. These conventions have developed over a long period of time, and they represent a consensus about what parts are necessary to a good research report and how they should be ordered. The consensus is not inviolable law, though. Each report-writing book suggests its own unique format, and every report writer has to pick and choose the parts and the order that work best for the project at hand. Many companies or universities also have an in-house, suggested report format or writing guide that researchers should be aware of. Thus the suggested format given here is the basis for the discussion in this chapter, and a beginning point from which the writer can shape his or her own appropriate format.[4] The **report format** is listed here and shown graphically in Exhibits 23.3 and 23.4:

1. Title page (sometimes preceded by title fly page)
2. Letter of transmittal
3. Letter of authorization
4. Table of contents (and lists of figures and tables)
5. Summary
   5.1   Objectives
   5.2   Results
   5.3   Conclusions
   5.4   Recommendations

EXHIBIT   23.4

The Report Format

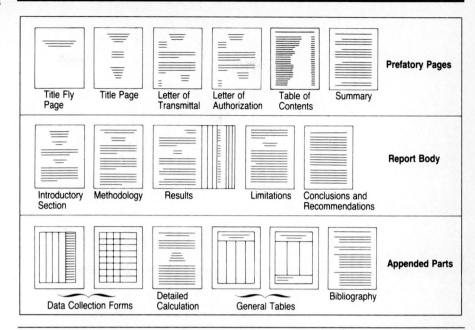

Prefatory Pages

Title Fly Page | Title Page | Letter of Transmittal | Letter of Authorization | Table of Contents | Summary

Report Body

Introductory Section | Methodology | Results | Limitations | Conclusions and Recommendations

Appended Parts

Data Collection Forms | Detailed Calculation | General Tables | Bibliography

Source: Adapted from David M. Robinson, *Writing Reports for Management Decisions* (Columbus, Ohio: Merrill, 1969), p. 301. Adapted with permission.

6. Body
    6.1 Introduction
        6.11   Background
        6.12   Objectives
    6.2 Methodology
    6.3 Results
    6.4 Limitations
    6.5 Conclusions and recommendations
7. Appendix
    7.1 Data collection forms
    7.2 Detailed calculations
    7.3 General tables
    7.4 Bibliography
    7.5 Other support material

Tailoring the Format to the Project

The format may need adjustment for two reasons: (1) to obtain the proper level of formality and (2) to alter the complexity of the report. The format given here is for the most formal type, such as a report for a large project done within an organization or a report from a research agency to a client company. This sort

E X H I B I T   2 3 . 5   **Adapting Format to Level of Formality**

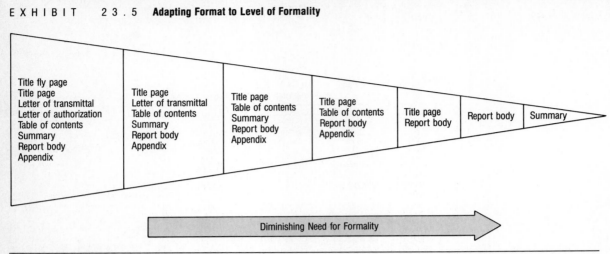

Title fly page
Title page
Letter of transmittal
Letter of authorization
Table of contents
Summary
Report body
Appendix

Title page
Letter of transmittal
Table of contents
Summary
Report body
Appendix

Title page
Table of contents
Summary
Report body
Appendix

Title page
Table of contents
Report body
Appendix

Title page
Report body

Report body

Summary

Diminishing Need for Formality

Source: David M. Robinson, *Writing Reports for Management Decisions* (Columbus, Ohio: Merrill, 1969), p. 295. Adapted with permission.

of report would probably be bound with a fancy cover and could be hundreds of pages long.

For less formal reports, each part would be shorter, and some parts would be omitted. Exhibit 23.5 illustrates how the format is adapted to shorter and less formal reports. The change may be compared to variations in clothing according to the formality of the occasion. The most formal report is, so to speak, in white tie and tails (or long evening gown).[5] It includes the full assortment of prefatory parts—the title fly page, title page, and letters of transmittal and authorization.

The next level of formality would be like a regular business suit, dropping those parts of the prefatory material not needed in this situation and reducing the complexity of the body material. In general, as the report goes down through the sport coat, slacks, and blue jeans stages, the prefatory parts are dropped and the complexity and length of the report body are reduced.

How does the researcher decide on the appropriate level of formality? The general rule is to include all the parts needed for effective communication in the particular circumstances, and no more.[6] This factor relates to how far up in management the report is expected to go and to how routine the matter is. The researcher's immediate supervisor doesn't need a 100-page full-dress report on a routine project. On the other hand, the board of directors doesn't want a one-page "blue jeans" report on a big project backing a major expansion program. Note that the white-tie-and-tails report to top management may later be stripped of some of the prefatory parts (and thus reduced in formality) for wider circulation in the company.

Parts of the Report

Title Page.   The title page will include the title of the report, whom the report was prepared for, whom it was prepared by, and the date of release or presentation. The title should be chosen to give a brief but complete indication of the purpose of the research project. Addresses and titles of the preparer and recipient may also be included. On reports of a confidential nature a list of the people to whom it should be circulated may be supplied. For the most formal reports a title fly page will precede the title page. On this page only the title appears.

Letter of Transmittal.   This element is included in relatively formal to very formal reports. Its purpose is to release or deliver the report to the recipient. It also serves to establish some rapport between the reader and the writer. This is the one part of the formal report where a personal, or even a slightly informal, tone should be used. The transmittal should not dive into report findings except in the broadest terms.

A sample letter of transmittal is given in Exhibit 23.6. Note that the opening releases the report and briefly identifies the factors of authorization. The letter comments generally on findings and matters of interest about the research. The closing section expresses the writer's personal interest in the project just completed and in doing additional related work.[7]

Letter of Authorization.   This is a letter to the researcher approving the project, detailing who has responsibility for the project and indicating what resources are available to support it. Because the researcher would not write this personally, writing guidelines will not be discussed here.[8] In many situations, referring to the authorization in the letter of transmittal is sufficient. If so, the letter of authorization need not be included in the report. In some cases, though, the readers may be unfamiliar with the authorization or may need detailed information about the authorization factors. In such cases the letter should be included, preferably in an exact reproduction of the original.

Table of Contents.   The table of contents is essential to any report more than a few pages long. It should list the divisions and subdivisions of the report with page references. The table of contents is based on the final outline of the report, but it should include only the first-level subdivisions. In short reports inclusion of only the main divisions will be sufficient. If the report includes many figures or tables, a list of these should also be included immediately following the table of contents.

Summary.   The summary briefly tells why the research project was conducted, what aspects of the problem were considered, what the outcome was, and what should be done. It is a vital part of the report. Studies have indicated that most managers always read a report's summary, whereas only a minority read the rest of the report.[9] Thus the only chance a writer may have for an impact may be in the summary.

SOFTPROOF LEATHER PRODUCTS COMPANY, INC.
KENT, OHIO 44240

December 1, 19XX

Mr. Carl M. Wheeler
Vice President for Marketing
Home Office

Subject: Presentation of Report on Study of Small-Volume Customers

Dear Mr. Wheeler:

Here is my report on the study of small-volume customers. This report, the
subject of our conference today, was prepared according to your authorization
memorandum dated April 21, 19XX.

As we suspected would be the case when we started the study, the report
recommends that we take a very careful new look at our present attitude toward
serving customers whose volumes are less than $20,000 per year. Some of the
experienced salesmen whom we contacted in personal interviews gave us some
excellent suggestions about what our new attitude should be.

The returns from our mail survey of small-volume customers were not as high
as we wanted them to be. We do believe, though, that the questionnaires
returned are representative of the customers involved in the study. The
follow-up survey of a sample of customers who did not return the first
questionnaire was most reassuring on this point.

As is perhaps typical of a research department, we discovered during this
study another problem area which might bear investigation. This area is
that of redefining the boundaries of our sales territories. We are now doing
some preliminary thinking about this problem. Should we decide research is
warranted, we later will make our recommendations to you.

We are grateful to you, Mr. Wheeler, for your cooperation in this important
study. Your keeping the president informally up to date on our progress
should pave the way toward his accepting the recommendations made in the
report.

Sincerely,

Harold M. Johnson

Harold M. Johnson
Associate Analyst
Sales Analysis Section

Approved:
December 1, 19XX

T. T. Landham
Director and Senior Analyst
Sales Analysis Section

Source: Adapted from David M. Robinson, *Writing Reports for Management Decisions* (Columbus, Ohio: Merrill, 1969), p. 340. Adapted with permission.

The summary should be written only after the rest of the report is completed. It represents the essence of the report. Its length will be one page (or at most two), so the writer must carefully sort out what is important enough to appear in it. As Exhibit 23.7 illustrates, several pages of the full report may have to be condensed into one summary sentence. It should be noted that different parts of the report may be condensed more than others—the number of words in the summary will not be in proportion to the relative lengths of the sections. The summary should be written to be self-sufficient. In fact, it is

EXHIBIT   23.7

**Condensing Full Report
into Summary**

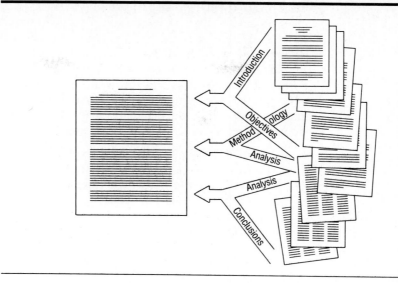

not uncommon for a summary to be detached from the report and circulated by itself.

The summary contains four elements. First, the objectives of the report are stated, including the most important background and the specific purposes of the project. Then the major results are presented. The key results regarding each purpose should be included. Next come the conclusions. These are opinions, based on the results, and constitute an interpretation of what the results say. Finally come recommendations, or suggestions for action, based on the conclusions. In many cases managers prefer not to have recommendations included in the report or summary. Whether or not recommendations are to be included should be clear from the particular context of the report.

Body.   The body constitutes the bulk of the report. It begins with an introduction that sets out both the background factors that make the project necessary and the objectives of the report. It continues with discussions of the methodology, results, and limitations of the study. It finishes with conclusions and recommendations based on the results.

The introduction explains why the project was undertaken and what it aimed to discover. It should include the basic authorization and submittal data. The relevant background will come next. There should be enough background to explain why the project was worth doing, but nonessential historical factors should be omitted. The question of how much is enough should be answered by reference to the needs of the audience. A government report that will be made widely available requires more background than a company's internal report on employee satisfaction. The last part of the introduction explains just what this particular project tried to discover. It discusses the statement of the problem and research questions in a manner similar to the way they were stated in the research proposal. Each purpose presented here should have a corresponding section of results later in the report.

The second division of the body explains the **research methodology.** This part is a challenge to write, because technical procedures must be explained in a way appropriate for the audience. It may be useful to supplement the material in this section with more detailed explanations in the appendix, or to include a glossary of technical terms. This division should address five areas:

1. *Research design.* Was the study exploratory, descriptive, or causal? Why was this particular design suited to the study?
2. *Data collection methods.* Did the data come from primary or secondary sources? Were results collected by survey, observation, or experiment? A copy of the survey questionnaire or observation form should be included in the appendix.
3. *Sampling.* What was the target population? What sampling frame was used? What sample units were used? How were they selected? Detailed computations supporting these explanations should be reserved for the appendix.
4. *Fieldwork.* How many and what types of field-workers were used? What training and supervision did they receive? Was the work verified? This section is important for establishing the degree of accuracy of the results.
5. *Analysis.* This section should outline the general statistical methods used in the study but should not overlap with the findings.

The presentation of *results* will occupy the bulk of the report. It presents those findings of the project that bear on the objectives in some logical order. The results should be organized as a continuous narrative, designed to be convincing but not to oversell the project. Summary tables and charts should be used to aid the discussion. Tables and charts may serve as points of reference to the data being discussed. They allow the prose to be free from an excess of facts and figures. Comprehensive or detailed charts should be reserved for the appendix.

No report is perfect; so it is important to indicate its limitations. If there were problems with nonresponse error or sampling procedures, they should be discussed. The discussion of limitations should avoid overemphasizing the weaknesses, though. Its aim should be to provide a realistic basis for assessing the results.

The last division of the body of the report presents the conclusions and recommendations based on the results. As was mentioned above, conclusions are opinions based on the results, whereas recommendations are suggestions for action. The conclusions and recommendations are presented here in more detail than in the summary, with whatever justification is needed.

Appendix.   The appendix presents the "too" material. Any material that is too technical or too detailed to go in the body should appear in the appendix. This includes materials of interest only to some readers, or subsidiary materials not directly related to the objectives. Some examples of appendix material are data collection forms, detailed calculations, discussions of highly technical questions, detailed or comprehensive tables of results, and a bibliography (if appropriate).

EFFECTIVE USE OF GRAPHIC AIDS

The person who first said "a picture is worth a thousand words" probably had graphic aids in mind. Used properly, **graphic (visual) aids** can clarify complex points or emphasize a message, but if used improperly or sloppily, graphics can be distracting or misleading. The key to effective use of graphic aids is to make them an integral part of the text. The graphics should always be interpreted in the text. This doesn't mean the writer should exhaustively explain an obvious chart or table. It *does* mean the key points should be pointed out and related to the discussion in progress in the text.

Several types of graphic aids may be useful in research reports, such as tables, charts, maps, and diagrams. The discussion below will briefly cover the most common ones—tables and various sorts of charts. The writer interested in other types should consult more specialized sources.[10]

Tables

Tables are most useful for presenting numerical information, especially when several pieces of information have been gathered about each item discussed. For example, consider how hard it would be to follow all the information in Table 23.1 if it were presented in narrative form. Using figures allows the writer to point out significant features without getting bogged down in detail. The tables that should be included in the body of the report are relatively short summary tables. Comprehensive tables should be reserved for the appendix.

Each table should include:

1. *Table number.* A table number allows for simple reference from the text to the table. If there are many tables, a list of tables should be included just after the table of contents.
2. *Title.* The title should indicate the contents of the table and be complete enough to be intelligible without the text. The table number and title are generally placed at the top, since the table is read from top down.
3. *Boxhead and stubhead.* The boxhead (or bannerhead) contains the captions for the columns of the table, the stubhead those for the rows.
4. *Footnotes.* Any explanations or qualifications for particular figures or sections should be given in footnotes.
5. *Source.* If a table is based on material from a secondary source, not on new data generated by the project, the source should be acknowledged, usually below the table following the footnotes.

Table 23.2 presents a typical table from a survey research report. It shows a cross-tabulation of demographics with survey responses. Table 23.3 shows how data from a statistical test might be reported in table format.

TABLE   23.1   **The Parts of a Table**

Table Number   Title

No. 795. Consumer Price Indexes, by Major Groups: 1950 to 1984

[1967 = 100. Annual averages of monthly figures, except as indicated. Prior to 1965, excludes Alaska and Hawaii. Through 1977 represents buying patterns of wage earners and clerical workers, beginning 1978, reflects buying patterns of all urban consumers in the 1970's. See text, p. 468 for details regarding other periods. See also *Historical Statistics, Colonial Times to 1970,* series E 135–173]

YEAR	All items	FOOD Total	FOOD Away from home	SHELTER Total	Rent, residential	Fuel oil and coal[1]	Gas and electricity	Apparel and upkeep	TRANSPORTATION Private	TRANSPORTATION Public	Medical care	All commodities	All services
1950	72.1	74.5	(NA)	(NA)	70.4	72.7	81.2	79.0	72.5	48.9	53.7	78.8	58.7
1951	77.8	82.8	(NA)	(NA)	73.2	76.5	81.5	86.1	75.8	54.0	56.3	85.9	61.8
1952	79.5	84.3	(NA)	(NA)	76.2	78.0	82.6	85.3	80.8	57.5	59.3	87.0	64.5
1953	80.1	83.0	(NA)	76.5	80.3	81.5	84.2	84.6	82.4	61.3	61.4	86.7	67.3
1954	80.5	82.8	70.1	78.2	83.2	81.2	85.3	84.5	80.3	65.5	63.4	85.9	69.5
1955	80.2	81.6	70.8	79.1	84.3	82.3	87.5	84.1	78.9	67.4	64.8	85.1	70.9
1956	81.4	82.2	72.2	80.4	85.9	85.9	88.4	85.8	80.1	70.0	67.2	85.9	72.7
1957	84.3	84.9	74.9	83.4	87.5	90.3	89.3	87.3	84.7	72.7	69.9	88.6	75.6
1958	86.6	88.5	77.2	85.1	89.1	88.7	92.4	87.5	87.4	76.1	73.2	90.6	78.5
1959	87.3	87.1	79.3	86.0	90.4	89.8	94.7	88.2	91.1	78.3	76.4	90.7	80.8
1960	88.7	88.0	81.4	87.8	91.7	89.2	98.6	89.6	90.6	81.0	79.1	91.5	83.5
1961	89.6	89.1	83.2	88.5	92.9	91.0	99.4	90.4	91.3	84.6	81.4	92.0	85.2
1962	90.6	89.9	85.4	89.6	94.0	91.5	99.4	90.9	93.0	87.4	83.5	92.8	86.8
1963	91.7	91.2	87.3	90.7	95.0	93.2	99.4	91.9	93.4	88.5	85.6	93.6	88.5
1964	92.9	92.4	88.9	92.2	95.9	92.7	99.4	92.7	94.7	90.1	87.3	94.6	90.2
1965	94.5	94.4	90.9	93.8	96.9	94.6	99.4	93.7	96.3	91.9	89.5	95.7	92.2
1966	97.2	99.1	95.1	96.8	98.2	97.0	99.6	96.1	97.5	95.2	93.4	98.2	95.8
1967	100.0	100.0	100.0	100.0	100.0	100.0	100.0	100.0	100.0	100.0	100.0	100.0	100.0
1968	104.2	103.6	105.2	104.8	102.4	103.1	100.9	105.4	103.0	104.6	106.1	103.7	105.2
1969	109.8	108.9	111.6	113.3	105.7	105.6	102.8	111.5	106.5	112.7	113.4	108.4	112.5
1970	116.3	114.9	119.9	123.6	110.1	110.1	107.3	116.1	111.1	128.5	120.6	113.5	121.6
1971	121.3	118.4	126.1	128.8	115.2	117.5	114.7	119.8	116.6	137.7	128.4	117.4	128.4
1972	125.3	123.5	131.1	134.5	119.2	118.5	120.5	122.3	117.5	143.4	132.5	120.9	133.3
1973	133.1	141.4	141.4	140.7	124.3	136.0	126.4	126.8	121.5	144.8	137.7	129.9	139.1
1974	147.7	161.7	159.4	154.4	130.6	214.6	145.8	136.2	136.6	148.0	150.5	145.5	152.1
1975	161.2	175.4	174.3	169.7	137.3	235.3	169.6	142.3	149.8	158.6	168.6	158.4	166.6
1976	170.5	180.8	186.1	179.0	144.7	250.8	189.0	147.6	164.6	174.2	184.7	165.2	180.4
1977	181.5	192.2	200.3	191.1	153.5	283.4	213.4	154.2	176.6	182.4	202.4	174.7	194.3
1978	195.4	211.4	218.4	210.4	164.0	298.3	232.6	159.6	185.0	187.8	219.4	187.1	210.9
1979	217.4	234.5	242.9	239.7	176.0	403.1	257.8	166.6	212.3	200.3	239.7	208.4	234.2
1980	246.8	254.6	267.0	281.7	191.6	556.0	301.8	178.4	249.2	251.6	265.9	233.9	270.3
1981	272.4	274.6	291.0	314.7	208.2	675.9	345.9	186.9	277.5	312.0	294.5	253.6	305.7
1982	289.1	285.7	306.5	337.0	224.0	667.9	393.8	191.8	287.5	346.0	328.7	263.8	333.3
1983	298.4	291.7	319.9	334.8	236.9	628.0	428.7	196.5	293.9	362.6	357.3	271.5	344.9
1984	311.1	302.9	333.4	361.7	249.3	641.8	445.2	200.2	306.6	385.2	379.5	280.7	363.0

Stubhead

Boxhead

Footnotes

NA   Not available   [1] Includes bottled gas.

Source: U.S. Bureau of Labor Statistics, *Monthly Labor Review* and *Handbook of Labor Statistics,* annual.

━━━ **Source**

Source: Table used as illustration from U.S. Department of Commerce, Bureau of the Census, *Statistical Abstract of the United States:* 1986, 106th ed. (Washington, DC: U.S. Government Printing Office, 1986), 477.

T A B L E   2 3 . 2

**Reporting Format for
a Typical Survey**

Which subjects did your household disagree or argue about in the past 12 months?

	Age			
	Under 35 Years	35–49 Years	50–64 Years	65 Years or More
Argued about something	79%	80%	58%	37%
Money	54	45	25	12
Children	33	43	24	6
Household chores	35	35	17	8
Diets/health	22	25	21	16
Job decisions	28	20	8	3
In-laws	24	15	10	4
Sex	20	19	7	4
Where to live	24	9	9	7
Vacations	12	12	10	6
Politics	8	6	7	4
Religion	10	6	4	3
Did not argue about anything	21	20	42	63

Source: Americans and Their Money/4, the fourth national survey from *Money* magazine 1986, p. 49.

T A B L E   2 3 . 3

Reporting a Statistical Test

**Will investors be more cautious about buying stock
in companies with questionable advertising?**

	Business	Advertising Management
Yes	57%	46%
No	27	35
Not sure	16	19
	n = 177	n = 154

$$\chi^2 = 4.933 \qquad d.f. = 2 \qquad p < .08$$

Source: A report to the Federal Trade Commission on the Effects of the STP "Public Notice" Advertising Campaign, June 1979.

Charts

Charts translate numerical information into visual form so that relationships may be easily grasped. The accuracy of the numbers is reduced to gain this advantage.

Each chart should include:

1. *Figure number.* Charts (and other illustrative material) should be numbered in a series separate from tables. The number allows for easy reference from the text. If there are many figures, a list of them should be included after the table of contents.

2. *Title.* The title should indicate the contents of the chart and be independent of the text explanation. The figure number and title are usually placed at the bottom of the figure.

Changing the Visual Image
Contracting or expanding vertical (amount) scale or horizontal
(time) scale tends to change the visual picture

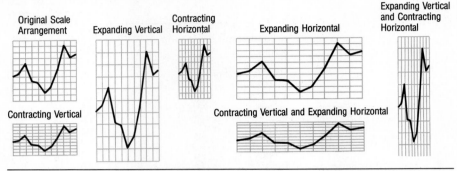

Source: Adapted from Mary Eleanor Spear, *Practical Charting Techniques* (New York: McGraw-Hill, 1969), p. 56.
Adapted with permission.

3.   *Explanatory legends.* Enough explanation should be put on the chart to guide the reader without reference to the accompanying text. Such explanations would include labels for axes, scale numbers, a key to the different quantities being graphed, and so on.

4.   *Source and footnotes.* Any secondary source for the data should be acknowledged. If footnotes are needed to explain items, they may also be used, although they are less common for charts than for tables.

Charts are subject to distortion, whether unintentional or deliberate.[11] Exhibit 23.8 shows how altering the scale changes the impression of the data. A particularly severe type of distortion comes from treating unequal intervals as if they were equal. This generally results from a deliberate attempt to distort data. Exhibit 23.9 shows this sort of distortion, where someone attempted to make the rise on the chart more dramatic by compressing the portion where there is little change.

Another common distortion is to begin the vertical scale at some value larger than zero. Note in Exhibit 23.10 how this exaggerates the amount of change in the period covered. This kind of broken scale is often used in published reports of stock price movements. In this case it is assumed that the readers are mostly interested in the changes and are aware of the exaggeration of a broken scale. For most research reports this will not be the case. Graphs should start at zero on the vertical axis.

Pie Charts.   One of the most useful kinds of charts is the **pie chart.** It shows the composition of some total quantity at a particular time. Each angle, or "slice," is proportional to its percentage of the whole, and it should be labeled with its description and percentage of the whole. Do not try to include too many small

EXHIBIT   23.9

**Distortion from
Treating Unequal Time
Intervals as Equal**

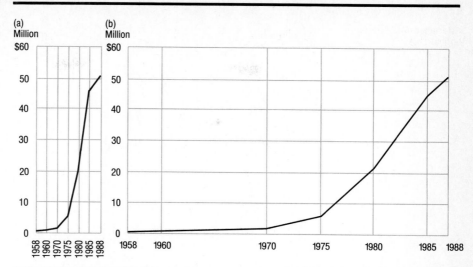

(a)
Million

(b)
Million

Source: Adapted from Mary Eleanor Spear, *Practical Charting Techniques* (New York: McGraw-Hill, 1969), p. 57.
Adapted with permission.

slices—about six slices is the usual maximum. Pie charts are commonly used by organizations to show the sources of their income and how their revenues have been used (as in Exhibit 23.11), what assets they hold, or the composition of their sales.

Line Graphs.   Line graphs are used to show the relationship of one variable to another. The dependent variable is generally shown on the vertical axis, and the independent variable is shown on the horizontal axis. The most common independent variable for such charts is time, but it is by no means the only one. Exhibit 23.12 depicts a simple line graph. Other variants of line graphs are also useful. The multiple-line graph (Exhibit 23.13) shows the relationship of more than one dependent variable to the independent variable. The lines for each dependent variable need to be in contrasting colors or patterns and should be clearly labeled. Do not try to squeeze in too many variables; this can quickly lead to confusion, not clarification. A second variation is the stratum chart (Exhibit 23.14), which shows the composition of a total quantity and its changes as the independent variable changes. The cautions that apply to the multiple-line graph should also be observed here.

Bar Charts.   Bar charts show changes in the dependent variable (again on the vertical axis) at discrete intervals of the independent variable (horizontal axis). A simple bar chart is shown in Exhibit 23.15. A common variant is the sub-divided bar chart (Exhibit 23.16). It is much like the stratum chart, showing

EXHIBIT 23.10

**Distortion from Broken
Vertical Lines**

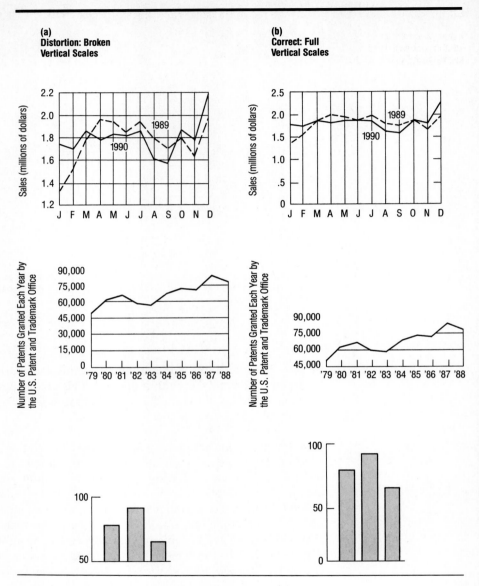

**(a)
Distortion: Broken
Vertical Scales**

**(b)
Correct: Full
Vertical Scales**

the composition of the whole quantity. Bar charts may be horizontal as well as vertical. For example, Exhibit 23.17 shows the horizontal form. The multiple-bar chart in this exhibit shows how multiple variables are related to the primary variable. Each variable needs to be clearly identified by using a different color or pattern for each. Do not try to use too many divisions or dependent variables. Too much detail obscures the essential advantage of charts, which is to make relationships easy to visualize.

EXHIBIT 23.11

**A Pie Chart with
Too Many Slices
Loses Its Effectiveness**

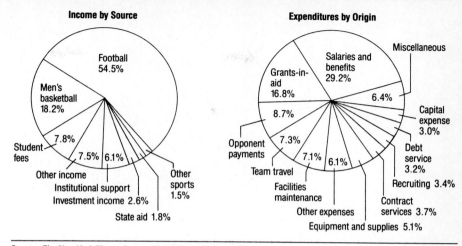

Income by Source

Expenditures by Origin

Source: *The New York Times*, August 13, 1989, y-29. Copyright © 1989 by The New York Times Company. Reprinted with permission.

EXHIBIT 23.12

Simple Line Graph

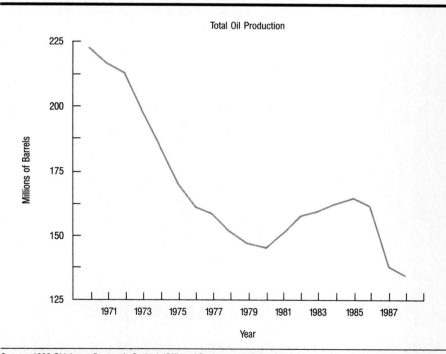

Total Oil Production

Source: *1989 Oklahoma Economic Outlook* (Office of Business and Economic Research, College of Business Administration, Oklahoma State University, 1989), 9.

E X H I B I T 2 3 . 1 3

Multiple-Line Graph

Ton–Miles of Domestic Intercity Freight Traffic—Percent Distribution
by Type of Transportation, 1960 to 1980

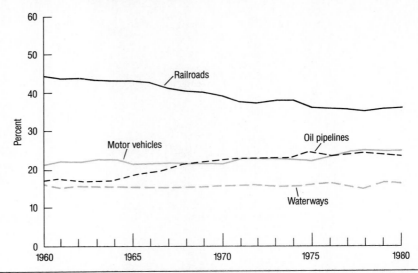

Source: U.S. Department of Commerce, Bureau of the Census, *Statistical Abstract of the United States: 1982–1983*,
103rd ed. (Washington, DC: U.S. Government Printing Office, 1983), 602.

E X H I B I T 2 3 . 1 4

Stratum Chart

Research and Development, Funds Used: 1970 to 1982

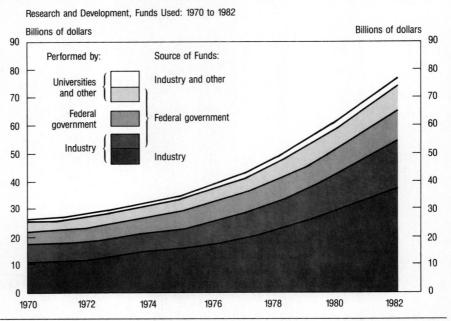

Source: U.S. Department of Commerce, Bureau of the Census, *Statistical Abstract of the United States: 1982–1983*,
103rd ed. (Washington, DC: U.S. Government Printing Office, 1983), 590.

EXHIBIT   23.15   **Simple Bar Chart**

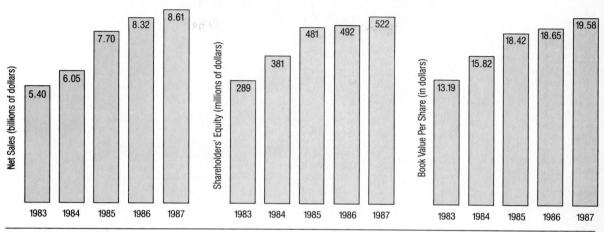

Source: 1987 Annual Report Fleming Foods.

EXHIBIT   23.16

Subdivided Bar Chart

Immigrants Admitted to the United States

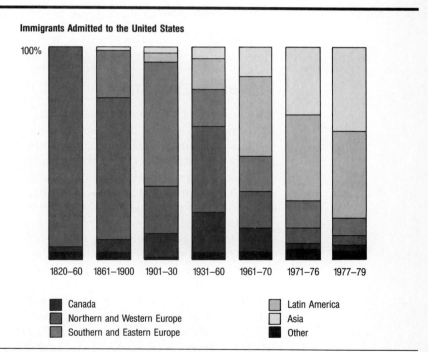

Source: "Immigrants Admitted to the United States," *The Wilson Quarterly, New Year's 1983*, 114.

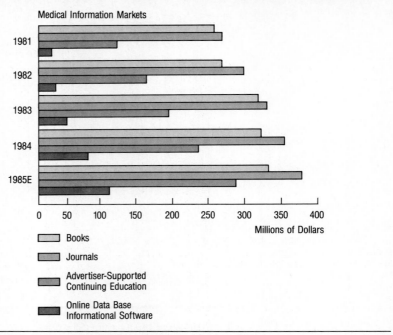

Source: *1985 CBS Annual Report to Shareholders*, p. 24. Reprinted courtesy of CBS, Inc.

THE ORAL PRESENTATION

The conclusions and recommendations of most research reports will be presented orally as well as in writing. The purpose of an oral presentation is to highlight the most important findings and to provide clients or line managers with the opportunity to clarify any ambiguous issues by asking questions.

The **oral presentation** may be as simple as a short conference with the researcher's immediate supervisor, or it may be a formal report to the board of directors. The key to effective presentation in either situation is preparation. The researcher should select the three or four most important findings for emphasis and rely on the written report for a full summary. The researcher needs to be ready to defend the results. This is not the same as being defensive. Rather, it means being prepared to deal with the questions that will arise in a confident, competent manner. Remember that even the most reliable, valid research project is worthless if the managers who must act on its results are not convinced of its importance.

As with the written report, a key to an effective oral presentation is adaptation to the audience. Delivering an hour-long formal speech when a ten-minute discussion is called for (or vice versa) reflects poorly on both the presenter and the report. Many business researchers view themselves as technicians whose purpose is to generate numbers using sophisticated research designs and statistical techniques. As a result, unfortunately, some researchers' oral presentations are organized around technical details rather than being directed toward the satisfaction of management's or the client's needs.

A comparison has been made between weather reporters and business researchers. The average person watching a TV weather reporter wants to know whether he or she needs to take an umbrella to work the next day. The weather reporter provides enormous amounts of information: It's snowing in Washington, sunny in San Diego, and raining in Texas. Maps full of lines showing fronts, high- and low-pressure areas, and other weather facts are extraneous information to the person who simply does not want to risk getting wet. Fortunately, most weather reporters eventually let us know if rain is forecasted. In a similar vein, if the client only wants an executive summary, the oral presentation should emphasize material that one would expect to be contained in the summary section of the written report. Managers can always ask for additional detail about the methodology or clarification of the data analysis.

The principles of good speech making apply when making a research presentation. Lecturing or reading to the audience is sure to impede communication at any level of formality. The presenter should avoid reading his material word for word by relying on brief notes, being familiar with the subject, and rehearsing as much as the occasion calls for. The presenter should avoid research jargon and should use short, simple words. The speaker should maintain eye contact and should repeat the main points. Often, because the audience cannot go back and replay what the speaker has said, the presentation should be organized around the standard adage: "Tell them what you are going to tell them, tell them, then tell them what you just told them."

Graphic and other visual aids can be as useful in an oral presentation as in a written one. Again, the presenter needs to interpret these aids for the audience by pointing out the key elements that are related to the discussion. There is a variety of media for presenting research results in an oral presentation. Slides or overhead projector acetates will be useful for large audiences or formal presentations. For smaller audiences the researcher may have the visual aids put on posters or flip charts. Another possibility is to duplicate copies of the charts for each participant, possibly supplemented by one of the other forms of graphic presentation.

Whatever medium is chosen, the visual aids should be designed to convey a simple, attention-getting message that supports a point on which the audience should focus its thinking. The best slides are easily read and quickly interpreted. Large typeface, multiple colors, highlighting bullets, and other artistic devices should be considered as means to enhance the readability of charts and other graphics.

THE RESEARCH FOLLOW-UP

Research reports and oral presentations should communicate the research findings in a manner that will allow managers to make a business decision. In many cases the manager who receives the research report is unable to interpret the information and draw conclusions relevant to his or her managerial decision. For this reason effective researchers do not see the report as the end of the research process. The **research follow-up** is a recontacting of decision makers and /or clients after they have had a chance to read over the research report. Its purpose is to determine if the researchers need to provide additional information or can clarify some issues that may concern management.

SUMMARY

Report preparation is the final stage of the research project. It is a key stage because the project can guide management decisions only if it is effectively communicated. The theory of communication emphasizes that the writer (communicator) must tailor the report (message) so that it will be understood by the manager (audience) who has a different field of experience. The research report is defined as the presentation of the research findings directed to a specific audience to accomplish a specific purpose.

The generally accepted format for research reports includes certain prefatory parts, the body of the report, and appended parts. The report format should be adapted to suit the level of formality of the particular report situation.

The prefatory parts of a formal report include a title page, letters of transmittal and authorization, a table of contents, and a summary. The summary is the most often read part of a report, and it should include a brief statement of the objectives, results, conclusions, and recommendations. The report body includes an introduction that gives the background and objectives, a statement of methodology, the results, their limitations, and appropriate conclusions and recommendations. The appendix includes various material that is too specialized to appear in the body of the report.

Effective use of graphic aids enhances the presentation. Tables present large amounts of numerical information in a concise manner. Charts present numerical data in a way that highlights their relationships. Pie charts, line graphs, and bar charts are useful forms of charts, with variants for special purposes.

Because most research projects will be reported orally as well as in writing, the researcher needs to prepare an oral presentation. The preparation should defend the results without being defensive. It is vital to tailor the presentation to the situation and audience. Graphic aids are also useful supplements to the oral report.

The research follow-up is a recontacting of decision makers after the report has been submitted so that any issues of concern to management may be clarified.

Key Terms

communication process

research report

report format

research methodology

graphic (visual) aids

table

chart   bar chart

pie chart   oral presentation

line graph   research follow-up

Questions

1. Why is it important to view the research report from a communications perspective?
2. As a manager, what degree of formality would you like from your research department?
3. What type of tables might be used to describe some of the various statistical tests discussed in previous chapters?
4. Do you believe that computer graphics will have an impact on the research report-writing format? Explain.
5. Try to find some research reports in your library. How do they meet the standards set forth in this chapter?
6. How does the oral presentation of research results differ from the written research report?

References

[1] This chapter was written by John Bush, Oklahoma State University.

[2] Thomas C. Kinnear and James R. Taylor, *Marketing Research: An Applied Approach* (New York: McGraw-Hill, 1979), 564.

[3] For some discussion of other written or oral communications that may be required during the report, see David M. Robinson, *Writing Reports for Management Decisions* (Columbus, OH: Merrill, 1969), 65–76, 99–102, 353–362. For discussion of shorter reports, see Jessamon Dawe and William Jackson Lord, Jr., *Functional Business Communication*, 2nd ed. (Englewood Cliffs, NJ: Prentice-Hall, 1974), 512–546.

[4] To see some of the similarities and variations in suggested formats, refer to Gilbert A. Churchill, *Marketing Research: Methodological Foundations* (Hinsdale, IL: Dryden Press, 1979), 611–612; Thomas C. Kinnear and James R. Taylor, *Marketing Research: An Applied Approach* (New York: McGraw-Hill, 1979), 567; Harper W. Boyd, Jr., Ralph Westfall, and Stanley F. Stasch, *Marketing Research: Text and Cases* (Homewood, IL: Irwin, 1977), 543; Jessamon Dawe and William Jackson Lord, Jr., *Functional Business Communication*, 2nd ed. (Englewood Cliffs, NJ: Prentice-Hall, 1974), 289, 402, 454; David M. Robinson, *Writing Reports for Management Decisions* (Columbus, OH: Merrill, 1969), 300–302; William J. Gallagher, *Report Writing for Management* (Reading, MA: Addison-Wesley, 1969), 52. The format given here is adapted from Robinson and from Dawe and Lord.

[5] Robinson, *Writing Reports for Management Decisions*, 294.

[6] Ibid., 297.

[7] Discussion based on ibid., 300, 338–339, and Dawe and Lord, *Functional Business Communication*, 414.

[8] Those interested in guidelines for writing letters of authorization should see Robinson, 72–74, or Dawe and Lord, 407–413.

[9] Gallagher, *Report Writing for Management*, 51–52.

[10] Mary Eleanor Spear, *Practical Charting Techniques* (New York: McGraw-Hill, 1969).

[11] The charts in this section have been adapted from Spear, *Practical Charting Techniques*.

The Writing Process

ORGANIZING THE REPORT

The writing process is outlined in Exhibit 23A.1. The first step in writing the report is organizing the way the material is to be presented. To a large degree, the organization flows from the earlier stages of the project. This is especially true of a well-organized project. If, in a major project, the researcher moved from exploratory and secondary research to a clear statement of the objectives of the main project, then designed a study specifically to meet them, there is a considerable organizational advantage when it comes time to report on the project. Suppose, on the other hand, that a researcher never did the preliminary work needed to clarify the research problems. Instead, questionnaires were sent out only in the hope of getting some sort of results. This will certainly cause difficulty in analyzing the results; it will also be a barrier to finding a coherent framework for reporting results.

Nevertheless, even after the best-run project has been completed, writing a report calls for consideration of how to organize the presentation effectively. The major sections are usually set up by general custom in the discipline or by organizational practice (see the report format in Exhibit 23.4). The writer's job is to make those blocks a coherent whole—a piece of writing that is unified from the first page to the last. "The readers should be able to read the objectives, turn to the conclusions section, and find specific conclusions relative to each objective."[1] They should also be able to turn to the results section, or the methodology section, or the letter of authorization—in fact, any part of the report—and see the whole tied together by concern with one problem, stated in terms of a small number of interrelated objectives.

A unified theme helps the reader understand what has been accomplished. A report with the results section organized one way and the conclusions in a different way, where neither seems to relate back to the objectives, is like a disassembled color television set. All the parts may be there, but until they are put together they will never be capable of showing a football game or

The Writing Process

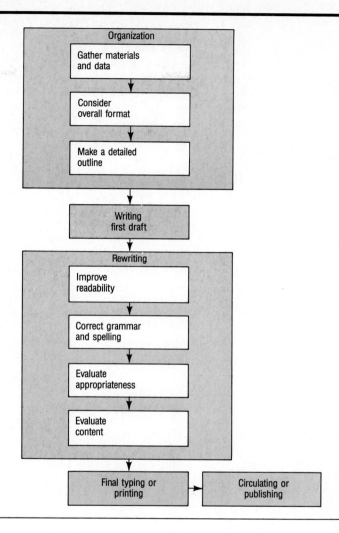

Organization
- Gather materials and data
- Consider overall format
- Make a detailed outline

Writing first draft

Rewriting
- Improve readability
- Correct grammar and spelling
- Evaluate appropriateness
- Evaluate content

Final typing or printing → Circulating or publishing

soap opera. Of course, during a project there are often dead ends and detours, as well as reassessments of what is and is not important. These should not be obscured in the report. If the research did not produce a conclusion on a point, the writer should say so. Since the report is written after the fact, it can take all these factors into consideration and show how they are interrelated.

Good organization is achieved by outlining. Many people resist using outlines for various reasons. Some may have had teachers who insisted on a detailed outline when it wasn't needed. Others may have found that no matter how they outlined, they ended up altering the outline in the course of writing. However, the research report is a long and complex piece of writing. Even someone who has been connected with the project from the start finds it hard to sit down and, without planning, produce a well-structured account of the project. Instead, he or she will probably leave out important parts and realize it later, or talk in circles, or repeat things over and over, or give undue emphasis to minor matters. If, on the other hand, the writer plans ahead, looking at the relationship of ideas and the order in which they should be presented, the report will usually be better organized. A better plan might still be discovered halfway through the first draft, but more often it will be discovered in the original outlining process.

The Outline

The outline has two main functions: (1) to show the order of presentation and (2) to show the way the parts relate to each other—particularly how small parts go together to form larger ones. The first is shown by order on the page, the second by indentation of subordinate parts.

There are, also, two major sorts of outline notation. The traditional method uses alternating letters and numbers to show levels of subordination whereas the newer method uses a decimal system, with successive places to the right of the decimal showing lower and lower levels of subordination:

Traditional Form
I. Main division
   A. First-level subdivision
      1. Second-level subdivision
         a. Third-level subdivision
         b. Third-level subdivision
      2. Second-level subdivision
   B. First-level subdivision
II. Second main division
     etc.

Decimal Form
I. Main division
   1.1 First-level subdivision
     1.11 Second-level subdivision
       1.111 Third-level subdivision
       1.112 Third-level subdivision
     1.12 Second-level subdivision
   1.2 First-level subdivision
II. Second main division
     etc.

These three levels of subordination are usually all that will be needed for most reports. Note that there should not be any single subdivisions. A subdivision implies that an idea is being broken into parts. When there is only one subsidiary point you want to make about a segment of the report, rewrite the segment caption to include it. For example:

2.31 Costs
    2.311 Cost overruns

could be recast as:

2.31 Costs and cost overruns

or:

2.31 Costs
    2.311 High basic cost
    2.312 Cost overruns

In preparing a working outline for your own use, there is little need to worry about whether the outline is a topic or sentence type. Also, the conventions of capitalization and punctuation are not overly important. The outline is a means to the end. It is not a goal in itself.

Attention to good practices in classification is useful in developing good outlines. First, at each level use only one basis for organization. This basis should include all the topics to be discussed. The following is an example of a mixed classification for part of a business research report on an experimental shampoo formula.

    I. Exploratory studies (*type of study*)
    II. New York City survey (*geographic location*)
    III. Characteristics (*attributes of subject studied*)

Each of the three parts uses a different basis of classification. They don't seem to belong together in a coherent whole. Suppose, instead, the basis of organization for classification was by type of study:

    I. Exploratory studies
    II. City surveys
    III. Consumer usage study

Or it could be organized geographically:

    I. New York City survey
    II. Chicago survey
    III. Los Angeles survey

Or it could be classified by the characteristics of the shampoo:

    I. Cleaning
    II. Physical form
        A. Color
        B. Odor
        C. Package

Of course, none of these schemes is comprehensive. Each includes points the others leave out. A full outline could employ all three, but each on a different level:

I. Exploratory studies (*type of study*)
II. City surveys (*type of study*)
   A. New York City ⎫
   B. Chicago   ⎬ (*geographic location*)
   C. Los Angeles   ⎭
III. Consumer usage study (*type of study*)
   A. Cleaning
   B. Physical form
      1. Color   ⎫
      2. Odor   ⎬ (*attributes of shampoo*)
      3. Package ⎭

The writer must decide which classification principle to use at which level. The above example might be appropriate if the writer wanted to report the results of the three different studies. Suppose the writer, instead, wanted to stress the characteristics of the product rather than the individual studies. The shampoo attributes could be promoted to the first level of classification, and the type of study demoted to a subordinate level:

I. Cleaning (*attributes of shampoo*)
   A. Exploratory studies ⎫
   B. City surveys   ⎬ (*type of study*)
   C. Consumer usage study ⎭
II. Physical form (*attributes of shampoo*)
   A. Color
      1. Exploratory studies ⎫
      2. City surveys   ⎬ (*type of study*)
      3. Consumer usage studies ⎭
   B. Odor
      etc.

For further discussion of outlining, see a good basic composition textbook.[2]

WRITING THE FIRST DRAFT

Joe B. Researcher, who works for Bigg Enterprises Inc., has just completed a research project. It is Monday morning, and his boss wants to have the report sometime Friday so he can read it over the weekend, before a major staff conference early next week. Joe feels his project has come up with good results, and he has already prepared the outline for the report. He tells his secretary to hold all calls, then gets out a yellow pad and a pen and gets ready to write.

But as he looks at the empty pad, he can't decide how to start. All the bright ideas in his head seem to disappear as he puts his pen to the paper. Finally, he writes a sentence, then looks at it, rips the page off, crumples it up, and tosses it at the wastebasket (he misses). He glances at the clock and sees that, somehow, it's already ten o'clock—time for coffee break! When he goes on break, a couple of his staff need to talk to him, so he doesn't get back to the office for an hour. When he is back, there are a dozen phone calls he needs to return. The whole afternoon is scheduled with meetings, and Joe knows no writing will get done that day.

That's the way it goes the whole week. Joe can't get to it Tuesday. Wednesday he tries writing at home, but the kids keep making noise. On Thursday Joe's secretary asks when the report will be ready to type and Joe snaps "How should I know!" As 5 o'clock rolls around, Joe calls his wife, telling her he'll be very late, because he still has to get the (censored) report written. By the time the sun comes up the next morning, Joe has finally gotten most of the report done, impelled by sheer desperation. As he looks at it, he knows it is not his best work. It is incoherent in places, includes unexplained technical language in a couple of spots, and has several redundancies. He knows a lot of the language and sentence structure could be worked over for better clarity. But the job is finally done, and Joe stretches out on his office couch to get an hour of sleep before the workday starts again.

This example is a bit exaggerated, but it's not too far from what many writers do. Some of them, unlike Joe, look at the mess they've just produced with indulgent eyes. They overlook all the problems and take any criticism personally. However, a first draft can almost always be improved. Often it needs major work, but doing that work is much easier than writing the draft in the first place. Every research writer, indeed every writer, should memorize two maxims: "Easy writing is hard reading" and "Good writing comes from good rewriting."

Why is this so? Trying to produce a perfect job on the first draft means combining creation and criticism. It's bound to be hard to write anything when you're continually crossing it out in your head before it gets on paper. Trying to create and criticize simultaneously makes it almost impossible to write anything. What seems clear in thought evaporates into vagueness the moment the pen touches the paper. All the underlying assumptions and experiences have to be made explicit on paper. In the written report the only chance we have for clarifications is in rewriting, before the reader ever sees it. But rewriting a first draft is almost always easier than getting down the first draft to begin with. (The next section deals with some of the "hows" of effective rewriting. The discussion here concerns ways to overcome the difficulties of writing the first draft.)

The key to getting the first draft down, before that last-minute desperation, is suppressing the critical "internal editor" and releasing the creative side. Some suggestions:

1. Consolidate your time. There is usually wasted motion in getting started. Once started, don't stop prematurely. Most writers accomplish more in two hours of uninterrupted work than in four half-hour sessions spread over a day or week.

2. If you have trouble getting started, set your pen on the paper and keep it going, writing anything that hits your mind—connected or not. You may have to write: "I can't think, I hate writing," and so on for a few minutes before you relax enough to move into your subject. Later, you can cross out the irrelevant. The job now is *to get started*.

3.   The introduction is one of the hardest parts to write, but that's where many writers start. Instead, try writing a later section that you're very sure of. If you move from the sections that are easy for you to the others, you have the reassurance that you are making progress. This suggestion assumes you have an outline, so that you know how all the sections "look" together. If you use this technique, pay special attention to transitions in rewriting.

4.   Don't keep shifting gears from writing to revising. You may make some false starts that have to be crossed out, but don't take the time for extensive revision or rewriting during the first draft. You may want to make marginal notes to yourself to use in revision, but don't stop now, or valuable thoughts may escape.

5.   Many writers find it easier to "talk" the first draft into a tape recorder. Most people speak more easily than they write, and the result may be more natural. This approach will also overcome the tendency to stop and revise while creation is in progress. When revising, you need to pay special attention to phrasings that are appropriate for speech but not for writing. That doesn't mean, however, that you write in stilted, strait-jacketed, polysyllabic prose.[3]

CRITICIZING AND REWRITING

The professional writer who doesn't make extensive revisions is a rarity. As an authority on business communications points out, "All good writers revise diligently; many great ones revised almost endlessly. Victor Hugo, for example, revised one novel eleven times; Hemingway rewrote the final page of *A Farewell to Arms* 39 times; Thomas Jefferson spent 18 days writing and rewriting the Declaration of Independence; and Voltaire frequently spent an entire night laboring over a single sentence."[4] When we read their works, they seem to fit together naturally, but the "naturalness" is achieved as the end product of careful rewriting. The report writer's aim is different from the novelist's, poet's, or statesman's, but the tools of revision in shaping rough work into a final product are just as useful.

The key to effective revision is objectivity. In writing the first draft, the challenge is to suppress the critical side and be creative. In revision the task is to look at the work as a self-editor. Feelings that "it's mine, and to change it is a slap in my face" or "I'll never get any sense out of this mess" both get in the way. One of the best ways to achieve objectivity is to put the first draft aside for a while before revising it. A day or two is good, but even an hour or two will help you to gain a critical distance from the work. Another suggestion is to let someone else look at it, and to encourage that person not to withhold suggestions for fear of offending you.

A Revision Inventory

But how do you go about doing the revision? What do you watch for? The best way to learn is to become sensitive to the qualities of good and bad writing you encounter, imitating the good and purging the bad in your own writing. Even so, writers on writing invariably say, "Be concise, be clear, be forceful."[5] Often the person who reads such advice doesn't find it very helpful. It's like being told "Be brave, be beautiful, be happy." No one questions the desirability of these attributes, but if writers knew how to realize them, they probably wouldn't need the advice.

The revision inventory in Exhibit 23A.2 is an attempt to overcome the problem of vagueness.[6] It presents details to check in a framework of four general criteria: readability, correctness, appropriateness, and thought. These criteria may be considered one at a time in successive reviews of the report, or all together, depending on what the individual writer finds most effective. Note that the criteria are related to the communications model presented earlier in Chapter 23.

The readability criterion refers to factors that facilitate or block the transition from the writer's field of experience to the reader's. The correctness criterion refers to the way the message has been put into the code of the medium—written English. The appropriateness criterion emphasizes consideration of the audience. Finally, the thought criterion refers to the message itself, the set of meanings the report is to convey.

Revising for Readability

This criterion concerns the clarity of the writing. In research reports the style should be transparent, making the content clear and never calling attention to itself. Whenever readers give their attention to the *way* something is said, they are no longer concentrating on *what* is being said. The first elements here refer to tailoring the report to the reader's field of experience. First, the report should be aimed at the reader's level of understanding. It should not insult the reader by talking down to him or her, belaboring the obvious. Nor should it assume too much. The reader usually has less technical background in the field being reported on than does the writer. The language employed must be appropriate.

The hardest of the three listed language problems to overcome is improper use of jargon. Jargon amounts to "shop talk," and among those who understand it, it speeds and clarifies communication. When spoken or written to an outsider, however, it lowers comprehension. If the report is aimed at an audience without the proper technical background, technical words should be translated or used only after they have been clearly defined.

Next come the elements of sentence and paragraph construction. The *sentence* part refers to the choice among appropriate grammatical structures, not to grammatical correctness itself (which is considered in the next criterion). The aim should be an appropriate variety of long and short, of simple, compound, and complex sentences. The average length should be reduced in difficult, technical passages, and increased in less difficult ones. Also watch out for overuse of the passive voice ("The report *was prepared* by Butch Gemin") and "there" or "it" constructions ("*There* was no real need for the report," "*It* could be seen that the report was pointless"). These add wasteful words and invert the normal sentence order, forcing the reader to search for the meaning.

E X H I B I T   2 3 A . 2   **A Revision Inventory**

READABILITY

Reader's Level

☐ Too specialized in approach
☐ Assumes too great a knowledge of subject
☐ So underestimates the reader that it belabors the obvious

Familiarity of Words

☐ Inappropriate jargon
☐ Pretentious language
☐ Unnecessarily abstract

Sentence Construction

☐ Unnecessarily long in difficult material
☐ Subject-verb-object word order too rarely used
☐ Choppy, overly simple style (in simple material)

Paragraph Construction

☐ Lack of topic sentences
☐ Too many ideas in single paragraph
☐ Too long

Reader Direction

☐ Lack of "framing" (i.e., failure to tell the reader about purpose and direction of forthcoming discussion)
☐ Inadequate transitions between paragraphs
☐ Absence of subconclusions to summarize reader's progress at end of divisions in the discussion

Focus

☐ Unclear as to subject of communication
☐ Unclear as to purpose of message

CORRECTNESS

Mechanics

☐ Shaky grammar
☐ Faulty punctuation
☐ Serious or abundant spelling errors

Format

☐ Careless appearance of documents
☐ Failure to use accepted company form

Coherence

☐ Sentences seem awkward owing to illogical and ungrammatical yoking of unrelated ideas
☐ Failure to develop a logical progression of ideas through coherent, logically juxtaposed paragraphs

APPROPRIATENESS

**A. Internal Reports
(Researcher to Superior)**

Tact

☐ Failure to recognize differences in position between writer and receiver
☐ Impolite tone to brusque, argumentative, or insulting

Attitude

☐ Too obvious a desire to please superior
☐ Too defensive in the face of authority
☐ Too fearful to be able to do best work

**B. External Reports
(Researcher to Client)**

Diplomacy

☐ Unmindfulness that messages are representative of company
☐ Failure to recognize needs and rights of client
☐ Failure to adopt managerial decision-oriented perspective—narrowly technical viewpoint

Attitude

☐ Unfavorable results slanted or suppressed to gain favor of recipient
☐ Too defensive about technical purity of study
☐ Obviously attempting to use this report to gain further assignments from client

C. Common to Both

Supporting Detail

☐ Inadequate support for statements
☐ Too much undigested detail for busy reader

Opinion

☐ Adequate research but too great an intrusion of opinion
☐ Too few facts (and too little research) to entitle drawing of conclusions
☐ Presence of unasked for but clearly implied recommendations

THOUGHT

Preparation

☐ Inadequate thought given to purpose of communication prior to its final completion
☐ Inadequate preparation or use of data known to be available

Competence

☐ Subject beyond intellectual capabilities of writer
☐ Subject beyond experience of writer

Fidelity to Assignment

☐ Failure to stick to job assigned
☐ Too much made of routine assignment
☐ Too little made of assignment

Analysis

☐ Superficial examination of data leading to unconscious overlooking of important pieces of evidence
☐ Failure to draw obvious conclusions from data presented
☐ Presentation of conclusions unjustified by evidence
☐ Failure to qualify tenuous assertions
☐ Failure to identify and justify assumptions used
☐ Bias, conscious or unconscious, which leads to distorted interpretation of data

Persuasiveness

☐ Seems more convincing than facts warrant
☐ Seems less convincing than facts warrant
☐ Too obvious an attempt to sell ideas
☐ Lacks action-orientation and managerial viewpoint
☐ Too blunt an approach where subtlety and finesse called for

Source: Adapted and reprinted by permission of *Harvard Business Review.* An exhibit from "What Do You Mean I Can't Write?" by John S. Fielden (May–June 1964), 147. Copyright © 1964 by the President and Fellows of Harvard College; all rights reserved.

In revising paragraphs, aim for unity. Each paragraph should have only one topic. Stating the topic in the first sentence will help the writer focus the paragraph and will help the reader grasp the main idea. Keep the paragraphs to a reasonable length. The reader will be daunted by paragraphs that go on for pages. Long paragraphs usually contain too many main ideas and lack unity.

Finally, *reader direction* and *focus* refer to showing the report's goal and how the writer is moving toward that goal. The introduction should state the aim of the report and how it will be reached. The body should follow the plan laid out in the introduction, and the conclusion should show that the aim has been reached. It is like giving the reader a road map at the beginning of the report, then putting in mileposts and directional signs through it, and showing the reader the destination has been reached as the report closes.

Revising for Correctness

Correctness is necessary for a report to be acceptable, but it is not sufficient to ensure that it will be acceptable. Even the best report, one that meets the other criteria, will not be received well if it is full of grammatical, punctuation, or spelling errors. These mechanical errors indicate that the writer has approached the work casually. Every writer should have (and use) a good English handbook and a standard college dictionary.

Proper format is another ingredient of correctness. Many companies and universities have a standard report format that should be followed or adapted to the individual report. Another consideration here is the "correctness" of such elements as margins, section heading format, figure and table titles, and so on. Such factors as neat and accurate typing are also included here. Many writers dismiss these things as not their responsibility, expecting their secretaries or typists to handle them. Typists and secretaries are indispensable, of course, but the writer also needs to pay attention to these factors in preparing the draft for final typing, giving directions, proofreading, and inspecting the final product—after all, the writer's, not the typist's, name is associated with the report.[7]

The final element of correctness is less cut and dried. Coherence comes from putting related sentences and paragraphs together, and making clear the transitions between unrelated ideas.

Revising for Appropriateness

This criterion refers to the "tone" of the report, which reflects the writer's attitude toward the report and the person for whom it is written. Research reports usually are written either for a superior in the writer's organization or for a client in another organization.[8] In either case the report should balance detail and generalization, and focus on facts, not opinions. The report should not include recommendations, unless they were requested in the assignment; rather, it should present reasonable conclusions from the facts assembled.

In reports to superiors the writer needs to strike a balance between too much familiarity and too much fear of the boss. Either extreme will reduce the credibility of the report and lead the reader to question its objectivity. In reports to outside clients the writer needs to be aware that the report represents the organization as well as the writer. The report needs to be oriented to the needs of the client, to the decisions to be made, not to the technical questions with which the writer is probably most familiar. Attitude can also be a problem here: The findings must be presented objectively, not slanted toward what the writer thinks the client wants to hear.

Evaluation of Thought

Here we turn from concentration on form to concentration on content. Remember that the two are really inseparable: The one way that the "content" can be learned is through the "form." We artificially separate the two here only for convenience. The report will miss the mark if it is based on inadequate preparation, if the project was beyond the researcher's competence, if it doesn't fulfill the assignment, or if it reflects too little analysis or an improper persuasiveness. Many of these problems come from the project stages before the report was prepared. If they haven't been done properly, it will be too late to make up the lack in the report.

SUMMARY

The report-writing process begins by effectively organizing the material to be presented. Organization helps develop consistency throughout the report. The first stage in the writing process is outlining, which shows the order of presentation and the subordination of subdivisions to major sections. The second stage is writing the first draft. At this point the key is to suppress the "internal editor" and get an initial version of the report in writing. Finally, the first draft is rewritten, possibly several times, to produce the final draft.

The key to rewriting is objectivity. A revision inventory is presented as an aid to effective revision. It covers the evaluation of readability, correctness, appropriateness, and thought.

References

[1] Harper W. Boyd, Jr., Ralph Westfall, and Stanley F. Stasch, *Marketing Research: Text and Cases,* 4th ed. (Homewood, IL: Richard D. Irwin, 1977), 546.

[2] John C. Hodges and Mary E. Whitten, *Harbrace College Handbook* (New York: Harcourt Brace Jovanovich, 1977), 336–350; or Frederick Crews, *The Random House Handbook* (New York: Random House, 1977), 35–44; or a business writing book, such as William J. Gallagher, *Report Writing for Management* (Reading, MA: Addison-Wesley, 1969), 60–68; or David M. Robinson, *Writing Reports for Management Decisions* (Columbus, OH: Merrill, 1969), 212–217.

[3] Some suggestions from Gallagher, *Report Writing for Management,* 69–74. People particularly afflicted with writer's block should see James W. Miller, Jr., *Word, Self, Reality: The Rhetoric of Imagination* (New York: Dodd, Mead, 1972). This book deals with the whole flow of language, not with rules and restrictions, and offers numerous exercises useful in learning to let out the words locked within one's head.

[4] Gallagher, *Report Writing for Management,* 84.

[5] Jessamon Dawe and William Jackson Lord, Jr., *Functional Business Communication* (Englewood Cliffs, NJ: Prentice-Hall, 1968), 495.

[6] The following discussion is indebted to John Fielden, "What Do You Mean I Can't Write?" *Harvard Business Review* (May/June 1964).

[7] Dawe and Lord, *Functional Business Communication,* Chapters 10 and 11; also see Robinson, *Writing Reports for Management Decisions,* 302–312.

[8] Thus this section has been adapted from the original division into categories for upward and downward communications. The interested reader may want to refer to the original inventory, by Fielden, in "What Do You Mean I Can't Write?" 147.

PART 7

A Special Topic

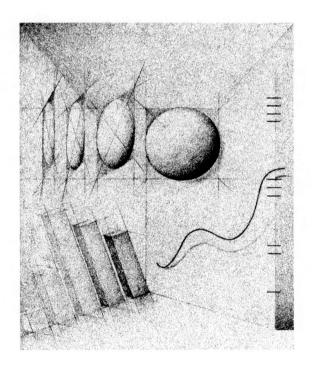

Ethical Issues in Business Research

What you will learn in this chapter:

To explain why ethical questions are philosophical questions.

To define societal norms.

To describe the three parties involved in most research situations and discuss how the interaction among these parties may identify a series of ethical questions.

To discuss the rights and obligations of the respondent.

To discuss the rights and obligations of the researcher.

To discuss the rights and obligations of the client sponsor.

To take each of the three parties' perspectives and discuss selected issues such as deception, privacy, and advocacy research.

To discuss the role of codes of ethics.

Executives of a firm interested in acquiring information concerning union members' attitudes toward management put a hidden microphone (attached to a tape recorder) in the employees' coffee room so that the union members' conversations might be observed unobtrusively. Is there a moral question to be decided here?

An accounting researcher who has sampled 100 organizations in a survey on CPA firms' accounting practices believes that a particular CPA firm in the sample is inefficiently managed. He discards its questionnaires, eliminating the firm from the analysis. Is this proper?

A number of West Coast residents believe that national television news networks making early projections about presidential races before their local polls close has an impact on their voting behavior, especially turnout. Are early election projections an ethical practice?

The personnel manager of a large bank tries to persuade a researcher to undertake a project with "political purposes." Is this in the organization's best interest?

Each of these situations illustrates an ethical issue in business research. Just as there are ethical aspects concerning all human interaction, there are some ethical questions about business research. Throughout this book selected ethical and moral issues have arisen concerning fair business dealings, proper research techniques, and appropriate utilization of research results. This chapter addresses the growing concern in recent years about the ethical implications of business research.

■

ETHICAL QUESTIONS ARE PHILOSOPHICAL QUESTIONS

Ethical questions are philosophical questions. There is no general agreement among philosophers about the answers to such questions. However, the rights and obligations of individuals are generally dictated by the norms of society.

Societal norms are codes of behavior adopted by a group; they suggest what a member of a group ought to do under given circumstances.[1] This chapter reflects the author's perceptions of the norms of our society (and undoubtedly his own values to some extent).[2]

GENERAL RIGHTS AND OBLIGATIONS OF CONCERNED PARTIES

In most research situations three parties are involved: the *researcher,* the *sponsoring client (user),* and the *respondent (subject).* The interaction of each of these parties with one or both of the other two parties identifies a series of ethical questions. Consciously or unconsciously, each party expects certain rights and feels certain obligations toward the other party. Exhibit 24.1 diagrams this relationship. Within any society there is a set of normatively prescribed expectations of behavior (including rights and obligations) associated with a social role, such as researcher, and another, reciprocal role, such as respondent. Certain ethical behaviors may be expected only in certain specific situations, while other expectations may be more generalized. If there are conflicting perspectives about behavioral expectations, ethical problems may arise. For instance, several ethical issues concern the researcher's expected rights versus those of the respondent/subject. A number of questions arise because researchers believe they have the right to seek information, but subjects believe they have a certain right to privacy. A respondent who says "I don't care to answer your question about my income" believes that he or she has the right to refuse to participate. Yet some researchers will persist in trying to get that information. In general, a field-worker is not expected to overstep the boundary society places on individuals' privacy.

For each of the subject's rights there is a corresponding obligation on the part of the researcher. For example, the individual's right to privacy dictates that the researcher has an obligation to protect the anonymity of the respon-

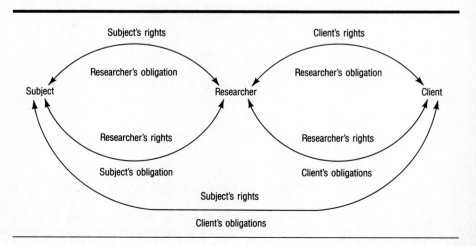

E X H I B I T   2 4 . 1

Interaction of Rights and Obligations

dent. When that respondent discloses information about personal matters, it is assumed that such information will be guarded from all people other than the researcher.

RIGHTS AND OBLIGATIONS OF THE RESPONDENT

The ethical issues vary somewhat depending on whether or not the participant has given willing and informed consent. In an unobtrusive observation study, the participant's rights differ from a survey respondent's rights because he or she has not willingly consented to be a subject of the research.

The Obligation to Be Truthful

When a subject provides willing consent to participate, it is generally expected that he or she will provide truthful answers. Honest cooperation is the main obligation of the respondent or subject.

Privacy

Americans relish their privacy. A major polling organization indicates that almost 80 percent of Americans believe that the collecting and giving out of personal information without their knowledge is a serious violation of their privacy.[3] Hence the right to privacy is an important question in business research. This issue involves the subject's freedom to choose whether or not to comply with the investigator's request.[4] Traditionally, researchers have assumed that individuals make an informed choice. However, critics have argued that the old, the poor, the poorly educated, and other underprivileged individuals may not be aware of their right to choose. Further, they have argued that the interview may begin with some vague explanation of its purpose, initially ask questions that are relatively innocuous, and then move to questions of a highly personal nature. It has been suggested that subjects be informed of their right to be left alone or to break off the interview at any given time. Researchers should not follow the tendency to "hold on" to busy respondents. However, this view is definitely not universally accepted in the research community.[5]

Another aspect of the privacy issue is illustrated by the question "Is the telephone call that interrupts someone's favorite television program an invasion of privacy?" The answer to this issue—and to most privacy questions—lies in the dilemma of determining where the rights of the individual end and the needs of society for better scientific information on citizen preference take over.[6] Generally, certain standards of common courtesy have been set by interviewing firms—for example, not to interview late in the evening and at other inconvenient times. However, there are several critics who may never be appeased. The computerized interviewer ("junk phone call") has stimulated increased debate over this aspect of the privacy issue. As a practical matter, respondents may feel more relaxed about privacy issues if they know who is conducting a survey. Thus it is generally recommended that field interviewers indicate that they are legitimate researchers by passing out business cards, wearing name tags, or in other ways identifying the name of their company.

In an observation study the major ethical issues concern whether the observed behavior is public or private. Generally it is believed that unobtrusive observation of public behavior in such places as stores, airports, and museums is not a serious invasion of privacy. However, recording private behavior with hidden cameras and the like does represent a violation of this right. For example, in a survey of research directors and executives, the practice of observing women putting on brassieres through a two-way mirror was disapproved by approximately 80 percent of the executives.[7]

Deception

In a number of situations the researcher creates a false impression by disguising the purpose of the research. The researcher, at least at the outset of the research, is not open and honest. Bluntly stated, to avoid possible biased reactions, the subject is lied to. Deception or concealment is the result of the researcher's lack of opportunity to observe or straightforwardly ask about the phenomena of interest, and hold all other factors constant, without partially deceiving the respondent. Generally, such deception is justified under two conditions: (1) Investigators assume that no physical danger or psychological harm will be caused by the deception, and (2) the researcher takes personal responsibility for informing the respondent of the concealment or deception after the research project ends. This issue is interrelated with the subject's right to be informed.

The issue of deception concerns the means-to-an-end philosophical issue. The major question is: Does a small deception substantially increase the value of the research? Suppose a survey research project must contact busy executives. Pretending to be calling long distance might improve the response rate—but is this a justifiable means to this end?

A distinction has been made between deception and discreet silence. The ethical question concerning the manifest content of a questionnaire versus the true purpose of the research has been cleverly stated as follows:

> *Must we really explain, when we ask the respondent to agree or disagree with the statement, "prison is too good for sex criminals; they should be publicly whipped or worse," it is really the authoritarianism of his personality we are investigating, and not the public opinion on crime and punishment?*[8]

Observation methods prevent a number of problems concerning the deception of subjects. Some people might see contrived observation as entrapment. To entrap means to deceive or trick into difficulty, which is clearly an abusive action. The difficulty is one of balancing values. If the researcher obtains permission, the subject may not act in a typical manner. Thus the researcher has to determine his or her own view of the ethics involved and determine if the usefulness of the information is worth telling a "white" lie.

The Right to Be Informed

It has been argued that subjects have a right to be informed of all aspects of the research, including information about its purpose and sponsorship. The argument for the researcher's obligation to protect this right is based on the aca-

E X H I B I T   2 4 . 2

**An Extreme Example of
Lack of Debriefing**

In an experiment conducted in a natural setting—independent food merchants in a number of Dutch towns were brought together for group meetings, in the course of which they were informed that a large organization was planning to open up a series of supermarkets in the Netherlands. In the High Threat condition, subjects were told that there was a high probability that their town would be selected as a site for such markets, and that the advent of these markets would cause a considerable drop in their business. On the advice of the executives of the shopkeepers' organizations, who had helped to arrange the group meetings, the investigators did not reveal the experimental manipulations to their subjects. I have been worried about these Dutch merchants ever since I heard about this study for the first time. Did some of them go out of business in anticipation of the heavy competition? Do some of them have an anxiety reaction every time they see a bulldozer? Chances are that they soon forgot about this threat (unless, of course, supermarkets actually did move into town) and that it became just one of the many little moments of anxiety that must occur in every shopkeeper's life. Do we have a right, however, to add to life's little anxieties and to risk the possibility of more extensive anxiety purely for the purposes of our experiments, particularly since deception deprives the subject of the opportunity to choose whether or not he wishes to expose himself to the risks that might be entailed?

Source: Herbert L. Kelman, "Human Use of Human Subjects: The Problem of Deception in Social Psychological Experiments," *Psychological Bulletin* (January 1967): 1–11.

demic tradition of informing and enlightening the public. Further, debriefing experimental subjects may relieve stress resulting from deception or other questionable procedures. Debriefing the subject by communicating the purpose of the experiment and the researcher's hypotheses about the nature of human behavior counteracts any negative effects of deception and/or stress and provides an educational experience for the subject.

> *Proper debriefing allows the subject to save face by uncovering the truth for himself. The experimenter should begin by asking the subject if he has any questions or if he found any part of the experiment odd, confusing, or disturbing. This question provides a check on the subject's suspiciousness and effectiveness of manipulations. The experimenter continues to provide the subject cues to the deception until the subject states that he believes there was more to the experiment than met the eye. At this time the purpose and procedure of the experiment is revealed.*[9]

When there is clear-cut deception or when the researcher perceives that there may be psychological harm in participating in an experiment (a rarity in business research), debriefing is often performed. However, if the researcher does not foresee potentially harmful consequences in participation, this process is often eliminated due to time and cost considerations. See Exhibit 24.2 for an example of what may occur if there is no debriefing.

A pragmatic argument for providing respondents with information about the nature of the study concerns the long-run ability of researchers to gain cooperation from respondents. If the public understands why survey or experimental information has been collected and that the researchers may be trusted with private information, it may be easier in the long run to conduct research. Several research suppliers have suggested that public relations work is needed to sell the public on the research industry story.

RIGHTS AND OBLIGATIONS OF THE RESEARCHER

General business ethics should be a standard for business research firms and business research departments. Our concern is not with issues such as bribery or the welfare and safety of one's employees but with ethical issues that are specifically germane to business research practices.

More has been written about the ethics of researchers than about those of the other two parties because this group's purpose is clearly identifiable. Exhibit 24.1 illustrates that researchers have obligations to both subjects and clients as well as the corresponding rights. A number of professional associations have developed standards and operating procedures for ethical practice by researchers. Exhibit 24.3 is the **code of ethics** for the American Association for Public Opinion Research. This code shows several major issues exist that should be further explored in this book. Students contemplating entering business research should check for codes of ethics set out by their professional associations.

The Purpose of Research Is Research

Businesspersons are expected not to misrepresent a sales tactic as business research. The Federal Trade Commission has indicated that it is illegal to use any plan, scheme, or ruse that misrepresents the true status of the person making the call as a door-opener to gain admission to a prospect's home, office, or other establishment.[10] This sales ploy is considered to be unethical as well as illegal. No research firm should engage in any practice other than scientific investigation.

Objectivity

Throughout this book the need for objectivity and scientific investigation to ensure accuracy has been stressed. Researchers should maintain high standards to ensure that the data are accurate. Further, they must not intentionally try to prove a particular point for political purposes.

An example of the lack of objectivity in research was observed when managers inspected focus group interviews conducted by a research supplier they used for several product lines. They noticed that some of the respondents looked familiar. A review of the video recordings of the session found that the focus group moderator had solicited subjects who had in the past been found to be very articulate and willing to cooperate. It was questionable whether these subjects could have remained aloof from the role of expert.

RESEARCH INSIGHT
Les Sondages

Political polls are referred to as *Les Sondages* in France. One of the juiciest French tales of creative lying, totally unconfirmed, of course, recounts how Jacques Chirac, mayor of Paris, hoisted Valerie Giscard d'Estaing into the presidential race by citing a nonexistent *Sondage* which proved that Giscard would make a better candidate than **the favorite, Jacques Chaban Delmas.**

It is accepted wisdom that without this coup someone else would have been elected president of France. Despite repeated demands, this crucially important *Sondage* could never be produced.

Source: Carolyn Pfaff, "French Take Poll-tampering in Stride," *Advertising Age*, Jan. 15, 1979, 81.

Misrepresentation of Research

Research companies (and clients) should not misrepresent the statistical accuracy of their data, nor should they overstate the significance of the results by altering the findings. Basically, it is assumed that the researcher has the obligation to both the client and the subjects to analyze the data honestly and to report correctly the actual data collection methods. For example, the failure to report a variation from the technically correct probability sampling procedure is ethically questionable. Similarly, any major error that has occurred during the course of the study should not be kept secret from management or the client sponsor. Hiding errors or variations from the proper procedures tends to distort or shade the results. A more blatant breach of the researcher's responsibilities would be the outright distortion of data.

Protecting the Right to Confidentiality of Both Subjects and Clients

A number of clients might be very desirous of a list of favorable industrial prospects generated from a research survey. It is the researcher's responsibility to ensure that the privacy and anonymity of the respondents are preserved. If the respondent's name and address are known, this information should not under any circumstances be forwarded to the sponsoring organization.

Information that a research supplier obtains about a client's general business affairs should not be disseminated to other clients or third parties. The client or users of business research have a number of rights and obligations. Their primary right is to expect objective and accurate data from the research supplier. They should also expect that their instructions relating to confidentiality have been carried out.

Dissemination of Faulty Conclusions

Another ethical issue concerns the dissemination of faulty conclusions. A research project may be conducted and then the researcher or decision maker may disseminate conclusions from the research project that are inconsistent

E X H I B I T   2 4 . 3   **Code of Professional Ethics and Practices: American Association for Public Opinion Research**

We, the members of the American Association for Public Opinion Research, subscribe to the principles expressed in the following code. Our goals are to support sound and ethical practice in the conduct of public opinion research and in the use of such research for policy and decision-making in the public and private sectors, as well as to improve public understanding of opinion research methods and the proper use of opinion research results.

We pledge ourselves to maintain high standards of scientific competence and integrity in conducting, analyzing, and reporting our work and in our relations with survey respondents, with our clients, with those who eventually use the research for decision-making purposes, and with the general public. We further pledge ourselves to reject all tasks or assignments that would require activities inconsistent with the principles of this code.

The Code
I. Principles of Professional Practice in the Conduct of Our Work
A. We shall exercise due care in developing research designs and survey instruments, and in collecting, processing, and analyzing data, taking all reasonable steps to assure the reliability and validity of results.
   1. We shall recommend and employ only those tools and methods of analysis which, in our professional judgment, are well suited to the research problem at hand.
   2. We shall not select research tools and methods of analysis because of their capacity to yield misleading conclusions.
   3. We shall not knowingly make interpretations of research results, nor shall we tacitly permit interpretations that are inconsistent with the data available.
   4. We shall not knowingly imply that interpretations should be accorded greater confidence than the data actually warrant.
B. We shall describe our methods and findings accurately and in appropriate detail in all research reports, adhering to the standards for minimal disclosure specified in Section III, below.
C. If any of our work becomes the subject of a formal investigation of an alleged violation of this Code, undertaken with the approval of the AAPOR Executive Council, we shall provide additional information on the survey in such detail that a fellow survey practitioner would be able to conduct a professional evaluation of the survey.

II. Principles of Professional Responsibility in Our Dealings with People
A. *The Public:*
   1. If we become aware of the appearance in public of serious distortions of our research, we shall publicly disclose what is required to correct these distortions, including, as appropriate, a statement to the public media, legislative body, regulatory agency, or other appropriate group, in or before which the distorted findings were presented.
B. *Clients or Sponsors:*
   1. When undertaking work for a private client, we shall hold confidential all proprietary information obtained about the client and about the conduct and findings of the research undertaken for the

client, except when the dissemination of the information is expressly authorized by the client, or when disclosure becomes necessary under terms of Section I-C or II-A of this Code.

    2. We shall be mindful of the limitations of our techniques and capabilities and shall accept only those research assignments which we can reasonably expect to accomplish within these limitations.

C. *The Profession:*

    1. We recognize our responsibility to contribute to the science of public opinion research and to disseminate as freely as possible the ideas and findings which emerge from our research.

    2. We shall not cite our membership in the Association as evidence of professional competence, since the association does not so certify any persons or organizations.

D. *The Respondent:*

    1. We shall strive to avoid the use of practices or methods that may harm, humiliate, or seriously mislead survey respondents.

    2. Unless the respondent waives confidentiality for specified uses, we shall hold as privileged and confidential all information that might identify a respondent with his or her responses. We shall also not disclose or use the names of respondents for nonresearch purposes unless the respondents grant us permission to do so.

III. Standards for Minimal Disclosure

Good professional practice imposes the obligation upon all public opinion researchers to include, in any report of research results, or to make available when that report is released, certain essential information about how the research was conducted. At a minimum, the following items should be disclosed:

1. Who sponsored the survey, and who conducted it.

2. The exact wording of questions asked, including the text of any preceding instruction or explanation to the interviewer or respondent that might reasonably be expected to affect the response.

3. A definition of the population under study, and a description of the sampling frame used to identify this population.

4. A description of the sample selection procedure, giving a clear indication of the method by which the respondents were selected by the researcher, or whether the respondents were entirely self-selected.

5. Size of sample and, if applicable, completion rates and information on eligibility criteria and screening procedures.

6. A discussion of the precision of the findings, including, if appropriate, estimates of sampling error, and a description of any weighting or estimating procedures used.

7. Which results are based on parts of the sample, rather than on the total sample.

8. Method, location, and dates of data collection.

with or not warranted by the data. Most research professionals consider this to be improper.

A dramatic example of violation of this principle is given in an advertisement of a cigarette smoker study. The advertisement compared two brands and stated that "of those expressing a preference, over 65 percent preferred" the advertised brand to a competitive brand. The misleading portion of this reported result was that most of the respondents did not express a preference; they indicated that both brands tasted about the same. Thus only a very small percentage of those studied actually revealed a preference, and the results were somewhat misleading. Such shading of the results is not in line with the obligation to report accurate findings.

Consider the client who has solicited several bids for a business research project. The research supplier that wins the bid is asked by the client to appropriate ideas from the proposal of a competing research supplier and include them in the research study to be done for the client. This is generally regarded as unethical.[11]

RIGHTS AND OBLIGATIONS OF THE SPONSORING CLIENT (USER)

Ethics between Buyer and Seller

The general business ethics expected to exist between a purchasing agent and a sales representative should exist in the business research situation. For example, if the purchasing agent has already decided to purchase a product (or research proposal) from a friend, it is generally considered unethical for him to solicit competitive bids that have no chance of being accepted just to fulfill a corporate purchasing policy stating that a bid must be put out to three competitors. The typical business and other commitments unrelated to a specific business research situation are ethical questions not dealt with here.

An Open Relationship with Research Suppliers

The sponsoring client has the obligation to encourage the research supplier to seek out the truth objectively. To encourage this objectivity, a full and open statement of the problem, explication of time and money constraints, and any other insights that may help the supplier anticipate costs and problems should be provided.[12] In other words, the research sponsor should encourage efforts to reduce bias and to listen to the voice of the public.

An Open Relationship with Interested Parties

Conclusions should be based on the data. A user of research should not knowingly disseminate conclusions from a given research project or service that are inconsistent with the data or are not warranted by them.[13] Violation of this principle is perhaps the greatest transgression that a client can commit. Justifying a political position that is not warranted from the data poses serious ethical questions. Indicating that data show something so that a sale can be made is also a serious matter.

Privacy

A mailing list company is offering a mailing list that has been compiled by screening millions of households to obtain the necessary brand-usage information. The information would be extremely valuable to your firm. You suspect a fake survey was conducted to obtain the data. Is it ethical to purchase the mailing list? If respondents have been deceived about the purpose of a survey and then their names are sold as part of a user mailing list, this practice is certainly unethical. The client as well as the research supplier has the obligation to maintain the respondents' privacy.

Sales managers who know that a survey of their customers has been keyed to increase response rate must resist the temptation to seek those accounts that are the hottest prospects.

Commitment to Research

Some potential clients have been known to request research proposals from a research supplier when there is a low probability that the research will be conducted. For example, obtaining an outsider's opinion of the company problem via a research proposal provides an inexpensive consultation. If the information supports a given manager's position in an intracompany debate, it could be used politically rather than as a basis for research. A research consultant's opinion may be solicited even though management is not really planning research and funds have not been allocated for the project. Because the research supplier must spend considerable effort planning a custom-designed study, most research practitioners believe that the client has the obligation to be serious about considering a project before soliciting proposals.

Pseudo–Pilot Studies

It has already been stated that it is important for clients to be open about the business problem to be investigated. However, there is a special case of this problem that should be explained. Sometimes a client will suggest that a more comprehensive study is in the planning stages and that the proposal the research supplier is bidding on is a pilot study. This can be best phrased by the statement "I don't want to promise anything, but you should know that this is the first in a very ambitious series of studies we are planning to undertake, and if you sharpen your pencil in estimating cost. . . ."[14] The research consultant is told that if a good job is performed during the pilot study stages there will be an additional major contract down the line. Too often these pilot studies are "come-ons"—the comprehensive study never materializes, and the consultant must absorb a loss.

ADVOCACY RESEARCH

Recently the brand name Monopoly became a generic name. Parker Brothers' trademark was lost when the courts ruled that the name Monopoly primarily denoted a product, not the product's producer. The primary evidence submitted to the Ninth Circuit Court was a consumer survey that had tested the motivation of buyers. Do people buy Monopoly because Parker Brothers, a General Mills subsidiary, makes it? Or would they buy the same game from any manufacturer? Some 65 percent of the sample indicated that they were motivated to buy Monopoly because they wanted to play the game, not because it was produced by a certain company. This is an example of **advocacy research.**

With increased legal activity relating to health and safety issues, consumerism, and other changes in the business environment, such advocacy research as claim substantiation has increased substantially. Advocacy research differs from research that has traditionally been intended for internal use only.[15] The traditional factors, such as sample size, people to be interviewed, and questions to be asked, are weighed against cost when making an internal decision. In advocacy research the court's opinion of the value of the research may be based exclusively on sampling design and validity processes. Thus the slightest variation from technically correct sampling procedures may be magnified by an attorney until a standard business research project no longer appears adequate in the judge's eye.

The ethics of advocacy research present a number of serious questions. Consider the following quote:

> *Almost never do you see a researcher who appears as an independent witness, quite unbiased. You almost always see a witness appearing either for the FTC or for the industry. You can almost predict what is going to be concluded by the witness for the FTC. And you can almost predict what will be concluded by the witness for industry. That says that research in this setting is not after full truth and it is not dispassionate in nature. And for those of us who consider ourselves to be researchers, that is a serious quandary.*[16]

Researchers doing advocacy research do not necessarily bias results intentionally. However, attorneys in an advocacy research trial rarely will submit research evidence that does not support the client's position.

The question of advocacy research is one of objectivity: Can the researcher search out the truth when the legal client wishes to support its position at a trial? The ethical question stems from a conflict between legal ethics and research ethics, and perhaps only the individual researcher can resolve this question.

A POSSIBLE FUTURE ISSUE

The Privacy Act of 1974 has lent itself to various interpretations. One question that remains unanswered deals with the act's stipulation that information about an individual cannot be extracted without securing his or her informed, expressed consent.[17] Certain privacy advocates have suggested that this provision indicates that written consent of the respondent is required. If this becomes the case, it is very likely that potential respondents may be reluctant to cooperate if they are required to sign some type of agreement.

A FINAL NOTE ON ETHICS

There is no question that there are unethical researchers in the world and that a number of shady dealings occur. The business researcher's honesty is no different from any other aspect of business ethics, or of personal morality, for that matter. One may occasionally run across the case of a researcher who produces a report on fabricated findings, just as there are occasional cases of interviewers who cheat by filling out the questionnaires themselves. In pre-Castro Cuba there was at least one firm that, for a fee, would provide a handsomely engraved certificate attesting that the Court of Public Opinion held the client or the client's products in whatever kind of high esteem might be desired (with no extra charge for percentages).[18] Under some circumstances even good researchers take shortcuts, some of which may be ethically questionable. However, like most businesspeople, researchers are generally ethical people. Of course, the answer to the question "What is ethical?" is not easy—only one's conscience operates to inhibit any questionable practice.[19]

A FINAL NOTE ON BUSINESS RESEARCH

Business research is not a panacea or a substitute for judgment—it is only a tool. Yet business research, properly conducted and utilized by management, can play an indispensable role in better decision making. It is hoped that the student will have gained a greater appreciation of the diverse nature of business research from reading this textbook. Business research is not a black-and-white area in which there is always a correct technique for solving a given problem. It is a gray area that in many cases requires considerable experience, a bit of skill, and the touch of an artist. It is further hoped that the student will be interested in exploration of the more complex aspects of business research now that the basics have been mastered.

Key Terms
societal norms

code of ethics

advocacy research

Questions
1. Is it ethical for a manufacturing company that wishes to remain anonymous in a mail survey to invent a fictitious research company name and print that name on letterhead paper for the survey? For example, a firm in Ohio wishing to disguise the sponsor of its survey might choose a name such as North Central Research Corporation with which to survey its own distributors.
2. A mouthwash company learns that a competitor is test marketing a new lemon-flavored mouthwash in an Arizona city. The research department of a competing firm is told to read the results of the test market, and the

marketing manager is told to lower the price of the competing product to disrupt the test market. Is this ethical?

3.   You have solicited research proposals from several firms. The lowest bidder has the best questionnaire and proposal. However, you particularly like one feature from a firm that will not receive the bid. How should you handle this situation?

4.   A researcher investigating attitudes toward her company notices that one individual answers all image questions at one end of a bipolar scale. Should she throw this questionnaire out and not use it in the data analysis?

5.   Page through your local newspaper to find some stories derived from survey research results. Was the study's methodology indicated for this news item? Could the research have been termed advocacy research?

6.   How might the business research industry take action to ensure that the public believes that research is a legitimate activity and that firms that misrepresent and deceive the public using business research as a sales ploy are not "true" business researchers?

7.   Comment on the ethics of the following situations:

   a.   A researcher plans to code questionnaires in an employee survey by using invisible ink. Is this ethical?

   b.   A researcher is planning to visually record (videotape) test users' reactions to a new product in a simulated kitchen environment from behind a two-way mirror.

   c.   A food warehouse (box store) advertises "savings up to 30 percent" after a survey showed a range of savings from 2 percent to 30 percent below that of an average shopping trip for selected items.

   d.   A radio station broadcasts the following message during a syndicated rating service's rating period: "Please fill out your diary."

   e.   A researcher pretends to be a member of a business firm's secretarial pool and observes workers without the workers realizing that they are part of a research study.

   f.   A researcher tells a potential respondent that the interview will last 10 minutes rather than the 30 minutes the researcher actually anticipates.

8.   Name some research practices that are ethically questionable.

9.   The American Testing Institute (also known as the U.S. Testing Authority) utilizes the mails to conduct what it calls a television survey. A questionnaire is sent to a respondent, who is asked to complete it and mail it back along with a check for $14.80. In return for answering eight questions on viewing habits, the institute promises to send the respondent one of 20 prizes ranging from $200 to $2,000 in value. These prizes include video recorders, diamond watches, a lifetime supply of camera film, color televisions, and two nights of hotel accommodations at a land development resort community. The institute lists the odds of winning as 1 in 150,000 on all prizes except the hotel stay, for which the odds are 149,981 out of 150,000. During a three-month period the institute sends out 200,000 questionnaires. What are the ethical issues in this situation?

References

[1] Don Martindale, *The Nature and Types of Sociological Theory* (Boston: Houghton Mifflin, 1960), 478–480.

[2] For an alternative perspective, see Kenneth C. Schneider's excellent article "Marketing Research Industry Isn't Moving Toward Professionalism," *Marketing Educator* (Winter 1984): 1, 6.

[3] Lawrence D. Wiseman, "The Present Value of Future Studies," speech to the Advertising Research Foundation, March 1980.

[4] Alice M. Tybout and Gerald Zaltman, "Ethics in Marketing Research: Their Practical Relevance," *Journal of Marketing Research* (November 1974): 357–368.

[5] Robert L. Day, "A Comment on Ethics in Marketing Research," *Journal of Marketing Research* (May 1975): 232–233.

[6] Robert O. Carlson, "The Issue of Privacy in Public Opinion Research," *Public Opinion Quarterly* (Spring 1967): 1–8.

[7] C. Merle Crawford, "Attitudes of Marketing Executives Toward Ethics in Marketing Research," *Journal of Marketing* (April 1970): 46–52.

[8] Leo Bogart, "The Researcher's Dilemma," *Journal of Marketing* (January 1962): 6–11.

[9] Tybout and Zaltman, "Ethics in Marketing Research," 357–368.

[10] C. J. Frey and T. C. Kinnear, "Legal Constraints in Marketing Research: Review and Call to Action," *Journal of Marketing Research* (August 1979): 259.

[11] Sidney Hollander, Jr., "Ethics in Marketing Research," in *Handbook of Marketing Research*, ed. Robert Ferber (New York: McGraw-Hill, 1974), 1–11.

[12] Lawrence D. Gibson, "Use of Marketing Research Contractors," in *Handbook of Marketing Research*, ed. Robert Ferber (New York: McGraw-Hill, 1974), 129.

[13] Marketing Research Standards Committee, *Marketing Research Code of Ethics* (Chicago: American Marketing Association, 1972).

[14] Robert Bezilla, Joel B. Haynes, and Clifford Elliot, "Ethics in Marketing Research," *Business Horizons* (April 1976): 83–86.

[15] "New Market Research Guides Urged," *Advertising Age,* Apr. 30, 1979, 54.

[16] H. Keith Hunt, "The Ethics of Research in the Consumer Interests: Panel Summary," ed. Norleen M. Ackerman, Proceedings of the American Council of Consumer Interests Conference, 1979, 152.

[17] Frey and Kinnear, "Legal Constraints in Marketing Research," 295–302.

[18] Bogart, "The Researcher's Dilemma," 6–11.

[19] Crawford, "Attitudes of Marketing Executives," 46–52; and Shelby D. Hunt, Lawrence B. Chonko, and James D. Wilcox, "Ethical Problems of Marketing Researchers," *Journal of Marketing Research* (August 1984): 309–324.

PART 8

Cases

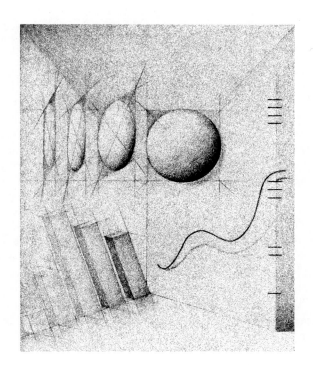

C A S E   **1**

Tulsa's Central Business District (A): Developing a Research Proposal

When Bob Griffin, vice-president of Williams Realty Corporation, asked the Metropolitan Tulsa Chamber of Commerce to meet with him, he had spent much time thinking how downtown Tulsa was changing. Only a year ago, construction had begun on a $2.6 million central pedestrian mall system. Mayor Robert LaFortune said that the carrying out of the downtown revitalization project reflected the solid "partnership of public and private interests. . . . We have to see great things emerge both in private development and general use of this facility by all Tulsans."

The project called for improving Main Street from Third to Sixth Streets and Fifth Street from Boston to Denver, including landscaping, a multilevel fountain at Fifth and Main, and brick paving. Throughout the mall there would be rest areas, drinking fountains, and other facilities, such as telephone booths and a postal service center. The concept of the central pedestrian system was expected to strengthen the "Main Street" segment as the prime rental area in downtown Tulsa.

NEW WILLIAMS CENTER COMPLEX

One of the most obvious symbols of what was happening downtown was the 52-story Bank of Oklahoma (BOK) Tower, the focal point of the "new" Tulsa skyline. The Williams Companies had constructed the $18 million tower, the state's tallest building, and office space was beginning to be leased. This was the first of several Williams Center projects to be completed.

The Williams Center was planned as a $50 million complex located in the heart of downtown, consisting of a 50-story office building, a hotel, a shopping center, and a performing arts center.

Twenty-five thousand square feet would be given over to food service establishments. There would be a cafeteria and several fast-food places on the first floor; on the second floor, overlooking the rink from the west end, would be a restaurant that would likely specialize in crepes. A first-rate restaurant would be on the third, or plaza, level—the same level as Bank of Oklahoma's main banking facilities.

In addition to casual shoppers, the retail area was expected to draw from 7,000 persons working in the BOK Tower plus 500 guests of the hotel.

PLANNING FOR REVITALIZATION

Bob Griffin had asked two members of the Metropolitan Tulsa Chamber of Commerce—Don Wolfe, manager of community relations, and John Piercey, manager of research—to meet with him in his office. Griffin was responsible for the development of the Williams Center.

The Williams Company was incorporated on February 3, 1949, as the Williams Brothers Company, the successor to an oil-related business established in 1908. Its headquarters were in Tulsa. The company was primarily engaged in the chemical fertilizer, energy, and metals business. In its chemical fertilizer business, the company manufactured and marketed chemical fertilizer materials worldwide (Agrico Chemical Company). Its energy-related activities included owning and operating the largest independently owned pipeline system in the United States (Williams Pipeline Company), retailing and wholesaling liquefied petroleum gas (Williams Energy Company), exploring for and developing oil and gas properties (Williams Exploration Company), and owning and operating an intrastate natural gas pipeline in Louisiana. In its metals business the company purchased, processed, and distributed steel and other metals, principally on the East Coast (Edgecomb Steel Company) and in the Midwest (Steel Sales Corporation). The company's activities also included investing in short-term-paper marketable securities and equity interests. The Williams Realty Corporation's primary purpose was to develop a major area of downtown Tulsa.

The company had a rich history. In 1908 two young brothers were sent by their employer, a Kansas City contractor, to begin a highway paving job. When the bond issue for this project was delayed, the contractor decided to move on— but not David R. and S. Miller Williams, Jr. The brothers persuaded their employer to accept their note for the equipment and supplies and agreed to perform the city's program piecemeal as funds permitted. Thus the Williams Brothers Company was founded.

The company's first pipeline venture, in 1915, established Williams Brothers as the principal builder in this new field. Ever since, the name "Williams" has been synonymous with pipelines.

Williams Brothers expanded to work outside of Canada and the United States in the late 1930s. An important milestone occurred when the company purchased the assets of the 6,200-mile Great Lakes Pipe Line Company in 1966 and subsequently expanded this system to provide more complete coverage of its upper Midwest distribution area.

The Williams Companies consisted of the founding organization, Williams Pipeline, Williams Energy, Williams Exploration Company, Agrico Fertilizer Company, and Williams Realty.

WILLIAMS REALTY WORKS WITH THE CHAMBER OF COMMERCE

Bob Griffin's chief responsibility as vice-president of Williams Realty was to sell the idea that downtown Tulsa was revitalizing and the Williams Center in particular would be a good place to locate offices and a shopping center.

At the meeting, after the usual informal chitchat about goings-on in the city, Griffin addressed the group. "I've found out many things since the Williams Companies made the decision to develop the Williams Center. One is that we need to know more about the central business district. As I speak to prospective occupants of our space, one question almost universally asked is "How many people work in the downtown area?" I have been able to do some rough computations by estimating the average number of workers per square foot and then multiplying that figure times our estimate of the square footage in the downtown area. That is the answer I give these people. Nevertheless, we do not have a reliable estimate of how many people work in the downtown area. Knowing how many people work here is only the tip of the information iceberg. There are a number of other things I'd like to know about the downtown area."

John Piercey commented, "You know, Bob, the future of Tulsa's central business district has been a topic of concern for many years. Its present conditions and its future are perceived to be an indication of the vitality and future of the entire city. Just a few years ago, Tulsa's CBD was in a state of decline. At that time there was every indication that Tulsa's downtown was going the way of those in so many other cities. But the Chamber of Commerce and Downtown Tulsa Unlimited started revitalization plans, hoping to reverse the declining trend. Many major private investments have been made in the last few years. But most of these efforts have been made on the basis of intuitive feelings about the CBD. I think you're right. The lack of timely information is hampering industrial decision making and commercial marketing efforts in the downtown area. If the Chamber of Commerce is going to help the central business district, we have to eliminate the information gap about the central business district. Information such as (1) the quantity and nature of the downtown population, (2) commercial enterprise (and vacancy) inventory, (3) business' opinions about the CBD, and (4) shoppers' opinions about the CBD is needed."

Don Wolfe suggested that many downtown firms might be interested in the type of information that the Williams Companies desired. He said, "I believe the Chamber of Commerce should develop a statement of information needs and determine our research objectives; then we can see if a number of their firms in the central business district would be willing to support some research."

John Piercey added, "I think this is going to be an extremely big task. The Chamber's research department is not going to be able to collect such massive amounts of data. Perhaps we can utilize the source of an outside consultant, perhaps one of the universities in the area."

Don Wolfe said, "Yes, I believe we need someone who could help us out substantially in defining our research objectives and collection of the data."

Bob Griffin said, "Fine, gentlemen, I think we've made an important decision."

The Chamber of Commerce decided that the project would require extensive fieldwork in four interrelated areas. These areas were:

1. A survey of the central business district employers and employees (characteristics, work habits, and attitudes).
2. A survey of commercial establishments and off-street parking facilities (type, size, and location).
3. A survey of commercial vacancies (concentrating on ground-floor space but with some consideration given to multistory commercial buildings).
4. An on-the-street *sample* survey of shopping attitudes and preferences (this would also address attitudes toward working and living downtown).

Questions

1. Do you agree with the Chamber of Commerce's research objectives and proposed methods of data collection? Why or why not?
2. Briefly outline a research proposal by listing the appropriate techniques for collection of these data.

C A S E **2**

Hamilton Power Tools Corporation

On July 13, 1983, Mr. Campagna, the marketing manager for Hamilton Power Tools, was anxiously awaiting his meeting with the business research firm. He felt the findings from the business research would change Hamilton from a sales-oriented company to a firm that would adopt the consumer-oriented philosophy of the marketing concept.

For more than 35 years Hamilton Power Tools had been marketing industrial products by catering to the construction and industrial tool

Source: This case is modified from the original case that appeared in William G. Zikmund and William J. Lundstrom, *Outstanding Cases in Marketing Management* (St. Paul: West Publishing, 1979). Copyright 1979 by William G. Zikmund. All names are fictitious to ensure confidentiality.

markets. Its construction product lines included power trowels, concrete vibrators, generators, and powder-actuated tools. Its industrial products were primarily pneumatic tools: drills, screwdrivers, etc. One of its products, the gasoline-powered chain saw, was somewhat different from traditional construction and industrial tools. The chain saw line had been added in 1949, when John Hamilton, Sr., had the opportunity to acquire a small chain saw manufacturer. Hamilton believed that construction workers would have a need for gasoline-powered chain saws. He acquired the business in order to diversify the company into other markets.

During the late 1970s and early 1980s the

chain saw market was rapidly changing, and Hamilton Power Tool executives began to realize they needed some expert marketing advice. Mr. Campagna, marketing manager, felt that a major change in the company's direction was on the horizon. Campagna had been in the chain saw business for 15 years. Reports from trade publications, statistics from the Chain Saw Manufacturers Association, and personal experience had led him to believe that the recent chain saw industry was composed of roughly the following markets: professionals (lumberjacks), farmers, institutions, and casual users (home or estate owners with many trees on their lots). The casual user segment was considered to be the future growth market. Campagna wished to ensure that Hamilton would not make any mistakes in marketing its product to this segment of "weekend woodcutters" who once or twice a year used a chain saw to cut firewood or to prune trees in the backyard.

In March 1983, when chain saw sales began to slow down because of the seasonal nature of the business, Campagna and Ray Johnson, the chain saw sales manager, had a meeting with John Hamilton, Sr. Although Hamilton believed they had been doing well enough in chain saw sales over the past decade, Campagna and Johnson were able to persuade the aging executive that some consumer research was necessary. After talking with several business research firms, Hamilton Power Tools hired Consumer Metrics of Chicago to perform two research projects. The first was a Thematic Apperception Test (TAT).

The TAT research was completed the first week of July. Campagna arranged for a meeting with the business research firm the following week. As Dale Conway and Frank Baggins made their presentation of the results of the survey of chain saw users, Campagna thought back to the day Consumer Metrics had originally suggested the idea of a TAT to John Hamilton. Conway had sold him on the idea with his argument that motivational research was widely used in consumer studies to uncover people's buying motives. Conway had mentioned that Consumer Metrics had recently hired a young, bright MBA. This MBA—Baggins, as it turned out—had specialized in con-

sumer psychology and business research at a major state university. Conway had thought that Baggins was one of the best-qualified people to work on this type of project. Since Hamilton Power Tools had had no experience in consumer research, Campagna had been eager to proceed with the in-depth thematic apperception test (TAT).

Conway told Campagna, Hamilton, and Johnson that in the TAT respondents are shown a series of pictures and are asked to tell their feelings concerning the people in the pictures. He told Campagna that although the present study was exploratory, it could be used to gain insights into the reasons people make certain purchases. He also suggested that the test would be a means for gaining the flavor of the language people use in talking about chain saws, and it could be a source of new ideas for copywriting.

Campagna remembered that at one time he had thought this project wouldn't be very worthwhile; however, he also realized he did not know that much about the consumer market. During the initial meeting with the research firm, it had been proposed that an exploratory research project be conducted within the states of Illinois and Wisconsin to obtain some indication of the attitudes of potential casual users toward chain saws. The researcher had suggested a TAT. Campagna had not known much about this type of research and needed time to think. After a week's deliberation, he called Conway and told the researchers to go ahead with the project. Case Exhibit 2.1 shows the TAT used by the researchers.

At the meeting, Conway and Baggins carefully presented the research results. They pointed out that in the TAT study several screening questions were asked at the beginning of the interview. The findings of this study were based on those respondents who either planned to purchase a chain saw in the next 12 months, already owned a chain saw, or had used a chain saw in the past. The presentation closely followed the written report submitted to Campagna. The findings were as follows.

The first picture (Exhibit A of Case Exhibit 2.1) shown to the respondent pictured a man standing looking at a tree. The interviewer asked the respondent the following question:

CASE EXHIBIT   2 . 1

Hamilton TAT Study

Exhibit A

Exhibit B

Exhibit C

Exhibit D

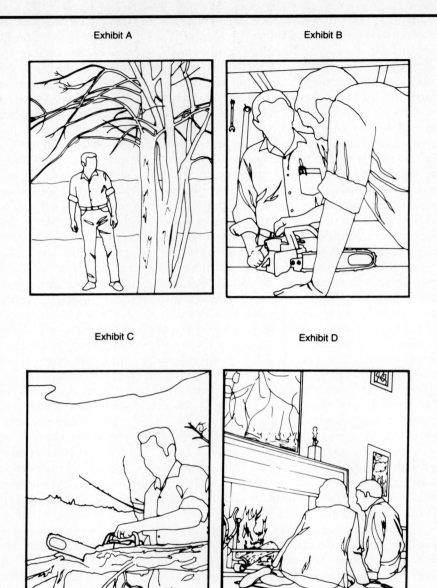

Source: Reproduced by permission from A Collection of Outstanding Cases in Marketing Management by William G. Zikmund and William J. Lundstrom. Copyright © 1979 by West Publishing Company. All rights reserved.

I have a problem which you may find interesting. Here's a picture of a man who is thinking about the purchase of a chain saw. Suppose that such a man is your neighbor. What do you suppose he is thinking about?

After the respondent's initial answer, the following probing question was asked:

Now, if he came to you for advice and you really wanted to help him, what would you tell him to do? Why do you think this would be the best thing for him to do?

Initial responses seemed to center around what the man would do with the tree. Many respondents expressed an interest in the tree and were concerned with preservation. It seemed that pride in having a tree that beautified the owner's property was important to some respondents. Some of the typical responses given are as follows:

He's thinking about cutting the tree down.
Why cut a whole tree when you can save part of it?
He could trim out part of those trees and save some of them.
We lose trees due to disease and storm damage. Trees beautify property and make it more valuable.
I don't like to destroy trees.

Considering the alternatives to buying a chain saw was the next step many of the respondents took. Basically, the ultimate consumer sees the alternatives to the purchase of a chain saw as:

1. Using a hand saw.
2. Hiring a tree surgeon.
3. Renting or borrowing a chain saw.

These alternatives were in the respondents' minds partly because they were concerned about the cost of doing the job. They seemed to be worried about the investment in a chain saw, about whether it paid to buy one for a small, single-application job. (Another reason for the alternatives came out in responses to a later picture.) Some quotations illustrating these points are as follows:

He's thinking how to go about it. He will use his hand saw.

He doesn't have to invest in a chain saw for only one tree.
He's thinking about how to get the tree down— the cost of doing it himself versus having someone else do it. Have him cut it down himself, it's not too big a tree. He'll save the cost.
He's thinking whether it pays for a couple of trees. If it would be worth it. How much longer with an axe.
He's thinking whether he should do it himself or get someone else to do it for him. Get someone who knows what he is doing.
He's thinking he'll rent a chain saw for a small area and would buy one for a large area.
The best way to get a job done. Chain saw is faster, but a hand saw is cheaper. Depends on how much work he has to do.

An interesting comment made by two respondents was "He's thinking about Dutch elm disease." The area had recently been hit by that disease. The respondents were projecting their situations into the TAT pictures.

Other statements were made concerning the ease and speed of using a chain saw. Some questions regarding the characteristic performance of a chain saw were raised in response to this question; however, Exhibit B covered this area more adequately. This picture showed two men standing in a chain saw store looking at a chain saw. The question asked went as follows:

Here is a picture of the same man in a chain saw store. Suppose he's a friend of yours— your next-door neighbor, perhaps. Tell me what you think he will talk about with the chain saw clerk.

The issue most frequently raised was how the chain saw worked. An equal number of respondents wanted to know first how much it cost. Weight (lightness) was the next most frequently raised issue. Horsepower was of concern among many of the respondents. Other subjects they thought the man would talk about with the clerk were maintenance and availability of repair, performance (what size tree the chain saw would cut), durability and expected life, safety (what safety features the chain saw had), and ease of starting the chain saw. In relation to price, comments were made such as:

Well, price is the most important, of course. He's wondering how he will pay for it.

One respondent said, "He's not considering price; price means nothing in regard to safety." One individual was concerned whether the chain would come off the "blade" (respondents referred to the guide bar as a "blade" rather than a "guide bar").

Various other issues were raised by respondents. These are as follows:

Ease of handling
Length of blade
Which was the best brand?
Whether it had direct drive
Whether it had a gas protector
Self-lubrication
The warranty (guarantee)
Ease of controls
Specifications
Availability of credit
Possibility of mixing oil and gas

The third picture (Exhibit C) showed a man cutting a felled tree with the chain saw. The question asked was as follows:

The man in the picture is the same man as in the last picture. He purchased the chain saw he was looking at. Knowing that he purchased the chain saw, what can you tell me about him? Can you tell me anything about the character and personality of this man?

A follow-up question was:

What do you suppose this man is thinking about while he's using his chain saw?

A common response was that the man was satisfied. Typical responses were: "He's pleased," "He's happy he bought the chain saw," "Lots of time saved," and "He's happy with the chain saw; he made the right decision." Many favorable overtones to using a chain saw were given, for example:

Sure beats bucking with an axe.
He's thinking about speed of getting through, time saved.

How much easier it is to cut a tree down with a chain saw than a hand saw.
He seems to be saying, "Why didn't I buy a chain saw sooner?"

Respondents in general seemed to think the man was using the chain saw for the first time.

Very prominent in many respondents' answers was the fear of using a chain saw—it seemed to be a major reason why people would not purchase one. Some typical comments were:

He's a little frightened. He doesn't know how to go about it, but he's willing to learn.
If he gets caught in that blade. . . .
He's watching what he's doing—he could lose a limb.
He might be somewhat apprehensive about the use of it.
He looks scared of it.
He better think safety.

In general the test, as it is designed to do, made the respondents project their own personalities and backgrounds onto the character of the man. A wide variety of responses were given describing the man. He was described as a blue-collar worker, an office worker laboring after hours and on weekends, a somewhat wealthy man able to afford a chain saw, and a homeowner. A number of responses indicated that he was a do-it-yourselfer, a man who liked to "do his own thing." "Farmer" was another more than scattered response. Associations with an outdoorsman, a man who liked to keep in shape, were also indicated. One quotation seems to sum it all up:

This seems to be his first job. He seems to be happy about it. He seems to think the chain saw will lighten his work load. He looks like he has not owned many power tools. He looks excited. He seems like he will be able to do a lot of cleanup work that he would not have been able to do without the chain saw. The chain saw is sure an improvement over the hand saw. It's faster, easier to use.

The fourth picture (Exhibit D) showed a man and woman seated before a fireplace. The question read,

Here's a picture of the same man as in the previous pictures, sitting and talking with a woman; what do you suppose they're talking about?

An analysis of the fourth picture in the projection test showed that respondents felt the man and woman in the picture were happy, content, cozy, and enjoying the fireplace. The man was "enjoying the fruits of his labor." It came out very strongly that a man who uses a chain saw is proud of himself after he cuts the wood; he thinks his cutting of wood with a chain saw is a job well done. Some typical comments concerning this were:

> *He's very happy to cut his own wood for his fireplace—real proud of himself.*
> *He's telling her how much he saved by cutting it himself.*
> *They're talking about the logs, how pleased he is with himself.*
> *He's thinking about the beauty of the fire, fire logs he himself sawed from their property.*

The people projecting their feelings into the picture seemed to think that because the job was well done, purchasing a chain saw was worthwhile:

> *The man in the picture is saying, "The chain saw pays for itself. There's a $200 job, and you will be able to use the chain saw afterwards."*
> *Work's done, and there's enough for winter, and he has trees for winters to come.*
> *What a good buy that chain saw was. Cut wood costs, save money.*

The woman in the picture was also very happy; she was satisfied and probably thinking about the future. But most of all she was very proud of her husband. This came out very strongly. For example,

> *The woman is looking to the enjoyment of the fireside and of the money saved because they*

cut their own wood. She might have questioned the investment before this, before sitting in front of the fireplace.
She is proud of her husband.
She is pleased the tree is down.
The woman is probably proud of the fireplace and starting the fire. He's probably thinking about the wood he sawed.
The man and woman are congratulating each other on finally getting around to buying a chain saw and cutting firewood.
She is complimenting him on his ability and on how handy it is to have a man around the house. She is also thinking that possibly it was easier for her husband to use a chain saw.

The woman didn't care about the chain saw, but she was satisfied. The husband's concern over his wife's approval of this investment was also brought out by this picture—evidently men were worried that their wives would not see the value of a chain saw purchase. Also, there were implications that the man should be tired after using the chain saw—"and he had to work hard in the afternoon to get the logs for the fireplace."

After the presentation, Campagna was reasonably impressed. He asked Hamilton what his opinion was. Hamilton said, "This is all very interesting, but I don't see how it can lead to greater profits in our chain saw division."

Questions

1. How should Conway and Baggins respond to Hamilton's question?

2. Is Hamilton investigating the casual-user market segment correctly?

3. What conclusions would you draw from the thematic apperception test? Do you feel this is a valid and reliable test?

4. What specific recommendations would you make to Campagna concerning the casual-user chain saw market?

C A S E   **3**

Middlemist Precision Tool Company

Dennis Middlemist was a weekend do-it-your-selfer. A hobby he particularly enjoyed was custom building furniture for his own home. After many years of frustration with trial-and-error adjustment of his radial arm saw (using a T square and trial cuts), Middlemist decided that he needed to invent an alignment device for his radial arm saw.

It wasn't long thereafter that Middlemist had designed a solution. A custom prototype was built at a local engineering job shop. When Middlemist tested the device, it seemed to work perfectly for his needs. The proud inventor sought out an attorney to patent the device, and it looked as if a patent would be available. At this point Middlemist started to dream about the possibility of the Middlemist Precision Tool Company and the vast empire he would leave to his children. But in reality he did not know much about marketing and wondered what market information he would

need before getting serious about manufacturing the device, such as what the market potential would be. He thought the best place to start would be to determine how many radial arm saws there were in the United States and how many prospective customers there might be for his invention.

Questions

1. If you were a research consultant called in to help Middlemist define his business problem, what information do you think would be most important to him?
2. Middlemist has decided to see what information about the radial arm saw market can be found in secondary data sources. Go to your library and find what you can about radial arm saws and/or any related information that might be of value to Middlemist.

C A S E   **4**

Tulsa's Central Business District (B)

The Metropolitan Tulsa Chamber of Commerce recognized that there was a critical gap between the availability of timely information about the central business district (CBD) and the need for this information for investment decision making, commercial marketing efforts, and the continued pursuit of the goal of downtown revitalization. The Chamber of Commerce undertook four separate research projects to gather information about

the CBD. One project was a physical inventory of the existing downtown commercial base. The objectives of the study were to determine what types of establishments were operating in the CBD and the number of vacancies there and to generally profile the commercial geography of the CBD. The researchers found that the CBD was based on the U.S. Bureau of the Census classification scheme. The CBD was identified as the area en-

CASE EXHIBIT   4.1

**Census Blocks in
Census Tract 25**

U.S. Bureau of the Census.

compassed by the inner dispersal loop (a system of expressways), which corresponded identically with Census Tract 25 (see Case Exhibit 4.1).

A team of ten pedestrian field-workers covered each block in the inner dispersal loop. Field-workers utilized the observation form in Case Exhibit 4.2 to record the company name, address, primary business activity, estimated frontage, and other relevant information about each building site or office. Standard Industrial Classification (SIC) codes for retailers were recorded by the field-workers. SIC codes for all other establish-

ments were recorded by research assistants after the data were collected. All the data were identified by census block.

Questions

1. Evaluate the research design in this case.
2. What changes, if any, would you make in the observation form?
3. What problems would you expect in the data collection stage?
4. What techniques would you use to analyze the data?

CASE EXHIBIT 4 . 2

Observation Study Questionnaire

Company Name _____

Address _____
_____
_____

Tulsa, Oklahoma

Activities: __1 Vacant __2 Retail __3 Wholesale __4 Manufacturing
__5 Service __6 Other (Specify) _____

Retail SIC __52 __53 __54 __55 __56 __57 __58
__59 __60

Other activities (describe) _____

Is the building: __1 For sale?
__2 For rent?
Leasable space _____
Realtor's name _____
Realtor's phone _____
Rent (per sq. foot) _____
Is the building being: __1 Restored?
__2 Remodeled?
Estimated frontage (feet) _____
Estimated number of stories _____
Comments _____
_____
_____

CASE 5

Tulsa's Central Business District (C)

Case 1, Tulsa's Central Business District (A), indicated the Metropolitan Tulsa Chamber of Commerce had recognized that there was an absence of timely information about the Central Business District (CBD). There was a great need for information for investment decision making, commercial efforts, and continued revitalization of the downtown area. One of the research projects was a survey of chief executives of business firms in the CBD. The purpose of this survey was to gather information concerning the number of employees working in downtown Tulsa, employees' salary distributions, proposed future investment in downtown Tulsa, and executive attitude toward a variety of dimensions of the downtown area.

For the purposes of this research, downtown Tulsa was defined as coinciding with Census Tract 25 and the inner dispersal loop [see Tulsa's Central Business District (B)].

A mail survey of the chief executives of business firms within the inner dispersal loop was conducted. The questionnaire appears in Case Exhibit 5.1.

In order to ensure a representative picture of executives' opinions of downtown Tulsa, each firm within the CBD was given the opportunity to

CASE EXHIBIT   5 . 1   **Survey of Tulsa Executives**

INSTRUCTIONS

This is a survey concerning firms in *Tulsa's Central Business District (CBD)*. Technically, we are referring to the area within the *inner dispersal loop* and not "suburban" Tulsa. As you respond to this questionnaire, answer only about your firm's *Central Business District (downtown)* operations.

> Is the person to whom this letter was addressed the "right" person to answer the questionnaire? If not, will you please give the letter and questionnaire to the person who is best able to respond to the questions and ask him or her to complete the questionnaire for us?

(continued)

EXECUTIVE OPINION SURVEY

First, we would like to ask you some *general* questions about Tulsa's Central Business District (CBD). Please check (✔) your answer.

1. Overall, how would you rate business conditions in Tulsa's Central Business District?
   ☐ Excellent   ☐ Good   ☐ Fair   ☐ Poor   ☐ Very poor

2. Would you say Tulsa's Central Business District is more or less suitable for your business now than it was five years ago? (If not in operation five years ago, use the date when you started your business.)
   ☐ More suitable   ☐ Same   ☐ Less suitable   ☐ No opinion

3. If past trends continue, would you predict there will be fewer, more, or the same number of firms in Tulsa's Central Business District next year?
   ☐ Fewer   ☐ More   ☐ Same

The following statements are things that some businessmen have said about Tulsa's Central Business District.

Please indicate your degree of agreement with the statement below. Please *circle* if you strongly agree, mildly agree, neither agree nor disagree, mildly disagree, or strongly disagree.

4. Tulsa's Central Business District is an active retail center (shopping complex).

Strongly Agree	Mildly Agree	Neither Agree nor Disagree	Mildly Disagree	Strongly Disagree

5. The future of Tulsa's Central Business District looks very bright.

Strongly Agree	Mildly Agree	Neither Agree nor Disagree	Mildly Disagree	Strongly Disagree

6. One major problem in the Tulsa Central Business District is an increasing crime rate.

Strongly Agree	Mildly Agree	Neither Agree nor Disagree	Mildly Disagree	Strongly Disagree

7. In the next five years there will be a decreasing emphasis on the Tulsa Central Business District as a retail shopping complex.

Strongly Agree	Mildly Agree	Neither Agree nor Disagree	Mildly Disagree	Strongly Disagree

8. Occupying an office in the Central Business District rather than elsewhere in the city has more advantages than disadvantages.

Strongly Agree	Mildly Agree	Neither Agree nor Disagree	Mildly Disagree	Strongly Disagree

9. Off-street parking in the Tulsa Central Business District is inadequate.

Strongly Agree	Mildly Agree	Neither Agree nor Disagree	Mildly Disagree	Strongly Disagree

10. In the next five years the Central Business District will lose its share of occupied office space to other parts of the city.

Strongly Agree	Mildly Agree	Neither Agree nor Disagree	Mildly Disagree	Strongly Disagree

11. The new Williams Center will be a major stimulus to downtown Tulsa and its financial future.

Strongly Agree	Mildly Agree	Neither Agree nor Disagree	Mildly Disagree	Strongly Disagree

12. In the next five years your business will move out of Tulsa's Central Business District.

Strongly Agree	Mildly Agree	Neither Agree nor Disagree	Mildly Disagree	Strongly Disagree

13. The Tulsa city government is very willing to respond to problems in Tulsa's Central Business District.

Strongly Agree	Mildly Agree	Neither Agree nor Disagree	Mildly Disagree	Strongly Disagree

We would now like to ask you about your firm's business activity in the *Central Business District.*

If your company has offices, warehouses, factories, etc. at other locations, please provide *only* the information about your operation in the *Tulsa Central Business District.*

To determine what actions are needed to improve business conditions in your business district, it is essential that we know more about the current level of business activity in Tulsa's CBD. The remaining questions are similar to those asked by the Bureau of the Census.

Responses will be kept CONFIDENTIAL and used only to analyze the entire business area and for classification purposes (e.g., small vs. large firms). The data will NOT be used in any way that will allow determination of individual firms or the competitive position of your type of firm.

14. What is your primary business activity?

☐ Manufacturing   ☐ Services   ☐ Transportation and public utilities

☐ Retail trade   ☐ Construction

☐ Wholesale trade   ☐ Agriculture, forestry, fishing   ☐ Other (please specify)

☐ Finance, insurance, real estate   ☐ Mining   _____

15. What was your average number of paid *full-time* employees in the Tulsa Central Business District last year? _____

16. Please estimate how many of these employees are managerial and how many are nonmanagerial.

_____ Number of managerial employees

_____ Number of nonmanagerial employees

17. What was your *average monthly payroll* for the firm (before deductions) in the Tulsa Central Business District last year? _____

18. What was the distribution of your firm's payroll to *full-time* employees in the Central Business District?

Annual Salary/Wage Range	Number of Employees
Under $10,000	_____
$10,000–$19,999	_____
$20,000–$29,999	_____
$30,000–$49,999	_____
$50,000 or over	_____

19. Approximately how much *office space* does your company or business organization *occupy* in the Tulsa Central Business District?

_____ Office space in square feet

_____ Other space in square feet

20. Does your business operation in the Tulsa Central Business District generate sales revenue from customers buying *within* the Central Business District?

☐ Yes (Go to Question 21)

☐ No (Go to Question 22)

21. If yes, please estimate your dollar sales volume for the last fiscal year from customers buying within Tulsa's Central Business District.

$_____

22. In what year did you start operating your business in the Tulsa Central Business District?

_____

23. Do you intend to invest in capital improvement for expansion or remodeling of your Central Business District facility in the next five years?

_____ Yes (Go to Question 24)

_____ No (Thank you for completing the questionnaire.)

_____ Uncertain (Thank you for completing the questionnaire.)

24. If yes, approximately how much do you intend to invest?

$_____

Thank you very much for your cooperation. Please return the completed questionnaire in the postage-paid envelope at your earliest convenience.

CASE TABLE 5.1

Response Patterns

	Number Sent Out	Number Returned	Percentage of Number Sent Out	Percentage of Total Number Returned
Pretest	36	24	66.7%	11.0%
Main test[a]	325	144	44.3	65.7
Follow-up	181	51	28.2	23.3
Total	361	219	60.7	100.0

[a] Excluding 11 undeliverable.

CASE TABLE 5.2

Response Patterns by Strata

	Number Returned	Percentage of Number Sent Out	Percentage of Respondents
Strata 1: "Major" firms	101	63.125%	46.119%
Strata 2: "Random" firms	118	55.660	53.881
Total	219	*	100.000

be selected in the sample. However, as the larger firms were expected to have a greater impact on the future of downtown, a stratified sample was selected. Prior to sampling, these larger firms were identified on the basis of information gleaned from the Oklahoma Employment Security Commission and a proprietary source listing the square footage of firms in the CBD. Several additional firms were included after consultation with the Metropolitan Tulsa Chamber of Commerce. The stratum of larger firms consisted of 154 major firms within the inner dispersal loop. The first stratum was broken into two parts labeled *key firms* for the "largest" 40 firms and *other major firms* for the remaining 114 firms of major importance in the CBD. Every firm on this list of major firms was sent a questionnaire. The other strata consisted of all other firms in the CBD.

A systematic random sample of the firms in the second stratum was selected from *Polk's City of Tulsa Directory* (reverse directory). The sample size for this strata was 218. Together, then, the total sample had 372 elements.

Of the 372 questionnaires sent out, 11 were undeliverable or otherwise unusable, leaving a true sample size of 361. Two hundred and nineteen of the 361 remaining questionnaires were filled out and returned. Thus approximately a 61 percent response rate resulted. Case Table 5.1 indicates the pattern of responses according to pretest, main test, and follow-up. Case Table 5.2 indicates the composition of the respondents according to designation by strata.

To ensure a high response rate, an advance notification letter was sent to all firms selected in the sample. Then a cover letter from the president of the Chamber of Commerce was included with a questionnaire (see Case Exhibit 5.1). If firms did not respond after three weeks had elapsed, a follow-up letter (with second questionnaire included) was sent to those firms that did not respond. For certain key firms that did not respond after six weeks had elapsed, telephone calls were made by the researchers asking if the questionnaires had been received and if they could be completed and returned.

Questions

1. Is a mail survey the best way to contact business executives in this situation?

2. Evaluate the sampling design in this case.

3. Does the questionnaire appear to satisfy the research objective? Why or why not?

CASE 6

Money Magazine: The Best Places to Live

If you could live anywhere in the United States, where would it be? San Francisco? New York City? Plains, Georgia? Various surveys, such as Rand McNally's *Places Rated Almanac,* have attempted to identify the most livable metropolitan areas. But those previous lists have a serious flaw: They do not give extra weight to the key characteristics—such as safety, the weather, the local economy—that are most important to the public. Instead, they assume everyone cares equally about all factors.

In reality, of course, different factors do matter more to different people. With that in mind, *Money*'s editors set out to determine what characteristics our readers prize. We then ranked 300 metropolitan areas by their preferences. Specifically, *Money*'s poll asked a representative sample of 226 readers (median age, 42; median household income, $56,000) to score each of 60 variables on a scale of 1 to 10. Their three most important variables: safety of property, personal safety, and likelihood that houses will appreciate in value. The three least important: proximity to an Amtrak station, availability of household help, and closeness to a bus terminal.

We then gathered data about the largest Metropolitan Statistical Areas, as the Census Bureau calls them, using both government and private sources. Working closely with Bert Sperling, a Portland, Oregon, researcher who designed a computer software package called Places, U.S.A.,

we awarded the appropriate amount of points to each area.

The winner was Nashua, New Hampshire, and its neighboring towns, primarily because of the area's strong economy, first-rate schools, and proximity to both Boston and the bountiful recreation spots in New Hampshire's White Mountains. Only one criterion required a subjective judgment: the definition of good weather. We decided the ideal was in San Diego, where the sun shines about 270 days a year, and it never snows. Undoubtedly, this choice helped boost two California areas into our top 10 list: Oxnard/Ventura and Anaheim/Santa Ana.

A strong local economy mattered enormously to our respondents. Therefore, it was no surprise that 7 of our best 10 places are in the booming Northeast, in or near large metropolitan areas. Unemployment is 3 to 4 percent in many Northeastern cities. And house prices appreciated 10 to 25 percent in 1986 in most of the area, compared with 7.4 percent nationwide.

Our two top 10 surprises are Wheeling, West Virginia, and Scranton, Pennsylvania, where the local economies are sluggish at best. Both areas, however, boast low crime rates (fewer than three murders per 100,000 residents annually) and inexpensive houses ($20,000 to $80,000 for typical three-bedroom units).

Case Exhibit 6.1 lists the top 100 places to live, while Case Exhibit 6.2 shows how each of

CASE EXHIBIT 6 . 1 **The Top 100 Places to Live**

1. Nashua, N.H.
2. Norwalk, Conn.
3. Wheeling, W. Va.
4. Beaver County, Pa.
5. Danbury, Conn.
6. Long Island, N.Y.
7. Oxnard/Ventura, Calif.
8. Boston's North Shore, Mass.
9. Scranton/Wilkes-Barre, Pa.
10. Anaheim/Santa Ana, Calif.
11. Houma/Thibodaux, La.
12. San Francisco
13. Central New Jersey
14. Rochester, Minn.
15. Cumberland, Md.
16. Johnstown, Pa.
17. Los Angeles
18. Burlington, Vt.
19. Johnson City/Kingsport, Tenn.
20. Binghamton, N.Y.
21. San Jose
22. San Diego
23. Monmouth/Ocean counties, N.J.
24. Danville, Va.
25. Stamford, Conn.
26. Lancaster, Pa.
27. Southeastern New Hampshire
28. Fargo, N.D.
29. Riverside/San Bernardino, Calif.
30. St. Cloud, Minn.
31. Altoona, Pa.
32. Wausau, Wis.
33. Santa Cruz, Calif.
34. Utica-Rome, N.Y.
35. Manchester, N.H.
36. Bismarck, N.D.
37. Bridgeport/Milford, Conn.
38. Orange County, N.Y.
39. Bergen/Passaic counties, N.J.
40. Eau Claire, Wis.
41. York, Pa.
42. Lafayette, Ind.
43. Pittsburgh
44. Santa Rosa/Petaluma, Calif.
45. Boston
46. Oakland, Calif.
47. Duluth, Minn.
48. Chicago
49. Parkersburg, W. Va.
50. Sioux Falls, S.D.
51. Green Bay
52. Vallejo/Fairfield/Napa, Calif.
53. Appleton/Oshkosh, Wis.
54. Williamsport, Pa.
55. Philadelphia
56. Steubenville, Ohio
57. Bangor, Maine
58. Honolulu
59. Provo/Orem, Utah
60. Seattle
61. Fort Walton Beach, Fla.
62. Florence, Ala.
63. Minneapolis/St. Paul
64. La Crosse, Wis.
65. Harrisburg, Pa.
66. Fayetteville, Ark.
67. Olympia, Wash.
68. Newark, N.J.
69. Milwaukee
70. Washington, D.C.
71. Asheville, N.C.
72. Lowell, Mass.
73. Allentown/Bethlehem, Pa.
74. Knoxville, Tenn.
75. Reading, Pa.
76. Lorain/Elyria, Ohio
77. Madison, Wis.
78. Kenosha, Wis.
79. State College, Pa.
80. Albany/Schenectady, N.Y.
81. Dallas
82. New York City
83. Cleveland
84. Ann Arbor
85. Lake County, Ill.
86. Raleigh/Durham, N.C.
87. Bremerton, Wash.
88. Lawrence, Mass.
89. Charlottesville, Va.
90. Worcester, Mass.
91. Jersey City, N.J.
92. Gary/Hammond, Ind.
93. Aurora/Elgin, Ill.
94. Santa Barbara
95. New Orleans
96. Buffalo
97. For Meyers, Fla.
98. Atlanta
99. Lafayette, La.
100. Wilmington

CASE EXHIBIT 6 . 2 **The Top 10: How They Rate Head to Head**

Place	Crime	Economy	Housing	Health	Weather	Lesiure	Arts	Education	Transit	Ranking
Nashua, N.H.	73	87	11	64	34	33	38	61	36	100
Norwalk, Conn.	53	64	2	95	36	84	83	55	34	98
Wheeling, W. Va.	100	43	62	22	37	7	1	56	31	98
Beaver County, Pa.	100	19	22	41	38	11	18	37	29	96
Danbury, Conn.	56	55	7	95	27	84	83	56	27	96
Long Island, N.Y.	53	44	10	90	35	91	84	64	11	94
Oxnard/Ventura, Calif.	33	47	13	72	96	79	49	38	19	93
Boston's North Shore, Mass.	70	45	10	70	35	39	40	56	32	92
Scranton/Wilkes-Barre, Pa.	89	30	29	34	35	10	6	65	51	90
Anaheim/Santa Ana, Calif.	24	50	11	75	96	87	58	45	33	90

the ten best places ranks in nine categories. The best possible score for each category, as well as the overall ranking, is 100. High scores in the crime column signify safety. High scores in housing signify low housing costs. Some places, such as Nashua and Norwalk, scored well in several categories. Others, such as Beaver County, had one or more particular strengths but were weak in many other areas.

Questions

1. Do you believe that this measure is reliable? Why or why not? What measures of reliability might be used to test reliability?

2. Do you believe that this measure is valid? Why or why not? What procedures might be used to test validity?

C A S E   7

Omar's Fast Freight

Omar's Fast Freight, a regional truck transportation company, had eight offices and accompanying truck docks located in a four-state area. Trucks arrived daily with inbound freight that had to be unloaded onto the truck dock and then reloaded onto smaller trucks for city delivery. The process for outbound freight was similar: The city trucks picked up the local freight that had to be unloaded onto the truck dock and then loaded onto outbound trucks going to the other cities serviced by Omar's Fast Freight.

The nature of the transportation business required Omar's Fast Freight to operate its truck docks on a round-the-clock basis. Dock workers worked on a rotating shift basis. There were three shifts:

- Day (8:00 a.m. to 3:30 p.m.)
- Evening (3:30 p.m. to midnight)
- Night (midnight to 8:00 a.m.)

Mr. Weslow, the personnel manager, had heard of some grumblings about shift work from the dock workers. He wanted to learn what the workers thought about working the rotating shift, so he decided to conduct a survey. The questionnaire used in his survey appears in Case Exhibit 7.1.

Mr. Weslow personally designed the questionnaire items concerning the rotating shift. He also thought it would be a good idea to ask some questions concerning job satisfaction. He went to the library to learn about this subject.

During his library research he found an apparently valid and reliable eight-question scale on identification with the work organization.[1] Because he didn't want to make the questionnaire too long, he selected only three of the best questions for inclusion in his survey.

Because Mr. Weslow also thought that some of the workers might be drinking on the job, he decided that some questions concerning the consumption of alcohol would be of value. He suspected that asking directly if workers drank on the job wouldn't get truthful answers. He disguised the questions by asking if individuals knew someone else who frequently consumes alcohol on the job.

Mr. Weslow wanted to impress the workers that it was important to complete the questionnaire. Therefore he personally handed out the questionnaires at the end of the evening and night shifts, asking the workers to return them the following day.

QUESTIONNAIRE

1. What part of your rotating shift are you working this week? Please check below.
   Day   _____
   Evening   _____
   Night   _____

2. Compared to working steady days, do you feel that shift work is in conflict with your activities and responsibilities as a husband (accompanying wife in her activities, protecting her at home, etc.) such that you decide not to go on job that day?

Evening:	Very often	Often	Occasionally	Rarely	Never
Night:	Very often	Often	Occasionally	Rarely	Never

3. Compared to working steady days, do you feel that shift work is in conflict with your activities as a friend (enjoying the company of your friends, attending weddings, reunions of family and/or friends, and other get-togethers) such that you decide not to go on job that day?

Evening:	Very often	Often	Occasionally	Rarely	Never
Night:	Very often	Often	Occasionally	Rarely	Never

4. Compared to working steady days, do you feel that shift work is in conflict with your activities and responsibilities as a father (teaching your children, spending time with them, taking them to children's programs, etc.) such that you decide not to go on job that day?

Evening:	Very often	Often	Occasionally	Rarely	Never
Night:	Very often	Often	Occasionally	Rarely	Never

5. Compared to working steady days, do you feel that shift work is in conflict with your activities as a member of social organizations (attending meetings, sports events, etc.) such that you decide not to go on job that day?

Evening:	Very often	Often	Occasionally	Rarely	Never
Night:	Very often	Often	Occasionally	Rarely	Never

Now we would like to ask some questions about the psychological and physical effects of shift work.

Psychological: related to your esteem, status ego, anxiety over shift work, etc.

Physical: related to your health and bodily functions.

In Questions 6 and 7 two shift workers are expressing their views about shift work. Read both views, evaluate your position regarding them, and then check the appropriate box.

6.   Tom   Dick

Tom	Dick
Shift workers are not only out of sight but also out of mind of management. In shifts we lose our visibility to management and thus chances of growth. Working in shifts make me feel that I am a part of a rotating machine and completely divorced of my status as a social being. One way to show my dissatisfaction with shifts is to be more and more absent.	Our work is always visible to our assessors and being constantly evaluated. Good performance and regularity improves our chances of growth. Shift staff is very important to the plant and as such enjoys a special status. I try to be regular in my job for my good and for the good of the company.

Check one box:

I am like Tom.	I am more like Tom than Dick.	I am halfway between Tom and Dick.	I am more like Dick than Tom.	I am like Dick.

7.   Bob   Pat

Shift work offers more problems than it solves. It is damaging rather than adding to our social status. On occasions (for example, at a party) I do not like people to know that I have an abnormal life routine. On such occasions I prefer skipping the job to show that shifts are no limitations on my social life.	I like shift work. It facilitates me more than it hinders my activities. Although it makes life routine somewhat abnormal, people have a clear recognition and appreciation of the contribution we are making to national growth. As such I am not facing any psychological problems in shift work.

Check one box:

I am like Bob.	I am more like Bob than Pat.	I am halfway between Bob and Pat.	I am more like Pat than Bob.	I am like Pat.

8. Compared to working steady days, how often does getting proper sleep or rest become so difficult that you decide not to go on job that day?

| Evening: | Very often | Often | Occasionally | Rarely | Never |
| Night: | Very often | Often | Occasionally | Rarely | Never |

9. Compared to working steady days, while working in shifts, how often do you not feel sufficiently well physically (stomach upsets, bowel problems, loss of appetite) and physical disturbance is so severe that you decide not to go on job that day?

| Evening: | Very often | Often | Occasionally | Rarely | Never |
| Night: | Very often | Often | Occasionally | Rarely | Never |

10. How much satisfied are you with your work schedule, that is, with the present arrangement of your hours for work? Check one.
_____ Completely satisfied with my schedule.
_____ Very well satisfied.
_____ I do not care what my working hours are.
_____ Dissatisfied a little.
_____ Very dissatisfied with my schedule.

11. If you could begin working over again in the same occupation that you are in now, how likely would you be to choose Omar's as a place to work? Check one.
(1) _____ Definitely would choose another place over Omar's.
(2) _____ Probably would choose another place over Omar's.
(3) _____ Wouldn't care much whether it was Omar's or some other place.
(4) _____ Probably would choose Omar's over another place.
(5) _____ Definitely would choose Omar's over another place.

12. How do you feel when you hear (or read about) someone criticizing Omar's or comparing Omar's unfavorably to other trucking companies? Check one.
(1) _____ It doesn't really bother me; I don't care much what other people think of Omar's.
(2) _____ It bothers me a little.
(3) _____ It bothers me quite a bit; I'm anxious to have people think well of Omar's.
(4) _____ I never hear or read such criticism.

13. How often do you leave the truck dock during lunch break?
Always _____ Very often _____ Occasionally _____ Never _____

(continued)

CASE EXHIBIT   7 . 1   *(continued)*

14. Have you worked around someone who frequently consumed alcohol on the job?
    Yes _____ No _____
15. If yes, do you ever worry about your safety?
    Always _____ Sometimes _____ Never _____
16. How would you try to deal with employees drinking on the job?
    _____
    _____
    _____

17. In your opinion, which one of these suggestions would be most appropriate for dealing with the situation?
    _____ Employees should not be permitted to leave the plant during lunch break unless authorized.
    _____ More employee awareness through educational programs.
    _____ Adoption of stricter rules in dealing with the problem.
18. How satisfied are you with your earnings?
    _____
    _____
    _____

19. What is your age? _____
20. What is your marital status? _____
21. Name of respondent _____
22. Job position _____

Questions

1. Evaluate the research design in this case.
2. Are there any improvements that could be made in the questionnaire?

References

[1] M. Patchen, *Some Questionnaire Measures of Employee Motivation and Morale: A Report on the Reliability and Validity* (Ann Arbor: University of Michigan, Institute for Social Research, 1965).

C A S E   **8**

Canterbury Travels

Hometown is located in the east north central United States and has a population of about 50,000. There were two travel agencies in Hometown before Canterbury Travels opened its doors.

Canterbury Travels was in its second month of operation. Veronica Ewert had expected to have more business than she actually had. She decided that she needed to conduct a survey to determine how much business there was in Hometown. She also wanted to learn if people were aware of Canterbury Travels; she thought that this survey would determine the effectiveness of her advertising.

The questionnaire that Veronica Ewert designed is shown in Case Exhibit 8.1.

Questions

1. Critically evaluate the questionnaire.
2. Will the information that Canterbury Travels needs be gained after the survey has been conducted?

CASE EXHIBIT   8 . 1   **Travel Questionnaire**

QUESTIONNAIRE

The following questionnaire pertains to a project being conducted by a local travel agency. The intent of the study is to better understand the needs and attitudes of Hometown residents towards travel agencies. The questionnaire will take only 10 to 15 minutes to fill out at your convenience. Your name will in no way be connected with the questionnaire.

1. Have you traveled out of state?
   ___ Yes ___ No

2. If yes, do you travel for:
   ___ Business
   ___ Pleasure
   ___ Both

3. How often do you travel for the above?
   ___ 0–1 times per month   ___ 0–1 times per year
   ___ 2–3 times per month   ___ 2–3 times per year
   ___ 4–5 times per month   ___ 4–5 times per year
   ___ 6 or more times per month ___ 6 or more times per year

4. How do you make your travel arrangements:
   ___ Airline
   ___ Travel agency
   ___ Other (please specify) _____

5. Did you know that travel agencies do not charge the customer for their services?
   ___ Yes ___ No

6. Please rate the following qualities that would be most important to you in the selection of a travel agency:

	Good				**Bad**
Free services (reservations, advice, and delivery of tickets and literature)	___	___	___	___	___
Convenient location	___	___	___	___	___
Knowledgeable personnel	___	___	___	___	___
Friendly personnel	___	___	___	___	___
Casual atmosphere	___	___	___	___	___
Revolving charge account	___	___	___	___	___
Reputation	___	___	___	___	___
Personal sales calls	___	___	___	___	___

(continued)

CASE EXHIBIT 8 . 1 *(continued)*

7. Are you satisfied with your present travel agency?

	Very Satisfied				Very Dissatisfied
Holiday Travel	____	____	____	____	____
Leisure Tours	____	____	____	____	____
Canterbury Travels	____	____	____	____	____
Other _____	____	____	____	____	____

8. If no, what are you dissatisfied with about your travel agency?

	Good				Bad
Free services (reservations, advice, and delivery of tickets and literature)	____	____	____	____	____
Convenient location	____	____	____	____	____
Knowledgeable personnel	____	____	____	____	____
Friendly personnel	____	____	____	____	____
Casual atmosphere	____	____	____	____	____
Revolving charge account	____	____	____	____	____
Reputation	____	____	____	____	____
Personal sales calls	____	____	____	____	____

9. Did you know that there is a new travel agency in Hometown?
   ___ Yes   ___ No

10. Can you list the travel agencies in Hometown and their locations?
    _____
    _____
    _____

11. Do you use the same travel agency repeatedly?

	0—1 times per month	2—3 times per month	4—5 times per month	6 or more times per month	0—1 times per year	2—3 times per year	4—5 times per year	6 or more times per year
Holiday Travel								
Leisure Tours								
Canterbury Travels								
Other (please specify)								

12. Have you visited the new travel agency in Hometown?
    ___ Yes   ___ No

13. If yes, what is its name? _____

14. How do you pay for your travel expenses?
    ___ Cash   ___ Company charge
    ___ Check   ___ Personal charge
    ___ Credit card   ___ Other _____

15. Which of these have you seen advertising for?
___ Holiday Travel
___ Leisure Tours
___ Canterbury Travels
___ Other _____
16. If yes, where have you seen or heard this advertisement?
17. Would you consider changing travel agencies?
___ Yes   ___ No

The following are some personal questions about you that will be used for statistical purposes only. Your answers will be held in the strictest confidence.

18. What is your age?
___ 19−25   ___ 46−55
___ 26−35   ___ 56−65
___ 36−45   ___ Over 65
19. What is your sex?
___ Male   ___ Female
20. What is your marital status?
___ Single   ___ Divorced
___ Married   ___ Widowed
21. How long have you lived in Hometown?
___ 0−6 months   ___ 5−10 years
___ 7−12 months   ___ 11−15 years
___ 1−4 years   ___ Over 15 years
22. What is your present occupation?
___ Business and professional
___ Salaried and semiprofessional
___ Skilled worker
___ Laborer
___ Student
23. What is the highest level of education you have completed?
___ Elementary school   ___ 1−2 years of college
___ Junior high school   ___ 3−4 years of college
___ Senior high school   ___ More than 4 years of college
___ Trade or vocational school
24. What is your yearly household income?
___ $0−$5,000   ___ $30,001−$45,000
___ $5,001−$10,000   ___ $45,001−$70,000
___ $10,001−$20,000   ___ $70,000 and above
___ $20,001−$30,000

CASE   9

Professional Recruiters*

Professional Recruiters, a consulting firm that specializes in helping large corporations improve their recruiting efforts among college students, decided it needed sound information about some job-rating criteria for MBA students. More specifically, they wanted to examine selected evaluation criteria utilized by college graduates when considering jobs and job offers encountered in the recruiting process. What are students looking for when they consider their future careers? What really motivates acceptance of a job offer?

In particular, the consulting firm hypothesized that there was an increased interest among college students in the place of business in society. Professional recruiters questioned whether the social responsibility exhibited by a firm could be a significant influence in the job selection process. They wanted to know if corporate recruiters should stress salary or their firms' social responsibility. After reviewing some academic literature in the organizational behavior field, professional recruiters concluded that the *nature of the work, opportunity for advancement,* and *salary,* in that order, are the major factors influencing students as they make their job selections.

The researchers noted that past research dealing with the factors influencing job selection had been primarily based on the findings from survey research. They thought using a research format that merely asks the students which factors are important in job selection may be biased by the social desirability of certain answers. For example, rating the firm's social responsibility as an important job determinant factor has some potential for response bias due to the obvious desirability of positive answers. The researchers chose to utilize an experimental method to provide better control of the variables influencing job selection and to secure information on relation-

ships among selected factors expected to influence job selection.

The subjects for the experiment were 36 male MBA students at a prestigious state university. The sample was selected because researching MBA students offers the best chance of comparing experimental results with past findings. Only MBA students then currently interviewing for positions in anticipation of graduation at the conclusion of the spring or summer term were included in the study.

Each subject participated in four separate experiments. The subjects were presented with a series of job offers to which they indicated their probability of acceptance. In each situation two of the variables of interest were paired.

The four situational pairings were: salary—interesting work, salary—social responsibility, interesting work—social responsibility, and interesting work—opportunity for advancement. Three levels of monthly salary ($2,450, $3,000, and $3,450) and two values (high and low) of interesting work, opportunity for advancement, and social responsibility were utilized.

Thus the design produced a 3×2 matrix when salary was one of the paired variables. In other cases, because all other variables had two values, a 2×2 matrix resulted. Six subjects were placed in each cell of the 3×2 matrix and nine subjects in each cell of the 2×2 matrix. For example, a student might be asked to respond to a situation in which the work was *interesting* but the company was *low in social responsibility:*

> You have been offered a position with a well-known company in your area of academic specialization or interest. The salary appears to be competitive. From the interview you have gained some impressions about what your future activities would consist of. It appears that the job will be challenging and the nature of your proposed future activities appeals to you.

---

*All names in this case are fictitious.

After the interview you discussed the job with one of your friends, who had also interviewed with this company. He has informed you that the company has recently been in the news because it is being sued for water and air pollution.

The MBA students were then asked to indicate their estimate of the chance of their accepting a position:

___ 100% (Certain) I will accept

___ 90% (Almost sure) I will accept

___ 80% (Very big chance) I will accept

___ 70% (Big chance) I will accept

___ 60% (Not so big a chance) I will accept

___ 50% (About even) I will accept

___ 40% (Smaller chance) I will accept

___ 30% (Small chance) I will accept

___ 20% (Very small chance) I will accept

___ 10% (Almost certainly not) I will accept

___ 0 (Certain not) I will accept

Descriptions of job offers for several other situational pairings are given below.

Low Salary—Low Interesting Work:

You have been offered a position in your area of academic specialization or interest at a starting salary of $2,450 per month with a well-known company. Before your interview with the company, you looked into the organization and found that it was well established in its industrial classification and all indications were that it would actually be expanding its activities in the future. During the interview itself, you got the impression from both the job description and the discussion with the company's representative that your particular job does not appear to be a great challenge and the nature of the work does not really appeal to you.

High Salary—High Social Responsibility:

A well-known company has offered you a job at a salary of $3,450 per month in your area of academic specialization or interest. Because of your recent interest in the company, you have noticed a series of articles in newspapers covering its activities. The company seems assured of stability in the near future because of good consumer acceptance of its most recent product line. You have also noticed that the company has a good record of social responsibility and has actively led civic campaigns to clean up the environment.

High Opportunity for Advancement—Low Interesting Work:

A well-known company has offered you a position in your area of academic specialization or interest. The salary is competitive. At the campus interview, you got the impression that the opportunity for advancement is high and you are assured of moving up the ladder quickly. From the interview it also appears that the job is not challenging and your proposed future activities do not appeal to you.

Questions

1. What type of experimental design is this?
2. Evaluate the research design in this case.
3. What type of statistical analysis would be required to analyze the data obtained from this experiment?

CASE **10**

Effects of Newspaper Endorsements on Election Outcomes: An Experiment

The decline of party and the rise of candidate-oriented election campaigns have underscored the importance of the question of what impact campaign events have on election outcomes. This case reports the results of a study of a newspaper's candidate endorsements.

BACKGROUND

The election we focus attention on is the November 1977 contest in Suffolk County, New York, for the office of County District Attorney. Located on eastern Long Island, Suffolk County is classified as a suburb of New York City, and its one and one-third million residents make it the second most populous county in the state outside the city. Because the population is scattered over hundreds of small communities (school districts, hamlets, housing developments), because city newspapers are read each morning, and because most radio and television sets are tuned to city stations, there is no easy way of communication for the local office holder or candidate.

The 1977 district attorney race was characterized by two unusual circumstances. First, the incumbent district attorney, Henry O'Brien, was a Democrat, an extraordinary occurrence in a county which traditionally has been heavily Republican. Second, O'Brien's three years in office had been marked by a running feud with the county police commissioner. After O'Brien publicly levied charges of "corruption" against the commissioner and his department, the police produced a witness who swore that O'Brien was a homosexual. Although the witness subsequently

recanted his testimony, the charge of homosexuality against O'Brien, a bachelor, was not easily forgotten.

Since neither *Newsday,* the island's only newspaper, nor the *New York Times,* which includes occasional but brief coverage of Suffolk County, took an editorial position or endorsed one of the candidates, the general newspaper reader had to decide for himself whether to vote for the reelection of O'Brien, or whether to vote for his Republican opponent, Patrick Henry, a name which added additional color to the contest.

There was one newspaper, however, whose editorial stand throughout the feud had been outspokenly pro-O'Brien. *Suffolk Life* is a twice-weekly newspaper published from offices located in the extreme eastern part of the county. The paper has a high circulation because, sustained by advertisements, it is delivered *free* to the doorstep of virtually every house—the paper claims 98 percent coverage—in the six easternmost towns and small parts of two of the other four towns. Altogether, the circulation covers an area which contained 43.9 percent of the November 1977 registered voters. The hallmark of the paper is its blatantly outspoken editorials which, although often seemingly conservative (e.g., it opposed the Panama Canal Treaty), are best described as anti-establishment (unions, corporations, government). The editor is scathing in his denunciation of many Republican officials, yet nothing angers him more than "liberal Democrats." The editor happened to be a long-time friend of O'Brien. Hence, throughout O'Brien's feud with the police, editorials decried the fact that a district attorney who "had the courage to expose corruption in high places" was paying the price of having his personal morality questioned. Several times the full details of O'Brien's family life were spelled

Source: This case was prepared by Howard A. Scarrow with Steve Borman. Reprinted by permission of the publisher from *Public Opinion Quarterly*, vol. 43 (3), pp. 388–393. Copyright © 1979 by The Trustees of Columbia University.

out, details which were said to explain why O'Brien had never married. On the weekend preceding the election the paper's front-page editorial carried the headline "IS O'BRIEN QUEER?" Anyone who had read the paper over the preceding months knew the editor's negative answer to that question.

THE EXPERIMENT

We have, then, the beginnings of an unusually good set of experimental conditions to test the effectiveness of a newspaper's candidate endorsement: an election for an office about which the public usually knows or cares very little, the absence of any countywide media endorsements, and the circulation within one part of the electorate and only one part, of a newspaper which carried a well-publicized endorsement. Two additional factors complete the experimental setting: the basic similarity of the two parts of the county, and the presence of a control variable.

Both sections of the county are heavily Republican in voter registration. In the eastern part of the county where *Suffolk Life* circulates—hereafter referred to as the east—the ratio of registered Republicans to registered Democrats was, at the time of the election, 65 percent to 35 percent; in the western part of the county the ratio was 59 percent Republican to 41 percent Democratic. There is another method of measuring the partisan complexion of the two parts of the county, made possible by the fact that on the same ballot as the district attorney race was the contest for two vacancies on the family court. As sometimes happens in these judicial races, the Republican and Democratic parties backed the same two candidates. For each vacancy on the court, therefore, the one name appeared on the ballot twice—once on the Republican row and once again on the Democratic row. It may be presumed that when a voter recorded his preference for the name as it appeared on the Republican row, that voter was Republican in orientation. Similarly, if he voted for that candidate as the name appeared on the Democratic row, that voter may be presumed to

be a Democrat. Using this method, then, the ratio of Republicans to Democrats was identical in both parts of the county, viz., 53 percent to 47 percent.

Finally, the conditions for an experimental setting are completed by the presence of a control variable. There was one additional countywide office to be filled in the November election—the office of county clerk. Like the office of district attorney, this post is usually of low visibility and tends to be lost among the many other local offices which clutter the election machine. For our purposes, however, it presents a valuable control: *Suffolk Life* made no endorsement among the competing candidates. If *Suffolk Life*'s endorsement of O'Brien made a difference in the district attorney contest, we would expect that difference to be reflected *only* in that contest and *not* in the county clerk contest.

RESULTS

The election was won by the Republican Patrick Henry, who polled 53.4 percent of the valid vote.[1] *Suffolk Life*'s favored candidate, Henry O'Brien, thus lost the election. But for our purposes the important question is whether the election outcome differed in the two parts of the county in such a way that we may infer that the newspaper's efforts on behalf of O'Brien made a difference. And if it made a difference, how much of a difference?

There are two ways we can compare the election outcomes in the two parts of the county: (1) comparison of the raw vote totals, and (2) comparison of the extent to which each district attorney candidate "ran ahead" or "ran behind" the average of his party's totals in the two family court races.

In terms of raw percentages of the two-party totals,[2] within *Suffolk Life*'s circulation area O'Brien beat Henry 54.9 percent to 45.1 percent. In the western end of the county the result was nearly the exact opposite: Henry beat O'Brien 54.5 percent to 45.5 percent. In terms of the candidates' "excess" or "deficit" votes, the same pattern was apparent. In the east there was a plus eight percentage point difference between O'Brien's share of the two-party vote (54.9 percent) and the Democratic court candidates' vote share (46.9 percent). In contrast, in the west the difference between O'Brien's vote share and the judicial candidates' vote share was a minus 1.8 percentage points (45.5 percent contrasted to 47.3 percent). Henry's vote percentages were, of course, the reciprocals of these figures. By both methods of analysis, therefore, the conclusion seems inescapable that *Suffolk Life*'s endorsement of O'Brien made a difference.[3]

How much difference? We note that in the western part of the county, where *Suffolk Life*'s influence could *not* be felt, O'Brien still managed to outpoll his fellow judicial candidates by 2 percent (59,481 compared to 58,292). If we assume that in the east, without *Suffolk Life*, there still would have been this 2 percent difference, and then if we compare this hypothetical eastern result with the actual eastern result, we may infer that *Suffolk Life* accounted for over 20 percent of O'Brien's eastern vote.[4] That percentage "boost" is sufficiently large that had it been present in the west as well, O'Brien would easily have won the election.

But, the skeptic may well ask, how do we know that these east–west differentials are not the result of some other factor common to all Democratic candidates, and not the influence of *Suffolk Life*'s pro-O'Brien editorials? The best way to answer this question is to look at the east–west totals for the office of county clerk, an office for which *Suffolk Life* made no candidate endorsement. These results show that the Democratic candidate for county clerk lost out to his Republi-can opponent in both parts of the county, the margins of defeat being about the same in both areas.[5]

There seems no question, therefore, that O'Brien's exceptionally strong showing in the east stemmed from some factor which was peculiar to the district attorney contest.

Questions

1. Evaluate the experiment in this case. What type of experiment is it?
2. What types of experimental controls were utilized?
3. What other factors might have accounted for the difference between Henry and O'Brien?

References

[1] Henry's total was 143,961, made up of 122,498 on the Republican row and 21,463 on the Conservative row. O'Brien's total was 125,812, made up of 121,904 on the Democratic row and an additional 4,908 on a separate Independent row.

[2] To facilitate comparisons with the family court totals, these and the following percentages are based on the Republican and Democratic votes only. The Conservatives put up only one candidate in the two family court posts.

[3] An analysis of Henry's 21,000 Conservative votes reveals the same pattern as his 122,000 Republican votes, i.e., a better performance in the west (relative to one Conservative judicial candidate) than in the east.

[4] The arithmetic is as follows:
   2 percent of 47,596 (Democratic judicial vote in east) = 952
   O'Brien's hypothetical eastern vote = 47,596 + 952 = 48,548
   O'Brien's actual eastern vote = 62,423
   Difference = 13,875, or 22.2 percent of 62,424

[5] 44.9 percent to 55.1 percent in the east; 47.6 percent to 52.4 percent in the west. In terms of "excess" or "deficit," the Democratic clerk performance was a minus 2.0 percentage points in the east, a plus 0.3 percentage points in the west.

CASE **11**

The Business Forms Industry (A)

The business forms industry is heavily dependent on personal selling. Case Exhibit 11.1 shows a sampling frame containing a list of 200 salespeople in the business forms industry.

The first column is an identification number associated with the salesperson listed in Column 2. Column 3 indicates the salesperson's gender. Column 4 indicates the number of sales calls the salesperson has made during the last month. Column 5 gives the name of the company where the salesperson works. The last column is used for snowball sampling. During the snowballing sampling procedure, the researcher must select a first-stage sample of nominators. The nominators then point out the salespeople whom they know, and these elements are also included in the sample. For example, T. Montz (I.D. number 14) knows four respondents—I.D. number 1, A. Abbott; I.D. number 170, C. R. Gemelli; I.D. number 194, S. T. Siwula; and I.D. number 200, J. Zorilla.

A sales manager wishes to determine the mean number of sales calls made per month.

ADDITIONAL INFORMATION

The data from this case are stored in a computerized database. Your instructor will provide information about the floppy disk if this material is part of the case assignment.

Source: This case is based on materials supplied by Scott Burton, Louisiana State University, and George M. Zinkham, Conn Professor of Marketing, University of Houston. Used with permission.

Questions

1. Using a table of random numbers, draw a simple random sample (number of observations equal to 15). Discuss the step-by-step procedure that was implemented to draw the simple random sample. For the number of sales calls, calculate the sample mean and standard deviation for your sample. Calculate the proportion of women in the industry.

2. Using the results from Question 1, determine what sample size would be necessary if the researcher wanted to be 95 percent confident and have a range of error no larger than two sales calls.

3. Draw a systematic sample of the sample size that you calculated in Question 2. Calculate the sample mean and a 95 percent confidence interval for the mean.

4. Draw a snowball sample (n = 20) using a random numbers table to determine the nominators.

5. Draw a two-stage cluster sample (n = 20) using each company as a single cluster. At the first stage randomly select one of the clusters (or companies). At the second stage use a random numbers table to select four elements (or salespeople) from each of the five clusters selected at Stage 1. Calculate the sample mean in a 95 percent confidence interval.

CASE EXHIBIT 1 1 . 1   **Sampling Frame**

Identification Number	Salesperson Name	Gender	Number of Sales Calls	Company	Snowball Referral
1	Abbot, A.	M	42	Formcraft	14, 34, 47, 48, 154
2	Barton, R.	M	20	Formcraft	199, 186, 82
3	Brinson, C.	F	30	Formcraft	13, 35, 168
4	Butler, D.	M	41	Formcraft	12
5	Chafin, J.	M	24	Formcraft	150, 151, 197, 18
6	Ciliberti, R.	F	42	Formcraft	7, 93, 106, 167
7	Dunn, P.	M	37	Formcraft	6, 169, 180, 197
8	Gallin, F.	M	37	Formcraft	9, 180, 76, 91, 110
9	Hicks, G.	F	39	Formcraft	8, 188, 95, 96, 106
10	Howard, C.	M	42	Formcraft	108, 116, 119, 130
11	Knoclel, D.	M	40	Formcraft	None
12	Leverick, W.	M	23	Formcraft	4, 146
13	Mahon, J.	F	40	Formcraft	3, 139, 175
14	Montz, T.	M	40	Formcraft	1, 170, 194, 200
15	Nelson, P.	M	40	Formcraft	17, 29, 44
16	Porras, F.	M	39	Formcraft	26, 38, 72, 60
17	Riddell, G.	F	41	Formcraft	15, 68, 74, 89
18	Stevens, W.	F	40	Formcraft	28, 83, 89, 136
19	Traweek, S.	F	30	Formcraft	20, 135, 149, 164, 194
20	Young, B.	M	37	Formcraft	19, 151
21	Aaron, A.	M	37	Western Business Forms	39, 43, 79
22	Abud, M.	M	39	Western Business Forms	None
23	Atkinson, O. R.	F	41	Western Business Forms	85
24	Barnett, J. J.	M	41	Western Business Forms	27, 111
25	Battels, L.	M	38	Western Business Forms	38, 59, 134
26	Chen, S.	M	37	Western Business Forms	16, 27, 141
27	Craft, T.	M	38	Western Business Forms	24, 158, 161, 179
28	Davis, A.	M	39	Western Business Forms	18, 36, 45
29	Floyd, P.	F	39	Western Business Forms	15, 181, 182
30	Gentry, D.	M	41	Western Business Forms	25, 31, 48, 181
31	Holmes, S.	F	33	Western Business Forms	30, 186
32	Jones, C.	F	39	Western Business Forms	42, 43, 198, 49, 58
33	Lee, K.	M	41	Western Business Forms	41, 53, 62, 87
34	Lyon, D.	M	41	Western Business Forms	84
35	Olm, K.	M	38	Western Business Forms	3, 40, 90
36	Rawlings, D.	M	13	Western Business Forms	4, 28, 108, 136
37	Salazar, A.	M	33	Western Business Forms	None
38	Ullman, L.	M	40	Western Business Forms	16, 143, 152, 200
39	Wood, F.	M	33	Western Business Forms	21, 44, 138, 145, 149
40	Zapalac, J.	M	40	Western Business Forms	35, 158, 161
41	Allen, M.	M	41	McGregor Printing	33, 57, 70, 71
42	Bell, R.	F	37	McGregor Printing	32, 80, 81
43	Branch, K.	F	34	McGregor Printing	21, 32
44	Diaz, A.	M	38	McGregor Printing	15, 39, 98, 165
45	Ellis, J.	M	31	McGregor Printing	28, 47, 56, 65
46	Fagan, D.	F	34	McGregor Printing	None
47	Gonzalez, E.	M	40	McGregor Printing	1, 45, 195
48	Hestings, O.	M	34	McGregor Printing	1, 30, 46, 66
49	Lang, D.	F	40	McGregor Printing	50, 51, 52, 53
50	Lorenz, K.	F	42	McGregor Printing	49, 64, 77, 100, 114, 140, 172
51	Meek, J.	M	28	McGregor Printing	52, 49
52	Morris, N.	F	42	McGregor Printing	55, 67, 101, 102
53	Newman, P.	M	25	McGregor Printing	33, 49, 54, 71
54	Parker, L.	M	38	McGregor Printing	53, 110
55	Potter, H.	M	38	McGregor Printing	52, 56, 109, 111
56	Roy, M.	F	34	McGregor Printing	45, 55, 167

Identification Number	Salesperson Name	Gender	Number of Sales Calls	Company	Snowball Referral
57	Scott, D.	F	31	McGregor Printing	41, 195
58	Stone, M.	M	37	McGregor Printing	32, 172, 173
59	Trimble, L.	F	39	McGregor Printing	25, 61, 73, 112
60	Williams, W.	F	25	McGregor Printing	16, 63, 69, 108
61	Antill, J.	M	40	Control Business Forms	59, 118, 183
62	Ashley, K.	F	41	Control Business Forms	33, 184
63	Berker, L.	F	41	Control Business Forms	60, 74, 184, 197
64	Burton, S.	M	41	Control Business Forms	50, 69, 187
65	Carter, J.	M	40	Control Business Forms	45, 185
66	Edwards, K.	M	32	Control Business Forms	48
67	Finger, T.	M	37	Control Business Forms	52, 189, 190, 191
68	Ganesh, G.	M	38	Control Business Forms	17, 193
69	Green, W.	F	38	Control Business Forms	64, 192, 193, 196
70	Ivey, T.	M	33	Control Business Forms	41, 78
71	Johnson, C.	F	34	Control Business Forms	53, 86, 92, 93
72	Jones, F.	M	41	Control Business Forms	16, 88, 89, 136, 143
73	Landry, T.	M	36	Control Business Forms	59, 63, 82
74	Lewis, C.	F	34	Control Business Forms	17, 89, 90, 104
75	Matthews, M.	M	38	Control Business Forms	None
76	O'Neil, J.	F	41	Control Business Forms	8, 77, 138
77	Rice, J.	F	38	Control Business Forms	50, 76, 94, 137
78	Sanchez, M.	F	38	Control Business Forms	70, 1, 82
79	Welch, B.	M	33	Control Business Forms	21
80	Zeff, S.	M	42	Control Business Forms	42, 142, 143, 144, 145
81	Bishop, N.	F	39	Brunswick Press	42, 115, 140
82	Bryan, W.	M	37	Brunswick Press	2, 73, 144
83	Cloud, P.	M	40	Brunswick Press	18, 7, 117
84	Dyer, P.	F	36	Brunswick Press	34
85	Elliott, G.	M	36	Brunswick Press	23, 11, 147, 155, 156
86	Gray, J.	M	38	Brunswick Press	71, 157, 163, 187
87	Hale, K.	M	41	Brunswick Press	33, 88
88	Keller, J.	F	41	Brunswick Press	72, 87, 89
89	Kramer, C.	F	38	Brunswick Press	18, 74, 90, 91
90	Love, S.	M	32	Brunswick Press	35, 89, 91
91	Morse, H.	M	41	Brunswick Press	8, 89, 90, 196
92	Palmer, G.	M	36	Brunswick Press	71, 104, 105, 120
93	Pyle, G.	M	39	Brunswick Press	6, 71, 121, 133, 147, 148
94	Riley, T.	M	29	Brunswick Press	77, 123
95	Summer, V.	M	32	Brunswick Press	9, 122, 123, 132, 146
96	Thompson, L.	M	34	Brunswick Press	9, 98, 104
97	Trahan, J. R.	F	32	Brunswick Press	None
98	White, E.	M	37	Brunswick Press	44, 96, 106, 9, 104, 195
99	Wilson, F. A.	M	40	Brunswick Press	None
100	York, H.	F	39	Brunswick Press	50
101	Bizek, R.	M	32	Arnold Corporation	52, 102
102	Blais, D. R.	M	40	Arnold Corporation	52, 103, 101
103	Harp, V.	M	41	Arnold Corporation	192
104	Hines, A.	M	40	Arnold Corporation	74, 92, 126, 127
105	Moore, A. A.	F	38	Arnold Corporation	92, 107, 119
106	Payne, R. L.	M	36	Arnold Corporation	6, 9, 98, 17, 107
107	Payne, W.	M	30	Arnold Corporation	105, 106, 128
108	Peters, B.	M	37	Arnold Corporation	60, 128, 115, 116
109	Peters, L. R.	M	33	Arnold Corporation	55, 129
110	Raines, C.	M	24	Arnold Corporation	54, 159, 170
111	Richards, A. L.	M	39	Arnold Corporation	55, 112
112	Rogers, R.	M	36	Arnold Corporation	59, 111

(continued)

CASE EXHIBIT 1 1 . 1 *(continued)*

Identification Number	Salesperson Name	Gender	Number of Sales Calls	Company	Snowball Referral
113	Samad, I.	M	36	Arnold Corporation	24, 174, 176, 184
114	Scruggs, J.	M	36	Arnold Corporation	50, 117, 130
115	Simmons, E. M.	F	41	Arnold Corporation	81, 108, 139, 140
116	Smith, R. J.	M	36	Arnold Corporation	10, 108
117	Starks, T. W.	M	36	Arnold Corporation	83, 114, 6, 182
118	Tomey, E. L.	M	36	Arnold Corporation	61, 131, 141, 142, 184
119	Vail, M.	M	40	Arnold Corporation	10, 105
120	Walker, K. L.	F	36	Arnold Corporation	92, 121, 134, 191
121	Abbott, J.	F	39	Moore Business Forms	93, 120, 134, 191, 192
122	Author, R. L.	F	36	Moore Business Forms	95, 142, 143
123	Bough, M.	F	36	Moore Business Forms	94, 124, 149, 152
124	Coleman, W.	M	35	Moore Business Forms	24, 123, 149, 152, 161
125	Collins, O. L.	F	35	Moore Business Forms	None
126	Eades, A. M.	M	35	Moore Business Forms	104, 127
127	Enloe, S. D.	M	35	Moore Business Forms	104, 126, 128
128	Fisher, N.	M	41	Moore Business Forms	107, 106, 170
129	Holifield, W. B.	F	35	Moore Business Forms	109
130	Lott, M.	M	35	Moore Business Forms	10, 114, 176, 131, 118
131	Love, A. J.	M	35	Moore Business Forms	118, 130, 139, 3
132	Lucas, D.	F	39	Moore Business Forms	95, 80, 118, 141, 122, 133, 93, 17
133	Norris, L. A.	F	35	Moore Business Forms	93, 132, 122, 118
134	Rouse, J.	F	38	Moore Business Forms	24, 120, 121, 142, 80
135	Rouwalk, C.	M	38	Moore Business Forms	19, 142, 148, 151, 152
136	Taynor, S. A.	M	38	Moore Business Forms	72, 137, 77, 153
137	Teel, B.	M	38	Moore Business Forms	77, 136, 72, 167, 6, 7, 93
138	Waters, J.	M	42	Moore Business Forms	39, 115, 166, 167
139	White, K.	M	42	Moore Business Forms	3, 140, 50
140	Willis, R.	M	40	Moore Business Forms	50, 139, 6, 56, 137
141	Argo, M.	F	42	Taylor-Made Forms	26, 118, 142, 80, 122
142	Aris, B.	M	42	Taylor-Made Forms	80, 118, 141, 122, 134, 135, 143
143	Baird, R. S.	M	42	Taylor-Made Forms	80, 142, 95, 142
144	Balinski, J.	F	39	Taylor-Made Forms	82, 142, 146
145	Brancheau, C. C.	F	39	Taylor-Made Forms	80, 169, 147, 148
146	Brown, S.	M	39	Taylor-Made Forms	4, 95
147	Brugnoli, G. A.	M	34	Taylor-Made Forms	85, 145
148	Brunt, R.	M	34	Taylor-Made Forms	93, 145
149	Bybee, W. D.	F	42	Taylor-Made Forms	19, 123, 124, 150
150	Cupps, T.	M	40	Taylor-Made Forms	5, 149
151	Gurun, L.	F	14	Taylor-Made Forms	20
152	Kondelka, F.	F	15	Taylor-Made Forms	136
153	Kovalcik, A.	F	16	Taylor-Made Forms	136, 152, 159, 154, 1, 142
154	Kowis, M.	F	40	Taylor-Made Forms	1, 142, 153, 155
155	McZeal, E.	F	42	Taylor-Made Forms	85, 145, 153, 154, 180
156	Meduris, C. A.	M	27	Taylor-Made Forms	85, 145
157	Peters, W.	M	31	Taylor-Made Forms	86, 163, 189, 190
158	Searl, S.	F	42	Taylor-Made Forms	27, 35, 40
159	Teziano, E.	M	39	Taylor-Made Forms	110, 54, 145, 153, 164, 174
160	Thiede, C.	M	42	Taylor-Made Forms	145
161	Avalos, H.	F	37	Key Printing	27, 40, 163, 86
162	Awl, J. N.	F	37	Key Printing	145
163	Baird, D.	F	37	Key Printing	86, 157, 161, 40
164	Balderas, O. L.	M	37	Key Printing	19, 159, 16, 165
165	Bekins, J. B.	M	37	Key Printing	44, 145, 164, 19
166	Bivin, W.	M	37	Key Printing	138, 167, 145, 168
167	Breda, H.	M	42	Key Printing	6, 56, 137
168	Freeman, J. F.	M	35	Key Printing	3, 145, 176

Identification Number	Salesperson Name	Gender	Number of Sales Calls	Company	Snowball Referral
169	Gekeler, D.	M	35	Key Printing	7, 145, 176
170	Gemelli, C. R.	M	42	Key Printing	14, 110, 193, 68
171	Goss, E.	M	33	Key Printing	142
172	Gulick, R. W.	M	41	Key Printing	58, 173
173	Hansen, C.	M	41	Key Printing	58, 172, 178
174	Kostelic, P. P.	M	33	Key Printing	113, 180, 181, 8
175	Nowacki, D.	F	40	Key Printing	13, 142
176	Pesl, J. V.	M	42	Key Printing	142, 145, 169, 178, 173
177	Smith, R. A.	M	42	Key Printing	None
178	Tomey, T. S.	M	42	Key Printing	173, 145, 176, 142
179	Usrey, B.	M	42	Key Printing	27, 145
180	Vader, L.	F	42	Key Printing	8, 174, 181, 196
181	Blake, P.	M	19	Form Tech	29, 174, 180, 182, 117
182	Brechtel, W. J.	M	39	Form Tech	29, 117, 181, 188, 8, 189
183	Burks, R.	M	35	Form Tech	61, 145, 184, 62, 113
184	Chirco, S. J.	M	35	Form Tech	62, 113, 183
185	Distefano, E.	M	36	Form Tech	None
186	Duong, C. V.	M	36	Form Tech	30, 198, 26
187	Dupka, A.	M	41	Form Tech	86, 142, 192, 13
188	Fournier, P.	M	32	Form Tech	8, 67, 189
189	Gomez, J. G.	M	33	Form Tech	67, 157, 182, 8
190	Harlar, C.	M	34	Form Tech	67, 189, 157, 194
191	Lomax, J.	M	35	Form Tech	192, 134, 121, 142, 186, 187
192	Manos, E. P.	F	42	Form Tech	86, 142, 187
193	McAdoo, R. O.	F	37	Form Tech	68, 145, 170, 14, 110
194	Siwula, S. T.	F	38	Form Tech	14, 145, 190, 67
195	Stanzel, J. Z.	M	39	Form Tech	41
196	Stubbs, D.	M	40	Form Tech	91, 180, 197, 5, 7
197	Wacpeng, L.	M	41	Form Tech	5, 7, 142
198	Wu, A.	F	42	Form Tech	32, 145, 187, 199, 2
199	Young, P. P.	M	39	Form Tech	2, 145, 189, 32, 186
200	Zorilla, J.	M	21	Form Tech	14, 142

C A S E   12

Immigration Reform and Control Study

The Immigration Reform and Control Act of 1986 established civil and criminal penalties for employers who knowingly hire unauthorized aliens. Furthermore, the antidiscrimination provision of the law requires employers to ask all job applicants for documents verifying that they either are

citizens or are authorized to work in the United States. The Immigration and Naturalization Service is responsible for enforcement of this act. The General Accounting Office (GAO) is responsible for the annual reporting to Congress if there is "widespread discrimination caused solely by this law." The GAO, as part of its responsibility, has conducted many research projects on this issue, one of which was an employer survey.

Source: Adapted from U.S. General Accounting Office, Report to the Congress, *Immigration Reform: Status of Implementing Employer Sanctions after Second Year*, November 1988.

The GAO developed a questionnaire on the act's implementation that was sent to a stratified random sample of U.S. employers in late 1987. The GAO surveyed employers anonymously to gather information on their (1) understanding of the law, (2) employment practices, and (3) costs to comply with the I-9 form requirements.[1] To help ensure an adequate response rate to the survey, the GAO deliberately avoided explicit questions about illegal activities by employers. For example, it consciously did not ask employers if they discriminated against authorized workers because of employer sanctions.

For its sample the GAO used a private commercial firm's mailing list of over 6 million employers. It selected the sample from the firm's database as it was constituted on September 15, 1987.

To draw the sample, the GAO first stratified the universe of employers into a 36-cell matrix. The stratification was a mix of the high-alien-population states (California, Texas, Florida, New York, and Illinois contain approximately 80 percent of the alien population) and all other (low-alien-population) states; and of high-alien-population industries (agriculture, restaurants and hotels, construction, garment, and food processing) and all other (low-alien-population) industries. (See Case Table 12.1.)

Because of technical difficulties and issues concerning proprietary rights, the GAO agreed to have the commercial firm draw the sample and certify that its sample selection procedure was a random one. The GAO did not verify the procedure that the private mailing-list service used.

The GAO based cell sample sizes on a confidence level of 95 percent ±10 percent. Generally, this resulted in required sample sizes of between 90 and 100 employers per cell. The GAO oversampled in each cell by approximately 30 percent, being aware that all mail surveys experience some degree of nonresponse and considering it important to maintain the 10 percent error level. The 30 percent oversampling represented the researchers' best judgment as to the percentage of nonrespondents they could expect for this type of mail instrument. The resulting cell sizes for the sample were generally between 126 and 137 employers. Because of the size of the populations for the other-industries-and-states category, the GAO deliberately oversampled (779) in this category in case a more detailed analysis of the responses from this group was necessary.

In addition to the sample employers drawn for the 36-cell matrix, the GAO had the commercial mailing-list service draw an additional random sample of 500 employers from the population of approximately 6,000,000. The GAO had originally intended this sample to be used for test purposes, but subsequently decided that the test was not necessary. Because the 500 employers had been randomly selected, the researchers included them in the mail-out to the sample of employers. The practice effect of including them was to raise the sample sizes in the matrix, especially in the other-industries-and-states category.

CASE TABLE 12.1

Sampling Plan

Industries	States						Total
	CA	FL	TX	NY	IL	Other	
Agriculture	137	135	136	133	136	139	816
Restaurant/hotel	137	137	137	151	137	123	822
Construction	133	136	136	137	135	137	814
Garment	134	130	128	136	126	135	789
Food processing	134	126	129	129	128	136	782
Other	137	137	135	137	135	1,294	1,975
Totals	**812**	**801**	**801**	**823**	**797**	**1,964**	**5,998**

The GAO initially mailed the questionnaire to 5,998 employers across the country in November 1987. Follow-up mailings were sent in January 1988 and March 1988. Finally, researchers tried to telephone all nonrespondents in April 1988.

Employers were requested to separately return a postcard acknowledging that they had responded to the questionnaire. Although this enabled the GAO to determine the nonrespondents, the GAO had no way to associate specific employers with their questionnaires.

Of the 5,998 questionnaires mailed, 3,230 completed questionnaires were returned. The GAO dropped 1,956 questionnaires from the sample: 1,714 were returned because they were out of business, that is, the addressees could not be located, and 242 were dropped because the respondents said they had no employees. The adjusted sample (subtracting the number that researchers considered to be no longer in business and the number that indicated they had no employees from the original sample) was 4,042. Of the 3,230 questionnaires received, 61 were excluded because, when projected, the estimates for the number of employees in each respondent's company exceeded Census Bureau estimates of the number of employees in an industry in a given state, or 1,000,000. In these instances the GAO assumed that the employers had provided the number of employees in the entire company rather than the number employed at the specific location. The number of completed and usable questionnaires returned (3,169) provided a response rate of 78 percent. The final estimates indicated that the results projected to a population of about 4,200,000 employers out of the firm's list of 6,000,000 employers.

Questions

1. The federal government has many lists of businesses (U.S. Census Bureau, Internal Revenue Service, Small Business Administration, etc.). Why would the General Accounting Office use a commercial mailing-list service?
2. Evaluate the sample design.
3. Do you think the sample size was adequate? Why or why not? How much sampling error do you expect there was in this study?
4. What nonsampling errors would you expect in this study?
5. Evaluate the questionnaire.

References

[1] For all employees hired after November 6, 1986, employers are required to examine documents that show the person is authorized to work in the United States and complete a federal form I-9, which records employment eligibility verification.

CASE 13

CETA

The CETA Title III program served the Native American population of a city of 700,000 and the nearby Indian reservations. The clients on whom the study in this case focused had all received training in secretarial work. The purpose of the study was to determine the success of this occupational training and to determine what demographic variables and work experience characteristics were associated with success in the occupation. The criteria of success were defined as (1) a "satisfactory" rating by the employer and (2) a 12-week minimum length of employment. The success rate was close to 50 percent, and a random sample of 34 client records was pulled. Case Table 13.1 shows the data for the successful group of clients. Case Table 13.2 shows the data for the unsuccessful group.

Source: Adapted from R. Dennis Middlemist, *Client-Oriented Effectiveness Evaluation* (Stillwater, OK: Native American Training Project, 1977), 28–37.

C A S E T A B L E   1 3 . 1   **Successful Group of Clients**

			Client Characteristics			
Client Number	Sex	Marital Status[a,b]	Age	Education	Number of Weeks Unemployed	Number of Dependents
1	F	M	21	11	1	1
2	F	S	24	12	1	2
3	F	D	32	10	26	5
4	F	W	24	13	2	5
5	F	S	18	12	8	1
6	F	D	33	12	1	3
7	F	.	24	12	56	1
8	F	M	33	12	6	1
9	F	W	25	9	12	2
10	F	M	25	12	20	3
11	F	M	32	12	68	1
12	F	.	22	13	1	1
13	F	.	25	12	1	2
14	F	S	24	12	52	2
15	F	M	22	12	52	1
16	F	D	25	14	2	3
17	F	S	18	12	1	1

[a] . = information not recorded. A missing value for an Edu-Stat variable is represented by a period (.).
[b] S = single, M = married, D = divorced, W = widowed.

C A S E T A B L E   1 3 . 2   **Unsuccessful Group of Clients**

			Client Characteristics			
Client Number	Sex	Marital Status[a,b]	Age	Education	Number of Weeks Unemployed	Number of Dependents
1	F	S	20	12	.	1
2	F	.	20	11	.	1
3	F	D	28	12	32	2
4	F	.	28	12	8	1
5	F	M	21	11	.	1
6	M	.	20	13	104	3
7	F	S	28	14	.	2
8	F	.	19	12	28	1
9	F	S	20	12	.	1
10	M	S	26	12	108	1
11	F	S	20	11	10	1
12	F	.	18	12	12	1
13	F	S	19	10	.	1
14	F	.	42	12	.	1
15	F	S	20	12	2	1
16	F	W	30	16	24	3
17	F	S	21	13	52	1

[a] . = information not recorded. A missing value for an Edu-Stat variable is represented by a period (.).
[b] S = single, M = married, D = divorced, W = widowed.

Client Characteristics		Program Services				Outcome Criteria	
Previous Wage	Own Transporation	Training Site	Type of Training[c]	Weekly Allowance	Other Support	Number of Weeks Employed	Employer Rating
2.90	Yes	B	OJT	100	No	12	S
2.25	No	B	WE	100	No	12	S
2.50	No	A	C/T	63	C	12	S
2.00	Yes	B	OJT	100	No	12	S
2.19	Yes	B	OJT	100	No	12	S
2.25	Yes	A	C/T	63	B	12	S
2.50	No	B	OJT	160	No	12	S
2.10	Yes	B	OJT	126	No	12	S
2.50	•	C	OJT	84	No	12	S
2.80	Yes	C	OJT	90	No	12	S
2.00	•	C	C/T	63	No	12	S
2.30	Yes	C	OJT	63	No	12	S
2.50	•	A	C/T	63	B	12	S
2.10	Yes	A	OJT	63	A	12	S
•	Yes	C	C/T	100	No	12	S
2.40	•	A	C/T	63	A	12	S
2.30	Yes	B	WE	92	No	12	S

[c] OJT = on-the-job training; WE = work experience, similar to OJT except CETA arranged with the employer to share the trainee's salary; C/T = classroom training; and PSE = public-sector experience, in which the trainee was hired on a temporary basis with a government agency and received training similar to on-the-job training.

Client Characteristics		Program Services				Outcome Criteria	
Previous Wage	Own Transporation	Training Site	Type of Training[c]	Weekly Allowance	Other Support	Number of Weeks Employed	Employer Rating
2.10	No	B	WE	84	No	6	U
1.00	•	A	C/T	90	No	8	U
2.00	Yes	A	C/T	30	No	3	U
2.61	•	A	C/T	0	No	9	U
2.25	•	A	OJT	100	No	2	U
1.05	Yes	A	OJT	100	No	1	U
2.50	•	B	WE	100	No	4	U
•	Yes	A	OJT	100	No	10	U
•	•	A	C/T	63	A	8	U
1.00	•	A	C/T	63	A	3	U
1.00	•	A	C/T	63	No	7	U
2.00	•	A	C/T	63	No	5	U
1.95	•	A	C/T	63	No	9	U
2.50	•	B	WE	82	No	2	U
2.95	Yes	A	C/T	63	A	1	U
4.00	Yes	B	WE	92	No	4	U
2.85	•	B	OJT	120	No	4	U

[c] OJT = on-the-job training; WE = work experience, similar to OJT except CETA arranged with the employer to share the trainee's salary; C/T = classroom training; and PSE = public-sector experience, in which the trainee was hired on a temporary basis with a government agency and received training similar to on-the-job training.

CASE EXHIBIT 1 3 . 1

**Variable Names in the
CETA Dataset**

Variable Name	Label
SEX	Respondent's gender
MARITAL	Marital status
AGE	Respondent's age
EDLEVEL	Respondent's education
UNEMP	Number of weeks unemployed
DEPENDS	Number of dependents
WAGE	Previous wage
TRANS	Own transport
TRAINING	Training site
TRTYPE	Training type
ALLANCE	Weekly allowance
OTHER	Other support
EMP	Number of weeks employed
RATING*	Employee rating

*For the variable RATING, U = unsuccessful; S = successful. Some Edu-Stat programs require numeric coding so this variable is also coded 1 = unsuccessful; 2 = successful for the variable name SUCCESS.

ADDITIONAL INFORMATION

The data from this case are stored in a computerized database. Your instructor will provide information about the floppy disk if this material is part of the case assignment. Case Exhibit 13.1 lists the Edu-Stat variable names.

Questions

1. Calculate the appropriate descriptive statistics to compare the two groups.

2. What bivariate statistical techniques are appropriate?

3. Formulate statistical hypotheses and perform the appropriate statistical tests.

C A S E   **14**

Fleming Companies 🔳

Fleming is the nation's largest wholesale food distributor. The firm supplies complete product lines and operational services to more than 5,200 retail grocery stores in 36 states. In some regions of the country it also operates retail stores.

Case Exhibit 14.1 lists the many variables that are stored on a floppy disk that your instructor will make available to you. The database includes two general categories of data: (1) financial

data from the Fleming Companies' annual reports and (2) economic data for the United States. Both sets of data are for the ten-year period between 1979 and 1988.

Questions

1. If you were researching the Fleming Companies, how would you use the data provided?

2. Select three variables from the financial data set and calculate their means.

3. Select three variables from the economic

Source: *Fleming Companies Annual Report 1988* and *Fleming Companies Annual Report 1989*.

data set and determine if they are highly interrelated.

4. Formulate a statistical hypothesis and test it.

5. Forecast sales for the upcoming year.

6. What are the limitations of the data for forecasting purposes?

CASE EXHIBIT 14.1 **Variables in the Fleming Companies Data Set**

Financial Variables

YEAR	Year of data	SALES	Net sales
COST	Cost of sales	INT	Interest
EBIT	Earnings before income taxes	TAX	Federal and state income taxes
OPEARN	Earnings from continued operations	NETEARN	Net earnings
EPS	Primary earnings per share	NEPS	Net earnings per share
DIVPS	Cash dividends paid per share	BVPS	Book value per share
INV	Inventories	WORKCAP	Working capital
CAPEX	Capital expenditures	EQUITY	Shareholders' equity
REINVEST	Earnings reinvested in business	CASHDIV	Cash dividends paid
DEP	Depreciation and amortization	CFLOW	Cash flow
EQRETURN	Percent return on average equity	CAPRET	Percent return on average total capitalization
RATIO	Current ratio	INVTURN	Inventory turnover
RECTURN	Receivable turnover	OUTSTAND	Shares outstanding at year-end
AVROUT	Weighted average shares outstanding	SHOLDERS	Shareholders of record

Economic Variables

GNP	Gross national product—billions	C	Personal consumption expenditure
I	Gross private domestic investment	G	Government purchases of goods and services
X	Exports of goods and services		
XLESSM	Net exports	M	Imports of goods and services
PT	Personal taxes	PI	Personal income
DPI	Disposable personal income	PS	Personal savings
DPICAP	Disposable personal income per capita	APS	Average propensity to spend
LABOR	Civilian labor force	DEFICIT	Federal deficit on NIPA basis
PRMEN	Adult male participation rate	UNEMPT	Civilian unemployment rate
PROD	Hourly business productivity	PRFEM	Adult female participation rate
COMP	Hourly business compensation	FARM	Hourly farm productivity
CPI	Consumer price index	FRB	Federal Reserve Board % manufacturing capital utilized
FPI	Farm price index	PPI	Producer price index
R3MO	Mean yield on 3-month bill	CHGPI	Change in consumer price index
PRIME	Prime rate charged by U.S. banks	RBOND	Mean yield on Aaa bond
CDEBT	Consumer installment debt	DJIA	Dow average of 30 stocks
MDEBT	Mortgage debt by all holders	FDEBT	Federal government debt

C A S E   **15**

Hampton Mayoral Survey

THE PROBLEM

In the early weeks of the 1983 mayoral campaign, most party leaders felt that Frank Wagner's many accomplishments as mayor of Hampton virtually assured his election as a second-term Democratic mayor. By early October of that year, John Adams, Wagner's campaign manager, was not as confident due to what he believed was a subtle but observable shift in voter preferences towards the Republican candidate and past mayor, Bill Lucking. Adams was bothered by the number of Democratic precinct workers who had reported residents' caustic comments concerning Mayor Wagner's integrity and leadership style. He partially attributed these remarks to a series of damaging editorials and political advertisements which accused Mayor Wagner of being a dictatorial administrator. Reporters frequently labeled Wagner's leadership style as autocratic although the majority of the city administrators viewed him as an impatient man who too frequently lacked tact when dealing with controversial issues. Nevertheless, his rather direct manner did convey an image of rigidity to the press, and this conveyed image was not improving his re-election chances.

Bill Lucking's public image was the opposite of Wagner's because of his relaxed, laid-back approach to city governance. Former Mayor Lucking avoided politically sensitive issues and gave the county and city branches of government almost complete autonomy over their operations. This lack of centralized planning caused frequent coordination problems among city and county officials and often resulted in delayed and unfinished projects. Even though Lucking was a congenial individual and a popular politician in

Source: Presented at Midwest Society for Case Research Workshop, 1984, and accepted by referees of the Midwest Society for Case Research for international distribution. Copyright © 1985 by Dr. Robert J. Listman, Associate Professor of Marketing, Valparaiso University. Reprinted with permission.

Hampton, his lack of accomplishments did lead to his defeat by Frank Wagner, who ran on a reform platform. Wagner delivered his campaign promises and was successful in obtaining many civic improvements for Hampton residents. His principal accomplishments were: installing storm and flood control sewers in the low-lying areas of Hampton; securing new equipment for the fire department; obtaining passage of a controversial tax referendum for improvement of the city parks; enlarging the city ambulance fleet; installing curbs and sidewalks in older areas of the city; improving county and city roads; and facilitating the selection of Hampton as the location of the state-funded job-training facility and the site of the North County Hospital Annex. Unfortunately, these accomplishments did not come without political conflict, and Wagner was frequently involved in political infighting with other county and local administrators. His terse manner and tenacious approach to these problems made him a favorite target of reporters in spite of his many successes.

Approximately five weeks before the election, a minority faction of the opposing Republican party strategically leaked to the *Hampton Chronicle* the accusation that Wagner owned the land upon which the proposed North County Hospital Annex was to be built. The paper published the accusation which was later proved to be false, but it did hurt Wagner's image because he had publicly fought for the location of the Hospital Annex at this site. The newspaper printed a retraction, but, in spite of this, most party leaders felt that Wagner's image was severely damaged. Wagner himself was greatly disheartened over this latest turn of events, because he felt that the people of Hampton should see through what he termed a "shabby political assault."

After weighing Wagner's many accomplishments against his further tarnished image, Adams had to conclude that the election was going to be a lot closer than originally had been predicted. Lucking was an astute politician, and he was quite adept at publicly exaggerating Wagner's seemingly autocratic manner. However, the real concern was what did the voters believe and how would these beliefs affect their voting behavior? Adams felt that business research could help in assessing Mayor Wagner's image and in determining his re-election chance. Therefore, he asked for and received authorization to commission a political poll.

THE STUDY

Upon authorization by the re-election committee, Adams was able to divert $3,200 from the promotional budget to fund the needed research. Penton Research Associates, a local business research firm, was commissioned to complete the survey. After thoroughly reviewing the problem with the re-election committee, Joe Meyers, the Penton account executive, concluded that answers were needed to three key questions:

1. How do potential voters evaluate Frank Wagner as opposed to Bill Lucking on the dimensions of (a) job performance as mayor, (b) success in obtaining civic improvements, (c) honesty and integrity, and (d) overall concern for the welfare of Hampton residents?
2. Would Wagner or Lucking win the election and, specifically, which precincts would each carry?
3. What factors would influence the way in which Hampton residents would vote in this election?

For issue number three, Adams hypothesized that the key vote determinants would be the critical factors of political affiliation, candidates' stands on community issues, their previous performances in office, and the voters' perceptions concerning the honesty and integrity of the candidates. Adams reasoned that since there had been many controversial community issues over the past four years, respondents should not be given

a lengthy list from which to select. Both Adams and Meyers concluded that a response bias might likely occur if the respondents were asked to select issues from a list because they might frequently select issues which were not key determinants to them, but merely remembered issues. It was, therefore, agreed that if respondents identified the category, local issues, as a primary factor affecting their vote, then they would be directed to state the issue(s). Later a frequency distribution could be developed, and the most influencing issues could be easily identified.

Adams believed answers to these three questions would allow him to predict the results of the election on a citywide and precinct basis and also to access the present image of Mayor Wagner. If a re-election problem did exist, then an intensified "promotional blitz" in select precincts would be undertaken with the intent of changing voters' preferences in the remaining three weeks of the campaign.

RESEARCH METHODOLOGY

Both Adams and Meyers believed the answers to the three research questions could be more effectively obtained by conducting a large telephone survey rather than by conducting time-consuming and expensive personal interviews. Their rationale was based upon the advantages of telephone surveys, which included an obvious cost efficiency, specific control over selection of the sample, speed in completing the survey, and a higher degree of supervisory control over the actual interviewing. Meyers felt this last point was extremely important, because if interviewers varied on the phrasing of key questions, then a substantial but unquantifiable response bias could occur.

After discussing how to control interviewer bias, Joe Meyers raised the issue of sampling error. In explaining sampling error to Adams, Meyers stated, "The precision of data obtained through survey research is directly related to the size of the sample because the larger the sample, the more likely you are to reduce sampling error. In practice, however, a sample size is a compromise between some acceptable level of precision

CASE EXHIBIT 1 5 . 1   Sampling Error Table at 90 Percent Confidence Level

Sample Size	1% or 99%	2% or 98%	3% or 97%	4% or 96%	5% or 95%	6% or 94%	8% or 92%	10% or 90%	12% or 88%	15% or 85%	20% or 80%	25% or 75%	30% or 70%	35% or 65%	40% or 60%	45% or 55%	50%
25	3.3	4.6	5.6	6.5	7.2	7.8	9.0	9.9	10.7	11.8	13.2	14.3	15.1	15.7	16.2	16.4	16.5
50	2.3	3.3	4.0	4.6	5.1	5.5	6.3	7.0	7.6	8.3	9.3	10.1	10.7	11.1	11.4	11.6	11.7
75	1.9	2.7	3.3	3.7	4.2	4.5	5.2	5.7	6.2	6.8	7.6	8.3	8.7	9.1	9.3	9.5	9.5
100	1.6	2.3	2.8	3.2	3.6	3.9	4.5	4.9	5.4	5.9	6.6	7.1	7.6	7.9	8.1	8.2	8.3
150	1.3	1.9	2.3	2.6	2.9	3.2	3.7	4.0	4.4	4.8	5.4	5.8	6.2	6.4	6.6	6.7	6.7
200	1.2	1.6	2.0	2.3	2.5	2.8	3.2	3.5	3.8	4.2	4.7	5.1	5.3	5.6	5.7	5.8	5.8
250	1.0	1.5	1.8	2.0	2.3	2.5	2.8	3.1	3.4	3.7	4.2	4.5	4.8	5.0	5.1	5.2	5.2
300	0.9	1.3	1.6	1.9	2.1	2.3	2.6	2.9	3.1	3.4	3.8	4.1	4.4	4.5	4.7	4.7	4.8
400	0.8	1.2	1.4	1.6	1.8	2.0	2.2	2.5	2.7	2.9	3.3	3.6	3.8	3.9	4.0	4.1	4.1
500	0.7	1.0	1.3	1.4	1.6	1.8	2.0	2.2	2.4	2.6	3.0	3.2	3.4	3.5	3.6	3.7	3.7
600	0.7	0.9	1.1	1.3	1.5	1.6	1.8	2.0	2.2	2.4	2.7	2.9	3.1	3.2	3.3	3.4	3.4
800	0.6	0.8	1.0	1.1	1.3	1.4	1.6	1.8	1.9	2.1	2.3	2.5	2.7	2.8	2.9	2.9	2.9
1,000	0.5	0.7	0.9	1.0	1.1	1.2	1.4	1.6	1.7	1.9	2.1	2.3	2.4	2.5	2.6	2.6	2.6
1,200	0.5	0.7	0.8	0.9	1.0	1.1	1.3	1.4	1.5	1.7	1.9	2.1	2.2	2.3	2.3	2.4	2.4
1,500	0.4	0.6	0.7	0.8	0.9	1.0	1.2	1.3	1.4	1.5	1.7	1.8	2.0	2.0	2.1	2.1	2.1
2,000	0.4	0.5	0.6	0.7	0.8	0.9	1.0	1.1	1.2	1.3	1.5	1.6	1.7	1.8	1.8	1.8	1.8
2,500	0.3	0.5	0.6	0.6	0.7	0.8	0.9	1.0	1.1	1.2	1.3	1.4	1.5	1.6	1.6	1.6	1.6
3,000	0.3	0.4	0.5	0.6	0.7	0.7	0.8	0.9	1.0	1.1	1.2	1.3	1.4	1.4	1.5	1.5	1.5
4,000	0.3	0.4	0.4	0.5	0.6	0.6	0.7	0.8	0.8	0.9	1.0	1.1	1.2	1.2	1.3	1.3	1.3
5,000	0.2	0.3	0.4	0.5	0.5	0.6	0.6	0.7	0.8	0.8	0.9	1.0	1.1	1.1	1.1	1.2	1.2
7,500	0.2	0.3	0.3	0.4	0.4	0.5	0.5	0.6	0.6	0.7	0.8	0.8	0.9	0.9	0.9	0.9	1.0
10,000	0.2	0.2	0.3	0.3	0.4	0.4	0.4	0.5	0.5	0.6	0.7	0.7	0.8	0.8	0.8	0.8	0.8

and restricting budgetary constraints. So, John, you have to evaluate precision against increased costs in selecting sampling parameters which are used to determine the actual sample size. Precision could be increased and sampling error reduced by selecting more statistically stringent parameters, such as a 99 percent versus a 90 percent confidence level, and/or by stipulating a smaller error range, such as ±2 versus ±5 percentage points from any given survey mean or percentage. This increased precision would result in a large and, therefore, more expensive sample."

Adams interrupted and said, "Joe, is there any relationship between cost and precision?"

Meyers replied, "As a rule of thumb, doubling the sample size for surveys like this one would increase cost by 60 percent, but if you cut the sample size in half, costs would only decrease 25 to 35 percent due to high fixed expenses."

Adams looked somewhat confused and asked, "Does this mean that if I double the sample size, I will cut the sampling error in half?"

"Unfortunately, no," replied Meyers. "Precision increases in proportion to the square root of the increase in sample size. Let's look at a standard error of a proportion table, John, and you can see what I mean. (Refer to Case Exhibit 15.1.) Assume we have a 50/50 proportional split and a stipulated error range of 5.8 percent at the 90 percent confidence level. This gives us a calculated sample size of 200. Doubling the sample size to 400 will only reduce the error range from ±5.8 to ±4.1 percentage points. It would require a sample size four times as large, or 800, to cut error in half to 2.9 percentage points. This would result in a cost increase of 250 to 300 percent higher than the original survey of 200."

Adams appeared to be satisfied with this response, although he was getting impatient because of all these "scientific uncertainties," as he labeled them. He wanted to begin the survey immediately and cut back upon the time spent in drawing a sample by employing the local telephone directory as the sampling frame. He believed he could reduce both time and cost with this approach. Meyers disagreed and strongly rec-

ommended that the sampling frame be registered voters and be proportionately stratified by the percentage of registered voters within each political precinct. Although he did agree that approximately 150 fewer calls could be made for the projected five hours of time it would take to select about 900 respondents, Joe Meyers projected that the actual sample size would be between 400 and 500, but he felt they should obtain 900 phone numbers to obtain double the sample size ratio needed for political polls. Meyers eventually obtained agreement to adopt his sampling frame, but he knew Adams believed that the result of this selection was a net loss of 150 calls!

In order to minimize further conflict, Meyers cautiously raised the last sampling issue. "John, I am glad that you approved the sampling frame of registered voters, but there still remains an additional source of sampling error which we must discuss."

Adams's reaction was immediate and abrupt. "Listen, Joe, if you are trying to sell me on a larger or more expensive survey, forget it."

Meyers was rather surprised by Adams's autocratic response, so he cautiously added. "Well, John, we both know that customarily only 60 percent of eligible voters actually vote in local elections, which gives us a built-in nonresponse error. What we need is a way of subdividing our survey respondents into homogeneous groups representing their probability of voting in this election. We could easily accomplish this by including filtering questions in the questionnaire which would assess respondents' interests in local politics, their interest in this campaign, and their past frequency of voting in local elections. After completing the interviews, we can weight and score each question, create an index of anticipated voter behavior, and, based upon composite scores, group the respondents."

"O.K., Joe, you have my interest. What would you do then?" replied Adams.

"Well, assume we end up with three groups which have a high, moderate, and low probability of voting in this election. By analyzing the grouped responses, we could more precisely predict the results of the election and more accurately identify the campaign issues of greatest importance to those individuals most likely to vote."

Adams responded: "How much is this going to cost?"

Meyers replied: "Assuming an extra two and one-half minutes for each questionnaire times approximately 400 questions gives us almost 17 additional hours of survey time. To this product, we should add the cost of six hours of account executive time in formulating the filtering questions, calculating the index, and interpreting the results. In total, this should add approximately $950 to the research bill."

Adams started shaking his head and emphatically said: "Well, you lost my interest with that $950 projection, Joe, but maybe we can still reach an agreement. Adopt my original sampling frame, which will give us 150 additional respondents, and I think I can convince the election board to add the $950 to the survey costs."

Joe Meyers quickly responded: "No, John, I can't support that approach because all we will accomplish is to reintroduce our original sampling problem."

"O.K., Joe, you are the expert," replied Adams, "but it is my money, and I don't think it is worth $950 merely to break down our findings into three additional categories of responses, so I am going to say no!"

After fifteen minutes of further discussion, Joe Meyers was unable to persuade John Adams to approve the addition of filtering questions. Since Adams was becoming progressively more agitated, Meyers reluctantly concluded that the issue was a stalemate which would not be resolved in an amicable fashion.

Therefore, Meyers left this issue and moved to the problem of determining a specific sample size. The sampling parameters of $\pm$ 4 percentage points at the 90 percent confidence level, with an assumed voter split of 45/55 in favor of Wagner, were agreed upon. This resulted in a calculated sample size of 400, which was possible to obtain for a cost of $3,000. However, Meyers believed that if the election was going to be that close (45/55 split), then a more statistically stringent

and, therefore, larger sample was warranted. However, the subject was quickly dropped when Adams, who was obviously agitated, said, "Look, if you need a larger sample, then adopt my sampling approach and we will be able to survey 150 more people." Since Meyers did not wish another confrontation at this stage of the project, he dropped the issue.

The next day Penton personnel started the research project. Joe Meyers developed, pretested, and refined the telephone questionnaire while other Penton employees randomly selected a pool of 800 respondents from the precinct listings. Case Exhibit 15.2 contains a copy of the survey instrument used in the study. The actual selection process did not attempt to further stratify the sample by political affiliation even though most registered voters declared their political affiliation in the primaries as either Democratic or Republican. In fact, only 60 percent of the registered voters even voted in past mayoral elections, and the majority of these voted a straight party ticket.

Penton personnel were instructed to select twice the number of needed calls for each precinct. All numbers were randomly selected from precinct listings so any biasing periodicities in the alphabetized listings were eliminated.

Interviewers were directed to speak to only the registered voters within the surveyed households, and all interviews were conducted between the hours of 6:30 and 9:30 p.m. over a three-day period. Interviewers were assigned specific precincts and a supervisor was present to monitor the quality of the phone interviewers. If a phone number was busy or there was no answer, then repeated callbacks were made in an effort to reach that household.

RESULTS OF THE STUDY

In total, 629 calls had to be made in order to obtain the requisite sample size of 400. In several precincts, the number of nonrespondents (those who refused to participate in the survey) approximated the needed quota of calls in that precinct. Of the 402 completed interviews, approximately 43 percent (171) were males while 57 percent

CASE EXHIBIT 1 5 . 2   **Telephone Questionnaire**

Precinct ID Number _____   Telephone Number: _____

Good Evening, this is Penton Research Associates and we are conducting a very brief *randomized survey* of Hampton residents to determine their opinions of the two candidates running for mayor of Hampton. May I speak to __[insert name]__ ? All responses are, of course, treated anonymously and confidentially. Thank you. [Check space below.]

____ Participated   ____ Male   ____ Female   ____ Did not participate

Question 1:   I will read four reasons which could likely affect the way people will vote in this election. *After* I state all four reasons, select the *one primary* reason which will influence your vote the *most.* [Interviewers: Mark 1 after that response, and if they identify another primary factor, describe it below.]

____ Candidate's political affiliation

____ Candidate's personal integrity and honesty

____ Candidate's previous performance as mayor

____ Local community issues (ask following question)

Other _____

Of the remaining three reasons (read again), please identify any *secondary reason* which will *significantly influence* your vote. [Interviewers: Code 2 (secondary) after each choice. If none, leave blank.]

Question 2:   Please describe the *community issues* which you believe will influence your vote in this election. [Describe below.]

_____

_____

Question 3:   In your opinion, who do you believe has done the best job as mayor?

____ A   The present mayor, Frank Wagner

____ B   The previous mayor, Bill Lucking

____ C   There is no difference between the two

____ D   Don't know or no opinion (do not give as an option)

Question 4:   How do you believe Bill Lucking compares to Frank Wagner on the following points? *After* I read each point, indicate which candidate is superior to the other *by stating the name of the candidate you prefer.* If you have no preference, respond *no preference.* [Interviewers: If respondents are unable to make a decision, check the don't know column.]

   Qualifications:
   1.   Successful in obtaining community improvements for Hampton residents
   2.   Personal integrity and honesty
   3.   Concern for welfare of Hampton residents
   4.   Candidate's overall performance as mayor of Hampton

	Lucking	Wagner	No Preference	Don't Know
1.	____	____	____	____
2.	____	____	____	____
3.	____	____	____	____
4.	____	____	____	____

Question 5:   If the vote were tomorrow, would you vote for [check one]:

____ Bill Lucking   ____ Frank Wagner   ____ Undecided [Interviewers: Do not give as an option but check if respondents can't decide.]

Question 6:   Would you classify your political affiliation as:

____ Democratic   ____ Republican   ____ Independent

CASE TABLE 15.1

Precinct Sampling Statistics

Precinct	Sample Size	Completed Calls	Would Not Participate in Survey	Total Contacts
2	24	24	8	32
3	24	24	14	48
5	20	20	19	39
6	16	16	8	24
7	28	28	10	38
8	20	20	7	27
9	24	25	13	39
12	13	13	9	22
13	16	16	13	29
14	20	20	9	29
17	17	17	7	24
18	20	20	12	32
20[a]	20	16	18	34
21	29	29	13	42
22	20	21	13	34
23	16	16	6	22
24	20	21	8	24
25	20	20	13	33
26	20	22	18	40
27	13	13	9	22
Totals	400	402	227	629

[a]Fifty numbers were supplied; however, after repeated callbacks, only 34 out of the 50 could be reached.

CASE TABLE 15.2

Breakdown by Political Affiliation and Gender

Political Affiliation[a]	Count	Percentage
Democratic	128	31.84%
Republican	72	17.91
Independent	198	49.25
Would not respond	4	1.00

Gender	Number of Surveys	Percentage
Male	171	42.54%
Female	231	57.46
Total	402	100.00%

[a]Many respondents register in primaries as Democratic or Republican but vote the issues or person. Consequently, they classify themselves as independent even though they may have registered as a member of a political party.

(231) were females. Case Tables 15.1–15.3 contain these and other descriptive statistics concerning the sampling distributions.

The findings indicate that the primary reasons affecting voters' preferences (Case Table 15.4) were voters' perceptions of the candidates' integrity/honesty and the candidates' past performances as mayor. The data also suggest that candidates' political affiliation and community issues were not as important in this election as the preceding two reasons. Approximately 18 percent of the surveyed voters indicated that local commu-

CASE TABLE 15.3

Cross-Tabulation—Political
Affiliation by Precinct

Precinct	Political Affiliation of Respondents			Would Not Respond	Total
	Democratic	Republican	Independent		
2	8 33.33%	5 20.83%	9 37.50%	2 8.33%	24 5.97%
3	9 37.50%	3 12.50%	12 50.00%	0 0.00%	24 5.97%
5	5 25.00%	2 10.00%	13 65.00%	0 0.00%	20 4.98%
6	6 37.50%	5 31.25%	5 31.25%	0 0.00%	16 3.98%
7	8 28.57%	3 10.71%	17 60.71%	0 0.00%	28 6.97%
8	7 35.00%	1 5.00%	12 60.00%	0 0.00%	20 4.98%
9	7 26.92%	8 30.77%	11 42.31%	0 0.00%	25 6.47%
12	1 7.69%	3 23.08%	9 69.23%	0 0.00%	13 3.23%
13	4 25.00%	2 12.50%	10 62.50%	0 0.00%	16 3.98%
14	4 20%	3 15.00%	12 60.00%	1 5.00%	20 4.98%
17	9 52.94%	4 23.53%	4 23.53%	0 0.00%	17 4.23%
18	10 50.00%	1 5.00%	9 45.00%	0 0.00%	20 4.98%
20	5 31.25%	3 18.75%	7 43.75%	1 6.75%	16 3.98%
21	5 17.24%	7 24.14%	17 58.62%	0 0.00%	29 7.21%
22	6 28.57%	5 23.81%	10 47.62%	0 0.00%	21 5.22%
23	6 37.50%	0 0.00%	10 62.50%	0 0.00%	16 3.98%
24	8 38.10%	4 19.05%	9 42.86%	0 0.00%	21 5.22%
25	10 50.00%	3 15.00%	7 35.00%	0 0.00%	20 4.98%
26	6 27.27%	8 36.36%	8 36.36%	0 0.00%	22 5.47%
27	4 30.77%	2 15.38%	7 53.85%	0 0.00%	13 3.23%
Totals	128 31.84%	72 17.91%	198 49.25%	4 1.00%	402 100.00%

Reason	Bill Lucking	Frank Wagner	Undecided	Would Not Respond	Total
Political affiliation	6 26.09%	13 56.52%	2 8.70%	2 8.70%	23 5.72%
Personal integrity/ honesty of candidate	64 42.11%	52 34.21%	30 19.74%	6 3.95%	152 37.81%
Previous performance as mayor	52 35.62%	71 48.63%	18 12.33%	5 3.42%	146 36.32%
Local issues	28 39.44%	24 33.80%	14 19.72%	5 7.04%	71 17.66%
Could not identify any primary reason	2 20.00%	5 50.00%	1 10.00%	2 20.00%	10 2.49%
Totals	152 37.81%	165 41.04%	65 16.17%	20 4.98%	402 100.00%

Frequency distributions of the secondary reasons affecting voting decision:

Question	Count	Percentage
Political affiliation	42	10.45%
Personal integrity and honesty	76	18.91
Previous performance as mayor	109	27.11
Local community issues	107	26.62
Could not identify any secondary reason	68	16.92

Summary results of voter preference and question 5:

Choice	Count	Percentage
Bill Lucking	152	37.81%
Frank Wagner	165	41.04
Undecided	65	16.17
Would not respond	20	4.98

1. Need for sidewalks and curbs—29
2. Need for hospital in community—17
3. Drainage and/or flood control—15
4. Controversy over hospital land issue—10
5. Police point system—6
6. Firehouse equipment needs—5
7. Frank Wagner's autocratic image—2
8. *Examples of other reasons:*
   Improved management—3
   Cleaner city—3
   School busing program—2
   Job-training facility and attracting business to Hampton—3
   Nepotism—3
   Park/tax increases—10
   City/road improvements—6
   Ambulance—5
   Miscellaneous—4
9. Would not state any specific community issue—40

[a]Some respondents cited more than one reason, so the tallies do not represent number of respondents.

CASE TABLE 15.5

**Breakdown of Opinion
of Best Job as Mayor
(Question 3)**

Preference	Count	Percentage
Frank Wagner	129	32.09%
Bill Lucking	101	25.12
No difference between the two	94	23.38
Don't know or no opinion	78	19.40

CASE TABLE 15.6

**Candidates'
Qualifications
(Question 4)**

1. **Comparison of success in obtaining community civic improvements for Hampton residents:**

Preference	Count	Percentage
Bill Lucking	81	20.15%
Frank Wagner	158	39.30
No preference	114	28.36
Don't know	49	12.19

2. **Comparison of personal integrity and honesty:**

Preference	Count	Percentage
Bill Lucking	130	32.34%
Frank Wagner	97	24.13
No preference	136	33.83
Don't know	39	9.70

3. **Comparison of concern for welfare of Hampton residents:**

Preference	Count	Percentage
Bill Lucking	117	29.10%
Frank Wagner	122	30.35
No preference	122	30.35
Don't know	41	10.20

4. **Comparison of candidates' previous performance as mayor of Hampton:**

Preference	Count	Percentage
Bill Lucking	115	28.61%
Frank Wagner	133	33.08
No preference	104	25.87
Don't know	50	12.44

nity issues were a primary factor and 27 percent indicated they were a secondary factor. Case Exhibit 15.3 contains a listing of these identified community issues.

The summary results of voters' preferences contained in Case Table 15.4 suggest that Frank Wagner is slightly preferred over Bill Lucking.

However, 21 percent of the registered voters classified their preference as still undecided or would not respond. Case Tables 15.5–15.8 contain summaries of cross-tabulations of registered voters' preferences by (1) candidates' qualifications, (2) gender, (3) precinct, (4) political affiliation, and (5) candidates' past performance as mayor.

CASE TABLE 15.7

Cross-Tabulation—Voter Preference by Precinct

Precinct	Bill Lucking	Frank Wagner	Presently Undecided	Would Not Respond	Precinct Total
2	9 37.50%	11 45.83%	3 12.50%	1 4.17%	24 5.97%
3	8 33.33%	10 41.67%	6 25.00%	0 0.00%	24 5.97%
5	10 50.00%	6 30.00%	1 5.00%	3 15.00%	19 4.98%
6	4 25.00%	6 37.50%	3 18.75%	3 18.75%	16 3.98%
7	7 25.00%	13 46.43%	7 25.00%	1 3.57%	28 6.97%
8	4 20.00%	11 55.00%	4 20.00%	1 5.00%	20 4.98%
9	15 57.69%	7 26.92%	3 11.54%	1 3.85%	26 6.47%
12	6 46.15%	3 23.08%	2 15.38%	2 15.38%	13 3.23%
13	7 43.75%	3 18.75%	6 37.50%	0 0.00%	16 3.98%
14	8 40.00%	6 30.00%	5 25.00%	1 5.00%	20 4.98%
17	7 41.18%	8 47.06%	2 11.76%	0 0.00%	17 4.23%
18	6 30.00%	13 65.00%	1 5.00%	0 0.00%	20 4.23%
20	3 18.75%	6 37.50%	6 37.50%	1 6.25%	16 3.98%
21	17 58.62%	8 27.59%	3 10.34%	1 3.45%	29 7.21%
22	12 57.14%	7 33.33%	2 9.52%	0 0.00%	21 5.22%
23	3 18.75%	10 62.50%	2 12.50%	1 6.25%	16 3.89%
24	5 23.81%	12 57.14%	2 9.52%	2 9.52%	21 5.22%
25	7 35.00%	10 50.00%	3 15.00%	0 0.00%	20 4.98%
26	9 40.91%	9 40.91%	2 9.09%	2 9.09%	22 5.47%
27	5 38.46%	6 46.15%	2 15.38%	0 0.00%	13 3.23%
Totals	152 37.81%	165 41.04%	65 16.17%	20 4.98%	402 100.00%

CASE TABLE 15.8

Cross-Tabulations—
Voter Preference by
Political Affiliation/
Past Performance as
Mayor/and Gender

Voter preference by political affiliation:

	Bill Lucking	Frank Wagner	Undecided	Would Not Respond	Total
Democratic	21 16.41%	85 66.41%	16 2.50%	6 4.69%	128 31.84%
Republican	52 72.22%	12 16.67%	7 9.72%	1 1.39%	72 17.91%
Independent	78 39.39%	67 34.34%	40 20.20%	12 6.06%	198 49.25%
Would not respond	1 25.00%	0 0.00%	2 50.00%	1 25.00%	4 1.00%
Totals	152 37.81%	165 41.04%	65 16.17%	20 4.98%	402 100.00%

Voter preference by past performance as mayor:

	Bill Lucking	Frank Wagner	Undecided	Would Not Respond	Total
Frank Wagner	5 3.88%	112 86.82%	10 7.75%	2 1.55%	129 32.09%
Bill Lucking	95 94.06%	2 1.98%	2 1.98%	2 1.98%	101 25.12%
No difference	31 32.98%	21 22.34%	31 32.98%	11 11.70%	94 23.38%
No opinion	21 26.92%	30 38.46%	22 28.21%	5 6.41%	78 19.40%
Totals	152 37.81%	165 41.04%	65 16.17%	20 4.98%	402 100.00%

Voter preference by gender:

	Bill Lucking	Frank Wagner	Undecided	Would Not Respond	Total
Male	65 38.01%	67 39.18%	23 13.45%	16 9.36%	171 42.54%
Female	87 37.66%	98 42.42%	42 18.18%	4 1.73%	231 57.46%
Totals	152 37.81%	165 41.04%	65 16.17%	20 4.98%	402 100.00%

INTERPRETING THE FINDINGS

In reviewing all of this data, Adams concluded that the election would be very close but that Wagner would win by a narrow margin. He based this conclusion upon the assumption that the undecideds would vote in approximately the same proportion as those who were able to state their preference. He saw no data refuting this conclusion; therefore, he felt it was a valid assumption to make.

On the other hand, Meyers felt that the results were not very conclusive because he believed the high undecided factor could easily reverse the narrow margin Wagner presently enjoyed. He was also bothered by the fact that a large percentage of area voters would not respond to the poll. John Adams listened to Meyers's concerns but said, "Joe, don't be so pessimistic; your people did a good job and your worries are really unwarranted. After all, the calculated sample size was obtained and the respondents were selected at random." Therefore, Adams saw no reason to assume that the opinions of the nonrespondents or undecideds would deviate significantly from the findings of the survey. He was further encouraged by the fact that Wagner appeared to carry twelve of the twenty precincts and was slightly trailing or equal to Lucking in two, while clearly losing in only six. Case Table 15.7 contains a summary of voter preferences by precincts.

John Adams did realize that the election was not a "shoo-in" for Wagner, but he felt that concentrating the promotional blitz in precincts 5, 9, 12, 13, 14, 21, 22, and 26 would help to increase Wagner's narrow margin because these were the precincts Wagner was losing or trailing in. Joe Meyers felt intimidated by Adams's optimistic interpretation of the findings. He believed that Penton provided the Democratic Party with a scientific poll free from biased questions, and he did not wish to conclude the engagement by discrediting the findings and the efforts of his staff. Maybe his concerns were unwarranted, but he believed that Adams's interpretation of the findings was not entirely valid and that the election could go either way. He wondered if he was professionally justified in accepting the commission for this study when he had reservations concerning what he felt was a built-in sampling problem. Meyers knew that he informed the client about this problem and repeatedly tried to convince Adams of the need for the filtering questions. There was personal conflict in this engagement, and Meyers further believed that Adams did not fully understand the technical justification for his suggestions, but he did not want to admit this to John or take the time to listen to John's rationale. Meyers sadly concluded that this was a classic example of a line decision maker not understanding the technical reasons underpinning a "staff" person's suggestions. Unfortunately, as is often the case, this resulted in study findings which could be interpreted in a variety of ways, depending upon one's perspective.

Questions

1. Was the sampling methodology (frame, size, and selection process) that Joe Meyers used better than the methodology that John Adams preferred? State your preference and substantiate your conclusion.

2. Evaluate the questionnaire used in this study. Did it provide answers to the research questions? Was any pertinent information lacking which you feel should have been included? What questions, if any, would you have deleted or changed? Be specific in your suggestions.

3. Explain why the findings of this study could or could not predict the results of the election. Do you agree with Adams's conclusions concerning: (a) the election outcome, (b) the assumed patterning of the nonrespondents' opinions, and (c) the selection of specific precincts for the promotional blitz?

4. Identify any additional cross-tabulations of questionnaire responses necessary to strengthen the predictability of the findings.

CASE   **16**

Sunbelt Energy Corporation 🔒

Sunbelt Energy Corporation is a diversified petroleum company engaged in producing and marketing gasoline, motor oil, petrochemicals, and a number of other energy-related activities such as coal mining, uranium extraction, and atomic-power generation. Sunbelt markets its petroleum products though its own retail outlets and independent suppliers in a 25-state area within the continental United States. Sunbelt's company-owned service stations are the latest in station design and automation. Sunbelt's retail marketing strategy emphasizes modern station designs and continually works to improve the appearance of both its company-owned and independent-owned retail outlets. A research study to investigate the consumers' reaction to a new method of payment was conducted in a single city in which the company owns all stations. The company investigated the use of automated payment machines (using the same technology as automated teller machines used by banks) and gasoline credit cards for payment of gasoline services.

The specific objectives of the research were to determine the following:

1.   The overall percentage of customers who use the automated payment machines.
2.   What machine features are liked by people who use the automated payment machines.
3.   What improvements to the machine could be made to assist the current users of these machines.
4.   What improvements to the automated payment machine could be made to cause nonusers to use the machines.
5.   The percentage of people who not only purchase gasoline but who also purchase something else at the station.
6.   The percentage of people who pay using cash, a Sunbelt credit card, or a bank credit card.

The research was conducted in a Southwestern city where the company owns all retail outlets and each station has automated payment machines. Respondents were interviewed as they filled their cars with gasoline. The personal interview lasted only a few minutes, because most people wish to purchase gasoline and then leave as quickly as possible. This time frame restricted the number of questions that could be asked. All questions were short and to the point.

Four stations in the town had automated teller machines. Fifty interviews were conducted at each station for a total of 200 personal interviews. The stations were:

Station Number 1—Limestone
Station Number 2—Boulevard
Station Number 3—Performance Plaza
Station Number 4—Madison Convenient
              Store

SAMPLING

Every automobile that entered the service station in the self-service lanes was considered a member of the sampling frame. After a car arrived, the interviewer waited until the customer got out of his or her car and made a selection at the pump. As the gasoline was being pumped into the tank, interviewers introduced themselves and conducted the interviews. Only one individual refused to grant an interview. The questionnaire is shown in Case Exhibit 16.1.

Source: Based on research by George L. Bazin II. The company name is fictitious in order to protect confidentiality. The data are adjusted slightly for the same purpose. Reprinted with permission.

**Personal Interview
Questionnaire**

"Hello, my name is _____. In cooperation with Sunbelt, I am conducting a survey on how Sunbelt can better serve you. I'd like to ask you a few short questions."

Question 1
To start off, did you know that this station has an automated teller machine?
Yes _____   No _____

Question 2
In addition to a gasoline purchase, are you planning to purchase anything else, such as a soft drink, motor oil, or cigarettes?
Yes _____   No _____

Question 3
For today's purchase, are you planning to pay using the automated teller machine, or are you planning to go inside and pay the station attendant?
Go inside and pay attendant _____   Use the automated teller machine _____
(Skip to Question 9)   (Proceed to Questions 4, 5, 6, 7, and 8)

Question 4
Have you ever used the automated teller machine to pay for your gasoline purchase?
Yes _____   No _____
(Proceed to next question)   (Go to Question 8)

Question 5
What features of the automated teller machine do you like?
_____
_____
_____
_____
_____

Question 6
What features of the automated teller machine do you dislike?
_____
_____
_____
_____
_____

Question 7
From your viewpoint, are these any improvements that could be made to make it easier to use the automated teller machine?
_____
_____
_____
_____
_____

Question 8
Up to today, what features of the automated teller machine have caused you not to use it?
_____
_____
_____
_____
_____

(Skip to the observation section)

Question 9
Will you be paying for your purchase in cash, or will you be using a credit card?

Pay with cash _____   Pay with a credit card _____
(Skip to observation part)   (Proceed to Question 10)

Question 10
Will you use a Sunbelt credit card, or will you use a Visa or Mastercard for payment?

    Sunbelt card _____   Use other type _____
    (Proceed to Question 11)   (Skip to observation section)

Question 11
Have you ever used the automated teller machine for your purchase?

    Yes _____   No _____
    (Proceed to Questions 12, 13, and 14)   (Skip to Question 15)

Question 12
What features of the automated teller machine do you like?

_____
_____
_____
_____
_____

Question 13
What features of the automated teller machine do you dislike?

_____
_____
_____
_____
_____

Question 14
From your viewpoint, are there any improvements that could be made to make it easier to use the automated teller machine?

_____
_____
_____
_____
_____

(Skip to observation section)

Question 15
What features of the automated teller machine have caused you not to use it?

_____
_____
_____
_____
_____

(Skip to the observation section)

Observation Section
On behalf of Sunbelt, I thank you for your time and comments.

Is the driver of the vehicle male or female?	Male _____	Female _____
Is the driver under or over 40?	Under _____	Over _____
Are there any passengers in the vehicle?	Yes _____	No _____
Does the vehicle have Washington County tags?	Yes _____	No _____

CASE EXHIBIT 1 6 . 2

**Variable Names in the
Sunbelt Dataset**

Variable Name	Label
ATM	Auto teller knowledge
ELSE	Purchase anything else
USE	Use ATM to pay
USEGAS	Use ATM to pay for gas
CASH	Pay with cash or credit card
SUNBELT	Use Sunbelt credit card
EVER	Ever use ATM for purchase
SEX	Male or female
AGE	Under or over 40
PASS	Passengers: yes or no
TAGS	Washington county tags

ADDITIONAL INFORMATION

Several of the questions below require the use of a computerized database. Your instructor will provide information about the floppy disk if this material is part of the case assignment. Case Exhibit 16.2 lists the variable names.

Questions

1. Evaluate the research objectives.
2. Evaluate the research design in the light of the stated research objectives.
3. Using the computerized database, obtain simple frequencies for the answers to each question (the answers to the open-ended questions are not included on the database).
4. Perform the appropriate cross-tabulations.
5. Perform the appropriate univariate and bivariate statistical tests after you develop hypotheses for these particular tests.

C A S E   **17**

Employees Federal Credit Union

Employees Federal Credit Union is the credit union for a Fortune 500 firm. Any employee of the organization is eligible for membership in the credit union.

Over the past few years the Employees Federal Credit Union (EFCU) has accumulated a large amount of surplus cash funds, which have been invested in certificates of deposit. It has also experienced a lower loan/share ratio than other

Source: This case was prepared by John H. Walkup. Reprinted with permission.

credit unions of similar size. Because of these factors, the Credit Union's average earnings on its investments have slowly declined and its profit margins are being squeezed. As a result, the EFCU Board of Directors decided that a research project should be conducted to determine why its members are not borrowing money from the Credit Union. More specifically, the research project was mandated to answer the question of why the members are borrowing money from other alternative sources instead of the Credit Union.

In addition to the above, the EFCU Board of Directors expressed its desire to determine what the membership's attitudes were toward the overall management and operations of the Credit Union. Also, it was determined that the following questions should be addressed as well:

How informed is the membership about the services provided by the Credit Union?

Do any differences in opinion toward borrowing funds and the services provided by the Credit Union exist between headquarters-based and non-headquarters-based members?

RESEARCH OBJECTIVES

To respond to the questions raised by the Board, the following objectives were developed. The research design was formulated to address each of the objectives stated below:

To determine the reasons why people join the Credit Union.

To determine the reasons why members use other financial institutions when they need to borrow funds.

To measure member attitudes and beliefs about the proficiencies of the Credit Union employees.

To determine whether there are any perceived differences between headquarters-based and non-headquarters-based members.

To determine member awareness of the services offered by the Credit Union.

To measure member attitudes and beliefs about how effectively the Credit Union is operated.

RESEARCH DESIGN AND DATA COLLECTION METHOD

The research data were collected by a mail questionnaire survey. This technique was determined to be the best method for collecting the research data for the following reasons:

The wide geographic dispersion of the Credit Union membership

The minimization of the cost of conducting the research

The sensitivity of several of the questions asked in the questionnaire

The flexibility of being able to wait for the survey results before taking any actions

A copy of the questionnaire used to gather the research data is provided in Case Exhibit 17.1. Most of the questions were designed as structured questions because of the variation in the educational backgrounds, job functions, and interests of the members surveyed. However, the respondents were given the flexibility to answer several key questions in an unstructured format. The Likert scale was principally used where attitude measurements were requested.

SAMPLING PROCEDURES

The population of the EFCU is well defined; consequently, a simple random sample of the membership was selected. A sample size of 300 was calculated using the estimated population standard deviation based on the responses from 15 members to Question 37 of the questionnaire. Question 37 was used because it capsulized the essence of the research project.

The random numbers used in making the selection of the sampling units were generated with the help of a personal computer. The sampling frame used was the January 31, 1987, trial balance listing of the EFCU membership. According to the sampling frame, the EFCU had 3,531 members on that date. As a result, the 300 random numbers were generated within the range of 1 to 3,531. The random numbers were matched to a corresponding number in the sampling frame, and those individuals were selected to receive copies of the survey questionnaire.

FIELDWORK

Most of the fieldwork for the research project, including all of the editing and coding of the survey

1. Are you currently a member of the Employees Federal Credit Union (EFCU)?
   Yes ( )   No ( )
   If no, please have the member of your household who is a member of the EFCU complete the questionnaire. If no one in your household is a member, please return the questinnaire in the enclosed prepaid envelope.

2. Why did you join the Credit Union? (Check as many answers as are applicable.)
   _____ Convenience
   _____ Higher interest rates on my savings than other financial institutions pay
   _____ More personal than other facilities
   _____ Wanted a readily available source for borrowing money
   _____ Adverisements prompted me to join
   _____ Other—please explain:
   _____
   _____

Statements 3 through 6 ask for your opinion of the Credit Union employees. Check the response that best describes your rating of the Credit Union employees in each category. Please check only one response for each statement.

3. The Credit Union employees are courteous.

Strongly disagree	Disagree	Uncertain	Agree	Strongly agree
( )	( )	( )	( )	( )

4. The Credit Union employees are helpful.

Strongly disagree	Disagree	Uncertain	Agree	Strongly agree
( )	( )	( )	( )	( )

5. The Credit Union employees are professional.

Strongly disagree	Disagree	Uncertain	Agree	Strongly agree
( )	( )	( )	( )	( )

6. The Credit Union employees are always available.

Strongly disagree	Disagree	Uncertain	Agree	Strongly agree
( )	( )	( )	( )	( )

7. What is your opinion about the rates the Credit Union is paying on its share (members/savings) accounts?
   A. Very high _____   B. High _____   C. Average _____
   D. Low _____   E. Very low _____   F. No opinion _____

8. What is your opinion about the rates the Credit Union is charging its members to borrow funds?
   A. Very high _____   B. High _____   C. Average _____
   D. Low _____   E. Very low _____   F. No opinion _____

9. How often do you receive a financial statement of your account activity?

Too often	Very often	About right	Not often enough	Never
( )	( )	( )	( )	( )

10. How would you rate the accuracy of your statements?

Excellent	Good	Fair	Poor
( )	( )	( )	( )

11. Are they easy to understand?
    Yes ( )   No ( )

12. Do you feel that the Credit Union maintains your account information in a confidential manner?
    Yes ( )   No ( )

The next set of questions is important in determining how effective the Credit Union has been in communicating its different services to the members. Please answer each question honestly—remember, there are no right or wrong answers.

Circle the response that best describes your awareness of the services offered by the Credit Union.

Circle 1—If you were aware of the service and have used it.
Circle 2—If you were aware of the service but have not used it.
Circle 3—If you did not know this service was offered by the Credit Union.

		Aware and Have Used	Aware but Have Not Used	Unaware of Service
13.	Regular share accounts	1	2	3
14.	Special subaccounts	1	2	3
15.	Christmas club accounts	1	2	3
16.	Individual retirement accounts	1	2	3
17.	Mastercard credit cards	1	2	3
18.	Signature loans	1	2	3
19.	New-car loans	1	2	3
20.	Late model car loans	1	2	3
21.	Older model car loans	1	2	3
22.	Household goods/appliance loans	1	2	3
23.	Recreational loans	1	2	3
24.	Share collateralized loans	1	2	3
25.	IRA loans	1	2	3
26.	Line of credit loans	1	2	3

27. Do you currently have a loan with the Credit Union?
    Yes ( )   No ( )

28. During the past year, have you borrowed money from a bank or other lending source other than the Credit Union?
    Yes ( )   No ( )
    If no, go to Question 30.

29. Why did you go to a source other than the Credit Union?
    _____ My loan application at the Credit Union was not approved.
    _____ The Credit Union did not offer this type of credit.
    _____ I found better loan rates elsewhere.
    _____ I have an established credit line elsewhere.
    _____ I prefer to use a local financial institution.
    _____ Other: _____
    _____

(continued)

For Statements 30 through 34, check the response that best describes your feelings about the statements. Check only one response for each statement given.

30. The Credit Union's loan rates are lower than those offered by other institutions.

Strongly disagree	Disagree	Uncertain	Agree	Strongly agree
( )	( )	( )	( )	( )

31. The Credit Union personnel will keep my personal financial information confidential.

Strongly disagree	Disagree	Uncertain	Agree	Strongly agree
( )	( )	( )	( )	( )

32. The Credit Union is prompt in processing loan applications.

Strongly disagree	Disagree	Uncertain	Agree	Strongly agree
( )	( )	( )	( )	( )

33. The current financial services provided by the Credit Union meet the needs of its members.

Strongly disagree	Disagree	Uncertain	Agree	Strongly agree
( )	( )	( )	( )	( )

34. The loan applications used by the Credit Union are simple and easy to complete.

Strongly disagree	Disagree	Uncertain	Agree	Strongly agree
( )	( )	( )	( )	( )

35. Which of the services provided by the Credit Union do you like best?

36. Which of the services provided by the Credit Union do you like least?

37. Overall, how do you feel the Credit Union is being managed and operated?
    A. Excellent _____   B. Good _____   C. Average _____
    D. Poor _____   E. Very poor _____   F. No opinion _____

38. Do you live in the Headquarters area?
    Yes ( )   No ( )
    If yes, go to Question 40.

39. Do you feel the Credit Union meets your needs as well as those of members who live in the Headquarters area?
    Yes ( )   No ( )
    If no, please explain:
    _____
    _____

40. If you were managing the Credit Union, what changes would you make and what additional services, if any, would you provide?
    _____
    _____
    _____
    _____
    _____

I sincerely appreciate the time and effort you made in completing this questionnaire. Thank you for your help.

data, was performed by the supervisory committee chairperson. The following is a list of the (much appreciated) assistance received during the field procedures:

>Bob Perkins obtained a copy of the most currently available listing of the membership of the EFCU.

>The payroll department prepared mailing labels for all the members in the sample who were having withholding for the credit union made out of their payroll checks.

>The Credit Union clerks obtained the addresses and prepared mailing labels for all the remaining individuals selected in the sample.

>Administrative assistants helped in copying and collating the survey questionnaires and preparing them for mailing.

>Ron Walker mailed all of the survey questionnaires.

The survey data from the structured questions were coded based on classifications established by the researcher. The codes were input into a series of databases using an IBM personal computer and a statistical software package.

Of the 125 returned questionnaires, two were not included in the survey results. One of the questionnaires was returned without the first two pages attached, and the other questionnaire appeared to be deliberately falsified. Not only were all the responses of the falsified questionnaire at the extremes, but a number of noted contradictions existed as well.

ADDITIONAL INFORMATION

Several of the questions below require the use of a computerized database. Your instructor will provide information about the floppy disk if this material is part of the case assignment. Each variable name is coded by its question number. Q1 is the variable name for Question 1, "Are you a member of the Employees Federal Credit Union?" Q2 is the variable name for Question 2, and so on.

Questions

1. Evaluate the research objectives.
2. Evaluate the research design in the light of the stated research objectives.
3. Using the computerized database, obtain simple frequencies for the answers to each question (the answers to the open-ended questions are not included on the database).
4. Perform the appropriate cross-tabulations.
5. Perform the appropriate univariate and bivariate statistical tests after you develop hypotheses for these particular tests.

C A S E   **18**

University Van Pool

Oklahoma State University is a major university in the state of Oklahoma. Its main campus in Stillwater is located an equal distance (approximately 75 miles) from Oklahoma City and Tulsa, the

Source: This case was prepared by Clifford E. Young and William G. Zikmund to be used with the Edu-Stat system (copyright 1989).

state's two largest metropolitan areas. More than 20,000 students are enrolled in classes on the Stillwater campus.

It was suggested that because many OSU students commute from Oklahoma City (approximately 500) or Tulsa (approximately 700), a van-

CASE EXHIBIT 1 8 . 1

**Cost Association
with Van Pooling**

An example of a cost analysis on a per-trip basis for vans is presented below. This analysis assumes that a van can carry 15 people but on the average will be carrying 10 people ($\frac{2}{3}$ load factor) plus the driver. We also assume that we don't have to pay for the driver, i.e., he or she is a student and will drive instead of paying for the ride. Using the per-trip cost of the van, we figure that we would need to charge each person $4.50 per trip in order to break even.

Cost of van	$12,000.00		
Less trade-in	$ 4,000.00		
Net cost of van	$ 8,000.00		
Useful life of van		80,000 miles	
Net cost of van per mile			$ 0.10
Gasoline cost	$1.25/gal.		
Fuel efficiency of van		12.5 mpg	
Net cost of gasoline per mile			0.10
Insurance and maintenance per mile			0.10
Total cost of van per mile			$ 0.30
Number of miles per van per trip		150 miles	
Cost per van per trip			$45.00
Load factor estimate		10 people/van	
Cost per person per trip			$ 4.50

pooling system could be a viable operation. The basic concept was to have central locations in both Tulsa and Oklahoma City where students could board the van (or bus) and ride to the university campus. Students would be dropped off at the same location on the return trip. A commuter student would be the driver of the van, which would substantially reduce the cost of operating the service. Case Exhibit 18.1 provides additional information about the cost associated with operating this service.

THE SURVEY RESEARCH PROJECT

A telephone survey was conducted to determine how many OSU students were regular commuters and to estimate the demand for the commuting service. The questionnaire used in the study appears in Case Exhibit 18.2. The student directory served as a sampling frame. Initially, pages from the directory were randomly selected. For each page selected as a primary sampling unit, an interviewer was instructed to call every name that listed Tulsa or Oklahoma City as the student's address. The first question on the questionnaire determined if the student was actually commuting. This resulted in a sample size of 224 commuting students.

The data from the survey were edited and coded to be analyzed using the Edu-Stat computer program. The variables from the data set are listed in Case Exhibit 18.3.[1]

CASE EXHIBIT 18.2   **Research Questionnaire: Commuting Service to Oklahoma State University**

Hello, I'm _____ your name _____. We are conducting a survey to find out if it would be feasible for OSU to establish a van or bus commuting service for students commuting to school in Stillwater.

1. Do you commute to attend classes?   _____ Yes   _____ No

   If yes, continue with the interview.

   If no, terminate and try again.

2. How many times a week do you travel to Stillwater to attend classes?

   _____ times per week

3. How do you get to Stillwater? Drive your own car, pool with other students, or some other method?

   __1__ Drives own car

   __2__ Rides in pool

   __3__ Other

If student rides in a pool:

4. What percentage of the time are you the driver in your car pool?   _____%

5. What mileage does your car get on the road?   _____ mpg

6. What do you think is your total cost per month to commute to OSU? $_____

Two alternative methods available for providing a commuting service to OSU are providing a van or a bus. A bus would be similar to riding commercially in that it would depart early in the morning to be at school by 8:00 a.m. and would return after 12:00 noon. A second bus would depart so as to arrive by 12:30 p.m. and would return after 5:00 p.m. A licensed driver would be hired by the university to drive the bus. A van would have similar departure times but arrangements would be made so that the commuters would do the driving on a rotating basis.

I am going to make a number of statements about these possible methods of commuting and would like you to indicate your agreement or disagreement with each of the statements. When I give you the statement, I would like you to either strongly agree, agree, slightly agree, indicate no feeling, slightly disagree, disagree, or strongly disagree.

Go over this with the respondent to be sure he or she understands what you are trying to do.

7. The inconvenience of commuting by bus or van outweighs the advantages.

   __7__ SA __6__ A __5__ SA __4__ N __3__ SD __2__ D __1__ SD

8. I could use the time riding over to Stillwater to study.

   __7__ SA __6__ A __5__ SA __4__ N __3__ SD __2__ D __1__ SD

9. I would rather be able to come and go as I please.

   __7__ SA __6__ A __5__ SA __4__ N __3__ SD __2__ D __1__ SD

10. Having to wait for the van or bus coming home would take too much time.

   __7__ SA __6__ A __5__ SA __4__ N __3__ SD __2__ D __1__ SD

11. I don't like riding a bus because they are so uncomfortable.

   __7__ SA __6__ A __5__ SA __4__ N __3__ SD __2__ D __1__ SD

12. Riding a van would be better than riding a bus.

   __7__ SA __6__ A __5__ SA __4__ N __3__ SD __2__ D __1__ SD

13. If I were in a van pool, I would be willing to do some of the driving.

   __7__ SA __6__ A __5__ SA __4__ N __3__ SD __2__ D __1__ SD

14. Having to drive to the pickup point is too much of a bother.

   __7__ SA __6__ A __5__ SA __4__ N __3__ SD __2__ D __1__ SD

15. Driving myself is getting too expensive.

   __7__ SA __6__ A __5__ SA __4__ N __3__ SD __2__ D __1__ SD

(continued)

CASE EXHIBIT 18.2 *(continued)*

16. I would worry too much about the dependability of a van or bus.
   __7__ SA __6__ A __5__ SA __4__ N __3__ SD __2__ D __1__ SD

17. I could save money by taking a van or bus.
   __7__ SA __6__ A __5__ SA __4__ N __3__ SD __2__ D __1__ SD

18. If a bus were available, I would use it.
   __7__ SA __6__ A __5__ SA __4__ N __3__ SD __2__ D __1__ SD

19. If a van were available, I would use it.
   __7__ SA __6__ A __5__ SA __4__ N __3__ SD __2__ D __1__ SD

20. I don't like riding in a van because they are so uncomfortable.
   __7__ SA __6__ A __5__ SA __4__ N __3__ SD __2__ D __1__ SD

21. In a van, I would be concerned about the driving by others.
   __7__ SA __6__ A __5__ SA __4__ N __3__ SD __2__ D __1__ SD

22. Taking a van or bus is too much hassle.
   __7__ SA __6__ A __5__ SA __4__ N __3__ SD __2__ D __1__ SD

Finally, I have some questions about you as a student. This survey is stricly confidential and your name will never be used in any results.

23. What is your class status? __1__ Fresh __2__ Soph __3__ Jr __4__ Sr __5__ Grad

24. Do you consider yourself full or part time? __1__ Full __2__ Part

25. Are you also employed? __1__ Yes __2__ No
   If yes:

26. Full or part time? __1__ Full __2__ Part

27. Your age? _____

28. Sex __1__ Male __2__ Female (You should be able to figure that out.)

29. Are you married? __1__ Yes __2__ No

30. How are you financing your education?
   __1__ Own funds __2__ Parents __3__ Scholarship __4__ GI Bill __5__ Other

31. What percentage savings would you need to realize before you would be interested in riding a bus?
   _____% _____ Wouldn't ride a bus.

32. What percentage savings would you need to realize before you would be interested in riding a van?
   _____% _____ Wouldn't ride a van.

Thank you very much for your time in responding to this survey.

Questions

1. Evaluate the research design.
2. What variables in the available data set will be most important in solving the problem? Identify which of these are dependent variables and which are independent variables.
3. Using Edu-Stat (or another computer program), demonstrate that you can perform descriptive analyses such as calculation of frequency distributions and calculation of means.
4. Using cross-tabulation analysis, determine which market segment is most likely to use the van pool.
5. Is the van pool economically feasible in Tulsa? In Oklahoma City?

Notes

[1] In Edu-Stat a missing value is represented by a period.

CASE EXHIBIT 1 8 . 3   Variables in the Commuter Data Set

ID	Identification number	HASSLE	Van or bus too much hassle
CITY	1 = Tulsa, 2 = OKC	STATUS	1 = freshman, 5 = grad student
—	Question 1 not coded	FULLTIME	1 = full time, 2 = part time
FREQ	Frequency per week (Question 2)	EMPLOYED	1 = yes, 2 = no
METHOD	1 = own car, 2 = pool, 3 = other	EMPFULL	1 = full, 2 = part time employed
PDRIVE	% drive own car	AGE	Age
MILEAGE	Car mileage, mpg	SEX	1 = male, 2 = female
ESTCOST	Estimated cost per month	MARRIED	1 = yes, 2 = no
INCONV	Inconvenience	FINANCE	1 = own, 2 = parents, 3 = school, 4 = GI bill, 5 = other
STUDY	I could study	PSAVBUS	% savings bus
COMEGO	Come and go	RBUS	1 = wouldn't ride bus at all
TIME	Too much time	PSAVVAN	% savings van
BUSCOMF	Bus is uncomfortable	RVAN	1 = wouldn't ride van at all
VANBUS	Van better than bus	ASAVBUS[a]	Amount bus savings needed
DRIVEV	Would drive van	ASAVVAN	Amount van savings needed
PICKUP	Pickup is a bother	GASCOST	Computed gas cost
EXPENSE	Driving is expensive	DIFF	Estimate computed gas cost
DEPEND	Worry about dependability	COSTT	Cost per trip
SAVE	I could save money	BUSSAVT	Bus savings needed per trip
USEBUS	I would use a bus	VANSAVT	Van savings needed per trip
USEVAN	I would use a van	MAXBUS	Maximum price for bus
VANCOMF	Van is uncomfortable	MAXVAN	Maximum price for van
CONCERN	Concern about drivers	VRIDER	Van rider; 1 = yes, 2 = no

[a]Variables through RVAN are directly from the raw data taken from the questionnaire. The rest of the variables were calculated from the original variables as follows:

$$ASAVBUS = PSAVBUS \times ESTCOST$$
$$ASAVVAN = PSAVVAN \times ESTCOST$$
$$GASCOST = FREQ \times PDRIVE/100 \times 52/12 \times 150 \times 1.25/MILEAGE$$
$$DIFF = ESTCOST - GASCOST$$
$$COSTT^{b} = ESTCOST/(FREQ \times 52/12)$$
$$BUSSAVT = ASAVBUS/(FREQ \times 52/12)$$
$$VANSAVT = ASAVVAN/(FREQ \times 52/12)$$
$$MAXBUS = COSTT - BUSSAVT$$
$$MAXVAN = COSTT - VANSAVT$$
IF MAXVAN $>$ 4.5 THEN VRIDER = 1, ELSE IF MAXVAN $\neq$ .1 THEN VRIDER = 2

[b]GASCOST is an estimate of what the marginal cost of the trip to and from Stillwater to Tulsa or Oklahoma City would be for gasoline alone. It assumes a gasoline price of $1.25 per gallon and a 150-mile round trip (75 miles to the pickup location in the heart of each city).

Statistical Tables

Random Digits

37751	04998	66038	63480	98442	22245	83538	62351	74514	90497
50915	64152	82981	15796	27102	71635	34470	13608	26360	76285
99142	35021	01032	57907	80545	54112	15150	36856	03247	40392
70720	10033	25191	62358	03784	74377	88150	25567	87457	49512
18460	64947	32958	08752	96366	89092	23597	74308	00881	88976
65763	41133	60950	35372	06782	81451	78764	52645	19841	50083
83769	52570	60133	25211	87384	90182	84990	26400	39128	97043
58900	78420	98579	33665	10718	39342	46346	14401	13503	46525
54746	71115	78219	64314	11227	41702	54517	87676	14078	45317
56819	27340	07200	52663	57864	85159	15460	97564	29637	27742
34990	62122	38223	28526	37006	22774	46026	15981	87291	56946
02269	22795	87593	81830	95383	67823	20196	54850	46779	64519
43042	53600	45738	00261	31100	67239	02004	70698	53597	62617
92565	12211	06868	87786	59576	61382	33972	13161	47208	96604
67424	32620	60841	86848	85000	04835	48576	33884	10101	84129
04015	77148	09535	10743	97871	55919	45274	38304	93125	91847
85226	19763	46105	25289	26714	73253	85922	21785	42624	92741
03360	07457	75131	41209	50451	23472	07438	08375	29312	62264
72460	99682	27970	25632	34096	17656	12736	27476	21938	67305
66960	55780	71778	52629	51692	71442	36130	70425	39874	62035
14824	95631	00697	65462	24815	13930	02938	54619	28909	53950
34001	05618	41900	23303	19928	60755	61404	56947	91441	19299
77718	83830	29781	72917	10840	74182	08293	62588	99625	22088
60930	05091	35726	07414	49211	69586	20226	08274	28167	65279
94180	62151	08112	26646	07617	42954	22521	09395	43561	45692
81073	85543	47650	93830	07377	87995	35084	39386	93141	88309
18467	39689	60801	46828	38670	88243	89042	78452	08032	72566
60643	59399	79740	17295	50094	66436	92677	68345	24025	36489
73372	61697	85728	90779	13235	83114	70728	32093	74306	08325
18395	18482	83245	54942	51905	09534	70839	91073	42193	81199
07261	28720	71244	05064	84873	68020	39037	68981	00670	86291
61679	81529	83725	33269	45958	74265	87460	60525	42539	25605
11815	48679	00556	96871	39835	83055	84949	11681	51687	55896
99007	35050	86440	44280	20320	97527	28138	01088	49037	85430
06446	65608	79291	16624	06135	30622	56133	33998	32308	29434

(continued)

APPENDIX   Statistical Tables

TABLE 1

(continued)

37913	83900	49166	00249	53178	72307	72190	75931	77613	20172
89444	98195	46733	37201	71901	55023	54570	83126	09462	93979
12582	41940	36060	56756	07999	64138	06492	25815	19518	86938
50494	80008	64774	51382	08059	66448	16437	91579	39197	43798
78301	66128	12840	22254	15193	81210	95747	47344	33660	41707
79457	31686	94486	27386	41641	72199	67265	51794	81521	01556
49337	10475	49588	79338	32156	47732	29464	92835	09498	81902
92540	56528	21200	87462	08924	56993	57330	85069	10903	80904
17729	61914	74616	20433	59474	21270	96406	13090	94308	02072
24003	80475	19793	71578	52010	72216	15692	96689	80452	46312
16129	49245	21693	20946	60873	82451	32516	23823	30046	06870
05453	03060	83621	43443	17082	04401	15299	64642	73497	88426
67711	70526	46700	00171	55077	11440	95932	91116	17259	19645
76306	39287	31026	49379	30267	68885	98147	70311	43856	37376
81300	17782	76403	00972	12558	46140	19818	20440	83967	61036

TABLE 2

Area under the Normal Curve

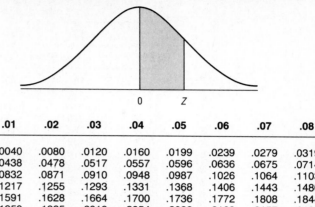

z	.00	.01	.02	.03	.04	.05	.06	.07	.08	.09
0.0	.0000	.0040	.0080	.0120	.0160	.0199	.0239	.0279	.0319	.0359
0.1	.0398	.0438	.0478	.0517	.0557	.0596	.0636	.0675	.0714	.0753
0.2	.0793	.0832	.0871	.0910	.0948	.0987	.1026	.1064	.1103	.1141
0.3	.1179	.1217	.1255	.1293	.1331	.1368	.1406	.1443	.1480	.1517
0.4	.1554	.1591	.1628	.1664	.1700	.1736	.1772	.1808	.1844	.1879
0.5	.1915	.1950	.1985	.2019	.2054	.2088	.2123	.2157	.2190	.2224
0.6	.2257	.2291	.2324	.2357	.2389	.2422	.2454	.2486	.2518	.2549
0.7	.2580	.2612	.2642	.2673	.2704	.2734	.2764	.2794	.2823	.2852
0.8	.2881	.2910	.2939	.2967	.2995	.3023	.3051	.3078	.3106	.3133
0.9	.3159	.3186	.3212	.3238	.3264	.3289	.3315	.3340	.3365	.3389
1.0	.3413	.3438	.3461	.3485	.3508	.3531	.3554	.3577	.3599	.3621
1.1	.3643	.3665	.3686	.3708	.3729	.3749	.3770	.3790	.3810	.3830
1.2	.3849	.3869	.3888	.3907	.3925	.3944	.3962	.3980	.3997	.4015
1.3	.4032	.4049	.4066	.4082	.4099	.4115	.4131	.4147	.4162	.4177
1.4	.4192	.4207	.4222	.4236	.4251	.4265	.4279	.4292	.4306	.4319
1.5	.4332	.4345	.4357	.4370	.4382	.4394	.4406	.4418	.4429	.4441
1.6	.4452	.4463	.4474	.4484	.4495	.4505	.4515	.4525	.4535	.4545
1.7	.4554	.4564	.4573	.4582	.4591	.4599	.4608	.4616	.4625	.4633
1.8	.4641	.4649	.4656	.4664	.4671	.4678	.4686	.4693	.4699	.4706
1.9	.4713	.4719	.4726	.4732	.4738	.4744	.4750	.4756	.4761	.4767
2.0	.4772	.4778	.4783	.4788	.4793	.4798	.4803	.4808	.4812	.4817
2.1	.4821	.4826	.4830	.4834	.4838	.4842	.4846	.4850	.4854	.4857
2.2	.4861	.4864	.4868	.4871	.4875	.4878	.4881	.4884	.4887	.4890
2.3	.4893	.4896	.4898	.4901	.4904	.4906	.4909	.4911	.4913	.4916
2.4	.4918	.4920	.4922	.4925	.4927	.4929	.4931	.4932	.4934	.4936
2.5	.4938	.4940	.4941	.4943	.4945	.4946	.4948	.4949	.4951	.4952
2.6	.4953	.4955	.4956	.4957	.4959	.4960	.4961	.4962	.4963	.4964
2.7	.4965	.4966	.4967	.4968	.4969	.4970	.4971	.4972	.4973	.4974
2.8	.4974	.4975	.4976	.4977	.4977	.4978	.4979	.4979	.4980	.4981
2.9	.4981	.4982	.4982	.4983	.4984	.4984	.4985	.4985	.4986	.4986
3.0	.49865	.4987	.4987	.4988	.4988	.4989	.4989	.4989	.4990	.4990
4.0	.49997									

Source: Chaiho Kim, *Statistical Analysis for Induction and Decision.* Copyright © 1973 by The Dryden Press, a division of Holt, Rinehart and Winston, Inc. Reprinted by permission of Holt, Rinehart and Winston.

TABLE 3

Distribution of t for Given Probability Levels

	Level of Significance for One-Tailed Test					
	.10	.05	.025	.01	.005	.0005
	Level of Significance for Two-Tailed Test					
d.f.	.20	.10	.05	.02	.01	.001
1	3.078	6.314	12.706	31.821	63.657	636.619
2	1.886	2.920	4.303	6.965	9.925	31.598
3	1.638	2.353	3.182	4.541	5.841	12.941
4	1.533	2.132	2.776	3.747	4.604	8.610
5	1.476	2.015	2.571	3.365	4.032	6.859
6	1.440	1.943	2.447	3.143	3.707	5.959
7	1.415	1.895	2.365	2.998	3.499	5.405
8	1.397	1.860	2.306	2.896	3.355	5.041
9	1.383	1.833	2.262	2.821	3.250	4.781
10	1.372	1.812	2.228	2.764	3.169	4.587
11	1.363	1.796	2.201	2.718	3.106	4.437
12	1.356	1.782	2.179	2.681	3.055	4.318
13	1.350	1.771	2.160	2.650	3.012	4.221
14	1.345	1.761	2.145	2.624	2.977	4.140
15	1.341	1.753	2.131	2.602	2.947	4.073
16	1.337	1.746	2.120	2.583	2.921	4.015
17	1.333	1.740	2.110	2.567	2.898	3.965
18	1.330	1.734	2.101	2.552	2.878	3.992
19	1.328	1.729	2.093	2.539	2.861	3.883
20	1.325	1.725	2.086	2.528	2.845	3.850
21	1.323	1.721	2.080	2.518	2.831	3.819
22	1.321	1.717	2.074	2.508	2.819	3.792
23	1.319	1.714	2.069	2.500	2.807	3.767
24	1.318	1.711	2.064	2.492	2.797	3.745
25	1.316	1.708	2.060	2.485	2.787	3.725
26	1.315	1.706	2.056	2.479	2.779	3.707
27	1.314	1.703	2.052	2.473	2.771	3.690
28	1.313	1.701	2.048	2.467	2.763	3.674
29	1.311	1.699	2.045	2.462	2.756	3.659
30	1.310	1.697	2.042	2.457	2.750	3.646
40	1.303	1.684	2.021	2.423	2.704	3.551
60	1.296	1.671	2.000	2.390	2.660	3.460
120	1.289	1.658	1.980	2.358	2.617	3.373
∞	1.282	1.645	1.960	2.326	2.576	3.291

Source: Abridged from Table III of R. A. Fisher and F. Yates. *Statistical Tables for Biological, Agricultural, and Medical Research*, published by Longman Group, Ltd., London (previously published by Oliver & Boyd, Ltd., Edinburgh). Abridged with the permission of the publishers.

T A B L E   4

Chi-Square Distribution

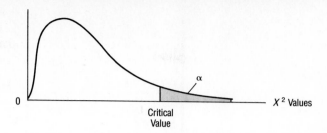

Degrees of Freedom (d.f.)	Area in Shaded Right Tail (α)		
	.10	.05	.01
1	2.706	3.841	6.635
2	4.605	5.991	9.210
3	6.251	7.815	11.345
4	7.779	9.488	13.277
5	9.236	11.070	15.086
6	10.645	12.592	16.812
7	12.017	14.067	18.475
8	13.362	15.507	20.090
9	14.684	16.919	21.666
10	15.987	18.307	23.209
11	17.275	19.675	24.725
12	18.549	21.026	26.217
13	19.812	22.362	27.688
14	21.064	23.685	29.141
15	22.307	24.996	30.578
16	23.542	26.296	32.000
17	24.769	27.587	33.409
18	25.989	28.869	34.805
19	27.204	30.144	36.191
20	28.412	31.410	37.566
21	29.615	32.671	38.932
22	30.813	33.924	40.289
23	32.007	35.172	41.638
24	33.196	36.415	42.980
25	34.382	37.652	44.314
26	35.563	38.885	45.642
27	36.741	40.113	46.963
28	37.916	41.337	48.278
29	39.087	42.557	49.588
30	40.256	43.773	50.892

Example of how to use this table: In a chi-square distribution with 6 degrees of freedom (d.f.), the area to the right of a critical value of 12.592—i.e., the α area—is 0.05.

Source: Abridged from Table IV of R. A. Fisher and F. Yates, *Statistical Tables for Biological, Agricultural, and Medical Research,* published by Longman Group, Ltd., London (previously published by Oliver & Boyd Ltd., Edinburgh). Abridged with the permission of the publishers.

T A B L E   5   Critical Values of F_{v_1, v_2} for $\alpha = .05$

v_1 = Degrees of Freedom for Numerator

v_2 = Degrees of Freedom for Denominator

	1	2	3	4	5	6	7	8	9	10	12	15	20	24	30	40	60	120	—
1	161	200	216	225	230	234	237	239	241	242	244	246	248	249	250	251	252	253	254
2	18.5	19.0	19.2	19.2	19.3	19.3	19.4	19.4	19.4	19.4	19.4	19.4	19.4	19.5	19.5	19.5	19.5	19.5	19.5
3	10.1	9.55	9.28	9.12	9.01	8.94	8.89	8.85	8.81	8.79	8.74	8.70	8.66	8.64	8.62	8.59	8.57	8.55	8.53
4	7.71	6.94	6.59	6.39	6.26	6.16	6.09	6.04	6.00	5.96	5.91	5.86	5.80	5.77	5.75	5.72	5.69	5.66	5.63
5	6.61	5.79	5.41	5.19	5.05	4.95	4.88	4.82	4.77	4.74	4.68	4.62	4.56	4.53	4.50	4.46	4.43	4.40	4.37
6	5.99	5.14	4.76	4.53	4.39	4.28	4.21	4.15	4.10	4.06	4.00	3.94	3.87	3.84	3.81	3.77	3.74	3.70	3.67
7	5.59	4.74	4.35	4.12	3.97	3.87	3.79	3.73	3.68	3.64	3.57	3.51	3.44	3.41	3.38	3.34	3.30	3.27	3.23
8	5.32	4.46	4.07	3.84	3.69	3.58	3.50	3.44	3.39	3.35	3.28	3.22	3.15	3.12	3.08	3.04	3.01	2.97	2.93
9	5.12	4.26	3.86	3.63	3.48	3.37	3.29	3.23	3.18	3.14	3.07	3.01	2.94	2.90	2.86	2.83	2.79	2.75	2.71
10	4.96	4.10	3.71	3.48	3.33	3.22	3.14	3.07	3.02	2.98	2.91	2.85	2.77	2.74	2.70	2.66	2.62	2.58	2.54
11	4.84	3.98	3.59	3.36	3.20	3.09	3.01	2.95	2.90	2.85	2.79	2.72	2.65	2.61	2.57	2.53	2.49	2.45	2.40
12	4.75	3.89	3.49	3.26	3.11	3.00	2.91	2.85	2.80	2.75	2.69	2.62	2.54	2.51	2.47	2.43	2.38	2.34	2.30
13	4.67	3.81	3.41	3.18	3.03	2.92	2.83	2.77	2.71	2.67	2.60	2.53	2.46	2.42	2.38	2.34	2.30	2.25	2.21
14	4.60	3.74	3.34	3.11	2.96	2.85	2.76	2.70	2.65	2.60	2.53	2.46	2.39	2.35	2.31	2.27	2.22	2.18	2.13
15	4.54	3.68	3.29	3.06	2.90	2.79	2.71	2.64	2.59	2.54	2.48	2.40	2.33	2.29	2.25	2.20	2.16	2.11	2.07

16	4.49	3.63	3.24	3.01	2.85	2.74	2.66	2.59	2.54	2.49	2.42	2.35	2.28	2.24	2.19	2.15	2.11	2.06	2.01
17	4.45	3.59	3.20	2.96	2.81	2.70	2.61	2.55	2.49	2.45	2.38	2.31	2.23	2.19	2.15	2.10	2.06	2.01	1.96
18	4.41	3.55	3.16	2.93	2.77	2.66	2.58	2.51	2.46	2.41	2.34	2.27	2.19	2.15	2.11	2.06	2.02	1.97	1.92
19	4.38	3.52	3.13	2.90	2.74	2.63	2.54	2.48	2.42	2.38	2.31	2.23	2.16	2.11	2.07	2.03	1.98	1.93	1.88
20	4.35	3.49	3.10	2.87	2.71	2.60	2.51	2.45	2.39	2.35	2.28	2.20	2.12	2.08	2.04	1.99	1.95	1.90	1.84
21	4.32	3.47	3.07	2.84	2.68	2.57	2.49	2.42	2.37	2.32	2.25	2.18	2.10	2.05	2.01	1.96	1.92	1.87	1.81
22	4.30	3.44	3.05	2.82	2.66	2.55	2.46	2.40	2.34	2.30	2.23	2.15	2.07	2.03	1.98	1.94	1.89	1.84	1.78
23	4.28	3.42	3.03	2.80	2.64	2.53	2.44	2.37	2.32	2.27	2.20	2.13	2.05	2.01	1.96	1.91	1.86	1.81	1.76
24	4.26	3.40	3.01	2.78	2.62	2.51	2.42	2.36	2.30	2.25	2.18	2.11	2.03	1.98	1.94	1.89	1.84	1.79	1.73
25	4.24	3.39	2.99	2.76	2.60	2.49	2.40	2.34	2.28	2.24	2.16	2.09	2.01	1.96	1.92	1.87	1.82	1.77	1.71
30	4.17	3.32	2.92	2.69	2.53	2.42	2.33	2.27	2.21	2.16	2.09	2.01	1.93	1.89	1.84	1.79	1.74	1.68	1.62
40	4.08	3.23	2.84	2.61	2.45	2.34	2.25	2.18	2.12	2.08	2.00	1.92	1.84	1.79	1.74	1.69	1.64	1.58	1.51
60	4.00	3.15	2.76	2.53	2.37	2.25	2.17	2.10	2.04	1.99	1.92	1.84	1.75	1.70	1.65	1.59	1.53	1.47	1.39
120	3.92	3.07	2.68	2.45	2.29	2.18	2.09	2.02	1.96	1.91	1.83	1.75	1.66	1.61	1.55	1.50	1.43	1.35	1.25
—	3.84	3.00	2.60	2.37	2.21	2.10	2.01	1.94	1.88	1.83	1.75	1.67	1.57	1.52	1.46	1.39	1.32	1.22	1.00

Source: Maxine Merrington and Catherine M. Thompson, "Tables of the Percentage Points of the Inverted F-Distribution," *Biometrika* 33 (1943): 73–78. Reprinted with the permission of the Biometrika Trustees.

T A B L E   6   Critical Values of F_{v_1, v_2} for $\alpha = .01$

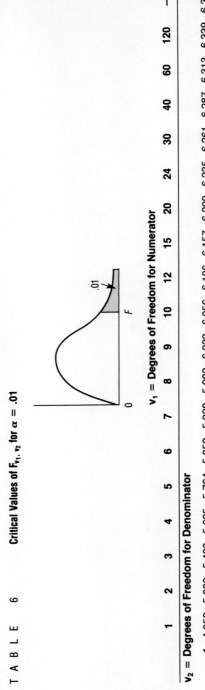

v_1 = Degrees of Freedom for Numerator

v_2 = Degrees of Freedom for Denominator

	1	2	3	4	5	6	7	8	9	10	12	15	20	24	30	40	60	120	—
1	4,052	5,000	5,403	5,625	5,764	5,859	5,928	5,982	6,023	6,056	6,106	6,157	6,209	6,235	6,261	6,287	6,313	6,339	6,366
2	98.5	99.0	99.2	99.2	99.3	99.3	99.4	99.4	99.4	99.4	99.4	99.4	99.4	99.5	99.5	99.5	99.5	99.5	99.5
3	34.1	30.8	29.5	28.7	28.2	27.9	27.7	27.5	27.3	27.2	27.1	26.9	26.7	26.6	26.5	26.4	26.3	26.2	26.1
4	21.2	18.0	16.7	16.0	15.5	15.2	15.0	14.8	14.7	14.5	14.4	14.2	14.0	13.9	13.8	13.7	13.7	13.6	13.5
5	16.3	13.3	12.1	11.4	11.0	10.7	10.5	10.3	10.2	10.1	9.89	9.72	9.55	9.47	9.38	9.29	9.20	9.11	9.02
6	13.7	10.9	9.78	9.15	8.75	8.47	8.26	8.10	7.98	7.87	7.72	7.56	7.40	7.31	7.23	7.14	7.06	6.97	6.88
7	12.2	9.55	8.45	7.85	7.46	7.19	6.99	6.84	6.72	6.62	6.47	6.31	6.16	6.07	5.99	5.91	5.82	5.74	5.65
8	11.3	8.65	7.59	7.01	6.63	6.37	6.18	6.03	5.91	5.81	5.67	5.52	5.36	5.28	5.20	5.12	5.03	4.95	4.86
9	10.6	8.02	6.99	6.42	6.06	5.80	5.61	5.47	5.35	5.26	5.11	4.96	4.81	4.73	4.65	4.57	4.48	4.40	4.31
10	10.0	7.56	6.55	5.99	5.64	5.39	5.20	5.06	4.94	4.85	4.71	4.56	4.41	4.33	4.25	4.17	4.08	4.00	3.91
11	9.65	7.21	6.22	5.67	5.32	5.07	4.89	4.74	4.63	4.54	4.40	4.25	4.10	4.02	3.94	3.86	3.78	3.69	3.60
12	9.33	6.93	5.95	5.41	5.06	4.82	4.64	4.50	4.39	4.30	4.16	4.01	3.86	3.78	3.70	3.62	3.54	3.45	3.36
13	9.07	6.70	5.74	5.21	4.86	4.62	4.44	4.30	4.19	4.10	3.96	3.82	3.66	3.59	3.51	3.43	3.34	3.25	3.17
14	8.86	6.51	5.56	5.04	4.70	4.46	4.28	4.14	4.03	3.94	3.80	3.66	3.51	3.43	3.35	3.27	3.18	3.09	3.00
15	8.68	6.36	5.42	4.89	4.56	4.32	4.14	4.00	3.89	3.80	3.67	3.52	3.37	3.29	3.21	3.13	3.05	2.96	2.87

16	8.53	6.23	5.29	4.77	4.44	4.20	4.03	3.89	3.78	3.69	3.55	3.41	3.26	3.18	3.10	3.02	2.93	2.84	2.75
17	8.40	6.11	5.19	4.67	4.34	4.10	3.93	3.79	3.68	3.59	3.46	3.31	3.16	3.08	3.00	2.92	2.83	2.75	2.65
18	8.29	6.01	5.09	4.58	4.25	4.01	3.84	3.71	3.60	3.51	3.37	3.23	3.08	3.00	2.92	2.84	2.75	2.66	2.57
19	8.19	5.93	5.01	4.50	4.17	3.94	3.77	3.63	3.52	3.43	3.30	3.15	3.00	2.92	2.84	2.76	2.67	2.58	2.49
20	8.10	5.85	4.94	4.43	4.10	3.87	3.70	3.56	3.46	3.37	3.23	3.09	2.94	2.86	2.78	2.69	2.61	2.52	2.42
21	8.02	5.78	4.87	4.37	4.04	3.81	3.64	3.51	3.40	3.31	3.17	3.03	2.88	2.80	2.72	2.64	2.55	2.46	2.36
22	7.96	5.72	4.82	4.31	3.99	3.76	3.59	3.45	3.35	3.26	3.12	2.98	2.83	2.75	2.67	2.58	2.50	2.40	2.31
23	7.88	5.66	4.76	4.26	3.94	3.71	3.54	3.41	3.30	3.21	3.07	2.93	2.78	2.70	2.62	2.54	2.45	2.35	2.26
24	7.82	5.61	4.72	4.22	3.90	3.67	3.50	3.36	3.26	3.17	3.03	2.89	2.74	2.66	2.58	2.49	2.40	2.31	2.21
25	7.77	5.57	4.68	4.18	3.86	3.63	3.46	3.32	3.22	3.13	2.99	2.85	2.70	2.62	2.53	2.45	2.36	2.27	2.17
30	7.58	5.39	4.51	4.02	3.70	3.47	3.30	3.17	3.07	2.98	2.84	2.70	2.55	2.47	2.39	2.30	2.21	2.11	2.01
40	7.31	5.18	4.31	3.83	3.51	3.29	3.12	2.99	2.89	2.80	2.66	2.52	2.37	2.29	2.20	2.11	2.02	1.92	1.80
60	7.08	4.98	4.13	3.65	3.34	3.12	2.95	2.82	2.72	2.63	2.50	2.35	2.20	2.12	2.03	1.94	1.84	1.73	1.60
120	6.85	4.79	3.95	3.48	3.17	2.96	2.79	2.66	2.56	2.47	2.34	2.19	2.03	1.95	1.86	1.76	1.66	1.53	1.38
—	6.63	4.61	3.78	3.32	3.02	2.80	2.64	2.51	2.41	2.32	2.18	2.04	1.88	1.79	1.70	1.59	1.47	1.32	1.00

Source: Maxine Merrington and Catherine M. Thompson, "Tables of the Percentage Points of the Inverted F-Distribution," *Biometrica* 33 (1943): 73–78. Reprinted with the permission of the Biometrica Trustees.

TABLE 7

Critical Values of the Pearson Correlation Coefficient

	Level of Significance for One-Tailed Test			
	.05	.025	.01	.005
	Level of Significance for Two-Tailed Test			
d.f.	.10	.05	.02	.01
1	.988	.997	.9995	.9999
2	.900	.950	.980	.990
3	.805	.878	.934	.959
4	.729	.811	.882	.917
5	.669	.754	.833	.874
6	.622	.707	.789	.834
7	.582	.666	.750	.798
8	.549	.632	.716	.765
9	.521	.602	.685	.735
10	.497	.576	.658	.708
11	.576	.553	.634	.684
12	.458	.532	.612	.661
13	.441	.514	.592	.641
14	.426	.497	.574	.623
15	.412	.482	.558	.606
16	.400	.468	.542	.590
17	.389	.456	.528	.575
18	.378	.444	.516	.561
19	.369	.433	.503	.549
20	.360	.423	.492	.537
21	.352	.413	.482	.526
22	.344	.404	.472	.515
23	.337	.396	.462	.505
24	.330	.388	.453	.496
25	.323	.381	.445	.487
26	.317	.374	.437	.479
27	.311	.367	.430	.471
28	.306	.361	.423	.463
29	.301	.355	.416	.486
30	.296	.349	.409	.449
35	.275	.325	.381	.418
40	.257	.304	.358	.393
45	.243	.288	.338	.372
50	.231	.273	.322	.354
60	.211	.250	.295	.325
70	.195	.232	.274	.303
80	.183	.217	.256	.283
90	.173	.205	.242	.267
100	.164	.195	.230	.254

Source: Abridged from Table IV of R. A. Fisher and F. Yates, *Statistical Tables for Biological, Agricultural, and Medical Research*, published by Longman Group, Ltd., London (previously published by Oliver & Boyd, Ltd., Edinburgh). Abridged with the permission of the publishers.

T A B L E   8

**Critical Values of T in the
Wilcoxon Matched-Pairs,
Signed-Ranks Test**

	Level of Significance for Two-Tailed Test		
N	**.05**	**.02**	**.01**
6	1	—	—
7	2	0	—
8	4	2	0
9	6	3	2
10	8	5	3
11	11	7	5
12	14	10	7
13	17	13	10
14	21	16	13
15	25	20	16
16	30	24	19
17	35	28	23
18	40	33	28
19	46	38	32
20	52	43	37
21	59	49	43
22	66	56	49
23	73	62	55
24	81	69	61
25	90	77	68

Adapted from Table 2 of Frank Wilcoxon and Roberta A. Wilcox, 1964. *Some Rapid Approximate Statistical Procedures.* New York: American Cyanamid Company, p. 28.

Glossary of Frequently Used Symbols

Greek Letters

α **(alpha)**   level of significance or probability of a Type I error

β **(beta)**   probability of a Type II error or the slope of the regression line

μ **(mu)**   population mean

ρ **(rho)**   population Pearson correlation coefficient

Σ **(summation)**   take the sum of

π **(pi)**   population proportion

σ **(sigma)**   population standard deviation

χ^2 chi-square statistic

English Letters

d.f.   number of degrees of freedom

F   F-statistic

n   sample size

p   sample proportion

Pr ( )   probability of the outcome in the parentheses

r   sample Pearson correlation coefficient

$\mathbf{r}^2$ coefficient of determination (squared correlation coefficient)

S   sample standard deviation (inferential statistics)

$\mathbf{S}_{\bar{X}}$ estimated standard error of the mean

$\mathbf{S}_p$ estimated standard error of the proportion

$\mathbf{S}^2$ sample variance (inferential statistics)

t   t-statistic

X   a variable or any unspecified observation

$\bar{\mathbf{X}}$ sample mean

Y   any unspecified observation on a second variable, usually the dependent variable

$\hat{\mathbf{Y}}$ predicted score

Z   standardized score (descriptive statistics) or Z-statistic

Glossary of Terms

Abstract level In theory development, the level of knowledge expressing a concept that exists only as an idea or a quality apart from an object.

Acquiescence bias A category of response bias in which individuals have a tendency to agree with all questions or to indicate a positive connotation.

Administrative error An error caused by the improper administration or execution of a research task.

Advocacy research Research undertaken to support a specific claim in a legal action.

Affective component The component of attitude that reflects an individual's general feelings or emotions toward an object.

Alternative hypothesis A statement indicating the opposite of the null hypothesis.

Analysis of dependence A collective term to describe any multivariate statistical technique that attempts to explain or predict the dependent variable on the basis of two or more independent variables.

Analysis of interdependence A collective term to describe any multivariate statistical technique that attempts to give meaning to a set of variables to seek to group things together.

Analysis of variance (ANOVA) Analysis of the effects of one treatment variable on an interval-scaled or ratio-scaled dependent variable; a technique to determine if statistically significant differences of means occur between two or more groups.

Analytical models system A decision support subsystem that contains statistical software systems, spreadsheet software, and decision model banks that combine and restructure databases, diagnose relationships, estimate variables, and otherwise analyze the data within the system.

Applied research Research undertaken to answer questions about specific problems or to make decisions about a particular course of action or policy decision.

Area sample A cluster sample in which the primary sampling unit is a geographic area.

Attitude An enduring disposition to consistently respond in a given manner to various aspects of the world; composed of affective, cognitive, and behavioral components.

Attitude rating scale Measures used to rate attitudes, e.g., the Likert scale, semantic differential, and Stapel scale.

Attribute A single characteristic or fundamental feature pertaining to an object, person, situation, or issue.

Auspices bias Bias in the responses of subjects caused by the respondents being influenced by the organization conducting the study.

Automatic interaction detection (ID) A clustering method used to investigate the interaction of a large set of independent variables; a method of breaking a large heterogeneous group into various homogeneous subgroups.

Average deviation A measure of dispersion that is computed by calculating the deviation score of each observation value, summing up each deviation score, and dividing by the sample size.

Backward linkage A term implying that the late stages of the research process will have an influence on the early stages.

Balanced rating scale A fixed-alternative rating scale that has an equal number of positive and negative categories; a neutral or indifference point is at the center of the scale.

Bar chart A graphic aid that shows changes in a variable at discrete intervals.

Base (base number) The number of respondents or observations that indicate a total; used as a basis for computing percentages in each column or row in a cross-tabulation table.

Basic experimental design An experimental design in which a single independent variable is manipulated in order to observe its effect on another single dependent variable.

Basic (pure) research Research that is intended to expand the boundaries of knowledge itself; conducted to verify the acceptability of a given theory.

Behavioral component The component of attitude that reflects buying intentions and behavioral expectations; reflects a predisposition to action.

Behavioral differential An instrument developed to measure the behavioral intentions of subjects toward any object or category of objects.

Between-group variance Variation of scores between groups due either to the manipulation of an independent variable or to characteristics of the independent variable.

Bivariate data analysis Data analysis and hypothesis testing when the investigation concerns simultaneous investigation of two variables; test of differences or measures of association between two variables at a time.

Bivariate linear regression A measure of linear association that investigates a straight-line relationship of the type $Y = a + \beta X$, where Y is the dependent variable, X is the independent variable, and a and β are two constants to be estimated.

Bivariate statistics Tests of differences or measures of association between two variables at a time.

Blinding A technique used to control subjects' knowledge of whether or not they have been given a particular experimental treatment.

Briefing session A training session to ensure that all interviewers are provided with common information.

Business research The systematic and objective process of gathering, recording, and analyzing data for aid in making business decisions.

Callback An attempt to recontact an individual selected for the sample.

Canonical correlation analysis A technique used to determine the degree of linear association between two sets of variables, each consisting of several variables.

Case study method An exploratory research technique that intensively investigates one or a few situations similar to the researcher's problem situation.

Categorical variable Any variable that has a limited number of distinct values.

Category scale An attitude scale consisting of several response categories to provide the respondent with alternative ratings.

Causal research Research conducted to identify cause-and-effect relationships among variables where the research problem has already been narrowly defined.

Cell Section of a table representing a specific combination of two variables or a specific value of a variable.

Census An investigation of all the individual elements making up a population.

Central-limit theorem A proposition stating that as a sample size increases, the distribution of sample means of size n, randomly selected, approaches a normal distribution.

Central location interviewing Telephone interviews conducted from a central location; it allows effective supervision and control of the quality of interviewing.

Chart A graphic aid used to translate numerical information into visual form so that relationships may be easily understood.

Checklist question A type of fixed-alternative question that allows the respondent to provide multiple answers to a single question.

Chi-square (χ^2) test A test that statistically determines significance in the analysis of frequency distribution.

Choice technique A measurement task that identifies preferences by requiring respondents to choose between two or more alternatives.

Classificatory variable An independent variable representing some classifiable or qualitative aspect of management strategy. See also *Categorical variable*.

Cluster analysis An analysis that classifies individuals or objects into a small number of mutually exclusive groups, ensuring that there will be as much likeness within groups and as much difference among groups as possible.

Cluster sampling An economically efficient sampling technique in which the primary sampling unit is not the individual element in the population but a large cluster of elements.

Code A rule used for interpreting, classifying, and recording data in the coding processes; the actual numerical or other character symbol.

Code book A book identifying each variable in a study and its position on the disk, tape, or other input medium. The book is used to identify a variable's description, code name, and field.

Code of ethics A statement of principles and operating procedures for ethical practice.

Coding The process of identifying and classifying each answer with a numerical score or other character symbol.

Coding sheet A ruled sheet of paper used to transfer data from questionnaires or data collection forms after data have been collected.

Coefficient of correlation A statistical measure of the covariation or association between two variables. There are several correlation techniques that may provide information on whether two or more variables are interrelated or associated.

Coefficient of determination (r^2) A measure of that portion of the total variance of a variable that is accounted for by knowing the value of another variable.

Coefficient of multiple determination In multiple regression, the percentage of the variance in the dependent variable that is explained by the variation in the independent variables.

Cognitive component The component of attitude that represents one's awareness of and knowledge about an object.

Cohort effect A change in the dependent variable resulting from members of one experimental condition experiencing historical situations different from those of members of other experimental conditions.

Communality In factor analysis, a measure of the percentage of a variable's variation that is explained by the factors.

Communication process The process by which one person or source sends a message to an audience or receiver and then receives feedback about the message.

Comparative rating scale Any measure of attitudes that asks respondents to rate a concept in comparison with a benchmark explicitly used as a frame of reference.

Completely randomized design An experimental design that uses a random process to assign experimental units to treatments in order to investigate the effects of a single independent variable.

Compromise design An approximation of an experimental design; such a design may fall short of the requirements of random assignment of subjects or treatments to groups.

Computer-assisted telephone interviewing (CATI) A type of telephone interview in which the interviewer reads questions from a

computer screen and enters the respondent's answers directly into a computer.

Computer interactive survey A survey in which the respondent completes a self-administered questionnaire displayed on the monitor of a microcomputer. Respondents interact directly with a computer programmed to ask questions in a sequence determined by respondents' previous answers.

Computer mapping The portrayal of demographic data on two- or three-dimensional maps generated by a computer.

Computer voice-activated telephone interview A form of computer-assisted interviewing in which a voice-synthesized module enables the sponsor to register a caller's single-word response on a tape.

Concept A generalized idea about a class of objects; an abstraction of reality that is the basic unit for theory development.

Concept testing A form of research that tests some sort of stimulus as a proxy for a new or revised program, product, or service.

Conceptual definition A verbal explanation of the meaning of a concept. It defines the domain of the concept, and it may explain what the concept is not.

Concomitant variation The occurrence of two phenomena or events varying together.

Concurrent validity A classification of criterion validity whereby a new measure correlates with a criterion measure taken at the same time.

Confidence interval A specified range of numbers within which a population mean should lie; the set of acceptable hypotheses or the level of probability associated with an interval estimate.

Confidence level A percentage or decimal value that tells how confident a researcher can be about being correct. It states the long-run percentage of confidence intervals, including the true population mean.

Constancy of conditions A procedure in which subjects in experimental groups are exposed to situations identical except for differing conditions of the independent variable.

Constant error An error that occurs in the same experimental condition every time the basic experiment is repeated.

Constant-sum scale A measure of attitudes in which respondents are asked to divide a constant sum to indicate the relative importance of attributes.

Construct validity The ability of a measure to confirm a network of related hypotheses generated from a theory based on the concepts.

Consumer panel A sample of individuals or households that records their attitudes, behavior, or purchasing habits in a diary over time.

Content analysis A research technique for the objective, systematic, and quantitative description of the manifest content of communication.

Contingency table The results of a cross-tabulation of two variables, such as survey questions.

Continuous variable Any variable that has an infinite number of values.

Contrived observation Observation in which the investigator creates an artificial environment in order to test a hypothesis.

Control group A group of individuals who are exposed to the control condition in an experiment; subjects not exposed to the experimental treatment.

Convenience sampling The sampling procedure used to obtain those units or people most conveniently available.

Correlation coefficient A statistical measure of the covariation or association between two variables.

Correlation matrix The standard form of reporting correlational results.

Counterbiasing statement An introductory statement or preface to a question that reduces a respondent's reluctance to answer potentially embarrassing questions.

Cover letter A letter that accompanies the questionnaire in a mail survey. It generally has the purpose of inducing the reader to complete and return the questionnaire.

Criterion validity The ability of some measure to correlate with other measures of the same construct.

Critical values The values that lie exactly on the boundary of the region of rejection.

Cross-checks Comparison of data from one organization with data from another source.

Cross-sectional study A study in which various segments of a population are sampled at a single point in time.

Cross-tabulation A technique organizing data by groups, categories, or classes, thus facilitating comparisons; a joint frequency distribution of observations on two or more sets of variables.

Cumulative percentage A percentage (or percentage distribution) that has increased by successive additions.

Data Recorded measures of certain phenomena.

Database A collection of raw data or information arranged in a logical manner and organized in a form that can be stored and processed by a computer.

Database retrieval system A computerized system that permits investigation into the existence of certain data and the retrieval of that data.

Data conversion The process of changing the original form of the data to a format suitable to achieve the research objective.

Data matrix A rectangular arrangement of data into rows and columns.

Data processing error A category of administrative error that occurs because of incorrect data entry, incorrect computer programming, or other error during the analysis stage.

Decision support system A computer-based system that helps decision makers confront problems through direct interaction with databases and analytical models.

Deductive reasoning The logical process of deriving a conclusion from a known premise or something known to be true.

Degrees of freedom The number of degrees of freedom is equal to the number of observations minus the number of constraints or assumptions needed to calculate a statistical term.

Demand characteristics Experimental design procedures that unintentionally hint to subjects about the experimenter's hypothesis; situational aspects of an experiment that demand the participant to respond in a particular way.

Dependence method Any multivariate statistical technique used to explain one or more dependent variables on the basis of two or more independent variables. Multiple regression analysis is a dependence method.

Dependent variable The criterion or standard by which the results of an experiment are judged. It is so named because it is expected to be dependent on the experimenter's manipulation.

Depth interview A relatively unstructured, extensive interview used in the primary stages of the research process.

Descriptive analysis The transformation of raw data into a form that will make them easy to understand and interpret; rearranging, ordering, manipulating data to provide descriptive information.

Descriptive research Research designed to describe characteristics of a population or a phenomenon.

Descriptive statistics Statistics used to describe or summarize information about a population or sample.

Determinant-choice question A type of fixed-alternative question that requires a respondent to choose one (and only one) response from among several possible alternatives.

Diagnostic analysis Posterior analysis used to understand findings, such as explanations respondents give for a behavior or attitude. See also *Elaboration analysis*.

Direct data entry The use of an online computer terminal as an input device for data storage.

Direct observation A straightforward attempt to observe and record what naturally occurs; the investigator does not create an artificial situation.

Discriminant analysis A statistical tool for determining linear combinations of independent variables that show large differences in group means. The intent is to predict the probability of objects belonging in two or more mutually exclusive categories based on several independent variables.

Discriminant validity The ability of some measure to have a low correlation with measures of dissimilar concepts.

Disguised question An indirect question that assumes the purpose of the study must be hidden from the respondent.

Disproportional stratified sample A stratified sample in which the sample size for each stratum is allocated according to analytical considerations.

Door-in-the-face compliance technique A two-step method for securing a high response rate to research. In Step 1 an initial request, so large that nearly everyone refuses it, is made. In Step 2 a second request is made for a smaller favor; respondents are expected to comply with this more reasonable request.

Door-to-door interview Personal interview conducted at the respondent's home or place of business.

Double-barreled question A question that may induce bias because it covers two issues at once.

Double-blind design A technique in which neither the subjects nor the experimenter knows which are the experimental and which are the controlled conditions.

Drop-off method A method of distributing self-administered questionnaires whereby an interviewer drops off the questionnaire and picks it up at a later time.

Dummy table Representation of an actual table that will be in the findings section of the final report; used to gain a better understanding of what the actual outcome of the research will be.

Editing The process of making data ready for coding and transfer to data storage. Its purpose is to ensure completeness, consistency, and reliability of data.

Elaboration analysis An analysis of the basic cross-tabulation for each level of another variable, perhaps subgroups of the sample.

Empirical level Level of knowledge reflecting that which is verifiable by experience or observation.

Equivalent-form method A method that measures the correlation between alternative instruments, designed to be as equivalent as possible, administered to the same group of subjects.

Evaluation research The formal, objective measurement and appraisal of the extent to which a given action, activity, or program has achieved its objectives.

Experience survey An exploratory research technique in which individuals who are knowledgeable about a particular research problem are surveyed.

Experiment A research investigation in which conditions are controlled so that one or more variables can be manipulated in order to test a hypothesis. *Experimentation* is a research method that, by manipulating only one variable, allows evaluation of causal relationships among variables.

Experimental group The group of subjects exposed to an experimental treatment.

Experimental treatment Alternative manipulation of the independent variable being investigated.

Exploratory research Initial research conducted to clarify and define the nature of a problem.

External validity The ability of an experiment to generalize the results to the external environment.

Extremity bias A category of response bias that results from response styles varying from person to person; some individuals tend to use extremes when responding to questions.

Eye-tracking equipment Any of a number of devices that record how the subject views a stimulus, such as an advertisement, and how much time is spent looking at the various parts of the stimulus.

Face (content) validity Professional agreement that a scale logically appears to be accurately reflecting what was intended to be measured.

Factor analysis A type of analysis used to discern the underlying dimensions or regularity in phenomena. Its general purpose is to summarize the information contained in a large number of variables into a smaller number of factors. There

are a number of factor-analytical techniques.

Factor loading A measure of the importance of a variable in measuring a factor; a means for interpreting and labeling a factor.

Factorial experimental design An experimental design that investigates the interaction of two or more independent variables.

Feedback A reverse flow of communication that may be used to modify subsequent communication.

Field A collection of characters that represents a single type of data.

Field editing Preliminary editing by a field supervisor on the same day as the interview; its purpose is to catch technical omissions, check legibility of handwriting, and clarify responses that are logically or conceptually inconsistent.

Field experiment An experiment conducted in a natural setting, often for a long period of time.

Field interviewing service A research supplier that specializes in data gathering.

Field-worker An individual responsible for gathering data "in the field." For example, a personal interviewer administering a door-to-door questionnaire.

File A collection of related records.

Filter question A question in a questionnaire that screens out respondents not qualified to answer a second question.

Fixed-alternative question A question in which the respondent is given specific limited alternative responses and asked to choose the one closest to his or her own viewpoint.

Focus group interview An unstructured, free-flowing interview with a small group of people.

Follow-up A letter or postcard reminder requesting that a respondent return the questionnaire.

Foot-in-the-door compliance technique Based on foot-in-the-door theory, which attempts to explain compliance with a large or difficult task on the basis of the respondent's compliance with an earlier, smaller request.

Forced-choice scale A fixed-alternative rating scale that requires respondents to choose one of the fixed alternatives.

Forward linkage A term implying that the early stages of the research process will influence the design of the later stages.

Frequency determination question A type of fixed-alternative question that asks for an answer about the general frequency of occurrence.

Frequency distribution Organizing a set of data by summarizing the number of times a particular value of a variable occurs.

F-statistic A test statistic that measures the ratio of one sample variance to another sample variance, such as the variance between groups to the variance within groups.

F-test A procedure used to determine if there is more variability in the scores of one sample than in the scores of another sample.

Funnel technique A procedure whereby general questions are asked before specific questions in order to obtain unbiased responses.

Graphic aid A picture or diagram used to clarify a complex point or to emphasize a message.

Graphic rating scale A measure of attitude consisting of a graphic continuum that allows respondents to rate an object by choosing any point on the continuum.

Guinea pig effect An effect on the results of an experiment caused by subjects changing their normal behavior or attitudes in order to cooperate with an experimenter.

Hawthorne effect An unintended effect on the results of a research experiment caused by the subjects knowing that they are participants.

Hidden observation Situation in which the subject is unaware that observation is taking place.

History effect Specific events in the external environment occurring between the first and second measurements that are beyond the control of the experimenter and that affect the validity of an experiment.

Hypothesis An unproven proposition or supposition that tentatively explains certain facts or phenomena; a proposition that is empirically testable.

Hypothetical construct A variable that is not directly observable but is measured by an indirect means, such as verbal expression or overt behavior.

Iceberg principle The principle indicating the dangerous part of many business problems is neither visible to nor understood by business managers.

Independent variable In an experimental design, the variable that can be manipulated to be whatever the experimenter wishes. Its value may be changed or altered independently of any other variable.

Index (composite) measures Multi-itemed instruments constructed to measure a single concept; also called *composite measures.*

Inductive reasoning The logical process of establishing a general proposition on the basis of observation of particular facts.

Inferential statistics Statistics used to make inferences or judgments about a population on the basis of a sample.

Information A body of facts that are in a format suitable for decision making.

In-house editing A rigorous editing job performed by a centralized office staff.

In-house interviewer A field-worker who is employed by the client company rather than by a research supplier.

Instrument A data collection form, such as a questionnaire, or other measuring device.

Instrumentation effect An effect on the results of an experiment caused by a change in the wording of questions, a change in interviewers, or other changes in procedures to measure the dependent variable.

Interaction effect The influence on a dependent variable by combinations of two or more independent variables.

Interdependence methods A category of multivariate statistical techniques. Independence methods give meaning to a set of variables or seek to group things together.

Internal records and reports system A data collection subsystem that establishes orderly procedures to ensure that cost data, shipment data, inventory data, sales data, and other recurrent data are routinely collected and entered into the computer.

Internal source Source of secondary data that is found inside the organization.

Internal validity Validity determined by whether an experimental treatment was the sole cause of changes in a dependent variable.

Interpretation The process of making pertinent inferences and drawing conclusions concerning the meaning and implications of a research investigation.

Interval scale A scale that not only arranges objects according to their magnitude but also distinguishes this ordered arrangement in units of equal intervals.

Interviewer bias Bias in the responses of subjects due to the influence of the interviewer.

Interviewer cheating The practice of filling in fake answers or falsifying interviews by field-workers.

Intuitive decision making Decision making based on direct knowledge without evident rational thought or inference.

Item nonresponse The technical term for an unanswered question on an otherwise complete questionnaire.

Judgment (purposive) sampling A nonprobability sampling technique in which an experienced researcher selects the sample based upon some appropriate characteristic of the sample members.

Laboratory experiment Experiment conducted in a laboratory or artificial setting to obtain almost complete control over the research setting.

Latin square design A balanced two-way classification scheme that attempts to control or block out the effect of two or more extraneous factors by restricting randomization with respect to the row and column effects.

Leading question A question that suggests or implies certain answers.

Least-squares method A mathematical technique ensuring that the regression line will best represent the linear relationship between X and Y.

Likert scale A measure of attitudes ranging from very positive to very negative designed to allow respondents to indicate how strongly they agree or disagree with carefully constructed statements relating to an attitudinal object.

Line graph A graphic aid showing the relationship of one variable to another. The dependent variable is generally shown on the vertical axis and the independent variable on the horizontal axis.

Loaded question A question that suggests social-desirability answers or is emotionally charged.

Longitudinal study A survey of respondents at different points in time, thus allowing analysis of continuity and changes over time.

Magnitude of error The confidence interval that indicates how precise an estimate must be.

Mail survey A self-administered questionnaire sent through the mail to respondents.

Mailing list A list giving the names, addresses, and phone numbers of specific populations.

Main effect The influence on a dependent variable by each independent variable (separately).

Mall intercept interview A personal interview conducted in a shopping mall or other high-traffic area.

Marginals Row and column totals in a contingency table.

Market tracking The observation and analysis of trends in industry volume and brand share over time.

Matching A procedure for the assignment of subjects to groups; it ensures each group of respondents is matched on the basis of pertinent characteristics.

Maturation effect An effect on the results of a research experiment caused by changes in the experimental subjects over time. For example, subjects become hungry during the course of an experiment.

Mean A measure of central tendency; the arithmetic average.

Mechanical observation Situations in which video cameras, traffic counters, and other machines help observe and record behavior.

Median A measure of central tendency that is the midpoint, the value below which half the values in a sample fall.

Mode A measure of central tendency; the value that occurs most often.

Model A decision-making aid that draws actionable knowledge from sets of data.

Moderator variable A third variable that, when introduced into an analysis, alters or has a contingent effect on the relationship between an independent variable and a dependent variable.

Monadic rating scale Any measure of attitudes that asks respondents about a single concept in isolation.

Mortality effect Sample attrition that occurs when some subjects withdraw from an experiment before it is completed, thus affecting the validity of the experiment.

Multidimensional scaling A technique that measures objects in multidimensional space on the basis of respondents' similarity judgments of objects.

Multiple regression analysis An analysis of association that simultaneously investigates the effect of two or more independent variables on a single, interval-scaled or ratio-scaled dependent variable.

Multistage area sampling Sampling that involves using a combination of other probability sampling techniques.

Multivariate analysis of variance (MANOVA) A statistical technique that provides a simultaneous significance test of mean difference between groups, made for two or more dependent variables.

Multivariate data analysis Statistical methods that allow the simultaneous investigation of more than two variables.

Nominal scale A scale in which the numbers or letters assigned to the object serve as labels for identification or classification; a measurement scale of the simplest type.

Nonforce-choice scale A fixed-alternative rating scale that provides a no-opinion category or that allows respondents to indicate they cannot say which alternative is their choice.

Nonparametric statistics Statistical procedures that use nominal- or ordinal-scaled data and make no assumptions about the distribution of the population (or sampling distribution).

Nonprobability sampling A sampling technique in which units of the sample are selected on the basis of personal judgment or convenience.

Nonrespondents People who are not contacted or who refuse to cooperate in a research project.

Nonresponse error The statistical difference between a survey that includes only those who responded and a survey that also includes those who failed to respond.

Normal distribution A symmetrical, bell-shaped distribution that describes the expected probability distribution of many chance occurrences.

Not-at-home A person not at home on the first or second attempt at contact.

Null hypothesis A statement about a status quo that asserts that any change from what has been thought to be true will be due entirely to random error.

Numerical scale An attitude rating scale similar to a semantic differential except that it uses numbers as response options to identify response positions instead of verbal descriptions.

Observation The systematic recording of nonverbal as well as verbal behavior and communication.

Observer bias A distortion of measurement resulting from the cognitive behavior or actions of the witnessing observer.

Oculometer A technologically advanced machine that helps in the measuring of unconscious eye movements.

One-group pretest-posttest design A quasi-experimental design in which the subjects in the experimental group are measured before and after the treatment is administered but in which there is no control group.

One-shot design An after-only design in which a single measure is recorded after the treatment is administered.

Open-ended response questions Questions that pose some problem and ask the respondent to answer in his or her own words.

Operational definition A definition that gives meaning to a concept by specifying the activities or operations necessary in order to measure it.

Optical scanning system A data-processing input device that directly reads material from mark-sensed questionnaires onto magnetic tape.

Optimum allocation stratified sample A sampling procedure in which both the size and the variation of each stratum are considered.

Oral presentation A verbal summary of the major findings, conclusions, and recommendations given to clients or line managers to provide them with the opportunity to clarify any ambiguous issues by asking questions.

Order bias Bias caused by the influence of earlier questions in a questionnaire or by an answer's position in a set of answers.

Ordinal scale A scale that arranges objects or alternatives according to their magnitude.

Paired comparison A measurement technique that consists of presenting the respondent with two objects and asking the respondent to pick the preferred object. Two or more objects may be presented, but comparisons are made in pairs.

Panel study A longitudinal study that involves collecting data from the same sample of individuals over time.

Parameter A variable or measured characteristic of a population.

Parametric statistics Statistical procedures that use interval-scaled or ratio-scaled data and assume populations or sampling distributions with normal distributions.

Participant observation Situations in which an observer gains firsthand knowledge by being in or around the social setting being investigated.

Percentage A part of a whole expressed in hundredths.

Percentage distribution The organization of a frequency distribution into a table (or graph) that summarizes percentage values associated with particular values of a variable.

Performance-monitoring research Research that regularly, perhaps routinely, provides feedback for evaluation and control of business activity.

Periodicity A problem that occurs in systematic sampling when the original list has a systematic pattern.

Personal interview The gathering of information through face-to-face contact with individuals.

Physical-trace evidence A visible mark of some past occurrence.

Picture frustration A version of the thematic apperception test that uses a cartoon drawing in which the respondent suggests dialogue that the cartoon characters might make.

Pie chart   A graphic aid that shows the composition of some total quantity at a particular time; each angle or "slice" is proportional to its percentage of the whole.

Pilot study   Any small-scale exploratory research technique that uses sampling but does not apply rigorous standards.

Pivot question   A filter question used to determine which version of a second question will be asked.

Plug value   An answer inserted according to a predetermined decision rule, if an editor finds a missing answer where there can be no missing values.

Point estimate   An estimate of the population mean using a single value, usually the sample mean.

Pooled estimate of the standard error   An estimate of the standard error based on the assumption that variances of both groups (populations) are equal.

Population   A complete group of entities sharing some common set of characteristics.

Population distribution   A frequency distribution of the elements of a population.

Population element   An individual member of a specific population.

Population parameter   The variables in a population or measured characteristics of the population.

Postcoding   Determination of a framework for classifying responses to questions where categories cannot be established before data collection.

Posttest-only control group design   An after-only design in which the experimental group is tested after exposure to the treatment, and the control group is tested at the same time without having been exposed to the treatment; no premeasure is taken.

Predictive validity   A classification of criterion validity whereby a new measure predicts a future event or correlates with a criterion measure administered at a later time.

Preliminary tabulation   Tabulation of the results of a pretest.

Pretest   A trial run with a group of respondents used to screen out problems in the design of a questionnaire.

Pretesting   The administration of a questionnaire to a small group of respondents in order to detect ambiguity or bias in the questions.

Pretest-posttest control group design   A true experimental design in which the experimental group is tested before and after exposure to the treatment, and the control group is tested at the same two times without being exposed to the experimental treatment.

Primary data   Data gathered and assembled specifically for the research project at hand.

Primary sampling unit (PSU)   A unit selected in the first stage of sampling.

Probability distribution   The organization of probability values associated with particular values of a variable into a table (or graph).

Probability sampling   A sampling technique in which every member of the population will have a known, nonzero probability of selection.

Probing   The verbal prompts made by a field-worker when the respondent must be motivated to communicate his or her answer more fully. Probes encourage respondents to enlarge on, clarify, or explain answers.

Problem definition   The indication of a specific business decision area that will be clarified by answering some research questions.

Production coding   The physical activity of transferring the data from the questionnaire or data collection form after the data have been collected.

Program strategy   The overall plan to utilize a series of business research projects; a planning activity that places each project into the company's business plan.

Projective technique   An indirect means of questioning that enables a respondent to "project" beliefs and feelings onto a third party, onto an inanimate object, or into a task situation.

Proportion   The percentage of population elements that successfully meet some criterion.

Proportional stratified sample   A stratified sample in which the number of sampling units drawn from each stratum is in proportion to the relative population size of that stratum.

Proposition   A statement concerned with the relationships among concepts; assertion of a universal connection between events that have certain properties.

Pseudo-research   Research conducted for the purpose of organizational politics rather than an objective gathering of information for business decisions.

Psychogalvanometer A device that measures galvanic skin response, a measure of involuntary changes in the electrical resistance of the skin.

Psychographics A basis for market segmentation stressing consumer life-style characteristics and buying patterns in pursuit of life goals.

Pupilometer A device used to observe and record changes in the diameter of a subject's pupils.

Quota sampling A nonprobability sampling procedure that ensures that certain characteristics of a population sample will be represented to the exact extent that the investigator desires.

Random-digit dialing A method of obtaining a representative sample in a telephone interview by using a random number table to generate telephone numbers.

Random error An error in which repetitions of the basic experiment sometimes favor one experimental condition and sometimes the other on a chance basis. See also *Random sampling error.*

Random sampling error The difference between the result of a sample and the result of a census conducted using identical procedures; a statistical fluctuation that occurs because of chance variation in the elements selected for a sample.

Randomization A procedure in which the assignment of subjects and treatments to groups is based on chance.

Randomized block design An extension of the completely randomized design in which a single extraneous variable that might affect test

units' response to the treatment has been identified and the effects of this variable are isolated by blocking out its effects.

Randomized response questions A research procedure for dealing with sensitive topics that uses a random procedure to determine which of two questions a respondent will be asked to answer.

Range The distance between the smallest and largest values of a frequency distribution.

Ranking A measurement task that requires that the respondents rank-order a small number of activities, events, or objects in overall preference or on the basis of some characteristic of the stimulus.

Rating A measurement task that requires the respondent to estimate the magnitude of a characteristic or quality that an object possesses.

Ratio scale A scale having absolute rather than relative quantities and possessing an absolute zero where there is an absence of a given attribute.

Record A collection of related fields.

Refusal A person who is unwilling to participate in the research.

Region of rejection An area with values that are very unlikely to occur if the null hypothesis is true but relatively probable if the alternative hypothesis is true.

Regression (bivariate) analysis A technique that attempts to predict the values of a continuous, interval-scaled or ratio-scaled dependent variable from the specific values of the independent variable.

Reliability The degree to which measures are free from error and therefore yield consistent results.

Repeat purchase rate Percentage of purchasers making a second or repeat purchase.

Repeated measures Exposure of the same subjects to all experimental treatments in order to eliminate any problems due to subject differences.

Report format The general plan of organization for the parts of a written or oral research report.

Research design A master plan specifying the methods and procedures for collecting and analyzing needed information.

Research follow-up A recontacting of decision makers and/or clients after they have had a chance to read the research report.

Research objective The purpose of the research in measurable terms; the definition of what the research should accomplish.

Research project A specific research investigation; a study that completes or is planned to follow the stages in the research process.

Research proposal A written statement of the research design that includes a statement explaining the purpose of the study and a detailed, systematic outline of a particular research methodology.

Research report The presentation of research findings directed to a specific audience to accomplish a specific purpose.

Research report summary A summary of a research report containing (1) objectives of the report,

(2) results, (3) conclusions, and (4) recommendations.

Research supplier A commercial business research service that conducts business research activity for clients. The research supplier may be thought of as a business research consulting company.

Respondent The person who answers an interviewer's questions or the person who provides answers to written questions in self-administered surveys.

Respondent error A classification of sample biases resulting from some respondent action or inaction such as nonresponse or response bias.

Response bias Error that occurs when respondents tend to answer questions in a certain direction. Examples of response bias are acquiescence bias, extremity bias, interviewer bias, auspices bias, and social desirability bias.

Response latency The amount of time necessary to make a choice between two alternatives; used as a measure of the strength of preference.

Response rate The number of questionnaires returned or completed, divided by the total number of eligible people who were contacted or requested to participate in the survey.

Reverse directory A directory similar to a telephone directory in which listings may be found by city and street address and/or telephone numbers rather than in alphabetical order of surnames.

Role playing An exploratory research technique that requires the subject to act out someone else's behavior in a particular setting.

Rotation In factor analysis, the changing of the geometric axes which represent each factor to contemplate a new problem solution having fewer or more factors.

Sample A subset or some part of a larger population.

Sample bias A persistent tendency for the results of a sample to deviate in one direction from the true value of the population parameter.

Sample distribution A frequency distribution of the elements of a population sample.

Sample selection error An administrative procedural error caused by improper selection of a sample, thus introducing bias.

Sample size The size of a sample; the number of observations or cases specified by (1) the estimated variance of the population, (2) the magnitude of acceptable error, and (3) the confidence level.

Sample statistics Variables in a sample or measures computed from sample data.

Sample survey Formal term for survey; it indicates that the purpose of contacting respondents is to obtain a representative sample of the target population.

Sampling The process of using a small number of items or parts of a larger population to make conclusions about the whole population.

Sampling distribution A theoretical probability distribution of all possible samples of a certain size drawn from a particular population.

Sampling frame The list of elements from which a sample may be drawn; also called *working population*.

Sampling frame error Error that occurs when certain sample elements are not listed or available and are not represented in the sample frame.

Sampling interval The number of population elements between the units selected for the sample.

Sampling unit A single element or group of elements subject to selection in the sample.

Scale Any series of items that are progressively arranged according to value or magnitude; a series into which an item can be placed according to its quantification.

Scanner data Product and brand sales data collected through optical character-recognition systems.

Scientific method Techniques or procedures used to analyze empirical evidence in an attempt to confirm or disprove prior conceptions.

Scientific observation The systematic process of recording the behavioral patterns of people, objects, and occurrences without questioning or communicating with them.

Secondary data Data that have been previously collected for some project other than the one at hand.

Secondary sampling unit A unit selected in the second stage of sampling.

Selection effect A sample bias resulting in differential selection of respondents for the comparison groups.

Self-administered questionnaire A questionnaire, such as a mail questionnaire, that is filled in by the respondent rather than an interviewer.

Self-selection bias A bias that occurs because people who feel strongly about a subject are more likely to respond than people who feel indifferent about that subject.

Semantic differential An attitude measure consisting of a series of seven-point bipolar rating scales allowing response to a "concept."

Sensitivity A measurement instrument's ability to acutely measure variability in stimuli or responses.

Sentence completion The projective technique in which respondents are required to complete a number of partial sentences with the first word or phrase that comes to mind.

Significance level The critical probability in choosing between the null and alternative hypotheses; the probability level that is too low to warrant support of a null hypothesis.

Simple correlation coefficient A statistical measure of the covariation of or association between two variables.

Simple-dichotomy question A fixed-alternative question that requires the respondent to choose one of two dichotomous alternatives.

Simple random sampling A sampling procedure that assures each element in the population an equal chance of being included in the sample.

Simple tabulation A count of the number of responses to a question and placement of them in a frequency distribution.

Situation analysis The informal gathering of background information to familiarize researchers or managers with the decision area.

Slope The change in the variable on the vertical axis of a line divided by the change in the variable on the horizontal axis.

Snowball sampling A sampling procedure in which initial respondents are selected by probability methods, and then additional respondents are obtained from information provided by the initial respondents.

Social desirability bias Bias in the responses of subjects caused by respondents' desire, either consciously or unconsciously, to gain prestige or to appear in a different social role.

Societal norms Codes of behavior adopted by a group, suggesting what a member of the group ought to do under given circumstances.

Solomon four-group design A true experimental design that combines both the pretest-posttest with control group and the posttest-only with control group designs, thereby providing a means for controlling the interactive testing effect and other sources of extraneous variation.

Sorting A measurement technique that presents a respondent with several product concepts and requires the respondent to arrange the cards into a number of piles or to otherwise classify the product concepts.

Split-ballot technique A technique used to control for response bias. Two alternative phrasings of the same questions are utilized for respective halves of the sample to yield a more accurate total response than would be possible if only a single phrasing were utilized.

Split-half method A method that measures the degree of internal consistency by checking one half of the results of a set of scaled items against the other half.

Spurious relationship When the relationship between two variables is not authentic apparently because an elaboration analysis with a third variable has not yet been conducted.

Standard deviation A quantitative index of a distribution's spread or variability; the square root of the variance for distribution.

Standard error of the mean The standard deviation of the sampling distribution of the mean.

Standard error of the proportion The standard deviation of the sampling distribution of the proportion.

Standardized normal distribution (curve) A normal curve with a mean of zero and a standard deviation of one. It is a theoretical probability distribution.

Stapel scale An attitude measure that places a single adjective in the center of an even-number range of numerical values.

Static group design An after-only design in which subjects in the experimental group are measured after being exposed to the experimental treatment, and the control group is measured without having been exposed to the experimental treatment; no premeasure is taken.

Stratified sampling A probability sampling procedure in which subsamples are drawn from samples within different strata that are more or less equal on some characteristic.

Structured question A question that imposes a limit on the number of allowable responses.

Survey A research technique in which information is gathered from a sample of people by use of a questionnaire; a method of data collection based on communication with a representative sample of individuals.

Syndicated service A business research supplier that provides standardized information for many clients, as, for example, the A. C. Nielsen Retail Index.

Systematic (nonsampling) error Error resulting from some imperfect aspect of the research design that causes response error or from a mistake in the execution of the research; error that comes from such sources as sample bias, mistakes in recording responses, and nonresponses from persons not contacted or refusing to participate.

Systematic sampling A sampling procedure in which an initial starting point is selected by a random process, and then every nth number on the list is selected.

Table A graphic aid generally used for presenting numerical information, especially when several pieces of information can be systematically arranged in rows and columns.

Tabulation The orderly arrangement of data in a table or other summary format.

Tachistoscope A device that controls the amount of time a visual image is exposed to a subject.

Target population The specific, complete group relevant to the research project.

t-distribution A family of symmetrical, bell-shaped distributions with a mean of zero and a unit standard deviation, used when the population standard deviation is unknown or when testing a hypothesis with a small sample size.

Telephone survey The data collection method that uses telephone interviewing to collect the data.

Test marketing The scientific testing and controlled experimental procedure that provides an opportunity to test a new product or a new marketing plan under realistic marketing conditions to obtain a measure of sales or profit potentials.

Test tabulation During the coding process a small sample of the total number of replies to a particular question may be tallied in order to construct coding categories. This is a test tabulation.

Test unit A subject whose responses to experimental treatments are observed and measured.

Testing effect The effect of pretesting in a before-and-after study may sensitize the respondent or subjects when taking a test for the second time, thus affecting the validity of an experiment.

Test-retest method The administering of the same scale or measure to the same respondents at two separate points in time in order to test for reliability.

Tests of differences Investigation of hypotheses that state that two (or more) groups differ with respect to measures on a variable.

Thematic apperception test (TAT) A test consisting of a series of pictures shown to research subjects who are then asked to provide a description of the pictures. The researcher analyzes the content of these descriptions in an effort to clarify a research problem.

Theory A coherent set of general propositions used to explain the apparent relationships among certain observed phenomena. Theories allow generalizations *beyond* individual facts or situations.

Third-person technique The exploratory research technique in which the respondent is asked why a third person does what he or she does or what he or she thinks about an object, event, person, or activity. The respondent is expected to transfer his or her attitudes to the third person.

Thurstone scale An attitude measure in which judges assign scale values to the attitudinal statements and then subjects are asked to respond to these statements.

Time series design An experimental design utilized when experiments are conducted over long periods of time. It allows researchers to distinguish between temporary and permanent changes in dependent variables.

t-test A univariate hypothesis test using the t-distribution rather than the Z-distribution. It is used when the population standard deviation is unknown and the sample size is small.

t-test for difference of means A technique used to test the hypothesis that the mean scores on some variable will be significantly different for two independent samples or groups assuming interval data.

Total variance In analysis of variance, the combination of within-group variance and between-group variance.

Type I error An error caused by rejecting the null hypothesis when it is true.

Type II error An error caused by failing to reject the null hypothesis when the alternative hypothesis is true.

Unbalanced rating scale A fixed-alternative rating scale that has more response categories piled up at one end of the scale; the number of positive and negative categories are unequal.

Undisguised question A straightforward question that assumes the respondent is willing to reveal the answer.

Univariate data analysis Analysis that assesses the statistical significance of a hypothesis about a single variable.

Universal product code (UPC) A system of mechanical observation through which optical character recognition systems record product and brand sales information.

Unstructured question A question that does not restrict the respondents' answers.

User interaction system A subsystem in the decision support system; computer software written to manage the interface between the user and the system.

Validity The ability of a scale or measuring instrument to measure what is intended to be measured.

Variable Anything that may assume different numerical values.

Variance A measure of variability or dispersion. The square root of the standard deviation.

Verification The quality control procedures used in fieldwork to ensure that interviewers are following the sampling procedures; the method used to determine if interviewers are falsifying interviews.

Visible observation Situations in which the observer's presence is known to the subject.

Voice-pitch analysis A physiological measurement technique that records abnormal frequencies in the voice that are supposed to reflect emotional reactions to various stimuli.

Within-group variance Variation of scores due to random error or individual difference.

Word association test The exploratory research technique in which the subject is presented with a list of words, one at a time, and asked to respond with the first word that comes to mind.

Z-test A univariate hypothesis test using the standardized normal distribution which is the distribution of Z.

Z-test for differences of proportions When the observed statistic is a proportion, this technique is used to test the hypothesis that the two proportions will be significantly different for two independent samples or groups.

Index